STUMBLING GIANT

TIMOTHY BEARDSON founded Crosby Financial Holdings, at the time the largest independent investment bank in the Far East and the first to be licensed in China. He speaks frequently on economic and strategic issues at such events as the World Economic Forum in Davos and is chairman of the internet magazine China Outlook. He is a permanent resident of Hong Kong.

Website: www.timothy-beardson.com

Twitter: @timothybeardson

TIMOTHY BEARDSON

STUMBLING GIANT

THE THREATS TO CHINA'S FUTURE

YALE UNIVERSITY PRESS
NEW HAVEN AND LONDON

For information about this and other Yale University Press publications, please contact:

U.S. Office: sales.press@yale.edu   www.yalebooks.com
Europe Office: sales@yaleup.co.uk   www.yalebooks.co.uk

Set in Minion Pro by IDSUK (DataConnection) Ltd.
Printed in Great Britain by Hobbs the Printers, Totton, Hampshire

Library of Congress Cataloging-in-Publication Data

Beardson, Timothy.
   Stumbling giant: the threats to China's future/Timothy Beardson.
      pages; cm
   ISBN 978-0-300-16542-5 (cl: alk. paper)
1. China—Economic conditions—2000.   2. China—Politics and government—21st century.   3. China—Foreign relations—21st century.   I. Title.
   HC427.95.B42 2013
   330.951—dc23

                                                                              2013002119

A catalogue record for this book is available from the British Library.

ISBN 978-0-300-20532-9 (pbk)

10 9 8 7 6 5 4 3 2 1

Contents

Acknowledgements

I would like to thank many friends and acquaintances for their advice, comment and contributions. In the traditional manner, I hasten to say that I am indebted to them for their assistance but any errors and all opinions are my own. In fact many of them hold quite different views to mine and would not share all the conclusions I have drawn. In a number of countries, some people have asked not to be acknowledged owing to sensitivities. Advice and opinion have been given at many points over the years since my first visit to China in 1978 and have helped to form my evolving understanding of the country's dramatic development and potential destiny. Some people I met early on others more recently.

I should thank Zhou Xiaochuan, Liu Hongru, then Vice Governor at the People's Bank of China, Wang Ruipu at the Communist Party Central School, Li Yining, the late Jing Shuping at CITIC and Ma Hong at the Development Research Centre of the State Council, amongst many, for their early perspectives in the 1980s. Later I benefited from Liu Mingkang's views. I would like to thank Robbie Lyle for encouraging me to expand my interest in China. In particular, I would like to thank Cheng Siwei, previously Vice Chairman of the Standing Committee of the National People's Congress. I gained from speaking with Professors Kang Shaobang, Gong Li and Qin Zhilai of the Communist Party Central School, Zhang Weiying at Peking University, Ding Ningning of the Development Research Centre at the State Council, Andrew Goudie, formerly of the Oxford University China Centre, Wu Qidi, formerly Vice Minister of Education, Li Peilin and Wang Zhimou of the Chinese Academy of Social Sciences (CASS) and Michael Pettis at Peking University. I should mention Felipe Larrain from the Catholic University of Chile, now Chilean Minister of Finance, for his input on R&D and innovation, Zhu Min, then at the Bank of China, Li Ruogu at the State Export-Import Bank for his ever-robust views, Manmohan Singh, the Prime Minister of India, Shaukat Aziz, formerly Prime Minister of Pakistan, Bob Tuttle, President George W. Bush's ambassador to London, Thomas Rawski at Pittsburgh University, Alexei Pushkov in Moscow, John Harrison, then Vice-Chairman of KPMG, Philip Snow, the historian, Frank Dikotter at Hong Kong University for his illumination of Chinese economic and social history, particularly during the Republican period, Ben Simpfendorfer, now at Silk Road Associates, Larry Lau, then President of the Chinese University of Hong Kong, Carsten Holz, then at Hong Kong University of Science and Technology, Bob Mundell at Columbia University, Anthony Chow of the CPPCC, Rick Levin, Zhiwu Chen and Jeff Prescott at Yale University, Ali Allawi, formerly Minister of Finance and Defence in Iraq, Serge Michailof, a leading specialist in aid and reconstruction, and Nick Shenton of Polar Capital in London. I would like to thank Weili Fan in Beijing, Hugues Maury in Paris, Rana Mitter in Oxford, Anthony Pettifer in Hong Kong, Xiaodi Bell and Verne Grinstead in London and Charles Elwell in Madrid for their advice on the text. I should particularly mention Nick Fielding for the extensive efforts he made to advise on the whole draft. I am indebted to Julian and the late Christine Gaisford-St Lawrence in Ireland for giving me the opportunity at short notice to exchange some views and think in peace. Some people made brief points, which registered with me, others provided more discursive contributions. No matter how distinguished the advice, mistakes on my part are regrettably inevitable.

In particular, I would like to give posthumous thanks to Wang Daohan in Shanghai who kindly encouraged and sponsored my early involvement in the development of capital markets in China in the 1980s and 1990s and taught me much of what I understand of modern China.

I still have the original copy of Mao's 'Red Book' which was given to me by the Chinese Embassy in London in the 1960s and so it was a particularly poignant moment when the investment bank I had founded was the only foreign institution invited onto the working party to set up the Shanghai stock exchange and became the first foreign firm to be authorised by the People's Bank of China to open up in the country in 1989. I should probably say here that, although the opinions expressed are not closely aligned to official views, I am putting them forward as an old friend who has spent over thirty years working with China and who wishes it well.

I would like to thank my wife Clair for her steadfast support and wise advice throughout this project, inspired, I am sure, through her love of China and its culture. It is with no hesitation that I dedicate this book to China which has had such terrible nineteenth and twentieth centuries and which fully deserves a prosperous, successful and happy twenty-first century.

Abbreviations

ADB	Asian Development Bank
AFP	Agence France Presse
AP	Arunachal Pradesh
APSCO	Asia Pacific Space Cooperation Organisation
ASEAN	Association of South East Asian Nations
BMJ	*British Medical Journal*
BRICS	Brazil, Russia, India, China and South Africa
CASS	Chinese Academy of Social Sciences
CCP	Chinese Communist Party
CPPCC	Chinese Peoples' Political Consultative Conference
CCTV	China Central Television
CIC	China Investment Corporation
CIS	Commonwealth of Independent States
CMC	Central Military Commission
CSM	*Christian Science Monitor*
CSTO	Collective Security Treaty Organisation
DPJ	Democratic Party of Japan
DPP	Democratic Progressive Party [Taiwan]
EAS	East Asia Summit
EC	*The Economist*
ETIM	East Turkestan Islamic Movement
FAO	Food and Agriculture Organization
FDA	[US] Food and Drug Administration
FDI	foreign direct investment
FT	*Financial Times*
GDP	gross domestic product
GDFCF	gross domestic fixed capital formation

GONGO	government-organised non-governmental organisation
ICC	International Criminal Court
ICOR	Incremental Capital–Output Ratio
IHT	*International Herald Tribune*
IMF	International Monetary Fund
IPO	initial public offering
Jane's	*Jane's Defence Weekly*
LA	*(Daily Times): Los Angeles (Daily) Times*
NATO	North Atlantic Treaty Organization
NBS	National Bureau of Statistics
NDRC	National Development and Reform Commission
NGO	non-governmental organisation
NIEs	newly industrialising economies
NPC	National People's Congress
NRI	non-resident Indian
NYT	*New York Times*
OECD	Organisation for Economic Cooperation and Development
OEM	original equipment manufacturing
PBC	People's Bank of China
PLA	People's Liberation Army
PRC	People's Republic of China
PRD	Pearl River Delta
PPP	purchasing power parity
R&D	research and development
RMB	*renminbi*
SCMP	*South China Morning Post*
SCO	Shanghai Cooperation Organization
SEPA	State Environmental Protection Agency
SLEs	state-linked enterprises
SMEs	small and medium-sized enterprises
SMH	*Sydney Morning Herald*
SOEs	state-owned enterprises
SIPRI	Stockholm International Peace Research Institute
TI	Transparency International
TVEs	town and village enterprises
UNCTAD	United Nations Conference on Trade and Development
UNDP	United Nations Development Programme
UNESCO	United Nations Educational, Scientific and Cultural Organization
USCESRC	US–China Economic and Security Review Commission

UWSA	United Wa State Army [Burma]
WHO	World Health Organization
WSJ	*Wall Street Journal*
WTO	World Trade Organization

Introduction:
Facing Multiple Challenges

The question of whether, and when, China might replace the United States as the superpower is one that occupies much time and attention.[1]

China has been, bar none, the country that has changed fastest over the last thirty years. To take a quarter of the world's population from communism to an essentially market-based economy in such a short period – without a civil war – is the largest and most peaceful counter-revolution in human history.

The Chinese government and its people share a common aspiration to build a modern, prosperous, strong and respected country. They also possess an age-old cultural heritage that values society over the individual. China is certainly not the only country in Asia – or elsewhere – to do this; but it is often the basis for many of the misapprehensions and fears about China.

To understand China's true position, we must appreciate its history and consider in detail matters internal and external – from education to the economy. We must address and, often, reject existing assumptions and conclusions. It will be argued that China is weaker than it appears; that its future rise is surrounded by threats; and that, although it can and probably will rise further, it will *not replace America as the superpower* – at least not in this century.

That is not to underestimate the emergence of China on to the international stage: it is probably the most important world development since the birth of communism in the nineteenth century. However, China's rise is of more consequence, for it is likely to last far longer than the seventy or so years between the start of Communist rule in 1917 and its effective end in every major country by 1989.

It has been estimated that China represented 26 per cent of the world's GDP in the year AD 1 and 29 per cent in 1600.[2] These statistics are significant, suggesting as they do some kind of dominance; but that is not in fact the case. Henry Kissinger's reference to 'the reestablishment of a central role for China in . . . world affairs' is wrong and misleading.[3] China's sphere of influence has always been limited. Its soldiers never went further than the eastern shores of the Caspian, and – though its silk eventually reached Ancient Rome and it undertook some voyages to Africa's east coast in the early fifteenth century – China was, at its height, never more than a very large regional power. The Roman and British empires were intercontinental; China was not. As a result, it is more appropriate to talk of China's *emergence* on to the world stage rather than the fashionable (and dramatic) 're-emergence'.

The recent history of China's growth is interesting, but the outlook is even more so. According to Global Language Monitor in Texas, which tracks print and internet news stories, the rise of China has been the most widely read subject of the last decade.[4] And yet, all too often, the factors most likely to determine the outcome are not those that are most closely followed: some write as if the story were exclusively economic.

The last half-century has seen a wide variety of candidates for world leadership: in the 1960s it was suggested that Germany would replace America; in the 1980s that Japan would; we have entered the (rather ambivalent) Pacific Century; we have had books entitled *When China Rules the World* (2012) – and others that have predicted *The Coming Collapse of China* (2003).

China faced a major challenge after the death of Mao Zedong in 1976 and the end of the Cultural Revolution: where was it going? Now we know; but how the changes came about (and why) is less clear. We are in what is likely to be a phase of fundamental and profound change in the country's development. In order to consider and predict what this will look like, it is worth examining what lessons can be drawn from China's history. Here I trace some of the events that led to the creation of today's China, look at the reasons for its success, and identify certain themes I believe are relevant to an understanding of its future. After a period of sustained growth, China is facing challenges almost as testing as those at the end of the Cultural Revolution. New challenges – such as a demographic crisis at home and regime collapse on its borders – are arising. China has demonstrated considerable problem-solving skills, and these talents are now being severely tested by the new, emerging challenges of public health issues, national integrity, regime survival – and how the world will react to the rise of China.

It is useful to consider how China sees itself at this crucial juncture, and to examine how (and how fast) it is changing. In 2013, the US-based Pew Survey asked what issues were important to the Chinese. The responses highlighted rising prices, corrupt officials, income inequality, air pollution, water pollution and food safety.[5] It is interesting to see what concerns the Chinese public today, but also what threats will confront China tomorrow.

Then President Hu Jintao said in 2012 that corruption could test the grip of the Chinese Communist Party (CCP). But there are many other issues – from unemployment, through the Party's mandate to rule, to demography, the country's place in the world economy, and instability inside and outside its borders. China's people will have to consider how their country will look ethnically (and thus geographically), and how its society and economy will function. Is it a nation state or is it an empire? Will China's extensive ecological devastation pollute foreign countries? Is the world's largest population facing a period of mounting instability? Is the world right to be frightened by its research advances? How will China behave should its rise continue?

China has a strong record in recent history of meeting and solving challenges. The one-child policy was a brave political decision (although its results can be debated). Its nuclear and space projects were carried off with éclat; and few would have expected a quadrupling of the economy between 1980 and 2000.

Some 500 million people have been lifted out of poverty. Leaving aside the vagaries of Maoist utopianism, government by the Communist Party has proved highly successful in terms of achieving what might objectively be regarded as broad national aspirations. This is not to overlook, or diminish, the fact that some of the achievements came at huge human cost.

Much international attention has focused on how China survived the recent Western financial crisis and the ensuing uncertainty. Whether the country will buckle under the weight of a new round of non-performing loans or will navigate this period is of great interest to those in the West who are looking for stability in the world economy. Some speculate that China has found a better way of harnessing market forces and might be well placed to assist the West in its economic and financial travails. However, an economic slowdown and a decoupling of the link between the economy and employment might bring instability. Whatever one's political orientation, few would wish to see an internecine struggle in which the country shatters.

Thus China faces several major challenges; but it is not possible to mention every source of stress, and I will focus only on those with the greatest potential impact. The principal challenges facing China today are serious. They embrace the environment, welfare, demography, employment, frontiers, resources, science and stability – factors that frequently overlap. China is often criticised for its political system; it is not, after all, a liberal democracy. However, just two hundred years ago, many of the planks on which China's current system is based would not have seemed unusual in the West: historically, the liberal democratic values of today are not universal human values – even in the West. The pursuit of economic and social development goals can conceivably take priority over political reform. Chinese leaders – at least in the last thirty years – have had to tackle issues of a scale and significance beyond anything ever encountered by most Western leaders. The achievements of Chinese administrations in recent decades place them amongst the most successful governments ever.

This book looks at the background to today's China, how it got where it is and the lessons we can draw for the future. We will examine how the economy grew to its current level, as well as the challenges it faces, particularly of structural unemployment and a weak economic model of low-cost manufacturing. China suffers from both rising wages and endemic unemployment. Its principal economic challenge is whether it can change its model – either by building an innovation economy or by becoming more consumption-driven. This is proving much harder than expected, and we will look at the reasons for this – including educational, cultural, moral and political factors.

Many of the issues covered in this book can be resolved with imagination and will. It is important to examine the identity of the Communist Party and the state, how they have adapted and how they need to adapt further to support a continuation of the country's rise. The post-communist party will need to find a new ideology that can rally support in the twenty-first century; those groups apparently in opposition can be co-opted; and even the borders of the state might be shrunk in order to create internal cultural harmony.

It is essential to examine China's relationships with the world, and for that we must also look at what is happening with the world's current greatest power, America: it is down but not out. The other great powers that have fractious relationships with China – India, Russia and Japan – are considered for the challenges they present.

The greatest risks to regional relations will, I argue, come from China's plan to divert Tibetan-sourced waters to northern China (which is creating anxiety in South East Asia, India and Russia) and from Beijing's militant stance on maritime border issues. Thus Beijing's own policies could lead to regional conflict. Developments in Central Asia also pose risks to China, in the form of potential Taliban rule in Afghanistan extending to the borders of China's Muslim Xinjiang province (with the threat of insurrection); and the possibility of state collapse in Pakistan, which could place the world's fastest-growing nuclear arsenal in radical Islamic hands.

How a more powerful China behaves in the world (including in the arcane cyber world) and whether its aggressiveness could make it go too far are important questions.

If we seek to judge a society, we should consider where it was before, all that has been achieved – good and ill – and the financial and human cost of getting to where it is now. China is a very large and diverse society and, as a result, many of the easier generalisations do not hold (although others certainly do). Does a catalogue of fifty or a hundred appalling incidents necessarily indicate that the form of society is inherently wrong? Or might it suggest that the society is complex but could still be heading broadly in the right direction? It behoves the critic to look first at his own country's behaviour – not just its principles.

Chinese statistics are of vital importance in painting a picture, but there is a woeful lack of clarity about the numbers. It is not so much that information is being concealed as that the facts are not accurately known. Statistics can lack credibility either because they are contradictory (e.g. every province might report a GDP growth rate above the national average) or because they are eerily the same year after year. Thus scholars learn not to take official data as sacrosanct.

Much attention is paid in China to the unsanctioned disclosure of 'state secrets'. Rather than focus on the loss of state secrets, the government would be better advised to concentrate on the acquisition and distribution of state knowledge: economic policy discussion in government would be far more effective if accompanied by accurate data. Whether we talk of 10 per cent economic growth, millions of unemployed or, worse, millions of deaths, we need to remember that the data presented here are *purely illustrative*. Government data are often contradictory, and officials, academics and the government media often cite figures that do not fit the data. The facts and figures are not to be wholly relied upon.

Sometimes there are no official numbers with which to agree or disagree. In many countries, an official might say one thing and an academic something else: both statements would be correct, but the interpretation is substantially different. Truths are multiple but understanding is unitary. In China it is different because often one does not know which data are true. There tends to be an official 'echo effect': a statement made by a national leader will be authoritatively echoed by other officials, even though often there were no solid grounds for the original statement.

A key point to bear in mind is the problem of scale. China has over 1.3 billion people; so inevitably, there is a lot of everything there – of poverty, road deaths, corruption ... But America has the same *proportion* of poverty and almost the same level of income inequality as China. Driving is more dangerous per capita in Russia and several other countries than in China. China's level of corruption is appalling, yet the country is ranked in the 'better' half of the world's countries.

One could reduce everything to four key ideas: Stability, Prosperity, Identity and Honour. Stability is the provision of social calm and the avoidance of secession, large-scale dissidence or external threat. Prosperity covers adequate employment levels, social security, economic development and rising incomes. Identity revolves around what kind of society China is, what its values are, what the Party stands for, and what its 'contract' with the public is. Perhaps one should also include the future scope and scale of its military. Honour is how the Chinese feel they treat, and are treated by, the world and how their government performs in this field.

This is not an encyclopaedia of modern Chinese civilisation. It does not celebrate all the many achievements of China in science and medicine, contemporary art, commerce, cuisine, sport or space. Neither is this a foreign relations handbook. It treats China's relationship with some countries, where challenges are identified, but not with other, equally important, countries where no similarly contentious issues appear to exist. It assesses China's relationship with other world powers in the first decades of the twenty-first century. China has an impressive history of identifying issues and dealing with them, and few of the challenges identified here cannot be solved. However, solutions may require radical changes of policy.

So will China solve all the issues facing it? I do not believe it will and I do not believe it will overtake the US this century. China's demographic outlook is dire: extreme gender disparity, remorseless ageing, a falling population and a declining labour force, all of which will affect stability and make high economic growth unsustainable. Instability is a threat to growth. Because of its falling population, China has a limited window of opportunity – maybe twenty years – to make its economic breakthrough. Otherwise it risks being caught in a 'middle income' trap. The China–America population ratio is projected to fall from over 4:1 now to 1.5:1 or even below by 2100. (The critical factor here is US immigration policy.) This will radically shift the global power balance from one influenced by scale to one driven by technology.

As will be argued in this book, other severe threats to China's growth and future leadership include a devastated environment; a low-tech economy that is failing to innovate; the absence of an effective welfare safety net, which deters consumer spending; and an ossified and warped governance structure. The country also faces the challenge of radical Islam on its borders. It has a historically scarred national psyche, which encourages deeply unpopular external behaviour; and it is experiencing a rising annual number of large-scale violent riots.

In the face of these threats, Chinese policy-makers do not act with sufficient urgency; they appear to be thinking in terms of centuries, whereas they need to plan in terms of years. The threats will outweigh the opportunities. China will become a society that is brittle at home and brusque overseas.

CHAPTER ONE

The Making of Today's China

China's history offers several insights into why the country is the way it is today and how it might behave tomorrow. I briefly examine the last thousand years, and then look more closely at China's two centuries of disastrous history – from around the 1770s until the 1970s. I would suggest that what has happened to China – and what the Chinese have done to themselves – has shaped and will shape their character and their future. This is a recurring theme in this book. As the contemporary writer Xiao Jiansheng has said:

> the most important thing is that we Chinese strive to understand the truth about our own history in an objective fashion. This will help us to reform our own political system and improve our own quality as a people.[1]

Whose China?

There is a common perception that China was a great country that was at the centre of world affairs; that over the millennia it has had periods of glory and periods of weakness, but – apart from the foreign incursions from the 1840s to the 1940s – was never conquered. However, this perception is inaccurate: it has never been at the centre of world affairs and it has spent much of its history under foreign domination.

China had a succession of imperial dynasties, each of which generally ruled for several centuries. A thousand years ago, the Song dynasty (960–1279) ruled for the first half of its history in a large part of 'China proper'. Many races have always lived in what is today's China, but the largest is the ethnic Chinese, or 'Han'. The Song dynasty was Han, although it coexisted with contiguous empires ruled by non-Han races. At various times these other dynasties occupied large parts of the Chinese 'heartland'. The Song's initial northern neighbours were the Kitan empire and the Tangut state. It was soon fighting both.

The Song was militarily inept and generally favoured peaceful solutions. From 1004 it paid tribute to the Kitan and from 1044 to the Tangut. By 1142, the Song had lost the northern part of its empire to a new foreign power – the Jin. So weak was the Song dynasty that, on the eve of the Jin invasion in 1126, the Song soldiers had their right arms tattooed to deter them from deserting.[2] The Jin dynasty was founded by tribesmen from the far north (in today's Russia) called the Jurchen. The Kitan also came from the area where Manchuria and Mongolia meet. They were, like the Jurchen, of Tungusic stock. The Tangut were likewise non-Han. Thus the Song were surrounded by non-Han states.

Military weakness led the Song dynasty to pay off those non-Han states.[3] In fact, 'at the risk of oversimplification one could say that the military history of the Song's 319 years is a record of retreat and defeat broken only by intervals of purchased peace.'[4] Almost throughout its existence, then, the Song dynasty accepted a subordinate position and paid tribute either to the Kitan empire (from 1004), the Tangut state (from 1044) or the Jin empire (from 1142, after the loss of Hangzhou).[5] In 1207, the Song had to increase their tribute to the Jin and the Emperor had to refer to himself as the 'nephew emperor' in addressing himself to the Jin 'uncle emperor'.[6] This might be compared with current Chinese histories, which invariably refer to the Han people as the 'elder brother' of the other ethnic groups.

The origins of the Tangut are disputed, but they are probably Tibetan or quasi-Tibetan. One view is that they descend from the Qiang, who inhabited eastern Tibet; another is that they were a Mongol tribe that had long resided adjacent to Tibet. Many historians simply call them Tibetan. It seems that at various times Tibetan people and Chinese both gave and received tribute. This weakens contemporary suggestions that paramountcy between Tibet and China has been one-way.[7]

Table 1.1: **Dynasties Ruling Areas of the Chinese Heartland**

Kitan dynasty	916–1125
Tangut state	982–1227
Jin dynasty	1115–1234
Song dynasty	960–1279

It was under Jin rule that the habit began of foreign invaders ruling China from Beijing. The city had the advantage of not being in the traditional Chinese heartland, and it was close to the Jin's non-Chinese homelands. From the time

China was unified (in 221 BC) until 1911, for 70 per cent of the time Beijing was not the capital. And when it was, for two-thirds of the time this was because it suited foreign rulers. It has been observed that 'the past has been so successfully rewritten that most Chinese are not consciously aware of the role Beijing played in their history ... Beijing owes its origins to the place where the Chinese came to deliver their tribute to their uncivilized neighbours'.[8] Native Han dynasties (and Chiang Kai-shek) preferred cities such as Xi'an, Kaifeng or Nanjing, in the heartland. The ethnic Han Taiping rebels in the nineteenth century, rejecting the alien Manchu, chose Nanjing as their capital.[9]

If modern China bases its self-image partly on China's history, then we should reflect on that history. The dynasty that ruled for longest in the last thousand years was the Song. A critical feature of the Song is that it paid tribute to its non-Han neighbours and never received tribute. For 70 per cent of its three-century hold on power, the dynasty acknowledged its subordination to a succession of non-Han neighbouring states.

The Song dynasty was finally ended by Khubilai Khan, founder of the new Yuan dynasty and grandson of the Mongol leader Genghis Khan, who invaded and progressively conquered all of China proper. The ground had been prepared in 1215 by Genghis, when he destroyed ninety cities and left Beijing burning for a month.[10] The widespread acceptance by the Han elites of non-Han rule over China was to dismay subsequent generations of Chinese historians.[11] Under the Yuan dynasty the Han found their role in government severely circumscribed:[12] they retained few positions other than as local officials, and were largely out of national power for a century. Khubilai regarded race as a potential source of disloyalty and preferred not to rely on Han elites in government.[13] The Yuan dynasty created a vast multiracial and syncretistic pan-Asian empire, and it brought artists from all of West and Central Asia to interact with their Chinese peers to produce a great flowering of artistic innovation, resulting in 'the creation of new art forms that would provide models for the arts of China in all subsequent periods until the twentieth century'.[14]

The Yuan were dethroned in 1368 by the Han founder of the native Ming dynasty. Hongwu had grown up in an anti-Mongol Buddhist sect, and the Ming dynasty consciously represented ethnic renewal. It acknowledged no foreign superior, but the dynasty lived in constant fear of another invasion from the north and its heavy spending on the Great Wall undermined its rule. When the Ming dynasty was ended by the invasion of the Manchus, who inaugurated the Qing dynasty in 1644, foreign rule over China resumed and lasted until 1912. If we want to ask the pertinent question of how does China behave when it is powerful, rich – and governed independently by Chinese – the only time we can find in the last thousand years is during the first half of the Ming dynasty – a period of scarcely over a hundred years. The answer was a continual series of wars against neighbours. The entire dynasty, across both strong and weak periods, engaged in an average of 1.12 wars per year.[15] Alastair Johnston at Harvard notes that Chinese strategic culture 'places a high degree of value on the use of pure violence to resolve security conflicts'.[16]

The differences between Han and non-Han dynasties were not minor ones. The language of the non-Han rulers was not a variant of Chinese but derived from a different root. They were not only racially different from the Chinese but usually originated in lands to the north which even today China does not claim as Chinese. Accordingly, they were not ethnic rebels emerging from Chinese soil, but were from lands outside who invaded China and consciously imposed foreign rule. The new rulers may have co-opted Confucian, or Chinese imperial, practices, but this was purely to consolidate and perpetuate their non-Han rule.

Table 1.2: **The Dynasties and their Relationships with Foreigners**

Song	960–1279	Paid tribute to foreigners and accepted vassal status
Jin	1115–1234	Foreign
Yuan	1271–1368	Foreign
Ming	1368–1644	Han Chinese, spending hugely to avoid invasion
Qing	1644–1912	Foreign

China bore a marked resemblance to Italy: for a millennium all sorts of powers – Saracens, Normans, Spanish, French, Austrians – ruled over large parts of Italy, and the greater part of Italy was under the rule of non-Italians until the late nineteenth century. Similarly China was under foreign rule for two-thirds of the last thousand years of imperial history.

When not under foreign rule, namely during the Ming dynasty, China was so obsessed by the fear of invasion that it conducted one of the most remarkable – and yet ultimately futile – exercises in world history: construction of the Great Wall. It did not immure today's Inner Mongolia, Manchuria, a significant part of the Yellow River, or indeed anything much north of Beijing.[17]

Only with the Mongol conquest of China did suggestions of an international cultural superiority and political supremacy emerge; the Song could not have asserted it.[18] The Ming maintained this congenial line of thought, and it was further developed by the Manchus. In fact it was not so much a Han construct as a belief easily held by strong (largely non-Han) emperors who governed most of China as well as other territories. In the last thousand years, periods of Han cultural achievement frequently occurred at odd times, such as during the weak reign of the Song or the foreign occupation by the Yuan.[19] Perhaps an analogy might be Robert Brasillach or Jean-Paul Sartre happily writing in 1940s German-occupied Paris.

The fact that China's neighbours may have been occasionally militarily formidable, but were frequently culturally less advanced, fed the growing sense of superiority of the inhabitants of empire, regardless of their rulers' origins. This, combined with the curious Chinese habit of treating foreign traders as though they were paying tribute, erected an edifice of superiority which largely prevented the reciprocal cultural exchange that developed in Europe.[20] This self-proclaimed superiority and lack of stimulating neighbourly competitors have been a weakness in China's scientific development.[21]

The Manchu Seize China

Who were the Manchu? In the seventeenth century, the Jurchen chief Nurhaci merged a number of Jurchen tribes north of the Ming dynasty's protective Liaodong Wall and north-west of today's Vladivostok. The Jurchen had ruled much of northern China as the Jin empire, following their final defeat of the northern Song in 1126. In 1235 they were themselves crushed by Khubilai Khan's Mongols. Nurhaci called his reign the Later Jin dynasty, renamed the people Manchu and then, in 1636, renamed the dynasty 'Qing' (meaning 'pure'), before riding south to invade and conquer China again.

If the Manchu were originally Jurchen, who were the Jurchen? They probably descended from Korean, Mohe and Merkit stock. The Mohe lived in what is now Primorsky Krai, in the Russian Far East, and the Merkit lived between Lake Baikal and the Sea of Okhotsk, in today's Siberia, where they opposed Genghis Khan's Mongol expansion. None of these areas is currently part of China, or claimed by China. The Jurchen spoke Tungusic, an Altaic language. They later came to inhabit the Mongol empire of the Kitan but rebelled in 1113 and established their own state, which expanded southward, and eventually invaded China. There was nothing Chinese about either the Jurchen empire of the twelfth and thirteenth centuries or their later descendants the Manchus.

The Great Wall did not impede the Manchus, and they also benefited from a Han peasant uprising. Ming finances had sharply deteriorated for a variety of reasons: self-imposed interdictions on trade with Japan and the Philippines, wars and the cost of constructing the Great Wall. Financial pressure caused the Ming to raise taxation sharply, which undermined their support. Corruption among severely underpaid officials further intensified the dynasty's unpopularity.[22] To make matters worse, record cold and devastating drought accompanied famine, which even led to cannibalism.[23]

When the Qing conquered, they maintained much of the traditional culture and policy bequeathed by previous dynasties. When new leaders take power anywhere they often assume the characteristics of their predecessors. This is particularly true of new foreign rulers. However, these non-Han rulers decided to embark on conquest to create a larger empire that would not be as ethnically Han as the Ming had been.

The China ruled by the Han Chinese Ming dynasty had been a shrivelled version of the China ruled by the alien Yuan dynasty: Ming borders on the north-west, north, north-east and south-west had been withdrawn by between 160 and 600 miles.[24] This was the only Chinese sovereign state between the tenth and the twentieth centuries. The subsequent Qing empire grew to almost twice the size of the Ming and lost the features of a nation state (though China was scarcely even familiar with the concept). Not being Chinese, the Qing risked nothing by building an imperial state transcending racial defini-tion. The dynasty pursued successful military campaigns in Xinjiang and Tibet, and against Burma and Nepal. At its height, the Qing empire 'constituted one of the largest and most sophisticated empires in the world at that time (along with the Ottoman and Mughal empires)'.[25] Paradoxically, the Qing and other foreign rulers' colonial wars often form a basis for contemporary Chinese claims to sovereignty. What is a mystery is how China today decides which of its previous foreign rulers' subordinate territories to claim and which not to claim.

The broad tenor of Qing society had been set during previous dynasties. The emphasis was on order over innovation, stability over development. The country was large and populous even then and rulers chose to prioritise control over experimentation. Little changed over the decades, and at the end of the eighteenth century society was still largely agrarian, with pockets of industry and banking.[26] Overseas travel was discouraged, although regional maritime trade blossomed, and the sale to Europe of tea, porcelain and lacquer goods is estimated to have led to half of all the silver shipped from Mexico and South America to Europe between 1600 and 1800 going on to China.[27] It has been noted that 'in the 1840s more tonnage passed through the port of Shanghai' than through the port of London.[28] Life expectancy of a Chinese at birth was 28 and at ten was 42.[29] Socially and politically there was quiescence. The Qing and Chinese inheritance customs discouraged manorial estates, and the Qing instituted a system of generational degradation of aristocratic rank that avoided the rise of a hereditary Chinese aristocracy independent of the throne.[30]

Distrust of strong and independent private interests is not just a communist characteristic; it is often the hallmark of proponents of the mighty state –

imperial, Napoleonic or Marxist. The Qing justice system resembled post-1949 China: there was no independent judiciary, torture was practised and confession generally preceded trial. Magistrates were judge and jury.[31]

Features of Foreign Rule

There are certain recurring features of foreign dynastic rule in China from Kitan in the tenth century to Qing in the twentieth. For instance, there was a tendency to exclude or restrict Han in government. The Jin would employ Han, but normally only if they had served the Kitan empire. The Mongols, plagued by illiteracy, employed West Asians – 'Uighur Turks', Arabs and even some Europeans – and Chinese who had served the foreign Jin dynasty, but carefully avoided using southern Chinese from the Song state who might have had independent interests.[32] (The southern gentry were in any case unenthusiastic about serving a foreign regime.)

When the old civil service examinations were resumed by the Mongols in 1315, the Chinese were treated differently: they constituted most of the successful candidates but were appointed to minor posts in offices of no importance. In all cases, the occupiers were far less numerous than the indigenous Han, and yet the foreign rulers maintained their reign for prolonged periods. The Chinese gentry tended to spend their lives in literary pursuits out of public life (rather like the nineteenth-century *émigration intérieure* of the French aristocracy). Probably the only benefit of this is that we have more scholarly works than if the authors had been engaged in government.

The dynasties naturally wished to maintain the use of their own language alongside Chinese. In Qing times, 'much important documentation was in Manchu.'[33] However, there were strains owing to the sheer weight of literature in Chinese as opposed to, say, the Tungusic languages, such as Manchu. 'Eventually the formula was to have capable Chinese do the work and loyal Manchus check up on them.'[34] The occupying and occupied races were treated differently: Manchu males were not allowed to marry Chinese women, and strict segregation was enforced between the victorious 'banner people' – Manchu, Mongol and descendants of pre-1644 Chinese adherents – and the defeated Chinese.

When the Qing forces captured the Ming capital [Beijing] in the seventeenth century, they expelled all of the residents of the Inner City, which they took over entirely for their own people, and they relegated the Han and other non-banner people to the old walled addition to the south known as the Outer (or 'Chinese') City.[35]

Domestic Thought

For most of China's history until 1911, it was under the influence of Confucianism, with an admixture of Daoism, Legalism and Buddhism. This intellectual regime discouraged commerce and technology, but also critical thinking. The Sinitic world has been compared with Marxism–Leninism in its disdain for objectivity. Similarly, the predominant absence of religion in the culture led to a utopian interest in realising heaven upon earth. Indeed, the neo-Confucian Wang Anshi in the eleventh century was an inspiration to the French utopian socialists, who in turn inspired Karl Marx. The Qing followed the Ming and the Yuan in denigrating commerce. While arguably demonstrating a certain moral superiority, Confucian China suffered a decided technological weakness.

Waking up to a Buffet Breakfast

Modern China originates in the years running up to 1800. For almost four hundred years – since the Ming closed the doors on the outside world – China had existed as a largely inward-focused culture, generally ignoring the developments shaping Europe and North America. Under this placid surface, however, social and economic problems were simmering. After a period of sharply falling population, birth rates were again rising and putting pressure on land-holding and crop production. The population trebled to about 300 million in the century and a half between the Qing victory and 1800.[36] Meanwhile, plots of land were small and were regularly subdivided for inheritance. As well as their immediate devastating effects, famines led to rising female infanticide and a consequent increase in embittered unmarried males (a recurring theme in Chinese history right up to the present day).

By the latter years of the eighteenth century, there was rising concern about the underpinnings of the state. The Wang Lun rebellion of 1774, frequently ascribed to the White Lotus sect – 'a Buddhist millenarian lay sect'[37] – caused shock, as did other rebellions, such as those of the Muslims in Gansu and the Miao tribe in the south-west.[38] An expedition to Vietnam to restore the ruling Le family was defeated. The nineteenth century also started badly with an increasingly serious revolt, again by the White Lotus Society. Secret societies had participated in most peasant risings, right back to the Yellow Turbans in the second century,[39] but the White Lotus seems to have been particularly prominent throughout much of Chinese history.[40] The founder of the Ming dynasty in the fourteenth century is said to have been an associate, as possibly were the Boxers in the twentieth.[41] The White Lotus was an avowedly racial group (and at this time specifically anti-Manchu).[42] They used the slogan 'To restore the Han and annihilate the Manchus'.[43] The rebellion became a serious challenge in 1799, when it beat an imperial force. Eventually, the imperial army ended the insurrection in 1804, but real damage had been done: it heralded the end of Manchu military dominance and the sense of Qing invincibility.

After a long sleep of several decades, Imperial China woke up in 1800 to find it had become old and weak. Various attempts to invigorate and rebuild the dynasty during the 1800s failed, and throughout the century calamity followed disaster: famine, domestic revolt and, once again, foreign incursion – this time by the Europeans. The century from the 1840s to the 1940s was to be an embarrassment for China (or, as the Chinese put it, a 'humiliation'), but the serious damage had already been wrought.

The First Opium War began in 1839. By 1842 China had been defeated and the Nanjing Treaty opened up coastal treaty ports for foreigners to trade and ceded Hong Kong to Britain. In 1844, America and France secured similar agreements with China. While the Empire was dealing with foreign commercial demands, there was a growing storm in the interior. The Taiping movement drew strongly on Protestant Christian elements, but it transformed itself from a purely religious force into a combined ethnic, religious and military rebellion, which swept across central China.[44] Fighting lasted from 1850 until the mid-1860s, and with an estimated death toll of between 20 and 30 million, the Taiping rebellion has been described as the world's bloodiest civil war of the last thousand years. The Taiping was the largest but not the only domestic distraction for the Qing. Almost simultaneously, there were Muslim rebellions in Yunnan in the south-west, and in Xinjiang in the north-west. There was also the Nien rebellion, which featured angry youths unable to find wives owing to the famine-induced gender imbalance. These and smaller revolts collectively occupied much of the imperial military between the 1840s and the 1870s. This combination alone would have kept the Qing distracted until the late 1870s – even without the Second Opium War.

From 1856 until victory in 1860, Anglo-French forces waged war on Qing China in what is also known as the Second Anglo-Chinese War. The Chinese imperial troops were still largely Manchus (though from the late eighteenth century it appears that the Manchu warriors gradually lost their martial vigour, so increasingly the Empire had to ask Chinese officers to take over). Presumably drawing no distinction between an English alien and a Manchu one, the Chinese helped both sides: one Chinese governor rented campsites to the British forces and another sold them mules.[45]

One irony of the Second Anglo-Chinese War was that, before it was over, in August 1860, Britain was in alliance with the Empire against the Taiping in southern China, even as it was fighting the Empire in the north,[46] and indeed a

British officer, General Gordon, led the 'Ever-Victorious Army' – a unit of imperial forces which contributed to the smashing of the Taiping rebellion.[47] After the 1860 Anglo-French victory, the Treaty of Beijing awarded 3.75 square miles of Kowloon and Stonecutters Island to Britain, property-purchase rights to French priests and additional indemnities beyond those from the first war. However, the surprise winner was Russia, which arrived in a quasi-mediatorial role and left with confirmation of its de facto occupation of 300,000 square miles of the old Manchu province of East Tartary (which now embrace the cities of Khabarovsk and Vladivostok).

It is paradoxical and somewhat puzzling that China should have inveighed so much against the 'unequal treaty' of Nanjing and the cession of Hong Kong and 3 square miles of Kowloon to Britain, and yet complained so little about this massive concession to Russia. Mao made an issue of the lost lands in the 1960s. Deng merely mentioned it to Gorbachev in 1989. The Tahcheng Protocol of 1864 ceded another 167,000 square miles around Lake Balkhash to Russia, and in 1871 Russia invaded the Yili district of Turkestan. The Treaty of St Petersburg with Russia in 1881 did return part of the Yili district, but caused China to lose a net 20,000 square miles there, in what is now Kazakhstan, and confirmed the cession of the Lake Balkhash territory.

In 1879 Japan took the Ryukyu Islands, and in 1884 France sank an entire Chinese fleet in a sovereignty dispute over Vietnam. In 1885, Britain assumed control over Burma, which had previously acknowledged Chinese suzerainty. In 1894 Japan started infiltrating Qing territory and appointed a regent in the Kingdom of Korea, the northern part of which had been under China during the Han dynasty (207 BC–AD 220) and even the Yuan dynasty. The 1894–95 Sino-Japanese War ended with the Treaty of Shimonoseki, which ceded Taiwan, part of Manchuria and four more ports, including Chongqing, way up the Yangtze. In 1898–99 there was a further round of foreign encroachment, through the granting of leases: Britain at Weihaiwei and expanding in Hong Kong; France in south-western China; Russia in Manchuria; and Japan in a number of areas. China's internal and external sovereignty was crumbling.

The late 1890s witnessed the violent Boxer rising. Academics dispute the movement's intentions but it probably originated in a hatred for foreign missionary activity in northern China, increasingly permitted through the treaty conditions imposed on the Qing. Dowager Empress Cixi ultimately declared support for the Boxers and war on the foreigners in 1900. China's subsequent defeat led to the 'Boxer Protocol' of 1901, which included the granting of first-time concessions in Tianjin to Austria-Hungary, Italy and later Belgium. It seems extraordinary today to think that Italy, which then lacked even fifty years' history as a country, could gain a piece of China.

While serial foreign military incursions shredded China's territorial integrity and rebellions caused internal disruption, natural disasters also took their toll.[48] The first half of the nineteenth century witnessed four famines, with a possible death toll of 45 million. The middle of the century saw more natural disasters, coinciding with the Taiping and other revolts: in 1853, the Yellow River burst its banks (and yet again changed course, this time by 500 miles);[49] the drought and famine in 1876–79 claimed around 10 million lives; and floods in 1887 killed another million. The century ended with the 1896–97 famine. It is estimated that between 1820 and 1890 there was no net population growth, and that the economy actually contracted.[50]

There is a myth that modern Chinese nationalism was born with the May 4th Movement in 1919. However, from at least 1901 there was a series of popular protests, generally led by students. They opposed the Russian occupation of Manchuria, American immigration laws felt to be anti-Chinese, French aggression in southern China and opium availability, and they supported domestic reforms.[51] The 1905 anti-American campaign, in particular, was virulent and employed many modern methods of agitation.[52]

Even after two centuries of Qing rule, native Han antipathy to the Manchu had not waned, and in fact became stronger after 1840.[53] The Taiping leader Hong Xiuquan rose up against the 'alien' Qing rulers,[54] as did the Nien.[55] The Boxers, too, were originally anti-Manchu.[56] Organised opposition to the Manchu started with the formation by Sun Yat-sen of the Xingzhonghui organisation in Honolulu in 1894 and in Hong Kong in 1895. The three bedrock objectives were clear: 'Expelling the Manchus, restoring China to the Chinese, and creating a republic.'[57] Expelling the Manchus and reverting to Chinese self-rule were central themes to the Xingzhonghui and its successor the Tongmenghui. Between 1900 and 1905, those who were opposed to the Qing shifted from sullen unhappiness to active plotting.

But the original opposition of secret societies and Christian activists, coordinated by Sun Yat-sen, did not have sufficient traction. The opposition's real opportunity came when intellectuals participated. The Qing late reform drive encouraged education and sent students to Japan, but these same students soon engaged in dissident activity. Overseas Chinese students played a leading part in the anti-Qing movement, particularly in Japan. In 1904, Sun Yat-sen gave several speeches in San Francisco 'on the issue of the Han (Chinese) people versus the Manchu race.'[58] Sun declared that 'the Han people should be loyal to China and not to the Ch'ing government.' Huan Xing, one of the leading revolutionaries, believed they were fighting for a 'racial revolution' (i.e. Han versus Manchu).[59] The revolutionaries grumbled that Chinese people were not developing patriotism, nationalism or xenophobia, and thus were not feeling and thinking like a nation. It is, of course, quite understandable why such traits were not inculcated – for the very same reason as they were not encouraged in the contemporaneous Austro-Hungarian Empire. These were multiracial empires which did not wish to encourage – indeed would have been mortally threatened by – any racial or nationalist thinking. The revolutionaries' goals were clear: to expel the alien Manchus and establish rule over China by Han people. As there was no Ming claimant, a republic would be required, but this was of secondary importance.

Historians have suggested that the late attempts to strengthen the Qing state could have been successful and that the state was not as closed to external technology and ideas as is commonly stated. For example, the Qing took a great interest in the suffering of Chinese indentured labourers overseas: a study of labour conditions in Cuba in 1873–74 led directly to the opening of a consulate in Havana.[60] There is a notion that the Qing 'bid for survival' nearly succeeded, but this seems like rosy revisionism. In fact, the Qing was probably doomed from the first half of the 1800s – not because it was not a market-driven state built on universal suffrage (rather an anachronism), but because the Empire was incessantly assailed by forces that it was unable to dispel. Its economy was damaged, its social compact fractured, its political credibility eroded and most inhabitants felt no affection for Qing rule. However, China was not a closed and backward society or economy. In the late nineteenth century it was very open to new ideas and products.[61]

The 'Sinicisation' Argument

A gloss is often put on the centuries of foreign occupation. As the Mongols or Manchus were not obviously Han, the next-best tactic has been to suggest that they were 'sinicised' after decades of living in China. Some claim the foreign emperors became sinicised because they employed the Chinese language to promulgate laws or for communication involving Han officials. It is also noted that they often adopted a Confucian world-view and appreciated Chinese art and craftsmanship.[62] However, language is merely a tool of rule and objects are simply loot. We cannot judge the rulers' disposition from an inclination to accept the parallel use of Chinese or to own Chinese objects. When Germany invaded France in the Second World War, it did not abolish all French laws, nor did it insist on the sole use of the German language. The German occupiers also took French paintings. However, no one has claimed that the invaders became 'gallicised'.

The convenient theory of sinicisation is undermined by a series of facts: for example, the failure to use Han officials in central government proportionately to their share of the population; the Yuan dynasty's predominant use of non-Han as officials; the Qing laws against intermarriage which existed right up until 1902; the fact that many important documents were written in Manchu throughout the Qing dynasty; the call by Sun Yat-sen's colleagues in the 1900s for a 'racial revolution' against the Qing. There are 10 million items written in Manchu in the Qing archives, about a fifth of the total, and 'the picture of the Qing that emerges when one has access to Manchu sources differs markedly from the one drawn from Chinese sources'.[63] The Han generally disliked their foreign rulers. This was as true after 250 years as it was after one year: the anti-Manchu bloodshed in 1911 demonstrates that. The new foreign governing elites each time borrowed from Confucian thinking and classical imperial practice; however, this was not because the rulers were becoming sinicised but because these were conveniently neutral tools, which promoted order and control. The foreign rulers and their Han court intellectuals would maintain that such non-Han dynasties could foster the Confucian culture of China and this was because that culture is essentially *déraciné*, not nationalist. Indeed the Song emphasis on the universal nature of their values and beliefs only assisted in their dispersion. If and when needed, there were always Han intellectuals who would serve the foreign master, and neo-Confucian thought assisted this by encouraging harmony, hierarchy and submission to authority. The Jin established the intellectual basis for a multiracial empire, which was developed further by the Qing. In certain respects the Qing in the eighteenth and nineteenth centuries were wrestling with the same kind of issues as the contemporary Habsburgs in justifying a multi-ethnic empire during the rise of the nation state. The Qing both assumed the role of wise Confucian ruler and at the same time patronised Lamaist Buddhism.[64]

'Inhabiting multiple cultural worlds was no novel thing to the Manchu Qing rulers . . . and it is well known that the Qianlong Emperor opted to have himself represented in portraiture variously as a Confucian scholar, Daoist adept, Tibetan Buddhist Bodhisattva, patron of Islam, and Western science enthusiast.'[65] They were aware that theirs was a multicultural state and they thus had different constituencies.

Second-millennium China was like St Andrews or Wimbledon. It supplied many of the rules and processes of government, sometimes the officials and the ground on which rulers competed, but it offered few champions, or rulers, itself.

The Han Position in China

The Kitan from Inner Mongolia are believed by many scholars to have lent their name to the word Cathay. One of China's ambiguities – both a positive and a negative – is that the Chinese name for China – *zhongguo* – means 'Middle Kingdom' or central country. There is nothing to mark it as belonging to any particular race; it is not, for example, called 'Land of the Han'. 'China' does not denote a nation state based upon Han ethnicity; it is, to use the language of Metternich, simply a geographical expression. It has been the name of the country or empire of whoever was ruling at the time, regardless of ethnicity.

When threatened by the foreign Jin dynasty, Li Quan, the Shandong bandit leader, said, 'I'd rather be a southern Chinese ghost than serve as a Jin official.' During the Yuan dynasty, we are told, the Mongols were despised: 'Chinese liked to say that they stank so that you could smell them downwind.'[66] In the Qing period foreign observers noted that 'in China under the Manchus Chinese scholars might hate Qing rule but leave no record of the fact.'[67] The British Consul General in Hankow (now Wuhan) said an official 'hates the Manchus as do all Chinese officials I have met'.[68]

Although the relationship was rebarbative, at least seen from below, there was cooperation more than resistance under occupation (as was also the case during the Second World War in France or in the second half of the twentieth century in Soviet-occupied Eastern Europe). That the Qing were non-Han might account for the particularly violent insurrections that they faced compared with the rebellions during the preceding Ming dynasty. However, the argument shouldn't be exaggerated. The Ming downfall was, practically, engendered by a peasant rising.

The Manchu–Han Relationship

Like the Jin and the Yuan, the Qing dynasty acted as an occupying power. Right up until 1912, the Manchu, with some other racial minorities – the 'banner people' – were treated as a hereditary military caste. They received government stipends and did not work, though they were allowed to be officials and sometimes farmers; instead their duty was to fight for the dynasty, although (as noted above) these warriors gradually lost their effectiveness and had to rely on Han recruits. The Manchu lived in separate garrisons or 'Manchu cities', spacious and calm, while the Han were strictly segregated and there were restrictions governing acquisition by them of land from Manchus. Even after 1900 they were still excluded from certain parts of Manchuria, which were reserved for the Manchu.[69]

A system of dyarchy meant that, for most important national bodies, there were two top officials, a Manchu and a Han. Considering that the Manchu made up only 1–3 per cent of the population during the dynasty, the system of joint government, which lasted almost to the end, led to the Manchu being disproportionately represented in official posts. From 1906, the dyarchy was restructured, supposedly to ensure greater equality, but eight of the top thirteen posts went to Manchu and other banner people of the 'conquest elite'. In the regions it was different: governors and even the powerful Governors-General (who were lower in the hierarchy than the Beijing officials) were mostly Han. The conquest dynasties established by non-Han people, ethnic background of consorts was also emphasized to maintain the ethnic purity of the ruling house.[70]

As the Qing limited the number of Chinese who could become officials and restricted intermarriage, the latter were subordinate in their own land. The Chinese were obliged to adopt the Manchu hairstyle, or queue (which was widely resented), and Chinese officials were pressured to adopt Manchu costume. There were two attempts to change Manchu–Han relations by imperial edict – in 1865 and in 1898 – but neither was enforced. The latter was doomed by the palace coup of the Dowager Empress Cixi in September 1898. Although Cixi did eventually announce reforms in 1901, the electoral changes did not take effect before the dynasty fell. (The result of the national elections, aborted owing to the revolution of 1911, would have been interesting.)[71] It was widely believed that Associate Grand Secretary Gangyi had said, at the time of Cixi's coup, that he would rather hand the Empire over to 'neighbouring friends' than to 'household slaves'[72] – a glimpse of how the Manchu were believed to view the Chinese.

Reflections on the Legacy of Occupation

The long foreign rule over China was not perceived by the Han as self-rule: it had a lasting effect on the Chinese psyche and on Chinese interaction with foreigners, and probably strengthened nationalistic feeling and militarist sentiment. The Han character has been scarred by the occupation centuries. The noted writer Lu Xun in the early 1900s said that foreign occupation had caused the Chinese to lack honesty and integrity.[73] The origins of modern Chinese nationalism lie not in the hated '100 years of humiliation' at the hands of the West, but rather in the thousand years of humiliation of having rulers who originated – ethnically and geographically – from outside China. That the foreigners were seen as uncultured barbarians made matters worse. These centuries of subservience heighten China's emotional attitude towards sovereignty issues. What China holds and what it claims are of such importance because of the regular emasculation of its sovereignty over a thousand years. This is neither surprising nor reprehensible, but problems arise when this emotion clashes with modern ideas such as self-determination.

A schizophrenia exists in Han culture that can both deplore the victorious invasions of China by the Manchu and the Mongol Khubilai Khan, and then vicariously exult in their subsequent external military victories. It is odd that

today's Chinese desire to retain non-Han peoples and their lands stems from
conquests by non-Han rulers of China.

Republic Replaces Empire

After the disastrous and destabilising floods of 1910 and 1911, the Republic
finally replaced the Empire in 1912. It is suggested that the Qing dynasty
collapsed through internal decay and lack of support, but it was not that simple.
There was a wave of anti-Manchu violence, including genocidal slaughters in
Manchu garrison towns. In Wuchang in October 1911, for example, four
leading Manchu families were slaughtered. A brief counter-attack by loyalists
was followed by a purge of surviving Manchu. The Hubei revolutionary government declared that the Manchu 'have seized our lands and taken away our
rights. Now in order to seek our revenge, we rightly ought to exterminate them
with all our might.' On formation, this radical administration announced its
objective to 'elevate the Han and exterminate the Manchus'.[74]

Again in October, Xi'an's Manchu city fell. According to a British missionary,
'Old and young, men and women, little children, were alike butchered.'[75] One
of the most horrifying incidents was the Nanjing massacre of December 1911:
the Manchu city was razed and it is said the killings were 'incalculable'. A
visiting French scholar found that 'not one stone is left standing'. It didn't
matter if Manchus had been reformers or conservatives: race was what
mattered, even after 260 years of so-called 'sinicisation'.

The 1911 rising was more about race than form of government. This
is emphasised by the sudden disappearance of many Manchus after 1912.
It wasn't that they had all left the country or been exterminated, but that,
even though bannermen's stipends were still being paid into the late 1920s,
discrimination and fear caused them to assimilate. The reported size of the
community and the use of spoken Manchu therefore did not increase to reflect
population growth in the following century. Moreover, many Manchus suffered
appallingly during the Cultural Revolution and were treated as 'spies'.[76] By
2007, it was estimated that barely a hundred people still spoke Manchu.[77]
Nonetheless they were by 2010 frequently the objects of merciless attack by
Han nationalists using such expressions as the Manchus are 'the Jews of China'.[78]

In 1912 the Tongmenghui merged with other groups to form the
Guomindang, with Sun Yat-sen as its leader. The new government was led by
Yuan Shikai, a former Qing general, who subsequently spent much of his time
suppressing the Guomindang. Sun had to flee China, and Yuan tried to make
himself Emperor before he died in 1916. Subsequently, China experienced the
rule of competing warlords until 1928, when Chiang Kai-shek, Sun's successor

as leader of the Guomindang, managed to unite significant parts of the country and strike alliances with warlords ruling other parts.

Although China had been among the victors in the First World War, it did not benefit; at Versailles in 1919 it was revealed that its government had privately agreed a further territorial concession to reward Japan for joining the war. This caused student anti-government protests on 4 May 1919. The May 4th Movement has influenced subsequent Chinese history: governments try to avoid being judged as weak in confronting challenges to national honour, lest they be taken to task in the streets by patriotic students. Hence government caution since the 1990s towards popular protests over perceived slights to national pride by Japan, Taiwan or America.

One criticism of the republic was that it did not jettison sovereignty over the non-Han lands. This was a clear opportunity to create a modern and united Han nation state. Turkey went in this direction after its defeat in the First World War and built a successful nation state around Turkish race, language and religion.[79] In China's case, some territories did depart, but there was no clearly thought-out plan. Tuva and Mongolia broke away. Although the Chinese governed Tuva again in 1920–21, it is not now claimed. Confusingly, Manchuria was retained: this was the last stop on the Manchu road south from their ancestral lands, and much of Manchuria had been technically closed to Han residents until 1907. And yet it was retained by China on the dissolution of the Qing empire.[80] In fact, from 1895 until 1905 Manchuria was substantially under Russian occupation; after that, Japanese influence gradually increased.[81]

Today, accordingly, China's borders contain an uneasy amalgam of Han and certain ethnic groups conquered at various times, but not others. The minorities are castaways, stranded as the imperial tide receded: the Uighurs and Tibetans are in, but most Koreans, the Burmese and the Vietnamese are out. There is no obvious logic to today's mix. Modern China's borders are the result of accident, rather than principle or logic.

There is a consensus that in 1912 a worn-out dynasty was replaced by a corrupt and inefficient Nationalist republic, which would inevitably, in its turn, fall to a vigorous proletarian revolutionary Communist movement, strong enough to purge, unify and clean up the country. It sounds crisp and clear, but this linear and quasi-Marxist interpretation of history is being challenged. The nationalist Guomindang, although active in rebellions against the Qing, didn't gain power until 1928. As a modern ideological force, the Nationalists had a powerful relationship with the Soviet Union, on whose Communist Party they modelled their party discipline. Indeed they were seen by many as Bolsheviks, and their chief adviser was the rather sinister Soviet representative, Mikhail Borodin (whose wife was believed to be related to the Hollywood comedian

Buster Keaton).[82] In fact Barlow, the deputy chief manager of the Hong Kong and Shanghai Bank, wrote in 1924: 'I cannot think that Bolshevism will ever take great hold in China . . . Sun [Yat-sen] himself dare not put his Bolshevist theories into practice'.[83] The British Foreign Office also called the Guomindang Bolshevists until it embarked on rapprochement in 1927.[84]

The 1911 revolution enhanced the continuing opening up to ideas, trade and foreign investment. By 1949, this powerful trend, which began under the Qing and continued throughout the Nationalist Republican period, had made China's economy and society one of the world's more open.[85] The absence of strong and stable government between 1911 and 1949 underlines the fact that economic and social progress don't require a strong state but merely the absence of legislative malice: the open society of the Republic existed not because of any ideological drive towards openness but because there was no desire to be closed. Foreign ideas and foreign-invented products permeated the country, both in the coastal cities and in the rural heartland. In the 1940s one could buy suits, hats and shoes of foreign design in remote villages in the interior.[86] China did not just import them: if they were thought useful, entrepreneurs would manufacture them. There was a proliferation of schools and non-governmental societies, creating a rich social fabric. A westerner, in 1945, made the observation: 'Crooked and narrow ways and winding, evil-smelling alleys are swallowed up in the fine straight roads, so that a traveller returning after a few months' absence can scarcely find his home.' [87] This observation will be familiar to anyone who has regularly visited Beijing or Shanghai in recent decades.

The presence on Chinese soil of foreign concessions where China's laws and sovereignty did not apply was widely deplored, but they did provide considerable social and economic benefits:

> With hindsight, the emergence of huge complex international concessions in Shanghai and Tianjin within less than a century must have constituted the largest cultural transfer in human history, comparable to the transplantation of whole metropoles from Europe to China, from skyscrapers and department stores down to pavement slabs and sash windows, and it is unlikely that such transfer could have taken place, at least initially, without the extraterritorial rights allowing business to be conducted outside of the jurisdiction of native authorities.[88]

In retrospect, there is an impression that Nationalist China was an economic playpen for foreigners. However, research suggests that by 1933 foreign interests were responsible for only 2.5 per cent of economic output (GDP).[89] Chinese banks pressed the foreign banks hard.[90]

Businessmen salivate over books published today on how to tap a billion customers in China. But the 1938 book *400 Million Customers* evoked the same excitement and had the same themes.[91] Although the economy may have experienced slow growth between 1911 and 1936, presumably because it had such a large agricultural component, what is striking is the investment in gross domestic fixed capital formation (GDFCF) – capital investment in creating the building blocks of a modern economy. The share of GDFCF in annual economic output rose in the period, from under 1 per cent to almost 4 per cent.[92] By 1952, it had passed 10 per cent.[93] This indicates rapid modernisation throughout the Republican period and across the industrial base – from transport to textiles. 'The economy was not "stagnant" or "regressing" from 1870 to 1930 but steadily growing and thriving, even in the countryside.'[94] Despite all the uncertainties from the 1920s to the 1940s, the modern economy was being born.

The Republican diplomats Wellington Koo and Alfred Sze got the Japanese to leave their Shandong concession in 1921–22 and the British to cede extraterritoriality in Hankou and Jiujiang in 1927 and to return Weihaiwei in 1930.[95] Furthermore, the Nationalist government pushed hard to recover the other foreign concessions and made considerable progress. Britain and America both relinquished extraterritoriality in 1943. In 1925 the Guomindang government coordinated anti-British strikes and boycotts in Guangzhou,[96] and in the 1930s they successfully faced down the British banks.[97] The Nationalists thus honoured their name and pursued nationalist policies.

What is, however, true is that rural life was miserable through incessant natural calamity. The years 1928, 1931, 1936 and 1941 brought a succession of droughts, floods and famine, with an average death toll of 3.5 million each time. The first decade of Guomindang government is credited with reasonably prudent monetary policy, compared with the preceding early Republican era and the late Qing.[98] However, this was succeeded by catastrophic wartime inflation. 'From 1937 to 1941 retail prices rose 15-fold in Shanghai and 37-fold in Chungking [Chongqing]. At the end of the war prices were 2,500 times as high as in 1937 in Chungking.'[99] The scale is disputed, but scholars agree that inflation undermined the Republic. However, equally we can say that bad money weakened the Song, the Yuan, the Ming and the Qing; in other words, it has been a problem for more than a millennium.[100] Like the Qing dynasty, the Nationalist government in the 1930s and 1940s had to contend simultaneously with natural disasters, a foreign invasion and a domestic insurrection. These led to measures which engendered inflation.

China endured 'incidents' with Japan from 1928 until 1937, at which point war began. Many Chinese Communist Party supporters were not communist, but were patriotic and disillusioned with the Nationalists, who seemed uncertain whether to defend the country against the invasion or quell the insurrection. By standing back and allowing the Nationalists to be the principal anti-Japanese force, the Communists ensured a weak Nationalist military capability by 1945. The government was successfully demonised as unable to prioritise national interests.

One comparison of the governments before and after 1949 is that:

> The sufferings of the people after 1911 occurred despite the post-revolutionary governments, but the sufferings under Communist leadership were the direct result of policies devised by the party or its top leader ... The other basic difference was that the 1911 revolution intended to deliver democracy to China, but it failed, whereas the 1949 revolution never intended to bring about democratisation.[101]

Not everyone will agree that the Kuomintang really planned democracy either, but the view is an interesting one.

The Guomindang, or Nationalist, period produced some great successes: foreign concessions were regained and extraterritoriality terminated; there were some important improvements in public health;[102] an open economy was maintained through great difficulties; and the base was laid for the modern economy. In fact it was a subtle policy success to reduce foreign concessions and still maintain a fully open economy and society. That the Nationalists nonetheless lost the civil war is a fact permanently lodged in the mind of the CCP as it apprehensively plans its future strategy.

The 1912–49 Republican era has been distorted, with the bad features aggravated and the good ignored. However, with appalling natural disasters, the Japanese war, and a Communist insurrection, stable government was not easy. Every revolutionary movement, whether of the Left or the Right, requires its mythology, and the CCP version was certainly powerful. This served it well in the revolutionary war and in the decades following victory. Whatever the real performance of the Nationalist Republic, the CCP indisputably won the propaganda war. Its interpretation and its case dominated, paved the way to victory and is the received view today.

The Rural Revolution

History tends to focus on conquered cities, and particularly capital cities – national control is regarded as changing hands when the capital is seized. But during the 1940s much was going on in China's rural areas. And developments were occurring at different times in different regions. There may have been a Nationalist Republic until 1949, when Beijing (and the Nationalist capital of Nanjing) fell to the Communists, but the Communist Party had been reorganising production methods much earlier in large parts of rural China, particularly in the north – and even behind Japanese lines.

There are many misconceptions about farming conditions before 1949. One important point is that there had been a steady fall in land per capita ever since the eleventh century. Given patchy trends in yield, this meant a steady reduction in crop production per capita.[103] 'Most farms were very small and few were more than twice the average. Tenants were not generally much poorer than owners.'[104] The standard of living on farms had progressively increased from 1870 until the early 1930s.[105] The 1930–35 world depression caused serious problems in China, but fortunately was not as steep or prolonged as in America.

From 1937, the Japanese War damaged rural communities. For many peasants it could be said that the years from the early 1940s until the early 1950s constituted a quiet period, in which they were in practice under local Communist authority but were left alone by the Party to manage their own lives. Between 1943 and 1953 many cooperative farms were created. In Communist-held China, early efforts prioritised voluntary participation in cooperative farming. Such farms were managed by the participants along market economy lines, had many profitable sidelines to boost income, and were governed through internally driven and fully democratic processes. People on successful cooperatives lived better than those on unsuccessful ones. But from 1953, the authorities imposed compulsory collective and communal farming, and market-related elements were progressively squeezed out. Successful units had to share their success with unsuccessful units, sideline activities were discouraged, decision-making was by external officials and, most important of all, participation became mandatory. Much of Communist China was like Imperial China, but with more precise, logical and zealous implementation – for example, the inward-looking character of the Ming, the communal revenue-sharing of the Qing or the *hukou* system of household registration, which requires people to live where they were born and has its roots in the early dynasties.

Documents and eyewitness accounts of China's momentous rural development between 1940 and 2000 offer valuable – albeit inevitably differing – insights. At one end of the spectrum is the unambiguously titled study, 'The State's Revolutionary War on Tillers'.[106] An opposing view comes from the expatriate academic Gao Mobo who, drawing on youthful memories, depicts the Mao era as a quasi-Aboriginal dreamtime where all was wonderful. The year 1953 was a critical date when the grain market was nationalised and thus peasants were obliged to sell at artificially low prices – a recurring theme. Membership of cooperatives was enforced and then collectives became mandatory with no voluntary departure permitted.

> . . . It became clear early on that the collectives were not intended as a means of achieving higher standards of living but as a way for the state to extract ever more wealth from the rural sector in order to finance urban industrial development . . . in reality the peasants were not demanding collectives and the collectivization drive represented an intensification of the war on peasants . . . initiated in 1953 with the nationalization of the grain market. Mao was treating peasants like enemies, not like the allies who had brought him to power.[107]

There are clear similarities between how Mao treated the peasants in the 1950s and how Stalin treated the Russian peasants in the 1930s.

After scrapping the cooperatives by compulsorily introducing the collectives and communal farming in the 1950s, in the late 1970s it was decided that the system was rotten. The compulsory communes were abandoned in favour of the 'household responsibility system' of private contractual farming. Many rural commentators felt that the cooperative system had worked in the late 1940s and early 1950s, but had been needlessly terminated for ideological reasons, and that in the late 1970s and 1980s there was another ideological move away from any form of cooperation. This reinforced the belief that the urban state made decisions about rural life with no consultation and little knowledge. However, the World Bank said in 2009 that introducing the household responsibility system 'was arguably the single most important reason for the rapid decline in poverty China experienced in the first half of the 1980s'.[108]

The early cooperatives had nurtured rural democratic decision-making, rather than top-down diktats, and this could have laid the foundations for political reform. But as one academic who spent thirty years studying rural life in China, says:

> Mao was the commander in chief of the war on peasants, that is, the relentless campaign to squeeze as much as possible out of the rural economy to fund urban industrialization and to maintain peasant consumption at bare subsistence levels – or worse.[109]

Virtually throughout the history of the People's Republic, 'a critical protest voice was being expressed by peasants'.[110] There was a 'war waged on local rural communities by the socialist state and socialist state-imposed collectives'[111] and 'an uninterrupted war waged by contemptuous urban bureaucrats on

hardworking rural people who sought only to raise their standards of living.'
Even following what many regard as the successful transition to private farming
in China after 1979, 'tensions between state and village in the early twenty first
century are shockingly explosive.'[112] While this might seem to be extreme in the
sedate environment of China forty years after the Cultural Revolution, one
should note this 2013 report on land expropriation:

> Zheng Enchong [said] 'Every year, China's farmers lose at least 2 trillion yuan
> worth of land and 20 million urban residents are forced into poverty by
> having their homes demolished and being forced to move. China is worse
> than the Soviet Union. Through these violent seizures of land and homes,
> the ruling party has lost the hearts of the people, even more than through
> its handling of [the Tiananmen Square crackdown of] June 4 and of
> Falun Gong,' he said.[113]

Few would seriously challenge the view that urban areas subsidise rural
areas; indeed, many maintain the reverse. And state media show that violent
mass incidents are rife in the countryside.

There is a more cautious view of the interaction of peasants and the
state. This suggests that from the beginning they resisted state coercion,
initially using methods that had been employed in the pre-Communist era.
Later, those who had become familiar with the new ways, such as Party
members, doctors, teachers and former soldiers, used the state's own weapons
against it to protect their interests.

There is an entrenched view that all dynasties have fallen to peasant
insurrection and thus government must control the rural population.
Furthermore, 'the evidence of history indicates that no vigorous agrarian
movement takes place unless the owners of the land have turned to living in
cities and their way of living has become urbanized.'[114] This development
became increasingly evident amongst intellectuals in China after the post-1900
modernisations.[115]

An associated theme is that rural income is being depressed in order to
fund the urban and industrial economy. In 1994, the influential book *Looking
at China through a Third Eye* argued that China has financed its industries
by exploiting the peasantry, and that allowing peasants to farm their own
land without social and political controls, and to come to the cities as migrant
workers, was letting the genie out of the bottle.[116] The then 800 million
peasants were 'China's active volcano'. Mao's solution had been to chain them to
the land. To allow them to travel in droves over the landscape is a recipe for
chaos or 'social cataclysm'. When farmers leave the land and reach the towns,

crimes such as 'armed robberies' will multiply, and this will threaten the Party's authority. A 'mass assault of farmers on the cities' will be the result of five decades of 'discrimination against the countryside'. The book asserts that China has followed other socialist countries in capitalising its industry by disadvantaging its rural population through deliberate social neglect and underpayment. Li Ruogu, one of China's leading economic thinkers, openly supports this statement:

> Price scissors of industrial and agricultural products: due to the low foundation of the China economy, capital accumulation had to be realized by bringing down the prices of agricultural products. Of the value of 100 Yuan created by the agricultural sector, the portion transferred, through price mechanism, to the industrial and commercial sectors was 17.9Y in 1952, 23Y in 1957 and 25Y in 1978.[117]

There is even a strong belief that rural people are prone to defective behaviour – social, sexual and intellectual – and that this needs to be controlled.

China has gone from revolution won through the support of the farmers to what some call the state's war against the farmers and it has moved from notions of egalitarianism to a reality of fast cultural change and inequality. Rural China has been compared to a 'Third World' marked by traditional methods and values, underdeveloped and outdated. Urban China is fast becoming identified by town planning, technology and the consumer. There is a clear danger of two societies – as different as Europe and Africa – emerging with different endowments and different rights. The values appreciated today are not those encapsulated by the age-old considerations of rural life.

The Communist Victory

There are many different views of the years from 1949 until Mao's death in 1976. From the declared victory of the Communist Party until the end of the Cultural Revolution in 1976, it is variously estimated that well over 50 million died either deliberately or as collateral damage resulting from a succession of ruthlessly applied agricultural, industrial and ideological policies (leaving aside births which didn't happen): the counter-revolutionary and land reform purges from before 1949 into the 1950s; the series of 'anti-rightist' campaigns between 1957 and 1959; the economic 'Great Leap Forward' of 1958–61 (which is estimated to have resulted in up to 45 million deaths on its own).[118]

Furthermore, approximately 7 per cent of the deaths, over 3 million, were not accidental but clear cases of murder.[119] The 'Great Hunger' of 1959–61, which occurred in the midst of the Great Leap Forward, is blamed for 20–36 million government-inflicted deaths, caused by stubborn and cruelly unrealistic agricultural and industrial policies. Yang Jisheng, a reporter for the official Xinhua news agency, used access to official archives to calculate 36 million deaths: 'There was no war. No disease. The weather was quite normal. But 35 to 40 million people just disappeared.'[120] It is a source of some dispute whether nature played a part or if weather conditions were benign and the disaster wholly anthropogenic. President Liu Shao Qi, who later died in the Cultural Revolution, is quoted saying that it was 'three parts nature and seven parts man'.[121]

The situation was not helped by the fact that the authorities chose not to import significant amounts of grain until 1961, and it was exacerbated when they increased the proportion of the (diminished) harvest that they would appropriate – from 21 per cent in 1958 to 28 per cent in 1959.[122] Additionally, it has recently been suggested that perhaps 40 per cent of housing in rural China was destroyed during this period.[123] In a research paper in *China Rights Forum* magazine in September 2005 it is said that Mao was personally involved in these campaigns and even set 'killing quotas'.[124] One could argue that for most people in China the fifty years from the late 1920s to the late 1970s were a period of upheaval, fighting and the prospect of death. The only plausibly calm time for China as a whole might have been the decade from 1949 until the anti-rightist campaigns broke out; calm, that is, provided one was not from a land-holding family and was not seen as a 'counter-revolutionary', on which grounds significant numbers of Chinese people were executed.[125] The Western analysis of the whole three decades from 1949 is unremittingly bleak. It is redeemed only by a widely held view that what went before was institutionally corrupt and deserved to be swept away.

The 'secret speech' by Khrushchev in 1956 criticising Stalin's crimes led to the Sino-Soviet split, which laid the basis for the gradual Sino-American rapprochement. Mao stated that Khrushchev was on a wrong, revisionist, path. In 1969, China fought a localised war against the Soviet Union across the Amur-Ussuri River (with several hundred casualties). Soon after, in 1971, China and America established a relationship and gradually a common under-standing about circumscribing the hegemonism of the USSR. Despite China's subsequent opening up, espousal of legal rights and development of economic reform, the CCP cannot yet admit that Mao erred in this hostility to Soviet revision of communism. Perhaps too many of the founders of post-1978 China were implicated in his stand.

The official CCP view is that Mao went astray for about two decades – from the late 1950s until the late 1970s. This is a difficult view to articulate as – at the very least – it suggests that the Party was in error for around two-thirds of the period after its victory. Most Chinese statistics start from 1978, and there is an unspoken belief that society since then has been very different. Chinese officials appear to have no interest in defending pre-1979 history, providing direct criticism of the Party and the mythology of the 1949 Revolution is avoided. Eventually history will regard the three decades of Mao in 'New China' as a disaster and New China will be dated from the 'opening up' in 1979, not from the closing down in 1949.

Why the Cultural Revolution?

The Cultural Revolution was announced by Mao in 1966 and lasted until his death. It turned China upside down. What was Mao's motivation? The likely explanation is that he felt constrained by a new establishment, drawn from the successful revolutionaries, which expected to govern through a formal process in which their collective views would be weighed and weighted. The winners wanted to enjoy their victory and rule a stable kingdom. Many of the military and political leaders had joined the Party because they were repelled by the Guomindang regime of Chiang Kai-shek and hated the Japanese occupation. They were not all from proletarian families. They might be more accurately regarded as fundamental patriots rather than social radicals, anxious to restore national integrity in both the moral and the geographical sense. It is frequently suggested that Mao had more freedom of unilateral decision-making as a revolutionary leader than after he had won, when a vast government system and some due process were needed. He was pushed aside twice in the 1950s, the second time at the An Lushan conference in 1959. The Cultural Revolution of the 1960s was probably an attempt to assert untrammelled authority after his return to power.[126]

I think we could go further and say that the 'bourgeoisification' – or adaptation from revolution to government – of the Communist Party probably bored him. He could have been driven by some of the same reactions experienced by Che Guevara after the victory in Cuba. The difference was perhaps that Mao was not the number two and was not going to go off and risk 'dying beautifully' (as Soviet President Anastas Mikoyan put it) in a second revolution in Bolivia.[127]

Mao did not just dislike the tedium of institutional government but perhaps he also had an arrogance in disdaining circumscription by rules. His senior colleagues annoyed him by seeking to curtail his power and his policies so he stayed at home and turned upside down the worlds of the new bureaucrats who had betrayed the legacy of his idealised revolution, probably didn't believe in it and tried to make him obey rules. He is likely to have seen himself as Nietzschean Man, who had made his revolution and was not going to end up subservient to his own creation.

During the first stages of the Cultural Revolution, until a directive was received from Beijing in September 1967, the People's Liberation Army (PLA) had its hands tied and could not uphold order or even defend its men and its arms effectively. Zhou Enlai is said to have remarked that the army suffered 'hundreds of thousands' of casualties (though it should be pointed out that there is a similar Chinese expression which just means 'many, many').[128] Rival groups of Red Guards plundered military arsenals and fought pitched battles with armaments including machine guns and artillery. The September directive 'issued orders to the PLA giving it sweeping powers to use force to re-establish law and order'.[129]

Why was there no *coup d'état* by the army to bring down Mao, who was clearly responsible for the chaos and violence? There are two principal answers. The first is the extraordinary personal loyalty which senior officers felt to Mao after the civil war. Though the Communist Party had technically had seven leaders before him, and although he only took over in 1943, Mao had been regarded as its leading figure and guiding spirit from substantially earlier on. Second, unlike in other countries, the military leaders and the government leaders overlapped so much that few would have seen themselves as 'military men' alone. Most of the military leaders of that time – unlike now – such as Marshal Lin Biao, were members of the party organs as well as the military ones. Both Mao and Zhou Enlai had military credentials as well as political standing. The PLA leadership was the Party.[130] This meant that military leaders, technically, were collectively co-responsible for permitting the chaos and violence. Moreover, it might also be said that the conception of 'people's war' was so ingrained that it was probably difficult for the PLA to disarm the civilian paramilitaries.

How Revolutionary Was the Communist Revolution?

A minor theme of this book is that much of post-1949 China echoes earlier history. While destroying the immediate antecedents, much of post-1949 Communist rule emulated aspects of Imperial China. We should note the comments of Professor Hugh Trevor-Roper in the teeth of the Cultural Revolution in 1968:

> Theoretically, the Chinese communist revolution is a repudiation of the millennial history of China. Communist China has broken decisively with its past, loudly and explicitly disowned its long and splendid history. The recent 'cultural revolution' has emphasized and exaggerated that breach. The deposit of 4000 years has now been repudiated in its totality; everything that is old

has been discarded; and all things, we are told, have been made new. But in
fact, what has happened? The inheritance of the Kuomintang, of the Chinese
republic, has indeed been rejected, but the older inheritance of the Manchus,
of the Chinese Empire, has returned to fill the void.[131]

We could say that even elements of the Kuomintang heritage have been
retained.

The *hukou* system was resurrected to chain the peasants to their villages;
compulsory land reform followed the Qing in ensuring that civil society threw
up no large landowners who could be authority figures and challenge the status
of the government; and the judicial system had many similarities to that of
the Qing. In 1979 the most sweeping measure, the one-child policy, was
introduced, but the minority races were excluded (echoing the Qing after their
victory, when they exempted the minorities from wearing the queue). The
discouragement by the Party of non-governmental organisations echoes Qing
prohibitions.

The Communist victory introduced a society which eventually resembled
the preferred system of the neo-Confucian Wang Anshi, the eleventh-century
Song dynasty chancellor and poet, who argued that politics and society
should be fused together. Inequality of wealth should be eliminated by means
of a comprehensive state economic policy. Private wealth might support opposition, and opposition is not moral, so private wealth should be sapped so that
all rely on the state. Families should be weakened and should not mediate
between society and the state. While Wang's poetry might have occasionally
celebrated dissidence, his policies were centralising. However, both were
utopian: this vision of the omnipotent state, imbued with correct moral values
and occupying all corners of social life, is totalitarian and utopian. It was the
philosophy underpinning the French Revolutionary terror and Stalinism. In
building utopia – or heaven on earth – secularism is a normal precondition,
but is not essential (as we saw with the Taiping rebellion). In this respect,
Confucianism provided fertile soil. Because the cause is right, the means are
justified. Parallels have been noted between the neo-Confucians and the
latter-day 'neocons' in the West, many of whom originated in the hard Left.
Eventually, the Song dynasty rejected the radical utopianism of Wang Anshi for
the pragmatic conservatism of Sima Guang – just as, much later, reformist
China rejected Mao's utopianism for the pragmatic politics of Deng Xiaoping.

The 1949 Communist victory closed China's doors, just as the Ming
had done. Purges were as pervasive as under the early Ming. Objective
scientific inquiry was discouraged by Confucianism and again by Marxism–
Leninism. The Song dynasty 'community compact' meetings have been cited as

a model for self-criticism sessions under Mao. Similarly, one might say, the occasional self-criticism of the emperors. The Party after 1949 frequently obliged business owners, both domestic and foreign, to sell their enterprises in lieu of 'back taxes' – which was a method also used by the Han dynasty.[132] Today Ai Weiwei, the prominent artist, is accused of tax offences rather than of speaking out. The Xia dynasty's (c. 2070–1600 BC) family registers have been cited as one foundation of today's *hukou* system, which the Communist Party strengthened in 1958 in order to manage population flows.[133] Intervening dynasties contributed additional elements to the system, which was mirrored in Taiwan, South Korea and Vietnam.[134] The *hukou* system echoes the Song Confucian philosophers' desire for individuals to remain in their communities.[135] The Communist Party Organisation Department ostensibly makes official appointments and personnel evaluations, as did the Yuan dynasty's Ministry of Personnel, and it echoes the Tang dynasty's (AD 618–907) grading of officials. The system of political commissars borrowed not only from the Soviet Union but also from imperial history, when emperors sent representatives to evaluate their generals' loyalty. The legal system of torture-induced confession and lack of independent judiciary echoes that in Lord Macartney's description of the Qing legal system.[136]

'China is more radical than the Soviet Union was,' says Yuan Weishi, the historian.[137] This is because it wants to control everything – right down to the lowest level – and every aspect of society. Radical perhaps, but not new, and always borrowing from its past. Religion is as minutely organised and controlled in contemporary society as were Buddhism and Daoism under the Ming. There is no private freehold land today, as there was none under the Sui dynasty in the eighth century.[138] The Party echoes the detailed supervision of individuals which existed in the Qin period around 340 BC, *baojia* (or *pao chia*), which continued during the Ming, and the neighbourhood responsibility systems under the Qing.[139] As Hugh Trevor-Roper argued in 1968, 'New China' may have erased the openness of the Republican period, but it was not so much new as a rejection of the open and plural society of the first half of the twentieth century and a reassertion of the state-ordained moral codes and order of Imperial China.

Even the mass mobilisation, polarising campaigns and vicious objectification had historical roots. Traditional religion offers a basis for the Cultural Revolution. The charismatic style of Mao's leadership was grounded in Chinese culture, and violent struggle also draws deeply on the same traditional culture which possesses a 'demonological paradigm and its messianic correlate'.[140] This goes back at least to the early Qing, when messianic cults were associated with opposition and the demonising of the Manchu conquerors. The frenzied hostility exemplified by the White Lotus and the Taiping against demons (in the form of the Manchus), and by the Boxers against demons (in the form of Western missionaries) was finally brought to bear on class enemies in the Mao years. This long tradition of 'quite brutal violence' is important to understanding contemporary history.[141]

One could debate whether Mao was a radical peasant leader who came from the country to turn the city upside down, in the style of the Taiping and others, or an urbanite manqué who used the peasants to gain power and then ruthlessly imposed a metropolitan agenda. His policies suggest that he shared the traditional urban concern about the dangers of rural chaos and its corollary: the need to manage the peasants. Mao's Communist Party was a Leninist party, not so different from its predecessor, the Nationalist Guomindang, which was itself modelled on Leninist discipline. One could go further and suggest that both drew deeply on the authoritarianism, or despotism, of the imperial dynasties.

Mao appears to have shared much of the radical thinking of the May 4th Movement – a disdain for traditional language, Confucian values and rural life. On the other hand, he certainly did not replace the despised elements with Western or Enlightenment values, as many of the May 4th intellectuals proposed. Instead he exhibited some of the inward-looking features of the Ming dynasty. He began language reforms but didn't complete them. He curbed Confucianism but didn't replace it. He subjugated the countryside for urban benefit but then traumatised the cities for personal reasons. Mao might best be seen as one of those rarest of creatures – a violent middle-of-the-roader, a radical centralist. He could countenance seeing his country degenerate into violent chaos in order for him to escape the constraints of collective leadership. However, he left the PLA largely unscathed to ensure the survival of the nuclear capability and an elementary institutional structure. He was one of the greatest polemicists of his age who has bequeathed no serious intellectual movement.

Step Back from the Brink: The Slow Coup

The year 1976 was a momentous one. First, Zhou Enlai, Mao Zedong's faithful premier, died in January. There then followed large demonstrations in April at Tiananmen Square, a significant gathering place in Chinese history. These ostensibly mourned Zhou but, responding to public security intervention, were later seen also as critical of the leading political group, the radical leftist 'Gang of Four', which included Jiang Qing, Mao's wife. It has been estimated that 200–400 demonstrators were executed.[142] The 'incident' was branded as counter-revolutionary and Deng Xiaoping was blamed. He was stripped of his roles and sent into the countryside for a second time. In September, Mao died. In October, a group of Party leaders arranged the arrest of the Gang of Four. Hua Guofeng, Mao's presumed nominee, came to power. Mao's policies largely continued, with a change of drivers and some distancing from the Cultural Revolution. In 1977, Deng was reinstated amongst Party leaders against Hua's wishes, and this was followed by a gradual process of replacing leading officials with Deng's sympathisers. By early 1979, Deng was indisputably the leader, and the policies and guiding principles were being unceremoniously changed. The Tiananmen Square demonstrations of 1976 were declared not to have been counter-revolutionary, and reforms began. We could call the period of two and a half years after Mao's death 'the slow coup', in which radical change took place in slow motion but consistently in the same 'rightist' direction.

The protracted counter-revolution between 1976 and 1979 led to a recasting of national history. The victors usually write the history and so the mainstream domestic analysis of the Cultural Revolution years and, to an extent, some of the earlier phases, is influenced by the perspectives of those who took power in the late 1970s. The present leaders are in power because their predecessors changed the course of Chinese history in two senses: they changed the political direction of the country and they changed the way it is described in the history books. Illogically but understandably, they did not reverse the verdict on events with which they might not later agree but with which they were personally associated.

The official view is that Mao was a great revolutionary leader who held the Party together, inspired the wartime fight against the Japanese and the Nationalists and brought military victory and the building of the New China. His behaviour from the late 1950s became increasingly aberrational, culminating in the chaos of the Cultural Revolution, the rise to influence of the Gang of Four and then his death. The Dengist line was not that Mao's thirty years in power were a mistake – that would undermine too much of the wider polity and risk the legitimacy of the Party. A balancing act was needed. The line was that Mao had pursued sound policies from assuming the leadership until about 1957, when he started to go wrong.

In 1981, the Party's Central Committee, at its Sixth Plenary Session, adopted a resolution on 'Certain Questions in the History of our Party'.[143] Deng himself presided over this document's production. It condemned the Cultural Revolution and re-evaluated Mao, affirming that 'his merits are primary and his errors secondary'.[144] It stressed the need to uphold and develop Mao Zedong Thought and distinguished it from the mistakes Mao made in his later years. The anti-rightist campaign of 1957 was partially criticised for excess. The Great Leap Forward was criticised for being overly ambitious. Mao's increasingly autocratic tendencies, regular and excessive labelling and persecution of 'rightists' and growing personality cult were condemned. The decade from the late 1950s until 1966 was judged by the Party to have contained dreadful mistakes, while the subsequent decade of the Cultural Revolution was felt to be almost entirely disastrous, with only a handful of redeeming features.

It would be helpful to have a clearer public debate as to who might be responsible for – say – the 35–40 million deaths of the Great Hunger and why it is only Mao who is criticised in passing. Should every leader of that time share the blame for the millions of deaths in the 1950s, '60s and '70s? It is not evident, as it is not discussed. China's government has a collective leadership and thus in theory a collective responsibility.

The Reform Years

Reforms began with the agricultural changes in late 1978, led by officials like Zhao Ziyang. It is difficult to overestimate the significance of the changes in thinking that began then. As Li Ruogu puts it:

> Before and after the reform and opening-up, major changes occurred in guiding thoughts and basic line of the Party. Before 1978, we 'took class struggle as the basic task', placed politics in command, and placed economic development in a secondary position. Therefore sluggish economy was inevitable . . .[145]

These changes led rapidly to the institution of household responsibility in agricultural production. Rural reform was followed by reforms in many economic areas. The reform period created dramatic change in people's lives. In cities, the ubiquitous bicycle gave way to the car in the late 1990s, although not for all. Travelling through the Pearl River Delta (PRD) in the late 1980s it seemed to me that every Party secretary wanted three things for his community – a five star hotel, a power station and a stock exchange. Indeed there was a danger that local officials, unleashed to create growth across the economy, would open scores of stock markets throughout the nation in a confused dash for modernity.

For many years after 1978, most foreign China watchers were uncertain whether China would continue to reform or return to Mao's policies. The debate between Deng and fellow party elder and leading economist Chen Yun about the appropriate degree of economic freedom was widely misunderstood as a discussion about whether to go forward or backward. Chen Yun had been advocating using market influence in the economy since the 1950s. He had been exiled from Beijing and sent to factory work during the 1970s. After the arrest of the Gang of Four, he took the lead in demanding that the Party go further and condemn the entire Cultural Revolution. The overseas media in the 1980s delighted in depicting China as engaged in a Manichaean struggle between reformers and Maoists, exemplified often in the forms of Deng and Chen. The latter would have been horrified to be seen as anything resembling a restorer of Cultural Revolution policies.

The international media then enjoyed employing the expression 'two steps forward, one step back' in relation to the apparent dithering nature of the reforms. In fact, it is true to say that there was not a single year from 1978 until 2000 in which China had less reform in December than it had in January – not even 1989. The consistency was clear. Even as recently as the early years of this century there was still widespread international misgiving about the nature of post-Maoist China. This was best exemplified by the lingering questions from westerners about how Hong Kong had changed after the 1997 handover. The high growth derived from the reforms surprised overseas analysts by arising in a self-described Communist country. The West should not be entirely blamed for this: considerable culpability should be placed on the Chinese system, where much policy debate is in private and there is a culture disposed to threaten those who reveal even innocuous information. Such a society is more likely to be misrepresented than one which conducts itself transparently.

It has been under-appreciated that those who arrested the Gang of Four, scrapped Mao's policies and later executed the coup against his chosen successor were mostly individuals who had suffered badly under the chaotic, cruel and indeed deadly Cultural Revolution and were firmly opposed to its return. Deng Xiaoping's principal contribution, as Chinese leader, was to seek quietly to drop ideology and adopt pragmatism as guiding policy. Formal use of ideology and the old rhetoric continues, however. This is partly because the Party has not adopted a new ideology. The Chinese Communist Party is still the party in government and Marxism–Leninism is still taught to aspiring political leaders. The economic reform strategy is referred to as introducing 'socialism with Chinese characteristics'. However, there is a huge gap between textbook theory and the reality of government policies.

The Liberal Historical Outlook

The dominant Western view is to see little value in the Cultural Revolution – a dark combination of tragedy and farce – and to hail the Deng years as a new Long March but in a positive direction. Outside the country, recent history is analysed with inherent assumptions of the inevitability of China modernising and therefore more closely resembling the West. Internally there is also a deep-seated belief that China is moving towards a more modern, strong nationhood which will see it more resemble the West (particularly America), while still being recognisably Chinese. Of course, 'Westernness' is a buffet: different guests select different dishes. Many do not choose democracy and human rights. They prefer the taste of science and technology. For many Chinese, to resemble America is to be strong, dominating – and perhaps arrogant – but not necessarily to be liberal.

The mainstream analysis – both domestically and internationally – applauds China's modern historical development when it approximates structures and forms familiar to the West and deplores it when it does not. Judging a country's past by the standards of the present is quite common in history. Butterfield wrote eloquently of 'The Whig Interpretation of History' in England:

> Real historical understanding is not achieved by the subordination of the past to the present, but rather by our making the past our present and attempting to see life with the eyes of another century than our own . . . It is not reached by assuming our own age is the absolute . . . and their generation are only relative; it is only reached by fully accepting the fact that their generation was as valid as our generation, their issues as momentous as our issues and their day as full and as vital to them as our day is to us.[146]

Goering observed flatly at Nuremberg that those who lose in battle are inevitably judged by those who win. So it is for the Mao years. Much of the legacy has been swept away, whether good or bad, as it didn't fit the thinking of the new reformed China. Any other values have been airbrushed out of history. One of historiography's critical issues is the selection of material. There is usually so much to choose from that what is chosen will generally determine the message which emerges. Once one knows what one expects from history, it becomes easier to select the material to illustrate it.

The idea that history continually charts an upward course, as the advanced specimens of mankind battle the evil and the backward in the interests of human progress and fulfilment, is a fundamentally liberal position. If where we are is desirable, and more desirable than anything in the past, then the winners of the battles and confrontations in the past have generally been on the side of progress and the losers have been the enemies of a better world. A more sophisticated adjunct to this view is that when we examine the past we can recognise those who fought for a world which more closely resembles ours and see them as the heroes. This world-view sits particularly comfortably in the United States and Northern Europe, and with Protestants more than Catholics.

However, such a view of history may not be shared by an Aborigine or a Red Indian – or indeed by wide sections of the population in modern China. This thinking creates the framework which historians have found most convenient. It is the framework or context in which most writers have approached China's recent past. This approach is strongly challenged by thinkers such as Butterfield and recently Gao Mobo. An alternative view is that each civilisation is unique and contributes differently to humanity.

It is richly paradoxical that both Marxists and those liberals who rejoice in Marxism's end suffer from similar beliefs: that history is a movement with a purpose, tends to operate with some inevitability and is generally moving towards a better world. There are many who appear to believe history has a direction and a purpose, and that it is a warm and gentle one. As John Gray said:

> In intellectual terms the cold war was a competition between two ideologies, Marxism and liberalism, that had a great deal in common ... Both were Enlightenment ideologies that looked forward to a universal civilisation. Both interpreted history in reductive terms, viewing technological and economic development as primary and religion as a secondary factor of dwindling importance.[147]

Every culture in every era tends to have its own distinctive mythology, to which most citizens subscribe, but from which a few dissent. In the West, currently, it is liberal democracy, however defined. In China, it might be modernisation and prosperity.

One lesson of history – sad though it might be – is that there is never anything special about the particular time in which one lives. History has neither improved century by century until today, as the liberals like to feel, nor has it deteriorated since the days of Pericles, as Georges Sorel stated. There are good periods and bad periods: the West's 'Dark Ages' had their saints and martyrs; the twenty-first century has the Congo. Mass murders occur in every era. A death in the tenth century is as sad as a death in the twentieth.

The Revisionist Counter-attack

There is always an alternative analysis to the mainstream one. Many of those who had a different class background remember the latter Mao years as a period when anything could be tried, a period of exhilaration for the ordinary man, a period when he might feel he was treated almost as an equal of the officials, the officers and the directors. There is a whole cultural underworld which perpetuates positive memories of the Cultural Revolution and often associates this with a radical leftist perspective and a corollary criticism of the economic and social conditions of today's China. Much of this work is by old men using young tools; meaning it is frequently older people utilising internet sites to create virtual shrines to that period. Then there is the *zhiqing* experience, which refers to those 'educated youth' who were encouraged by Mao to leave the towns and go to the countryside. During the Cultural Revolution, the process was mandatory for many. The United Nations estimates that 18 million went between 1962 and 1978.[148] It was a transformative time and is generally the most important experience they ever had. Many still mourn that period, which gave them a sense of purpose.

There is a significant historiographical attack on the perceived wisdom that the later Mao years were aberrational and that China is now progressing. The revisionist view is that Mao has been traduced. First, the charge that China was brought to its knees industrially and agriculturally, and socially exhausted by the endless campaigns culminating in the threat to life and limb of the Cultural Revolution, is refuted. It is argued that China improved economically almost every year after 1949 and evidence is cited, for example that US authorities recognised it, and that China was a better society for the most ordinary agricultural worker (though not for the expendable landlord or land-owning peasant).[149] Certainly the reported per capita GDP from 1950 until 1973, in the latter years of the Cultural Revolution, grew faster than in the USA – by a cumulative 93 per cent to the USA's 73 per cent. The authorities announced GDP growth in the decade before reforms (1969–78) at an average 8.4 per cent. Popular science flourished, gender equality and public health improved, literacy and longevity increased. The 'people' were put squarely at the centre of culture and society. But the data are riddled with error and untruth. The frenzied campaigns for improvement obliged officials to announce development success regardless of reality. The numbers cannot be taken as fact.

A report on the nation's healthcare in May 2009 makes a clear and unflattering comparison of the situation after thirty years of reform, compared with the pre-reform years:

> the failings of China's health system are the dark side of the past three decades of economic reforms. Under Mao Zedong, improvements in health-care were one of the main achievements. The strengths of the Maoist system are often exaggerated – the 'barefoot doctors' sent out to work in villages were often barely educated and poorly prepared to provide medical treatment. But with the introduction of simple antibiotics and improvements in

public hygiene, the results were impressive. Life expectancy rose from 35 in 1952 to 68 in 1982. But in the 1980s – when China started reforming its economy – this system was in effect dismantled. Clinics on farm communes were often closed when land was redistributed. In the cities, state-owned companies and other public sector organisations started pulling out of providing healthcare. The government also put less focus on health spending, which fell from 3 per cent of GDP in the Mao era to below 2 per cent by the late 1990s.[150]

It is argued that China has – since 1978 – taken the wrong road and grown economically while leaving its people behind. A 2008 report, by an alliance of trades unions, NGOs and labour groups, stated that 47 per cent of the population earns less than $2 per day.[151] Here, we need to look beyond numbers. One US dollar one year can be half of a sterling pound, or at another date the same as a pound. In other words, the data move around. Multinational authorities can deem poverty to be life on $1 or $2 a day. Even more confusion comes from purchasing power parity (or PPP), which is the method of valuing money in different countries, based upon what it will buy. In some parts of rural China $2 can buy ample food, but many have suffered, and are still suffering, from the withdrawal of the 'iron rice bowl' – the provision by the work unit of jobs and welfare services for all. If they could be heard, these people might express a different view of China's success than today's articulate middle classes.

Within fifty years of Mao assuming power, no part of China would be either under foreign sovereignty or ceded to foreign control – the first time this had been the case for four hundred years. Eventually all alienated areas returned to Han rule (with the arguable exceptions of Taiwan, which is ruled by Chinese people, and areas now under Russia, which Mao regarded as unfinished business). He could therefore be regarded as a nationalist hero.

Mao's sympathisers say he is falsely accused of planning the murder of millions of people: even though there may have been many deaths, they were not deliberately planned by him. This is close to framing a charge narrowly in order to rebut it. That most of the deaths were not centrally planned, despite firm charges of 'killing quotas', is true. A rational charge would be that – from 1966 with the 'Bombard the Headquarters' poster campaign – Mao consciously willed a partial breakdown of the state and the rise of radical 'Red Guard' groups with extreme perspectives. These unsupervised groups, expressing harsh rhetoric (often that of Mao), unleashed widespread chaos, damage and death. He may be said to have caused the societal breakdown: he encouraged the radicals, reviewed them often in Tiananmen Square, was aware of what they wrought and chose not to restrain them. It cannot reasonably be maintained that he was unaware of what was being done in his name.

The revisionist view of history suggests that Mao was right to be apprehensive of the motives of what were then called the rightists or the 'capitalist roaders' as, despite the conservatism of much of their rhetoric, they later moved China profoundly in a capitalist direction, allowed inequality to flourish and – possibly worst of all – built a society based on prosperity and stability rather than revolutionary zeal. One could argue that such principles encourage social stability at the expense of radical renewal. The revisionists feel that the Mao years had China moving forward; that they saw a radical, refreshing effort to build a new China, at ease with itself – a China that could stand as different from but equal to the West. This has been broken and lost.

An Appraisal

When we contrast the three Maoist decades with the thirty years influenced by Deng, the chiaroscuro is not so sharply defined. The huge significance of the 1976–79 coup is that ideologically-based policy gave way to pragmatic policy, and economics was prioritised over ideology. Politics derived from a search for utopia – whether Wang Anshi in eleventh-century China, the seventeenth-century Great Rebellion in England, the French Revolution or Mao – will inevitably seek to change men to meet a social vision. This is extremely uncomfortable for those being changed. Pragmatic politicians approach affairs differently. If they enjoy stability in power and can pursue their policies, they will generally not interfere with personal beliefs or normal pursuits. Policies derive from consideration of what works. While arguably less romantic, this is less exhausting for those governed. There is nothing as dangerous as politicians who know they are right. It is not surprising that one of contemporary China's neo-Maoist websites is called 'Utopia'.[152] After five decades of mass campaigns and upheaval, many Chinese were quite responsive to the theme of peace and prosperity.

Deng's verdict on the Mao period of '70 per cent good, 30 per cent bad' was entirely pragmatic and the formula of 70:30 has extensive roots in Chinese culture. The verdict was not based on honest objectivity. There is, however, something casually extreme about noted Chinese history writer Yuan Tengfei saying 'The only correct thing Mao Zedong did after 1949 was to die.'[153] There were drastically bad results and some good results from Mao. It is difficult for the objective observer not to be repelled by the campaigns and the killing, the objectification and the slaughter. There were redeeming features: some foundations were laid for the later modernisation; women were encouraged into the labour force; there was some healthcare innovation, as well as increasing longevity; the industrial base was developed, as were good primary and secondary education and literacy; perhaps even making China a nuclear power. My verdict on Mao would be almost the opposite of Deng's: perhaps 80 per cent bad, 20 per cent good.

In the years immediately after the 1949 Communist victory, many non-political Chinese took extraordinary pride in the building of a 'new China'. Indeed Chinese flooded back from exile to help. During the 1950s it became clear that New China did not welcome everyone. Divisive campaigns undermined national enthusiasm and identified whole groups as enemies in their homeland. People were objectified by their family or class, or as intellectuals. This led eventually to the Cultural Revolution in 1966 when the state itself almost seized up and violent chaos seemed an invited guest at the dining table for a decade. Thirty essentially confrontational years since the 1949 revolution have now been followed by thirty constructive years of domestic growth, rising prosperity for most, largely passive foreign policy and, above all, relative stability. The stability has been relative because for redundant state enterprise workers, for those who lost their social security or were victims of compulsory property acquisition (whether corrupt or above board), for those suffering polluted air and water, with lead poisoning for their children, the reform years have provided jarring instability. China has metamorphosed from social stability with political instability to political stability with distinct elements of social instability. To say that the reform years have provided more stability underlines how unstable the prior decades were.

China is known internationally to have had rapid long-term growth, but it has actually reported average growth of 10 per cent annually over the thirty years since it started the reforms. This means that, for the greater part of most people's lives, it has been the world's fastest-growing significant economy and the world's fastest-changing major country.

The last three decades, ushered in by Deng, have been mixed. For all the successes, there have been blemishes. Chinese income inequality has increased so much that it rivals or exceeds that of America. Official corruption is an admitted problem. Industrial growth has been assisted by an unenthusiastic concern for environmental or labour conditions. The limited social safety net is increasingly becoming problematic. Beijing's announcement allowing journalists certain reporting freedoms during the 2008 Olympics underlined the fact that freedom is not the norm. International calls for self-determination in Tibet and Taiwan, Xinjiang and (to a much lesser extent) Inner Mongolia have caused anger amongst Han in China. Chinese actions in these areas cause equally strong opposite reactions overseas – whether it is redeveloping Lhasa or pointing warheads at Taipei. According to state media, peaceful petitioners have been consigned to mental treatment.[154] There are international campaigns for Chinese human rights and political prisoners. Beijing's language to its neighbours is becoming increasingly harsh. Ministers say violent mass riots occur frequently.

In October 2009 the Chinese government celebrated the 60th anniversary of the Communist revolution. However, if one considers two facts this might look odd. First, 1949 was when China shut itself off from the world and severed its links. Only in recent decades has it started the rightly celebrated 'reform and opening up' process. What isn't entirely understood is that what we have been witnessing is reform of the 1949 system and an opening up of China after the 1949 closing down. Second, and linked, we should note that most of Mao's years in power are directly criticised by today's China, and this is exemplified by the fact that most statistics offered today only start in 1979, when 'reform China' began. We might recognise this and say that China's 2009 celebration was not of the 60th anniversary of its closing down, but of the 30th anniversary of its opening up again.

Reflections on China's System

China has had a politically and militarily unhappy last thousand years, and yet it has achieved cultural successes in abundance. There may well be some remarkable results from its serial occupation by other races. This could lead to a fiercely nationalistic foreign and domestic policy, which may have damaging results, or may lead to a strong and peaceful drive to be highly successful. Whichever direction is eventually taken, I believe the judgement of history would have to be that China today is an incontrovertibly better place than it was thirty years ago. The World Bank tells us that, using purchasing power parity – if we must – the proportion of Chinese living on under $2 a day declined from 98 per cent in 1981 to 36 per cent in 2005.

It can be debated whether China should have changed faster, given greater priority to other policies, tried more personal freedoms. However, against all this is the deep concern of many Chinese who lived through the twentieth century, and the Cultural Revolution in particular, to prioritise the avoidance of violent upheaval over everything. Displeasing though it is in the West, I believe this explains the unpleasant phenomenon of the shootings in Tiananmen Square, the summary of Mao Zedong by Deng as '70 per cent good and 30 per cent bad' and the fact that such a man is still on the national banknotes.

The recent national priorities for most Chinese could – if ever formulated – best be described as stability and rising income. We need to look at whether these priorities might be changing. The country has been held together. This government has delivered these objectives handsomely.

The Pew Survey of Global Attitudes taken in 2013 showed that 80 per cent of Chinese believed their economy would be better in a year.[155] This was higher than in any of the 38 other countries polled in 2013. Furthermore 82 per cent feel their children will be more prosperous than they are. This again is an opinion held more strongly by Chinese than by citizens of any other country surveyed by Pew. China tends each year to have the highest degree of satisfaction with its general direction. When it comes to financial competence in government, a 2009 poll asked people in many major countries how confident they were in their government's ability to deal with the global crisis. China came top with 72 per cent confidence in the government (compared with the US and its 47 per cent confidence in the Obama administration). Clearly censorship and news management play their part here, but nonetheless public opinion is clear.

Table 1.3: **Countries' Confidence in their Governments' Handling of the Global Crisis, 2009 (score out of 10)**

China	7.2
India	6.3
USA	4.7
Great Britain	3.3

Source: *Guardian*, 20 August 2009.

Beijing receives considerable criticism for lacking participatory elections on Western lines. However, officials spend much time studying public opinion, and policies are adopted in this context. Liberal consciences may understandably be affronted by some things that happen in China, but for a country where sons and daughters can remember their parents' harrowing tales of the Cultural Revolution, the regime has delivered. Bearing in mind the challenges that confronted the authorities over the last thirty years, this must be regarded as one of the most competent governments worldwide. If China had had free elections in 2008, before the recent downturn, I believe the government would have won handsomely. I think this still holds true today. Now we need to look forward. What does the past tell us about the future?

A Legacy of History

The cumulative impact of the last two hundred years has been particularly noteworthy. Many and varied examples could be given:

> The untold suffering of the Chinese people – caused by Western imperialism, the Taiping Rebellion, the collapse of the Manchu dynasty, the internecine struggle of the warlords, Japanese aggression, the conflict between the Nationalists and the Communists, and the misguided policies of the People's Republic of China – contextualized the meaning of Chineseness in a new symbolic structure. Marginality, rootlessness, amnesia, anger, frustration, alienation, and helplessness have gained much salience in characterizing the collective psyche of the modem Chinese.[156]

A leading intellectual, Ai Weiwei, writes about helping to rescue a warehouse full of abused cats, and concludes that the Chinese people will always lack respect for other forms of life.[157] A Henan province delegate to the National People's Congress/Chinese People's Political Consultative Conference, Hu Baosen, 'sees a lack of moral education in the Chinese society'.[158]

I have examined China's recent history over the last millennium for some insights into its future. The national character does seem to have been affected by the many traumas and the long centuries of occupation and foreign authority. The Chinese seem strikingly nationalistic as a race, perhaps because of an innate anger, with all the foreign policy risks this implies. When, rarely, the Chinese have been independent of foreign control and also rich and powerful, most typically during the early Ming period, there has been a regular resort to war against the neighbours. There is a strategic culture of prioritising force in disputes when finance permits. This is the only real evidence we have of Han foreign policy culture. Past prominence, albeit under foreign leadership, appears to justify a sense of entitlement to, if not the inevitability of, future great power status. And yet, *pace* Mussolini, tenuous Italian or Greek relationships with classical empires do not imbue a similar sense of entitlement.

So many of the features of what the Communist Party calls the New China, post-1949, are actually reflections of Imperial China. Even the closing down of China in 1949 mirrors the turn to inward focus of the Ming. Through this history there has been a continuing alternation between the passive permitting of openness and the conscious imposition of harmony and conformity.

Many of the themes in this book return to a deficiency in the moral core of today's China. This is even noted by officials. Some writers ascribe it to the last two hundred years; others to the centuries of foreign occupation. What is clear is that dozens of perceptive Chinese – as well as foreign – observers have noted a lack of honesty, integrity and morality in contemporary society. This has not only a social impact, but repercussions in culture, technology, foreign affairs and governance. And it will constrain growth and affect how China is appreciated in the world.

CHAPTER TWO

The Broken Economic Model

Internationally, the impression of the Chinese economy is of an unstoppable juggernaut rolling towards global domination. But this is not quite correct: China faces internal and external challenges and needs to make major changes in her economy.

The Background: The Reform Years

By 1978, China's leaders knew they must introduce serious measures to restructure the country. However, reforms were politically sensitive; Mao had only been dead two years. Deng Xiaoping and his colleagues presided over some of the most radical reforms in modern history, but they displayed a curious reticence at this time. Reform was mentioned seldom, and the Maoist communes were actually praised. There was disagreement among the leaders, policy discussion, but not much action for many years. Considering the results, it is ironic that those who did so much to drive reform are now not publicly acknowledged: Hu Yaobang and Zhao Ziyang. In his memoir, Zhao depicted the policy debates then and showed how much reform came from below rather than above.[1] The two biggest economic reforms involved dismantling most of the state enterprise system and the state housing system, but these took almost twenty years to complete. This is paradoxical, since 1979 saw one of the world's most radical *social* reforms introduced: the one-child policy. It was politically easier to propose drastic – but inclusive – social policies than drastic economic policies which sacrificed 'equalitarianism'.

Nonetheless, China was a genuine pioneer. Chinese economic reforms started six months before the 'Thatcher revolution', and Chinese officials always interested themselves in the British prime minister's actions. At Deng Xiaoping's direct behest, the military budget was cut by almost a quarter between 1979 and 1981 to generate funding for economic growth.[2] Communes were allowed to wither away after 1979, and had virtually gone by 1984, when the system was declared redundant. However, as late as 1985, Chen Yun, a senior leader and economist, could say that China should have the 'planned economy as primary, market adjustments as auxiliary'.[3]

In 1980, Hu Yaobang, Communist Party Secretary General, called for the economy to quadruple in size in a mere twenty years. This was achieved with private sector leadership, and the Party experimented with introducing entrepreneurs to membership from the late 1980s – well before Jiang Zemin announced the policy in 2001. Generally, reform is discussed within the Party at one speed, is pursued more slowly, and is announced even more slowly. Many of China's reforms started with local action. They benefited from a combination of central benevolence and passivity until their success was evident, at which point the leadership decided the bus was going in the right direction and the seats were comfortable. Nonetheless, the length of the journey was still debated.

The first stop was agricultural reform, then the urban economy. China's prodigious economic success was built principally upon two engines of growth: domestic investment and manufactured exports – in that order. Domestic investment – capital investment in steel mills, cement plants, power plants, real estate – has dwarfed other economic areas. From 1997 to 2009, gross investment rose from a third of the economy to almost half. By the first half of 2009, on another estimate, state investment was 88 per cent of GDP – 'a share for which it is hard to find any parallel in any country, at any time'.[4] As early as 2005, not only did Asian ports handle two-thirds of global container traffic, but eight Chinese ports alone made up 25 per cent. China also became the low-cost international manufacturer. By 2007–9, it was the largest global producer of such diverse items as toys, garments, leather, solar panels, mobile phones, heparin (a blood thinner), video games, steel, sex toys, prawns, garlic and lighters. However, while domestic consumption has grown rapidly, it has fallen as a proportion of the economy.[5] This is largely because, as industry has shifted from being labour intensive to capital intensive, rising wages have made up a falling proportion of a faster-rising GDP.

In 2005, the *renminbi* (RMB), the Chinese currency, was allowed to rise in value, reflecting three things – the need to keep an eye on potential inflation, US political pressure and a desire to upgrade the economy. The result of the 20 per cent increase needs to be seen in context. This was a time of currency volatility. Importantly for China, many of its competitors saw their currencies fall sharply against the dollar. Thus, in pricing goods for the US market China was disadvantaged not by 20 per cent, but by up to 40 per cent. It was unfortunate timing and exporters complained.

However, we should note that in the four years up to appreciation (2000–4), when the currency was pegged to the dollar, exports rose more slowly than imports. During the three years (2005–8) in which the RMB rose 20 per cent against the dollar (and more against its rivals), exports rose much faster than imports. This is not the classical expectation, nor is it what Washington wants when it presses Beijing to appreciate its currency.

So what happened? It seems the margins of exporters, particularly private sector companies, were sharply squeezed, and there is some evidence that exporters responded by becoming more productive, increasing output per worker: China has enjoyed some of the highest productivity growth worldwide in recent years (though latterly this has diminished).

The economy has been transformed from one that was growing rapidly and providing commensurately rising employment to one that, through massive investment, is increasingly capital intensive. Output growth is no longer matched by employment growth, and we have seen 'jobless growth', a problem also apparent in the more developed West. The government will need to rethink its old-fashioned attachment to massive capital investment and heavy manufacturing; it now needs to foster the small and medium-sized enterprises (SMEs) and the service sector, which generate more employment and are often less environmentally damaging. The authorities' dilemma is that these sectors are more entrepreneurial and less state-linked. The state has a residual distrust of the private sector: as it is independent, officialdom cannot easily incorporate it into national economic plans. However, if this is the future, the challenge is to embrace it and decide how to encourage it.

The Accuracy of the GDP Numbers

The reported economic growth rates averaging 10 per cent annually for thirty years used to be generally accepted: except initially, by Thomas Rawski of Pittsburgh University. However, there are now many academics who publicly question the data. Chris Hall, at Macquarie Graduate School of Management in Australia, Carsten Holz, at the University of Southern California, and Arthur Kroeber at Dragonomics, in Beijing, have all described them as inaccurate. In 2007 Hall wrote:

> In the past, Chinese statistics have tended to be part reality and part imaginary. Statistics tended to be reworked to meet the targets set by the Central Committee. Consequently, if a given level of growth was a government target, the statistics were massaged to show that the growth target had been achieved.[6]

However, non-economic government targets are not massaged, and the targets for education, the environment, research and development, social welfare and curbing corruption are often not met. Also, if Britain can restate its GDP figures years later, we should not expect every Chinese official number, when announced, to be, prima facie, totally correct.

The mid-2009 GDP adjustments unleashed a gale of domestic criticism. The official newspaper *China Daily* stated bluntly that local officials were overwhelmingly more preoccupied with pleasing their bosses than with serving their community.[7] The Communist Party's *Global Times* reported that the public reacted to official wage data with 'banter and sarcasm', and it cited an online poll showing that 88 per cent did not believe official numbers.[8] The journal *Xiaokang* went further and reported a survey showing that local officials have very low credibility – just above real estate developers. Ninety-one per cent have no confidence in government data. *Xiaokang* wrote that, according to the public, the most trustworthy sectors of the community included soldiers, religious workers and prostitutes.[9] However, a 2009 survey conducted by Harris, measuring public confidence in official statistics in the West, found that 'Only one in eight adults believe official data are accurate and an equally small proportion feel that figures are produced without political interference . . . Just 6 per cent of people in Britain believe the government presents official figures honestly . . .'[10]

China's nominal economic growth since 2000 has tracked the emerging market average but it reports the highest inflation-adjusted growth. This implies China's inflation is about the lowest and is said to be due to minimising rising property prices. More accurate indices lower the GDP number by 10 per cent and "given the relative ease with which obvious statistical manipulation was found, it is quite likely that less obvious fraud is present in the CPI data".[11]

Certain commentators have been somewhat sarcastic about the NBS's ability to report the economic results of 1.3 billion people just fifteen days after the year end. John Makin of the American Enterprise Institute has observed that China's GDP data are calculated in a fundamentally different way, based on what goes in rather than, for example, on what is eventually sold (as in America). There is thus a basic accounting difference that stems from the state planning model.

It is suggested that this approach permits the authorities to report what they want by allocating credit and encouraging spending and production plans. Although statistical accounting is not yet Western-style, Makin overstates matters by implying that it has remained unchanged since the 1970s: China did significantly change its statistical accounting in 2003. However, it has not significantly changed its data collection, and that undermines the results.

A further difference lies between measuring accurately the growth rate of the economy and its size: measurements of size are probably distorted by consistently underestimating the SMEs, the service sector, the private sector and the 'shadow economy'. David Ogden, the US Deputy Attorney General, said in 2009 that organised crime is believed to contribute a further 15 per cent of global GDP; add to that all the window cleaners, maids, etc. and it is quite possible that the shadow economy in China might add a further 30 per cent to the officially reported economic activity. Then Premier Wen Jiabao stated that corruption was a top threat; this suggests large-scale activity and bolsters state media claims that it is normal to pay for government jobs or promotions. China also has large-scale organized crime, growing drug addiction, major underground gambling and illicit transfers of state assets into private hands. All countries have a shadow economy, but China's seems proportionately bigger.

Perhaps the best witness is Premier Le Keqiang, who, in 2007, told the US ambassador that the GDP numbers are 'unreliable'.[12] Common sense suggests that the official growth rates are inaccurate. However, the inaccuracy is less than it was before 1979, and the main point is that China has consistently shown a growth that would be enviable anywhere.

How Did the Economy Grow so Rapidly?

One of the main reasons for China's tremendous success in the three decades after 1979 is that for the previous thirty years it was outside the global economy. One should not exaggerate: the pre-reform economy did grow. However, while the industrialised world was developing after 1945, China barely participated. Success after 1979 came principally because it was catching up. It is idle, but fascinating, to speculate on where the economy would be today if Mao and his colleagues had not closed the door in 1949.

Domestic Factors

The domestic factors that enabled rapid growth included stable, low wages, rising productivity, high investment and savings rates, an inexhaustible supply of young – and eager – workers, a competitive currency, subsidised fuel and negligible social charges. Growth was also aided by the prolonged absence of union activity and labour regulations, and by political and social stability, huge and continuing state sector redundancy and a consistent sympathy towards foreign business and investment. It did not hurt that China had a policy of incentivising officials to achieve growth, which led to fierce competition between local party secretaries for investment. A slow recognition of property rights and private enterprise and the courage of proto-entrepreneurs in taking political risks in an undefined landscape also did much to encourage this growth, while a willingness to conduct quite radical experiments (such as special economic zones and the Meitan county experiment)[13] did not harm matters. There was also the constructive role of corruption in generating growth under a command economy,[14] minimal environmental regulation, low total government tax taken, low interest rates and cheap loans for exporters, a growing and effective infrastructure and the courage to reform extensively.

Critical amongst these factors was the reallocation of entrepreneurial talent from serving the state to private enterprise, which, according to Zhang Weiying of the Guanghua Management School, 'is unprecedented in Chinese history of the past two thousand years'.[15] In Zhang's words: 'The difference is that in a competitive market, success is determined by one's productivity, while in the government, success . . . is much dependent upon one's political performance, personal connection, and even damage-ability to others.'

The success of the agricultural reforms in 1978–79 had two main benefits: more efficient agriculture released surplus labour, and this encouraged the creation of the town and village enterprises (TVEs) which brought commercial activity into the countryside and drove economic growth in the 1980s. While not formally private, these were seedbeds for private enterprise, and by 1997 more than half of those in many large provinces had been privatized.[16] By 2006, some 28 per cent of all rural labour was off the farms and employed in TVEs,[17] and two thirds of all manufacturing workers are in TVEs rather than the cities.

In addition, the rural reform created a labour wave that migrated across China in search of (low-paid) work.[18] The same phenomenon had earlier assisted economic development in Taiwan, South Korea, Singapore and Japan, but the scale was different in China: more than 260 million underemployed workers migrated to the new factories.[19] This tide ensured that wages in the fast-growing 'informal' sector did not rise for twelve years. Cai, Du and Wang suggest that in 1982–97 one-fifth of growth resulted from internal migration.[20]

Low wages did not so much generate profit as permit the accumulation of an ever-increasing market share of exports, and Chinese products became highly competitive. After 1979 pragmatism replaced ideology. This led to a (somewhat timid) end to the interdiction on enterprise. With characteristic iconoclasm, Li Ruogu, Chairman of China's state Export–Import Bank, reflects that the pre-reform welfare structure had to end and income inequality needed to increase in order to create a savings-driven growth model. 'What the reform has to break first is equalitarianism.'[21]

External factors

There were of course also external factors which helped to shape the environment. Rising Western costs inclined businesses to outsource manufacturing to cheaper regions: China could offer low labour costs, acceptable quality and efficient delivery to port. Although not the principal driver of economic growth, exports rose rapidly as China integrated swiftly with world trade and found its natural position. Like India, China had a huge diaspora, but it seemed to have more businessmen – and more rich ones – willing to work with the global business chains and to invest. As Zhao Ziyang stressed, this compensated for a lack of domestic capital.[22]

China accessed substantial manufacturing know-how at a critical time. Hong Kong and Taiwanese businessmen's proximity made it easier for them to make investments and monitor them. Beijing understood that development needed skills that were lacking, so officials framed policies friendly to overseas companies. Initially offering 49 per cent participation, Beijing progressively relaxed ownership until foreign investors could own all of their investment. Foreign investing companies were given preferential tax rates for over two decades, and they now account for half of exports. Normally host countries prefer to benefit their nationals, but China made it as attractive as possible for overseas corporate investment. The *renminbi*, in 1980, as China opened up to foreign investors and trade, stood at 1.49 to the dollar; by 1994 it was 8.62, an over 80 per cent fall.

The world vastly increased its consumption of manufactured goods, and this was facilitated by debt. The extraordinary growth in Western debt was partly permitted by the originate-to-sell model in Anglo-Saxon banks which allowed credit provision on a wholly new scale. Second, it was supported by the expansion of activity by banks which had not hitherto been large-scale or cross-border participants, for example Icelandic or Irish banks. Third, the willingness of hedge funds and others to purchase parcels of securitised debt artificially expanded the banking system's lending capacity beyond what its capital base, growing through internal cash flow and capital raisings, would normally support. Fourth, rising house prices in the Anglo-Saxon world made people feel richer: American consumers were willing to reduce their low savings rate and further increase their consumption, encouraged by increasing property values and apparent economic growth.

The removal of ideological primacy in China was a precondition for success. Migration contributed as a ready supply of low-cost labour. Government-mandated artificial low interest rates enabled huge investment: a massive subsidy from consumers to producers. The 82 per cent currency decline in the first fifteen years of the open-door strategy assisted exports. The wooing of overseas manufacturing skill was essential, and the explosion of consumer credit in the West helped inflate the market. The emergence from nowhere of a vibrant private sector transformed the economy.

Private Sector Leadership

The economy comprises three principal sectors. In the early 1980s, the dominant component was the state-owned enterprises, followed by the fledgling joint ventures or foreign-funded enterprises, and then the unpopular private sector (often conflated with other enterprises in blurred categories such as 'small and middle-sized enterprises'). The advantages of private enterprises become clearer when compared with state enterprises, which are vividly described as

> still rigidly hierarchical organizations typified by imperious chief executives, poor promotional prospects, deficient R&D and low rates of innovation. Many of them are monopolies. There is a fear of failure, or loss of face, which permeates the educational system and acts as a significant barrier to entrepreneurialism and innovation. The Chinese are taught to work for others rather than themselves.[23]

We should begin this section on the private sector by reiterating that the data are very unclear, vary widely and are much disputed.[24] However, the developments since the early 1980s have been striking and the landscape is scarcely recognisable. In 1979 the private sector accounted for about 3 per cent of GDP; by 2005 it was estimated at 70 per cent,[25] and it was even put at 80 per cent in 2006.[26] The downturn meant that it probably weakened to 60–65 per cent by 2010, but it still provided 80 per cent of urban jobs.[27] By 2012, it represented one third of exports. The private sector has been the economic engine and has generally performed much better than the state sector.

In late 2011, Hou Junchun, a senior state researcher, said that SMEs accounted for 99 per cent of companies, 80 per cent of urban jobs, 70 per cent of national patents, 60 per cent of GDP and 50 per cent of corporate tax.[28] At the same time the State Administration for Industry and Commerce said there 'were nine million private enterprises employing 98 million at the end of June. In addition, there were 36 million self-employed people providing 73 million jobs.'[29] If we say that the economy grew from 1980 to 2010 by around 10 per cent annually in real terms, and that the private sector was 3 per cent of the economy in 1980 and 70 per cent in 2010, then this means that the private sector grew on average by over 21 per cent annually for three decades.[30] The data vary substantially but the thrust is consistent: 'This explosion of entrepreneurial businesses is unprecedented in human history.'[31] Interestingly, one of the drivers of the private economy is often said to have been the inability of those young urban dwellers sent into the country under the *zhiqing* programme to find jobs in the state economy when they returned (see Chapter 5).

Government has largely retreated from its desire to dominate the economy; it now seeks to dominate only a few exceptional fields that it considers strategic, such as banking, aviation and natural resources. It has achieved this by barring access to those sectors and merging state enterprises to create effective quasi-monopolies.

The pricing of bank credit favours state enterprises rather than the private sector.[32] Perhaps as a result, bank credit allocation has often been unsuccessful: 'The rate of investment in China consistently exceeded the share of capital income in GDP during 1992–2003. This implies that the rate of investment in China has been too high, and the Chinese economy is probably on a dynamically inefficient growth path.'[33] We might say that China's growth is of low quality and yet the private sector has succeeded despite having to struggle.

China's private sector success has gone against many of the classic assumptions: it did not appear to require clear ownership title, effective law of contract or indeed the rule of law (the occasional high-profile entrepreneur has been singled out and jailed). Access to the formal banking system and the capital markets has not been generally available to the successful private enterprises. By 2013, SMEs were estimated to have received only 20 per cent of all bank loans.[34] They were obliged to resort to the unofficial, or shadow, banking system or to fund their growth from internal cash flow. Academics estimate that the unofficial banking system is roughly 30 per cent the size of the official system. It is unregulated, illegal and essential. Given this environment, it is extraordinary to think that by 2012 China's private sector was almost as large as Japan's total economy.[35] However, the squeeze in interest rates in 2011 put severe pressure on private companies, as they could not access state bank credit, and in the unofficial banking system rates soared. Newsworthy bankruptcies occurred in Wenzhou, the fabled home city of private entrepreneurs.

Before becoming too impressed with the overall growth of the private sector, we should note that many private businessmen are Party members or related to Party members. Official Chinese research reported in 2007 showed that 88 per cent of those with assets over $14 million are children of high-ranking officials.[36] This seems to lend official support to the view that 'the mainland remained very unequal because wealth was concentrated in a small "red class" of those related to and associated with leaders of the party and the government, who hold many senior posts in the government, party, army and large state companies.[37] Moreover, we should reflect on the origins of these private businesses. Many were corruptly acquired during privatisation, by people with influence and access to money. 'In reality, publicly owned resources found their way into the pockets of rent seekers through corrupt (power for money) exchanges.'[38]

It is important not to confuse cause and effect. China has been economically successful and it has a large private sector, but that does not mean that national leaders are trying to create a market economy. They want China to be modern and to be strong, but they do not wish to lose control of the economy or the financial system, let alone political power. If market signals can be useful, they may be used; if state enterprises can be prioritised and made 'national champions', even better. The end is economic growth in a stable society. Beyond that, pragmatism plays a substantial role. Leaders feel absolutely no compulsion to follow any external development model, so long as they are clearly 'delivering the goods'.

In short, then, state companies have most of the assets, fill oligopolistic and thus profitable economic positions, receive virtually all bank credit (and at preferential rates), represent most of the stock market capitalisation and generate most of the profit. Private enterprises constitute most of the companies, provide most of the jobs, dominate exports, represent over two-thirds of economic activity and drive the economy. When analysed, this presents a rather unusual picture and demonstrates why there is a strong lobby against further economic reform.

Why Unemployment Has Become Systemic

China has had serious unemployment since the 1990s. The wave of factory closures and redundancies in the export areas has attracted widespread attention only since late 2008, but there have been factory closures every year in this wildest of free markets. Inefficient state enterprises underwent massive restructuring from 1995, and by 2005 68,000 state-owned enterprises (SOEs) – 58 per cent of the total – had closed.

Unemployment in China is not simply the result of global economic slowdown; there are important domestic reasons. Principal has been state industry reform: surplus labour has been shed and entire factories closed in order to streamline SOEs. From 1995 until 2005, state and collective enterprise employment almost halved (to only 30 per cent of urban employment); 70 million workers lost their jobs – almost half the workforce of urban state and collective enterprises (and twice the entire British labour market).[39] Fortunately, most of these workers found re-employment in the burgeoning private sector, which by

2008 accounted for two-thirds of jobs.[40] This trend of SOE restructuring has continued, and even in the period 2007–10 it was estimated that there were a further 2 million redundancies.

During the downturn, leaders kept repeating that 8 per cent growth was needed to absorb annual surplus labour. It even became a slogan: '*bao ba*' – 'protect eight'.[41] But this linkage between inflation-adjusted growth and job creation is false, particularly as the economy has become more capital intensive and less labour intensive: a decade ago, 1 per cent economic growth might have yielded 1 per cent employment growth, but today every extra 1 per cent economic growth is likely to produce little extra employment growth.

While wages have risen somewhat, they are not growing as quickly as the economy (which many economists would approve of) and the need for employees has faltered. China says, controversially, the labour force has peaked; what we are seeing is the absence of marked job growth.[42] Put simply, the available workforce has grown faster than the number of jobs. As the Asian Development Bank's Zhuang Jian has said:

> The economic structure is gradually shifting from labor-intensive industries to capital-intensive ones. Employment growth brought about by the same amount of capital will naturally decrease.[43]

The anti-pollution measures have also led to redundancies. Ten sectors of industry came in for scrutiny in 2007, including electricity, steel and iron, construction materials and coal mining. Around Lake Taihu alone, 1,000 factories were closed down and the National Development and Reform Commission (NDRC) predicted that 'mass unemployment' would result from this initiative.

Matters have not been helped by businesses leaving to operate overseas, impelled by rising labour costs and an appreciating currency. Sports shoe manufacturers such as Adidas and Reebok reduced their manufacturing in China several years ago. In 2008 there was another wave of departures. US-originated businesses in particular have been influenced by the rising *renminbi* rate against the collapsing Mexican peso. Others have gone to Vietnam, the Philippines and Bangladesh. In 2010, the hourly labour cost was $2.50 in China and 50 cents in Vietnam.[44] By 2012, Burma at $94 a month was half the wage of Vietnam.[45] There have been reports of Hong-Kong-funded businesses closing and relocating to Hong Kong, and manufacturing has returned to America, Britain and even France from China as cost differentials have narrowed.

Alongside all these contributory factors, there has been a structural change in employment: in 1986, employment was 313 million in the primary sector (agriculture, mining). This was unchanged twenty years later. Secondary sector (manufacturing) employment grew by 70 per cent, or just below 3 per cent annually. Tertiary sector (services) employment grew by 200 per cent, so that by 2009 it represented a third of recorded employment.

The problem has been intensified by factories leaving the coast, due to cheaper wages inland. We should be careful here, however: although 62,361 enterprises in Guangdong province terminated their business licences in the first nine months of 2008, some 100,634 were newly registered. This closing and reopening is often done to get around labour contract legislation and pollution controls by moving to areas with more amenable officials.

The country also suffers from growing graduate unemployment, with the number of people graduating each year increasing by over 700 per cent from 1998 to 2012. Graduate employment prospects weakened during the boom years and worsened further in the economic downturn. Youth unemployment is a global problem, but the surprise with China is that graduate unemployment is so high across both boom and recession. However, as the labour force eventually contracts, graduate unemployment may be absorbed but possibly in sub-graduate roles.

The impact of the various waves of unemployment has mostly been absorbed, however, through the continued expansion of the largely export-driven private sector. China could live with massive redundancy in the 1990s and the early 2000s: uncompetitive enterprises shed labour, while growing companies hired. But when the 2008–9 Western financial crisis hit, exports fell by 16 per cent – the first fall in over twenty years. Unfortunately, domestic demand also fell. Factories closed and redundancies soared.

The NBS has a curious set of numbers which suggests that the private sector was a net recruiter of employees throughout the period and more than covered the net loss of workers by the state and collective sectors. But of course, these numbers exclude the hundreds of millions of very vulnerable migrant labourers. Nevertheless, the data suggest that the private sector, deprived of credit and hard hit by the export decline, still kept going.

Establishing the real unemployment level is difficult. Official unemployment statistics show a rate of over 4 per cent. However, they don't measure unemployment – only workers who have already held a job, are under a certain age, are registered to live in an urban area and have registered to find a job. This is quite limiting: it largely excludes migrant workers, even though, by 2007, half of all urban workers were migrants.[46] Indeed most migrant labour worked informally, thus usually outside the statistics.[47] As unemployment is a continuing challenge, it is worth examining how bad it was during the downturn. Official data are scant and conflicting, and should not be relied upon except as broad illustration.

There are now over 260 million domestic migrant workers. This compares with an estimated 214 million international migrants worldwide.[48] As the number of migrant workers was long unknown, it was difficult to calculate how many were unemployed. Railway officials noticed an unusually early return of people to celebrate the 2009 Chinese New Year, and the Ministry of Social Security surmised that 10 per cent were redundant and had gone home early. The UNDP and the Chinese Academy of Social Sciences (CASS) maintain that two-thirds of migrant workers work informally – a statistical void.[49]

Factory closures should give an indication of migrant unemployment, but here there is little clarity: different officials give variably credible data for their cities or areas. The NDRC in 2008 calculated that 67,000 larger factories (with annual sales of over 5 million *renminbi* ($750,000)) had closed by June, making over 20 million workers redundant.[50] Smaller factories will also have closed during this period, and other factories made workers redundant without closing. Service industries are excluded, although service sector companies are often now more labour intensive than manufacturing. This omission is important because in 2009 China, according to the WTO, was the world's fifth-largest exporter of services. The later steep upward revisions of GDP (by up to 14 per cent) were largely based on service activity having previously been under-reported.

Given the rapid downturn in the second half of 2008, one might assume that total factory closures for the year were well over 150,000. It is not clear how many people an average factory employs. The Dongguan Association of Foreign-invested Enterprises predicted that 9,000 factories in that centre would have closed by spring 2009, with 2.7 million job losses. The prior data suggests an average of 300 workers per factory.

In late 2008, CASS estimated that urban unemployment was 9.4 per cent, versus the official rate of 4.5 per cent (though it is unclear what the definition was). The NBS showed an urban labour force of 294 million at December 2007. Using that figure and the CASS estimate suggests urban unemployment of virtually 28 million. This number presumably omits many unregistered urban workers.

In sum, then, the larger factory closures reported probably represented 20 million redundancies in the first half of 2008; unreported smaller factory closures probably added 5 million in the same period. There might have been a further 17 million in the second half of the year. That makes 42 million for the whole of 2008. Factories that laid workers off but did not close could account for 5 million more job losses. There was some re-employment, but net job losses by Christmas 2008 might have been 37 million. By early summer 2009, the figure was probably 47 million.

In November 2008 it was announced that 4 million pre-2008 graduates were still seeking work. That same year, CASS said 5.6 million students had graduated and 1.5 million (27 per cent) would still be unemployed by year end (in fact, it seems to have been over 30 per cent). Some 2 million 2009 graduates (again over 30 per cent) could not find a job; and in 2010, the Education Ministry revealed that over a quarter of that year's 6.3 million graduates were unemployed.[51]

The official line, then, is that about 30 per cent of graduates each year are unable to get a job in the months after graduation. As the system relies on the universities to report the figures, graduate unemployment is likely to be under-estimated, since it harms universities' reputations and so they try to obfuscate and even fabricate nominal occupations (such as unpaid research posts).

State media have argued that the true figures for graduate unemployment are much higher. The real rate could be up to 50 per cent. Many of the rest settle for non-graduate-level employment. We could be looking at up to 3 million unemployed in the months after graduation, with a hard core of 4 million long-term unemployed.

In March 2010 a vice minister stated that there had been 90 million unemployed migrant workers; it is estimated that there were at least 9 million unemployed registered urban workers and a minimum of 6 million unemployed graduates.

Table 2.1: **Rough Estimate of Recent Unemployment Peak in 2009 (in millions)**

Migrant workers	40–90
Registered urban workers	9–28
Graduates	6–10
Total	55–128

Source: author's estimate, using official data.

If we take some of the higher figures in Table 2.1, there could have been a peak of anywhere up to 128 million. The higher number would suggest that China's total unemployment was more than four times the entire British labour market.

In early 2009, China may have hit a peak of between 12 and 25 per cent national unemployment. That compares with America's average of 14.8 per cent in February 2009, using broad unemployment data.[52] Chinese academics have suggested high levels of total unemployment at other points: in mid-2002, an unexceptional year, Professor Hu Angang, a prominent Chinese economist, estimated that real urban unemployment was 8.5 per cent.[53] In mid-2006, Professor Zeng Yan Bo, of the Shanghai Academy of Social Sciences, estimated total unemployment at up to 20 per cent.[54]

There is some evidence, from early 2008, that redundant workers were still able to be re-employed in industries that were holding up. By mid-2009, orders had recovered in export areas, and soon after that short-term job opportunities created by stimulus money (see p.66 ff below) and railway construction, coupled with a recovery in export orders among the reduced number of factories, probably staunched unemployment, which by early 2010 may have fallen to 40 million. The data used to provide the estimates here on crisis unemployment are official, but the resulting totals far exceed those publicly declared.

Demography and the Employment Outlook

Paradoxically, we see in China both high unemployment and labour shortages. It is ironic that a country with one of the fastest-growing economies, whose population is ageing and whose workforce is verging on peaking, should be facing severe unemployment during a boom. This speaks eloquently of the education system. Graduates are not prized, as they lack experience, and migrant workers are often viewed similarly, unless there is a sudden need for pairs of hands. Skilled workers and professionals can be valued and comparatively well paid.

There are two schools of thought about unemployment. Some people worried about it in the short term, during the 2008–9 downturn, but following the recovery they argue that unemployment is no longer a problem and that the issue now is a demographically influenced labour shortage (while many experts expect the labour force to peak between 2013 and 2016, others believe it has already peaked).[55] The other school believes that the redundancies in state enterprises and the necessary closure of dangerous mines and polluting factories, the gross agricultural over-employment and the low levels of job creation all remain a cause of concern. The reality is that both are right: we should be worrying about unemployment and instability, but also about labour shortage and rising wages – in the same country and in the same year. There is famine in abundance.

Demography has changed profoundly. China's fertility rate has been on a downward trajectory for some decades, regardless of the 1979 one-child policy. The result is that the population is scarcely growing and, perhaps more importantly, is ageing. A quarter of the population of Shanghai, deemed China's first 'ageing city', is now over 60. The longer-term impact of ageing is that wages rise, labour becomes scarce and the welfare dependency rate deteriorates. Although estimates differ, the national workforce size should have peaked by 2016, and will then decline; by about 2025, only about 40 per cent of Chinese will be of working age.

A secondary effect of this trend is that China will be overtaken by India as the most populous country by about 2028. Well before then, this will encourage multinational companies to develop a clear India strategy, as most have hitherto had for China. That will affect global capital and resource allocation. The issue here is that by the 2040s a steep population fall will start, damaging the ability to generate growth.[56]

What we have seen is the unusual coexistence of unemployment, underemployment and labour shortage. These labour factors are not, however, all fungible: 40-year-old farm workers with little education cannot generally do what is needed in the coastal factories. And migrants prefer other industrial areas to the complex of manufacturing clusters in Guangdong province's Pearl River Delta for a number of reasons: the Hong Kong factories based there are unlikely to pay much above the minimum wage, a lot of overtime is required, and the migrants prefer to live closer to home. There are even isolated reports of foreign – usually Vietnamese or Cambodian – labour being brought into the PRD.[57]

Wages continue to rise, and this does suggest rising production costs in southern China. The much-heralded peak in the labour force numbers has mysteriously moved on, with some even forecasting that it will happen in 2017–20. It is difficult to understand why the estimates change so much, as the young people in question were already born by the 1990s. Once the labour force does peak (whenever that may be) it will start to decline, which is good news for unemployment, as is the fact that large-scale state enterprise redundancy is much reduced and is unlikely to return to the historic levels (though it will nevertheless be important).

In response to the financial crisis, the Ministry of Railways said in 2008 that 6 million new jobs would be created in 2009.[58] In 2010, 9.3 million urban jobs were created. In 2012 the government announced a plan to create 45 million new jobs between then and 2015, which sounds like over 11 million a year.[59]

The local authorities in migrants' home provinces allocated money to encourage returnees to start small businesses. As early as 2003–5, access to microcredit enabled 300,000 people successfully to start small businesses. The idea is good, but the rate will need to accelerate sharply to have any significant overall impact. Surprisingly, by world standards China is slightly underrepresented in small business ownership: it has 40–60 million SMEs (if one includes the self-employed). On average across the world, 5 per cent of the population owns an SME, so China could anticipate an entrepreneurial stratum of 67 million.

China is likely to have to wrestle with deep unemployment for some years; it will simultaneously have to confront the challenges of rapid ageing, a declining labour force and rising wages.

Stimulus Measures

Beijing moved swiftly, bravely and on a large scale to address the Western economic crisis. Policy-makers hoped that a cocktail of initiatives could resurrect exports and build domestic consumption.

The three most important measures announced to boost the economy were the stimulus package, the massive bank lending programme in 2009–10 and the planned healthcare initiative. Worth $586 billion, the scale of the financial stimulus package, initially unveiled in November 2008, surprised many commentators. It focused on infrastructure, such as railways, airports and earthquake reconstruction, and, to a lesser extent, on social initiatives.

State banks obediently supported the package with a mammoth $1.4 trillion of extra lending in 2009, and $1.2 trillion in 2010. Since banks are mostly now listed companies, with substantial overseas shareholders who might have been expected to cavil at massive government-supported infrastructure lending, the revelation that the leading banks are not transformed commercial institutions, but are still essentially government departments, could hit China hard in years to come. Most senior bankers are state-appointed Party members who circulate through government posts; they do not gain promotion by refusing requests from senior leaders. There is little evidence of restraining attempts by foreign shareholders, and any influence they have is likely to diminish, as overseas banks often sold their stakes in Chinese ones because of their own difficulties. Any moral suasion by overseas bankers has lost much of its traction since the debacle of Western banking.

Private enterprises will not have felt empowered to participate actively in stimulus arrangements, as they are heavily geared to exports during a trade collapse and have been largely excluded from bank credit. Some finance will have gone into construction and associated fields, and accelerated massive railway construction is under way. Jobs have been created, often in the interior of the country. China has spent heavily on infrastructure since 1979, but there has been much wasteful duplication and much provincial and local posturing. This is another example of China's 'rule of scale': because China is a very large place, there can be hundreds of examples of waste, yet investment overall has proved highly efficient. As a result one should always be wary of drawing conclusions from anecdotal evidence. Many investment projects were long overdue and much needed – for example the policy to link all 'qualified administrative villages' in the whole country by road. All such measures bring employment. The issue has more to do with the type of infrastructure, the balance between infrastructure and other measures, and the extent of subsequent bad loans.

The most eye-catching measure was the huge boost to bank lending during 2009–10. However, there is evidence that throughout this period much of the credit was used for other purposes, such as bank deposits, real estate, the stock market and perhaps even the Macau gaming tables. Some reports suggest that in 2009 up to 30 per cent found its way to the stock market,[60] and according to Wei Jianing, an economist at the State Council in Beijing, 15 per cent of loans 'were illegally invested in stocks'.[61] Certainly share prices and volumes rose markedly. We can assume that between a third and a half of the new lending over 2009 and 2010 went into the real economy, say $1 trillion. It is unfortunate that most economic growth and employment creation happen in the private sector because most bank lending went to the state sector. One can say that 'a rising tide floats all ships' but it does seem inefficient for a government-led banking system not to meet government objectives more effectively. It is unfortunate that when the state uses its coercive powers to oblige banks to increase lending substantially, it does not simultaneously mandate lending to the most productive borrowers.

Beijing had to supplement its original stimulus package with further measures. The November 2008 package was a fine first step, but was insufficient and too biased towards infrastructure spending. The economic crisis and the need for responses presented a real opportunity to change the economic model, rather than just await the return of good times for low-cost exporting. However, this opportunity was missed – or at least not fully grasped. Furthermore, government itself has some ability to play a direct role by borrowing and spending. It is in the position of having – formally – an under-leveraged balance sheet and a savings-rich state corporate sector. The healthcare initiative was welcome but it will require extensive application, and academics do not believe it is being rolled out swiftly enough. Unguided credit expansion and modest social security expansion did not represent the best package. In 2010, Guo Shuqing, then head of China's second-largest commercial bank, was gloomy. He said GDP growth of 9.5 per cent or above would

> be very problematic . . . It will mean more duplication of construction, more excess capacity and higher waste of capital . . . There [will] be a price to pay

for the flood of new state-directed bank lending that made up the bulk of China's economic stimulus package last year, when banks extended Rmb 9,600bn [\$1,400bn] in new loans – double the amount lent a year earlier . . . we are definitely going to pay some costs for that in the form of asset bubbles or rising inflation.[62]

The economy was in severe trouble in 2008–9 – the worst the country has seen, certainly since 1979. The challenge went beyond economics, as it threatened stability and was thus potentially political. The authorities appreciated this and responded with solutions which, although not fine-tuned to the most critical requirements, did have an effect. The stimulus money was not completely effective in creating employment, and – as Guo implies above – the price to pay may be significant risk of collateral damage in terms of future inflation and over-investment, stock market loan defaults, bad real estate debt and a large amount of general non-performing loans. However, most importantly, action was taken and crisis was averted.

Saving and Spending

Alongside the encouragement of innovation, domestic consumption offers the best prospect for restoring long-term economic growth. Having been about 6 per cent of GDP before reforms started in 1978, savings rose substantially and averaged around 20 per cent for the decade up to 2008. If household savings could be reduced and the money spent, policy-makers would be delighted with the impact on the economy. Growth, fuelled by fixed investment, has been high because consumption has been low; if we want consumption-driven growth, the model must change.

Lacking effective social security, most save for medicine, future hospital bills, school fees, their sons' dowries to their future wives' families, housing or retirement – 'precautionary saving'. Parents, often allowed only one child, face old age with reduced family support, and the unsophisticated nature of the financial system offers a limited and ineffective selection of financial products to provide social security. Social initiatives, particularly in health, would have a huge effect: as so much of the country's untapped household saving is for unpredictable events, such as illness or hospitalisation, some form of insurance against any such eventuality should release 10, 50 or 100 times as much savings as the same money spent on infrastructure.

Creating confidence in any new initiative will take time, and savings will not be spent quickly. House prices are so high that many young people cannot afford the 20–30 per cent down-payment that is needed, so many parents use their savings to help them. Spending was also constrained during and after the 2008–9 downturn because, with every factory closure or restructuring, people became increasingly nervous that they might join the tens of millions of unemployed. This was not the best climate for savers to start spending. During the boom years, the economy expanded but disposable income lagged behind, so workers felt they were not prospering as the economy grew. Indeed, wages as a percentage of GDP fell from 52 per cent in 1999 to 37 per cent at the end of 2008. This also reduces the impetus and ability to spend; hence, household consumption fell to 34 per cent by 2010 – surely the lowest share of consumption in any significant economy ever.

In China, household savings per person are not especially high by Asian standards, although in 2011 the IMF reported consistently rising urban savings rates, from 20 to 30 per cent of disposable income – the opposite of what is desired.[63] Furthermore, the level of household savings – in 2009 the average was $3,000 or so per capita – does not lend itself to a massive spending urge. Government-mandated low interest rates are a forced subsidy from household savers to industry. If we want households to spend, they might be encouraged by gaining greater income from their deposits. The current exchange rate of the *renminbi* is again a subsidy from households (which might otherwise buy imported goods and balance the trade flows) to industry, which wants to export.

More of China's high savings are to be found in the corporate sector, and particularly in the state sector, as its frequently quasi-monopolistic position and artificially cheap credit make it generally more profitable than the private sector. However, middle class households could spend more if persuaded.[64]

Given these factors – government failure to prioritise social provision, rising gender disparity, gloomy economic news, low currency value, low interest rates and low economic impact on wages – the domestic consumer economy is unlikely to boom in the near term. Further social programmes and implementation of previous announcements would be constructive. Even more useful would be for the authorities to take a radical look at the role of the currency and interest rates. Even in 1988, the government was choosing to keep interest rates low to benefit producers.[65] It should consider how much it wishes to run the economy for the producers rather than the consumers, especially when it is paranoid about threats of instability.

Productivity and Agriculture

At the end of the 1970s, China, America and India had the same investment efficiency, measured by the Incremental Capital–Output Ratio (ICOR): it required the equivalent of 6 per cent of the economy to be invested to produce

1 per cent economic growth. Since then, America has become less efficient (the figure required now is almost 8 per cent), while China and India have become more efficient (under 4 per cent at times).[66]

China has received substantial investment recently, but its efficiency has been debated, and sharp increases in 2009–11 in the ICOR (twenty-year highs of around 5.5 per cent in 2009–10, then 6 per cent in 2011 taking it back to the late 1970s) highlighted the issue: theoretically the economy is becoming less efficient.[67] It is disputed whether investment is calculated correctly and whether growth is under- or overstated (and even whether previous data are accurate). There has clearly been a sustained long-term increase in efficiency but there is now some evidence that it has ended. This should be combined with the fact of rising leverage yet lower rates of economic growth.

Jobs haven't grown much recently, but people continue migrating from the land to the urban areas. Over ten years (1997–2007) official figures reported that agricultural employment had fallen by 10 per cent, manufacturing had risen by 25 per cent and services by 35 per cent. These figures are quite under-stated, but they illustrate a trend. Overall, jobs have grown by 1 per cent per annum for the decade; roughly 43 per cent of the labour force works in agriculture, which is 11 per cent of the economy. Clearly agricultural productivity is low, and so each person who transfers from working in farming to working in commerce could contribute to a rise in GDP and productivity.

It is a national priority to maintain farming, but it is hugely labour intensive: American agriculture employs 1.5 people for every square mile of arable land; China employs 500. This is largely because China's farmland is often worked manually, without the use of animals. This will not change until farmers can raise sufficient funds to buy animals or equipment. That will depend on land registration finishing by 2019 and land rights trading and mortgaging being widely introduced.

If we apply the US agricultural labour intensity to Chinese agriculture, that would suggest there are up to 275 million farm workers who would be surplus to modern farming needs and theoretically freed to enter urban employment. However, it is normally the young who become migrant workers, there will be no immediate change to the way agriculture is financed, and so much of that potential pool will not migrate in the near future.

The 2006 agricultural census shows there are well over 7.5 smallholdings for every tractor. The NBS tells us there is scarcely over 1 acre of land for each of the 349 million agricultural labourers. This partially explains the labour intensity in farming. And the excess labour explains why, since the 1980s, young migrant workers have been flooding into towns and cities in search of work. The 2010 census shows 260 million migrants.

The question is whether the surplus has been absorbed. To try to answer this, CASS carried out a study in 2009.[68] Using a figure of 326 million agricultural workers, it estimated that only 44 million would probably migrate. It also examined migrants' wage rates and found that, since about 2004, wage rates had at long last started rising, again suggesting that the migrant labour supply was dwindling. An associated, politically sensitive, issue is whether Beijing needs to consider consolidation of land-holdings to create efficiencies of scale: 201 million separate farm holdings is suboptimal.

If agricultural efficiency continues to improve, then for many years there should be a net 8–10 million leaving the land to become migrant workers (probably nearer 10 million – possibly more). The urban areas will still produce several million people of their own who want jobs. Including the 7 million or so students who graduate each year, on average some 22 million of those currently aged 16–25 will emerge on to the national job market annually. We should probably assume that, say, 4 million of those join the dwindling agricultural workforce to replace the dead and retired.

According to the NBS, in the decade up to 2007 manufacturing and services in the cities and formal jobs in the rural areas generated an average of just over 11 million jobs a year. The years 2011-12 reported annual urban job growth averaged 12 million, although the quality is unclear.[69] Many informal jobs are not captured in the statistics, but it does look as if either the economy has to maintain high growth rates or unemployment will rise sharply. However, what we are seeing is reduced rates of growth and a reduced linkage between growth and jobs

Table 2.2: **Possible Annual Balance of Future Demand for Formal Employment**

Annual school-leavers and graduates	22 million
Potential transfer of current farm workers to factories	10 million
[Minus school-leavers going into farming	4 million]
Formal job-seekers each year	28 million
[Minus retirees	17 million]
Net annual job demand	11 million?
Average annual new urban job creation 2006–10	11.4 million

This leaves out currently unemployed migrants, unemployed urban residents, unemployed graduates, and future redundancies from further restructuring and pollution-related closures and informal job creation. Currently up to 17 million annually reach retirement age (50–5). Although the habit is often to take another job, they will die/retire at some point. If all labour surplus down to 20 times US intensity levels left farming, over 10 years a further 11 million would arrive annually in the cities.

It is estimated that half of today's urban jobs are informal: this includes the self-employed, micro enterprises, short-term contract workers, home workers and day labourers.[70] Many people end up in the informal sector, and thus slip through the statistics; but there will be little social protection for them.

Productivity is likely to continue improving as workers move from labour-intensive, inefficient agriculture to rather more efficient manufacturing or services. However, even there, productivity is much lower than in the West, and there is substantial room for improvement.

A major issue in agriculture has always been arable land per capita. This has been falling since the Song dynasty (see Chapter 1).[71] Chinese officials express considerable concern about the continuing loss of arable land to urbanisation or degradation and the accompanying fear that food self-sufficiency may end. Needless to say, the actual extent of cropland is unclear. While the loss of land is a steady process, new land is constantly being introduced in the further margins, such as Heilongjiang, Xinjiang and Inner Mongolia.[72] Unfortunately, the land lost to urbanisation was 80 per cent more productive than this new remote land.[73]

Total cropland is estimated to have increased by 42 per cent from 1700 to 2005.[74] However, from 1986 to 2000 – a period of rapid development – the net result was that although cultivated land increased, production scarcely changed. By 2005 cropland had decreased again.[75] In 2010, there was more land in cultivation than in 1935, but in per capita terms it had halved.[76] Beijing has set a 'red line' that it must retain 300 million acres of cropland (official calculations suggest that the actual figure now is around 305 million). The real problems are not acreage but official discouragement from growing what suits the soil (in favour of grains); inefficiently small plot sizes; water shortages; excessive farming intensity; and the progressive replacement of good land with poor land.

In 2008, a reform was enacted to allow farmers to lease out land and from 2009 loans were made against land use rights. At first no corporate money could participate, but by 2010 this constraint had apparently been lifted. If farmers get better land title and then borrow to acquire animals and tractors, they are likely to shed surplus labour faster. There may not be enough urban jobs for the swelling migrant population and formal job creation has been weakening. This puts huge reliance on the informal sector – private and services – to take up the slack.

Challenges to the Private Sector

State company quasi-monopolies have created huge profitability: the telecom company China Mobile was adding a customer base the size of Greater London every quarter.[77] Meanwhile, attempts to close smaller mines to consolidate the coal industry favour state enterprises, and drives to address pollution can appear biased against private companies: smaller mining companies may be guilty of more pollution or accidents than larger ones, but it is clearly arbitrary to close those producing less than 90,000 tons a year (as happened in 2006). One of the contemporary battles being quietly fought is between property-based rights and position-based rights (as in the powers of government officials). There is a slow acceptance of property rights but practical recognition lags behind constitutional change.[78]

When the *renminbi* appreciated in 2005–7, it became harder for firms to win orders. Companies with parents overseas in America, Japan or Europe probably continued to get a good flow of orders, but independent private and Hong Kong companies struggled and had to cut their margins severely. The real state of private enterprise is difficult to discern but since 2008 its dynamic expansion has probably been hampered by both thin margins and credit shortage. This could weaken China's economy, and Beijing is being pressed by bodies like the World Bank to encourage the private sector and boost the service sector. As a result, in 2010 and 2013 the authorities said they would open various hitherto closed sectors of the economy.[79]

Private companies have largely passed from being despised on political grounds to being disadvantaged through standing outside the state-sector relationship culture. Increasingly, Jiang Zemin's drive to attract entrepreneurs into the Party has not just benefited the Party, but has also provided entrepreneurs with political 'legitimacy' and contacts to bankers, regulators and other officials.

It is, though, still dangerous to attain conspicuous wealth. The richest businessman of 2008, Huang Guangyu, the owner of retail giant Gome, was jailed on insider dealing charges. The second-richest entrepreneur in 2008 lost control of his company to a state enterprise after claiming he had been denied bank credit and then becoming involved in a bribery case.[80] The long period before charges are filed and the lack of information make these incidents quite opaque. Is it a problem of becoming 'too big' for the taste of the authorities, or one of operating outside the Party networks? The individuals concerned might be guilty of crimes, but it is difficult to know.

It is estimated that one-third of private entrepreneurs are Party members, if one includes former state officials who have somehow acquired previously state-owned enterprises.[81] Li Shufu, the owner of the largest private car manufacturer, Geely, which in 2010 bought Volvo, is reportedly the secretary of his company's CCP branch.[82] Political protection is widely deemed necessary. However, given the 'contestation' between different business groups, protection alone is not enough: it is probably necessary to have *better protection* than one's competitors.

The Middle Income Trap

It is often observed that fast-rising economies can run out of steam, settle into a middle-income rut and fail to continue their rise to challenge for global pre-eminence. A common example given is South America in the 1960s and 1970s. A study sponsored by the Asian Development Bank suggests there is a good chance that China will encounter this phenomenon.[83]

The chances of this happening are much greater in economies which have highly undervalued exchange rates, as China has had. A shrinking ability to bring underemployed people into the economy and a reducing contribution from utilising acquired foreign technology contribute to this. Hence the Chinese government aspiration to build a knowledge-based economy to create 'indigenous innovation' and so power the country to continuing high growth. The study additionally cites the likely contribution of a slowdown in labour force growth, an undervalued exchange rate, the rise of capital stock and total factor productivity growth. Other critical factors are rising old-age dependency, and volatile and high inflation.

Also, and very importantly, it is apparently essential for China to attain 58 per cent of US GDP per capita – that represents some kind of turning point. But this becomes harder to achieve if the other factors induce a slowdown. With expected future growth rates of 6–7 per cent this decade and 5–6 per cent in the next, it is even harder for China to reach that 58 per cent figure. Even at 7 per cent, followed by 6 per cent growth, China won't reach 58 per cent of American per capita GDP until 2023–24. So perhaps what we shall see is a steady slowdown in the long-term Chinese growth rate.

Into Africa: Trade and Investment in the Developing World

A singular aspect of China's economic strategy is its drive into some of the remotest parts of the world. Government, banks and enterprises have made huge efforts, and overseas investment is rising rapidly. Outward foreign direct investment (FDI) rose nineteen-fold from 2000 to 2006 and sixfold from 2005 to 2012.[84] Total Chinese overseas FDI is estimated at $350 billion and projected to hit $1–$2 trillion by 2020. This is a serious element of the total economy and is focused mainly on the developing world.[85] Investment in Africa alone is estimated at $127 billion.[86] Beijing has signed energy deals with Brazil, Kazakhstan, Iraq, Sudan, Venezuela and Russia, and mining deals with the Congo and

Afghanistan. The strategy is also driven by a clear concern about the state of domestic grain production and thus national food security.

China has recognised the opportunities: 'Africa is in the stage of passing from a continent open and rural to a continent full and urban.'[87] Beijing has several reasons for engaging actively with developing countries. Africa has a tenth of proven global oil reserves and China buys a third of its oil there. (America plans to buy a quarter there by 2015.)[88]

In 2008, the OECD confirmed that China had invested in forty-eight African countries, and by 2009 over 2,000 enterprises were involved.[89] The ten largest external investors were all state-linked enterprises. Most of those firms which answered the government's call for commerce to 'Go Global' were in natural resources, but according to US officials small Chinese private investors have also put millions of dollars into factories, construction and agriculture.[90] Indeed, in 2010, one private firm planned to buy two of the world's largest molybdenum producers.[91] There has been a distinctly old-fashioned mercantilist aspect to attempts to buy energy, minerals and food.

China's African trade rose from $10 billion in 2000 to $198 billion in 2012, in which year it was estimated that there were 1 million Chinese in Africa.[92] It overtook Russia to become the largest arms supplier to Africa in 2005-8.[93] By 2009, it was South Africa's largest trade partner. Both the Chinese government and private sector have been supportive of the expansion outwards: since the 1980s, the number of Chinese institutions teaching Arabic has risen from two to over a hundred, with an estimated 10,000 students.[94]

Some very substantial energy deals were negotiated in Africa in 2009-10, particularly in Angola and Nigeria. China, which imports half its oil, invested heavily in Sudan's oilfields, and now Sudan and South Sudan theoretically provide 7-10 per cent of China's imported oil. Since South Sudan's independence, fighting has prejudiced this flow.[95]

China's participation in recent 'land grabs' has attracted comment. Countries and businesses have become concerned about food and energy security, as foreign states and private investors have signed deals with poor countries to take control of huge tracts in Africa and elsewhere to cultivate food crops and ethanol.

The UN warned in 2010 that China was losing 1.5 million acres of farmland annually and could face food insecurity.[96] In 2011, the Chinese Academy of Sciences suggested that within fifty years China could lose 40 per cent of its grain production owing to erosion of the black soil in the north-east.[97] With such predictions, it is hardly surprising that China has joined the land-buying. China's sovereign wealth fund (China Investment Corporation (CIC)) has acquired 15 per cent of the Noble Group, which has agricultural land in Argentina, Brazil and Uruguay. Chongqing, China's largest city, announced in 2009 its plan to spend $8 billion buying foreign assets, including attaining food security by acquiring almost 1 million acres of agricultural land. China has also negotiated with Zambia to acquire 5 million acres to plant jatropha, a cheap biofuel feedstock that needs little water, is long lasting and can be planted almost anywhere.

China's substantial investment in distant and volatile areas raises a number of important issues. Western countries criticise it for appearing to 'back' unattractive governments in Africa. This is because China does not link its investment, trade and aid to human rights and does not make value judgements (an approach that was familiar to Disraeli or Kissinger). Its non-interference can resemble overt support: it trains and arms the police of regimes which many find distasteful; South African port workers have refused to unload Chinese arms for the Zimbabwe police. In Niger, Zambia and the Congo Africans have also criticised allegedly harsh labour practices and Chinese unwillingness to employ locals except in the most junior capacity. Namibia has complained of bribery and loans tied to the purchase of Chinese goods. Furthermore, many of the African countries where China has acquired agricultural land are themselves at 'high risk' and 'extreme high risk' of food insecurity.[98]

However, we should note the 2010 coup in uranium-rich Niger, where China is a major investor. There the army deposed the dictator and began talking of good government. China didn't miss a beat and relations are as good as before. In fact, China is possibly less directly supportive of regimes than is France in countries like Gabon, Mauritania and Niger. Li Ruogu has been forthright about China's investment in Africa – it is a different development model, but, he believes, a superior one:

> ... without economic growth, development is but an empty word. However, economic growth is not everything. If economic growth fails to drive social progress in the end, such kind of growth is meaningless altogether.[99]

Li argues that the West left Africa with weak institutions and infrastructure, impeding its subsequent development. China is willing to invest in infrastructure and trade and to grant loans and aid without making political demands, and has no interest in the internal political affairs of countries. China works with all kinds of political systems – a policy approved by Senegal's then president, Abdoulaye Wade: 'China's approach to our needs is simply better adapted than the slow and sometimes patronizing post-colonial approach of European investors.'[100]

In an opinion piece 'Why we need the Chinese', President Kagame of Rwanda wrote in 2009 that trade and investment were better than aid, that African countries need to take responsibility for human rights, and that Europe and America should open their markets to African products: 'while helpful, aid has not delivered sustainable development, it is clear that trade and investment bring greater opportunity for wealth creation'.[101] Yoweri Museveni, the Ugandan president, suggested that 'the western ruling groups are conceited, full of themselves, ignorant of our conditions'.[102] Wade, Kagame and Museveni are regarded by the West as good African leaders. Ecobank CEO Arnold Ekpe says the Chinese 'are not setting out to do good. They are setting out to do business. It's actually much less demeaning.'[103] The Zambian economist Dambisa Moyo argues that drastic aid reduction would improve African governance.[104] It is perverse and hypocritical to single China out for specific criticism. Western accusations of 'neo-colonialism' should be more equitably distributed.

Of course, China does not stop with Africa: Australian farming and mining, Afghan copper, Iraqi oil, Swedish automobiles and South American agriculture, mining, railways and energy have been among its many targets. In Alaba, Nigeria, Africa's largest electronics market, 90 per cent of the appliances are Chinese, and China is the largest foreign investor in Brazil.[105] The overseas drive, particularly in the developing world, addresses China's need for food, energy and minerals security, but it also enables enterprises to find compensating custom during Western retrenchment. Worryingly, however, any regime changes or social disturbances abroad may jeopardise China's increasingly large investments.

What Now?

It is perhaps unsurprising that this chapter on the economy has been as much about employment as about growth. Employment is the political priority. Several key factors – domestic and external – that helped to make China so successful over thirty years are now changing. The old model is comprehensively broken and it faces multiple challenges. China is no longer the cheapest country in which to manufacture. Currency movements have disadvantaged it, wages have risen, social and environmental costs are increasing. Export margins were always thin, but with rising costs there is little buffer available to absorb the impact. The good news is that entrepreneurs continually seem to squeeze further productivity gains out of their businesses. Unemployment has risen but – paradoxically – so have labour shortages. The economy needs to generate adequate employment and rising incomes. China needs to handle deep unemployment and simultaneously reorient itself to address a declining labour force and a rising cost structure. If the old cheap export and fixed invest-ment model is broken, the alternative should be a combination of the long-awaited innovation and domestic consumption. However, the downturn showed that the country's technological and economic competitiveness still lags well behind world standards.[106]

China has proved resilient in the face of the Western slowdown. However, we might ponder the likelihood of adverse consequences from the credit boom. And the drive into Africa and elsewhere may present unpalatable political and security entanglements.

China experienced years of essentially Gladstonian capitalism, which worked. Now that instability is rising, working conditions must improve. The passive government unions have woken up. The social system needs upgrading. Beijing has had enough of pollution: it is imposing higher environmental standards. The Communist Party will not espouse socialism, but elements of what some might call 'social democracy' are appearing. Indeed, British Conservatives might be reminded of Disraeli's critique of industrial capitalism untempered by social justice. The formula for the future might be growth tempered with equity.

Does this mean 'farewell high growth'? Not necessarily. The old model will not endure: repairs have been made but the future requires real reform. If there is genuine desire to encourage consumer spending, measures might include increasing the value of the *renminbi* and raising interest rates. Further and comprehensive reform is needed, for example in water and energy pricing, land and credit supply. To create employment, the service sector must be opened to more competition – private competition; and the private sector needs measures to encourage it to continue as the motor of growth and employ-ment. Clearer property rights, less political risk for private business, an end to the regulation which restricts rural people's rights to become urban, deregula-tion and the dismantling of monopolies, encouraging businessmen to focus less on handling officials and more on innovation – all this could allow the economy to move up a gear.

Despite vested interests, most economic reforms will probably come about in the end; the process is fitful, but the message is accepted. The difficulties arise when economics overlaps with politics: property rights and state owner-ship are not academic economic debates but issues that affect political power. Such considerations affect the speed and scope of the economic reforms China needs to embrace. Unwillingness to widen reforms risks the nation's future. Failure to reform and an inability to create the innovation economy will directly prejudice China's long-term growth. The middle-income trap will beckon.

CHAPTER THREE

The Elusive Knowledge Economy

If it is to avoid being trapped by its rising wage costs, China needs to make a clear break from its old model of low-cost, low-margin manufacturing and to build a high-technology, innovative economy. The government has planned for several years to make China an innovation-driven economy. But can China upgrade and compete – not on price, but on quality and innovation? Second, the status of global superpower normally implies being the technological and intellectual leader of the world. How successful is China in this drive? There are some bright pockets, but overall the results are quite disappointing.

Beijing is convinced of the need for innovation, and considerable research has been done. The growth in the number of patents, for example, can be shown to have a causal relationship with GDP growth in advanced economies. Josheski and Koteski use a variety of statistical tests to demonstrate that there is a positive long-term relationship in G7 countries between patent growth and subsequent economic growth.[1] Although China has been able to grow as a developing economy for reasons not associated with technology and innovation, if it is to make the breakthrough as a developed economy it must now employ both.

China is highly active in research: it can build an aircraft carrier, a jet airliner, is a leader in stem-cell research and is getting almost as many citations in nanotechnology as America. Chinese scientists were the first to map the genome for rice. It has produced the world's fastest supercomputer and is becoming a leader in higher sciences. It is engaged in space exploration and cyber technology to the point where teams can hack into US military command programs (see Chapter 13). The world appears genuinely worried by China's scientific advances. However, I will argue that the platform is lacking for China to create an innovative economy. This is for reasons of education, history, culture, ethics and politics.

The country wants to upgrade from cheap manufacturing (or even assembling) for overseas customers, instead becoming the inventor of branded products that sell worldwide. To own the brand is to capture the margin. Can China move from assembling iPods to inventing the next big thing? As the chairman of the Chinese manufacturing company Konka said: 'We had worked very hard as a contract manufacturer . . . and we realized we had no money, nothing to show for it . . . like sewing a wedding dress for someone else's wedding.'[2] China must address this challenge if it is ever to match the American economy.

Margins have never been fat in China's export industries – a recent estimate put them at 3 per cent – and this has helped to make the exporters competitive in world markets.[3] They have competed not on innovation, but on price and delivery time.

The Aspiration

To become inherently profitable, and thus sustainable, the commercial sector must upgrade to value-added proprietary manufacturing and distribution. China must become more innovative, develop a knowledge-based society and a high level of technology – not just in one or two areas, but across the economy. Otherwise, the country is unlikely to be able to construct a sophisticated economy and achieve great power status. But demographic developments suggest time is running out (see Chapter 2).

Officials regarded the post-2005 rises in minimum wages and in the *renminbi* partly as policy tools to oblige companies to move up market (in an echo of Singapore's approach in the late 1980s). Unfortunately for China, the rises coincided with a downturn in global demand. This reduced the profitability of private companies, constrained their ability to raise their technical quality and even threatened their survival.

Beijing sees innovation as the key, and seeks to raise research spending and increase the number of patents, scientific citations, etc. There are far-reaching long-term official plans (such as the '863 project', which is China's 'premier strategic high-technology development program') and also long-range forecasts.[4] The thinking is that 'China wants to move away from the embarrassing situation of having to export 800 million shirts to pay for one imported airplane.'[5]

There are heterodox views that inventing products is not the best form of innovation, that research spending is wasted and patents often lie idle. Danny Breznitz at Georgia Tech in the US suggests in *Run of the Red Queen* that there is now so much dissociation within the invention, manufacturing and marketing process that no one can do everything.[6] Instead, clusters of excellence are emerging, where some firms, often neighbours, perform one function for many customers and do it excellently and cheaply, assisted by economies of scale. This suggests that Chinese business succeeded by being cost-effective and efficient in production. It has not followed the government-indicated path of inventing new products. Breznitz makes the point that Japan conquered the automobile industry by efficiently utilising other people's ideas; only later did it initiate original ideas. It seems that China can create a sustainable economy without invention but by continuing high-quality process innovation. However, despite such objections, Beijing has firmly embarked on the road of citations, research spending and patent application, and so we should look at how successful this is proving.

I would suggest that process innovation alone cannot upgrade companies sufficiently: sales and volumes could continue rising, and yet China might not prosper proportionately. There is a clear role for China to play in becoming ever better, more efficient and cheaper at manufacturing parts on an extensive scale within a much larger dissociated global production process, but the present margins of export manufacturers are extremely narrow. There is insufficient profit to make this an effective alternative central strategy to that of innovating new products. Moreover, as many of the China-based manufacturers are foreign owned, who benefits from their success?

The truth lies somewhere between the two views. While original invention and distribution are valuable, the vital element is brand ownership. Those who have the final customers can set the price; brand is the key. The potential for profit maximisation lies after manufacturing and before distribution.

Before the Western downturn, Chinese companies should have followed what their Asian cousins had done in Japan, Korea and Singapore – raised the quality and ownership of their product range. However, they were not ready. China is building brands, but it has insufficiently broad international distribution. Domestic products are improving all the time, but the picture is mixed. In 2009, China produced 12 per cent of the world's computer chips, and this is forecast to reach 21 per cent by 2012. This growth is assisted by large government expenditure and by the fact that since 2003 China has made up 41 per cent of all demand growth. However, the chips manufactured are 'two or more years behind' those of China's competitors. The challenge will be for Chinese companies to become designers of state-of-the-art chips.[7] Furthermore, four of the top five semiconductor manufacturers in China are actually foreign multinationals.

The Fallibility of Numbers

Before discussing research spending, we should first define what research and development (R&D) is. The Organisation for Economic Cooperation and Development (OECD) describes it rather grandiosely as: 'creative work undertaken on a systematic basis in order to increase the stock of knowledge, including knowledge of man, culture and society, and the use of this stock of knowledge to devise new applications'.[8]

Spending on R&D is hailed by politicians, academics and businessmen alike: it is a sign of modernity and dynamism. Unfortunately, as with so many statistics, the figures are often flawed. Governments can be subjective in constructing statistics, while private businesses might be very lax with their arithmetic in order to claim tax relief or boost their image. Frank Gannon, an academic who writes knowledgeably of the European Union bureaucracy, shows the scope available:

> The money a nation reports on R&D spending comes from a pot into which all sorts of unrelated ingredients are poured: building costs for research institutes, staff costs at all levels in the R&D chain, hospital laboratory costs, some clinical services, grants to industry to stimulate their research, costs to promote R&D, etc. And in reality, the list is even more heterogeneous, since the R&D spending is open to inventive interpretation.[9]

Real research costs in the context of the European Union might be only one-fifth of what is described as 'R&D expenditure'. Whenever the expression 'R&D expenditure' appears, let us assume that much of the money has been spent in distinctly unproductive ways. It is perhaps best if we use it reluctantly as an illustrative figure – a number that gives a sense of various countries' commitments to this laudable effort.

The OECD, while suggesting that data collection has improved in China, rather coyly implies there are problems with the balancing of 'China-specific characteristics and international comparability' – in other words, Chinese R&D data are not entirely comparable internationally.

Studies on China's Position in the World

Research and development expenditure is normally presented as a percentage of a country's annual economic output, or GDP, which is called 'R&D intensity'. Thus the resources committed by one country can be compared to those of another. In 2011 China spent 1.84 per cent of its GDP on R&D, compared with around 2.8 per cent in the US, 2.9 per cent in Germany and well over 3 per cent in Japan.[10] In 2012, China reached 1.98 per cent.[11] These are big differences. Moreover, unlike China, a quarter of US R&D is conducted overseas and thus is not counted.

Furthermore, because the figure is relative to the economy of each country, in absolute terms America probably spends about three times as much as China on research. China's R&D intensity is 40 per cent less than America's, though it is steadily rising (whereas the spending of US companies at home is not; their overseas spending is another matter). Countries that wish to overtake other, economically richer, nations by adopting a more innovative or research-based economic strategy inevitably need to have a greater R&D intensity than their competitors. The 2007/8 UNDP Human Development Report did not place China even in the top twenty countries for R&D intensity.[12]

The World Economic Forum's *Global Competitiveness Report 2013-2014* ranks China as the 29th most competitive economy in the world (out of 148), as it was in 2008.[13] It ranks China as the 26th most competitive economy in the world (out of 147) – up three places in three years. Factors that have held it back include: quality of scientific research institutions, managers' unwillingness to delegate, availability of financial services, lack of judicial independence, quality of the educational system, the efficacy of corporate boards, low education expenditure, secondary education enrolment, total tax rate including sales taxes, difficulties of starting a business, tariff barriers, firing, restriction on capital flows, and the availability of the latest technologies. China might be the second-largest economy, but it is very difficult to be the second most competitive economy when, in many respects, the advantages lie with smaller, more nimble countries: eight of the twelve most competitive economies had populations under 25 million.

INSEAD, the French business school, in its *Global Innovation Index 2013*, rates China as the 35th most innovative economy (of 142). In the 2011 report it was 29th. Adverse indicators have been include limited press freedom, low education expenditure and the whole political environment.[14] IMD, the Swiss business school, showed China in 20th place (out of 60), having fallen from 10th place in 2010 in terms of competitiveness.[15]

The OECD takes a rosier view of Chinese research. It focuses more on the rate of growth in research spending, but confuses matters by using purchasing power parity and constant dollars. It shows business contributing 70 per cent of research spending, but doesn't identify whether this is state or private business (because China doesn't analyse this well). According to the OECD, Chinese R&D spending is the third highest in the world, but only on the basis of PPP accounting – an economist's construct which seeks to recalibrate financial comparisons between countries that have varying costs of living; this may help to clarify relative living costs based on the cost of buying lunch in a rural Chinese village, but does not reflect the standard cost of buying laboratory equipment from Switzerland.[16] Ranking countries by money spent also suggests that they all spend equally wisely.

At the rather heterodox end of the spectrum, Booz Allen, the consulting firm, published a survey in 2005 of the world's top 1,000 corporate R&D spenders. It suggested that there was 'no discernible statistical relationship between R&D spending levels and nearly all measures of business success'.[17] Furthermore, Bart Becht, chief executive of Reckitt Benckiser, the Anglo-Dutch consumer cleaning products leader, also said in the same year that 'there is no correlation between the percentage of net revenue spent on R&D and the innovative capabilities of an organisation – none'.[18] A World Bank study from 1993 found that 'economic growth affects R&D activity rather than vice versa' and that developing countries that 'are behind grow by catching up technologically, not by advancing the technological frontier'.[19] These conclusions certainly suggest that much of the money committed to R&D is simply wasted.

One way of assessing scientific development is to count the number of citations by other scientists in scientific publications. Chinese research is increasingly cited, though less so in the most prestigious publications. Despite the quantity, the average Chinese scientific paper is cited on 30 per cent fewer occasions than the average paper from Japan, Hong Kong or Singapore.[20] For 2012, the website SJR Scimago ranked the most influential Chinese scientific magazine 484th in the world and Chinese scientific papers as among the least cited (behind more than 174 countries). This suggests that international scientists lack respect for their quality. In a 2010 report, the Chinese Institute of Scientific and Technical Information estimated that China ranked only 13th out of 19 major industrial economies in global scientific influence.[21]

State versus Private Spending on Research

Many problems arise from the state trying to be the R&D driver for the commercial sector. Milton Friedman observed that any state consumes at least twice as many resources in doing any given thing as the private sector. It adopts a top-down approach, deciding the programmes and priorities. It tries to pick the winners. This doesn't fit well with building success in a competitive global economy. Independent studies suggest that state sponsorship is not effective in driving commercially innovative research:

> Empirical research . . . results show that higher shares of government funding are associated with lower efficiency of R&D in improving total factor productivity. This may be attributed to source-of-fund effects on the research agenda and the incentive structure.[22]

Major countries tend to have low state and high private sector research funding, even if we acknowledge state subvention of private sector research. China cites high contribution rates to R&D from the business community: from 2000 to 2006, the share contributed by business enterprises to research spending rose from 60 per cent to 70 per cent. This looks good but, empirically, it seems unlikely. The traditional private sector cannot support R&D but a new private sector is arising which is technology-focused and contributing to R&D. Until recently, the private sector was starved of bank credit, it has chronically narrow margins, is culturally not research oriented and doesn't appear to be producing innovative new products.

Research suggests substantial commitment to projects that the government desires, rather than to projects which China's private sector would fund. No one suggests there is no serious role for government in research; the point is that suggestions of business sector leadership in Chinese research lack credibility. The official figures imply that private enterprise funds most research. What the NBS probably means to say is that *all business* – whether state enterprise, private or foreign – funds 70 per cent.

An increasing number of foreign-funded companies, such as Motorola (which in 2006 had sixteen R&D offices with 2,000 engineers), IBM and Microsoft, have set up and expanded R&D centres in China, since scientists are cheap (though salaries are rising rapidly thanks to competition) and it is an important market for future products.[23] By 2012, there were 3,000 foreign-owned research centres. In 2008, the OECD estimated that foreign contributions comprised a quarter of all business funding. Certainly US companies alone contributed over 2 per cent of total Chinese R&D spending in 2006, and that share should have risen.[24] These companies encounter some daunting hurdles, including human resources issues (stiff competition in hiring the best graduates and difficulties in retaining staff once they have been trained) and the problem of protecting their intellectual property – whether provided from their home base or developed in China – especially when staff leave. Thus human resources management is a two-edged sword: if access to sophisticated research work is permitted, the intellectual property may leave with the employee; if involvement in such programmes is denied, the employee may leave. Partly in recognition of such inherent difficulties, most multinationals circumscribe the research such facilities undertake:

Most R&D centers in China serve only in-country customer needs, but some companies have also set up branches of global technology-building networks that have the potential to boost regional growth in Asia. A growing number of companies are allowing their centers in China to work in both capacities.[25]

Multinationals conducting R&D do not necessarily transfer technology and aid the development of an innovative domestic economy. In fact, they are naturally protective of their intellectual property.

Around two-thirds of exports are from foreign-funded companies, as are 83 per cent of high-tech exports.[26] These levels are far higher than they were in Japan and Korea at similar points in those countries' development. This creates major concerns for China's 'national competitiveness and national security', which should parallel Washington's concern for the US. Beijing must groom its own globally competitive companies. State companies are probably funding many research projects on the government wish-list on a non-commercial basis.

The private sector funds about one-third of research. Of this, perhaps over half is by foreign enterprises such as Microsoft, which find Beijing pressing them to accept that when they do R&D in China, it counts as 'Chinese' R&D. China's domestic private sector contributes at most 10–15 per cent of total national R&D spending. This contrasts with the US, where it is 67 per cent, although some of that will be by foreign companies.[27] This is certainly supported by the figure that the Chinese domestic private sector contributes only about 12 per cent of new product development expenditure.[28]

Increasing Research Activity in China

In 2006, China overtook the US to become the largest exporter of high-tech products in the world, with a 17 per cent market share. However, as noted above, in 2009 some 83 per cent were made by foreign-funded enterprises.[29] Furthermore, the seemingly clear categorisation turns out to be less than clear: for example, 'high-tech products' can be high-tech components from overseas which are simply assembled to make a finished product. A 2008 study of high-tech industry in eight countries showed R&D expenditure to be between 11 per cent and 30 per cent of value added in seven of the countries; in China it was 4.6 per cent.[30] The study was tellingly entitled *Creative China?*.

In 1992, China spent 0.8 per cent of GDP on research, compared to the newly industrialising economies (NIEs) of Korea, Singapore, Hong Kong and Taiwan, which were spending 1.6 per cent. By 2002, China had reached 1.2 per cent intensity, but the NIEs' figure had increased to 2.2 per cent. China failed to hit its goal of 2 per cent by 2010. Even assuming that R&D intensity is of any significance, we should note that it is now not officially expected to reach 2 per cent until 2014.[31]

For Beijing, R&D is highly desirable in order to generate domestic innovation. Expenditure is rising rapidly (from a low base), but we should consider quality as well as quantity. Activity is perhaps too dominated by the multinationals and state-outsourced work, which means the fruits of the expenditure might be either unavailable or uncommercial. Chinese state-funded science culture evidences some of the worst aspects of government control, whereby the 'research and funding system is hierarchical and prizes seniority and connections over competence'.[32] China has a long road to travel before it overtakes Japan or America.

Patent Application and Grant

Domestic patent application has grown fast and this, according to academic studies, is due to economic growth, government encouragement, stronger patent protection, growth in inward FDI, greater industrial complexity and improved property rights. However, according to a survey by Thomson Reuters, 80 per cent of patent professionals believe Chinese patents are not of high quality.[33] Scepticism about the quality of patents is widespread.[34] There is even a view that much of China's rising patent application activity is designed merely to create bottlenecks and deterrents to innovative US companies.

The country has seen increasing intellectual property litigation: in 2011 there were 66,000 court cases. This shows growing interest both in new ideas and in defending them. What is less commendable is the suggestion that patent officials should gain bonuses for granting patents.[35]

The Availability of Scientists

By 2007, China had the same number of scientists as the US.[36] However, this has not yielded a research boom – presumably reflecting the scientists' quality, their resources, their projects and the culture and environment in which they operate.

A World Bank report on East Asia demonstrated a strong link between tertiary education for up to 8 per cent of the population and sharp rises in per capita income. After 8 per cent, there seem to be diminishing returns. China has already reached more than 25 per cent and has suffered massive graduate unemployment, even in boom periods (see Chapter 2). This suggests that what China needs is not more graduates, but better ones. In 2009 UNESCO reported on the growth of mass education: 'The "logic" of massification is inevitable and includes . . . generally an overall lowering of academic standards'.[37] The same report noted that increasing research intensity correlates well with raising GDP per person, but that after a certain stage of development it starts to produce diminishing returns. China has some time to reap these beneficial returns – if it can generate the research expenditure and direct it effectively.

China's under-performance in innovation might be explained not just by the level of research intensity but by other factors, such as human capital. In 2008, the World Economic Forum ranked China 52nd (out of 134 countries) for the availability of scientists and engineers. By 2009, it had risen to 36th place. Interestingly, a 2009 study, which draws on the experience of German companies in China, makes three critical points about R&D personnel: the average qualification level is below that of Western graduates in terms of practical experience and English-language skills (so great training effort is required); the turnover rates are very high (semiconductor manufacturers have reported median annual staff turnover of 29 per cent);[38] and salaries rise much more rapidly than in other countries.[39]

However, China has not only those scientists who currently reside there; it can also attempt to access the talents of the 700,000 or so highly skilled residents of OECD countries who are of Chinese origin (of whom over half live in the US). This is not to suggest that they would all move to China; however, some have, and others might be encouraged. Increasingly, after studying overseas, students have been returning home.[40] One difficulty is that the new environment and colleagues may not be so welcoming to those returning from overseas.[41] There are also quality issues surrounding domestic scientists: 'while the country's higher educational establishment is able to produce large quantities of science and engineering graduates to satisfy demand from both the civilian and defense economies, the quality of this talent pool is far from adequate'.[42]

Foreign Direct Investment

There is a good correlation between economic growth and the granting of patents, but there are other contributory factors. Academics refer to the 'spill-over' from business activities, such as the accumulation of knowledge derived by domestic companies from manufacturing foreign companies' products (original equipment manufacturing, or OEM) and the beneficial impact of foreign direct investment when it leads to the creation of factories or research facilities. China has historically been in the world's top tier of recipients of FDI funds. However, Swedish research based on 43,000 private SMEs in 2010 suggests that FDI suppresses China's ability to innovate.[43] The authorities previously expected FDI to flow principally from tax concessions. Indeed, in this context China was criticised for giving preference to foreign over domestic companies, and these concessions have been substantially reduced. Worldwide experience suggests that China was right to do this – an efficient working environment outweighs financial inducements:

> the World Bank's Investment Climate Surveys show that unreliable power supply, weak contract enforcement, corruption, and crime can impose costs several times greater than taxes. A Multilateral Investment Guarantee Agency (MIGA) survey of 191 companies with plans to expand operations found that only 18 percent in manufacturing and 9 percent in services considered grants and incentives to be influential in their choice of location. Of 75 Fortune 500 companies surveyed, only four identified them as influential.[44]

The aims of foreign company and host country can conflict. China wants to enforce a policy of 'autonomous innovation', which implies that, if intellectual innovation work is done in China, the process should be owned and patented in China. The US–China Business Council explains that the multinationals naturally resist:

> The effective management of IP [intellectual property] licensing rights is important for companies that want to maintain control over IP developed in China. Many companies ensure that IP developed by their R&D centers in China is owned by a larger entity . . . outside of China. This office . . . will contract the R&D center to complete fixed-term projects on a one-off basis. Doing so allows the company to manage its IP effectively and not unnecessarily expose IP to infringement risk in China. When gaining individual project approval from PRC government entities, such as local science and technology bureaus, it is important to be clear about to whom the resulting IP will be licensed and what the terms of the project in question are. Companies should also be aware that the PRC drive to promote 'autonomous innovation' could lead to future requirements that any IP significantly researched in China must be legally owned within China. For example, the Enterprise Income Tax Law (or corporate profit tax legislation) includes criteria for foreign-owned China entities to legally own core IP rather than have it licensed back to a parent company, per current standard practice.[45]

Local content rules for FDI were once seen by many countries, including China, as offering an opportunity to create technology 'spillover' to local industry. Such government policies do not of course encourage foreign investment in R&D in China. However, this often resulted in more expensive finished items, particularly China-produced cars. The attempt to insist on the creation of joint ventures rather than wholly owned foreign businesses had similar results: foreign firms are quite wary of sharing their technology with joint ventures. For example, Kodak invested six times as much in its sole wholly owned business in China as in all its various joint ventures combined. The joint ventures were required to produce basic film, while its subsidiary manufactured the most technically sophisticated film.

Chinese factories are often asked to assemble goods, and so their value added can be a handful of dollars on a product priced in three figures. Analysts in 2007 estimated that an assembly company in China received $4 for assembling a $299 iPod (and the profit on this sum would probably have been taken out of the country, as assemblers are generally foreign owned). Similarly, the Asian Development Bank reports that all components for an iPhone are bought in from outside China and has calculated that $6.50 is made in China by assembling the gadget, which is sold in the US for $179. Thus on 11 million units, $74 million revenue is booked to China, but a trade deficit of $2 billion is inferred. Again, the assembler which receives this sum is Taiwanese, and so not even the $74 million is gained by China.[46]

Research Decisions and Spending

So a disproportionate amount of China's R&D spending is by the government (or entities close to it), and the amount spent, relative to the country's economy, is far from impressive:

> China has been building up a network of national-level science and engineering laboratories since the mid-1980s to spearhead its technological modernization. But while more than 220 of these key state laboratories had been established by 2008, insufficient funding stunted their research performance. Between 1984 and 2004, total investment in these laboratories totalled a paltry Renminbi (RMB) 1.9 billion, much of which was spent on maintenance and salaries.[47]

We know very little about how the money is spent, but it is probably focused more on fulfilling government objectives than on meeting commercial requirements. Almost 80 per cent goes on product development and only 5 per cent on basic research, whereas in Japan, Korea and the US the latter figure is 13–19 per cent. This is an important point, as basic research promotes real inventiveness; there are signs that the level is now being raised. Most of the genuinely private sector spending is by multinational companies, which mainly develop existing products to target specifically Chinese customers. Multinationals remain determined to prevent the diffusion of any proprietary knowledge which they import or develop. A 2009 study by Booz & Co. found that firms which take a global approach to their research tend to outperform those that concentrate their research in their home market.[48] But very few of China's enterprises, apart from Huawei, the telecoms company, conduct research abroad. China urgently needs a more profitable domestic private sector with a greater interest in research.

If it is true that in the defence industry, which is a national priority, there are 'key structural barriers that include entrenched bureaucratic inertia, risk-averse decision making, institutional compartmentalization, and chronic project management problems that cause prolonged delays and cost overruns', how much more is this the case in the area of civilian government scientific research?[49]

History, Science and Plagiarism

There are serious issues to do with the history of science and the current state of science in China today. A glaring problem in the Chinese academic world is the amount of plagiarism. In 2007, for example, there was a flurry of well-publicised incidents, especially in university science and technology departments. This problem continues, but it extends far beyond claims of scientific discovery; there is pervasive fraud in the English and French language tests for entry to foreign universities, and in some areas the police have to supervise domestic university entrance exams.[50]

In academic circles there is a widespread culture of plagiarism. Fang Shimin, a molecular biologist who has assumed the role of plagiarism monitor, said in 2007 that he had found 'nearly 500 cases of plagiarism and other forms of misconduct at the country's leading universities'.[51] One professor exposed by Fang was charged in 2010 with arranging for a gang to attack him with a hammer.[52] *China Daily* reported in 2011 that 'academic plagiarism is rampant in Chinese universities, involving both students and staff. Academic papers are offered for sale on the Internet and some people specialize in helping others to write academic papers.'[53]

Plagiarism is clearly a global problem: it is, for example, widespread in the US. But a high proportion of students implicated in plagiarism in the US are Chinese: in 2007, Duke University expelled nine students – all from 'Asian countries'. A consultancy that advises US colleges on international students stated in 2010 that 'cheating is pervasive in China', with up to 'half of all applicants submitting forged transcripts and up to 90 per cent dummying up phony recommendations'. In 2010 Centenary College in New Jersey scrapped its entire MBA programme in Asia because of 'a plagiarism epidemic'.

Chinese intellectual tradition contributes to this phenomenon; classical scholars were trained to be 'compilers rather than composers': 'Having memorised vast sequences of the classics and histories, they constructed their own works by extensive cut-and-paste replication of phrases and passages from those sources. This unacknowledged quotation today would be called plagiarism.'[54] But they saw themselves as preservers rather than creators. There is a sense of paying 'tribute' to their predecessors. 'Confucius, be it remembered, claimed to be, not an originator or innovator, but a transmitter and restorer.'[55] Hegel made a different point in the nineteenth century: 'The Chinese have as a general characteristic, a remarkable skill in imitation.'[56] If one views China as having a different culture, where scholars seek knowledge, not self-promotion, and so can adopt an 'open source' approach to prior scholarship, perhaps the criticism of plagiarism can be overlooked. But this approach clashes with Chinese attempts to win a Nobel Prize in science.

This is by no means to overlook the breathtaking contributions to science over the centuries made by China, nor to ignore the tremendous influence that Chinese philosophy, for example, has had on Western thinking. Lou Marinoff at City University of New York has noted that scientific thinkers as diverse as the philosopher Gottfried Leibniz, the psychologist Carl Jung and the physicist Niels Bohr were all greatly indebted to Chinese philosophy. China's scientific future would benefit from distinguishing more clearly between utilisation and origination.

Arnold Toynbee, the historian, said that after 221 BC the configuration of China was that of 'intellectual torpidity and political unity punctuated by bouts of disunion that are abnormal and temporary'.[57] While not going that far, we might ask how it is that a society which, in ancient times, could invent paper, printing, canal locks, gunpowder and the compass could not continue innovating in modern science and technology.[58] China in the fourteenth century had a powered hemp-spinning machine similar to those introduced in France in the eighteenth century.[59] Song tax returns suggest that by 1078 iron production had reached 125,000 tons – a level Europe exceeded only in 1700.[60] In the eleventh century, the Chinese iron industry made the switch from charcoal to coal. Why did the industrial revolution take place in Britain rather than China? These questions have been termed the 'Needham Paradox' after the noted twentieth-century scholar Joseph Needham. He contested that China was a stagnant society, but conceded that it was 'homoeostatic', or prone to return to equilibrium after disturbance: China's inventions did not radicalise its own society, but they did others.[61]

A tension runs through the whole narrative of Chinese history. What is officially encouraged is the view that China was at its best when strong and united: what is respected is national integrity. But this was perhaps not China at its best. Xiao Jiansheng has made the observation that the Spring and Autumn and the Warring States periods (770–221 BC) were not nearly as negative a time as is suggested: 'Many competing schools of thought and philosophy competed in an open market of ideas.' On the other hand, 'many view the Emperor Qinshihuangdi's political unification of China in the Qin Dynasty as a great political act, even though it was a violently totalitarian state.'[62] Xiao observes that the weak Song dynasty produced the compass, gunpowder and moveable-type printing, but after that centralising governments took over and innovation waned.[63] This supports the point above made by Toynbee.

China seems to have followed very closely the path set by the Arab world – glorious scientific innovation, followed by rapid and almost complete somnolence. For the Arabs, the turning point came around the thirteenth century; for China it was between the thirteenth and the fifteenth centuries. Space precludes profound exploration of why this occurred, but some explanation for the decline of innovation in the Arab world might be found in the dispute between the scholar Averroës and al-Ghazali on the use of rational argument in Islam (Averroës favoured it and lost). Another contributory cause might be the Mongol invasion of the 1250s, which subsequently moved on to China. In the twelfth and early thirteenth centuries China seemed close to industrialisation, but, as Morris says: 'by the time Khubilai chased the last Song child-emperor into the sea in 1279, the complex infrastructure that had brought China to the verge of an industrial revolution was breaking down. Eastern social development went into free fall.'[64]

Reasons advanced for China's demise are diverse: there was no reward for success and no competition (internal or external); universities did not innovate, reason was not developed and mathematics was respected only for its practicality; the ethical system did not encourage science and inductive logic was not employed; there was no renaissance, no civilised neighbours, and no protection for intellectual property.[65] Moreover, the imperial examinations created barriers by focusing on the classics and literary skills (and therefore potentially excluding talented individuals without those skills); Confucianism was unenthusiastic about commerce,[66] and the culture did not encourage challenges to traditional thinking. There was no passionate pursuit of discovery and knowledge, and human endeavour was discouraged 'in its attempt to conquer Nature.'[67]

Even when Europe and China discovered the same things, Oswald Spengler draws a distinction: 'the Western strives to direct the world according to his will . . . the Chinese did not wrest, but wheedled, things out of Nature.'[68] Or, as Hegel said, 'in mentioning Chinese sciences we encounter a considerable clamour about their perfection and antiquity'; past findings were, in his view, reverently preserved, but 'there is wanting to them on the other side that free ground of subjectivity, and that properly scientific interest, which makes them a truly theoretical occupation of the mind'. Furthermore, 'what may be called scientific is of a merely empirical nature, and is made absolutely subservient to the Useful on behalf of the State'.[69] (This could have been written in the early twenty-first century.) As a result, science slept.

A specific case is the extraordinarily slow development of railways in China. They arrived only in 1876, with the Woosung railway near Shanghai, which was built by foreigners, bought by the Chinese and deliberately destroyed by them the following year.[70] Chinese officials had several concerns: they believed that increased mobility would assist foreign invaders; that the feng shui would be disturbed; and that the development of railways would raise unemployment.[71] They specifically believed that the large-scale and bloody Taiping rebellion had been started by transport workers rendered unemployed by innovation. Subsequently, in 1881, further railways were built, but at an average rate of only 18 miles a year until 1895.[72]

In the 1990s, Kenneth Pomeranz ascribed the West's superior economic development to its access to energy and colonies and its propensity to employ force to develop trade. He singles out the significance to the West of the presence of coal, the development of environmental knowledge (such as forest culture) and the arrival of the potato (though this rather downplays the arrival of the potato in China and its huge coal reserves).[73] By comparing the most developed regions of China with those of Europe, he allows himself to conclude that China might even have been more developed, more free and more market oriented than Europe in the late eighteenth century; but this approach ignores the fact that European clusters were often individual countries with their own national policies, whereas Chinese clusters were within a state which had a national policy that did not necessarily favour an open society.[74]

Horesh and Landes point out England's use of husbandry and chemicals in agriculture and water-milling in garment manufacture, China's weak institutional framework, the ubiquity of financial paper instruments and highly developed joint-stock companies in England. England's commercial law, government espousal of property rights and the ardent pursuit of scientific knowledge are all mentioned.[75] Wang Hui suggests that the industrial revolution came first to Europe because of the existence of a petty bourgeoisie, capital accumulated from trading with the East and the fact that there was a market for European products in the East (although this final point is somewhat questionable).[76] China's development of an agrarian-bureaucratic culture, rather than an industrial-commercial one, is blamed, as is the value system of Confucianism, with 'the Chinese tendency . . . to rule out neutrality and classify all things into the two categories of good and evil. This characteristic clearly indicated their lack of objectivity, and without such an attitude no science could develop.'[77]

Geography has been suggested as the main determining factor in the West achieving success. Indeed, Ian Morris claims it was much more important than people – 'maps not chaps'.[78] While the absence of civilised neighbours and cultural exchange may have affected China's inventiveness, it should be pointed out that the same absence existed before the fifteenth century, when China *was* inventive. The geography has not changed much in two thousand years. However, Morris's point is that at different stages of social development a different geography can prove beneficial – for example, access to rivers or to minerals:

> when the Atlantic rose to prominence in the seventeenth century . . . those people best placed to exploit it – at first chiefly the British, then their former colonists in America . . . created new kinds of empires and economies and unlocked the energy trapped in fossil fuels. And that I will argue is why the West rules.[79]

It is difficult to share the view that the Pacific was a great barrier to Chinese navigation. Although the Atlantic may have risen to prominence, the Pacific Ocean at the same time was not without commercial significance for China. It has been suggested that in the early nineteenth century the Yangtze enjoyed greater maritime trade than the Thames.[80] Looking further back, we should not disregard those vast Pacific voyages of thousands of miles undertaken by the Polynesians. Furthermore, China has some of the most extensive coal deposits in the world. Geography alone cannot explain the relative performance of civilisations; culture and character are not irrelevant. I believe there was a vigour and assertiveness in traders such as the English that was less evident in their Chinese contemporaries and that allowed them to expand their trade routes and fostered innovation.

Contemporary Chinese society emphasises harmony and respect for seniority over critical inquiry. It may be that Chinese science will remain principally derivative until reason and the critical faculty are further encouraged.

Branding, Innovation and Culture

Branding

Branding is another way of measuring the creation of a higher-value, higher-quality economy: the manufacturer of an item generally gains a lower percentage of the final price than does the brand-owner (see the example of the iPod, above). China wants to promote branding for its manufacturers' goods, so that they command higher margins. To go from manufacturing another company's branded products to making and selling one's own is appealing, and many manufacturers have shared this interest.

However, in the league tables produced on leading global brands, China scarcely rates a mention: the Interbrand survey of the best global brands in 2013 shows not a single Chinese company in the top 100.[81] According to the consultants Accenture, they are just not good at creating added value. An alternative approach would be to study a league table of reputable companies, such as the Reputation Institute 2012 survey. This shows Chinese companies in the same light: only one reached the top 100, and that was at number 95.

The Millward Brown global brands survey of 2012 paints a different picture: it suggests that more than a dozen Chinese brands are in the world's top 100.[82] This is rather encouraging – until one looks at the methodology, which is based on revenue. This approach produces rankings based on companies' oligopolistic position in controlled sectors of a domestic economy. They do not necessarily deserve the survey's accolade as 'trusted brands', since consumer choice is relatively limited. Furthermore, they cannot truly be called global. Of the top 380 companies in the world spending over $250 million annually on R&D, just ten are Chinese and virtually all of them are state companies.[83]

In 2013 *Marketing Week* in Britain produced a survey of the 100 top global brands which included 12 Chinese names, almost all of which were state enterprises with oligopolistic positions in their domestic market.[84] This makes them big domestic brands in a large country.

China's industry unfortunately does not spend enough (or have enough imagination) to develop strong global brands. The only companies with an impressive range of research and the resultant patents are Huawei, which is thought to be closely linked to the Chinese state, and ZTE, another Chinese telecoms company. ZTE applied for the largest number of Patent Cooperation Treaty (PCT), or multi-country, patents in the world in 2011,[85] and Huawei applied for the third-largest number. The consumer products company Haier is developing a very successful Third World strategy for its white goods; Lenovo is establishing itself with its personal computing products; and Snow beer is the best-selling beer in the world (though partly Western owned, it is not well known overseas).

There have been frequent optimistic forecasts of China's early arrival on the world stage as a manufacturer of quality brands. One reason this has not happened is that OEM manufacturers tend to think differently from own-brand manufacturers. At the most basic level, branding requires marketing, which is not an art for which China is renowned. Nor have quality and service really been treasured traditionally. Branding needs corporate leadership that is competent and comfortable with communication, marketing, design and sales. Brand leaders need to define their brand's proposition and constantly to reiterate it. The quality of graduates going into management is another hurdle and is visited elsewhere (see Chapter 5).

In the field of branding, image is critical and China's exports have consistently received more bad publicity than substandard exports from other countries. America has rejected substantial quantities of food consignments from China on public health grounds. One striking example involved mislabelled tins of monkfish, which the US Food and Drug Administration (FDA) reportedly said contained the poison tetrodotoxin and might well be poisonous pufferfish.[86]

Not only have goods been rejected on quality grounds, but there has been a systematic programme of mislabelling Chinese foodstuffs to circumvent FDA inspection. This severely damages international confidence in the quality of Chinese goods. As Alan Vandemolen, a leading US communications consultant, said in 2011, China's largest companies are 'viewed pretty direly in the US'. His company's annual 'trust barometer' had shown little improvement in their reputation in recent years.[87] International attention has also focused on the domestic melamine scandal in 2008, when some 300,000 children suffered after drinking adulterated milk.[88] As a World Health Organization (WHO) spokesman said, 'the large scale of this event shows that it was clearly not an isolated accident. It was a large-scale intentional activity to deceive consumers for simple, basic, short-term profits.'[89] The OECD's environment director forthrightly declared: 'If you have a reputation for being a polluted country, then you have a bad trademark abroad.'[90]

If scandals like the melamine one affect international buyers, they also have a substantial domestic impact: some consumers pursued an 'ABC' purchasing policy – 'Anything But Chinese'. This led to the much-reported practice of selling products as foreign when they were in fact home produced. Dr Li Zuming of China University of Political Science and Law said this 'played on people's faith in anything foreign'. As Professor Wang Hanwu of the China Brand Management Research Centre explained, there was a 'lack of faith in domestic brands because of shoddy products such as the melamine-tainted milk products that have totally crippled consumer confidence ... Many Chinese love the country, but they just can't take the chance of loving Chinese-made products.'[91] Even quite nationalistic Chinese will frequently choose to buy foreign products.

Stung by the outburst of public fury over adulterated food products, the authorities finally mounted one of their sustained campaigns. Between March and September 2011, officials closed down 5,000 companies and punished 2,000 people for introducing illegal food additives.[92] Laudable though it may be to take action, what is arresting is the fact that there were at least 5,000 companies in 2011 that were calmly adulterating consumer food products.

One of the debates in the corporate world is whether to create or acquire brands. Acquisition is quick, but treacherous. Although overseas acquisitions – often to gain foreign know-how and brands – have been much discussed and quite often pursued, the results have been disappointing. The financial sector is littered with cardiac arrest-inducing stakes bought by China in companies such as Barclays, Morgan Stanley and Blackstone. In 2008 the country only narrowly missed Bear Stearns. (There have been some successes, such as ICBC's purchase of a 20 per cent stake in Standard Bank of South Africa, which is reasonably untroubled and operates in a part of the world of considerable interest to China. However, it does not represent a brand acquisition.)

Manufacturing purchases often involve technology that the seller no longer wants, as in IBM's sale of its PC business to Lenovo. Prominent acquisitions in mining and resources have not been for knowledge or branding, but – in the mind of government – have represented a mercantilist dash for energy and resource security, and – in the eyes of industry – a chance to use state loans and cheap (for the seller) equity money to go international and become a producer. So China has not bought any very significant brands. Furthermore, even in fully 'developed' economies, studies suggest that over half of all acquisitions destroy value rather than create it. Creating a brand, on the other hand, requires some innovative thinking and much patient and thoughtful building.

Although China is not prominent in international brand positioning, it could foster the culture and skills to change that. The first challenge would be to recognise what is needed, and then plan how to create it. But uncertainty over property rights is likely to discourage the long-term investment required to build a brand. Second, there is a pervasive short-term mentality in many areas of Chinese business. Third, brand-building these days does require a degree of frankness, in order to build consumer confidence.

This is a fundamental cultural (or moral) issue that permeates Chinese history. Lu Xun, probably the most eminent Chinese writer of the last century, said that one of the features missing from contemporary society was honesty. Mao described him after his death as 'a man of unyielding integrity . . . a hero without parallel in our history'.[93] Hegel, in the nineteenth century, blamed the Qing political system for the lack of individual honour, which resulted in a society 'notorious for deceiving wherever they can. Friend deceives friend, and no one resents the attempt at deception on the part of another.'[94] Lu ascribed the lack of honesty and integrity to the fact that 'China had been twice occupied by foreigners: the Mongols who had established the Yuan dynasty (1279–1368) and the Manchus who established the Qing (1644–1912)'.[95] When responding in 2009 to the spate of academic plagiarism, Shandong University President Xu Xianming said 'it happens because of the lack of integrity in our society'.[96] In 2011, Professor Chu Huaizhi of the Law School of Peking University commented on contemporary proposals for laws to require ethical social behaviour: 'before we can establish a law to reward Good Samaritans and punish the heartless ones, we need to make sure our society is credible and its people can be honest'.[97] This is an issue that is constantly bewailed, even in the state media and by government officials. There is a moral deficit in contemporary Chinese culture, and it has many consequences, including economic.

Innovation

The Chinese government is committed to innovation, and there are signs of success in telecommunications, aviation, space and internet equipment. Haier has also shown some product innovation. But the situation in many areas is dismal. According to Booz and Co.'s 2012 Innovation 1000 study, measuring the world's most innovative companies, China had one company in the top 100 and that was the state oil company Petrochina, ranked at 70th. Furthermore, Booz made a strong point on the difference between companies which spent highly and those which achieved innovation.[98]

One practical domestic response to the problem of encouraging innovation has been to offer top foreign scientists large financial inducements to come to work in China.[99] Another approach has been for the government to encourage Chinese negotiators to require technology transfer in return for foreign companies winning contracts in China. Not surprisingly, that technology surfaces later in Chinese exports; but often foreign companies are confident that their technology is improving rapidly enough for China still to lag behind.

Writers such as Danny Breznitz and Graeme Maxton suggest that China's innovation need not be very sophisticated to be effective: it could be iterative and perhaps more associated with improving process manufacturing. One interesting feature of the innovation landscape is the *shanzhai* companies – firms which effectively 'reverse engineer' foreign products, but endeavour to make improvements. They might develop versions of foreign-manufactured high-tech products which are cheap enough to sell to migrant workers but contain extra features.[100] An example is the HiPhone, 'a knockoff iPhone that can accommodate two SIM cards, a feature popular with globetrotting Chinese travellers – and not available from the real thing'.[101] Some *shanzhai* firms have gone on to become quite prominent, particularly in the automobile and mobile telephone fields,[102] and by 2008 there were at least 10,000 *shanzhai* companies in China.[103]

Yet another approach has been to hack into foreign commercial internet systems to steal proprietary information. James A. Lewis, a former US diplomat now with the Center for Strategic and International Studies, said in 2011, 'they've identified innovation as crucial to future economic growth – but they're not sure they can do it . . . The easiest way to innovate is to plagiarize' by theft of foreign intellectual property.[104] The US intelligence claims not to seek commercial secrets were undermined by Director James Clapper being seen to lie to Congress.[105]

China has been criticised for encouraging intellectual piracy, but we should remember that this was exactly the intellectual activity which was chosen by the US in its early years. The US 'profited from international copyright piracy for a century'.[106]

Culture

In 2011, an organ of the Chinese state media lamented that 'our governments at various levels have been calling for the building of an innovation-oriented country. But we have seen few specific measures to pave the way for innovations.'[107] However, the scientific culture is not conducive to innovation: there is too much deference, hierarchy and centralised state control of research agendas and careers.[108] Even Wang Yang, a Politburo member, said in 2011 that China's students lacked the innovative spirit: 'Compared with students from developed countries, we still have a lot of room to improve.' He blamed the culture of exams and the age-old tendency to regard a teacher's answers as final.[109]

There is also little culture of product safety or integrity: 'imagine what it's like to be a consumer in China, where the authenticity and quality of everything in your life is suspect: the food you eat, the water you drink, the pills you put in your body, the building you live in, the computer you use, the airplane you fly in'.[110]

The tradition in China has always been to hide bad news. Intermittently, and increasingly, it is being recognised that bad news can get out and so it should be confronted. But still there are striking examples of unwillingness to confront and openly debate it. This was exemplified by SARS, the melamine-adulterated milk scandal and the 'tofu construction' claims of deficient building standards after the Sichuan earthquake. China is not alone in having these issues: India also has adulterated foods and spurious drugs, but there is a lack of openness about the issue in China.

The Pew Global Attitudes Survey 2008 tells us that only 16 per cent of Chinese people are aware of domestic product recalls. There is not yet the transparency and accountability in Chinese culture that would enable it to address global market demands in branded goods. The culture finds it difficult to confront criticism and controversy.

Rapid Development and Pervasive Negligence

Impressive success has been demonstrated by the country in many of its development projects, and the rapid growth has attracted global admiration. However, these achievements have been punctuated by a worrying number of incidents that indicate deficiencies in due care and attention. The high-speed train crash in Wenzhou in 2011, in which at least 39 people died and 200 were injured, seemed to bear out the warnings that a shortened construction period and dramatic scaling up based on 're-innovated' Japanese, Canadian and German technology carried severe risks.[111] There was a torrent of microblog invective against the authorities and even the state media were critical. One prominent television anchor, Qiu Qiming, for example, said: 'China, please slow down. If you're too fast, you may leave the souls of your people behind . . .'[112]

By the time of the Shanghai subway crash of September 2011, in which over 200 were injured, the state media were questioning the price of rapid development. The Party-owned *Global Times* wrote: 'Shanghai has already had the appearance of a developed city, but accidents such as the subway collision and the Shanghai fire last November reveal that it is still a developing city at its core.'[113] There were allegations of corruption and negligence against the railway management, and people recalled that earlier in the year the railways minister had been fired for large-scale corruption. Where there is a political imperative for hasty implementation and a lack of transparency in procurement, negligence and corruption are likely to appear. Both of these pave the way for public safety problems.

Or take the vast programme of dam-building in areas prone to earthquakes. There has been widespread criticism of the Three Gorges Project, the largest dam in the world, where subsequent landslides are said to have been dam-induced. And scientists have suggested that the Sichuan earthquake of 2008, which killed nearly 90,000 people, was not simply a random natural disaster but was induced by placing a dam on a fault line. Overseas, there has been criticism of the roads and housing built by Chinese companies in Angola.[114]

Such incidents call into question the likelihood that foreign countries will want to buy China's high-speed railway technology, for example. Given the billions of dollars sunk into these projects, this is of grave concern to the government. As a major exporter and an aspiring innovative economy, China must pay a heavy price if it starts to be seen to have the casual negligence of Vietnam or the institutionalised negligence notable in South Asia, Russia or Japan.[115] Unfortunately, in a Party state, negligence becomes a political subject in a way that it would not in a plural society. This is expressed clearly by the *Global Times*: 'It is obvious the country lacks experience in managing the construction and operation of big public projects. And the flaws which have been revealed so far have ruined the public's trust of the government.'[116]

The Intellectual Environment

China has a long history of rejecting innovation. Not only has there been a Confucian tradition of discouraging scientific inquiry, but the nineteenth century saw an unwillingness to go beyond human muscle to power economic development.[117]

By the middle of 2012, China had 538 million internet users – well over a third of its population.[118] This is the largest community in the world, and is more than the total population of the US. Over half of the users read blogs; it is estimated that there are over 340 million microblog accounts.[119] This suggests that one in every two internet users has a blog (though in fact some people will have six). Yet this does not seem to translate into commercial creativity. Perhaps what is missing are sufficient entrepreneurial, commercial and international skills to help differentiate a new, good marketable idea from a new, worthless idea.

There is a disturbing agenda in certain of the sciences, such as archaeology and anthropology. For example, the state wants to see the discovery of ancient human fossil remains that will support polygenist theories of the uniqueness of China's racial origins: 'The discovery at Xuchang supports the theory that modern Chinese man originated in what is present-day Chinese territory rather than Africa ... Extraordinary archaeological discoveries are critical to maintaining our national identity as well as the history of our ancient civilisation.'[120] Surprising discoveries, supposedly of sections of the Great Wall, in the controversial province of Xinjiang in 2001 can be employed to justify China's current political position there (see Chapter 1).[121]

In most leading countries, the state has no clear agenda or preference for scientific results. China, though, acts rather like Mormon archaeologists seeking to find certain remains in Central America that will underpin their religious beliefs, or climate-theory scientists who seek to censor peers who do not share their views. In 1995, China embarked on a project to show the antiquity of its civilisation. The Three Dynasty Chronology Project (or the Xia-Shang-Zhou Chronology Project) was reportedly initiated by Song Jian, a state councillor, who was piqued on a trip to Egypt to be told that the antiquities were pre-Chinese.[122] This vanity project apparently involved 200 experts and cost $2 million over four years. Published in 2000, the report received extensive criticism from overseas scientists.[123] The very fact that the country has an agenda weakens objectivity in the sciences and helps to create a climate uncongenial to free inquiry.

The education system is widely regarded as one of the main weaknesses in the quest for innovation. One Chinese state media journalist wrote in 2011 that 'the motivation for most students is a desire to pass examinations instead of seeing education as a journey of wonder and exploration', and that young people's 'brains are always occupied by a large amount of irrelevant, dogmatic and unproductive information. As a result, their imagination and sense of innovation are severely curtailed.'[124]

Forty years after the Cultural Revolution ended, political education still plays an important role in universities. After 1978, 'the primary aim of education was to serve political needs, train students ideologically, and enable all those who received an education to develop morally, intellectually and physically, so as to become well-educated workers imbued with a socialist consciousness'.[125] Tsinghua University, one of the country's elite institutions, has stated that 'the main task of political and ideological work in universities is to educate students with worldviews of patriotism, collectivism and socialism'.[126] The same message suffuses the political tracts imposed on schoolchildren.[127] The head of the mainland students' association at Shue Yan University in Hong Kong has remarked on the very different teaching styles in Hong Kong and China: 'On the mainland, we are used to a didactic teaching style, whereas here there is more emphasis on independent study.'[128] Mainland culture does not promote the single-minded pursuit of academic excellence. We should also, however, note that in China 90 per cent of the population regard scientists as role models, whereas amongst conservative Americans only 35 per cent have 'a great deal of trust' in science.[129]

Chinese university management teams have been actively participating in internationally organised programmes on how to run world-class universities. This is very laudable, and the participation is both wide and at a senior level: presidents and vice presidents and also Party secretaries. However, there is much misunderstanding. It is widely believed in China that taking a liberal arts course is sufficient to foster critical thinking. There is insufficient appreciation of the need to encourage analysis, criticism, judgement and debate. 'Qian Xuesen, one of China's most distinguished defense scientists, explained to Wen

Jiabao in 2005, one of the major issues holding back China's science and technology was that the country's universities were unable to produce innovative scientific and technical personnel.'[130] The future of Chinese university education depends on whether it follows the French route of deference or the Anglo-Saxon route of fostering critical debate.

There has been much discussion of China's mediocre showing in Nobel Prize rankings. Between the Communist victory in 1949 and 2010, some 584 Nobel prizes were awarded. Ethnic Chinese won ten of these; eight of these were in sciences. Unfortunately, all eight did their work in America or Europe – none performed their critical work in China. The other two prizes were for literature and peace. The winners were clearly born and raised in China and did most of their work there. Sadly, neither of them is approved of by the Chinese authorities: Gao Xingjiang's literary work is banned in China and he is in exile in France; Liu Xiaobo, a democracy and human rights advocate, is serving an eleven-year prison sentence for subversion.

It might be asked if there is Western bias, and if that is why science prizes are not awarded to Chinese resident scientists. Here the Shaw Prize is interesting. Established in 2004 by the noted Hong Kong-based Chinese film-maker and philanthropist Run-run Shaw, the Shaw Prize has, over the years, gained a stature not dissimilar to the Nobel Prize. Here there can be no racial bias. In the ten years to 2013, fifty-four prizes were awarded to illustrious scientists in the fields of astronomy, mathematical sciences, and medicine and the life sciences. Of those, one was awarded to a scientist who spent most of his life working in mainland China. It does seem as though the world genuinely does not view China-based science as in the same league as science in America, the UK, Europe or Japan. It is interesting to see a comment from a China-based weblog on this topic:

> As far as intelligence quotients are concerned, the Chinese people are no worse than any other people … We should discuss how the Chinese can re-establish the conditions to become creative … Clearly, the most important thing for a talented and creative person is to have an environment that allows him to create freely and it is definitely not about which nationality he has … Whether a person will win a Nobel prize depends first and foremost on whether he lives in an open country that encourages and protects creativity, or a country in which 'the academy is a bureaucracy' and 'a higher ranked bureaucrat is a better scholar.'[131]

From a cultural perspective, we might ask how easy it is for the authorities to encourage a spirit of inquiry, of innovation, of questioning in science, technology and marketing, given that such approaches are not always welcome in other areas of national life. Zhang Yimou, one of Beijing's favourite film directors, has admitted that his films are set in the past because otherwise they would be heavily censored.[132] Yin Li, a director of the China Film Group Corporation and a deputy to the Chinese People's Political Consultative Conference, has 'lambasted movie regulators, arguing that censorship was detrimental to creativity and left filmmakers little choice but to avoid contemporary issues and make films about historical events'.[133] The fact is that even views of history are censored. If an entire nation follows the practice of admiring the Emperor's new clothes and suspends normal judgement, there is a price to pay. If it is impossible to acknowledge facts in history or politics, it is hard to envisage a society endowed with critical thinking.

The Chinese and English Languages

What is the current role and future destiny of the Chinese language? Does it assist or impede China's technological rise?

There is a view which contends that the Chinese are simply innately clever and will eventually meet the challenges facing them. It is therefore interesting to look at Stanislas Dehaene's work on arithmetic.[134] This notes that:

(a) Memory works in short bursts: as the Chinese language is briefer in its expression of numbers than English, so numbers are better remembered.
(b) Chinese number forms are more regular ('ten one' for eleven, 'two ten eight' for twenty-eight, etc.) than English: twelve, thirteen, nineteen and twenty-one are quite irregular. This lends itself to faster arithmetic.

As a result, young Chinese can remember more and calculate quicker, quite possibly leading to more enjoyment and thus more short-term success. However, greater facility with maths does not demonstrate a better brain and may not indicate greater long-term success. Indeed, the leading fathers of modern algebra – Karl Popper, Thomas Kuhn and Jacob Klein – were from the West.

Chinese has more native speakers than any other language – particularly in the sense of speakers in one country. However, it has nowhere near the largest number of secondary, or non-native, speakers. English, French, Russian, Portuguese and probably Arabic all have more secondary speakers (20–190 million). Mandarin and Spanish are reported to have just 20 million non-native speakers. The point here is that part of being a world power historically has meant having a language which others learn in order to share the culture, technology or power of the society.

Official statistics are completely wrong here. In 2007, Chinese officials said that over 40 million foreigners were learning Chinese worldwide, and this would be 100 million by 2010.[135] In 2009 they again said that up to 40 million were learning Chinese and that it would be 100 million by 2010. This suggested no growth since 2007, but very steep anticipated growth in the subsequent twelve months. By the end of 2010, the same officials were saying that 40 million were learning Chinese, but they had dropped the target of 100 million. If close to 40 million people are learning Chinese, it would be interesting to know where they are.

In 2008, there were said to be over 200,000 people in the US learning Chinese (either in school or elsewhere) – largely ethnic Chinese people. This makes up 0.5 per cent of all those supposedly studying anywhere in the world, and yet the US has 6.6 per cent of the non-Chinese population of the world. So America is more than 90 per cent under-represented in this global movement. France (45,000 students) is similarly under-represented.[136] Also, we might imagine that the US and French educational systems are better able to teach languages to more of their secondary and tertiary students than are many countries in Africa or Asia. A 2006 survey of American higher education by the Modern Languages Association showed that there were 61,000 students taking Chinese – the seventh most popular language (behind American Sign Language). The fastest-growing foreign language was Arabic. Indeed, there were almost as many studying either Latin or Ancient Greek as Chinese (53,300 to 60,900). In the 1960s, more American students took Chinese than Japanese, but in every subsequent survey it has been the reverse.[137] In 2009, that was still the case and Arabic remained the fastest growing language studied.[138] It does look as though there has been quite a sharp increase in Chinese study in America, but it comes from a low starting base. The US Defense Department has estimated that about 60 per cent of those learning Chinese in American schools are ethnic Chinese.[139]

In 2010, the Chinese state media said there was a 'Chinese-learning fervour' in Russia and identified 12,000 students of Chinese there. Even if it was 30,000, Russia is 3 per cent of the world's population outside China. If Russia has 30,000 people studying Chinese, it suggests the whole world might have only 1 million people learning Chinese. I suspect nobody knows the true figure, but whatever it is, there were not 100 million foreigners studying Chinese in 2010; nor 40 million.

This tells us two things: the official target of 100 million was grossly unrealistic, and the seemingly factual statement that 40 million were learning Chinese has never been close to correct. It is worth pondering this, because it tells us a lot about official Chinese statistics in general.

To put things into perspective, well over 200 million Chinese schoolchildren were apparently studying English in 2007 (when under 250,000 American schoolchildren and university students – largely of Chinese origin – appear to have been learning Chinese). As English is being taught to people of all ages and is apparently quite popular, the total number learning English in China could be over 250 million; indeed, former Premier Wen estimated 300 million in 2009. Some Chinese even have surgery under their tongues to improve their pronunciation. This is the first time in history that an emerging superpower has been defined by the extent to which its people learn another country's language. Not enough non-Chinese people want to learn Chinese, so it is unlikely to become the world language. When we are told of the rapid growth of the use of Chinese on the internet, we need to appreciate that this is not foreign people deciding to communicate in Chinese, but more and more domestic Chinese getting on the internet. As such, as the penetration increases the growth rate is likely to slow. Indeed, during 2013, users only grew by 9.6 per cent.

It might be said that English has become today's medieval Latin or Enlightenment French. Divorced from its national roots, it has become a tool for educated people to use, regardless of origin. Swiss of different language communities often communicate with each other in English. This applies similarly to others who don't share a common language: Indian businessmen, Filipina servants and European Union officials. In fact, English has now become, alongside Arabic, Urdu and Persian, one of the key languages 'acting as a medium for expressing ideas in modern Islam'.[140]

If English has become as much a tool as a mobile phone or a computer, there are implications. Chinese is not being chosen by third parties as the means of communication between non-Chinese. Should China consider spreading its cultural offer in English? After all, in 1645 the Manchus made the fundamental decision not to impose their language on conquered China but instead learned Chinese to rule China (see Chapter 1). A hundred years ago Chinese students mostly went to Japan to imbibe Western knowledge. One culture does not require one language. Perhaps China will decide to use English in order to be 'dominant' in the world.

There is widespread academic debate over the impact of language on methods of thinking and even conclusions. A large body of opinion associates the features of language with intellectual results. Wally Olins, the branding specialist, told me that the Japanese language influences how people think and work, and at board level Japanese companies need their people to think and speak in American English.[141] In the nineteenth century, Hegel – discussing written Chinese – noted 'the obstacles which it presents to the advance of the sciences'.[142]

This is not a Eurocentric obsession. Domestic disenchantment with the Chinese language rose noticeably from the mid-nineteenth century, and by the first half of the twentieth century intellectual leaders viewed it as unsuitable for both its historic baggage and its deficient practical utility. Lu Xun is China's most revered twentieth-century writer. He was irritated by the deferential manner around him and his muscular and candid work is quite reminiscent of writers such as Wyndham Lewis and Roy Campbell. Chen Duxiu was Dean of the School of Arts and Sciences at Peking University, co-founder and first leader of the Chinese Communist Party. Both men were associated with the view that classical Chinese books should no longer be read, Chinese characters are a 'cancer' and Esperanto should be encouraged. They participated in the May 4th Movement in 1919 and were early advocates of writing in the vernacular. Of course this was not the first time such a view had been expressed. Zhu Xi, the twelfth-century neo-Confucian scholar, used the vernacular to reach the widest audience. However, it is not normally the case that the medium is the message.

The language reform debate in China in the early twentieth century was passionate and radical. Here are the words of some of the most prominent Chinese intellectuals of that period:[143]

> If we don't want China to perish, and if we want it to be a civilised nation in the twentieth century, the best thing to do would be to abandon Confucianism and Daoism, and the simplest way towards this end would be to abandon written Chinese. After written Chinese is abandoned . . . we should adopt Esperanto, an artificial language. (Qian Xuantong)

> In the period of transition (before the Chinese language is abandoned), we need to first abolish the Chinese script. The Chinese language may be maintained for the time being, but should be written in Roman script. (Chen Duxiu)

> There are many impediments to the dissemination of knowledge among the Chinese. Two of them have been disastrous. The first is having living human beings using the language of the dead; the second is the continuance in modern life of a script that is both primitive and clumsy . . . The origin of the Chinese script is extremely uncivilised, and its graphic shape very bizarre. It is extraordinarily difficult to learn, and uneconomical to use. Indeed, it is the clumsy, coarse script of monsters and demons, and the most inconvenient tool in the world. (Fu Sinian)

This antipathy manifested itself particularly with regard to Chinese characters. These writers were not eccentrics but leading members of the intellectual elite of China. Qian Xuantong was a noted philologist and leading member of the

May 4th Movement. Fu Sinian was a president of Peking University. Chen Duxiu was, as noted, the first leader of the Chinese Communist Party. Ping Chen, a specialist in linguistics, has said:

> perhaps at no other point in modern history has the intellectual and political elite of a major emerging nation seemed to hold its mother tongue in such apparent abhorrence, and used such strong depreciatory language in condemnation of the language. There were, to be sure, certain dissenting voices defending the Chinese language, but these were generally weak and few and far between, at least in the first half of the twentieth century.[144]

Subsequently, there were significant language reforms. Writers hurriedly discarded the classical style for the vernacular. Mao is cited as urging reform in 1936:

> We believe Latinization is a good instrument with which to overcome illiteracy. Chinese characters are so difficult to learn that even the best system of rudimentary characters ... does not equip the people with a really efficient and rich vocabulary. Sooner or later, we believe, we will have to abandon characters altogether if we are to create a new social culture in which the masses fully participate.[145]

In 1956 China introduced simplified characters. It did not, however, go as far as Latinised or phonetic script. The two main reasons were the existence of distinctly different dialects and the presence of many homonyms, which were not readily suited to phoneticisation.[146] Mao's long-range plan seems to have been to scrap Chinese characters and to move the Chinese language to a romanised alphabet. The debate in China has not finished.

In late nineteenth-century Turkey there was a similar debate about the use of Arabic script and Ottoman Turkish. These ideas were in ferment at exactly the same time as those of the *fin-de-siècle* intellectuals in China. Action was finally taken by Kemal Atatürk in 1928 to adopt both the Latin alphabet and an artificially regenerated pure Turkish, stripped of Arabic and Persian elements. Whether consciously or not, much of Atatürk's thinking echoed the ideas of Lu Xun and his contemporaries. The common idea was that language carries historical baggage, it shapes how one thinks and one can never be 'free' until one's tool of thinking and expression is fundamentally changed. However, Mao was not strong enough or sufficiently convinced to pursue the logic of Lu Xun and his generation. Against all his rhetoric, he acted as a reformer, not a revolutionary.

Chinese is categorised as an 'analytic' or 'isolating' language, whereas Greek-Latin- and Sanskrit-originated languages are largely treated as 'inflective' – they have 'endings'. Linguistic philosophers such as Gernet and Benveniste at the Collège de France have suggested that the inflective languages have lent themselves to forming 'ideas of transcendent and immutable realities', whereas Chinese language structure predisposes it more to 'transitory realities of the senses'.[147] Spengler, however, suggests that Chinese was once inflective.[148] The conclusion of Gernet and Benveniste seems to be that those who think/express themselves in different language structures will think differently. Not everyone will share this analysis.

It has been estimated that an ordinary Chinese knows 2–3,000 characters which would enable a 97 per cent understanding of the language.[149] Reading a newspaper in full probably requires about 4,000 characters (and indeed the 4,000 most frequently used characters represent about 99.6 per cent of all usage). University graduates might have 5,000 characters. However, two recent dictionaries include over 80,000 and over 100,000 characters, respectively, many of which have fallen into desuetude or are proper names. It is certainly true that many highly educated people today cannot make much of the classical poetry on the wall tablets of Suzhou formal gardens. There has been some discussion as to whether it is desirable to reintroduce the classical characters in order to preserve more of the national patrimony. Debate continues: one province has asked everyone to learn 500 traditional characters. In early 2009 the Chinese authorities introduced a list of modifications to correct 'oversimplifications', but it was formally decided not to reintroduce traditional characters:

> This will disappoint Pan Qinglin, a member of the consultative committee that advises China's government. In March he submitted a proposal to the government calling for a return within ten years to the greater expressiveness and 'artistic quality' of the traditional script. Others, however, will be pleased, including the internet commentator who recently compared reviving traditional characters to 'asking women to revive the practice of foot-binding'.[150]

For those who use even simplified Chinese regularly, there is the highly contemporary problem of 'character amnesia' or 'dysgraphia': constant use of computers, mobile phones and SMS messaging has affected their ability to recall and write characters.[151]

Overseas visitors to Beijing are frequently struck by two linguistic facts: taxis bear the word TAXI in roman script; and car registration plates use almost entirely Western script and numbers. Arguably it is important for the millions of tourists to know which cars they can hail, but it is harder to see why, in the largest country in the world, a domestic car registration plate should be written in an alien script. Thomas Rawski suggested to me that it might be related to the early introduction of computer records.[152] China is quite schizophrenic about its language identity. Perhaps radical language reform is one of the big reforms hanging over China, waiting for a strong and determined leader. It could prove more controversial than political reform.

Were the Chinese intellectual elite correct at the turn of the twentieth century? Will the use of Chinese slow the pace of the country's development? Certainly some Chinese parents have observed that their children seem to think more clearly when they go overseas and are taught in English. Japanese international executives, too, often remark that they 'think in English'. However, the leading Chinese intellectual Ai Weiwei, referring to the social networking medium Twitter, has said: 'In Chinese [in 140 characters] you can seduce a girl or write a constitution.' That is a ringing endorsement of the language. Nonetheless, might China decide that, in order to dominate the world, it will learn the world's language, English? This is no more unrealistic than Hu Yaobang saying in the 1980s that the Chinese should abandon chopsticks in favour of knives and forks.[153] Can we imagine China's rise without Chinese? If the Manchus could drop their language to rule China, and if the Protestant Henry of Navarre, when offered the French throne if he adopted Catholicism, could conclude that 'Paris is worth a mass', then perhaps China will decide that it is worth adopting the language of Shakespeare to become the world's superpower.

On the other hand, one of the striking findings of the Pew Global Attitudes Survey of 2008 is the sharp fall of Chinese respondents completely agreeing with the statement that 'children need to learn English to succeed' – down from 66 per cent in 2002 to 33 per cent. One-third is still a weighty figure, but as an indication of changes in priority it is interesting. This attitude will affect China's future. Will it sap its prospects of superpower status?

Migration and Talent

America is not an innovative, technological leader solely because of the skills of Americans: there is a history of talented people moving to America. Even in 1988, 45 per cent of all engineering doctorate students in the US were foreign-born,[154] and by 2008 foreigners (excluding those naturalised) represented over 60 per cent.[155] Bright, inventive, highly educated young people do not flock to China to study or work. Although there is a noticeable cult following for

Chinese films and contemporary art, not enough people 'buy into' becoming cultural dependants of China. Until that changes, China will find it hard to build a first-rank, innovative, knowledge-based economy. Societies rarely become cultural and technological leaders without some high-quality immigration and intellectual cross-fertilisation. An aspiring superpower should be expected to have a steady flow of the world's talented people, of all nationalities, coming to live in the world's future capital. Poets, professors, writers, architects, scientists, cooks should all come to live in Beijing, lured by the attraction of living in the world's up-and-coming super-city. This is simply not happening.

Those living in a foreign society tend to separate into two broad classes: a talented group, which brings the skills and knowledge that are in short supply in the host country; and a group that supplies labour which the host citizens prefer not to provide (e.g. agricultural workers in America or domestic and construction labourers in the Middle East). China has a large poor population and discourages the import of manual labour – even nannies. Accordingly, China takes in only the talented group, whereas the US takes in both. There are 38 million immigrants in America. Unscientifically (and doubtless rather unfairly), we might divide them by country of origin to guess their roles: 21 million are likely to be providing labour and 17 million to be offering talent.

A surprising 180 Chinese cities have announced their intention to become 'international metropolises', like Tokyo, New York or London.[156] It is likely that they have no real understanding of what it takes to reach that goal. Desirous of becoming an international city, the government of Shanghai has set a goal of having 5 per cent foreign residents in the population;[157] according to the 2010 census, it had 200,000 foreign residents (not even 1 per cent). Beijing had 100,000 foreign residents,[158] and there were just 600,000 in total in mainland China.[159] Although most of these would probably fall into the 'talent' category, this is a far cry from America's 17 million. For the sake of comparison, Tokyo is home to some 400,000 foreigners.

China is now the world's second most important economy, having supplanted Japan. It is tipped by some to become the superpower. So why don't more foreigners live there? Russian oligarchs and rich Indians buy houses in London and New York, not in Beijing. The rich appear to shun it, and the poor are not invited.

Is there a fear of restriction on expression and debate? China has so much to attract new residents. There is a distinct and stimulating policy discussion about potential directions for the country that is of overwhelming importance for the world's largest country, and indeed for the world. There is a cultural and artistic tradition and a vibrant contemporary arts world. There is world-class cuisine. Perhaps foreigners don't know enough about Beijing.

Most of them don't seem to want to find out. Is there a feeling that existence there is not enough? We don't hear much of high-achieving overseas ethnic Chinese taking up residence in Beijing, despite the excellent facilities that, for example, scientists would be offered. Chinese academics go to China as visiting professors, but generally do not move there permanently. This is even more the case with non-Chinese: there are more ethnic Chinese intellectuals in Washington than there are American intellectuals in Beijing. The prospect of China's coming greatness in culture and power is not attracting the world's intelligentsia. We do not yet see the outlines of New York, London or Ancient Rome.

Summary

So, China is failing in innovation. There is a long way to go before China can be expected to forge a higher-quality, knowledge-based economy. The government plans an attractive figure for R&D spending by 2020, which is laudable but begs some questions. Government may advise and exhort, but it is not really its function to manage the level of R&D spending unless it is government money and is probably spent by government agencies. As it happens, it is largely state money that is going into R&D and, although the level will rise, it is likely that the process will not be fully commercial. China may not reach its targets. Even if it does, there is the question of how the money is spent, and thus no guarantee of the desired results being achieved. China should define high technology and R&D more clearly; then it would see better where its economy stands now, could compare itself more accurately with other countries and could initiate better policies. There is a further need to refine the objectives. Innovation does not necessarily imply invention; it does imply a constant improvement and adaptation of technology and a commercial environment that seamlessly absorbs new ideas and stays ahead of the competition.

How quickly can China catch up with the technology of, say, the US? It has been suggested by Moses Abramovitz that

> differences among countries in productivity levels create a strong potentiality for subsequent convergence of levels, provided that countries have a 'social capability' adequate to absorb more advanced technologies. It reminds us, however, that the institutional and human capital components of social capability develop only slowly as education and organization respond to the requirements of technological opportunity and to experience in exploiting it.[160]

Abramovitz observes that social capability comprises many requirements, including certain forms of education, efficient mobilisation of capital and an openness to competition.

In other words, China may accumulate the funding, build the laboratories and staff them, but it might not possess a 'non-hierarchical scientific culture, fertile institutional framework and critical thinking' – the necessary soft skills. We must question whether China will rapidly develop these characteristics – or even if it wishes to.

Evidence from various countries suggests that the best innovation comes from research and development undertaken by the private sector, not by government. It is unlikely that China would be any different. Government direction can work for lengthy periods, but ultimately bureaucrats cannot guess better than the myriad interactions between producers and consumers. Hopes for success now must revolve principally around seeing a continuing improvement in the economy itself and also – which is not the same – sustained profitability. It would be exciting to see the private sector increase its focus on research, particularly on improving the quality of production and products, branding and service, marketing and sales. These can, by themselves, consti-tute a successful knowledge economy: branding, for example, is vital. Government can encourage some of this through fiscal policies and training, but innovation usually arises in an environment of free inquiry, stimulus, chal-lenge and debate. Efforts are needed to engender such a climate in China.

China's challenge is how to build an innovative economy, generate a reputa-tion for quality and imagination and develop a position of global intellectual leadership. Failure will not destroy the country, but without success it is diffi-cult to see China fulfilling the aspirations of its people to become a substan-tially more successful economy in these very competitive times – and, most importantly, a great power. Fortunately, China has the option of making radical changes to enable it to build a technology platform appropriate to a rising world power.

Building an innovative economy is a challenge, but it is one that can be met. The principal requirement is for more critical thinking. Is there any tension between encouraging the critical faculty and maintaining stability? China's leaders should be able to encourage enquiring minds without fostering insta-bility. If critical thinking and social stability are seen as opposites in a zero-sum game, China will be the loser. However, China can achieve much if it wills it.

CHAPTER FOUR

Finance

China's financial system contains many weaknesses and risks, and foreign exchange reserves, currency, government finance, the banking system and the stock market all present vulnerabilities.

Foreign Reserves

By end 2013, Beijing had $3.8 trillion of foreign exchange reserves – more than any other country. This would appear, on the face of it, to place China in an enviable position. There was, until 2013, ample liquidity in the domestic currency and so there has been little need to borrow overseas, which also puts China in a favourable position vis-à-vis other major economies.

These reserves are largely a result of the fact that, as Chinese enterprises export more than they import, they accumulate foreign currency, which the People's Bank of China (PBC), the central bank, normally purchases. Recent trade surpluses have magnified the reserves. Even the 2009 export downturn was matched by a reduction in imports, and so the surplus persisted. In addition, the government intervenes repeatedly in currency markets, selling *renminbi* to buy dollars in order to limit currency appreciation: it has been claimed that China has averaged intervention of US$1 billion a day for several years.[1] However, although the international market in *renminbi* has been growing, it is limited. Another factor that has contributed to the rising value of dollar reserves is the increase in the value of any yen, sterling or euro-denominated securities held during periods of dollar weakness. (Of course, weakness in the euro has the opposite effect.)

Thus the reserves principally arise from purchases by the PBC and are effectively funded by the state holding commercial banks' reserves (involuntary lending to the PBC), selling *renminbi* debt instruments or even printing currency. It was estimated that at the end of 2010 the PBC owed Chinese banks $2 trillion.[2] The fear of capital inflows swelling the domestic monetary base and thus building inflation is generally offset – or 'sterilised' – by absorbing domestic money through selling government bonds. Thus much of the $3.2 trillion of reserves is simply the obverse of the $3 trillion of domestic borrowing or money printing. We don't know exactly how much is borrowing rather than money creation (and hence inflationary risk), but by 2011 it looked like around 70 per cent. The authorities have clearly taken significant measures to 'sterilise' these capital inflows in order to reduce the prospect of inflationary pressures building up. This has taken the form of avoiding the negative impact of capital flowing into the Chinese currency by borrowing large amounts of Chinese currency to take it out of circulation.[3]

Government reserves are placed overseas, largely in dollar instruments. For example, China is the largest international holder of US Treasury bills, bonds and notes – $1.15 trillion in summer 2012. It also holds US agency instruments from issuers such as Freddie Mac and Fannie Mae, US corporate bonds, US equities and US deposits.

However, the over 30 per cent currency appreciation against the dollar between 2005 and 2010 meant a very large 'paper' loss for China on the holdings of US instruments. When Tim Geithner, the US Secretary of the Treasury, gave a speech in 2009 at Peking University, he assured the audience that China's investments in US government instruments were 'very safe'.[4] The students openly laughed.

The low interest received on the foreign (principally US) instruments acquired was estimated in 2011 at about 0.33 per cent, whereas the interest paid domestically in China on local bonds issued and reserves raised to buy them might range from 1.5 to 3 per cent. That 'spread loss' was estimated at $66 billion annually.[5] Since then Chinese rates have risen. If the *renminbi* appreciated by, say, 5 per cent, that would cause a further loss of $170 billion a year, resulting in an annual total of around $240 billion. It could become unsustainable.

Western economists and politicians had a warm feeling that Asia, and especially China, armed with superior economic performance and, in particular, blossoming reserves, could rescue the West's financial system. This is difficult to envisage. China's foreign reserves are largely committed in holding US and eurozone government bonds. Washington would be unlikely to encourage the dumping of US Treasury bills in favour of, for example, European bank equity or debt. Current holdings are largely short-term bonds, and thus theoretically one could sell by not buying more. However, the holdings are sufficiently large that even if Beijing decided to stop renewing them, it could negatively affect the value of their remaining holdings, the dollar and the US financial system.

When approached to bail out profligate eurozone economies, Chinese leaders have to consider that their resources are also needed to support their own economy.

Although Chinese leaders have talked about giving support to eurozone countries and their bonds, there is no evidence of any large-scale purchasing. Future experiments are more likely to be in the higher-potential emerging markets. Lou Jiwei, the chairman of sovereign wealth fund China Investment Corporation (CIC), said in 2008 that he was not then courageous enough to plough money into Wall Street and the City of London, he had no intention of saving the West from the financial crisis, and China would concentrate on resolving its own affairs. And in 2012, Gao Xiqing of CIC said they were interested in Europe but 'we don't want to buy any government bonds'.[6] This might have negative implications for the trillions of dollars' worth of government bonds to be issued by the US, British and European governments over the next few years. Perhaps Washington needs to reconsider its stance on large Chinese trade surpluses as they allow Beijing to support US government debt.

From media stories, we might imagine that China had bought the entire US Treasury market. In early 2009 it actually held around a quarter of all foreign holdings of US Treasuries, and 23 per cent in late 2013. Not only has the share not been growing, but this represented less than 11 per cent of America's total national debt.[7] China's role is not as dominant as is thought (certainly not when one thinks that the Federal Reserve Bank bought 77 per cent of all Federal debt sold in 2011).[8] However, for its holding to remain so large when the instruments are regularly maturing means that there is an active repurchase programme. China has been breathlessly called 'the Western world's biggest single source of sovereign credit'.[9]

The massive increase in US government debt concerns the Chinese, as well as American taxpayers. Japan and China, with well around $2.5 trillion between them in Treasuries alone, are the major creditors and they need to be considered. Beijing is clearly uncomfortable with its high dollar and US government exposure. In 2009, Kenneth Rogoff, former IMF chief economist, suggested that the 2008–9 financial crisis had reduced the remaining period of the dollar's primacy from 75 to 40 years, and if oil pricing moved to non-dollar currencies it would decline to 12 years or less.[10] In 2009, there were suggestions that the Gulf States, European countries and Japan were targeting this primacy. Although swiftly denied, this raises questions.

Will China and Japan continue to fund the US government budget? If not, there will need to be substantial further increases in domestic saving, another investor will have to be found (such as the Middle East oil producers), the Fed will have to buy even more of it (with worrying longer-term implications) or there will have to be a budget decrease. Any budget decrease threatens military spending (and possibly capability).[11] Given the substantial budgeted interest payments that must be maintained to avoid default, any decrease in the overall budget means sharp decreases in non-interest items. If China and Japan, the major foreign holders of US government bonds, continue to invest, they may give Washington guidance on spending.

On the face of it, China is enviably positioned with regard to these reserves; but there is vulnerability in owning so much foreign currency. If it wants to sell, it will be difficult to transfer that amount of dollars into *renminbi* without some exchange rate distortion. Macroeconomic considerations might make China encourage the consumer through higher interest rates and a higher *renminbi*, but this might also encourage speculative money into the currency, causing appreciation. Furthermore higher interest rates could increase the spread loss on the foreign reserves. This is uncomfortable for a country with over $3 trillion of foreign reserves.

Broadly speaking, Beijing is no richer for holding those vast reserves: it merely has more currency and interest rate exposure. Businesses are wealthier, but largely in *renminbi*. In fact we could go further and say that for China, with its potentially rising currency, to borrow domestically in order to place $3 trillion in someone else's – uncontrolled and potentially falling – currency makes it highly vulnerable. Taking such a large 'minority stake' in an insufficiently diversified portfolio with unhedged currency and interest rate exposure breaks many basic investment rules. It makes a country weaker, not stronger.

Currency

The valuation of the *renminbi* has drawn much criticism, particularly from America. The currency's history is remarkable. After the 1949 Communist victory, it stood at 2.5 to the dollar for twenty years. From 1970, it gradually appreciated until it reached 1.5 in 1980. After the reforms began, the *renminbi* gradually devalued, and by 1994 it had fallen 80 per cent, to 8.62 (see Chapter 2). This undoubtedly assisted the export take-off. It then appreciated modestly to 8.19, and remained at that rate until 2005.

America has pushed Beijing to allow *renminbi* appreciation in order to reduce China's trade surpluses, but Beijing cannot agree to quick, sharp loosening: that would run counter to the entrenched national concern over instability. Beijing officials recall the 1985 'Plaza Accord', when Tokyo agreed to appreciate the yen steeply against the dollar, and they associate it with Japan's subsequent twenty years of weakness. China responded to the US demands by freeing the trading bands of the currency in mid-2005, which meant, as we have seen, that by the end of 2013 it had appreciated by 35 per cent to 6.05. However, China has no interest in another Plaza Accord.

The appreciation was not solely to please America. Beijing believed that it would force an economic restructuring to higher-value exports and a move from exports to domestic consumption. However, the strategy encountered three problems: first, the *renminbi* might have risen against the dollar, but in 2008 this coincided with the currencies of many of China's export competitors falling sharply against the dollar. So, by mid-2008 the *renminbi* had risen since mid-2005 by 17 per cent against the dollar, but by over 25 per cent against the currencies of Korea and India; by 29 per cent against the Vietnamese currency; and by 65 per cent against the Mexican peso. These trends did not hit the head-lines but they damaged China's exports and caused many foreign manufac-turers to consider leaving China. The second factor was reduced world demand. And third, surging unemployment from failing export industries caused not more domestic spending but more household saving.

From 2007, US imports from China cost noticeably more, and this was ascribed to the cyclical rise in oil and raw material costs, to rising labour costs and to the appreciating *renminbi*. Exporters complained about the effect on their prices and margins – they have narrow margins and employ millions of rural migrants; any return to mass migrant unemployment will ring alarm bells in Beijing. Even the PBC has suffered from the falling *renminbi* value of its vast portfolio of US dollar bonds. Although productivity has increased, China's currency is less competitive in the US, UK and European markets against its direct competitors than it was in early 2008.

Subsequently, there was a period of ambiguity in China's foreign exchange policy. Beijing would not raise its currency sharply (because the US would like that), but it could do so gradually, because that could soften the impact of any inflation, make energy cheaper and encourage higher-value exports. Beijing officials have a particular aversion to radical change because it reminds them of the (American-recommended) 'shock therapy' which they feel caused so much damage socially, economically – and politically – in Russia and Eastern Europe after the fall of communism. Thus there is a possible strategy available of steady currency and interest rate rises to encourage consumption and innovation.

Separate from the currency level is its use. Beijing has tried to avoid it becoming rapidly used internationally. With the events of 2008–9 in the Western banking system, Chinese policy-makers have become more adven-turous. Privately, they say they are 'fed up' with the dollar. In 2010, Premier Wen and others uncharacteristically began commenting on US financial issues (on the reasonable basis that China had almost $2 trillion of US assets and was being asked by the US government to maintain, if not increase, them).

With a Democrat in the White House and a Democratic Congress in 2009, organised labour had IOUs to cash at Washington. This increased the pressure to confront China on currency and trade. In 2009, Tim Geithner narrowly avoided calling China a 'currency manipulator' (which under US law would require hostile executive action). This ignores the fact that both America and Britain have successfully manipulated their currencies through quantitative easing and thus low interest rate policies.[12]

For the Obama administration it was politically necessary to push China on currency, but it has found this harder to do than did the Bush administration. This is because the US is beholden to China as its banker (as it remorselessly increased its indebtedness by $4 trillion in just three years from 2009 to 2011) and because China has raised its exchange rate since 2005. Although China undertook this largely for its own strategic reasons (see p.119 above), it was painful and any such rapid move is unlikely to be repeated. China moved carefully from a managed rate to a managed float of the currency in mid-2010.

China clearly manages its currency, but despite the criticism it is not proven – especially from the results of 2005–8 – that a rising currency would reduce trade surpluses. The deal with America, negotiated or not, might be that China will only gradually appreciate its currency in the medium term, but will accumulate some further US Treasury holdings, providing its reserves continue increasing. That is not a given; there have occasionally been signs of outflows from China's reserves.

Government Finance

The 2009 Chinese budget was smaller than that of France or Germany and similar to that of Italy. China's economy is more than 50 per cent bigger than that of France, but its government has been spending less. There are believed, however, to be substantial undisclosed transfers. Compared to Western countries, China's state does not take as great a proportion of GDP in government taxes and other revenues (at 24 per cent, only about half the proportion), and there is a debate about reducing tax rates. Government expenditure to GDP has been separately estimated by a different source at 12 per cent (compared with 16 per cent for America and 22 per cent for the countries of the European Union).[13]

Another measure is to use general government final consumption expenditure as a proportion of GDP. China (at the bottom) spends 13 per cent while France (at the top) spends almost double, 23 per cent. The main point to be made is that China has a surprisingly small central government budget: it has one of the most decentralised governments in the world. Expenditure is largely at the local, rather than the national, level. The biggest item in the 2012 central government budget – 70 per cent – was tax rebates and transfers to local government. Indeed the low tax take, as was mentioned in Chapter 2, was one of the factors in the economic take-off after 1979 but on the other hand low taxation and imbalance between central and local government revenues received considerable criticism from intellectuals in the 1990s for creating a weak Chinese state.[14] Since then, the situation has not changed much.

However, the Open Budget Initiative, which rates countries for budget clarity and detail, was only able to give China 11 per cent and places it in the category of 'scant or no information' (along with Yemen). One reason is that China allows little public access to government information, including the budget, which 'has been codified into law, but it is frequently or always impossible in practice to obtain access.'[15]

According to the Chinese newspaper *Economic Observer*, in 2011, 'It's said that there are actually two systems for drafting fiscal budgets, and that only the non-public version shows how government money is really spent.'[16] But clarity of government financial information is not simply a political issue – it is also an economic one. There are strong commercial reasons for extensive financial information to be available to the business community. For example, it enables commercial enterprises to think of services and products that government, or society, might find beneficial. Beijing will eventually need a transparent budget to build its future.

At the local level, revenue arises substantially through transfers from Beijing (see p.121 above), sales of land and off-balance-sheet borrowing. National leaders have urged local government to increase pensions, unemployment pay and minimum wages, but often the money is not available.[17] This gives local government an incentive to embark on ambitious real estate projects, which depend on acquiring land (and removing it from use by citizens) at low compensation rates, employ dubious financial practices, and are at risk from fluctuating real estate values.

Local government spending has been deliberately unclear, as entities below the national level are forbidden to borrow (though there is now some experimental change).[18] However, there is widespread issuance of guarantees for off-balance-sheet loans, usually by 'investment companies' associated with local government. It now looks as if this practice of guarantees will be halted. If so, that raises questions about what will happen to the existing obligations. The China Bank Regulatory Commission has acknowledged debts of $1.1 trillion, with perhaps 20 per cent at risk of souring.[19] The National Audit Office estimated in 2013 total local government debt at $3 trillion.[20] Since much of the money went to fund infrastructure in the much-promoted $586 billion government stimulus package, and is effectively guaranteed, state banks probably did not evaluate the projects too closely. Mr Shih estimates that perhaps a quarter of these loans will fail. Thus up to a trillion dollars of bad loans, about to be unguaranteed, could become a liability of the banking system.[21] Central government concern about local government off-balance-sheet bank borrowing was dealt with, but in the first eight months of 2012 annualised corporate bond issuance – much of it by local government – rose by 90 per cent.[22] However, 60 per cent of these bonds were bought by banks. The problem continues.

There may be several reasons why China takes less revenue from its economy than other countries. Officially estimated tax evasion in 2007 was over $700 billion, or more than 75 per cent of government revenue.[23] In turn, there are numerous reasons for this: there is no taxation mentality and no history of taxing people in China because, until recently, all wealth and assets were state owned; there is no culture of accurate auditing; fiscal rectitude has not been widespread; government is not viewed as always better at spending money; tax collection is often inefficient. However, in my view, the main reason is the low profit margins. Businesses compete for contracts on razor-thin margins, and profit is too small a proportion of the economy.

Tax revenue rose well in the decade after 2000, despite the downturn – partly because of an improving economy and partly because of more effective collection. China has merged the discounted tax rate for foreign joint ventures and the higher rate for domestic enterprises into one equal rate. However, officials need to enhance tax revenues – not by increasing tax rates but through still more efficient collection. Even in boom times, central government revenues were lower than might have been expected for such a seemingly large economy.

Weak tax revenue is one reason for the slow development of social security programmes. A second is the substantial build-up in internal security capability. Another is the rapid growth in military expenditure, which has been rising at double-digit pace since the end of the Deng years. (The PLA, with 2.3 million staff, is probably the world's largest employer, slightly ahead of Walmart, with 2.1 million.)

The official Chinese figure for 2012 military expenditure was under 2 per cent of GDP, and China does not believe that to be excessive, particularly as it is geographically sandwiched between Russia and Japan, both of which have announced military expansion programmes. The world average is 2.5 per cent. However, US and British analysts suggest that China's spending could be as much as 4 per cent – the same as America's.[24] Tim Huxley of the International Institute for Strategic Studies in London suggests that the Chinese figures do not include weapons purchases from overseas, R&D spending, or revenue from China's own arms exports (although there are problems of double-counting here).[25]

Some of the suggestions for the possible scale of Chinese military expenditure are not convincing: is expenditure on space research commercial or military? America is a market economy. Normally, if the Department of Defense spends on satellites or space research, it can be called military. But in China it is much harder to separate the military and the commercial.

Beijing accounts for things very differently from Western countries – not for sinister but for historical reasons. The spending figures are probably not comparable, but nor are the GDP numbers. The Stockholm International Peace Research Institute (SIPRI), probably the most neutral observer, gave an estimate of \$166 billion for Beijing's 2012 military budget, versus Washington's \$685 billion. This would mean that China spent 2 per cent of GDP – still proportionately much less than America's 4.4 per cent.[26] On the other hand, low as China's military budget might be, it still generates calls in the National People's Congress – even from military delegates – for tighter financial controls and more auditing.[27]

China has many financial obligations. Its first response to the Western downturn was to announce a stimulus package of 4 trillion yuan (\$586 billion), which initially caught international attention (though later it became apparent that the amount was smaller than indicated and included projects already announced). With its relatively small budget and its reserves deployed in foreign bonds, China lacks the flexibility the world expects and is weaker than is widely assumed – especially if its trade surpluses cease to accumulate. One other reason for low government revenues has been the failure of SOE dividends in most cases to reach the Treasury. Most payments seem to have been recycled by State-owned Assets Supervision and Administration Commission (SASAC), the agency which controls them, back into SOE requirements.[28]

Pessimistic analysis of China's finances focuses on the prospect of another bad loan crisis, an overvalued stock market, out-of-control railway debt and a vulnerable property market – all tied in with the health of the banking system. Banking bailouts have had variable results in different countries: in Korea the net cost of the 1997 bank rescue was 23 per cent of GDP; similar exercises have cost 14 per cent in Japan and zero in Sweden. The difficulty is the sheer scale of the numbers, but China might be able to grow its way out of any problem; high growth did alleviate unemployment and seems to have enabled the non-performing loans of the 1990s to be absorbed. Furthermore Li Ruogu, with his customary insouciance, suggests that 'Bad loans are actually the cost of the financial system led by the state-owned banks in supporting the Chinese economic development.'[29]

Estimates of central government debt plus associated liabilities (such as railways and 'policy banks'),[30] local government debt and non-performing loan liabilities come to $3.5 trillion, or 59 per cent of GDP.[31] Other forecasts are up to 100 per cent of GDP. Local government debt estimates might not fully account for village debts. One problem is that village leaders are unsure what their debt is.[32] Around 60 per cent debt to GDP is much less than the figure for America and it is almost entirely domestically financed. However, academics have suggested that developing economies have a lower threshold for default than advanced economies:

> many emerging economies have exhibited historical tendencies to default on debt at much lower levels than those of advanced economies. For these economies, the projected rise in the aggregate net debt ratio to nearly 60 per cent of GDP by 2035 in some of the pessimistic scenarios represents a historically large increase in government debt.[33]

So China may already be there.

There is no set debt level that will precipitate crisis. It tends to be a sudden withdrawal of market confidence. China is unusual in facing severe demographic challenges: an ageing society, a falling labour force and a declining population. The practical case for incurring high public debt levels has been to benefit the next – larger – generation. Given China's anticipated diminution in population this century, to doom a *smaller* successor generation to its predecessor's debts could be disastrous. And it seems unlikely that heavy spending on public security, global military projection, remorseless local government 'investment' or a suboptimal education system will benefit the next generation.

Historically, China has been unenthusiastic about overseas borrowing to finance projects: it had estimated foreign debt in 2013 of just over $700 billion. There is a budget deficit, but at an estimated 1.5 per cent of GDP for 2013 it is smaller than those of Western governments; of course local government and off-balance-sheet deficits distort this. China's debt is much higher than generally recognised. However, markets have been oblivious to this. If China ignores the demographic threat and approaches the international bond markets, Western governments may find themselves 'crowded out' from the supply of investors' money, or having to pay higher rates, because of China's perceived better credit.

The Banking Sector

Financial markets will always have risks. Those risks must be managed, but it is equally important to seize the opportunities. China's financial system faces several challenges – but also several opportunities. Here are some of those challenges.

First, long before globalisation was an issue for Chinese banks, fundamental problems arose from how banking had for decades been conducted. It was frequently observed in the 1990s that China had non-performing loans that could dwarf the savings and loans (S&L) crisis in America. Back in 2005, Ernst and Young, an auditing firm, produced a report on non-performing loans which suggested they were much worse than stated and could rise to $911 billion. Shortly thereafter it disavowed the report, which is unusual for a leading professional firm. Although China has made major banking sector improvements, many large problems still exist. Premier Wen said in 2010 that bank capital adequacy stands at 11.1 per cent and the non-performing loans ratio at 2.8 per cent.[34] But many professionals feel that no one knows the quantity of bad loans; moreover, the newest wave of loans – those since late 2008 – is not yet troubled. By 2011, Standard & Poor's and bank analysts were suggesting that a 10 per cent bad loan ratio could emerge from local government financing, the real estate development slump and the SME crisis, which could prejudice up to half of bank equity.[35]

Second, China has instituted many of the elements of a modern bank supervisory system. However – consciously or not – it has effectively delegated much of the bank supervision to foreign institutions. Foreign banks have increasingly been allowed to operate in China in certain limited areas and on a limited scale. This provides competitive pressure, which has the effect of forcing domestic banks to improve their operations.

Foreign strategic partners have been allowed to buy substantial minority shareholdings in domestic banks: foreign bankers joined boards, IT and risk specialists were drafted in, and shareholder agreements were struck to allow the foreign banks to have some say in the running of the domestic banks. Senior Chinese officials imagined this would improve governance in their banks. However, looking at what Western banks have done recently with their own governance, one doubts it. Indeed, it would seem Western shareholders did not acquire much knowledge about the nature of the assets or the degree of risk after they invested. The foreign banks' substantial shareholdings have probably not encouraged them to undertake prudential supervision. They have evidently found it difficult to exercise adequate oversight, even if they can acquire adequate information. Overseas banks found that the information trails available in the banks in which they invested were flawed. Later, many of those foreign shareholders exited. In terms of value for money, China hoped for both money and advice. It received money, but not always useful input.

Third, Chinese banks have been allowed to list on overseas stock markets: Hong Kong and New York. This has obliged them to (try to) comply with onerous regulations requiring transparency and accountability. Having to meet the requirements of the New York Stock Exchange and of the Sarbanes–Oxley legislation should be sobering for the directors of a Chinese state bank. In addition, there is the discipline of being listed on a stock market, where investors and analysts scrutinise every piece of information and every line of each document, and then buy or sell the shares. We could call this 'the supervision of a million eyes'. Chinese managements, however, have not always chosen to be fully compliant.

What China did – while creating its own supervisory system – was in effect to contract out much of its bank supervision to foreigners. This is extraordinary, and the process did not develop as it might have done, but that it happened at all is fascinating (even if not actually planned by the Chinese authorities). This was a useful stratagem during the interim period: by encouraging overseas listings and strategic stakes, China co-opted foreigners into recapitalising the banking industry. With hindsight, however, this might be different. China got the capital, got the favourable atmosphere for a listing and got the stock market launches. What it probably didn't get from foreign investors was good supervision or better banks. It has been suggested that foreign banks which invested in Chinese banks with the promise of improving systems and management, and then sold out, will be eyed coolly if they return to China.[36]

A fourth issue is ownership of the domestic banking industry. Foreigners have certainly been allowed in – to be on the board, in management and to have influence – but only as minority shareholders. The state continues as the majority owner. The 2008 stimulus package underlined this clearly.

It is felt to be vital for the state to retain a majority shareholding. But why? Ownership is not the same as control. The state can control the share of revenues by taxing profits and dividends; it can influence lending policy through regulatory means; it can demand certain qualifications for bank officials; it can limit branch expansion or development overseas. The China Bank Regulatory Commission has already called for an expansion of lending to non-state companies, so there is no point in remaining a majority shareholder just to influence lending to the state sector. If foreign ownership of Chinese banks is feared, there can be statutory limits on this without the state needing to own. To confuse ownership with control is muddled and reflects the failed thinking of the 1960s.

State ownership has not guaranteed good corporate governance: in fact, it is positively bad for government to retain significant ownership of the major banks. To start with, there are better uses for the potential capital locked up in those shareholdings. It is expensive for the state to continue sharing in the recapitalisations of the balance sheets. Having state-appointed bank CEOs makes it difficult for the market, the shareholders (and the CEOs) to know whether they are officials or businessmen, and that does not foster a successful commercial strategy. Beijing may celebrate the banks' performance in the stimulus package; but (even if it is later shown to have worked) that doesn't require ownership. Having government as a major shareholder will also inevitably influence how the state regulates the banks: it is difficult simultaneously to be both a player and the referee. Finally, state ownership and control make it too easy for overseas countries to justify refusing Chinese acquisition of their assets.

Banking and Small and Medium-sized Enterprises

SMEs are usually private companies (indeed SME is often a synonym for 'private enterprise'). These have grown much faster than the state-linked enterprises (SLEs) or SOEs, and have thus been a major contributor to China's outstanding growth. They have absorbed labour by creating new jobs while many SOEs have been restructuring and shedding jobs. In the 1990s, two-thirds of all workers laid off by SOEs were subsequently re-employed by SMEs.

China has had substantial labour surpluses. However, in a society with a weak welfare network, the children of one-child families wish to work close to their ageing parents. As a result, labour is becoming less mobile. Two positive features of the SMEs are that they operate in the interior (as well as on the coast) and can affect any labour surplus, and that the more they grow, the more policy-makers will find the courage to restructure the SOEs, accepting the ensuing redundancies.

Many SMEs find it hard to obtain bank credit to expand (see Chapter 2).[37] In 2009, 60 per cent of all bank credit went to centrally controlled state enterprises (so excluding locally controlled state companies).[38] Originally this resulted from an institutional bias favouring the state sector. A 2006 IMF study concluded that state banks don't consider profitability in lending decisions.[39] More recently, officials have argued that SMEs have poor accounting, weak governance, borrow short term for small amounts and thus create costly loan administration (roughly five times that of normal loans). In addition county-level banks lack the skills to evaluate loans to them. Deputy PBC Governor Hu Xiaolian said in 2010: 'the lack of legitimate collateral is the real bottleneck. Approximately 70 percent of the credit collateral received by commercial banks in China is real estate, while more than 70 percent of the assets of SMEs are account receivables and inventory.'[40] However, private companies seem to be responsible for proportionately fewer non-performing loans.

Some private companies seem able to survive on cash flow, particularly if they are not capital intensive; others prefer the unofficial banking system. It has been suggested that the 'shadow banking system' – trust companies, underground banks and loan sharks – could provide half of all financing in China.[41] One estimate was that over 40 per cent of all credit in the country between the end of 2009 and mid-2011 was created by the unofficial banks – $2.6 trillion.[42] The combination of low official interest rates and high inflation caused depositor haemorrhage in favour of the shadow banking system with its higher rates, and by late 2011 it was estimated that the shadow banks were granting more credit than the formal banks.[43] One 2011 survey found that 53 per cent of SMEs questioned in the Pearl River Delta had only ever raised money through the unofficial banking system.[44]

Unofficial banks' activity exploded after the 2009 stimulus package which involved a $2.6 trillion expansion in lending. In 2011, government-mandated reductions in bank lending forced SMEs to rely even more on the much higher interest rates of the shadow banking market. This threatens the stability of many private enterprises and could lead to widespread bankruptcies. In 2011 it was reported that the most profitable activity by state-owned banks was not lending to businesses, but funding trusts and underground banks.[45] A good example is the $500 million near default in 2014 of a product issued by China Credit Trust and sold by ICBC. In the various crises, hundreds of entrepreneurs vanished, unable to pay wages or repay loans. Nevertheless, given the poor record of the state banks in mobilising capital for growth, there is a strong case for regulating the shadow banking market, rather than closing it.

A further approach to SME financing has involved the grey area of borrowing from state enterprises, which have better credit access (this has often meant an exchange of favours with 'friends' in state companies). Sometimes inaccurate documentation is presented to banks suggesting a relationship between an SME and a state enterprise.

The state banks operate differential lending rates. There are effectively four levels of interest rates: the highest applies to the private sector companies and the lowest to the SOEs. (In between come Hong Kong, Macau and Taiwan companies, and then other foreign-funded ventures.) A study by the Hong Kong Monetary Authority in 2009 found that in their test period, 2000–2005, private companies paid 2–2.5 per cent more interest on loans than similar state sector companies. It concluded: 'SOEs' profits would have been entirely wiped out if SOEs were made to pay the same interest rates as otherwise equivalent private enterprises.'[46] This research also discovered that most bad loans were from state enterprises. Thus there are few grounds for discriminating against private enterprises, and the bias towards lending to state enterprises actually harms the banks' balance sheets. A further observation is that: 'it is common knowledge that even those SOEs repaying their loans do so on favorable terms'.

A much greater drive is needed to increase SME lending. However the answer is not just to ask the banks to lend more, but to encourage them to learn the necessary skills to evaluate private sector loans, and to use their new pricing freedom to price for risk.

While SMEs accounted for just 5 per cent of the total lending increase during the early part of 2009, they accounted for 60–70 per cent of GDP, and for an even larger share of employment owing to their focus on labour-intensive industries. Minister of Industry and Information Technology Li Yizhong noted: 'No recovery in the medium and small enterprises, no recovery in the economy. No stability for them, no jobs for many and little stability for society'.[47]

By late 2011, state banks were accused of using their near-monopolistic position to force entrepreneurs to buy wealth management products in order to gain loans. In fact one newspaper suggested that banks sold more wealth products in the first half of 2011 than in the whole of 2010, or indeed than their total loan disbursements in 2010.[48] Wealth products aren't just higher-margin products to sell, but also (as they are often packages of bank loans) allow banks to pass on higher rates to their depositors than the law allows, since they are non-deposit products. They also permit banks to get loans off their balance sheets, which alleviates their reserve ratio requirements.

Disproportionate lending to the slow-growth state sector raises the serious issue of the quality of China's stimulated economic growth. A second strategic issue is what would happen to the economy if it followed logical, market reasoning and lent proportionately to the private sector. If more SMEs could obtain financing, there should be at least seven key results: (1) greater transparency in the SMEs; (2) diversification of bank credit risk between state and non-state sectors, thus increasing stability in the bank sector; (3) more job creation; (4) consequent encouragement for government to restructure state enterprises; (5) resulting redundancy; (6) an increase in declared taxable profit to justify loan applications; and (7) the stimulation of further high economic growth. It is in China's interest to rise to this challenge.

The government encouraged the banks to expand lending. Thus, until late 2010 the central bank consistently reduced reserve requirements to facilitate banks' credit growth again. Most of the important banks had foreign strategic shareholders, yet there was no apparent reluctance to support the authorities in this lending, despite the very weak economic climate. China benefited from the fact that bank chiefs are Party members, rely on the Party for promotion and are obedient to Party discipline. During the 2009–10 massive lending increase, which many felt underpinned a major economic recovery, the concomitant rise in bank deposits and share prices was evident. Taken together with anecdotal evidence, this suggests that perhaps 40 per cent of the loans were 'round-tripped' back into the banks rather than into the economy, and much of the balance was speculated on the stock market: in mid-2009, daily stock market volumes were three times the average of the previous five years.

A further observation is that the remaining money appears to have been lent to the slower-growth state companies rather than the private firms. By 2010 it was apparent that many loans had gone to heavy industry and even heavily polluting plants, both of which threatened the government's environmental targets.[49] No banker is likely to be sacked for making a loan to a state enterprise, even though the credit history of such enterprises has been poor and they often have no productive plan to use the funding.

Although the substantial increase in lending and liquidity aided real-estate prices and encouraged the more buoyant economic performance, it did represent an old-style *dirigiste* approach to the economy, which does not necessarily lead to the best companies receiving funding for the best projects. When the banks disbursed 20 per cent of the whole year's loan target in January 2010, the authorities had to rein things in and thus increased bank reserve ratios. All major banks have announced capital-raising because of the historic levels of new lending in 2009–10. This lending increase, especially when directed towards the state sector, could result in a flood of bad loans. Loans to stock market trading do not inspire particular confidence. The fact that delinquent loans can be renegotiated and thus become 'good' loans does not really change matters.

The challenges here are several: the lending increase was mandated only in scale, not in direction, and so the more productive private sectors of the economy experienced credit shortage; in this frenetic environment, large-scale bad loan decisions were made; financial services reforms, which could create new non-state-owned institutions and create new employment, were sidelined; continuing economic growth may mask the fact that historic bad loan problems have not necessarily been solved, but may have simply diminished as a proportion of all loans; and lastly, there is a social penalty from distorted loan priority to the state sector – state-induced corruption of the private sector in the search for funding. This places a moral dilemma at the heart of future economic growth.

Shanghai as a World-class International Financial Centre?

Becoming a financial centre requires more than ambition. It requires the rule of law. It requires the admission of foreign financial players on equal terms, free capital flows, domestic and foreign investment participation and liquidity, transparency and accountability. It requires confidence. A first-class port can operate on a surprisingly narrow platform if the trade flows are there. However, a first-class financial centre – where African companies float their initial public offerings (IPOs) to Swiss investors, Brazilian companies issue bonds to Belgian dentists and Australian companies arrange their loans from German banks – requires a wide and deep platform. Anything is possible, but for Shanghai to take on London or New York as the world's premier financial market requires deep structural change, which China does not currently wish to undertake. China's saving masses would need to be given choices. Curbs on foreign participation in domestic finance would have to be scrapped, and financial services opened to competition. Sound regulation is required – and it must be enforced. We should note that – even in its 1980s heyday – Tokyo was never even close to becoming a world financial centre.

The Chinese financial authorities might be fed up with being lectured by Anglo-Saxons on the superiority of their banking systems. While aghast at the carnage, they doubtless felt a degree of *Schadenfreude* at the downfall of these arrogant investment and commercial bankers. However, paradoxically, not long after, most of those same financial titans are plying their trade for vast reward in subsequent booms, while Chinese and European bankers look on in envy and astonishment. The Anglo-Saxon model might be cyclical, but it does broadly work. The lesson has been learned: avoid the scale and concentration of – unmeasured – risk that can endanger the system. Perhaps the answer is to return to Glass Steagall, US legislation of 1933 intended to restrict commercial banks and investment banks from engaging in each other's activities, and to impose capital ratios more accurately. While the Anglo-Saxons survived, learned and prospered again, the Chinese and Europeans are still pondering how to get into the game.

The Surprising Chinese Stock Market

Chinese stock markets opened in 1991 in Shanghai and Shenzhen. There were 'A shares' for local investors to buy, and 'B shares' for foreigners to buy. There tended to be many more A shares than B. However, in the early days there was little choice of companies, and rather volatile share price movements. The Chinese market did not attract wide interest, and gradually the authorities allowed foreign participation in the A share market. This encouraged those institutions which won such licences to promote the Chinese stock markets.

As the world woke up to China's reported average 10 per cent annual economic growth, investors started to participate in the stock markets, in the hope of sharing in the world's fastest growth. However (leaving aside some clever or lucky trading), investing rarely prospered. Even disregarding the unfortunate fall of 2008, there has been prolonged, disappointed surprise from international investors that participating in the stock market has not yielded results commensurate with steady inflation-adjusted 10 per cent annual growth.

The Chinese stock market has, over the long term, been a failure. In June 2001 the Shanghai Composite Index stood at 2,200; by January 2014 it was 1,991. There have been high points and low points but this is not a market which reflects the reported growth of the underlying economy. There are many unusual aspects to the Chinese stock markets. Chinese companies are frequently admired for being among the world's largest – which usually refers to their market capitalisation. However, there is an odd reason for this: most of the large companies listed have a very small stock market 'free float'. In other words, there is usually a dominant state shareholder in control of most of the shares: if a shareholder holds 80 per cent of the shares, the free float is 20 per cent. This means that normal investment interest affects the share prices more than might be expected. It could be said to account for higher than expected share prices.

However, we should regard the market in broad terms. We have noted that it has never matched the economy's reported 10 per cent growth. This is not surprising when one considers that the economy has three major elements: the state-linked enterprises, the joint ventures (or 'foreign-funded enterprises') and the private sector companies. The real engines of economic growth during the last thirty years have been the private companies (which have emerged from pariah status to near acceptability) and the foreign joint ventures. As an example, in 2006 the foreign-funded enterprises paid 21 per cent of all taxes of any kind paid in the country. Less impressive has been the performance of the state-linked enterprises. Their post-2000 profitability derives principally from oligopolistic status, and is heavily dependent on the absence of further reform.

The Chinese stock markets do not function as markets elsewhere, and private companies have found it virtually impossible to have a stock market listing. Officials used flotation as a capital-raising exercise for state enterprises and as a key element in their restructuring. The market was not open to all: over 80 per cent of major companies in 2013 were state-owned.[50] Listing permission is required from the NDRC. As it is responsible for a portfolio of state companies, it has understandably been more interested in getting them listed than in entertaining private sector applications. Such a conflict of interest is quite normal. New smaller boards have been designed to allow smaller and private companies better access to the stock market. Having been under 'examination' for a decade, these markets have now started. The project isn't progressing quickly.

As the private sector has powered China's economic growth over the last thirty years, it raises an interesting question: if bank loans and equity capital raising had been made readily available to the private sector throughout this period what would China's growth rate have been? Unfortunately, we shall never know.

State-linked companies may be in the economy's slow lane, but there also seems to be a casualness (to say the least) about their corporate ethics. In 2009, there was a domestic outcry about the large payouts to management of CNOOC, a major listed oil company. The state entity which controls CNOOC offered a placatory reply: the executive incentive scheme was merely a device to reassure foreign investors when listing overseas that management is adequately motivated. In fact, the Chinese public was told, these payments were returned to the company, and so no harm was done.[51] It didn't occur to the state entities that this involves making false declarations to overseas stock exchange authorities – not once but annually – with the express purpose of misleading foreign investors.

Many state companies have had option schemes, which managers dare not exercise without losing their actual standing, which derives from being not businessmen but senior government officials. It is not realised that as the CEOs of such organisations are generally members of the Party elite their next job might be outside the industry altogether. The situation was dramatically highlighted on 1 November 2004, when the heads of all three listed telecoms companies were shuffled around by the Party organisation department. The same situation arose again in 2011 with the state oil companies.[52] This makes a mockery of the boards' role in choosing senior management and the watchdog nature of independent non-executive directors. However, underwriters to IPOs have not highlighted the fact that Party committees and the organisation department might take the critical decisions affecting listed companies. Non-disclosure of such pertinent facts is pervasive.

Poor practice is not confined to state companies on the Chinese exchanges. There has been a trend over some years for private enterprises to list overseas, as they cannot easily list at home. In 2010 alone, 39 Chinese companies listed in New York. By 2011, there were estimated to be 350, often listed by reverse takeovers of shell companies (which reduces regulatory scrutiny). There were then serious complaints and investigations into charges of fraudulent accounting and other malpractice.[53]

State-linked enterprises reported indifferent profitability until about 2005, when the earlier decision to streamline them bore fruit. This had involved selling smaller enterprises and merging others so that they would become champions. The merged companies became quasi-monopolies and therefore more profitable. Later many of those companies involved in energy, raw materials and infrastructure benefited from global commodity inflation. There is no suggestion that these companies became better (or better managed): their profitability increased for largely external reasons. Indeed, any further economic reforms – such as opening up the service sector to greater competition or new ventures overseas – are likely to reduce the monopoly benefits of many of these companies. We should not expect the state sector to show such substantial earnings growth in the coming years.

By paying lower interest rates than its competitors, the state sector receives a huge subsidy from the banking system. This suggests that the real profitability of state enterprises is substantially lower (possibly negative), which indicates that share valuations have been further removed from reality than observers had feared. If banking eventually moves to unitary credit pricing, and if that reduces a state enterprise's profit by, say, 75 per cent, then the present market valuation of such a stock could change from 20 times annual earnings to 80 times, without the share price changing. This suggests there could be substantial future falls in stock market valuation, and thus share prices. The extraordinarily unilateral ownership complexion of listed companies is a weakness for the economy and financial system. If the authorities expedited the access of private companies to the market, they would probably increase interest in the stock exchanges and harness more household savings.

Greater private sector access to the stock market would reduce the pressure for corrupt practices. Greater transparency and accountability, allied with this growing liquidity, would bolster foreign institutional interest in the markets. Reducing state shareholdings in state-linked companies would increase liquidity and promote more accurate valuations. We should not confuse government selling 10 per cent of a state enterprise on the market with 'privatisation': critical decisions are still made by the Party. Many foreign investors were surprised in 2011 when Wu Bangguo, number two in the Party, 'said privatization was not under consideration'.[54] They thought they had seen much already.

The market could contribute more effectively to capital mobilisation if it were set on a more rational path. 'Reform' and 'opening up' are terms frequently used to describe economic policy over the last thirty years. It would be good to open up the stock market to the private sector and to reform the state sector through privatisation. However, we should have grave doubts about the likely scale of future privatisation when we see the sensitive role that many state enterprises are given in strategic investment and in R&D. The best example is the policy-driven quest to secure energy, mineral and food resources overseas. Powerful energy and resource companies that hold long-term contracts on behalf of the country are unlikely to feature among candidates for privatisation. We must assume that major parts of the stock market may never undergo meaningful structural reform. Furthermore, real reform of the stock markets would probably lead to reduced valuations, and thus substantial risk to the banking system.

The stock market level is often unjustifiably high, during both bull and bear phases, because of the distortion caused by limited free float. If the studies are correct and removing interest rate subsidy would cause the profits of state companies to halve, the stock market can clearly be vulnerable.

It might be argued that the state enterprises are paying the *correct* bank rate and the private sector is paying punitive rates. In that case, there would be no direct change in state sector profitability (and thus the stock market). However, the indirect change is that private sector companies would see the cost of capital fall and their profitability significantly rise. In areas where companies in both sectors compete, private sector firms should experience lower costs of doing business and thus be able to increase their market share at the expense of their state competitors. Either way, there are interesting challenges ahead.

Reflections on the Financial Challenges

Multilateral institutions frequently provide reports on developing countries, such as China, but are painfully polite to their hosts. However, this is what the IMF reported in mid-2011:

> The main near-term domestic risks to the financial system are four-fold:
> (i) the impact of the recent sharp credit expansion on banks' asset quality;
> (ii) the rise of off-balance-sheet exposures and of lending outside of the
> formal banking sector; (iii) the relatively high level of real estate prices; and
> (iv) the increase in imbalances due to the current economic growth pattern.[55]

While not exhaustive, this list at least has the benefit of being authoritative.

Each area of China's financial system has its vulnerabilities. The stock market and the banking markets do not do what they should normally do: mobilise capital to support healthy long-term economic growth. This misallocation of capital undoubtedly prejudices economic growth. Foreign exchange reserves are vulnerable to rises in the *renminbi* exchange rate and domestic interest rates, both of which are feasible. Government finance suffers from insufficient revenue for the size of the economy, which makes it difficult to build a strong military and security capability at the same time as developing a social welfare infrastructure. The level of domestic debt is higher than appreciated and local government finance is a mess. An under-utilised avenue for funding is external debt; however, if China enters the international bond markets it could have devastating results for debt-laden Western governments. The banking industry's excessive and uncritical focus on lending to state industry and capital investment leaves it vulnerable to a repeat of the large-scale non-performing loan crisis of the 1990s and has also created a crisis in the shadow banking sector. The stock market's large valuations rest on state enterprise oligopolistic positioning and subsidised interest rates, which are at risk from any resumption of economic and financial reform.

There have been attempts to introduce more efficient consumer finance. Consumer debt is less than 15 per cent of GDP, and more efficient instruments would help recycle household savings. Successful development of the new Growth Enterprise Market would be very constructive. If sound growing companies dominate the listings (rather than companies which benefit solely from relationships with officials), that would help financial stability, as well as the economy. It is also worth noting the moral challenge at the heart of the economy, where successful entrepreneurs must contemplate unethical practices if they are to survive and grow. The fact that everyone knows it, and officials accept it, undermines the rule of law and respect for the state.

China is a prisoner of its past. For a rising power, it has weak banking and capital markets – a vestige of the old command economy thinking. If it could substitute sensible regulatory oversight for dated conceptions of ownership and control, capital-raising would be larger and more efficient, and more likely to meet economic needs. Until then, the authorities will prefer to have government officials run the banks under Party supervision. Any sign of serious inflation, rising bad debt and capital write-offs as a result of the 2009–10 lending initiative might encourage reform. However, if China is successful, we may see little interest in further fundamental reform. Furthermore, the political implications of the next round of necessary change explain the leadership's timidity when faced with the need for reform. We have seen reform ideas mooted in late 2013 – hedged with restraints such as maintaining state dominance – but it is unclear how far they will be taken. Most importantly, unless reformed, government finance, stock market valuations, foreign reserves and the banking system all represent potential threats.

CHAPTER FIVE

Social Welfare: Missing Umbrella

The most intractable challenge China faces is that of demography. Everything has to be seen in the context of a long term, substantial and irreversible fall in total population. However, several other major social issues also loom.

Karl Marx predicted that as communism developed the state would 'wither away'. What happened in China in the 1980s was that the welfare state withered away. Since 1949, social services had been provided by the work unit, but this system broke down in the rush to market. The rolling redundancies since the early 1990s (which were exacerbated by the 2008–9 downturn) were just one of the stresses on an ailing system. Social security had to be created almost from nothing, at a time when the whole society was being radically transformed. Since the 1990s China has introduced social programmes and expanded education, but demand outstrips delivery. If these social demands cannot be satisfied, the consequences could be explosive and include widespread instability, which is a direct threat to growth.

China's need rapidly to develop far more comprehensive social programmes is driven by concern about stability and by a desire to encourage households to spend rather than to save; the country needs to establish a safety net to cope with endemic unemployment (or underemployment), population change, low charitable giving, changes in the structure of the family and increased expectations. Angry unemployed workers, with no safety net, can generate instability. Although officials recognise many of the challenges, the question remains whether their responses are quick or comprehensive enough. Ironically, this is reminiscent of a capitalist economy gingerly approaching socialism, rather than the reverse.

China went from a collectivist version of society, where all worked for and were supported by the state, to a rather murky polar opposite, where, at the very large, sharp end, a form of Gladstonian capitalism required most people to provide their own social security, and where a stay in hospital might cost a year's income. The iron rice bowl for most has been smashed. There are some social pockets where government still provides; however, it is now normal for the citizen to pay for kindergarten fees, private tuition, university loans, hospital treatment and medicine. School fees are common. This is in a society where, as late as 2010, there were still around 156 million living on under $1.25 a day.

As Margaret Thatcher and Ronald Reagan found, when the state is reduced, private philanthropy does not always step in. This is true in China, where the level of philanthropy is abysmal and has attracted government censure: Bain & Co., a global consulting firm, reckons it represents 0.1 per cent of GDP, compared with 0.3 per cent in Brazil, 0.6 per cent in India and 1.7 per cent in America.[1] There is much talk of billionaires and of the vast, fast-growing middle class in China, but philanthropy is not prominent. Disasters, such as earthquakes, have generated splendid generosity, but sustained charitable donation towards chronic issues is underdeveloped.

As noted above, it was not the state itself that used to provide assistance, but the work unit. Since the end of communes, there have been no agricultural state work units, and so most rural people are self-employed. In industry, the incorporation and flotation of state enterprises has meant there is little room on the balance sheet for workers' housing or crèches. Pay has undoubtedly risen substantially in the new market environment, but – as in the Soviet Union and Eastern Europe – there are those who have lost amid the new prosperity and are experiencing the living costs of a high-growth society that operates with exiguous social support.

Rural inhabitants often have limited disposable incomes. With such a large population, even a small percentage experiencing difficulties translates into a large number of victims.

Poverty

China is becoming richer, yet many people are poor. The wealth of information available is sometimes confusing and sometimes downright contradictory. The best study on poverty is probably the World Bank's 2009 report (which calculated – counter-intuitively – that in 2003, 43 per cent of those below the poverty line were actually saving money).[2] That report makes four clear points.[3] First, families might be above the poverty level at one point, but fall below it later. These families, described as 'vulnerable to poverty', make up twice the number of those counted as poor that year. Second, it showed that 99 per cent of poverty is in rural areas – underlining the observation that in China the cities look like Europe, but the countryside often resembles Africa.[4] Third, almost half of all poverty is in widely dispersed communities, and so attempts to resolve it through 'area-based targeting' – such as focusing on the Western provinces – no longer work well. And fourth, from 1981 to 2004, China took 500 million people out of poverty; in the same period the global number of impoverished fell from 1.5 billion to 1 billion. Thus, without China there would have been no reduction. We should note, however, that even in 2009 the Bank based its report on 2004 data.

China set its own official poverty level in 2007 at $0.57 per day, which could be described as conservative; it was certainly the lowest benchmark of the seventy-five countries compared. This is now $1 but the World Bank uses $1.25. The strategy seems to be to raise the threshold as prosperity grows, but not to bother with international benchmarks.[5] The Global Hunger Index of 2011 showed that, since 1990, China had improved from 11.6 to 5.5 (with normal being below 5), while South Africa, for example, showed no improvement between 6.5 in immediately post-apartheid 1996 and 6.4 in 2011.[6] Controversially, the Asian Development Bank calculated that by 2005 over half of China's population was 'middle class', as it could afford mobile phones and other assumed determinants. China would seem just to have 'lost' its working class, leaving nothing between the middle class and poverty.[7]

By comparison, almost a tenth of Britons are in 'deep poverty';[8] a fifth of New York schoolchildren rely on soup kitchens; and by 2012 a record 46 million Americans – over one in seven – were on food stamps[9] (the same percentage of Zimbabweans need food handouts).[10] So while China has been hauling millions out of poverty, America has seen food stamp beneficiaries double since 2003. Though definitions may differ, poverty levels are now quite similar in both countries – but they appear to be moving in different directions. The important point is that China has brought hundreds of millions out of poverty. This is an unparalleled achievement.

Education

China decided in 1993 to raise its education spending to 4 per cent of GDP by 2000, which is still low by world standards – the world average in 2008 was about 4.5 per cent; Mexico, for instance, spends 5.5 per cent.[11] Of course, as so often, there is no direct correlation between money spent and results achieved. Korea, for example, spends the same proportion of GDP on education as Argentina, but has a much higher reading score. In fact, in 2008 China was spending 3.5 per cent of GDP on education, and by 2011 it had still not reached its 4 per cent target – eighteen years after setting it. Furthermore, officials appear to prefer spending money on buildings than on people. There are many schools, even in rural areas, but not enough teachers.

A 2003 World Bank survey of government secondary education spending in developing countries placed China 36th out of 43, with spending of 0.8 per cent of GDP (the average was 1.8 per cent). Korea and Mexico each spent more money on secondary education than did China.[12] Teachers generally prefer urban life, and so in rural schools the education ministry has to rely on untrained (though educated) teachers.[13]

Schools often require family financial contributions (in different forms). Even the state media deplore the fact that 'parents usually have to pay large sums of sponsorship money, even for the nine-year term of compulsory education, which is supposed to be free'.[14] Non-governmental spending on pre-tertiary education in 2001 was 30 per cent of total spending (compared with 8 per cent in Japan and America). Primary and secondary education is seriously under-funded in many rural areas, and kindergarten fees are high. There is a popular desire for kindergarten education to become part of the compulsory state system. In 2011, one county in Shaanxi province announced it would begin offering free education between the ages of three and 15. In 2010, in the city of Shenzhen 98 per cent of kindergartens were private (and provided for just half the demand).[15]

Fees for higher education are widely regarded as unreasonable, given income levels. Universities are underfunded and so fees are elevated; meanwhile spending per student has reportedly fallen sharply – by over 60 per cent between 1997 and 2004.[16] State media have noted that 'the higher education system has also been widely criticized for putting expansion and larger student numbers ahead of quality'.[17] At Peking University, classes of below thirty are often not recognised for academic credits, and this discourages personal attention. In fact, 20 per cent of students in 2011 were attending private higher education institutions, where the fees were much higher.[18]

Until recently, rural residents have outnumbered urban but the proportion of rural students at Peking University fell by 2005 to 10 per cent and at Tsinghua to 17 per cent by 2010,[19] partly because, as already noted, qualified teachers want to work in the cities.[20] The 21st Century Education Research Institute in Beijing found that students at prestigious senior high schools who came from families of workers, farmers and migrant workers had dropped from 37.3 per cent in 1978 to 3.3 per cent in 2008.

China follows the pattern of the US and Australia, where non-government sources (usually the family) contribute more than half the cost of college education (in contrast to Europe, where the state funds most college education). As in Africa and India, there is a tendency in China for even the poor to pay for education.

The verdict on China's tertiary education is mixed; people overseas tend to feel fearful of it: then British Prime Minister Gordon Brown was concerned at the number of Chinese graduates – more than 3 million in 2006 (by 2013 it had reached 7 million). He was particularly concerned about the large number of engineering graduates.

However, there is a contradiction: millions of workers are left seeking jobs, and yet there is a lack of skilled workers for specific roles. Add to this the rising graduate unemployment (which has a long history) and serious questions arise about the education system. One major problem is the *gaokao* university entrance examination, which is based on rote learning. There is typically one correct answer and no opportunity for lateral thinking.[21] Secondary schools thus focus on teaching the answers to the questions. This distorts secondary education, producing undergraduates who lack the necessary educational skills or have insufficient intellectual curiosity.[22]

McKinsey asked HR professionals at multinational companies to evaluate Chinese graduates.[23] The verdict in 2005 was that over 85 per cent are unsuited to work in any international context, for three critical reasons: excessive reliance on rote learning, poor English and low mobility.[24] A survey of international universities prepared in 2012 by Shanghai Jiaotong University suggests one reason for this poor assessment: China does not have a university in the world's top 100.[25] The idea of 'universities in name only' has spread throughout the populist world, but according to Professor Ji Baocheng of Renmin University, a new university opened in China every three days for eight years.[26] An examination of these universities' research achievements might blunt any awe felt at China's supposed lead in producing top-flight graduates. Even Chinese companies deplore the quality of aspiring managers. One survey found that 44 per cent of domestic firms cite a shortage of managerial talent as the biggest constraint on expanding overseas.[27] Of course, China is not alone in having deficiencies in its educational system.

Education can be improved. In 2010, the State Council issued another plan to raise educational standards and expenditure. However, at college level, the focus seems to be on continuing the headlong increase in graduate numbers rather than the quality of teaching.[28] A Tsinghua University study in 2011 reported that 69 per cent of graduate entry-level salaries were below those of migrant workers.[29] Despite the huge and persistent graduate unemployment, the plan is to increase university graduates to 36 per cent of the population by 2020.

The Chinese often complain about rampant cheating in the *gaokao* exam, and the police are even called in to invigilate.[30] Reforms to the *gaokao* are being discussed, and one hopes these will encourage more critical thinking and less rote learning.[31] However, there are three concerns here: implementation of such plans is often slow, there is some doubt about how well critical thinking is understood and there is a deep concern amongst the public that any move away from a fact-based examination will allow greater corruption in the allocation of places.

Population Outlook and Implications

In 1979, when Beijing introduced the one-child policy it was generally not strictly applied, but later it was rigorously enforced for Han citizens. The fertility rate was falling in China in the 1970s (as in many other countries), and experts say that the policy itself has had no discernible impact on the birth rate.[32] However, the coercive nature of the one-child policy has affected the people's relationship with the state: there have been reports of forced abortions, and local officials have admitted that children over the permitted limit have been seized and sold for adoption overseas.[33] 'A popular perception is that China's low fertility is mostly a result of a restrictive policy, but the ultra low fertility observed in China also reflects a silent revolution in Chinese society.'[34] It has been noted that 'What now seems incontestable is that China's TFR [total fertility rate] has been below replacement level for almost two decades – since about 1990',[35] and that 'China has experienced a tectonic shift in its fertility regime: not only were there delays in marriage and childbearing, but more importantly there were fundamental changes in Chinese family values.'[36] The falling birth rate has had several damaging side-effects, such as gender disparity, an ageing of society and a reduction in the labour force.

Rural culture values boys more than girls, since girls leave the family on marriage and are thus unavailable to support their elderly parents. Boys, on the other hand, remain to farm the land. Confucianism also suggests some 'son-preference' (see Chapter 7). These factors have encouraged rural parents to use (illicit) ultrasound testing and to abort female foetuses. Although the national gender ratio across all age groups stayed constant between 1978 and 2006 (at 51.5 per cent male), for those born in 2010 the male–female birth ratio was above 54:46 (though it is possible that female births are under-reported by up to 3 million girl babies annually).[37] This ratio applied across all Chinese from birth to those aged 15 in 2010. The imbalance is even more pronounced in certain rural provinces: in some counties of Hubei, baby boys now exceed girls by 33 per cent.[38] While recent years have shown some reduction in the imbalances, the overall disparity is still pronounced. Interestingly, the Qing-era scholar Wang Shiduo recommended discouraging early marriage and encouraging compulsory abortion and female infanticide, particularly among lower-class families.[39]

Caring for parents and grandparents, who are living longer, is becoming a growing burden on the young. The McKinsey survey noted that a child's need to care for parents will reduce labour mobility, while population ageing could cause a massive pension deficit.

However, the main reduction in the birth rate (–50 per cent) came between 1949 and 1979 – before the one-child policy was instituted. Population control legislation was first introduced in 1957, and a birth control campaign operated from 1971. After 1979 there was a further one-third decrease in the birth rate. It took France 150 years to go from a total fertility rate (TFR, or the number of births per woman) of 5 to 2.5; China did it in twelve years. China's birth rate will probably shrink by another quarter by 2050.

Since minorities have no restrictions imposed on them, it is understandable that the birth rate in Tibet, Xinjiang and Inner Mongolia is more than double that in Shanghai and Beijing. Despite strong public support for the one-child policy, in a 2010 poll by *China Youth Daily*, one of the country's most influential newspapers, 75 per cent of respondents said they would have two children if allowed.[40] Because of the social pressures, it would not be surprising if China did re-evaluate the one-child policy and either scrap it or amend it to the Vietnamese version of two children per family. There is some internal debate on this among officials. In fact, Shanghai (which has drawn criticism for acting as 'an independent republic') and some provinces have substantially relaxed the policy, partly because the birth rate is falling, which is accelerating the ageing of society.[41]

Shanghai's population policy adjustment heralds change. Until recently, the stock response of officials was that policies do not change – yet they do. There is a clear internal debate on this, with most Chinese demographers arguing that the policy should end.[42] Sociologists see 2017 as a turning point, when the dependency ratio will sharply deteriorate. One solution to increasing longevity and deteriorating demography would be to delay retirement, but that could exacerbate youth unemployment.

The UNDP projects that China's total population will peak around 2026, and by 2050 will have fallen by about 3 per cent (or about 45 million) from its 2010 level. Indeed (for what it is worth), it has been estimated that, at the current rate of reproduction, China's population will have declined to zero by the year 3500.[43] India is poised – in about 2020 – to overtake China as the world's most populous country.[44] It is not that India is about to grow rapidly. But it (and America – see Table 5.1) will grow, while China's population will fall. Ebenstein and Jennings project a likely fall to a 550–700 million population by 2100.[45] The lower number could put the ratio at 1.15:1. However, by the end of the century, it does seem very likely that the Chinese–US population ratio will certainly be less than 2:1, and the second half of the twenty-first-century looks likely to be determined more by technological advantage than by dominance through scale. Societies with steadily falling populations do not normally have a sustained high rate of economic expansion. As China's population is estimated to peak around 2026 and then to fall, there is a narrowing window for China to continue its high economic growth rates.[46] The looming slowdown in labour force growth will raise wages. Demography is a factor which cannot respond quickly to government policy changes.

Table 5.1: **China–US Population Outlook: 2010–2050**

	China (millions)	US (millions)	Ratio
Population 2010	1,341	310	4.3:1
Population 2050 (est.)	1,296	403	3.2:1
Population 2100 (est.)	720	478	1.97:1

Data sourced from the UN: WUP Revision 2012.[47]

Fertility rates are declining globally, without one-child policies. This was the last and biggest of Mao's collectivist policy failures. Not only has it caused massive human rights damage but it did not even reduce fertility. Beijing couldn't adopt policies in the twentieth century to reduce population and won't find policies in the twenty-first to raise it.

Housing

Housing in China has been in transition since the 1980s. Before 1985, it is estimated that only 17 per cent of families were home-owning. In 1993, the Party announced the institution of a 'socialist market economy', leaving state enterprises to pursue individual strategies at their own risk, resulting in profitability or bankruptcy. Virtually all state firms liquidated their low-rent employee housing (which often yielded less than it cost to maintain). This enabled millions of employees to acquire their homes cheaply. Government continued to house its staff, not being subject to profit considerations. But in 1998, the incoming premier, Zhu Rongzhi, announced that economic growth would be based on building more housing, and that the welfare housing distribution system was abolished. Government then largely followed the state enterprises and sold off staff housing, often assisting employee purchase. Mortgage down-payments fell from 30 per cent to 20 per cent. (Over the years, this has proved quite a practical and effective policy tool: when necessary, the authorities raise the down-payment required in order to dampen speculation in the housing market, and when the market looks tired they reduce it to 20 per cent.)

In a 2002 survey, two-thirds of people who had bought their homes said they wanted to raise their living standards by buying a new house.[48] Rising incomes have often enabled the purchase of a new house but generally the old home is retained. This has led to the pervasive phenomenon of second home ownership, which contributes to high property prices.[49] However, the standards of the old factory employee housing were low, and much of the stock has been destroyed in huge inner-city development plans. This has thrown many people into an under-supplied urban housing market: there is now a shortage of both low-cost housing to rent and affordable middle-cost housing to buy. A very constructive development has been the gradual relaxation of restrictions on the resale of property originally bought from work units.

There are deficiencies and contradictions in ownership data. In early 2011 it was estimated nationwide that still only 32 per cent of homes were fully privately owned – i.e. with no strings attached.[50] This compares with 67 per cent in the USA, 70 per cent in Britain and 57 per cent in France. However, in 2012 state media issued highly contested survey results reporting 89 per cent home ownership. Much depends as always on definition.[51]

The Ministry of Construction says that the average permanent urban resident has 280 sq. ft of living space. On the face of it, this doesn't seem too bad, since it implies that a couple would have 560 sq. ft. By the standards of affluent (but land-starved) Hong Kong, where the average area per person in public housing is 135 sq. ft, it is positively attractive. However, the figures overlook the 260 million migrant workers, who are not 'permanent urban residents' and so are excluded from most statistics.

Housing loans rose from $80 billion in 2002 to $980 billion by 2012, this accounted for just 16 per cent of GDP. It was 12 per cent of all lending in 2011. By comparison, housing loans in Hong Kong can be over 30 per cent of lending. The delinquency rate at the end of 2008 was low (far below that of other loans), despite concern about falls of up to 30 per cent in property values in some cities. This is doubtless partly because of the relatively conservative collateralisation of mortgage loans. In the 2008–9 downturn, home ownership was favoured and various forms of assistance were offered. The mortgage down-payment was again lowered from 30 per cent to 20 per cent. This kept the housing market buoyant. In 2012, concerns revived.

The Chinese Academy for Social Sciences estimated in late 2009 that residential property was too expensive for 85 per cent of people.[52] This results from the government's policy on land provision and an unwillingness to regulate the development process. By late 2010, a home in the big cities cost 11.5 times the average income (but of course homes are not bought by average people).[53] However, the authorities are increasingly requiring developers to supply affordable housing, and in Beijing this makes up 15–30 per cent of projects.

Pensions

Demographic trends offer little comfort on the pensions front. First, as the 2010 census demonstrated, the population is not growing, but is rapidly ageing. Secondly, birth rates are creating inverse-pyramid families, with one child, two parents and four grandparents. Individuals come under huge pressure to support their parents and grandparents. The state is reluctant to assume the burden of providing institutional care or retirement funding. This will need to change.

The public retirement system suffers from being sub-scale, poorly designed and badly run. China launched its national pension scheme in 1997, with coverage depending largely on location. Most beneficiaries are urban workers, and virtually no rural residents or rural migrant labourers are included. Even in 2010, less than a third of employees were covered.[54] The system is supposed to cover all urban employees, but in practice contributions are made on behalf of 55 per cent. Compliance is low, as the contributions are high and there is little confidence in the system. The retirement age for urban workers is 50 for women and 55 for men; for professionals it is 55 for women and 60 for men.

The system is built on two approaches: fixed contributions from older workers in state industries, and individual retirement accounts for those working in the modern economy, whereby participants contribute 8 per cent of their wages to the individual funds. Unfortunately, in 2010 these accounts were virtually empty, owing to fraud and other problems.[55]

There is a myth that fast-developing economies have 'good' demographies. However, 'in 2000, every 9.1 work-age laborers supported one person aged 65 years or older in China, but the number of supporters is expected to shrink to 3.7 by 2030.'[56] Children under 14 constituted 19 per cent of the total population in 2008. This figure is falling, and in Shanghai they make up only 10 per cent. In 2005, China had almost twice as many under-14s as over-60s; by 2035 the figures will be reversed.

China has been called the world's fastest-ageing country, but this is not quite true: South Korea and Singapore are ageing even faster. Nor will China be among the ten most aged societies in 2050. However, by the 2040s it is expected to have more people over 65 than the *entire* US population. It will still have a better dependency ratio (i.e. working people to older people) than Japan. Even by 2050, China will not have the same proportion of over-65s as Japan, but it will have undergone the stress of sharply rising ageing.

Table 5.2: **Chinese and Japanese Demography: 2010–2035**

	China	Japan
2010		
Total population (millions)	1,354	127
Over-65s (millions)	111	29
Percentage	8	23
2035		
Total population (millions)	1,462	114
Over-65s (millions)	281	37
Percentage	19	32

Data sourced from the UN.

When the US, Japan and Korea hit roughly this level of ageing, they each had per capita GDP of around $15,000; the figure for China in 2011 was about $4,300. The average elderly person has less than one year's income in savings, and most rely on the extended family for support: almost 80 per cent of those over 85 rely on their children or relatives for financial support, and some 70 per cent of those over 60 live with their children or relatives. This is becoming unsustainable. In 2012, just over 1 per cent, or one million, lived in an institution;[57] by 2030 it could be 50 per cent, or around 150 million people.

Between 1995 and 2005, a net 108 million Chinese joined the workforce, and China is expected to lose a net 79 million from the workforce between 2025 and 2035. By 2050, the workforce is expected to have shrunk by almost a quarter, and a third of the population will be over 60.[58] Just as a rapid rise in household savings rates coincided with the fall in youth dependants, it is likely that savings will fall again in proportion to the rise in the ratio of aged dependants. Existing pension arrangements are inadequate, and most people need to save to support their parents – and perhaps later themselves – which undermines the government's aim of developing domestic consumer demand.

The pensions that do exist are not fully portable and thus threaten labour mobility (or it threatens them). The returns from the 'personal accounts' are also extremely low. It is all building towards a pension crisis, pressuring older people to continue working for as long as they can and putting huge funding pressure on the modest pension system. The solution is likely to involve introducing a wider pension system, administering it better and perhaps requiring people to work later (though high unemployment militates against raising the retirement age). At the moment, raising the retirement age to 65 would create 30–40 million extra workers; but as the labour force shrinks, theoretically the longer working ages and unemployment could both be absorbed. Shanghai, a regular incubator of reform, has already made working after retirement age more attractive financially. It has no choice: there 1.5 workers support every retiree. It is forecast that by 2020, 33 per cent will be over 65. The city pension fund is unsustainable.[59]

The World Bank in 2007 put the total funding need of the pension system – both 'legacy' claimants made redundant from state enterprises before the system began and those retiring subsequently – at $1.5 trillion.[60] The system is inadequately funded and the authorities have supplemented contributions with the proceeds of lottery ticket sales and overseas stock market flotations of state companies. From 2008, the government began trying harder to include migrant workers in the scheme, to share the cost of supporting current retirees. However, this strategy was damaged by the soaring redundancy of migrant workers in 2008–9. Most worryingly, some of China's provinces have been withdrawing funds from current workers' individual retirement accounts to compensate older retirees from the pre-pension era. Misallocation and actual fraud have caused a pension deficit – reported in 2000 at $4.5 billion and in 2010 at $200 billion.[61] As a result millions of personal retirement accounts contain no money and are forecast to fail to deliver the promised benefits.[62] A Fudan University report concludes that even if the retirement age is raised by seven years, by 2050 the pension fund deficit will cost 10 per cent of the total national budget.[63]

There is of course a global challenge to the pensions system, principally from demographic change: the European pensions gap, for example, is $2.5 trillion a year.[64] Chinese longevity is akin to that of Eastern Europe. It rose by six years between 1980 and 2010 and could rise further through improvements in medical care.[65] To deal with this growing problem, what is needed is effective funding, government regulation, professional management and adequate portability. Officials are already discussing the urgent need to reform a system which hasn't yet even been universally introduced. It has been remarked that China could be the first society to grow old before it grows rich.

Health

Healthcare is a challenge for China, as future need is unpredictable. The government of China contributes a smaller share of national health spending than the US government (even pre-Obama).[66] Chinese patients have been paying 60 per cent of the cost of healthcare themselves.[67] This is unusual for any advanced country: in America over half is privately funded, but in Europe, Canada, Britain and Japan the taxpayer foots over half the bill. In 2012, over a quarter of the Chinese population found paying for healthcare a key big problem.[68] 'One-third of people who had been told to go to hospital failed to do so – and of those, three-quarters blamed the cost.' [69]

In 2000, the World Health Organization rated China's health financing system as 'one of the most inequitable worldwide'; it ranked China 188th out of 191 countries.[70] The US spends 6.9 per cent of GDP on health; in China it is 1.8 per cent.[71] There is a target to ensure universal access to basic medical services by 2020, but it is not clear how achievable this is. The Indian approach of using less intensively trained workers for more routine medical procedures could be considered. Meanwhile, violence against medical staff is not uncommon: in 2006 (the last year for which there are official statistics) there were 5,500 cases, and in 2010 there were calls for police to be permanently stationed in hospitals to prevent violence. This is probably related to the rising violence in Chinese society in general. Professor Sun of Fudan University said in 2012 that 'those who lived through the 60s . . . feel today the only choice they have when things go wrong is to turn on the vulnerable.'[72]

The Rural Cooperative Medical Care System was launched in 2002, and the Health Ministry hoped it would be available to the entire rural population by the end of 2008. Through pressure and subsidy, 95 per cent participation was achieved in many rural areas by 2010. In 2011, the scheme paid 60 per cent of outpatient and 70 per cent of inpatient fees. However, many inpatients prefer to go to urban hospitals, where they expect better treatment but lower reimbursement.[73] Outpatient services are no more popular: prescription drugs are expensive and patients prefer the cheaper private drug providers (although a third of those drugs are counterfeit).[74] Despite this, the system has seen a sizeable take-up of inpatient services. That said, the pay-first principle and limited reimbursement mean that it is used less by the poor and more by the rich.[75] There are also many costs that are not covered (or covered inadequately) by the programme, including drugs for chronic complaints, and outpatient care.

A major complaint is that doctors are too frequently remunerated on revenues generated:

> Hospital management often incentivizes doctors by creating sales targets for pharmaceuticals and high-tech examinations. Departments that beat targets receive bonuses, to which doctors have been shown to respond. Other hospitals link doctors' pay directly to drug prescribing and CAT scanner use.[76]

Pilot projects are in place to see whether, and how, hospitals can manage without excess drug revenues.

In 2009, as part of the stimulus initiative, the authorities announced a welcome $120 billion healthcare initiative. Announcement was easy, but implementation is taking longer. As in education, officials focus on buildings rather than doctors and there is a tendency to prescribe high-margin drugs and handle high-profile diseases, rather than treat common ailments. Furthermore, Beijing pays 40 per cent of the package and the local authorities the balance. As Professor Liu Guoen, head of the Department of Health Economics at Peking University, says: 'I really don't know who is going to pay the remaining 500 billion yuan . . . Provincial governments may have some money, but county governments have no money.'[77]

The most recent available data (if somewhat old) indicate that China has fewer doctors, nurses and hospital beds per capita than the world average (or even than emerging markets on average). It has worse than average infant mortality, TB, cancer and other outcomes.[78] Life expectancy is below that of most advanced countries, and is at the level of Hungary or the Baltic states. The rising standard of living along with changing diet and lifestyle bring their own problems: less exercise, more male smoking, salty and sugared snacks all take their toll. China has under a quarter of the world's population, but a third of its smokers. Cereal consumption has declined, while consumption of meat, oils and fats has increased. The average adult spends 2.1 hours daily watching television, and only 15 per cent of urban adults exercise regularly. In line with these trends, there has been a pronounced shift from infectious diseases to chronic illnesses: by 2005, infectious diseases had plunged to 5 per cent and chronic diseases had risen to 74 per cent of diagnoses.[79]

Obesity is rising fast (though it has some way to go before it reaches the scale of the USA, where by 2018 one in every five dollars spent on healthcare will go on treating obesity). In 2010, 11.6 per cent of adults had diabetes, compared with 11.3 per cent in the US, and over half the population had either diabetes or pre-diabetes. The president of the International Diabetes Federation has said this is a catastrophe and could bankrupt the health system.[80] The *New England Journal of Medicine* suggests that over a quarter of all Chinese adults will be diabetic by 2030. High blood pressure has become a serious feature: almost a quarter of Shanghai's population is estimated to suffer from it. The leading cause of death in women is cardiovascular disease.[81] These are diseases of affluence: China seems to be facing the illnesses of the rich with the income levels of the poor.

Arresting though these statistics are, they depict trends which can be halted and redirected. National public health policy should focus urgently on the reduction of chronic disease growth.

According to the World Health Organization, mental illness has now overtaken heart disease and cancer as the biggest burden on the health system, representing 20 per cent of all costs.[82] A regional study led by the executive director of a WHO collaborating centre in Beijing found that 17.5 per cent of

Chinese diagnosed had some mental disorder. Nationally reflected, this would suggest 236 million people.[83] A major problem has been under-diagnosis: as recently as 2005, there were only 4,000 trained clinicians in the whole country.[84] A wave of murders in 2010 was blamed by officials on mentally ill people, and 550 new mental hospitals have been promised.

We need always to consider the political dimension. A study notes that 'gaps in health care due to privatisation have been cited as an important reason for growing anger towards the government in some rural districts and have led to increasingly frequent local riots and disturbances'.[85] Healthcare and insurance are some of the biggest issues today. Economists like to see this as a corollary to the economic impact of rising domestic consumption: if only we can solve healthcare, we can unchain domestic savings and, thus, consumption. Of course there are many reasons for private sector saving beyond the protection against unpredictable medical conditions. They include such considerations as dowries and 'bride price'.[86] Furthermore, we must be aware that the figure cited for Chinese savings often includes not only estimates of private sources of wealth but also Chinese state enterprises' accumulation. It is, as a result, a quite inexact figure.

The whole area of providing and funding healthcare, like pensions and other social benefits, would be greatly enhanced by introducing pilot schemes: overseas companies could offer products and services in association (or in competition) with domestic financial services businesses, in order to encourage innovation, price competition and customer service.

Labour Conditions

As we have seen, the Chinese state is no longer the monopoly employer; in fact, by 2010 SMEs employed over 80 per cent of urban labour.[87]

Working conditions do not particularly favour the workers, and wages have lagged behind growth. It is illustrative to look at the main export area, the Pearl River Delta, between Canton and Hong Kong. In the PRD, wages were static for about twelve years, but more recently, and certainly since 2004, they have averaged 11 per cent annual growth and in many parts are now growing much faster than that. As a proportion of GDP, however, wages have fallen, according to the World Bank – from 52 per cent in 1999 to 35 per cent in 2005 – and have stayed there at least until 2012. The PRD accounts for a third of China's exports. There, in the boom times, wages were characteristically paid late, not paid in full or not paid at all, and (despite power cuts) factory work weeks frequently exceeded 100 hours. In the year to April 2011 China had 21 times the per capita deaths through industrial accidents of the UK. Independent union activity is officially discouraged and there have been a number of violent labour incidents (which used to be enumerated and analysed each year by the Ministry of Public Security). The 2008 Olympics brought widespread complaints from international pressure groups, such as the Play Fair Alliance and the International Trade Union Confederation, about excessive working hours, underpayment of wages, deception of inspectors and frequent use of child labour.[88] Workers sometimes have no labour contracts, and one official admitted that the authorities had long been 'complicit' in the bad working conditions of foreign enterprises, hoping to attract overseas investment.

In 2007, the previously quiescent All-China Federation of Trades Unions began to encourage and lead collective bargaining for workers, particularly those in foreign-funded enterprises. By early 2009 it had 209 million members. Notably it forced Walmart to accept trade unions and collective bargaining. However, with the downturn in the economy, it prudently decided to back off while companies were struggling to survive. Recently it has become more active again. It has sought to address workers' grievances, but it has also tried to increase Party influence in multinational workforces. Labour legislation passed in 2008 to regulate such matters as redundancy pay has been largely enforced, even during the downturn. However, like much well-meaning Chinese legislation, it is often evaded by adroit lobbying. In the PRD, Hong Kong members of the National People's Congress (NPC), China's parliament, have reportedly lobbied to exempt Hong Kong companies from the requirements of the legislation.

In 2010, Guangdong and certain other provinces were rocked by a wave of strikes against pay and conditions. The authorities devised programmes to tackle such problems by requiring companies to appoint worker-directors and to engage in collective bargaining. After fierce lobbying in Beijing by Hong Kong employers, the plan was withdrawn for reconsideration.[89] However, there has been a trend in Guangdong for several years now of regulating for better labour conditions, pensions and unemployment payments. The germ of a new social and political philosophy is perhaps starting to emerge.

China is the largest coal producer in the world, mining 3.46 billion tons in 2011. It is a very controversial and fragmented industry, with the top three companies producing less than 15 per cent of the total. It is beset by poor management, antiquated equipment, under-investment and poor safety standards.[90] According to Michael Tien, a member of the National People's Congress, China produces 40 per cent of the world's coal, but accounts for 'about 80 per cent of mining deaths in the world'.[91] Reported fatalities were significantly down in 2011, but this is said to be due to official under-reporting, as well as better safety.[92]

Criticism can be made of both state and private mining companies: the 2010 flood at the state-owned Wangjialing mine typifies the poor safety conditions in the industry. The investigating authorities said the management didn't study the hydrogeology before starting the work; it sent too many workers in, and told them to beat the schedule; no managers went into the shaft; construction started before drainage had been arranged; and the managers did not respond to reports of leaks.

The government's response to the mining accidents is to close down smaller coal mines or amalgamate them with larger ones, on the grounds that the small mines are likely to have poor safety conditions. However, Wangjialing is not small. Closing smaller mines that have attracted no specific complaints hits private ownership. Despite substantial state ownership in the coal industry, it is popularly seen as dominated by excessively rich and insensitive private employers.

Violence has been a significant factor in labour disputes. Possibly the most extreme example was in summer 2009, when several thousand steelworkers in Jilin province rioted in the face of privatisation. The incoming factory manager was beaten to death and the roads were blocked to prevent medical assistance from arriving.[93] (To maintain some perspective, it is as well to recall – in the same period – the kidnapping of 'bosses' in France and the murder of a factory head in India.)

In 2010, sixteen workers committed suicide at the electronics firm Foxconn. The foreign press criticised poor labour conditions. Again, though, we should recall that in 2008 and 2009 some twenty-four workers linked to France Telecom committed suicide,[94] and there is some suggestion in academic circles that the Foxconn deaths were 'copycat' suicides. It is easy to blame working conditions, but the situation is more complex: at the time Foxconn employed 800,000 people in China, which makes its 2010 suicide rate 2 per 100,000. In Korea it is 31, in Russia it is 20, and in Denmark 12.[95] More tellingly, the official suicide rate in China ranges from 6.6 to 30 per 100,000 population (depending on which source one uses). In other words, workers at Foxconn are far *less* prone to suicide than is the average Chinese.

In its 2010 worldwide survey on workers' rights, Freedom House in Washington scores China only 2 (out of 5), placing it alongside Egypt and Singapore. Much of the material to support this verdict was several years old, but one point crops up again and again throughout our assessment of China: good laws are introduced but are simply not implemented.[96] New legislation has been brought in, and China is certainly making real progress in improving labour conditions; but there remains significant unhappiness on account of poor conditions, bad environment and evasion of the regulations. When faced with strict application of labour (or indeed environmental) legislation, factory owners often close down and open up somewhere more lenient: factories have shown they can be as mobile as labour. In the past, local Party officials were encouraged to work with factory owners and assist them in setting up and expanding, creating wealth and employment. They are now required to take a different approach, enforcing environmental regulations and labour laws, and restricting petitioning and rioting. It is an art to please all the people all the time, and not all local officials succeed.

Migrant Labour

Migration has been a factor at many points in Chinese history. However, in the nineteenth century it was migration from overpopulated to underpopulated land in more remote areas; in the last thirty years it has been migration from rural areas to urban areas. Most factory workers are migrants from rural provinces – usually younger and better-educated rural workers. According to CASS, the rural workers most likely to migrate are 16–20-year-olds with at least senior high school education (51 per cent likelihood). The least likely are those 50 and over with primary education or less (8 per cent).[97]

The *hukou* system has been used to impede free labour flow from rural to urban areas. It has been progressively relaxed, particularly since 1980, but it still deprives migrant workers of many social benefits: in the past one couldn't use schools or hospitals – or even buy food – outside one's district of residence, as recorded in the family *hukou*.

Because migrant workers have usually been unregistered in the counties where they work, their numbers were officially unknown, though the 2010 census estimates 260 million. Reform of the *hukou* system has been discussed for years. Premier Wen mentioned it again in 2009, and it was in the first 'Central Document' of 2010. With limited reforms, the system remains in place, bringing considerable comfort to China's urban middle classes (which are worried about the impact migrants would have on schools, hospitals, etc.) and local authorities, which are concerned about the financial liabilities that may arise from large-scale changes to the system. Reforms are likely to be moderate and gradual.

When migrants become redundant, the fact does not reach the unemployment statistics, as they are unofficial residents. The official national unemployment figure is usually only just over 4 per cent. However, on the cusp of the 2008–9 downturn CASS estimated the actual figure for urban unemployment, including migrants, to be over 9 per cent.[98] Still, this may not have captured the entire urban population: it is estimated that approximately two-thirds of rural migrants are employed 'informally' and are usually missing from official population databases. Over half of Shanghai's population are not permanent residents; the same goes for over three-quarters of Shenzhen's.[99] The mayor of Guangzhou

(Canton) lamented in 2011 that 'Guangzhou has 10.33 million registered residents... Targets and the scale of land use are based on this number. But in reality the actual population [including migrants] is about 15 million.'[100]

Migrants are often ineligible for medical and other benefits. For example, in 2004 the National Institute for Social Insurance said that just 443,000 migrants (of an estimated 120 million at the time) received unemployment income. If the migrants' families accompany them, the children may not be accepted into local schools (and if they are accepted, they seem not to thrive). If and when they sit the *gaokao* they have to travel back to their registered province. This goes some way to explaining the low proportion of rural migrant children at university.

Zhiqing

In 1955, Mao realised that the countryside was short of workers and began exhorting educated urban youth to go and work in the countryside (*zhiqing*). There were several reasons for this drive. Urban youth were synonymous with educated youth, and it was suggested that they could benefit the rural economy; also (a familiar story) China was producing more graduates than it needed. During the Cultural Revolution, it became compulsory for them to go to the country. By 1968 it was seen as good both for the countryside and for those who went. According to Mao: 'It is very essential for intellectual young people to go to the countryside to receive re-education from impoverished peasants.'[101]

Many found it such a transformative experience that even now they sometimes find meaning only in the company of others who went. Many have not prospered in the post-1978 competitive economic climate. They are frequently passed over for promotion, and have often experienced redundancy. Studies suggest that, in 1989, 75 per cent of urban unemployed were former *zhiqing*, and in 1998 they constituted about half the laid-off workforce. Communicating their experiences to younger generations has been difficult, and this frequently makes them feel isolated and marginalised. Some found it an uplifting experience, based on sacrifice, which goes unrecognised in today's materialist world. On the other hand there are those who view it as a compulsory, officially mandated, sacrifice of their youth which wrecked their lives.

It is estimated that 17 million were sent to the country during the Cultural Revolution itself, but the real number is higher, as the *zhiqing* movement lasted from 1955 until the early 1980s. As late as 1979, some 247,000 young people went.

In the post-2007 economic slowdown, the idea was revived that bright youngsters should go to the countryside and offer their services. This was not a resuscitation of Maoism; merely an attempt to find work for the excessive numbers of graduates. It fits well with plans to assist the less developed western provinces, but there is also a conscious historic resonance to these exhortations.

Income Inequality

Income inequality is measured by the Gini coefficient: the higher the Gini, the more unequal the society. When economic reforms began, they started with the rural workforce, and the gap between rural and urban incomes (using the Gini coefficient) closed significantly for the first decade – moving from 30 to 25. However, from about 1988 there has been increasing income disparity.[102] A 1999 survey showed a Gini of 39, though some experts said it was as high as 59, which again underlines how difficult domestic statistics are to use.

In a 2008 UNDP survey of 160 countries, China ranked 34th in terms of inequality. Apart from Malaysia and Nepal, all countries less equal were in Latin America or Africa.

Table 5.3: **UNDP Survey of Income Inequality, 2008**

34. China	46.9
56. USA	40.8
73. India	36.8
80. UK	36.0
101. France	32.7
116. Germany	28.3
125. Japan	24.9

It should be noted that neither were the data used those of 2007/8, nor were the above the only estimates. The rankings are out of 160 countries. Data sourced from UNDP Human Development Report 2007/8.

The Chinese government last produced a Gini figure in 2000 at 41.2. The above number of 46.9 was stated by the UNDP to be for 2005. The surveys and data differ, but the overall sense is consistent. One survey, which looked at 1978–2004 data, concluded that, per capita, urban residents were only 9 per cent better off (in total, not annually), but the urban population had risen from 18 per cent of the country to 42 per cent, and so urban wealth in aggregate had improved much faster.

A state research body said that in 2010 China had a Gini coefficient of 47 (the US Census Bureau estimates that America was on 47 in 2009).[103] CASS estimates that China hit 50 in 2008. In 2012, a semi-official survey by the Survey and Research Center for China Household Finance, a body linked to the Finance Research Institute of the People's Bank of China, announced that the Gini coefficient in 2011 was 70.[104] Academics tell us that a Gini coefficient above 40 or 50 can herald social instability. On that basis, China is close to trouble. Some believe that civil order may break down just as society is changing – and improving – as with France in 1789 and Russia in 1917. Indeed, many argue that revolutions occur only when the economy is developing. In 2010, Professor Ni Shoubin of Shanghai Institute for Foreign Trade said: 'the population is disgusted by how these rich people are becoming rich, and all society has started to hate rich people. And the rich people must feel that resentment, and it makes them feel insecure.'[105]

Interestingly, academic analysis focuses mainly on the monopoly industries (naturally state-dominated) and the inflated salaries paid to some state enterprise managers – up to 128 times average income. Officials and academics in China continually remark on 'the appalling income disparity' and note that the government 'has said more than it has done' to deal with it.[106] The fast-rising minimum wage is one government response. In 2011, at least twenty-one provinces raised their minimum wages by 22 per cent.[107] Shenyang city promised workers that the minimum wage would rise by 12 per cent for the next five years.[108] However, this doesn't seem to be having the effect of reducing income inequality.

As of 2013, there were some 262 dollar billionaires in China.[109] The increasing pool of great wealth is generating behaviour that may have social repercussions: a Tibetan mastiff was bought for $1.5 million by (needless to say) a mine owner from Shanxi; in 2012, a coal mine boss reportedly spent over $10 million on his daughter's wedding (including a dowry of six Ferraris); rich parents reportedly pay agencies up to $150,000 to coach their child for the entrance examinations at Oxford, Cambridge or top English schools. Mirroring Russia, over half of rich Chinese are contemplating emigration.[110] Meanwhile, the private security business has a turnover above $1.2 billion and provides employment for over 2 million guards.[111]

A Pew Center poll in 2012 shows that 48 per cent of all Chinese believe income inequality is a very big problem.[112] The other very big problems in the responses, as we have seen in the Introduction, include rising prices, corrupt officials and food safety. In 2011, the Communist Party's *People's Daily* carried a report on the wealth gap by Professor Zheng Gongcheng of Renmin University, who recommended that the government tackle the issue by cracking down on monopolies and corruption. There was no suggestion that high incomes in China were fairly derived.[113] The consistent message is that people are angry about this issue.

China and the US may have similar levels of inequality, but their public responses differ widely. There are two probable explanations. One is that, despite Deng Xiaoping's famous remark that some should get rich before others, China has an official culture that stresses equality and socialism as the desired states. Beijing might express French social platitudes, but it wants the American economy. It must change its rhetoric to match the realities. Otherwise it will create internal instability.

The other reason is quite simply, as we saw above from Professor Ni, an entrenched belief amongst the Chinese public that rich people have become rich through corrupt means. And that is in many cases correct.

A Two-class Society

A counter-intuitive aspect of contemporary China is its two-class structure. The *hukou* system is designed to keep rural people in the countryside; those who go to work in the cities are 'on loan'. As John Logan writes in *Urban China in Transition*:

> Official data as well as victim surveys do not include the huge number of non-registered migrants to the major cities, whose status resembles that of illegal immigrants. This group, which has to be regarded as most vulnerable to both violent and property crime, will neither report to the police nor be included in victimization surveys.[114]

So not only are migrant labourers the 'invisible' hands which perform the menial labour that 'full citizens' disdain, but their presence undermines crime, unemployment and other statistics.

Gender disparity is acute in certain rural provinces, and is exacerbated by rural women migrating to the cities (to work as maids or in factories) and finding a husband there. Dr Therese Hesketh, of University College, London, one of the leading researchers in this field, writes: 'In the past, migrants have tended to go back home to permanently settle. But women [now] are finding partners in urban areas and not going back. Men are unable to do that. Urban women will not marry a migrant man; men can't marry up.'[115] This ability of women to marry higher-status males – hypergamy, as it is called – increases the pressures on the surplus males and emphasises their lower status.[116] The hereditary nature of the residential distinction, coupled with the urban social embargo on marriage with rural males, means that the system is close to dividing society into a privileged class and a disenfranchised class on the basis of birthright. The distinctions between the two communities are enforced partly by the state (for example legal residence permits) and partly by society (for example limited intermarriage).

Those remaining in the countryside also suffer many disadvantages. During the 1990s, education spending was heavily decentralised. This led to more provincial decision-making and increasing differentiation in the amount spent per student between higher- and lower-spending provinces.[117] Dramatically lower investment in education in certain areas can perpetuate an underclass. In addition, though the practice has been officially banned, fees are charged for education in many regions.

There is a pervasive adherence to the principles of eugenics in the medical, judicial, police and political establishments. Poorer, rural, criminal, less educated and handicapped people are widely perceived as genetically prone to their destiny. Frank Dikotter, who discusses this extensively, writes:

> Whether scientific knowledge has replaced Communist ideology in China as an epistemological foundation for prescriptive claims about social order is open to debate, but available evidence shows that genetic ideas are increasingly used in the marginalisation of devalued social groups from poor farmers in Gansu province to minority people in Tibet.[118]

The rigid demarcation between urban and rural is starting to blur, however: some rural *hukou* holders have been allowed to become residents of small towns; some university graduates have been permitted to change their *hukou* to live and work legally in large cities; some migrant workers have made money and bought homes in the cities; and increasingly migrant workers are being allowed to participate in some of the social benefits available to urban residents. Further reform is being discussed. However, these changes are exceptions which highlight the rules.

Human Development

The UNDP human development indicators measure such factors as literacy, education, longevity and GDP per capita. The 2007 survey showed China as No. 93 in the world, with a score of 77.2, which placed it in the middle of 192 countries. Since 1980, China has improved faster than any other country bar Bangladesh. The fastest-improving countries are shown in Table 5.4, along with their rankings (out of 178 countries) in the 2010 Transparency International (TI) corruption survey.

Table 5.4: **Human Development Indicators: Progress 1980–2007**

Bangladesh	+66 per cent	(134)
China	+45 per cent	(78)
India	+43 per cent	(87)
Pakistan	+42 per cent	(143)
Egypt	+42 per cent	(98)
Indonesia	+41 per cent	(110)
Iran	+39 per cent	(146)
Morocco	+38 per cent	(85)
Guatemala	+33 per cent	(91)

Source: UNDP, Transparency International.

Note: Bracketed numbers are rankings for corruption: higher is worse.

Two interesting points emerge: first, the Transparency International data show that rampant corruption does not necessarily impede governments from rapidly enhancing public well-being; second, in this survey of fast global social advancement two countries stand out as having actually regressed – Russia since 1990 and South Africa since the end of apartheid. However, the main point is that China – on the criteria measured – is a leader in improving its socio-economic position, despite poor budgetary allocations.

Outlook

China's achievements have been tremendous, but so are the challenges facing it: poor working conditions, weak educational provision, poor housing, minimal public health services, widespread unemployment, deficient pension provision . . .

It has frequently been observed (rather tritely) that 8 per cent economic growth is needed to keep China standing still in its prosperity (or, in a recent rephrasing, 7 per cent is needed to avoid instability). But any calculation is largely meaningless, because growth does not relate closely to job creation. With increased economic sophistication, China will probably continue to grow, but in less job-intensive ways. The prospect now exists of below 7 per cent actual growth in the longer term, along with structural unemployment, at a time when the social safety net is poorly developed. This is potentially a recipe for instability.

Why hasn't China developed more of a social system? There are two main reasons. First, the priority has been growth. Government has believed that the critical objective was to raise living standards, and local officials have received

bonuses based on delivering growth. As Pavlov might have observed, it is difficult to give mixed messages and get clear results. The officials have provided
the growth.

Second, China cannot easily afford it. One reason is that the tax take is
surprisingly low (see Chapter 4): China's companies are just insufficiently
profitable to pay enough tax. Corporate profit has been low, especially in
exporting, and so corporate tax revenues have been thin. For many years, the
state sector was not particularly profitable. The private sector, starved of bank
lending and stock market access, has frequently relied on the informal banking
market, which has often been unattractively priced and has therefore eroded
margins. The result is that China's 2011 budget was virtually the same as
France's, though its economy is more than twice the size of France's.
Furthermore, defence and public security are believed to absorb a high
proportion of the budget. And historically, China has been wary of incurring
external debt, declining to borrow overseas to conduct substantial domestic
transformation (see Chapter 4). Each of these factors contributes to the
diminutive social budget. Given its passion for social harmony – not least for
regime survival – China is in urgent need of a coherent social policy and a
budget for it.

The demanding public debt levels of the developed world are certainly a
trap China wants to avoid. But there are numerous examples of lower-cost
welfare programmes in the developing world, from Brazil to Ethiopia. China
needs a frank national debate about its budgetary priorities. The conclusion
might be that a disciplined social welfare budget could prevent instability more
effectively than armed internal police, and that maintaining domestic stability
is more important than projecting military power overseas.

The record number of migrant workers in the cities presents the danger
that their return to the countryside could fuel resentment that different entitle-
ments are offered to citizens of different legal status. Urban–rural friction is
always a fear. If it is felt that social distinctions are entrenched, have hereditary
features and could create a permanent elite and an inescapable underclass, then
internal migration patterns could elicit an explosive public response.

The ability to fund basic welfare services might be achieved if prosperity
increases and priorities change. What is more alarming is the demographic
challenges, which China will find hard to avoid. The impending population
collapse will dominate policy in China in every field through to the end of the
century.

CHAPTER SIX

The Environment

Where Does China Stand Now?

Public health and rising prosperity are seriously threatened by large-scale pollution. Agriculture and industry are poisoning the rivers; factories and mines are polluting the air. China has badly depleted its reserves: its water supply is a quarter of the world average per capita, and in terms of forests it has scarcely more than half the world's average per capita.[1] The Blacksmith Institute in the US said in 2007 that six of the 30 most polluted places in the world are in China,[2] and according to the World Bank, so are 20 of the 30 most polluted cities.[3] Not only are health and prosperity endangered, but this ecological disaster angers the public and thus threatens stability – and even the survival of the regime.

China has the worst environment of any major country. This may seem surprising for an increasingly popular tourist destination, but it is a fact and comes despite China having first engaged the issue internationally at the 1972 UN Conference on the Human Environment. The degraded environment understandably causes public concern. As the Party claims credit for economic progress, it cannot be absolved from blame for environmental deterioration. I argue that this encourages widespread antipathy towards the Party.

The former socialist economic system has bequeathed the subsidisation of raw materials, causing gross inefficiency and wastefulness in the use of resources such as fuel and water. But the root cause goes back many centuries: 'as the numerous forms of environmental degradation that emerged in pre-modern China make evident, [the] "anthropocosmic" view of nature did not prevent people from ruthlessly exploiting nature as they harnessed its energies for their benefit'.[4]

The ecological disaster is not the Party's fault alone: it inherited a poor environment and degraded it. Traditional religions and ethical systems did not encourage preservation of the environment. As Professor Mark Elvin has remarked: 'classical Chinese culture was as hostile to forests as it was fond of individual trees'.[5] As early as 1737, there was a petition to protest about industrial pollution of water near Suzhou.[6] It is only amongst the intellectuals of the late twentieth-century New Confucian movement that we have seen a real drive to harness Confucian values to ecological imperatives.[7] Mao himself definitely saw nature as an enemy, and the Great Leap Forward caused widespread environmental damage.

Recent economic development has made the degradation extreme. Indeed, in the 1990s the combination of pollution and poor labour conditions created a beyond-Victorian dystopia (which, however, lacked the private charity networks that ameliorated life in nineteenth-century England). By 2007, China had overtaken the US in CO_2 emissions: 6,032 million tonnes versus 5,763 million tonnes, even though its economy was much less than half the size of the US's. By 2011 China's emissions reached 8,031 million tonnes, or over 50 per cent more than of those of the US at 5,277.[8] China's sulphur dioxide emissions (which contribute to acid rain) are the world's largest.[9] China tightened its air pollution standards in 2012, but they lag far behind other countries. Two-thirds of cities do not meet the standards, and Deputy Environment Minister Wu Xiaoqing has admitted it will be many years – even decades – before they do.[10]

Of course, China's per capita emissions appear much less striking; however, first we should probably not think per capita here but per unit of GDP and second we should note that many scientists believe the emissions data are understated.[11] The non-comparability (or the uncertain quality) of data also makes it hard to assess whether the trend is one of improvement or deterioration. But the statistics are shocking. In Yunnan, a province with 46 million people, 30 per cent of children have lead poisoning.[12] Only 1 per cent of China's urban population inhabit cities which meet the European Union air quality standards.[13] Linfen, a coal-mining city in Shanxi, has become notorious: there drivers need to use their car headlights at midday. Furthermore, China has contributed significantly to global pollution and to environmental distress far beyond its borders.

Cities are sinking into empty aquifers, fertilisers are poisoning rivers, and children are dying from pollution. However, positive results could be secured surprisingly rapidly in some areas – given the will. China's pollution takes diverse forms. Here we focus on just a few, by way of illustration.

Water Supply

Water is a serious problem globally: the world's demand is forecast to rise by over 50 per cent from 2010 to 2030. The demands of industry will be increasingly prominent, and it is estimated that by 2030 China will represent 40 per cent of the world's increased industrial requirement for water – largely a result of increased power generation.[14] Unfortunately, China is badly placed. Not only is water simply in short supply, but the country also faces poor geographical distribution, contamination, collapsing dams, empty aquifers causing cities to subside, desertification, changing rainfall patterns, marine 'dead zones' off the coast, blue algal bloom in lakes, new dams built on fault lines causing seismic quakes and frequent geological disasters.

Water in China is underpriced (which leads to inefficient use); officials are unwilling to compromise growth and employment by confronting companies that pollute; provincial finances are weak; there is poor oversight by (and of) local officials; and the authorities cannot be frank about engineering issues because they wish to avoid transparency and accountability.

Prices have been raised substantially, but the revenue has been poorly collected and the price rises have not always generated more efficient use.[15] It has been sporadically successful. Often farmers have sought private access through wells to avoid rising prices; the authorities have tried to discourage this practice. Government reform measures have been extensive, but they have not solved the problems. Because of its climate, China irrigates about half its farmland – five times as much as America. In 2011, the Ministry of Agriculture estimated that 55 per cent of water flowing through the irrigation system was being lost through leakage;[16] the 2015 target is only to cut that to 53 per cent.[17] Another example: in 2005, China used four times the world average of water for every unit of economic output, and twenty times the amount used in Europe and Japan.

The good news is that improvement is possible: China just needs to find the necessary educational programmes, pricing formulae, technology and political will.

Drought, Disaster and Responsibility

The years 2008–11 saw some of the worst drought in a century. In parts of Shandong it was the worst in 300 years.[18] China is the world's largest producer of wheat and rice, but in 2011 the UN Food and Agriculture Organisation (FAO) issued a warning that over a third of the country's wheat acreage had been damaged.[19]

Drought affected most regions and many crops: in northern China (the largest continuous piece of water-short land in the world) 7 million people were affected.[20] Rainfall in Guangdong province, on the southern coast, in 2009 was 13 per cent below average, owing to changing monsoon patterns.

Unfortunately, Guandong supplies Hong Kong with 60 per cent of its water. In 2010 Yunnan suffered its worst drought for a century and its main airport at Kunming developed cracks in the runway. According to the National Flood Prevention and Drought Relief headquarters in Beijing, over 25,000 square miles of China were affected by drought, and a quarter of that would produce no harvest at all. Between 2004 and 2007, 52 million acres of farmland (21 million hectares) were damaged by drought.[21] In 2010, alongside widespread drought came storms: a huge sandstorm affected 20 per cent of the country's population over 313,000 square miles.

Half of all China's water supply goes to irrigation of cropland devoted to grain. This is substantially in the dry north, where rainfall is low. In much of northern China, the water table is falling by over 3 feet annually (in Hebei it dropped by around 10 feet in 2010).[22]

The issue is not that China has natural disasters: it is that the same situations occur again and again – back in 1997, scientists were struggling to help drought-stricken provinces and the air force was being asked to shoot at clouds to induce rain. One gets a sense of structural societal impotence. The 2010 drought caused the Ministry of Agriculture to admit to a severe lack of investment in required projects and facilities. The Ministry of Water Resources said that by 2007 China had built over 87,000 water reservoirs but more than 40 per cent are now in need of repair.[23] The water resources bureau of Zunyi city, in the heart of the drought, said that the city's facilities are not functioning owing to most requiring maintenance. Lack of repair and maintenance recurs, decade after decade.

In times of crisis and deprivation, societies tend to blame their leaders. This is not just a problem for today's Communist Party leadership: the Ming dynasty collapsed in 1644 following seven years of drought.[24]

China's water consumption could be managed through an efficient pricing system (see p.164 above). Considerable attention has been devoted to this over the years and near-market pricing policies have been selectively introduced. Unfortunately, the results have been somewhat disappointing, owing to weak policy coordination, conflict between government units, poor staffing and, thus, poor implementation.[25] However, there were some clear signs of reduction between 2000 and 2007 in use per unit of GDP and per capita.[26]

Water Diversion

In 1952, Mao proposed diverting rivers to feed the north. Finally approved in 2002, the ambitious plans – named the South–North Water Diversion Project – to channel water from, for example, the source of the Mekong (in Tibet) to northern China should have alleviated the situation by 2010. However, the major part of the project was delayed, and the hope is now to complete it by 2014.[27] It was to be largely financed by local governments, but funding has been difficult and there have been serious environmental concerns. Yet the main problem has probably been the horrified reaction of downstream neighbours, such as Vietnam, whose people rely on the Mekong (see Chapter 14). Cambodia and Vietnam share a vulnerability, in that over half their water is sourced abroad. There is a 'fear that China's accelerating programme of damming every major river flowing from the Tibetan plateau will trigger natural disasters, degrade fragile ecologies, divert vital water supplies'.[28] This vast project potentially affects most of China's neighbours to the north, west and south. The Xiaogang dam on the upper reaches of the Mekong is estimated to exceed the height of the Eiffel Tower. It is believed that the next major project will be at Metog, on the Yarlung Tsangpo (which forms the upper reaches of the Brahmaputra River) – a dam that would be 50–100 per cent larger than the Three Gorges dam, in 2012 the world's largest-capacity hydroelectric power station.[29]

In its defence, Beijing says that the major rivers flowing on to China's neighbours receive 85 per cent of their water after leaving China.[30] Nevertheless, from Russia and Kazakhstan in the north and west to Vietnam and Laos in the south-east, there is deep regional anxiety. There is not only the abstraction of the water itself to consider, but also the impact on downstream biodiversity – and thus on environment, food and livelihood. We might, however, note that China's neighbours are themselves causing regional conflict by their own dams, downstream from China.

Water diversion is both a regional and a domestic issue: transborder diversion affects neighbours, but internally the demands of the engineering projects create a colossal cost burden. Although central or provincial government may pay the capital costs, there is a hefty operating cost. For example, diversion of the Yellow River finds the city of Taiyuan having its water pumped uphill at a cost of 5 CNY a cubic metre, and then treated and delivered at further cost. All this costs 8 CNY in total, but the people in the city pay under 3 CNY to buy it. Consequently, the water companies are losing money.[31]

Water Pollution

In 2007, 300 million people in China were drinking contaminated water, and almost 200 million were suffering from a water-related illness.[32] Sadly, the first statistic was true in 2012, too.[33] In 2006 it was judged that the water in half of China's major lakes was unfit for any use.[34] Since then the situation has improved in some respects: pollutants in surface water were down by 32 per cent between 2005 and 2010; but conditions are still dire.[35] In 2010, scientists bluntly stated that:

> the frequency of blue algal bloom has increased ... Nitrogen, phosphorus, organic compounds, and heavy metals are ubiquitous in China's rivers, with up to 80 per cent of urban rivers contaminated ... a situation that continues to deteriorate ... Over-exploitation has caused groundwater quality to deteriorate.[36]

Agriculture is now the biggest problem, generating nutrient pollution.[37] The urbanisation of farmland and its replacement with infertile land means that more chemical fertiliser is used, which often runs off into rivers and contaminates drinking supplies. In only 40 per cent of the 745 monitored stretches of river in the whole country is the water fit to drink – even after treatment.[38] (In fairness, we should note that in 2012 a third of Britain's beaches were deemed polluted.)[39]

A recurring concern has been a tendency by the authorities to obfuscate or deny water pollution incidents. In 2005, for example, when benzene poured into the Songhua River after a petrochemical plant explosion, local authorities announced that the water was being cut off for routine maintenance. It later transpired that benzene levels in the river were 108 times the safe limit.[40] In 2012, a cadmium spill in the Longjiang River resulted in the water containing 80 times the permissible level of that mineral. The Chinese magazine *Caixin* made the point that 'failed disclosure was the worst of the violations – and one that has stands [*sic*] as part of a pattern in heavy metal pollution accidents'.[41] It seems that year after year no lessons are learned.

One global phenomenon in which China fully plays its part is the steady increase in 'dead zones' in the ocean. These are marine areas where there is so little oxygen that life forms are almost absent, and they are caused by 'eutrophication', or the over-enrichment of waters by nutrients. By 2012, there were over 400 of these zones worldwide, covering an area the size of Britain. Probably the largest is off the Mississippi delta; it measures 7,700 square miles. China is believed to be the world's largest emitter of the nitrogen compounds which cause eutrophication.[42] The specific causes include fertiliser run-off into rivers, the burning of fossil fuels, animal waste and sewage disposal, which encourage the growth of bacteria. The bacteria consume the available oxygen, leading to hypoxia (lack of oxygen). Crabs, clams, fish and worms start to leave – or die.

In 2006, two of these zones were recorded off the coast of China – around the Yangtze and the Pearl rivers. In 2008, a third, measuring 280 square miles, was noted off the coast near Beijing. The other effect of eutrophication is harmful algal bloom or what (offshore) is often called the 'red tide' of marine algae. According to researchers at the World Resources Institute in 2013, various eutrophic and hypoxic events are recorded off China's coast; but the extent is difficult to measure, as much less research work is done on this in China than in the US. Indeed, in 2011 the State Ocean Administration said that 'China's oceanic environment was basically healthy in 2010, with 94 percent of the country's territorial waters being of the highest quality according to national standards.'[43] One of the problems is that China's national environmental standards are laxer than those of other leading countries. The World Resources Institute's map shows eight areas off China documented as hypoxic or eutrophic. These zones have been increasing rapidly in number.

In terms of identifying solutions to this pervasive and disastrous situation, scientists strike a gloomy note:

> Our scientific understanding of the mechanisms of water pollution is too limited to effectively control the problem in China. The complexity of the cumulative effects of water pollution requires the development and application of new technologies.[44]

The timetable required is depressing: systematic research is required 'over the next 5 to 15 years'.[45]

Subsidence

The issue of subsidence is a recurring one. It is caused principally by excessive groundwater extraction, but also by such factors as oil drilling and 'neotectonic movement'. It is 'slow, accumulative, irreversible'.[46] Subsidence seems to have been first identified in Shanghai and Tianjin in the 1920s, and in Beijing in 1935,[47] but now scientists refer to it as a 'nationally disastrous phenomenon'.[48] The area affected keeps expanding: Beijing, Tianjin, Xi'an, Shanghai, Kunming and areas of Tibet are all sinking, largely because the aquifers are being emptied. Guangdong, too – and Shenzhen in particular – suffers frequent subsidence. There are now signs of it in the oil and gas fields.

In 2006, scientists from the government's China Geology Survey reported that 'according to incomplete statistics, in the early 1990s the area affected by land subsidence was 48,700 sq km. In 2003 the land subsidence area had extended to 93,855 sq. km.'[49] This is over double the estimated area of subsidence in the similarly sized USA.

More than fifty cities have experienced subsidence of over 6 feet.[50] A subsidence monitoring system is being installed on the Beijing–Tianjin and Beijing–Shanghai railways, as well as on the Beijing subway (and in the city generally). Subsidence affected the high-speed railway west of Wuhan in 2012. Oil and gas are usually to be found at great depths, and so subsidence caused by extraction develops slowly. It is ominous that indications of subsidence have appeared in the oilfields of Daqing, Shengli and Huabei.[51]

There appear to be at least four independent factors at work in Shanghai's subsidence: rising sea levels, aquifer depletion, maritime erosion of the delta soil beneath the city, and silting up of rivers (which raises water levels). Shanghai's subsidence was arrested in the 1960s through water abstraction controls, but it has resumed since the 1990s owing to the construction boom. By 2006 Shanghai had over 5,000 high-rise buildings and the impact has been tremendous: today's Shanghai is reported to be less than 120 inches above sea level, but views differ about the rate of subsidence. Scientists estimate that between 1992 and 2002 the annual rate – rather unevenly – averaged just under half an inch. However, the areas worst hit were sinking by 80 per cent more than that. Furthermore, the rate of subsidence has apparently started rising again: in 2008, it was calculated that the maximum annual rate was 4.3 inches.[52] The phenomenon seems well correlated to the new, tall buildings: it is in the most modern parts of Shanghai that subsidence is worst. It was estimated in 2005 that subsidence damage had over forty years cost the city $35 billion.[53]

Tianjin, probably China's fourth-largest city, is in an even worse state. Virtually unconstrained water abstraction in the 1960s and 1970s contributed substantially to subsidence of 5 feet – at rates of up to 4 inches a year – before certain elementary controls were imposed. Unlike in Shanghai, the causes of subsidence in Tianjin also include natural tectonic shifts, which can't be easily arrested. Other contributing factors have been offshore oil exploration, under-consolidated soil that continues to compact, and rapid high-rise construction. Tianjin scientists found in 2005 that, although the rate of subsidence had slowed, the area affected had grown enormously and now covers five separate districts and a total of over 3,000 square miles.

Much of the devastation in China is human-induced. The over-exploitation of groundwater is relentlessly blamed, as are construction projects.[54] The government is taking action to recharge groundwater in order to avoid stress on aquifers; to introduce monitoring; and to consider the need for barrages and levees of a certain height in Shanghai. However, academics and policymakers are deeply concerned. The area of subsidence has increased by a third since the start of the 1990s,[55] and now an area of 60,000 square miles needs monitoring.[56] That is the equivalent of Bangladesh, or England and Wales.

There is a real danger that, with the steady expansion, several collapsed areas in the Yangtze delta will join together.

Collapse, Landslide and Debris Flow

Associated with subsidence is the phenomenon of landslides and debris flow, typically a consequence of engineering and mining, highway, railway and power station construction.[57] These hazards have become more frequent because of poor or negligent management and have been described by Chinese scientists as 'the most serious geo-environment problem'.[58] The landslides can be up to several million cubic metres and are usually triggered by heavy rain.

China has two slope areas: between the Tibetan plateau and the Yungui plateau, and between the Yungui plateau and the eastern near sea plain. These areas, the richest in minerals and hydropower, are where approximately 70 per cent of human-induced landslides have occurred since the 1980s.[59] They are likely to remain the most active areas for civil engineering and are home, for example, to the Three Gorges Project. In that project, millions were forcibly moved and many found their new homes were built on vulnerable sloping ground. Landslides have subsequently occurred.

Landslides can destroy dams, mines and mountains, and can block rivers. The incidents seem to increase with economic expansion. Academic criticism focuses on poor geological surveying, poor engineering management, and supervisory negligence. Ultimately – in a society led by one party – responsibility will be placed on the Party.

Infrastructure

In 2009, Water Resources Minister Chen Lei stated that 43 per cent of China's dams could collapse if there was heavy rainfall.[60] Ninety per cent of the dams are in Sichuan province and were badly shaken by the 2008 earthquake. In 2011, Water Resources Vice Minister Jiao Yong said that over 46,000 reservoirs needed to be rebuilt or reinforced to ensure that surrounding farmlands and communities would be safe.[61] The 2008–10 downturn left provinces financially weak. While some 'first aid' repair work has been done, much remains to do, and warning systems are often lacking: 'If a dam were to collapse, releasing floodwater, people living downstream would be unlikely to receive a warning. In many places the government was still using gongs and firecrackers to announce an impending flood.'[62]

Scientists draw clear linkages between dam construction and erosion. Since 1950, there have been about 45,000 large dams (of over 50 feet) built in the world, almost half in China.[63] In that period, about 50,000 dams of all sizes have been built on the Yangtze; they include fifteen that are taller than 300 feet. These dams have caused downstream channel erosion, and erosion of the Yangtze delta.[64]

Opposition to widespread dam construction is not new, but the issue became so controversial in the last decade that in 2004 construction was halted on at least thirty dams. However, by 2006 work had quietly resumed. Dam construction in south-west China has raised particular concern because of the earthquake-prone geology. Two geologists from the China Earthquake Administration published a study suggesting that the huge 2008 Sichuan earthquake was encouraged by the siting of a dam 600 yards from a fault line:

> the . . . paper said up to 320 million tonnes of water in the reservoir caused major seismic changes before the disaster . . . According to the paper, 'some clear correlations were verified between the local seismicity and stress change, thus we concluded that the impoundment of Zipingpu [the dam in question] clearly affected the local seismicity'. The paper also joined an appeal by a growing number of scientists that further study should be done on the possible dam–quake link.[65]

The particularly depressing feature for Sichuan, in south-west China, where so many of the dams are, is the apparent symbiotic correlation: earthquakes can destroy dams and dams can cause earthquakes ('reservoir-induced seismicity'). The Three Gorges dam, in Hubei province, occupies a huge site on the Yangtze River and abuts two fault lines. Conceived by Sun Yat-sen, it is now infamous for the forced resettlement of families (possibly up to 6 million people – the equivalent of the population of Denmark) and the environmental risks.[66] Problems have beset the project: the number of those forcibly resettled has spiralled; compensation was underestimated; the carrying capacity of the nearby land to which residents have been moved is inadequate; and the water has at times silted up. Yet critics of the project have been dissuaded from speaking out.[67]

A 2010 report by scientists from the Institute of Seismology noted that:

> in 2008 and 2009 . . . 22 earthquakes above 2.0 were recorded. The strongest was recorded as 4.1 . . . The frequency and intensity of seismic activity significantly increased in the Three Gorges reservoir area after the reservoir began to fill in June 2003, compared to the time period before the reservoir was filled.[68]

The US Geological Survey forecast in a 2008 report that the area could become unstable.[69] Now large seismically induced landslides have required mass evacuation.[70] After an unflinching political effort to drive the Three Gorges Project through (against strong activist opposition), in 2011 the State Council in Beijing finally acknowledged 'issues such as pollution, silt accumulation, ecological deterioration and geological hazards near the dam. It also points out the project's adverse effects on irrigation, water supply and shipping in downstream regions.'[71] The Ministry of Land Resources reported in 2012 that landslides and other disasters had increased by 70 per cent since the water level rose to its peak.[72]

China's history is littered with massive and costly hydrological engineering projects which although they had positive results were frequently expensive to maintain, were negatively affected by their environment and often had a damaging impact on their region.

Over eighty large dams are planned for the higher reaches of the Salween, the Yangtze and the Mekong.[73] Not only are the dams being placed in earthquake zones but their potential impact on water flows is a controversial challenge to China's many downstream neighbours. As Qiao Jianping, a geophysicist at the Chinese Academy of Sciences' Institute of Mountain Hazards and Environment in Chengdu, has said: 'It is an unbearable sight ... The way hydropower is developed in the region is totally unsustainable.'[74] Unfortunately there is an institutionalised fear of or disdain for Chinese scientific opinions.

Climate Change Through History

China is suffering from the adverse effects of climate change – and has done so throughout recorded history. The deleterious effect of wind erosion has been documented in China for 2,000 years.[75] Dust storms have been measured since AD 300 but really started increasing rapidly from 1100, with a further increase from the 1950s.[76] In 2000 BC, the area of today's Beijing supported a substantial elephant population, but by 1000 BC the climate had cooled and the elephants had gone.[77]

Climate scientists reckon that a thousand years ago there was a general global cooling and a weakening of the summer monsoon. The rise instead of strong winter monsoons from the eighth through the ninth centuries in both Central America and East Asia is understood to have led to lower rainfall, drier weather, crop failures and famine, hitting both the Tang dynasty and the Mayan civilisation.[78]

Climate change theorists no longer all predict global warming, but they certainly forecast increasingly volatile weather conditions. Ultimately it is not so important whether the change is cooling or warming: violent change in either direction is serious. In imperial times, the people would blame the

Emperor for extreme weather events. Now, the people can blame the Party for not being prepared. Drought, famine, floods, epidemics and food insecurity have all played their part in China's dramatic political history. Beijing today is understandably concerned to reduce their impact.

The Desert in China

Over 27 per cent of China's land mass (or 1 million square miles) is officially estimated to be desert.[79] The same figure has been quoted in 2000, 2007 and 2013. Since soil is 'nonrenewable on the human timescale',[80] the optimistic view is that the authorities are reclaiming land as fast as land is degrading to desert.

The mainstream view is that the desert is winning. The Food and Agriculture Organization has estimated the rate of desertification: a net annual increase of 600 square miles in the 1970s and of 800 square miles in the 1980s. In 2000, the BBC reported that total desert growth was 1,000 square miles a year. The estimates since then have mostly been substantially higher – between 1,400 and 2,500 square miles annually for (just) the Gobi; the Earth Policy Institute in Washington even claimed in 2004 that the Gobi was growing by 4,000 square miles a year. Incredibly, observers unanimously – and every year since at least 1997 – quote the same figure of 400 million people who are affected by desertification.[81] Only in China can 400 million people not be worth estimating more precisely or more than once in fifteen years while they confront what Minister of Forestry Zhao Shucong said in 2012 posed 'the greatest challenge of our generation'.[82] Li Tuo, the official in charge, said in 2011 that less than a third of the desert is salvageable, and 'at current rates [even that] would take 300 years to reclaim'.[83]

In the fifty years after 1950, 24,000 villages in northern and western China simply disappeared under the desert. The Tian Desert in Hebei province (which forms part of the Gobi) is now reported to be within 45 miles of Beijing. However, this looks like isolated drifts and not serious and continuous desert: a more accepted distance is about 70–90 miles. But it is estimated to be advancing on the capital by anything between 2 and 15 miles annually. The number of sandstorms seems to have reduced (which, officials claim, is the result of measures taken), but their ferocity appears to have increased.

So, amid this characteristic fog of contradiction the best guess is that the rate of desertification might have slowed down but it has not been reversed. Some areas are recovered and others succumb to the desert. What is disputed is the speed at which this is occurring. The problem, as always, lies in the definitions, as well as in China's confused statistics. Not all desert looks like a Caribbean beach; much of it is simply degraded land. Much of the country has been desert for a long time, such as the Taklamakan in Xinjiang, north-western China. There are other areas which have become a form of arid land, verging on desert, comparatively recently (such as the Gobi), and there has been wholesale degradation of large areas of arable and grass land by soil erosion, wind erosion, industrially generated devastation and salinisation.[84]

Sandstorms, whipped up by high-velocity winds, erode the topsoil, smother once productive agricultural land with choking sands and silt up reservoirs. Acid rain caused by industrial activity is another major cause of the degradation of arable land and of desertification. There is no general agreement on when degraded land becomes desert, but in 2002 there were seven areas of China where the desert was growing by more than 4 per cent a year (three of them in Inner Mongolia).

Very many factors are blamed for the phenomenon of desertification, including:

- Local population strains: although China has a one-child policy, it is not applied to the minorities. The Gobi (and the north-east generally) has many minorities, and annual population growth there is estimated as up to 2.8 per cent.
- Tree-planting drives (see pp.176–7 below): some environmentalists maintain that trees might be damaging, as they absorb part of the available groundwater.
- Climate change: the desert in Tibet has tripled in size in the last thirty years, apparently owing to glaciers retreating.
- Wind erosion: over-ploughing and over-grazing in northern China are creating a huge 'dust bowl'.[85] Unfortunate farming methods, combined with difficult topography, have rendered the rich farmland of the north-east prone to severe erosion.
- Water erosion: some two-fifths of the farmland is water-eroded. Another seventy-five years will see the topsoil reduced to perhaps 10 inches. This could reduce grain output by 40 per cent.[86]

The Communist Party did not begin desertification – it loomed large under the Ming and the Qing – but matters are continuing to deteriorate. No 'scientific socialism' has had much effect in slowing down the process.

Beijing's Future

US satellites show that over the last thirty years, thousands of lakes in China's north have disappeared. The aquifers under Beijing and Tianjin are depleted and the cities increasingly need to source water from the countryside. By 2012 Beijing had had, on some definitions, thirty-one years of drought,[87] and was reported by 2008 to have had 230 cubic metres of rainfall per capita – a 77 per cent fall since 1949.[88] Fortunately in 2012 there fell the heaviest rain in sixty-one years, yet by year end water resources were 119 cubic metres per capita.[89] The drought effectively continues. This makes Beijing one of the world's most water-short metropolises. The water table has fallen in the space of a decade from 36 feet below to 80 feet below sea level. In 2012, Beijing authorities sought to stop the use of private wells, of which there are some 800 in the city.[90] The water resources of nearby Hebei province have almost halved in recent years, and yet they are desperately needed by the capital. In 2009, Probe International, a leading development policy group, warned:

> the Chinese capital's water crisis is so critical that the city is facing economic collapse. Part of its population may need to be resettled in coming decades. Beijing could run out of water in five to 10 years ... Beijing would potentially have to start shutting down industry as the city would be incapable of supporting current levels of infrastructure or population.

Apparently the authorities had already discussed moving people out of the capital to other cities.[91]

The Chinese Dustbowl

Wind and water erosion now affect 37 per cent of the entire country.[92] It is estimated that in 1935 in the US 'dust bowl' 850 million tons of topsoil were blown away. In 2008, an official survey estimated that China was losing the equivalent of 4,500 million tons of topsoil annually.[93] Northern China has 'a fragile ecological system sensitive to human disturbance ... the increased wind erosion caused by human factors on average accounts for approximately 78 per cent of the total'.[94] The region has frequent and very severe dust storms. The US dustbowl in the 1930s obliged 2.5 million Oklahoma, Kansas and Texan farmers to leave the land and head west. A similar process is currently under way in China, only the numbers are even bigger and the people are heading east. The State Forestry Administration declared in 2008 that there were tens of millions of environmental refugees driven into the towns and cities as they could no longer live on the land. Drought may force 150 million people to move. We are seeing many of the characteristics of an ecological catastrophe.

The 'Green Great Wall'

The authorities have started to take the situation more seriously and have enacted several laws. In many areas they have limited the amount of livestock, or even banned farming and grazing. They are also trying to replace free-range sheep and goats with battery-farmed cattle.

They have tried to halt the desert's advance with a wall of trees – a new 'Green Great Wall of China' – reportedly spanning well over 2,000 miles across the country's north. This project will absorb a major part of the $100 billion Beijing has committed nationwide for afforestation.[95] It will cover over 40 per cent of the entire country and the project will last until 2074. China has planted more trees than the rest of the world combined,[96] and even cropland has been taken in parts of western China and forested, despite the national obsession with cropland shrinkage.[97] This is possibly the largest ecological project in history.

Unfortunately, some have observed that poor tree choice, poor planting, poor maintenance and pruning, drought, weather and corruption are undermining the strategy, and that three-quarters of the trees die. Apparently in 2008, winter storms destroyed a tenth of them. It also appears that the desert is killing the trees. In 2011, Beijing Forestry University estimated that 85 per cent of the plantings fail.[98] Since 2001, the authorities have been talking about releasing data on the project – such as tree survival rates – evaluated by foreign agencies. However, little progress has been made on that. The State Forestry Administration says that degradation is now being reversed but strong evidence contradicts this claim: low tree survival, increasing erosion and increasing desertification.[99] Indeed, if the 'Green Great Wall' strategy were to flourish, the trees could absorb much of the scarce available water, to the detriment of the general environment.[100] Jiang Gaoming of the Institute of Botany is one academic who is sceptical about the project: 'Do not get too excited by those recovered grasslands and forests you see alongside the highways. They only cover 10 percent of the total affected area. The other 90 percent causes the continuing sandstorms.'[101]

Tree canopies can also prevent the development of ground vegetation cover by decreasing surface roughness: this allows greater wind speed, which encourages wind erosion and sandstorms.

A team of Chinese and American scientists concluded in 2010 that:

> Current Chinese policy has not been tailored to local environmental conditions, leading to the use of inappropriate species and an overemphasis on tree and shrub planting, thereby compromising the ability to achieve

environmental policy goals. China's huge investment to increase forest cover seems likely to exacerbate environmental degradation in environmentally fragile areas.'[102]

This is quite a damning indictment of a $100 billion programme.

The Export of Pollution

The Vice President of Tsinghua University told me in 2007 that, in one 24-hour period, 320,000 tons of sand landed on Beijing. Sand can travel great distances: there are frequent complaints of sandstorms originating in the Gobi but wreaking havoc in Japan, Taiwan or Korea. The sand reaches Alaska and occasionally colours the sunsets in San Francisco. In 2008 it was reported that:

> Schools were forced to close in neighbouring Korea after being enveloped by a dust cloud that spread from over the Yellow Sea. Primary schools and kindergartens across the southeast were shut down when the cloud, laced with toxic residue, from northern China's industrial regions, covered all but two of the country's provinces ... The dust is whipped up by the wind from the Gobi desert in China and Mongolia. From there it spreads across East Asia, with Japan and Taiwan as well as the Korean peninsula regularly affected ...[103]

So the problem is also an international one – indeed intercontinental. Authoritative reports in America refer to high levels of Chinese-originated mercury threatening wildlife and watersheds in Oregon. Dust, soot, ozone, bacteria and nitrous oxide are driven from China at high altitude across the Pacific, and up to 25 per cent of the particulates in the air over Los Angeles come from China.[104] By 2030 it is predicted that China will emit twice as much carbon dioxide as all the other main industrialised nations put together.[105] Its economy, massive and inefficient in its resource usage, is gradually poisoning both the Pacific region and the Earth's atmosphere.

So much for China's export of environmental problems. What about its imports? In 2012, it was reported that more than half of the timber now shipped globally is destined for China.[106] China's largest supplier of wood is Russia (and China is Russia's biggest client). This logging trade is severely censured for its lack of sustainability. Unsustainable harvesting and illegal logging mean that China's other supplier nations have only another twenty years before their forests are commercially depleted. Hence Russia is crucial. China's increasing demand for foreign timber is spurred by a sharp decline in domestic forest resources, an increase in domestic consumption and growing demand in the US, Europe and elsewhere for the low-cost products manufactured in China.[107]

Resource Poverty and Choice of Fuel

China is remarkably deficient in resources. Timber and water have already been mentioned. But China also has less than 45 per cent of the world per capita average of arable land (and this figure is falling) and just 60 per cent of the world's average per capita energy reserves.

China is a disproportionately large consumer of coal: it accounts for two-thirds of the country's primary energy requirement. This is principally because, while it has 1 per cent of the world's gas reserves and 1 per cent of its oil reserves,[108] it has a full 13 per cent of the world's coal. Regrettably, coal is the most polluting of the fossil fuels: it produces 20 per cent more carbon dioxide than oil and 80 per cent more than natural gas. China's coal is generally of an unappealing quality, as it often has a high sulphur content. One surprising economic positive is that, because of the transport infrastructure, it is often cheaper to import less sulphurous coal from, say, Indonesia than it is to transport poor coal from northern to southern China.

Pollution-influenced lung cancer rates in Beijing rose 60 per cent during 2002–11. A World Bank study in 2009 estimated that outdoor air pollution causes 270,000 cases of chronic bronchitis annually, and 400,000 hospital admissions for respiratory or cardiovascular disease.[109] According to a 2009 Chinese report, more than one child in sixty in Beijing is born with physical defects that Chinese scientists have linked to pollution – almost double the rate of a decade earlier.[110] Shanxi province, dominated by heavy industry and China's top coal producer, has seen an incredible one child in five born with physical defects.[111] Nationwide, of children born with defects, 30 per cent die.

There is a continuing effort to diversify energy sources. Although plans to pipe natural gas from Russia to China are continually delayed, China plans to increase its off-take from the existing oil pipelines. However, it must compete with countries such as Japan and the US and reach a settlement with Moscow on the on-going price dispute. China is also advancing in renewable energy. It believes it can soon become the largest producer of wind energy and has been increasing its already large commitment to nuclear power. And yet, despite this, it will have to rely for a long time to come on its generally low-quality but abundant domestic coal.

China's initiatives are dramatic. In 2009, its nuclear plants provided 1.1 per cent of its energy; this is expected to rise to at least 5 per cent by 2020. As a result, it is engaged in the largest nuclear power programme in the world. In 2003, it accounted for 1 per cent of global solar power production; by 2007 it was 35 per cent and China is now the largest producer of photovoltaic cells. In October 2009 it announced the discovery of a large methane deposit in the Tibetan permafrost. Methane has been said to be a double gift for China: it helps with the energy deficit and also, by removing reliance on polluting coal, improves the environment. Unfortunately, though, many scientists inside and outside China worry about the 'greenhouse effect' of methane emissions.

Each of these advances comes with problems. There has always been concern about China's ability to construct and maintain its nuclear programme safely (a concern highlighted by Japan's Fukushima disaster of 2011), and about how it will find the large quantities of uranium necessary to supply it. The nuclear (and the solar power) industry makes huge demands on water resources, which might make it a less sustainable (and thus plausible) option in water-deprived China.[112]

Energy Efficiency

Though China has made great strides since 1980, it is still a very inefficient energy consumer. Carbon emissions are 70 per cent or so higher than they would be if the best modern technology were employed, and almost three-quarters of the country's industrial processes are at least 20 per cent (and sometimes 60 per cent) more energy intensive than in the developed world. There is a political reason for this: the price of fuel is subsidised. The prices of oil products, gas and electricity are government controlled and are generally below world levels.[113] However, there has been some reform, and by 2012 Chinese consumers were paying 20 per cent more for their petrol than consumers in America (in 2008 it had been 60 per cent of the US price).[114] That said, this is mainly the result of market prices falling below China's controlled domestic prices. Once consumers pay market (usually meaning higher) prices, it is likely they will be more careful in their energy use. This would help the government meet its fresh targets for 2000–2020 of quadrupling the economy (again) while merely doubling energy consumption.

In 2009, it was proposed that by 2050 China could grow its economy by 8–13 times while at the same time meeting reasonable carbon emission objectives by reducing its energy intensity by about 80 per cent. One major element in this strategy is the expected large place in the future economy that will be occupied by the service sector.[115] The problem for national economic planners is that this is the least understood sector – much of it being in private hands – so the planners consistently underestimate service sector growth (as it is an unplanned area).

Size makes China something of a victim in international debate on energy efficiency and pollution. For example, the International Transport Forum says China produces 228 tonnes of road CO_2, second only to the US. However, it has just 17 cars per 1,000 people. Its road CO_2 *per person* is 0.3 tonnes, compared to 1.76 in Japan, 1.99 in Britain and 5.16 in America. Perhaps emissions should be measured by rate of vehicle ownership. If China ever achieved the car ownership rate of America, the Chinese would own more cars than existed in the whole world in 2010. It does seem as if China's citizens are being told not to enjoy something they haven't attained yet. But China's underdevelopment in passenger motor transport is now being rewarded. It has been able to introduce stricter emissions standards than America, and it could incentivise the purchase of smaller cars, since it has fewer vested interests in its domestic automobile industry.

The Government's Response

How has the government reacted to the looming environmental crisis? Throughout the reform period, China's reaction to criticism of its environmental degradation has been that its top priority is to deliver rapidly a rising standard of living. As Li Ruogu reflected, with elegant understatement: 'we were unable to pay equal attention to the double objectives of development and environment'.[116]

The authorities are now taking the environment very seriously. One important reason has been a mounting awareness that the issue could cause instability; another was the realisation that gross energy inefficiency compromises energy security.[117]

The tendency to see investment in heavy industry as an easy proxy for economic growth is not only wrong, but deflects attention from development of the service sector, which is more labour intensive and also more environmentally friendly. China has a disproportionately industry-intensive economy. Recently, central leaders have taken the environment to heart. The World Bank and other institutions have been welcomed in to design and sponsor transformational development projects. Policies have been announced, supporting regulations have been introduced, investment rules, targets and timetables have been outlined. Between 2006 and 2009, small, inefficient coal-fired power plants with the combined equivalent output of all those in Australia were closed.[118] There has been a 90 per cent reduction in chlorofluorocarbons, or CFCs. Forest cover has been increased (albeit with too much single-species planting). There have been improvements in air quality (not always lasting). Fuel economy standards for motor vehicles are now amongst the most advanced in the world, although adverse lobbying by state energy companies is a hindrance.[119] A 20 per cent tax was levied on sports utility vehicles.

The authorities have introduced demanding energy efficiency standards in the building code and the energy consumption of new buildings is being halved. There is a full and compulsory system of energy-efficiency testing and labelling for household appliances. As a result, pollution controls are a rising cost for business. Government institutions, too, have for some time been encouraged to operate to certain standards. Unfortunately, in his 2012 work report the then prime minister failed to comment on the environmental objectives; the reason may be connected to the fact that the authorities had failed to achieve three of the seven targets.

In such a sprawling, decentralised government system, it is difficult to drive policy change rapidly. Even in sophisticated legal systems, attempts to improve the environment through legislation have encountered severe challenges; China's weak legal system makes matters even more difficult. There is a nervousness about criminalising wide swathes of the community, particularly important people. It is also a problem for a transitional economy, moving erratically from a command economy to a market system, to differentiate the regulated from the regulators. One study back in 2001 pointed out that laws do 'not necessarily take full account of the growing pluralisation of interests in society and the devolution of power from the center'.[120]

Questions arise, such as if rainfall in north China supplies only one-quarter of the water necessary for grain cultivation, would other crops be more suitable? The complication here is that the issue of food self-sufficiency (for which read 'grain') has returned, stoked by volatile commodity markets and overseas food riots. A further issue is the political reluctance to strengthen farmers' land rights and to facilitate financing for investment (for example in more efficient drip-irrigation equipment).

A constellation of events in 2008–9 led to substantial investment in the very parts of energy-intensive heavy industry which Beijing had been intending to de-emphasise. At the same time, in order to accelerate investment there was reduced focus on environmental audits of new projects. First of all, the economy was slowing down badly due to the Western recession. The authorities urgently wanted to rekindle growth: but in many quarters the idea of desirable growth meant heavy industry and new house building – both, alas, heavy energy consumers and polluters.[121] The country also needed to rebuild earthquake-damaged Sichuan province. A difficult choice had to be made between swift rebuilding and aesthetic, consumer-friendly, environmental and safety considerations. There was much criticism of the provincial (and indeed national) government for devoting insufficient attention to environmental considerations, but the authorities appeared to decide that their main responsibility was to get the destroyed homes rebuilt as quickly as possible.

The government's stimulus package did emphasise projects with a positive environmental impact (though many were going to happen anyway): there was substantial spending on the railways, the electricity grid (which will allow greater utilisation of renewable energy) and subsidies for manufacturers to develop alternative energy-fuelled cars. Although much of the extra lending went on unconstructive purposes, the sums were large enough for considerable good to be done.

Nuclear power is a massive commitment, as the authorities wish to address escalating demand for energy and simultaneously tackle emissions. Beijing has been debating whether to raise the target for installed nuclear capacity from the 40 GW agreed in 2005 to 70 GW by 2020. The country requires 2,000 tonnes of uranium annually. This figure is rising rapidly and the need to achieve it has led to a global search for sources and potential purchases of mining companies.

It is interesting to see more frequent public consultations in advance of major projects. The public is becoming increasingly vocal in the face of large-scale, potentially polluting projects. Beijing also accepts that China must be seen overseas to be acting responsibly regarding the environment.

Structure of Government Action

The State Environmental Protection Agency (SEPA) is charged with the execution of environmental policy. In 2000 it had a nominal staff of 130,000 but, characteristically of China, only 3,000 worked at the national level. So more staff are beholden to local officials than to the national leadership. Most local government operations are financed by local leadership and so, if they do not support the activity, funding will be constrained.

We need to accept the distinction between form and substance. Formally, much is going well. For example:

> . . . local governments are increasingly assessed with respect to their environmental performance . . . [the system] enables governments to design environmental responsibility contracts with local leaders for improvements in individual indicators, and to link these to assessments, financial incentives and promotion, encouraging town and village leaders to take environmental protection more seriously . . . local leaders are no longer judged only according to political and economic criteria, but also according to environmental results.[122]

This is the theory, but it is not universally applied. There is poor coordination between central government agencies, resistance by local governments (which often have no interest in tough environmental controls) and poor incentive arrangements for the local government and state enterprise level to follow national policy.

Environmental bodies have low status, particularly at the local level, vis-à-vis their economic counterparts. Often SEPA is not in charge of implementing environmental policies. Also breaching environmental laws is often less serious than going against administrative rules and programmes. Environmental laws are frequently vaguely drafted and are interpreted differently by local environmental policy bureaux, often influenced strongly by the mayor's office.

In contemporary China, environmental laws are commonly not enforced. In 2008, for example, legislation was enacted to require companies convicted of polluting to publish data on their emissions and discharges. But it was not clearly stated where such information should be published, and many companies do not comply. In 2009 Greenpeace reported that, in the first year of the legislation, ten major Chinese companies and eight leading multinationals were found to be polluting, but not one had subsequently complied with the requirement to disclose pollution levels. The multinationals were said to be Shell, Samsung Electronics, Nestlé, LG, Kraft, Motorola, Denso and Bridgestone.[123]

Aside from weak drafting and lax enforcement, the monitoring sources may be changed to improve the reported environmental results: for example, more upstream – and naturally cleaner – locations are allegedly being added to the river water monitoring system, and thus the percentage of stretches which provide drinkable water goes up.[124]

Tax breaks and discharge fees are the carrot and stick used to improve behaviour. Fees began in 1979 in certain regions, so there is a thirty-year history of selective and limited environmental action. However, this is less effective than using market forces to create financial incentives. Some large state companies, such as PetroChina, have become very conscious of environmental issues and standards through their extensive overseas operations, including joint ventures with Western multinationals. The need to adopt best practice overseas then influences domestic operations. It also affects the specifications for the equipment and parts which they buy: it makes little financial sense to buy two types of equipment – high-standard for overseas and low-standard domestically – so the decision is taken to operate at the higher standard everywhere. If international Chinese companies find they must operate to high standards inside China, they are likely to lobby for their purely domestic competitors to be required to raise their standards, too. Hence large state companies can, on strictly commercial grounds, become a force for good. On the other hand, there are many Chinese companies which have expanded into developing economies overseas and have exported their negligent environmental behaviour.

Not only have international Chinese enterprises had a real effect on standards within domestic industries, but the foreign environmental consultancies which accompany foreign development aid projects often remain in China and encourage further projects to which they can contribute. Multinational organisations, such as the World Bank, often make loans conditional on certain targets related either directly to the environment or to policy reforms affecting the environment. We then see incremental improvements.

China missed its environmental targets in the 2000–5 Five Year Plan. However, in its 2005–10 plan, Beijing met most of its objectives, including the energy efficiency of coal-powered electricity plants.[125] The difficulty with state-driven top-down targeting is that it is done by fiat and with some partiality: state-owned and politically connected enterprises are treated more leniently.[126] Although the government's target of a 20 per cent reduction in energy use relative to economic output was almost met in the five years to 2010, the target was reduced to a much less demanding 16 per cent for 2015. One effect of increasing energy efficiency is that it reduces costs and increases profitability, which can spur further production and thus boost aggregate energy consumption.

The Role of Civil Society

A significant but sensitive area of influence is that of NGOs. Because of the Party's apprehension about any independent activity, international environmental NGOs have had some difficulty in exercising influence. Domestic NGOs tend to be officially discouraged – unless they position themselves as industry experts, which can allow a degree of flexibility. Beijing has generally been more comfortable with the apparently oxymoronic phenomenon of 'government-organised NGOs' or GONGOs. By 2008, it was estimated that there were 508 officially registered independent grass-roots environmental NGOs. Increasingly, even some GONGOs are operating independently – organisationally and politically, as well as financially – of their government origins. Because they are making responsible and informed contributions to discussions on the environment and because the top leadership sympathises with their general thrust, they can have an impact.

Historically, the environment has been seen as a non-political issue, and thus open for discussion. However, in advocating environmental legislation, the environmental authorities cite public opinion: large-scale riots have been generated by environmental disasters, and these have 'the potential to pose very substantial questions of an intensely political nature with implications ... for ... Chinese authorities in general'.[127] Academics, too, can help to highlight problems: in 2008, Professor Hu Yali of Nanjing University linked pollution to a 40 per cent rise in the level of birth defects among children. The sharp increase was 'rather alarming', according to the Vice Minister of National Population and Family Planning.[128] But an effective channel for public participation is lacking, there is little legal provision for consulting public opinion, there is low public awareness of how to participate in civic affairs and it is hard for the public to monitor environmental developments. One exception has been the public hearings on proposed water price increases.[129] Of course, hearings potentially open the way for the middle class to be trained in political campaigning.

Because real NGOs are young, underdeveloped and not encouraged, they sometimes express themselves in a rather emotional manner, which can undermine their message. There was a mild relaxation of controls on NGOs in 2011, making it somewhat less difficult to set them up, but this move has not generally been felt to be very helpful.[130] However, they are growing in number and are slowly becoming more important.

The public does have opportunities to get involved, but this is usually through complaint mechanisms – and typically, of course, after the event. There has been little encouragement of public scrutiny in advance of, say, the construction of a chemical plant. Though not encouraged, there are sometimes public demonstrations: in 2007, between 8,000 and 20,000 people marched in protest at a petrochemical plant in Xiamen. Later there was a public hearing and subsequently the plant was resited.[131] Interestingly, the public were invited to offer to comment and there was a draw to determine who would be selected to give their views. However, this method of public expression is not encouraged on a national basis. There were two such demonstrations in 2012 which became violent and drew several thousand protesters. The entire environmental debate could be elevated and enhanced if the government was willing to trust the public. NGOs could be encouraged to do in China what they do elsewhere: persuade, lobby, publicise and criticise.

Beijing Goes to Copenhagen

While the national leadership appears to have accepted the need to repair the environment, it is not at all clear that it is in full accord with the – quite separate and rather controversial – Western climate change campaign. It broadly shares with India the view that developing countries should not arrest their development before they have caught up with the West. The NDRC report in 2007 on China's Climate Change Programme makes an interesting point:

> In the development history of human beings, there is no precedent where a high per capita GDP is achieved with low per capita energy consumption. With its ongoing economic development, China will inevitably be confronted with growing energy consumption and CO2 emissions.[132]

This influences all environmental policy. Furthermore, Chinese people are amongst the most sceptical in the world about climate change theory. While 85 per cent of Koreans and 72 per cent of Japanese feel climate change is their top threat, for the Chinese it is only 39 per cent.[133] The government's lukewarm activity in this area seems to reflect public opinion fully and accurately. We need to appreciate the profound difference between public scepticism towards climate change and powerful demands by the public to clean up the air and water. Beijing understands the distinction.

China's role at the 2009 Copenhagen climate change conference was controversial and it seems to have blocked many Western initiatives. One view is that Beijing does not want any external monitoring, as that would be a slippery slope towards infringement of national sovereignty. A more dramatic view is that China intended to flex its muscles and humiliate President Obama, confident that the NGO community will always blame the West for failure, never the developing countries. It was widely felt that China was enjoying its power on the world stage as American hegemony took another debilitating blow. Mark Lynas, environmental adviser to the president of the Maldives, claims to have been 'in the room' for the closed-door negotiations between heads of government. His subsequent description in the British *Guardian* newspaper is vivid: 'The truth is this: China wrecked the talks, intentionally humiliated Barack Obama, and insisted on an awful "deal" so western leaders would walk away carrying the blame.'[134]

Cadres and Targets

Officials are used to being rewarded annually on the basis of economic growth delivered in their district. This is very important, as pay and promotion are a natural and effective way of catching officials' attention and executing national policy priorities.

There are four fundamental problems with the way this system functions in contemporary China. First, in the past, targets such as economic growth – and,

to an extent, fiscal revenue, employment and lack of rioting – have been priorities. It is rather contradictory to require officials now, simultaneously, to
impose costly environmental restraints on production and still to produce high
levels of growth. It is unreasonable to give too many objectives, especially
conflicting ones. Officials are suffering from target fatigue. Top leaders should
construct a new set of simple, unambiguous targets on which officials will be
judged.

Second, cadres face problems of relationship as well as responsibility. There
are often close personal relationships between officials and the directors of
environmentally damaging factories in their areas. There are many issues for
officials to consider: they may not wish to cause problems for their friends and
associates; they may expect 'presents' – such as expensive watches – if they
keep quiet; they may worry that, if things get too difficult, factories might just
up sticks and move to a more accommodating part of China, leaving thousands
of unemployed to blight the county – and the career prospects of the official; or
they and their families might be shareholders in such factories.

Third, according to the state news agency Xinhua, it is 'an open secret that
local officials use bogus numbers to exaggerate local economic growth, impress
superiors and win promotions, while many employees at statistics offices
bowed to political pressure to report false data'.[135] Of course, that goes for data
in any area in any country.

Lastly, officials construct patronage networks, in which they cultivate their
seniors, seek mentors and lobby for support from similar-level officials. These
networking exercises seem to provide the decisive edge for promotion in at
least as many cases as those determined by the theoretical considerations of
performance against targets. As Professor Hu Xingdou, of Beijing University of
Technology, says: 'Canvassing for promotion or bribing people to garner
support is common among Chinese officials. Your promotion is under the
control of your superiors. Every cadre has to show "goodwill".'[136] When the
mayor of the important city of Shenzhen was sacked in 2009, one of the allegations against him was that he had bought his post. The *Financial Times* detailed
how government and Party posts are routinely bought; its report drew partly
on interviews and partly on leaked documents from the Communist Party
organisation department in Jilin province. Zhang Quanjing, who ran the
Organisation Department until 1999, admitted that 'the younger officials . . .
tend to think about themselves and are mainly after power, salary, status,
housing and medical care . . .This thinking encourages jealousy and encourages the buying of official posts to get promoted.'[137]

Sadly, the system strongly encourages lying. There is little penalty if one is
found out, and much reward if one is not. The result is the rotting of values.

Truth is not treasured, and indeed is often penalised. At best, this creates a moral vacuum; at worst, it constructs perverse incentives, with the wrong drivers for achieving ethical results. Unfortunately, national leaders cannot approach the overarching moral issues for the national culture without changing governance.

Government Action and Public Opinion

Despite many difficulties, government is now acting seriously to reduce pollution. But the results will not be immediately obvious. Officials showed initial interest in constructing a 'green GDP', but the idea was shelved because of inter-ministerial conflict and because no foreign country had achieved such a thing.

The environment is fast becoming a political issue: the 2012 Pew China Survey revealed water and air pollution to be two of the seven most important problems. As many 'mass incidents' are environmental protests, the authorities must focus more on pollution. Over 80 per cent of Chinese polled in 2009 said that environmental problems need to be addressed, even if the economy slows and unemployment rises.[138] China has been emboldened to chide the West and encourage faster action by developed countries on pollution control. Interestingly, even before the economic downturn the Hong Kong government reportedly lobbied the Chinese authorities, nationally and locally, to slow the imposition of environmental regulation in Guangdong province in order to ease financial pressure on the substantially Hong Kong-resident factory owners there.[139]

Official comment on the environment has been increasingly pointed, partly because of the public's reaction (which has ranged from polite, quiet marches against proposed developments to pitched battles or riots at polluting facilities). In 2006, there were reported to be 60,000 environment-related incidents:

> In July 2007 Zhou Shenxian, the leading minister of the State Environmental Protection Administration, publicly blamed the increasing instability across the country – reflected in riots, protests, and petitions – on the public's anger toward the polluted environment. He chided local officials for not confronting environmental polluters whom he blamed for the escalating 'mass incidents'.[140]

In 2011 Zhou said: 'If our homeland is destroyed and we lose our health, then what good does development do?'[141]

However, it is reported that the economic downturn led to a more flexible approach being taken by the environmental authorities, which were anxious not to arrest investment in plant that was part of the stimulus package. In 2009, Wu Xiaoqing, then SEPA Vice Minister, said that since the 2008 stimulus announcement his ministry had approved over 90 per cent of projects. It also accelerated the mandatory environmental impact studies. Some feel this indicates a relaxation of standards. In addition, in 2009, there was a 40 per cent cut in funding for pollution control.

Rather than passing legislation, one of the best ways of discouraging waste would be to change the pricing structure and eliminate subsidies. Ironically, though, a country that does not have elections must, in certain respects, be particularly sensitive to public opinion. Accordingly there is nervousness about reducing subsidies and raising prices. All governments wish to be popular, but those with an electoral mandate can occasionally do unpopular things; those without such a mandate live in greater fear.

Foreign observers tend to differentiate the central leadership's commitment to environment change from resistance by local officials:

> The Chinese central leadership has . . . demonstrated a strong commitment to deal with the environmental challenges ahead. This is reflected in the comprehensive corpus of environmental policies and laws that have been developed over the past decades; the increase in the environmental capacity through the steady build-up of environmental institutions and specialised staff; the rise in research and development of environmental technologies; and the state's relatively positive stance towards emerging green activism.[142]

The leaders have probably been won over; the problem is with the middle ranks. 'Over the last 15 years, China has written some of the prettiest laws in the world,' said Jin Zhong, editor of *Kaifeng* (Open) magazine in Hong Kong. 'But they are not enforced or enforceable. For that, you need institutions that oversee the police, the judiciary and the local governments and not a single source of power, as there is now.'[143]

China has a weak legal system; often it is the administrative units which enforce laws, rather than the judiciary, and courts often support local enterprises against the prosecution. The Party's Organisation Department needs to send clear and credible messages to officials across the country that the environment is a top consideration in their performance review. Furthermore, the authorities may be indulgent towards some civil activity in the environmental arena, but it is handicapped by general nervousness of activity by NGOs, which could otherwise play a major role in policing environmental performance. The authorities dislike encouraging activities which are not Party-led – even if they are completely aligned with state policy. This resulted in discouragement of the waves of volunteers who offered their help immediately after the Sichuan earthquake.[144]

Challenges for China

The polluted environment is a symptom of an underlying problem. That problem is essentially one of poor and weak governance. As the Party insists in leading all areas of national life, it claims the credit for success; but it must also accept the blame for failure.

The overwhelming public support for environmental protection (even over growth and jobs) means this is an area where the authorities cannot countenance failure. Top leaders are obviously aware of the need to confront environmental abuse. The problem appears to be an institutional one: laws cannot be implemented and senior leaders find it hard to impose their priorities on officials. This is a recurring problem throughout Chinese history. What is needed is reform of Party management and incentivisation of officials.

We have also seen clear evidence that, in any economic downturn, there is a loss of focus on the environment. Unfortunately, economic slowdown is highly likely in the coming years. Local officials must perceive that there is rising public unhappiness with the environment, and that it is possibly regarded today as a more important issue than the economy. If so, it is vital that the Party take this on board: it has not yet decided that further growth matters less than clean air and water. The lack of data makes it difficult to be precise about the current position and trends, but the situation is disastrous and there are only scattered signs of progress.

As for solutions, these fall into two categories: economic and governance. On the economic side, there need to be further and faster moves towards effective implementation of water and energy pricing; a shift in focus from manufacturing to the more labour-intensive but less resource-intense service sector; and definite progress in developing new environmental technologies and in building the knowledge economy. On the governance side, there must be encouragement of NGOs; greater attention to the rule of law and an independent judiciary; a radical overhaul of cadre management; and motivation for officials to follow national policy on the environment. The real threat for the Party may be that existing legislation cannot be implemented without radical reform of how the Party handles its power at all levels. This could prove an exercise too far. However, if the problem is not resolved, it could be the environment, rather than the economy, which topples the Party.

CHAPTER SEVEN

Threats to Social Stability

Stability is a major theme in China and threats to it are very important. After many centuries of upheaval – both foreign invasion and domestic insurrection – since 1979 the country has placed a high value on stability. It features constantly in the speeches of senior leaders, and many people prize it more than other possible 'goods', such as open elections or greater freedom of expression. Threats to stability can be divided into two categories. First, there are activities that in most societies would be regarded as criminal (or anti-social at the very least). These issues – which range from corruption to arms dealing – have a direct impact on society, and are thus threats to *social stability*. The second category covers activities of which the authorities in China do not currently approve (although many other states would find them acceptable). The groups involved are not against society, but they do dissent from one or more of the ruling party's present policies, some of which are of fundamental importance to the current Chinese state. I bring these activities together in Chapter 8 as threats to *civil stability*.

I accept that, for some, there may be a slender distinction between these. The authorities tend to use the word 'stability' interchangeably with the term 'social stability'. This is often the case where governments cannot see a distinction between their interests and those of wider society. However, it is useful to try to identify some differences.

Corruption

The frequent reporting of corruption by official media is alleged by regime opponents to indicate how bad things are. China's residents, native and foreign, regularly complain of corruption. It is certainly unacceptable; but it is worth stressing that many other countries are in a worse position. Nor should we think for a moment that corruption in China is solely caused by communism: it has been noted as a serious issue at most points in dynastic history. Emperors were aware of it; concerned that, if left unbridled, it might cause instability, they often sought to limit its scope. Corruption is, of course, nurtured in an environment which lacks both transparency and accountability. It flourishes in Chinese culture, which often pays greater regard to relationships than to the rule of law. We cannot blame the Party for the birth of corruption, but we can for imposing conditions which allow it to continue. If corruption is often noted by regime opponents, it is equally frequently highlighted by national leaders. Former Premier Wen Jiabao referred to this issue repeatedly: in 2009 he said 'this year efforts will be focused on investigation and handling of corruption';[1] in 2011, the *People's Daily* reported, 'Chinese Premier says corruption biggest threat to China';[2] in 2012, according to Wen, 'The biggest risk to the ruling party is corruption'. In the same year a Party member, Yang Jisheng, claimed that corruption was worse than at any time in China's history.[3] 2013 saw Xi Jinping observe that 'the fight against corruption is a long-term, complicated and arduous task'.

Scarcely a day passes without Xinhua reporting that one central leader or another has condemned corrupt practice amongst officials. In 2008, 2,687 officials were investigated for corruption and infringement of people's legal rights and 10,135 government workers for taking bribes. Somewhat confusingly, in 2010 it was announced that the previous year no fewer than 106,000 officials had been found guilty of corruption – an increase, it was said, of 2.5 per cent.[4] The number of officials caught embezzling over $150,000 was up 19 per cent – an increase that was ascribed to closer monitoring. The People's Bank of China released briefly on to its website in 2011 a report that between the mid-1990s and 2008 16–18,000 officials had smuggled $120 billion overseas.[5] In 2011, a former vice mayor got a life sentence for taking bribes of $3 million to approve conversion of farmland for development.

In 2009, Wen Jiabao posed a rhetorical question about why, in the midst of a financial crisis, such great importance was being attached to combating corruption. He went on to provide the answer: 'Because in my opinion, economic development, social justice and a clean government are the three pillars of social stability.' Of the three, went on Wen, clean government was the most important.[6]

A frequent criticism is that national leaders are willing selectively to stamp on low-ranking officials but refuse to make an example of more senior ones. Certainly the punishment of fifteen senior officials (apparently out of 106,000 guilty officials) would suggest that the focus is on the lower levels. Indeed, some say the problem is essentially a local one. However, investigations have gone up to provincial and ministerial level. According to Xinhua, in the year to November 2008 about 5,000 officials across the country above the county level were punished for corruption. The 2012 smuggling case involving the businessman Lai Changxing – described in state media as the biggest economic crime since 1949 – implicated Li Zhijou, the Vice Minister of Public Security, who received a suspended death sentence, the deputy mayor of Xiamen and, reportedly, the wife of a Politburo member.

Chongqing, with China's most extensive city government, was the centre of a huge investigation from 2009 to 2011, with up to 6,000 arrests. In 2009 it was announced that 50 officials, three billionaires, 24 gang leaders and countless policemen were being charged. A former chief of police was convicted in 2010 of receiving bribes and protecting criminals and organised crime. However, it seems much of this was linked with helping the career of the Chongqing party secretary, Bo Xilai. In the six months to April 2009, authorities arrested the former head of the Guangdong Higher People's Court, the vice president of the Supreme People's Court, the deputy party head of the Communist Party and head of police and judiciary for Guangdong, and a former Assistant Minister of Public Security.[7] A Supreme Court judge was sentenced in 2010 to life imprisonment for accepting bribes in exchange for giving favourable rulings in court cases. In 2011, the railways minister was sacked for 'severe disciplinary violations' involving corruption. While overall positive, it is regrettable the process is so lengthy.

In 2009, then Premier Wen Jiabao proposed that officials should be obliged to declare their assets. This has been followed up in a few areas, but not yet on a large scale. However, there is a steady drumbeat of demand for change. At the 2009 NPC meeting it was reported by state media that:

> While lawmakers hailed the country's anti-corruption progress, they also admitted that the country still has a long way to go. According to Hao Ruyu, vice president of the Beijing-based Capital University of Economics and Business and an NPC deputy, the lack of effective supervision against corruption has made the real estate, land management, finance and judiciary sector a hotbed for corruption.[8]

In 2009, a survey undertaken in major cities by Horizon Research found that the urban public believes corruption is the worst blemish on the country's international image – a view expressed by 59 per cent.[9] Real estate is a sore point for many people, who see their houses earmarked for destruction owing to corrupt deals between officials and developers. Lei Zhengfu, head of one of the districts of Chongqing, was fired in 2012 after a member of the public posted a video of him with a young girl, apparently provided by a businessman.

He had allegedly received protection from Bo Xilai. This is an example of a developing trend of 'citizen supervision' exercises.[10] These cases show that corruption is a serious issue that is nowhere close to eradication.

It was said at the 2009 NPC session that there should be a 'major focus' on preventing the stimulus package, at the time worth $586 billion, from 'falling prey to the corrupted'. Zhang Ping, Director of the National Development and Reform Commission, said that it had set up twenty-four teams to ensure that the money was spent correctly. Since officials later noted that much of this money went on illegal stock market activity and the casinos of Macau, these teams were evidently not effective. One deputy – a state prosecutor in Beijing – said: 'It is essential that the country's prosecuting authorities take anti-corruption as their focus of work' – apparently a demand for corruption to be prioritised over such issues as drugs or organised crime.[11]

An area which attracts considerable public censure is the abuse of government cars. When the Beijing Municipal Bureau of Finance announced that in 2010 there were 62,026 official cars in the city there was huge public scepticism, and a report by China Central Television concluded there were actually 700,000 official vehicles. In 2012, *Caixin* magazine reported that nationally there could be up to 3.5 million government cars, costing around $50 billion. It also said a National People's Congress researcher had worked out that government spent $300 billion annually on overseas travel, cars and receptions.[12]

In July 2011, Daniel Wu, a small entrepreneur and watch enthusiast, started a blog noting the various expensive watches worn by ministers and other officials. He posted the catalogue prices – for example $11,000 – next to photographs of the public-salaried officials. In September, Sina, the leading Chinese portal, closed down the blog.[13]

'Elite Hegemony'

Corruption in China is not a result of opening up to market forces. In 1952, two successive Tianjin Party secretaries were sentenced to death for corruption. In the 1960s Mao expressed his disgust at corruption amongst Party secretaries.[14] And as early as 1987, a survey by the Chinese Academy of Social Sciences found that 84 per cent of respondents felt corruption was the worst problem.[15] One of the principal factors is the sale of influence. Professor Michael Johnston uses the term 'elite hegemony' to describe a situation where

an entrenched political elite facing little political competition and few meaningful demands for accountability dominates and exploits economic opportunities, manipulating political access (a scarce and valuable commodity) in

return for further economic gains . . . In extreme cases, such as China's, political figures, bureaucrats and whole agencies go into business overtly or as
partners with entrepreneurs.[16]

In 2007, *Der Spiegel* published research from Chinese state institutions showing
that virtually all citizens with wealth above 100 million CNY ($14 million)
were related to senior Party officials (though it is not entirely clear how the
figures were arrived at).[17] The Party, too, seems concerned about family
involvement in corruption:

> A 2002 internal survey . . . suggested some 98 per cent of the spouses and
> children of high-level officials held senior government or business posts, with
> incomes as high as 120 times the national average . . . Moreover, they
> accounted for 78 per cent of suspects in fraud cases involving more than five
> million yuan and were the second-most cited cause of public grievances, after
> the police. More than 600 relatives of high-level officials had fled abroad after
> having been charged with graft.[18]

The culture of impunity among the children of Party leaders is underlined by
Xu Youyu, a liberal philosopher at CASS: 'the princelings enjoy virtually the
same political protection and status as the officials. They are above laws and
regulations and their business activities are off-limits to supervision or public
scrutiny.'[19]

It is depressing to look back and see what senior legal officials were saying
over a decade ago, in 1999:

> The President of the Supreme People's Court vowed yesterday to clean up
> corruption in the Judiciary and crack down hard on law-breakers to ensure
> social stability . . . 'The People's Court has made progress in the past year . . .
> But we must be somberly aware that our work is still far from meeting the
> development needs of the new situation.'[20]

This negligible progress in stemming corruption may be one of the reasons
why, in 2009, 2010 and 2011, a quarter of the National People's Congress
abstained or voted against the work reports of the President of the People's
Supreme Court and the Procurator General – in the Chinese context a very
telling condemnation. By 2011, Wang Xiaolu, deputy director of the National
Economic Research Institute, was obliged to admit that 'corruption is our
biggest challenge'.[21] The Party's *Global Times* acknowledged that 'grand
construction projects have often turned into pits of corruption. High-profile

scandals have been exposed in almost every grand project, including the construction that went into the Beijing Olympic Games.'[22] In other words, corruption has not declined since the 1980s, but has steadily increased. A Chinese friend of mine remarked in 2012 that mainland China is a feudal system where what many might call corruption is regarded by party leaders as merely reward or entitlement.

International Comparison

In the 2012 Pew China Survey, official corruption was regarded as the second most important issue facing Chinese people: half of them described it as a 'very big problem'. However, what may be surprising is that, in the 2013 survey of global corruption conducted by Transparency International, China was well up in the better half of countries surveyed, with a score (4.0) that was improved from 2007 (3.6 out of 10).[23] It is instructive to look at some of the results of TI's 2009–13 surveys (the latter of 178 countries), with marks out of 10 (Table 7.1).

Apart from the apparent improvement of Russia, Brazil, China and Morocco, not much has changed. This rather leads one to think that there is

Table 7.1: **Corruption Perceptions Index 2009–2013**

Scale: from 10 down to 1 (1 = most corrupt)

	2013	2011	2009
Denmark	9.1	9.4	9.3
USA	7.3	7.1	7.5
Italy	4.3	3.9	4.3
Brazil	4.2	3.8	3.7
Bulgaria	4.1	3.3	3.8
China	4.0	3.6	3.6
Greece	4.0	3.4	3.8
Morocco	3.7	3.4	3.3
India	3.6	3.1	3.4
Thailand	3.5	3.4	3.4
Mexico	3.4	3.0	3.3
Russia	2.8	2.4	2.2
Somalia	0.8	1.0	1.1

Source: Transparency International surveys.

nothing special about corruption in China – nothing especially good or bad. It is also important to make the point that, with the marginal exception of Brazil, China is the best-rated large developing country. Rated worse for corruption are: India, Indonesia, Mexico, Nigeria, Pakistan, the Philippines, Russia and Vietnam. In terms of corruption, it seems that the problem is not China, it is the world.

China performs somewhat differently on the World Bank Governance Indicators for 'Control of Corruption' in 2008–9. The selected countries in Table 7.2 (from a total of over 200) are rated between +2.5, least corrupt, and –2.5, most corrupt:

Table 7.2: **Control of Corruption: 2012**

Denmark	100
USA	89
Italy	58
Brazil	56
Bulgaria	52
Greece	51
Thailand	47
Mexico	43
Morocco	42
China	39
India	35
Somalia	0
Russia	N/A

Source: *World Bank, Governance Indicators 2013*

By 2011, China had gradually fallen in the rating to – 0.67. The World Bank rates China worse in absolute terms than does the TI survey, and the country is well into the bottom half of countries. While China's rating has been rising with TI, it has been falling with the World Bank, which suggests that all we know is that China is fairly corrupt but there are worse major countries. China has seen no material improvement (or deterioration) in absolute terms over the last twelve years (nor, indeed, has India).

Culture of Impunity

Too many officials still seem to benefit from a culture of impunity. Perhaps the scale of incidents in China is so large that it is difficult to investigate them all with the resources available. Nevertheless, the emphasis of investigation is on the lower levels. One of the disadvantages of China's being not a dictatorship but a large oligarchy is that government depends on widespread consensus, and there is probably insufficiently strong consensus to take on more of the senior officials. The zeal of officials in rooting out corruption probably also varies from area to area. Despite this, it does seem that investigations are increasing, and from time to time they do touch very senior officials (although it is said that the high officials charged are those who have lost in some factional struggle). Academics and officials seem to feel no compunction about recognising the problem and speaking out on it, and this seems a healthy trend. One official reason given for treating corruption as a very serious challenge is that it constitutes defiance of the state and therefore undermines authority.

Much is made of investigations of corruption amongst officials, but there seem to be far more cases that are ignored. The Carnegie Endowment in New York sponsored a study of corruption investigation in China from 1982 until 2007. Apparently 130,000–190,000 CCP members were disciplined and punished annually. Almost 80 per cent of them got no more than a warning:

> Only 20 per cent were expelled from the party. Less than 6 per cent were criminally prosecuted. In recent years, half of those convicted of corruption received suspended sentences and did not serve any jail time. Therefore, the odds of an average corrupt official going to jail are at most 3 out of 100, making corruption a high-return, low-risk activity.[24]

Even that low figure is 3 per cent *of those who are disciplined*: not all of those investigated will be found guilty and disciplined, and not all corrupt officials will be identified for investigation. However, the fact remains that courts do exist and petitions can be lodged. Officials are sacked, charged and even shot: Deng Xiaoping in 1983 emphasised the value of capital punishment in this regard, and harsh punishment for corruption is believed to be very popular with the public.

Of course, corruption does not necessarily involve the abuse of official authority for money. Two academics in Hong Kong did some interesting work in 2009 on the whole area of management corruption during the process of industrial restructuring.[25] They raise issues about the inability of the state to monitor and regulate restructuring because it does not effectively regulate the state enterprise sector. This leads to a drain of state assets or what one might term 'asset-stripping'. The late 1980s were marked by enterprise reform, the separation of political control and management. However, 'in the midst of this murky transition in rights, a majority of state-owned resources were transferred, legally and illegally, to benefit a small minority's economic interests'[26] – which suggests that China approached Yeltsin's Russia in this respect.

Implications of Corruption

Some party theoreticians suggest that corruption was a key factor in the collapse of Communist regimes in Russia and Eastern Europe. They also note that it weakens the economy, creates inefficiency, encourages crime and increases inequality. Zhao Ziyang, the General Secretary of the Chinese Communist Party until 1989, observed that 'If there is no independent enforcement of law, and the political party in power is able to intervene, then corruption can never be effectively resolved'.[27] Furthermore, as corruption provides – personally or collectively – private sources of wealth, it supplants loyalty to the Party and thus damages Party discipline. In other words, corruption is not just – as some Western critics would suggest – the fruits of a predatory system, but is actually a direct threat to the 'ruling capacity' of the Party.

Construction of a more market-driven economy may not lead automatically to Western-style democracy, but it does create new stakeholders who will make claims. They will inevitably want a stable and predictable relationship with other actors in the economy, such as the legal process, the banking system or regulators. Unless the market is rolled back, there is likely to be increasing pressure towards rule by law, which would probably circumscribe the freedom of political leaders to act unilaterally; the effects would then be felt rapidly in limitations on corruption.

Society has traditionally and to this day relied heavily on connections, or *guanxi*, to make things happen. This can weaken any attempt to modernise cadre management and base promotions for Party officials on merit; for example, we are told by state media that police in Chongqing and officials in Ningxia buy their promotions.[28] Buying positions seems to be widespread.[29] In such cases it might be difficult for superiors, having taken the money, to hold the officials to account. A further weakness is not social, but originally ideological. The continuing reluctance of state bank officials to grant funding to private companies forces some entrepreneurs who wish to grow their businesses to embark on 'grey transactions', by offering officials at state-linked companies inducements to borrow through their companies' credit access (see

Chapter 4). This exposes entrepreneurs to charges of corruption. Here the state is maintaining an environment in which corruption is almost inevitable.

However, the most telling point is that corruption is one principal cause of 'mass incidents' – violent riots. It was estimated by Professor Sun Liping of Tsinghua University that in 2010 there had been over 180,000 such incidents – four times the number in 2006. Corruption represents a severe and mounting threat to the stability and government of China.[30]

The Chinese authorities might do worse than consider the case of Chen Shui-bian, the former President of Taiwan, who was jailed for life on corruption charges in 2009. As he was a bête noire of the Chinese authorities, the mainland newspapers lapped the story up. However, Beijing should perhaps be concerned on two counts. First, the story demonstrated an implacable view that corruption in society must be pursued right to the summit of government and that there can be no immunity for the powerful (or recently powerful). Second, it suggests that Taiwan has a strong and free political system which has no fears about its stability when following justice as far as it needs to go. The fact that a Chinese society just a few miles from the mainland can be democratic and can apply the full rigour of the law to its leading citizen could well stand as a reproach to the People's Republic.

Population Imbalance

As this threat to stability arises from widespread social practices that are generally regarded as reprehensible (e.g. female abortion/infanticide, child trafficking) but are a by-product of a falling birth rate, I classify population imbalance as a social issue. However, in ten or twenty years' time, the consequences of the decisions taken in the past and unreversed today may be both social and civil threats to stability.

Emerging from the military and natural disasters of the 1930s and 1940s, the population grew rapidly after 1949 – something regarded by Mao Zedong as an asset to a modernising state. However, there were intermittent attempts by officials to encourage birth control. The birth rate had actually been falling for many years before 1979 and this was particularly evident between 1970 and 1979. Although it had already declined by 45 per cent from its post-1949 peak, there was a desire to reduce it further, so in 1979 China adopted the one-child policy. Since dubbed 'one of the most controversial social policies ever implemented,'[31] this sought to limit virtually all families to one child in order to control population growth. Exceptions were made at the outset for ethnic minorities such as Uighurs, Tibetans and Mongols (though strangely, their share of the national population has not since risen markedly: in the 2000 census minorities accounted for 8.41 per cent; in 2010 for 8.49 per cent; and yet the mid-term 2005 census seemed to show minority races at 9.44 per cent).[32] The overall national birth rate continued to fall after 1979, but more slowly. Social and cultural factors were driving in this direction independently of legislation.

During the 1980s, a striking effect began to emerge. The normal international gender ratio for babies is 103–107 boys to 100 girls. In the 1960s and most of the 1970s, China had a ratio of 106:100. When the policy was more strictly enforced in the 1980s it became clear that the ratio was beginning to lean increasingly towards male children, and by 1989 it was 113.8:100. A study in 2009 found that in the age range 1–4 years, the ratio was 124:100. A similar sharp upward trend was observed in the 1980s in Taiwan and Korea, too, though only China had the one-child policy.

Three interlinking factors can be associated with this phenomenon. First of all, something all these three Confucian-influenced societies have in common is 'son preference' – families want above all to have at least one son. In Chinese culture, sons are seen as economically more valuable (in working the land) and are more likely to take responsibility for their parents' welfare in old age, as daughters marry and leave to join a new family.

Second, for some decades there has been a trend to have smaller families. In China this was largely (though not exclusively) driven by legislation; in Korea and Taiwan, it was a growing social and economic objective – a goal that coincided with the availability of effective birth control methods. In the 1960s–80s, in all three societies the total fertility rate fell by over 60 per cent. Son preference matters little in societies with large families. However, if families have only one or two children, there is huge pressure to ensure that one is a boy. This led to the phenomenon of what academics call 'sex-selective abortion', or the frequent traditional practice of female infanticide.

A third factor was the growing accessibility of medical technology such as the ultrasound machine, which could distinguish gender prenatally. This led to gender-driven abortions of female foetuses to allow for the subsequent chance of a male child. Use of this technology has been made illegal, but it is widely used, particularly in the countryside.

By 2011, there had been small annual falls to bring the ratio for that year to just below 118 male children to every 100 girls. The figures are higher in the country areas. '[The] distorted sex ratio at birth is a new demographic phenomenon that accommodates both the parents' sex preference for [sons] and the small-family norm.'[33] In a few years' time, nationwide there will be such a shortage of women that one Chinese male in every five or six will not be able to marry (and in eight provinces the figure will exceed one man in four).

Understandably, the most 'normal' situation prevails in places such as Tibet and Xinjiang, where the exemption for minorities has allowed society to have balanced gender ratios. It is pointed out that there may be many cases of daughters' births simply going unrecorded (in order to allow a second attempt to have a son). However, it is unlikely that this happens sufficiently often to change the overall national picture very much. Any improvement in the situation is also likely to be cancelled out by the fact that many infant girls have been bought or abducted to supply the overseas adoption market: by 2005 girls constituted 95 per cent of all US adoptions of Chinese children.[34]

Gradually, further exceptions to the one-child policy have come to be made for only children marrying other only children; for the parents of a disabled child; in some provinces for families suffering hardship or who have only a girl; and now for parents who lost a child in the Sichuan earthquake. Shanghai, faced with a particularly ageing population, has introduced its own form of liberalisation, and eleven provinces allow a second child if only one parent is a single child. Even in 2007 – before the proposed 2013 adjustments – an official estimated that only 36 per cent of Chinese families were bound by the policy.[35] If it appears to extend to less than half the population, there may be more opposition to the one-child policy: why should a minority carry the burden of social planning for the whole nation? Furthermore, if – as demographers suggest – natural trends in fertility would have produced the same result, why apply the blunt force of the state?

Both the Pew Survey in 2008 and focus groups conducted by academics in 2009 show that there is broad public support in China for the policy. It is likely, though, that this consensus could break down. There is certainly limited debate on the policy, although the official line remains that change is inconceivable (despite the fact that the policy has already been modified). The situation is perhaps analogous to currency devaluation, where officials have to deny it until the day they announce it. Otherwise, it would be difficult for officials to enforce the policy on reluctant parents. Unusually, a senior official in Guangdong province said in 2010 that he believed the one-child policy would end when the national population peaks, currently estimated to be some time around 2030.

Implications for Stability

Whatever policy changes emerge, there is going to be a desperate shortage of girls in the age range 18–23. In 2010 the Chinese Academy of Social Sciences forecast that by 2020 there will be a shortfall of 24 million girls.[36] Furthermore, in 2012 Professor Dudley Poston at Texas A & M University estimated there were 41 million surplus men and if nothing is done to change the situation by 2020 there will be 55 million.[37]

The effects of this shortage include a rise in violent crime; young single men are held responsible for 25-33 per cent of the increase.[38] Some academics have established a link in India and Pakistan between unmarried young men and terrorist activity. The imbalance is likely to make young men angry and prone to violence – particularly sexual crimes and (possibly) terrorism. As Dr Therese Hesketh has observed:

> This trend could lead to increased levels of antisocial behaviour and violence, as gender is a well-established correlate of crime, and especially violent crime. Furthermore, when single young men congregate, the potential for more organised aggression is likely to increase substantially, and this has worrying implications for organised crime and terrorism.[39]

Prostitution, the trafficking of females and sexual disease are all increasing. China has a long history of stealing young boys, and there is now a mounting trade in female babies and young girls. State media estimate that the traffic in female babies and girls has reached 20,000 annually and continues to climb. There are even estimates of over 70,000 cases annually. There is a thriving cross-border trade in forcible abduction of Vietnamese, Burmese, Laotian and North Korean women.[40] North Korea is one of the few societies with average income below that of a poor uneducated Chinese peasant farmer. It is ironic that families do not want their own daughters, but they do want other people's – for their sons. And they want other people's sons if they only have a daughter. The shortage of girls has contributed to what Karl Gerth calls 'extreme markets': babies are stolen for adoption; women and girls are abducted for marriage or the sex trade; and virgins (both real and fabricated) are marketed.[41]

Since 1989, there has been a twentyfold increase in syphilis, which has reportedly reached 'epidemic proportions'.[42] In 2010, a paper stated that 'in 2008, an average of more than 1 baby per hour was born with congenital syphilis in China, for a total of 9,480 cases; the rate had increased by a factor of 12 during the previous 5 years'.[43] Public health is endangered by the social perception of deviancy among syphilis sufferers. This stigma results in a reluctance to seek treatment.

Then President Hu Jintao drew a parallel between the current gender imbalance and the shortage of available young women which was one of the causes of the Nien rebellion in 1851–68. Lasting seventeen years, it contributed to the eventual downfall of the Qing dynasty. Some historians have ascribed the rebellion principally to the fact that female infanticide had left a quarter of young men in the area unmarried.

In calculating that one in six of today's Chinese men will not find a wife, we should bear in mind that women tend to 'marry up' to more educated, handsome or affluent men. Thus, let's say, over one in three of China's poor, ugly or less educated men will not find a wife. That starts to look like transformational class oppression. If, in some provinces, a quarter of men on average will not get married, then simplistically we could say that half of the poorer males in certain rural provinces will not have families. This will begin to resemble the rule rather than the exception across swathes of rural China. There is some awareness of this issue, but very few potential policy initiatives. Exhortations to 'cherish daughters' are laudable, but rather long term. Professors at CASS have talked to me about encouraging 'intergenerational marriages', and one Central Party School academic has even recommended state-sponsored prostitution as a palliative.

Societies have had excesses of young males, for different reasons, at many times. A common policy response has been to engage them in military activities, but that normally requires some specific military action. Mao's response might have been to send them to the countryside; but that's where they already are. The assaults on China's society directly traceable to the one-child policy are multiple. It is quite likely that a future administration will decide that the good has largely been done and the results from now on are mostly negative.

China can change this gender disparity for coming generations. Korea's imbalance has improved substantially since the early 1990s, and lately there are signs that the situation is improving in certain urban parts of China.[44] Many factors have played a part: a greater sense of the worth of women, changes in inheritance laws and the strict illegality of ultrasound equipment. Continuing urbanisation might help (although it does not seem to have made much difference in Taiwan) although that comes at the price of increasing the population collapse. Other measures could include relaxing the one-child policy for farming families in rural areas, where there is the greatest incidence of abortions. In the very long term, a more balanced outlook can be induced. However, demography dictates that a long time will elapse before the trends and social impacts change significantly. The next two decades are bleak and inescapable.

Drugs

Drug use is perhaps even more covert in China than in Western countries, yet despite this it has attracted the attention of the authorities throughout the last decade. In 2002, Bai Jingfu, the Vice Minister of Public Security, said the situation was 'grim', and he was not very optimistic.[45]

There are three recognised forms of involvement in drugs: trans-shipment, manufacture and consumption. Originally Chinese citizens were involved in shipment from Burma, or the 'Golden Triangle' region. Washington says the large export volume, combined with poor official transparency, makes China an excellent drugs trans-shipment centre.[46] After trans-shipment, manufacture started. This particularly involved methamphetamine, because its main ingredient – ephedrine – is used in Chinese medicine. 'China is a major manufacturer of dual-use chemicals, primarily used for licit products, but also used for illicit drugs like methamphetamine. Organized crime diverts legitimately manufactured chemicals . . . from large chemical industries throughout China to produce illicit drugs.'[47] It is believed that consumption of illegal drugs followed some time after. Early on, it seemed to be concentrated in Yunnan province, on the Burmese border. Drugs are now popular with young people in clubs nationwide, and also among businessmen. They are smuggled across the border into Russia and are sold on internet websites. Considering the large number of people and the extent of policing of the internet, one can only assume that monitoring is given a low priority compared with political content.

It is difficult to gauge drug addiction rates from government statistics (for all the usual reasons). The National Narcotics Control Bureau issues many statements, but they do not engender clarity: it has mentioned the 'ever-increasing number of drug users', but then talked of around a million drug users or registered addicts (presumably two different-sized groups, as not all drug users will be registered as addicts) in 2003, 2004, 2007 and 2008 (compared to 901,000 in 2001). At the beginning of 2014 there were reported to be over 2 million registered drug users but there are estimates of over 12 million addicts.[48]

The UN World Drug Report for 2013 tells us that the world's largest seizure of methamphetamine (14 tons) was in China in 2011. In fact Lufeng in Guangdong province has probably been the principal global supplier.[49] But this could mean many things: it could mean the police are efficient; it could reflect the fact that China is close to the producing areas and is thus likely to see more shipments; or it could mean domestic consumption is rising.

A 2012 study described drug abuse as 'a substantial problem' in China.[50] That said, countries considered to be seriously affected by drug abuse generally have over 1 per cent of the population taking opiates, 2 per cent cocaine, 1 per cent amphetamines or 1 per cent Ecstasy, and unofficial Chinese estimates come nowhere near these levels. China does not report consumption; indeed China is not mentioned in the national statistics for individual drug use in the UN report. This absence suggests that the statistics are not efficiently collected – or that the authorities prefer not to announce them.

AIDS has now become, according to the Ministry of Health, the country's most deadly infectious disease. In 2006, 37 per cent of all cases of the disease were ascribed to drug abuse. In 2008 it was officially said to kill one person in China every hour. Unofficial sources estimate a rate three times higher. In 2011, officials announced that they had arrested over 12,000 people suspected of drug dealing over the internet and had confiscated over 650 lb of illegal drugs. Indeed after that, over 122 drug rings and 22 drug manufacturing plants were terminated.[51]

The overall impression gained is that drugs are an increasing problem in China, but they have not reached the pervasive levels of the West, Russia or Latin America.

Crime

A distinction should be drawn here between 'normal' criminal activity and the qualitatively different phenomenon of Chinese-style organised crime. The Chinese state media generally report 'Triad activity', with no specific Triad organisation mentioned. So does it simply mean any criminal gang, or does it imply membership of specific Triad organisations? In fact, the state media tend to use the expression to describe criminal gangs which are often armed and enjoy some degree of official protection. The term does not imply the whole panoply of classic Triad organisation, and these gangs cannot trace an unbroken lineage back to the Ming resistance after 1644, as the Triads once did. Yu Jianrong at CASS and some others prefer the term 'Mafia'. In today's China, any organised criminal gang that is armed is likely to be referred to as a 'Triad' gang or 'mafia'. Underground gambling is one favoured activity, but there are many others.

General Crime

General crime seems to have been rising significantly over the last thirty years, though the data are unclear. The use of targets to measure performance has tended to lead to police under-reporting (not an exclusively Chinese issue). Furthermore, a sizeable section of the community – around 260 million migrant workers – is largely omitted from the numbers. If they are victims of crime, they rarely find it expedient to report this.

It is entirely to be expected from any theory of sociology or criminology that times of rapid social change lead to increased crime. As one sociologist says, 'crime is one of the major costs of modernisation'.[52] Urban growth is generally linked to massive migration, and migration is generally linked by sociologists to crime: traditions of rural violence are imported; there are increasing rates of inequality; perceptions of surrounding affluence; and the mere concrete presence of valuable goods. Despite this, the published crime statistics – although rising – are lower than international criminologists would expect. The likely explanation is a combination of the social control and influence brought to bear by the state and under-reporting of the data. Indeed the combination of active state involvement, neighbourhood committees and 'moral guidance' has had the effect of under-emphasising the need for development of the rule of law.

Looking forward, we should anticipate a noticeable increase in crime levels as a consequence of the rising numbers of single (and thus not particularly happy) young men in the cities. This has already been pointed out as a key reason for recent increases in urban crime. We must also expect some diminution in the role of neighbourhood committees if the Party and state reduce their involvement in grass-roots society. Street children and youth gangs with links to organised crime are becoming a clear problem in Shanghai. Demography suggests that this pattern of young criminals has only just begun and is likely to intensify markedly.

Organised Crime

The Communist Party largely eradicated classic 'Triad' activity after seizing power in 1949. But the opening up of a market-based economy, private sector activity and some social loosening up have presented many opportunities for the criminally minded. Qiu Geping, a professor at East China University of Political Science and Law, has said the Triads of today are quite different from the crime organisations of the past: 'Traditionally, Triads are an enemy of the government because of their anarchic nature. But these days, they are born and grow in the fertile ground of government corruption.'[53]

It is not just the staple activities of drugs, prostitution, human trafficking, extortion and smuggling that Triad gangs engage in. New areas of opportunity include trafficking in historical relics and endangered species, credit card theft and identity fraud. Furthermore, in such a rapidly changing socio-economic environment, where legal specificity is deficient and codification slow, it is difficult for officials to be sure whether activities are legal, illegal or undefined: theft of intellectual property is a common activity of contemporary 'Triads'. Thirty years ago insider trading was not a crime in Western financial markets. Now it is.

However, some activities are fairly clearly wrong, and there are reports from various regions of criminal Triad activity. In Yanjiang, in Guangdong, two Triad leaders ran the whole local economy for ten years before being arrested.

Police declared that they had put an end to 1,221 gangs in Hebei between 2006 and 2009. In 2007, a Triad gang was arrested in Tangshan, in Hebei, and police seized thirty-eight guns, three armoured jeeps and an armoured personnel carrier.[54]

Probably the biggest example of Triad activity is the Chongqing campaign. After 2008, Bo Xilai, the then Party Secretary, led a massive crackdown on Triad activity there. By early 2010, more than 3,300 people were reported to have been apprehended, and over 1,700 guns seized. Those arrested included 24 Triad bosses from 'the fourteen key gangs', along with three billionaires, 50 government officials and six district police chiefs.[55] In the same year it was announced that 3,000 medium and high-ranking police officers would be required to resign and reapply for their jobs. Professor Chin Ko-lin of Rutgers University in New Jersey put this in context in 2010: 'I speak to the public security in many cities and they often talk about this – when there's a crackdown, when there's pressure, they have to come up with the numbers, the quotas . . . Often they go after the less powerful.'[56] The shooting of a PLA soldier in 2009 was described by some Chongqing residents as a payback from the Triads for Bo Xilai's campaign against them. We should not of course forget that in 2012 Bo himself was charged with corruption.

There has been a rising trend of violence against the rich, in the form of organised kidnapping, contract killing or just random attacks. Potential victims have started to take precautionary measures: according to the Ministry of Public Security, by the end of 2009 private security had become a US$1.2 billion business, with 2,767 companies employing over 2 million bodyguards.[57] In 2007, a national conference was held to discuss the chaos and crime erupting in rural areas. The public security ministry instructed rural cadres to report on 'Triad activity' in their areas, so it would seem that this exists in all parts of the country. It seems that organised crime is increasing, often operates with protection from officials and, in certain dramatic cases, with direct leadership from officials. This might be a result of two phenomena in contemporary China: the absence of strong and independent investigative media, and weak supervision by the centre of the use and abuse of political power in multiple fragmented localities.

Organised Crime Overseas

Chinese gangs are actively engaged in the rapid growth of illegal cannabis production in Britain.[58] They are also a force in such activities as the smuggling of counterfeit cigarettes into Europe,[59] and the manufacture of low-quality, fake pharmaceuticals. Through ports such as Naples, their fellow Chinese nationals import the cheap products, to be falsely branded and sold across Europe,[60] and supply the precursor drugs required for cocaine production. The US authorities have also charged Chinese gangs with the systematic corruption of Chinese-manufactured 'chip and pin' machines so that they pass on confidential data to criminals.[61]

Private Armaments

There is growing unofficial arms possession and trafficking throughout China. Occasional reference is made to guns hidden when the Nationalists lost the civil war in 1949–50, and substantial numbers of arms were seized by radical mass organisations from the PLA during the Cultural Revolution, but it is more recent developments that play the most important part.

There are arms illicitly imported into China, arms illicitly exported from China through neighbouring countries, arms illicitly produced in China for domestic use, and weapons from state arsenals that find their way into criminal hands. Unofficial domestic arms factories have been shut by the authorities and there have been successive waves of seizures of illegal domestic arms. It is estimated there are 40 million small arms illegally in civilian hands.[62] This is somewhat at variance with overseas impressions of China as a tightly controlled society.

For several years, China has been a major supplier to India – directly or indirectly – of small arms, particularly pistols, Kalashnikovs and M16s. The circulation of small arms has reached the point where India is estimated to have 46 million pieces not in official hands.[63] Naxalite guerrillas in India, considered the country's most important domestic security threat, receive a significant proportion of their substantial arms supply from China, and China is believed to be the main arms supplier to other Indian rebel forces. The main routes seem to be through Burma and Nepal. By 2008 China had replaced Cambodia and Thailand as the principal weapons supplier to the Naxalites and dissident forces in Burma.[64] In 2010 the BBC reported that guns 'are manufactured under "an informal franchise" that Burma's rebel United Wa State Army (UWSA) has managed to secure from Chinese ordnance factories'.[65] Bangladeshi and Indian intelligence officials confirmed to the BBC that South Asian rebels had been sourcing Chinese weaponry through the UWSA.

The trade in arms is very closely linked with the trade in opium. A 2006 report on the South Asian arms trade claimed that drugs and arms have a symbiotic relationship and often travel in opposite directions along the same trails, with one often being used to finance the other.[66] China has been assiduously courting the military junta in Burma for energy, logistical and strategic reasons. It is difficult to believe that Beijing would willingly prejudice such overtures, even if the arms sales to the rebels are substantial. It may be, then, that the managers of Chinese arms factories have an unofficial (indeed covert) foreign trade policy. Alternatively, organised criminal elements may be acting as intermediaries.

China has openly bought and legally imported substantial amounts of Russian military equipment for many years. It is believed to have been Russia's largest customer in this vital industry for the last twenty years, taking over a third of its conventional arms exports.[67] Russia has little that the world particularly wants, apart from energy, raw materials and arms. Accordingly, it has built up an extensive international arms trade. When energy prices are low, the arms trade becomes even more important.

The first Chinese gun control regulations were introduced in 1966 and there has been a progressive tightening of laws on gun ownership as well as regular campaigns to 'crack down' on illicit possession. In the country's biggest gun-smuggling case since 1949, four people were sentenced to death in 2005 for importing 900 guns from Pakistan. In a four-month period in 2006, 178,000 guns and 4.75 million bullets were seized nationwide. That year, a judge was arrested for selling guns on the internet.[68]

When the public security ministry announced a campaign (including gun amnesties) against illegal guns between March and October 2008, 79,000 guns and 5.75 million rounds of ammunition were retrieved. Between August and October there was a crackdown on the sale of guns over the internet: 381 people were arrested, over 1,000 websites were shut down and about 120,000 related web pages were deleted. The public security ministry reportedly claimed in 2009 to have confiscated 3.8 million guns in recent years; that is more guns than there are soldiers in the entire Chinese army.[69] Seizures continued regularly through 2012, when police detained 7,800 people from 180 gangs and captured 100,000 guns in 150 cities. State media say that occasionally criminal gangs arm themselves from arsenals holding decommissioned military weapons. Presumably government arsenals are guarded, so it must be assumed that the criminals either break in or bribe their way in. A growing gun culture is developing in China. This derives from a number of sources: criminals seek weapons to take on the police; criminal possession of weapons often appears linked to drug-related and Triad activity; and crime causes rich businesspeople to seek protection.

Gun enthusiasts also make up a significant interest group and the *Small Arms* magazine boasts 60,000 subscribers. Five of China's 51 gold medals in the Beijing Olympics were for shooting events. It is estimated that in America, where privately held guns are legal, there may be 223 million guns: nearly one for every man, woman and child. The difference is that in China private gun ownership is virtually illegal, and yet guns are still in wide circulation. That said, a foreigner strolling through one of China's cities would find it hard to imagine a safer environment. Anti-social gun activity is virtually entirely internecine.

Considerations

The noted American magazine *Foreign Policy*, in its 2010 survey of 'failed states', places China at No. 57. But the authors seem not to have chosen the best indicators, and the overall result is frankly bizarre. Anyone who suggests that China in 2009 was more 'failed' than Mexico, Albania or Russia is either labouring under some prejudice or trapped in faulty methodology. What this chapter demonstrates is that China has a serious drug problem, a noticeable nationwide revival of organised criminal activity, a developing gun culture (both criminal and enthusiast), pervasive corruption and a potentially destabilising gender imbalance. In other words, it has serious problems that are commensurate with the size of its population. However, most are no more than that.

The authorities are properly concerned and are showing reasonable determination to deal with most of the issues. Corrupt local officials do, in some cases, interfere with the pursuit of justice; sometimes they are caught, sometimes not. As might be expected in a population of over a billion, some incidents are quite egregious. However, the problems are not out of line proportionally with similar social problems in many other developed and developing countries. The state still functions.

Wen Jiabao, in a two-hour interactive internet discussion with citizens in February 2009, said he believed clean government was the most important requirement for society. Corruption is certainly serious and it does generate strong anti-government feeling. Unlike the former Premier, however, I believe the future collateral damage from today's gender imbalance will present a greater challenge to China's social stability. Corruption could bring down the Party, but gender disparity could destabilise the whole country. That is one real risk to China's rise.

CHAPTER EIGHT

Threats to Civil Stability

This chapter seeks to address the issues which can have an impact on regime stability. It will certainly be the view of many that the present government has been competent and has presided over extraordinary growth in social and economic well-being; thus threats to the government are threats to China's rise. Furthermore, they will note the absence of a formal opposition and claim that the alternative is a descent into chaos. This convenient analysis anathematises dissidence. One point to make at the outset, however, is that even under an authoritarian regime like China's, leaders have to consider their domestic political options.

While the majority of Chinese may not be implacably opposed to Party rule, there are strong minorities, occasionally even containing violent elements, which have been willing to contest certain issues physically on the streets. It would be important if those potentially violent minorities turn from opposing local officials to becoming an organised opposition to the Party's rule. The groups are very diverse; that is their weakness, but it also makes it hard for the Party to formulate policy. I believe this opposition can be won over and co-opted – if the appropriate tactics are employed. If properly handled, none of the issues need either bring down the regime or threaten the nation's rise.

One of the self-created challenges the Party faces is its lack of a driving ideology. Wang Hui, a leading leftist critic, laments 'China's current depoliticisation . . . characterised by the party elite's effort to transform itself into the representative of special interests while still holding onto political power'.[1] Depoliticisation is an understandable and continuing theme in Wang's critique of today's China.

The Pew surveys regularly find more than 80 per cent of Chinese believe the country is going in the right direction. However, even if 90 per cent support the government, no one wants to see the remaining 135 million people on the streets demonstrating a different view!

We need to put this in context: the only other countries to enjoy over 60 per cent public satisfaction ratings with the economy in recent years have been Australia (once) and Egypt (once). America, Britain and Japan have public satisfaction ratings of around 20–30 per cent. The management of information may well play a part; nevertheless, when we talk of dissidence and the public's attitude to government, we need to be aware that, in terms of the economy, China has by far the most satisfied body of international public opinion surveyed.

The Party and government are confronted by various groups which would like more rights: internet access, religious rights, language rights, implementation of rights in the constitution, the right to cleaner air and water – even outright independence for their region. These groups are not only separate, but are quite distinct. If asked, they are often hostile to each other's goals. A rare 'multi-theatre' exception was the 2008 letter from twenty-nine Chinese intellectuals calling for talks with the Dalai Lama and an end to 'aggressive nationalism'.[2] Usually, no individual issue causes widespread national manifestations of public support.

By no means all protest is based on a liberal democratic critique of today's society and government. Autonomy and separatism are issues that present challenges to parliamentary democracies such as Spain, France and Britain. And much of the violent disorder in China has been in connection with the restructuring of SOEs, rising unemployment, compulsory land acquisition and a deteriorating environment. It might be said that all these phenomena result from the headlong development of the economy, restructuring and the unleashing of market forces: that if China had retained its old Marxist system, those severe dislocations would not have occurred. I do not mean the old system could have survived; I simply note that much of the protest is not against Marxist society, but against the transformation of that society into a market economy. We should see violent confrontation not as signifying anger with the rule of the Party but as anger at the current direction of Party policy. In other words, the avant-garde of violence are the losers in the ascent from Marxism, not the winners. Professor Yu Jianrong has stated bluntly: 'the most notable characteristic of rights defense activities is that they are battles over financial interests, and are not battles over power. No one is going out in the streets saying that the Communist Party must hand over its political power.'[3]

Increases in public security spending have been targeted on the central and western provinces, where there is poverty, and Tibetan and Muslim populations that could prove restive. Xinjiang in 2009 proved this initiative prescient.

It is, however, a major commitment, as it is the same amount as central government spends on healthcare.[4] Public security expenditure in 2010 increased to $84 billion, placing it above military spending; in 2012 it was $111 billion and still above military expenditure. It exceeded the entire budget for health, diplomacy and financial oversight.[5]

So far the authorities have managed to keep the lid on social unrest by, on the one hand, being cautiously sensitive to popular wishes and, on the other (if we are to believe government media), employing a mixture of threats, house arrest, riot police, tear gas, imprisonment, labour re-education camps and compulsory psychiatric treatment. For example, in December 2008, the state-owned *Beijing News* reported that officials in Xintai city, Shandong, had for several years abducted citizens who had lodged petitions and sent them to mental hospitals.[6]

The Chinese authorities intently studied the fall of communism in Eastern Europe and the subsequent 'colour' revolutions. They identified NGOs and lawyers as playing an important role in these; consequently there is little easing of the controls on their activities. It may be that, until recently, the role of the Church – Catholic in Poland; Protestant in East Germany – was relatively overlooked.

We might identify two varieties of protest or dissidence in China. There are those movements – rural protest, protest against corruption and against property confiscation – which, particularly when they affect the working classes, tend to lead to violence. This could also cover autonomy activists. On the other hand, there are the essentially non-violent movements – those agitating for greater internet freedom, free speech or political reform; those urging the authorities to count the number of children lost in the Sichuan earthquake or to assist the victims of melamine-contaminated milk; or the environmental protesters.

It is paradoxical that most violent demonstrators are not against the state, whereas many peaceful ones are, and it could be argued that the threat to regime legitimacy from articulate and well-publicised peaceful arguments is greater than from workers rioting in far-flung provinces. That may be the way the authorities' minds were working when, on Christmas Eve 2009, they sentenced Liu Xiaobo, a Chinese dissident who was calling for greater freedom and an end to one-party rule – or was it observation of the constitution – to eleven years in jail for subversion. However, a promising Party strategy could include co-opting those peaceful dissidents who do not wish to subvert the state. It may not be too surprising if the authorities eventually decide that environmental protesters and religious activists – different though they may be – are acceptable.

International and Chinese Views and the Nature of Dissent

The following, from the United Nations Human Rights Commission in 2009, raises some interesting questions about contemporary China:

> The UN High Commissioner for Human Rights Navi Pillay said . . . she was deeply concerned about the verdict and extremely harsh sentence in the trial of the prominent Chinese writer and human rights defender Liu Xiaobo, adding that this represents a serious setback for the protection and promotion of human rights in China. 'The conviction and extremely harsh sentencing of Liu Xiaobo mark a *further severe restriction* on the scope of freedom of expression in China,' Pillay said [my italics].[7]

When the *Financial Times* reported the sentence, it drew attention to the rising number of such cases, and referred to 'official figures showing a sharp increase in the number of arrests and convictions for 'endangering state security' – these doubled in 2008 over 2007 and were nearly five times higher than in 2005'.[8] *Le Figaro* in Paris highlighted some other prominent cases: in 1994, Wei Jingsheng, the democracy campaigner, was sentenced to fifteen years for 'counter-revolutionary crime'; in 2005, the journalist Shi Tao was sentenced to ten years for 'divulging state secrets'; and the following year the blind activist Cheng Guangcheng received four years for 'subversion' and 'troubling public order'.[9]

But why has there in recent years been an average of over 1,000 cases annually of 'endangering state security'?[10] What kind of citizen wants to endanger the security of the state – and why? Why, after over sixty years, are the benefits of the Communist Party government not more obvious to its people?

The authorities have long had the objective of maintaining stability in the country – a policy that is broadly in tune with the wishes and needs of the vast majority of the people. I suggested in the previous chapter that many people prize stability more highly than, say, universal suffrage or freedom of expression, and it is conventionally believed that Chinese public opinion strongly prefers stability over innovation, order over political experiment. While the Party conflates stability of the nation with stability of Party rule and the public's asseveration of the importance of stability is to avoid a re-emergence of conditions such as the Cultural Revolution, it is of course an unspoken irony that it was the government by the Party and its leader Mao that gave China the Cultural Revolution. However, this presupposes that the situation is an either/or one. But the government has never made a clear case for why it must be so. If the government successfully provides stability, the conditions may arise where all is possible – as in most Western countries, or Japan or Brazil. How can we be sure that instability is so close to the surface in contemporary China that people must choose between stability and, say, freer expression?

If the Qing dynasty could announce in 1902 that there would be national elections in 1912 – as it turns out, after they were overthrown – why do today's rulers feel the people are not ready, over a century later? It is unfortunate that, after sixty years of Communist Party rule, China still cannot enjoy both stability and freedom of expression. Does this suggest a degree of policy failure since 1949? But perhaps the official analysis is wrong: maybe the government has been more successful than it thinks and China is more stable than the government believes. In any case, does introducing democracy necessarily weaken a country? Might it not strengthen it?

It is not surprising that most people in China welcome stability, prize it and are willing to make sacrifices to maintain it. There is a strong view that the entire system is focused on prioritising stability, so that there can never again be a Cultural Revolution. However, there are many groups today which are disaffected and would like change – although they do not necessarily desire instability.

Mass Incidents

There is sustained debate on the internet over what constitutes a 'mass incident' in China and how many are now taking place. Mass incidents used to be well documented and analysed in reports and statements by the Ministry of Public Security, the police ministry. It used to publish annual statistics on those involving over a hundred people and where there is violence – what many would describe as a riot. However, the method of reporting changed in 2005, since when there have only been sporadic statements, using different definitions each time.

Public order disturbances are different from mass incidents and are defined to include acts by individuals, and they cover activities as diverse as gambling, computer hacking and corpse desecration. Although there is no longer regular reporting of mass disturbances, references by officials or academics suggest the overall number continues to rise. Professor Wang Erping at CASS studies mass incidents. His definition is unclear, but he claims there were 80,000 in 2007, rising to 90,000 in 2008.[11] In August 2009 he said that 'they haven't gone down'.[12] Professor Yu Jianrong, also at CASS, said in Beijing in 2009 that mass incidents had risen from 8,709 in 1993 to over 90,000 in 2009.[13] It is clear that large-scale public violence over the last twenty years has risen. As noted in the previous chapter, Professor Sun Liping of Tsinghua University estimated that the figure in 2010 was over 180,000.

Yu Jianrong gave an interesting and colourful lecture at the Ministry of Finance to the Beijing Lawyers Association in December 2009. In it he said that 'what is key is the increase in especially large mass incidents'.[14] He observed that this increase troubles the leadership: 'On the surface, we have great buildings being constructed, great highways being opened up, and everyone has this feeling of orioles singing and swallows darting [a feeling of great prosperity]; however, in actuality, these things [large mass incidents] are shaking the view the rulers have about the future of China.'

He divides mass incidents into categories for analysis. The first is the defence of rights: largely farmers' rights, workers' rights and urban citizens' rights. He gives several examples of rural incidents and says that nowadays they largely focus on conflicts over land expropriation. In support, he cites information from the government's 'Focus Issue Call Centre', which people can telephone to express their grievances. In 2008, this anger helped spur the 'farm privatisation' movement in the north-east, which has unilaterally declared areas of farmland to be the private property of those who farm them.[15] Yu highlights the role of women, and particularly the elderly, in rural protest, because they act as a restraint on the officials, who might otherwise use excessive force against demonstrators. Apparently, in 80–90 per cent of cases, the 'Mafia' are involved to the extent of even shooting farmers (it seems that, rather like 'Triads', this term is used as a synonym for organised crime). He points out the political risk to the leadership from rural anger.

Workers' problems are different, more varied and more sophisticated, including late payment of wages and industrial restructuring that can cause wholesale redundancy. Yu claims that, according to his understanding of the Party and the philosophy of national leaders, a trade union which represents workers' interests is what is feared the most, and no such union may be established. Workers accordingly choose other, often quite sophisticated, ways to protest. One method is 'taking a walk'. The Anyuan coal miners, for example, tried requesting a pay rise; then they wrote to ask permission for a demonstration; then they sent a petition group to Beijing; but that group was detained by the police. Their final move was to arrange for 20,000 people to 'take a walk' to a nearby city. At that point the chairman of the company was removed by the police and the miners resumed work. Subsequently the technique has enjoyed some popularity, being used by environmental activists in Xiamen and Chengdu.

Sophisticated measures which avoid breaking the law are one approach. However, there has been a tendency towards greater violence in conflicts involving workers. The 2009 Tonghua Iron and Steel case is notorious: while the company was being restructured, the workers killed the general manager.

Afterwards it was not uncommon for protesting industrial workers elsewhere to shout slogans referring to Tonghua (and many bosses choose to be absent during restructuring). Urban residents' protests largely revolve around compulsory house demolition. Yu predicts that 'mass incidents sparked by city residents' rights defense activities will increase', adding ominously that 'everyone should pay close attention to this'.

The second form of mass incident is what Yu terms 'venting', or rising anger at officials and the rich. Such people are assailed verbally (and sometimes physically) – often for no clear reason. The characteristics of a 'venting incident' are that no specific demand is made, and there are no organisers: the event is spontaneous, sparked by something trivial. Police and government buildings may be damaged or destroyed, but crowds can disperse as quickly as they form. It bears some resemblance to the Western phenomenon of 'flash mobbing'.

The third category Yu terms 'rabble-rousing'. This might start with an event associated with the government that causes public anger, then spill over into attacks on unrelated parties, such as looting a supermarket. Yu refers to Tibetan and Xinjiang protest as rabble-rousing sparked by ideology. This is because victims of incidents can be quite unrelated to officialdom.

Yu develops the definitions further. Rights defence activity has a relatively clear material request and is directed at those who have inflicted harm and also at the government. Venting makes no material request and projects anger and resentment more towards government in general, but partly towards those who inflict specific harm. Venting freely violates the law, but not social morality: if you are not involved, you won't be harmed. Rabble-rousing targets completely unrelated parties: it violates the law and social morality.[16]

It is a popular exercise in the foreign media to link data on mass incidents with a consistent opposition to government authority. However, that is easily overdone: opposition to corruption, pollution or unpaid wages is directed not at the Party, but at employers or local officials. And any protest against local government is most unlikely to target the central leadership. The closest example of a national movement was the loosely coordinated series of urban taxi strikes which erupted in 2008 all the way from Chongqing to Guangzhou.

Some Individual Incidents in Recent Years

In 'the Dongzhou incident' in 2005, the state news agency Xinhua reported that 130 armed villagers led by a number of ringleaders used 'knives, steel, spears, sticks, dynamite powder, bottles filled with petroleum, and fishing detonators' to launch an attack on a Guangdong wind power plant.[17] They were protesting at local government land seizure. Three villagers were shot and a number were jailed. Human Rights Watch described this as 'the most serious government assault on public protesters since the Tiananmen massacre'.[18]

In 2008, there was a seemingly extraordinary event. A schoolgirl found dead in a river was widely believed to have been raped by relatives of an official. Local officials denied it and there were three successive autopsies. All found she had drowned. According to state media: 'Up to 30,000 people took part in the mass action in Weng'an county of Guizhou province on Saturday, torching government buildings and smashing and burning cars.'[19] Eventually the official verdict was confirmed as drowning, yet, in tacit acknowledgement of wrong-doing, four local officials were fired. What is arresting is that up to 30,000 people should riot in the presumed belief that officials were lying and covering up a murder. This indicates a low level of confidence in official integrity.

Further riots in 2008 also shook officials. Wudu town in remote Gansu province saw thousands of citizens stride through the streets with rocks, axes and iron bars to attack police in riot gear, and government offices. They were protesting over land redevelopment plans and claims of embezzlement of earthquake relief funds. A 2010 Tsinghua University report said: 'When fierce social protests occur, some local governments quickly put the police in the front line. This does not help to ease the conflict but adds fuel to the fire and leads to a confrontation between the people and the police. . .'[20]

Student Protest

Tiananmen Square

Although the events of Tiananmen Square occurred well over twenty years ago, in June 1989, their resonance does not fade, and the subject is brought up in any discussion of China and civil rights overseas.

To recap briefly: huge numbers of students and many workers had been demonstrating for days in Tiananmen Square and the area around, which leads in one direction to Zhongnanhai, the extensive walled compound where leading officials work. The conduct of government was impeded. There were also reportedly protests in 132 other cities.[21] The protests mixed demands for greater civil rights with concerns about official corruption and rising inflation. It would be quite wrong to see the movement as being solely about political reform. However, the pervasive perception of out-of-control corruption and abuse of power led to desire for political change. The demonstrators were unarmed but unwilling to obey the authorities. Workers got involved, including those from non-state companies like Stone Corporation. Every segment of society was represented there apart from the peasants.[22] The fact that the

Tiananmen dissidents received such extensive and favourable coverage in state media in April and May 1989 suggests that there may have been high-level support for their activism.

In 1989 Communist governments in Europe were showing signs of collapse and there was considerable nervousness in the ranks of China's leaders. The sons of some national leaders in Beijing were supposedly stockpiling arms at home in case of trouble – a story I heard from friends who knew the people involved. After days of dithering and mixed signals, the leaders eventually sent in troops to clear the square: tanks, armoured personnel carriers and troops with live ammunition. Of all the myriad estimates of casualties, to me the most realistic was from a professor who sympathised with the demonstrators and who was there that night. He put the figure at 775. This matches the 2012 statement of Chen Xitong, Beijing Party Secretary at the time, who was later jailed.[23]

Some officers and men refused to shoot unarmed civilians and were subsequently court-martialled – the most prominent being General Xu Qinxian of the 38th Army Group.[24] There were some '111 serious breaches of discipline by PLA officers at or above the level of company commanders . . . [and] in total 1,500–3,000 officers were investigated for possible breaches of discipline during the martial law period'.[25] Many Party members working in government were required to spend months attending ideological study classes after work to reinforce their awareness of the Party's views. Many who were deemed to have been insufficiently supportive through the upheaval were transferred to lesser positions. Interestingly, some have made it back to far higher positions today.

Without in any way minimising the event, we should not forget that just nineteen years before, in 1970, US National Guard troops had killed four unarmed students and wounded nine others at Kent State University in Ohio. No one seems to have given the order to fire there and no one was found guilty. Ten days later there was a similar incident at Jackson State University in Mississippi. While the number of victims in the US was a tiny fraction of the number in China, these armed attacks do raise some of the same issues associated with Tiananmen Square.

Memories of that night in Tiananmen Square live on down the years. The 4 June 2008 edition of the *Chengdu Evening News* contained a short classified advertisement: 'Saluting the strong-willed mothers of June 4th victims.' When interviewed, one such mother said:

The Government should realise that June 4th is a topic they can't cover up. For the past 18 years the authorities have adopted a policy of making people forget and that is why they are unaware. But the longer they cover it up, the higher will be the price they pay in the end.[26]

Despite the number of casualties, the overwhelming majority of middle-class Chinese seemed to take the view that mass protest and challenge to authority was something to be sternly faced down. This was doubtless part of the legacy of coming of age during the chaos of the Cultural Revolution.

To reiterate: stability is prized over many other things.

We don't know what the public response to a similar event would be today, after twenty years of prosperity and stability. In mainland China Tiananmen is rarely mentioned (in stark contrast to the West and, particularly, Hong Kong). But here we should remember the passage of time: today's Chinese students were mostly unborn in 1989. It is not a question of what they remember about Tiananmen Square; it is what they have been told or heard about it – or rather, perhaps, what they have not been told about it.

Where Did All the Students Go?

It is perhaps rather remarkable that, in an environment where general incidents of protest seem to have been increasing in number, student protest appears largely to have been quiescent. Since Tiananmen Square we have seen few mass student protests.

Anecdotal evidence suggests that the current calm amongst students – except for anti-Japanese irredentism – might be because economic imperatives trump political issues. In recent years, millions of graduates have found it impossible to get on the employment ladder. It is tempting to draw a parallel with Britain, where the absence of political protest tends to coincide with rising graduate unemployment. It does seem (possibly counter-intuitively) that students do not protest so much when they are faced with the prospect of unemployment as when they are confident. Indeed, the prospect of unemployment seems to raise the appeal for Chinese students of joining the Communist Party to assist their job hunt. Consciously or not, the Party may have got the conditions right by engineering a massive oversupply of graduates.

Currently student insurrection seems to present no serious challenge to the Party: graduate unemployment is likely to lead to more conventional behaviour. We should not, of course, equate rising Party membership in a high unemployment environment with growing political support (although we might expect some conformity). However, currently there seem to be no large areas of student dissatisfaction, aside from poor job prospects and a degree of nationalism. Anti-Japanese protest has been seen as licensed practising for 'the real thing'. Should youthful dissent rise, it may be associated with nationalist anger at some perceived weak government response to an overseas challenge or with a failure by the state to confront environmental disasters.

Autonomy and Independence

While some protest against corrupt local behaviour, others campaign for greater regional autonomy or even independence. It is sometimes difficult for westerners to comprehend the sharp official denunciations of those who demand autonomy or independence: they are called 'splittists' and are deemed guilty of 'subversion'. In Britain, the First Minister of Scotland heads a party dedicated to achieving Scottish independence, yet he has never been charged with any crime. It is not always clear to people in the West why, after several millennia of civilisation, China cannot have measured domestic debate about the location of frontiers, the question of secession or political reform.

The main pressure for autonomy and independence comes from the Tibetans, the Uighurs of Xinjiang and the Mongolians of Inner Mongolia (although this last group seems relatively peaceful). Here race, language and religion play important roles, and there are some passing references to democracy. The Tibetans and Mongolians are Buddhist, while the Uighurs are Muslim. Probably over half of all Tibetans live outside Tibet, and indeed the Sichuan earthquake occurred in a partly 'Tibetan' area. Strong indigenous feelings are roused by the Han Chinese practice of settling in Tibet, Inner Mongolia and Xinjiang. In the decade of the 1950s alone, immigration into Inner Mongolia was equivalent to a third of the then population;[27] by 2000, there were almost five Han to every Mongol. Demands for independence are treated as crimes against the state, and as such attract long sentences. But a lot of residents in Xinjiang and Tibet appear to feel that those regions are run by Han Chinese for the benefit of Han Chinese.

Xinjiang

The very name 'Xinjiang' can mean 'new dominion'.[28] From 104 BC until the eighth century the region was in fairly constant flux: sometimes the Chinese were in charge; at other times they were expelled. At the Battle of Talas River in 751, the Chinese were thrown out for good by a combined army of Arab, Uighur and Tibetan warriors. The Uighur royal house assisted the Tang dynasty in surviving the subsequent An Lushan rebellion, and this led to China paying tribute to the Uighurs.[29] Xinjiang was then alternately independent or under Kitan or Mongol sovereignty. In 1759, the Manchu Qing dynasty conquered Xinjiang. It was administered by a special office with no Chinese officials. There were various Uighur uprisings (the most important being put down by the Manchus only with the benefit of very large loans from the Hong Kong and Shanghai Bank).[30] Finally in 1884 Xinjiang was nominally integrated into occupied China.

When the Qing dynasty fell in 1912, Xinjiang found itself theoretically under Han government, though in effect it was an autonomous, non-democratic entity within republican China. The Uighurs and their fellow Muslims, the Hui, rose up in the 1930s and again in the 1940s to recover their independence, using the title 'East Turkestan'. However, these initiatives were later suppressed. Since then, there has been a history of separatist incidents: in the 1960s, the 1980s and the 1990s. The tempo increased after 2000. Following the 2001 World Trade Center attack in New York, China persuaded President Bush to classify the separatist East Turkestan Islamic Movement (ETIM) as a terrorist organisation, to encourage China to join 'the war against terror'.

Friction in Xinjiang seems to be associated with circumscription of language use and religious activity.[31] There are also grumbles about jobs going to Han migrants rather than local natives. The government's analysis of Uighur discontent focuses on economic issues. While these do have some relevance, the Party needs to get away from a purely Marxist analysis and understand that culture and religion can be of driving importance to people. It is clear, though, that Beijing's policy changes have contributed:

> Beginning in the mid-1980s, Beijing began to shift from cultural accommodation towards an overt policy of assimilation. This shift only served to reinforce both Uyghur nationalism and small separatist movements, with potential to undermine the territorial integrity of the PRC and the Chinese effort to build a modern Chinese nation. This policy shift has been counterproductive.[32]

Procuratorial Daily, an official newspaper in China, apparently disclosed that in the first eleven months of 2008 there were 1,295 arrests in Xinjiang alone for 'endangering state security' – roughly three times the number in 2007.[33] Over half of all such arrests were in Xinjiang province. China says it is battling three issues: separatism, terrorism and religious extremism. In 2008, an attack in Kashgar killed seventeen paramilitary officers and wounded fifteen others. Two militants were arrested. Afterwards, Wang Lequan, the then Party secretary for Xinjiang and a Politburo member, said the battle against the three forces was a 'life or death struggle'.[34] Given the substantial resources of the Chinese state, this suggests that there is serious support for the militants. In 2009, the government decided to increase security spending by over \$4 billion, mainly to strengthen security in Tibet and Xinjiang. Thus, the July 2009 outbreak of violence in Xinjiang, which saw around 200 people killed, was not unexpected.

What is going on in Xinjiang? Simon Shen, a Chinese professor in Hong Kong, compares Xinjiang and Algeria: in 1950s Algeria, many Muslims believed that adopting France's 'universal values' would entail sacrificing their own identity. The movement snowballed until independence. Internationally, reaction to the 2009 rioting was fairly muted. The responses from Muslim countries, such as Saudi Arabia and Iran, were probably restrained by their increasing trade and diplomatic ties with China. Turkey was the most outspoken, as it has cultural, linguistic and (possibly) ethnic links with the Uighurs: its trade minister suggested boycotting Chinese goods. As the power in charge, Beijing has the ability to set the terms of debate on Xinjiang's future. However, it seems to have been decided that there should be no inclusive debate. One major problem with not providing space for peaceful political opposition is that it encourages violent opposition.

Tibet

Chinese authority over Tibet has brought substantial change to the Tibetans' traditional way of life. It has also led to religious practice in their country being controlled by a political group that does not share their beliefs – and indeed claims to be atheist. When, in 1995, the Dalai Lama validated the choice of the Panchen Lama (the second most important figure in Tibetan Buddhism), the child was whisked away by the Chinese authorities and never shown in public again. Beijing then worked with some dissident monks to find an alternative.

In 2007, China enacted a law that all reincarnations of senior lamas were subject to Chinese government approval. This has sparked concern that Beijing will intervene in the selection of the Dalai Lama's successor. The Dalai Lama has said that he does not plan to be reincarnated in a country which is not free (though under the precepts of Buddhism it is uncertain how much influence he would have in the matter). He implied that his reincarnation could take place outside Tibet, could be as a woman, and could even occur before his death. The message appears to be that Tibetan Buddhists will probably look for his successor in India, and the Dalai Lama might have an important say in the choice. In 2007, the Chinese authorities stated that senior Tibetan Buddhists could not be reincarnated outside China and not without government recognition. It is not known if Buddhism allows anyone to dictate where reincarnation of a Dalai Lama (or any other senior Buddhist) will take place – whether Beijing or the current Dalai Lama.

As the most important Tibetan Buddhist monastery outside Chinese control, the Tawang monastery on the Chinese border with north-east India is likely to be critical in choosing the next Dalai Lama. This is helping to keep the Sino-Indian border issue simmering, as China eyes the territory around Tawang (see Chapter 11).

Unrest exploded in Tibet in 2008, but no neighbouring state will provide military support or sustenance for any insurrection. India provides a home for the Dalai Lama, but does not wish its borders to become a war zone. In fact, India would prefer to see a settlement of the disputed border area. It might later be offered a deal, provided it expels the Dalai Lama.

Inner Mongolia

Inner Mongolia has had a much less restive recent past. The main complaints there are about a curb on freedom of speech and use of the native language, and restrictions on the traditional livelihood of herding in the wake of measures to prevent the continuing spread of desertification. Some restriction seems reasonable. Da Lintai of CASS said in 2009 that the province has twice the number of animals it can reasonably support – 62 million cows, sheep and goats.[35] And environmentalists agree. In 2011, several thousand ethnic Mongolians protested about the lack of action over the killing of a herdsman who had been demonstrating against coal trucks destroying grassland.[36]

Summary

There is a high level of Han settlement in Tibet, Xinjiang and Inner Mongolia. Although they have a much higher birth rate, the feeling is common to all three indigenous communities that they will be outnumbered in their homelands by Han settlement. They believe that the increased prosperity has accrued more to the Han than to the local residents, but material development is not anyway necessarily their top aspiration.

In all three areas, we are likely to see intermittent hostilities for the foreseeable future (though probably at a much lower level in Inner Mongolia). As neither the Mongols nor the Tibetans have much realistic prospect of tangible external assistance in their aspirations for autonomy, they are unlikely to be any real challenge to the Chinese state. The only community which is likely to receive outside help in any direct action against the Chinese authorities is that of the Uighurs. China sees some evidence, but we should assume that any further deterioration of the situation in Central Asia will probably increase the likelihood of military and financial assistance to the Uighurs from externally based radical Islamic sources. As Abu Yahya al-Libi, a senior al-Qaeda official, said in autumn 2009: 'It is a duty for Muslims today to stand by their wounded and oppressed brothers in East Turkestan . . . and support them with all they can.'[37]

Although this hostility to the state of China may not immediately translate into action, the Quilliam Foundation, which promotes non-violent Muslim initiatives, noted in 2010 that 'China's Xinjiang province, as well as the Uighur diaspora, is being increasingly targeted by radical groups ranging from Hizb ut-Tahrir to al-Qaeda seeking to exploit the situation for their own ends.'[38]

It would be ironic if Beijing's policies actually serve to radicalise the Muslim population in Xinjiang.

The 2010 replacement of Wang Lequan, the long-standing Party secretary in Xinjiang, opened the way to a shift in policy. If Beijing could understand and address the local non-economic as well as economic needs, there was the chance to rewrite the relationship with the Muslim population and build a more stable and contented society.

Cantonese Dissidence

Here is a very different kind of dissidence – in the Han heartland. The summer of 2010 in Guangzhou, or Canton, was marked by demonstrations in support of Cantonese language, culture, architectural heritage and associated themes. Protests occurred on both sides of the Hong Kong border and neighbours crossed the border to participate jointly in the demonstrations. There was a clear political undertone. One professor from Sun Yat-sen University in Guangzhou said: 'It is no coincidence that the rallies in defence of Cantonese involved mostly the post-80s generation. I think this is exactly what Guangzhou has left to offer the rest of the country, that is, a civil society framework that is tolerant and liberal, embracing individual rights against a strong imposing force from above.'[39] Months later, young people were still being detained and interrogated for any knowledge they might have of the movement. Mobilisation of young people, whatever the purpose, causes distinct nervousness among the authorities.

Faith-based Dissidence

Religion is officially tolerated, but is supervised. It is divided into Catholicism (including Orthodoxy), Protestantism, Islam, Buddhism and Daoism. Government officials oversee worship, staffing, buildings and format. Many believers find this intolerable, but it is not unique to Communist Party rule: it happened under the Ming and the Qing, and happens today in many Muslim countries. In the nineteenth century, Hegel commented: '. . . true faith is possible only where individuals can seclude themselves – can exist for themselves independently of any external compulsory power. In China the individual has no such life; does not enjoy this independence.'[40]

There are reportedly 130,000 religious institutions in this officially atheist country. Some religions are seen as constituting a threat, others – for example

Daoism and Buddhism – are not. Confucianism, while not transcendental, is regarded by some as having some of the features of a religion. It is, however, envisaged by certain intellectuals as a potential future pillar of the state. I write here of those religions which are thought to present more of a challenge to the Party-state.

Islamic Cultural Protest

Estimates differ widely as to the number of Muslims in China – from 18 to 40 or more million.[41] Islam has, at times, been a highly influential element in society. Many governors and vice governors in the Yuan dynasty were Muslim; Khubilai Khan's architect who rebuilt Beijing was Muslim; even the native Ming dynasty employed Muslims in prominent positions. The great admiral Zheng He, who took China's fleet to East Africa, was Muslim. Now Islam languishes as a backwater of national statistics, with little discernible impact outside the provision of distinctive restaurants in most cities and an association with occasional incidents. Islam is not simply an issue in Xinjiang. It also provides a specific view of society, usually invisible but occasionally coming to the surface. For example, in 2010 several thousand Muslims in Gansu smashed a new clubhouse on the grounds that it offered offensive services such as prostitution.[42]

Any sympathy in the Islamic world for a perceived ill-treatment or marginalisation of Muslims in China has been successfully muted by China's economic emergence: it can be a big brother to Pakistan in its interminable struggle with India; it strikes energy deals with Iran and Saudi Arabia; and it is steadily increasing its involvement in Muslim Central Asia.

Christian Evangelicalism

Because it proselytises, Evangelical Protestantism is now the largest and fastest-growing form of Christianity in the country. It exists predominantly outside the state-sanctioned Christian organisation, which allows for Protestant or Catholic and Orthodox worship. Evangelical Protestantism tends to operate through informal 'house churches', which are occasionally suppressed but often tolerated by the authorities. Some have congregations of 4,000.[43] Harassment is unpredictable but severe. Landlords can be pressured to deny facilities, even when paid for, and congregations have been obliged to hold services in the snow.[44] People can be forcibly dispersed, merely for celebrating their religion.

Studies have been made of the success of this evangelicalism, and it appears that 60–90 per cent of new members may come as a result of pre-existing social networks: 'when the political environment is laden with uncertainty, as in a corroding state socialist regime, networks reduce risk'.[45] There are parallels here with the situation in Communist East Germany and Poland. Nonetheless, much recruitment is done amongst complete strangers. Evangelising can take place, and does, on university campuses, in hotels and in farming areas. There are underground Bible schools to help future leaders prepare themselves. Yu Jianrong thinks there may be 50 million participants.[46] He makes the excellent point that, because the house churches have to operate underground in secret (because they will not accept supervision), there is no awareness of what they are teaching and what they think. This is very dangerous. It is better for society that all elements operate openly. His view is that it would be safer for China to offer simple registration in return for becoming public – this need be no more onerous or intrusive than registering a church in Illinois with the Fire Department. A further concern of the authorities is that these churches are often attended by intellectuals and human rights lawyers who defend activists unpalatable to the state.

The official line on religion in general has metamorphosed: in 1949 the expectation was that it would die out; then it was accepted as a relic that needed to be controlled; now there is a move to harness it, to an extent, as a force for social good. But there is still unease as it, by definition, is centred on belief in a force which is more important than man or state – or Party. However, the Party seems to have decided that the two movements need not be on hostile terms. With the abatement of the Party's atheistic fervour, the evangelical movement could well be ripe for officials to consider co-opting it into the power structure.

Daoism

For interest, I mention here Daoism which is a religion felt to offer few challenges to the Party. In 2011, the Communist Party had discussions with Daoist officials for the first time about how traditional wisdom could be brought to bear on the rampant incidence of consumerism, social excess and moral failing in society. A senior official in the State Administration for Religious Affairs said: 'We can get some inspiration from Daoism in the period of globalization . . . We are concerned not just for environmental protection, but also for heart and soul protection.'[47] It is difficult to imagine this being said twenty years ago.

Falun Gong

Falun Gong is an avowedly non-religious movement, with no formal hierarchy – no priests and no churches. Based on meditation and breathing exercises, it was founded in the late 1980s by Li Hongzhi, a former clerk in the Grain

Bureau. In the late 1990s, government put membership at about 70 million, exceeding membership of the Party.[48] Hu Jintao, then the Vice President, said that, of 2.1 million adherents identified, a third were Party members.[49] As only about 5 per cent of the population belong to the Party, the movement appears to have appealed disproportionately strongly to Party members.

Falun Gong came to prominence in 1999, when 10–30,000 supporters surrounded the state leaders' compound, Zhongnanhai, in Beijing, close to Tiananmen Square. Members claim that the demonstration was impromptu and not organised by Li Hongzhi. It was to protest against critical press articles and growing restriction on the movement's activities: there appear to have been no demands of a political nature. 'Falun Gong is reactive, defensive and politically conservative. Like many forms of religious fundamentalism, it is not a purveyor of a "social project". Yet it turns out to be the most politicized and highly mobilized form of social contestation in post-1989 China.'[50] This was the first large-scale organised, non-official 'event' since Tiananmen Square, and Falun Gong found itself in a rather unconservative position.

There is perhaps a parallel with an incident in 1813, when around seventy-five peasants – adherents of the secret sect of the Eight Trigrams – broke into the Forbidden City with hidden knives and a plan to raise a rebellion.[51] Supreme power can never entirely rest easy. In 1999, the authorities reacted severely, even though the demonstrators were peaceful and did not break in. Falun Gong was declared illegal and – later – counter-revolutionary. A special office was set up solely to prosecute members.

Li Hongzhi is in exile in New York and Falun Gong is banned in China. Its sympathisers recanted, fled, went to ground or were jailed. Charges have been made that a number of imprisoned adherents have had their organs used for medical purposes. The American Embassy in Beijing investigated but could find no evidence of this.[52] Amnesty International has reported several cases of torture in detention, while the US State Department has noted that prisoners were 'subjected to harsh treatment in prisons and reeducation-through-labour camps, and there were credible reports of deaths due to torture and abuse'.[53]

The Chinese authorities have been successful at discrediting Falun Gong inside China and preventing association with other protest groups. The movement has, however, shown ability and innovation in challenging the state's media dominance, using subversive tactics such as hacking and replacing web content to convey opposing messages. The organisation had not been accused of any violent or subversive activities until it was banned. Its crime was to engage in a large-scale mobilisation right outside the leadership compound in Beijing. This looked to the Party like a direct challenge from a movement which had a mass membership. It was not the aims of Falun Gong or any ille-gality; it was the mere fact of its existence and scale that was the problem. The peaceful mass mobilisation in April 1999 simply crystallised the already growing concern among many leaders about the reach of this independent movement. Although there are supporters still 'at large' in China, and although it publishes a newspaper internationally, Falun Gong does not give the impres-sion of having the reach internally that it used to have.

Event-driven Protest

The Environment

Figures are not released every year, but the Ministry of Public Security has cited environmental pollution as one of the main causes of violent unrest, or mass incidents, in the country: for instance, there appear to have been 60,000 protests in 2006 connected with the environment.

People complain about planned chemical plants and railway developments; they also protest about the noxious results of some of the projects after they have commenced operations. The environment is one of the few issues to excite students on university campuses. The authorities' nervousness of above-board non-official NGO activity could lead to the creation of unmonitored organisa-tions. As with the house churches, if environmental NGOs are obliged to operate underground, and thus unobserved, their objectives may start to extend beyond the environment and they could be the starting point for a more broad-based protest movement. The environmental movement has certainly provided some quite radical activists in other countries.

While the Chinese government may broadly concur with many of the envi-ronmentalists' demands, it may not be able to deliver quickly enough and so could find itself under pressure. The ultimate challenge to the Party may not be democracy but the environment: one can live without the vote, but not without clean water or fresh air.

The Sichuan Earthquake

Natural disasters spark huge sympathy for the victims. After the 2008 Sichuan earthquake, which left up to 88,000 people dead or missing and around 5 million homeless, Chinese people gave large amounts of assistance in cash and kind. The Tangshan earthquake of 1976 was barely reported, but nowadays China is sufficiently open that it is difficult to hush up bad news. What is less well reported is that the parents of 58 of the 5,000 or more children who died when their classrooms and dormitories collapsed have taken contractors and officials to court for substandard construction – described by those involved as 'tofu construction'.

In June 2008, parents gathered in school grounds to grieve for their children. In one incident they shouted slogans about corrupt local politicians; in another they staged a sit-in; and in a third they were expelled by soldiers. In Dujiangyan, a dusty and nondescript Sichuan city, 600 people asked for justice for the dead and punishment for the contractors. In December it was reported that the courts had rejected the cases. There were claims that the plaintiffs had been threatened by local officials, nervous of charges of corruption. Parents have reportedly been warned that if they continue to seek compensation and to meet foreign journalists, they will be jailed.

Ai Weiwei, co-designer of the 'Birds' Nest' Olympic stadium in Beijing, announced in 2009 that he had set up a website to gather information and create an accurate tally of the children who died in the earthquake. He later stated that the children's deaths were a direct result of local officials diverting funds from school building programmes for their personal use.[54] When he sought to testify in a Sichuan court, he was beaten in his hotel room by police and suffered a brain haemorrhage (heroically, he said the beating was 'probably the result of local confusion').[55] This is quite typical. Across the country local officials are afraid to expose cases of suspected abuse to the scrutiny of the courts. Paradoxically, it is likely that top national leaders would be strengthened in popular esteem if they were more zealous in rooting out failings in the lower ranks of officials.

Rights, Expression and Participation

There is general concern about what happens to those who are detained by the authorities. Manfred Nowak, the UN Rapporteur on Torture, visited China in 2005 and said afterwards that he considered torture to be widespread.[56]

China engendered one of the more remarkable newspaper headlines of 2010: 'Police torture a sackable offence, new law says.'[57] In 2010, Nowak's report to the UN General Assembly detailed his criticisms of China for the prevalence of torture, but pointed out that many other countries have similar problems. These are usually poorer, developing countries.[58] However, it is worth noting that in 2006 some 1,300 people died from accident, suicide or homicide in US state or local prisons or (a third of them) in the course of arrest.

Chinese state media devoted quite a lot of attention during 2009 and 2010 to the number of deaths in detention centres and prisons. Reportedly, the Ministry of Justice is seeking control of detention centres currently run by the

Ministry of Public Security – a very powerful body in today's China. In March 2009, former Chinese Vice Minister of Justice Duan Zhengkun criticised torture in prisons after two prisoners were beaten to death.[59] In the first case, that of Li Qiaoming, the authorities initially claimed the prisoner had died in a game of 'hide and seek'. After an internet outcry, an official investigation revealed that he had been beaten to death. The excuses that the public security ministry has come up with for deaths in custody have made it an object of scorn inside and outside the country: people have purportedly perished after falling into a lavatory; they have drowned in a washbasin and have died after drinking boiling water while undergoing interrogation. According to Amnesty International, the famous activist against compulsory land seizures, Ni Yulan, had her kneecaps and feet broken in detention.[60] The outcry became so great that in 2010 Meng Jianzhu, Minister of Public Security, had to speak up: 'Recently, unnatural deaths occurred successively in certain places . . . This has seriously harmed the public's confidence in law enforcement by police authorities.'[61] Perhaps surprisingly, officials are willing to engage in measured conversations with overseas campaigners on behalf of dissidents who have been imprisoned in China. This doesn't mean they will take action, but they are willing to acknowledge and discuss individual cases. Cheng Lei, at the law school of the People's University in Beijing, has proposed 'an independent medical system that would examine detainees when they enter and leave the centres and make independent evaluations of deaths'.[62]

There are events from time to time which galvanise interest among intellectuals in subjects related to the expression of views or the political process. In 2008 an initiative called Charter 08 called for the 'rapid establishment of a free, democratic and constitutional country'. This doesn't seem particularly controversial but the authorities declared it 'counter-revolutionary' and all mention of the Charter is reportedly blocked from websites, search engines and even emails. After just a few months, over 8,000 intellectuals had signed the Charter. As well as calling for change, they put forward political analysis. Organisers of the initiative said of recent incidents (such as the threats to the Sichuan earthquake parents): 'As these conflicts and crises grow ever more intense . . . the decline of the current system has reached the point where change is no longer optional.' Indeed, they warn of 'the possibility of a violent conflict of disastrous proportions' if reform does not occur soon: one organiser, Liu Xiaobo, has (as mentioned earlier in this chapter) been jailed.

Controversial elements in the area of public order are the city administrators or *chengguan*, who enforce regulations amongst street vendors and assist in enforcing compulsory property acquisitions. *China Daily* ran a series of articles on the *chengguan* between 2006 and 2009. They are known for their violent assaults on street vendors: five were dismissed for beating a 28-year-old peddler, causing brain damage. Apparently a training manual for *chengguan* officers offered 'instructions' on how to 'physically subdue offenders as swiftly as possible without leaving bloodstains on their faces and bruises on their bodies'. The manager of a construction firm in Tianmen, Hubei province, was reportedly beaten to death after refusing to delete from his mobile phone a video recording of a confrontation between the officials and locals.[63] In 2011, hundreds rioted in Anshun, in Guizhou, after a one-legged street vendor was beaten to death by three *chengguan* officers as he resisted attempts to close his business. The Chinese website Youku showed photographs of bloodied demonstrators and heavily armed police.[64] One of the more surprising events was a violent clash in 2010, reported in the Party's *Global Times*, between *chengguan* and residents of a police dormitory due for demolition – the residents included members of the Ministry of Public Security.[65] We might think that the detailed circulation of news digests which goes to Party leaders would include such articles from *China Daily* and *Global Times* and they could form a view as to whether this is the society they wish to sponsor.

In 2011, a number of incidents in Beijing saw Western reporters – very unusually – being beaten in the streets. Foreign Minister Yang Jiechi chose to state that 'there is no such issue as Chinese police officers beating foreign journalists' – possibly rather unwisely, given the number of witnesses and the video footage circulating worldwide.[66]

Professor Jerome Cohen, a China legal specialist at New York University School of Law, has noted that, during Bo Xilai's Chongqing anti-corruption crackdown, police actually carried out 'a systematic and lengthy torture programme that coerced suspects caught up in the campaign against "gangsters" to confess even to crimes they may not have committed'.[67] Indeed there were reports that local Party secretary Bo had ordered several investigators (who viewed his wife as a murder suspect) to be tortured; three died.[68] The drive to restore law and order seemed to end in total lawlessness.

The Internet

The Open Net Initiative, co-sponsored by Harvard Law School, summarises internet control in China thus:

> As China's Internet community continues to grow exponentially, the government continues to refine its technical filtering system . . . including users, ISPs [internet service providers] and content providers, to limit the ability of its citizens to access and post content the state considers sensitive. A complex,

overlapping system of legal regulation, institutionalized practices, and informal methods has been extended from print and broadcast media to the Internet.[69]

In 2010, Google announced that it did not wish to continue censoring its services in China. Many analysts felt this stance was self-indulgent and deleterious to shareholders. Others hailed it as effectively a reality check for international companies doing business in China. Are they willing to operate under a repressive system? Does it not say something about China if it will not provide an environment in which a respected company such as Google is willing to work?

The catalyst for Google was that Gmail accounts, specifically those of human rights and other dissident activists, were hacked into. Google said that these attacks originated inside China, and there were reportedly indications that Chinese intelligence had been behind them.[70] According to *The Times*, the breadth and scope of the attacks indicated they were almost certainly the work of the Chinese state, and McAfee, the internet security company, said the attacks displayed a sophistication characteristic of a nation state.

China denied being behind the attacks and pointed out that hacking is illegal. The victims were left wondering who else would have the capability to launch a cyber attack of this sophistication from within China without the authorities noticing and prosecuting; who else would be interested in aggressively monitoring the activities of human rights activists; and, since it is a crime, what is the state doing about it? Google didn't seem to have been apprised of any investigation.

Of 780 Chinese scientists polled, 84 per cent said their research would be somewhat or significantly impaired by the withdrawal of Google.[71] One Chinese blogger wrote: 'It's not Google that is withdrawing from China – it's China that's withdrawing from the world.' Other companies didn't feel they needed to revisit their 'core corporate values'. Almost immediately after its announcement, Google started to dismantle its censoring filters. Ironically, it later needed China's official approval to acquire a company with a small operation in China: it is difficult to have complete freedom of action.

There is much contention on the internet. Columbia University's Yang Guobin notes that it falls principally into three areas: nationalist themes; concern over abuse of people's rights; and anger at abuses by rich people. These can evoke storms of online protest. However, he makes the point that internet contention 'is rarely directed at the national government; nor does it typically involve demands for wider political change'.[72] Large sections of the Chinese public are highly and emotionally nationalistic, and this may manifest itself in abusive campaigns across the internet, and even in public demonstrations against foreign targets – a Japanese embassy, an American consulate or a partly black singer. Domestic censorship of political events can have the beneficial effect of dampening domestic intemperance, giving the government flexibility to pursue non-extremist policies that are better aligned with the country's long-term interests. However counter-intuitive, Chinese political censorship could be regarded as a public good, allowing space for sober policy-making in a crisis.

The authorities aim to control pornography, violence and dissident content on the internet. Their internet-policing activities are reported to involve two million people, and they also pay people to post contributions in internet chat rooms in support of official views.[74]

CASS surveys on internet use over the last decade are very revealing. A strong majority (75–85 per cent) of Chinese respondents consistently say that there should be curbs on pornography. But in the 2003 survey, only 13 per cent thought political content should be controlled;[73] by the time of the 2005 survey, this had fallen to 8 per cent. However, the 2007 survey reveals a sharp change, with 41 per cent believing that political content on the internet should be controlled. The reasons for this change in public opinion are obscure, but may have to do with the choice of the Chinese word used for 'politics' in the survey: it has a fairly broad meaning, which can embrace moral and social issues.

The internet controls have been frequently described in the international media. It is possible to circumvent them; however, their very existence makes it harder to access prohibited material, which must discourage many. What is banned changes quite frequently, and this creates uncertainty: the existence of controls and punishment induces self-censorship. Overall the system probably works fairly satisfactorily for the authorities.

Two other interesting tendencies are highlighted in the 2007 CASS survey. First, Chinese people trust domestic sources of news much more than foreign sources; second, the proportion of Chinese using the internet to access international news has been progressively falling: 59 per cent in 2003, 40 per cent in 2005 and 31 per cent in 2007. This might suggest a declining interest in the outside world, but it is not really enough in itself to allow significant conclusions to be drawn. Of perhaps greater weight is the 2009 Pew Survey, which showed increasing Chinese public approval of the statement 'Our way of life needs to be protected against foreign influence': it rose steadily, from 64 per cent in 2002 to 81 per cent in 2009. Whenever there is a contentious debate on the political system within China, one argument that generally seems to help supporters of the status quo is that the proposed change is promoted and supported by foreigners.

The West has a tough job condemning all Chinese controls over the internet: the British manipulate search engines to reduce the chance of radical Islamic websites appearing in results, while the Americans are pushing judges to force open Twitter accounts to attack Wikileaks. But China is out in front in terms of intervention. Liu Xiaobo is reputed to have said that the internet is God's gift to China. It certainly played a part in the 2011 Arab Spring, but it can also assist an authoritarian regime by enabling citizens to raise complaints without bringing down the government – effectively operating as a safety valve.[75]

Rule of Law

It is often said – both inside and outside China – that an independent judiciary is essential if corruption is to be confronted or due process assured. But there is a major obstacle to this: the Party's ideology cannot easily countenance any independent body. Organs of power must be led by the Party (which is why NGOs are difficult to fit into the system). A re-examination of the state's ideological framework is needed if an independent judiciary is to function effectively.[76] In the meantime, genuine progress could be made by removing justice from local influence and at least making it report solely to central officials.

Despite concerns over the role of lawyers, development of the rule of law has been a stated objective of government for decades. The legal system has expanded massively since the 1980s. The number of law schools has grown from two to 600, and the number of lawyers from under 3,000 to over 200,000. The authorities want to enhance the rule of law in order to lay down rules for economic development, to prevent recurrence of the abuses which marked the Cultural Revolution, and to rein in arbitrary bureaucracies. The rule of law strengthens the fight against crime and corruption, responds to increasing public demand for rights and provides channels for the peaceful expression of grievances that arise from social change. It also develops legal arrangements based on international legal norms and provides popular recourse for grievances, as well as fairness and reliability to legitimize the state. There are many continuing problems, including corruption, poor training, limited judicial independence, torture and the lack of habeas corpus. For those charged, the conviction rate is a remarkable 99.9 per cent.[77] However, significant progress has occurred – in some areas. Commercial law, for instance, has made enormous strides in legislation and implementation; in the environmental area, though, there is a serious gap between law and implementation, and the same is true of civil rights.

Petitioning is a process whereby those who have a grievance against local officials can travel to the capital to seek relief from the central authorities. The tradition dates back at least as far as the Ming dynasty and is officially approved by today's government in Beijing. It is reported that in 2010 there were 9.7 million petitions.[78] However, the local officials can find their pay and promotion affected by petitions, and so an extrajudicial system has developed, involving the interception, imprisonment, torture and 'retrieval' of petitioners. Local officials pay unofficial gangs to seize petitioners and detain them illegally in what are called 'black jails'. Most petitioners are poor and vulnerable. Not only do their difficulties often go unaddressed at home, but their presence on the streets of Beijing is regarded as undesirable. Human Rights Watch has described the functioning of black jails in detail. In response, a spokesman for China's Ministry of Foreign Affairs angrily retorted that 'there are no black jails in China'. However, in 2009 *Liaowang*, a magazine for high-ranking officials, acknowledged the jails: 'in Beijing, a monstrous business network has emerged to feed, house, transport, man-hunt, detain, and retrieve petitioners'.[79]

According to a CASS survey, only 0.2 per cent of petition cases are satisfactorily resolved.[80] These tend to be resolved at the local level, usually by groups with social and economic leverage.[81] Interestingly, success is often achieved by breaking the regulations. Threatening to visit provincial leaders can lead local officials to bargain or cave in, and threatening social disorder may also work: the requirement to avoid local turmoil encourages cadres to buy off some protests. Thus a system which the state has encouraged for one purpose – monitoring and directing grievances into recognisable channels – can have unintended consequences, and it is said that petitioners develop hitherto unimagined skills in contending with the state.

The Chinese System and Western Opinion

China is widely criticised overseas for not copying Western democracy.[82] However, the authorities do monitor public opinion and use it in deciding policy. They govern as if they were running for election but the elections never come. There is an (unnegotiated) civil contract between state and individual: the state will seek to provide social stability and rising prosperity without unreasonable taxation or wealth redistribution; in return, the citizen should enter the political space only by invitation. The contract has worked well for hundreds of millions of people. Foreign critics of China are perhaps posing the wrong questions. After all, in spring 2012 the Pew Survey found that 82 per cent of Chinese were content with their country's direction. Even allowing for statistical errors, China does seem the happiest country. If Beijing is meeting popular aspirations, perhaps critics should ask not 'Do the Chinese people have the right government?' but rather 'Do the Chinese people have the right aspirations?'

If we take the frequent use of capital punishment, the Chinese military build-up, the pressure on Taiwan and the desire for superpower status – these may not be unpopular amongst the Chinese. Indeed, it is very likely that they accord with a highly nationalist sentiment amongst both grass-roots and educated Chinese people. Just consider the lyrics of the popular rock band Ordnance in its 2009 album *Rock City*, stating that China owns Taiwan and Tibet and that it would be disgraceful for China to compromise with the USA and Japan.

China may be becoming increasingly nationalist and 'democratic' – in the sense of being governed in a way that people want; but the West might not like what the Chinese people want. Another distinction between China and the West is the idea of opposition. In the West, the idea of opposition to government is culturally ingrained and almost obligatory. In China, opposition is almost, genuinely, an aberrational concept.

Western liberal opinion is close to employing double standards. Democracy sometimes produces results of which liberals cannot approve: Hitler 'won' the 1932 and 1933 elections in Germany; Italians regularly voted Silvio Berlusconi into power. Mainstream media like the *Financial Times* and the *Economist* had no hesitation in declaring that Italy gave the wrong result and that Berlusconi should go. How are Italians to know what is the right result if elected parliamentary majorities are inappropriate? China is, in some respects, akin to the pre-1832 political system in England. There is a feeling that power is restricted to 'responsible stakeholders'. The English Poor Laws restricted benefits to those remaining in their place of birth (reflecting the *hukou* system). The Party, particularly since Jiang Zemin, seeks to include in its ranks all 'advanced' sections of society: anti-government demonstrations are seen as 'hooligan' and subversive of established society. China partially reflects Edmund Burke's views on power and responsibility. It seems to be upholding conservative values akin to those of a nineteenth-century property-owning democracy, where influence accrues mainly to those with a stake in society.

Certain Asians suggest there is something called 'Asian values', which are at variance with those of the West, and specifically with Western democracy. Asian values are supposedly more collective than individual; more cooperative than confrontational. This view stresses the un-Asian character of formal opposition and the prioritisation of development goals rather than the fostering of a liberal society. Over a century ago, Hegel noted, during the Qing dynasty, that 'in China the Universal Will immediately commands what the Individual is to do, and the latter complies and obeys with proportionate renunciation of reflection and personal independence'.[83] Further back, in the fourth century BC, Aristotle said Asiatics were more 'slavish in character' than Europeans and 'submit without a murmur to their despotic government'.[84] A difficulty with this whole notion is that Taiwan, Japan and India are also Asian yet seem to be strangers to many such 'Asian values'.

Tens of thousands of intelligent young Chinese students study in the West each year. Many return to their homeland unconvinced of the merits of Western democracy. It is possible to acquire a liking for Disneyland but not democracy; to enjoy McDonald's food while caring nothing for the US constitution. Perhaps Western commentators should reflect on why bright young Chinese are not converted to their political system. Do intelligent people see Western democracy as being as flawed as their own political system? One young Chinese at Oxford told me he wanted democracy – 'no multi-parties, no universal suffrage, but an efficacious system to express the people's voice'.

The Party contends that any fully participatory democratic system would be inappropriate in China's contemporary stage of development. This ignores the small matter of India. Until recently, it was possible for Chinese authorities to argue that, although India had a democratic system with several hundred million voters, it was chaotic, requiring potentially unstable coalitions. Its policy-making was difficult, as evidenced by an anaemic growth rate. The emergence of a militarily strong, politically coherent and economically successful India would cause almost an 'existential threat' to the logic of an authoritarian China. That threat is looming, but it is not yet clear-cut. It is almost a zero-sum game that the success of India represents a failure for authoritarianism in China. But if an economically successful and stable democratic India would show that very large developing countries can successfully be democracies, the more immediate threat is Taiwan, where Chinese people are seen to be successfully managing a peaceful and stable democratic process. We could reasonably argue that the principal reason for seeking to extinguish Taiwan's independent status is less a desire for unification and more a longing to eliminate the standing rebuke to mainland China.

There is an area where China emulates Western participatory politics: village elections. Candidatures are generally Party-controlled but secret ballots are often used and independents occasionally win. One similarity to the West is that elected leaders frequently promise 'dividends' to the voters from village revenues. When revenues are insufficient – as they have been since 2008 – recourse is often had to debt, which has caused financial crisis in many villages (see Chapter 4).[85] Actions like this support conservative leaders, who argue that China is unprepared for a conventional democratic system.

China does, however, have a culture of public hearings, and this has been increasing rapidly. Hearings have been used to discuss electricity and water prices and a range of other local issues. They take place in both urban and rural areas. The problem with them is that frequently those participating are unrepresentative of the public. This makes the Zeguo experiments interesting. The local Party officials in this township in Zhejiang province asked the Center for

Deliberative Democracy at Stanford to conduct a series of 'deliberative polls', which were both representative and well informed, to decide on such issues as the prioritisation of infrastructure projects. James Fishkin from the Center observed that this process could prepare the ground for greater political participation or 'it could retard democratic development by contributing to the legitimacy of existing, less than fully democratic, institutional structures'.[86]

Western observers should perhaps accept that different societies may have their own approaches and values. The late Samuel Huntington who was a prominent political scientist at Harvard wrote that 'Western belief in the universality of Western culture suffers three problems: It is false, it is immoral and it is dangerous.'[87] Perhaps it is better to focus on encouraging the improvement of human rights in China than to demand democracy.

Consent

One of the weaknesses of a non-democratic political system is that consent by the governed is relatively hard to ascertain. However, it would be hasty to assume that it does not exist now in China. There are thousands of violent incidents each year, but I would strongly suggest that the violence is directed not against the current system of government, but against specific acts of government, policy outcomes or acts of omission. The main exceptions to this – where hostility to the state itself was demonstrated – were in the final stages of the Tiananmen events of 1989 and the posters plastered on the 'Democracy Wall' during the short-lived democracy movement in the winter of 1978–9. Those events, over twenty and thirty years ago, need to be weighed against the absence of similar events subsequently (plus the anecdotal evidence I have culled from many personal conversations).

Further evidence comes from opinion polls. There will be flaws in their processes, including the pervasive influence of state media; and yet the fact that they are international exercises, shaped by specialists independent of the Chinese authorities, makes their results interesting in a society lacking normal elections. This is important. The state today does not tax unduly; nor does it seek arbitrarily to redistribute citizens' wealth. This is an authoritarian, not a totalitarian, society.

> Anecdotal reports and survey research show a surprising degree of popular support for the existing political system and reform agenda ... Similarly, there is a widespread belief that democracy is not appropriate for China, at least not at its current level of economic and cultural development. This is, of course, the CCP's contention, and it is not challenged by most Chinese ...[88]

Whatever one thinks about harsh measures against dissidents, restricted rights of expression or limited participation in decision-making, it should always be remembered that this is a society which appears to consent to Party government – enthusiasm is not required. Indeed, throughout history, conservative philosophers have been wary of enthusiasm.

It would be a perversion of logic to say that, because there is censorship, a forceful state security apparatus and no evident demonstrations for democracy, then public opinion is prevented from free, private expression. Millions of foreigners visit China annually; it is not North Korea. Visitors are not normally followed, and there is ample opportunity for foreigners to have rational conversations in private with Chinese citizens both inside and outside the country. The overseas criticisms usually derive from those who see a political system which is different from theirs and wish to see it changed. The grumbles of most Chinese tend not to be structural and can be addressed through the current system. The nearest we can come to evidence of fragility and opposition to the state is the government's widespread jailing of dissidents and the frantic and ever higher expenditure on public security. The absence of political demonstrations against the system, of numerous expatriate political refugees and of pervasive private conversations that are critical of the system goes a long way towards indicating the broad acceptability of that system. This is not proof that it is loved: there may be cynicism, but there is little evidence that it is widely hated. Arguably, today's Chinese citizens offer an example of John Locke's 'tacit consent'.

Outlook

What would present a challenge to stability is the coming together of a number of different disaffected strands of society. Special interest groups (parents who believe their children died unnecessarily in the Sichuan earthquake or consumed poisoned milk in the melamine scandal) might coalesce with free-speech campaigners, unemployed industrial workers, advocates of Uighur, Mongolian or Tibetan autonomy, unhappy workers whose retirement date has been postponed on demographic grounds or whose pension fund has been plundered, villagers suffering from environmental degradation, and unemployed university graduates. A Tiananmen-style challenge to the authorities is possible, but on a much larger scale and at a time of harsher economic conditions. University graduates have a history of rising to the challenge of providing leadership to disaffected groups. Or the spark could come from a different direction – from rising nationalism.

Such groups need not constitute a majority. In Russia in 1917, a small minority could topple a government. More to the point, these groups have little in common and many actively dislike each other; coalescence is not predetermined. Interestingly, though, in Vietnam there is evidence of Catholic priests, Buddhist monks, democracy dissidents, environmental advocates and anti-Chinese activists joining together on some common platform. If this began in China it would be very serious. What troubles government officials (and large numbers of peaceful, comfortable citizens) is that the country could again fragment, with several internecine battlefields. This was partially seen in the Cultural Revolution, but even more startlingly a hundred years earlier, around the time of the Taiping rebellion: in a twenty-year period some 20–30 million people died (directly or indirectly) because of that event, the Nien rebellion, the Miao rising or the two separate uprisings by Muslims in different parts of the Empire.

There were several sensitive anniversaries in 2009: the 60th anniversary of the Communist victory, the 20th anniversary of Tiananmen and the 90th anniversary of 4 May 1919, which launched the powerful patriotic student movement that rejected concessions to the Japanese. The authorities were hyper-vigilant all year. Any of these anniversaries could have provided a match for a powder keg. But surprisingly, the main turmoil was the Xinjiang rioting.

Arab culture uses the system of *majlis*, or gatherings, to air opinions and complaints without needing to introduce democracy. Perhaps China can use the Zeguo process or develop a more high-tech approach to taking soundings and handling complaints. Good precursors are former Premier Wen's national internet interview or the 'Focus Issue Call Centre,' which the government instituted to handle grievances. The Party might even decide that it can cope with many of the demands of the disaffected, in order to strengthen its franchise and avoid a coalition of the alienated. It could co-opt some groups, while continuing to resist others. I don't mean a short-term thaw and then a return to the past, as with Lenin's New Economic Policy or Mao's Hundred Flowers Campaign: there could be a wholesale repositioning of the government to become a successful authoritarian administration for the twenty-first century, complete with managed outlets for civic complaint. This could be accompanied by a robust declaration that not all countries need to follow precisely in the steps of the West.

There are few obvious challenges to China's system that cannot be handled. It is quite possible that the wishes of the citizenry will substantially change, but even this would not automatically cause regime collapse. Providing the Party remains acute and sensitive, is willing to be flexible and provides government efficiently, it could sustain its rule for decades to come. Civil rights issues do not need to be a threat to China's rise.

CHAPTER NINE

Identity: Future of State and Party

So what is China and what is its guiding ideology? At first sight, the answers appear obvious. China is what we see on the map. The governing party is the Chinese Communist Party. The leadership school, the Central Party School, teaches Marxism–Leninism. The place it is most hostile towards is Taiwan, which is capitalist and democratic. The hammer and sickle is on the nation's flag and Mao is on the banknotes. Official rhetoric frequently contains Marxist references.

However, I suggest that both China and its ideology have changed much and will change more. Here I look at different options and possible futures for the Party, the state and the nation.

Incongruities

Incongruities abound: the largest and fastest-growing part of the economy has been the private sector; stock markets have existed for over twenty years; income inequality exceeds that in America;[1] entrepreneurs join the Communist Party; in 2013, there were 262 dollar billionaires in China.[2] Of the country's thousand richest, 157 are in the Communist Party Congress, the National People's Congress or the CPPCC.[3] The Party runs China but has no clear ideological identity.

Economic policy over thirty years ago went rapidly from socialist to pragmatic, with a broad (though not comprehensive) sympathy for market forces. Strikingly, the view is widespread that, when it comes, change will be towards *more* market influence, not less. In other words, the 'inevitability' argument has been reversed: instead of believing in the inevitability of communism (after messy compromises or phases of history), most officials more or less expect the market to triumph (inevitably). There is thus a difference between the 'real world' thinking of officials and the lingering Marxist rhetoric they still study for reasons of discipline. That the Cultural Revolution was disavowed, but not Mao, has created a straitjacket for officials: any economic liberalisation has to be justified by being cloaked in an archaic language of socialism and 'Chinese characteristics'. We must not confuse politics with economics, even if how wealth is created, to what extent it is shared and how government is financed are both economic and political issues.

There are vestiges of communism. The Party schools still teach Marxism–Leninism, but in the twenty years I have been visiting the Central Party School it never ceases to surprise me how little time is spent on it now – compared to other subjects and also compared to the late 1980s. Study of Marxism–Leninism is like a salute to a flag: the flag serves no concrete purpose, but it is a regime symbol. The Party is a disciplined, Leninist party (as was the nationalist Kuomintang), modelled on its one-time Soviet ally, the Communist Party of the Soviet Union.

Lessons Drawn

The Party has devoted much attention to studying how and why the Soviet and Eastern European communist systems collapsed and, more recently, to why the First World War broke out. But they have also studied many other organisations to discover the secrets of their longevity: the Catholic Church, the American Republican Party and the British Conservative Party, for example, as well as the Mexican PRI. Cuba is examined relentlessly to see how the regime there has survived – one lesson learnt is the beneficial populist impact of having America as the main public enemy, with the co-option of indigenous nationalism as a strengthening factor. Analysts frequently refer to the strong healthcare and education sectors in Cuba, though this hasn't inspired any decisive policy action in China to follow.

Academics frequently refer to the domestic ethnic conflict which sapped the Soviet Union.[4] The conclusion is that ethnic tensions should be treated as 'sensitive issues' with either economic or security solutions. An example of the former is the Chinese 'Go West' policy – a quasi-Marxist approach of investing in the economic development of the poorer distant interior provinces.

The analysts broadly recognise that military adventure, client states and arms races are to be avoided – and yet China is engaged in at least the latter two of these. Eventually, there may well be some debate over whether rapid military build-up is the best use of scarce national resources, but at the moment military development is fairly popular (probably because the public knows little about government finance limitations).

This is not an autistic party: it can be astute, particularly within a society that is introspective. Extensive analysis is made of critical issues which affect regime survival and success. NGOs and lawyers are seen as having been a malevolent force in the collapse of communism in Eastern Europe (see Chapter 8), and this influences how the Party views an independent judiciary and civil society. There are good commercial reasons why China could benefit from both, yet they are seen as threatening Party control. Exhaustive analysis of Western elections has produced examples of governments which have pursued the right policies and got the right results – and yet have still lost. Understandably, this curbs the Party's appetite for experimentation.

Communist Party Manifesto

The son of the influential Chinese leader Chen Yun said in the 1980s: 'We are the Communist Party and we will define what communism is.' In this section – to avoid such confusion – I compare China today with the policy prescriptions set out in the 1848 *Communist Manifesto* of Karl Marx and Friedrich Engels. This allows us to estimate clinically how communist China is today. The *Manifesto* had ten points, some of which were multifaceted. We might not regard the abolition of child labour as a distinguishing feature of communism, but I have taken each point at face value. Every clause in the original *Manifesto* is followed by a commentary comparing it with contemporary China; a percentage is proposed for the extent to which the programme has been fulfilled.

1. *Abolition of property in land and application of all rents of land to public purposes.* There is no freehold land but 70-year leases and private rents do exist and there is discussion of improving rural land rights. This is not so different from Hong Kong, which is seen as capitalist. **15 per cent**
2. *A heavy progressive or graduated income tax.* Dividend, interest and capital gains are taxed at a low flat rate. Salaries and wages attract a graduated tax. Thus, the middle class bears a progressive tax and the rich do not. **10 per cent**
3. *Abolition of all right of inheritance.* No, there is not even inheritance tax. **0 per cent**
4. *Confiscation of the property of all emigrants and rebels.* Mixed. Not emigrants but perhaps 'rebels'. **50 per cent**
5. *Centralisation of credit in the hands of the State, by means of a national bank with State capital and an exclusive monopoly.* Not really. Private banks, foreign banks, jointly owned banks and a large 'informal' banking system all exist. However, interest rates are officially driven. **20 per cent**
6. *Centralisation of the means of communication and transport in the hands of the State.* The internet and media growth and decentralisation coupled

with foreign airlines, domestic shipping and taxis mean this point does not apply well. **30 per cent**

7. *Extension of factories and instruments of production owned by the State; the bringing into cultivation of wastelands, and the improvement of the soil generally in accordance with a common plan.* State ownership of production is steadily diminishing. Wastelands are increasing with desertification. The soil is deteriorating. **20 per cent**

8. *Equal liability of all to labour. Establishment of industrial armies, especially for agriculture.* There is no equal liability to labour. There are no industrial armies. Agriculture has been privatised. **10 per cent**

9. *Combination of agriculture with manufacturing industries; gradual abolition of the distinction between town and country, by a more equitable distribution of the population over the country.* There is an increase in village enterprises. Suburbs and urbanisation are blunting the difference between town and country. However, the *hukou* system still maintains a rigid divide between rural and urban people. The benefits and income levels are different and the gap has grown. **10 per cent**

10. *Free education for all children in public schools. Abolition of children's factory labour in its present form. Combination of education with industrial production, etc.* Education in public schools is not free for all. Child labour is illegal below the age of 16 but reported as pervasive. There is no noticeable combination of education with production apart from apprenticeship schemes. **60 per cent**

Conclusion: It is difficult to summarise where some of these issues stand or to weigh one element of the programme against another. However, using the comments and the percentages for execution above, the mark I would give for contemporary China's adoption of the *Communist Manifesto* is 23 per cent. We might say the CCP follows Leninist organisation but not Marxist ideology.

Transformation and Continuity

The Party has undergone some fundamental transformations to move from its ideological basis before 1978 to the pragmatic approach it demonstrates today. Most of this was made possible by the forceful personality of Deng Xiaoping, but we should be clear that it is pragmatism that has been adopted – not market ideology. Reforms have been principally economic, not political, and now even economic reforms have stalled because the next wave inevitably has political implications. A critique of current Beijing thinking is that rather than introducing political reforms, the Party is wooing the people 'through consumerist modernization (economic developmentalism) and nationalist patriotism, the two poles of social participation now identified as the only possible forms of mass political practice'.[5] After the youthful romanticism of the 1980s, a more sober view formed that the choice for China is not either to remain mired in vestigial Marxism or make a confused dash for modernity, i.e. copying the US. There was a lot of reflection after Tiananmen Square. There was genuine shock that the US would bomb China's Belgrade Embassy, have her ships intercepted in third party countries[6] and above all seek to prevent her gaining the accolade of hosting the 2000 Olympics. The collapse and non-recovery of Russia was also influential. Opinion underwent a sea change during the 1990s. Themes that emerged included a preference for incremental policy-making over 'shock therapy'; allied with this is an increased appreciation for stability beyond simply the Party staying in power and additionally the feeling that China is important enough and has a strong enough culture that it need not simply approximate America but could find its own way to modernity.

Business and the Party

It was former President Jiang Zemin who initiated large-scale recruitment of entrepreneurs into the Party. By 2003 it was estimated that about a third of all entrepreneurs were Party members.[7] It suited the Party to have entrepreneurs well represented in its ranks for three reasons. First, if they did not join, they might support and finance dissident groups. In Russia, Putin dealt with the matter of independently rich entrepreneurs, 'oligarchs', by demanding that they stay out of politics; the CCP invited them to join. Second, Jiang believed the Party should openly seek to represent the advanced forces of society; in other words, those with a stake in society. Lastly, government research suggests many entrepreneurs are related to Party officials, and, of course, Party members became entrepreneurs. The Party now actively searches for entrepreneurs to join and even pays recruitment bonuses to facilitators. The fact that talented students and rising private entrepreneurs are wooed led one entrepreneur to say 'All the best people join the Party.'[8]

The Party also interests entrepreneurs: an opportunity to access credit and a degree of 'protection' can come from being a Party member. The case of Huang Guangyu is relevant here. In 2008, as chairman and major shareholder of the retail business Gome, he topped the list of the richest people in China, with estimated wealth of $6.3 billion. As noted in Chapter 2, by the end of 2008 he was in prison. He was held without charge until 2010, when he was indicted for bribery, illegal business dealings and insider trading. International media have suggested that officials are uncomfortable with someone independent of the

Party accumulating such substantial wealth.[9] The Huang case reflects – and may reinforce – the widely held public opinion that business is somehow unclean. Part of the problem is that the authorities want the jobs and economic growth that the private sector has created, but will not lay down a clear ethical and social framework for popular understanding and recognition of its public achievement. This is because of the Party's inability to formulate a coherent political and social philosophy in the twenty-first century. Thus the public is confused as to whether entrepreneurial activity is good or bad.

Of course, the Party pays a price for its alliance with the business world. 'In the marketisation process, the boundary between the political elite and the owners of capital grows gradually more indistinct. The political party is thus changing its class basis.'[10] Given that a large number of Party families are now directly or indirectly engaged in business, often as a result of non-transparent privatisations, it is somewhat unclear whether the Party now seeks to attract people from a different class, or whether the people the Party seeks to attract are the same but have simply changed their class.

A former senior official, now distinguished dissident, Bao Tong, makes an interesting distinction:

> There are two types of entrepreneurs: One type relies on himself and his own strength. Another type relies on the government, connections and backdoor favors. These two types of entrepreneurs have different hopes for China's future. Those who depend on the government's wealth, they like one-party rule … But independent entrepreneurs, who rely on their own ability to compete in the market – what they really want is equality and for the same rules of the game to be applied to everyone. Of course they cannot live very happily in a one-party state.[11]

Furthermore, if credit is routinely denied to entrepreneurs, as we noted in Chapter 4, it induces them to skirt the law. This causes a form of wish fulfilment: a particular group is marginalised and institutionalised into behaving in an anti-social manner, much as socialist theory originally suggested. A society that doesn't prioritise the rule of law encourages entrepreneurs to purchase protection. A society with many bad laws and policies encourages the evasion of laws.

Towards a 'Family State'?

We need to accept that corruption is deeply embedded in the Chinese state. Party Secretary Bo Xilai's campaign against corruption and organised crime in Chongqing exposed strong links between crime gang bosses and powerful officials, and also showed the pervasiveness of impunity and the substantial income generated within officialdom by the sale of promotions (see Chapter 7). The denouement saw Bo and his wife charged. Also in 2012 the *New York Times* reported allegedly huge wealth accumulation amongst the members of Wen Jiabo's family.[12] Leaders like Bo are often children of previous leaders. We should remember the hereditary aspect of political power: the privileged upbringing enjoyed by the child of a leader brings with it good education, high-level contacts, familiarity and good early job experience. Not surprisingly, such children can often compete for posts on merit.

It is important to reiterate that China is not corrupt because it is under Communist Party leadership. Corruption may be exacerbated by the Party, but in the nineteenth century, under the Qing, official corruption was rife.[13] And corruption goes back much further than the Qing. The point is that the Party has been unable to clean up China.

So is there debate within the senior levels of the Party on this issue? It is hard to be sure what is accepted and what is in dispute. Reference to family links amongst officials is a sensitive subject. On the one hand this is good, since it shows an awareness that some of the behaviour is wrong. However, it is uncertain whether there are moves by any group to end such practices. Perhaps the system is so permeated by blood and patronage links that it is difficult to reform. But corruption is one of the main targets for public excoriation. The Party cannot afford to pussyfoot around when public revulsion may overnight threaten regime survival.

Fundamental Change for the Party

One of the many great contributions of Deng Xiaoping to Party thinking was to support and articulate the move away from Maoist utopianism towards pragmatic politics. Deng carefully deconstructed Maoist thought through folk-like aphorisms: 'It doesn't matter whether the cat is white or black as long as it catches mice', 'Let some people become rich before others' and 'Seek the truth from facts'. These simple sayings helped officials manage the transition. But the Party was not changed by aphorism alone: the Gang of Four, including Mao's widow, were arrested at gunpoint.

The Party's movement from ideology to pragmatism shadows other tendencies in national history. Foreign ideas have shown a recurrent ability to become highly influential, but ultimately to fail to capture the heart of the people in the long term: Buddhism, Islam, Marxism ... Eventually immemorial China reasserts herself. Conformity at home can fit easily with rejection of values which many foreigners see as universal.

The Party is becoming younger. In 1990, only 1.2 per cent of college students were Party members; by 2012 it was 3.4 per cent.[14] Rather than a growing politicisation of youth, this might simply be a reaction to increasing graduate unemployment and an attempt to bolster the odds. Anecdotal reports from universities suggest that students joining the Party often come from poorer families and need more assistance to succeed in life.

Party Governance

The Party has adopted dramatic governance reform since Mao's time. It experimented with bringing in entrepreneurs as members, and then later embraced and trumpeted the policy. Its idea of representing the 'advanced forces of society' allows it to circumvent the theory that it has a strictly proletarian heritage (which was never entirely the case). It has also ceased to have leaders 'dying in the saddle': now leaders retire, and in fact there are term limits; presidents and premiers serve two five-year terms. At a lower level, officials are moved around the regions to reduce the chances of corruption. The American academic David Shambaugh noted the huge turnover of senior Party and government officials in 2002 and 2003, respectively: 'Never since the Bolshevik Revolution of 1917 has a communist party leadership experienced such wholesale elite turnover, absent a purge. More than half of the party's Central Committee, Politburo, and Standing Committee stood down from office. The turnover in the state and military leaderships were of a corresponding magnitude.'[15] And in 2007, it is said, 200,000 officials changed post.

At the national level, the incoming top leader is chosen not by the outgoing leader but by the collective wishes of the senior leaders. This is a genuine functioning oligarchy with some hereditary elements: the children of prominent parents might have some advantage, but there is no guarantee of a top job; ability is vital to reach the top. Loyalty to the system is also vital: there may be active internal debate on potential policies, but once a decision is taken officials must support it.

Zhou Ruijin, a retired deputy editor-in-chief of the Communist Party's *People's Daily,* discussed governance issues in an article for the reformist magazine *Yanhuang Chunqiu.* One-party rule, he claimed, causes 'an overconcentration of political power and the absence of checks and balances' and had 'helped cause rampant official and judicial corruption and given rise to irrational decisions and the blind pursuit of growth at the expense of people and the environment'. It could wreak 'immeasurable, irreversible havoc on society' at the cost of the government's remaining credibility.[16] Abrasive though these comments may be, the advice to the leadership is constructive. Hu Jintao, Wen Jiabao and others have pointed out how abuse of power by local officials and corruption threaten harmony; Zhou notes the background to the symptoms and explains why political reforms are needed. He also refers to the historically high numbers of petitions to government in 2010, and of mass incidents, 2011's ethnic riots in Guangzhou, Mongol unrest in Inner Mongolia and the three bombings in Anhui of government buildings. All of this gives the impression of mounting public anger with governance. If the Party is to respond constructively, it is not tear gas and water cannon that are required. Zhou even commends the transformation wrought by Chiang Ching-kuo in Taiwan in the 1980s, which laid the basis for democracy. The Party's new leadership of 2012 will eventually demonstrate whether new approaches can come to the surface.

The Party and Institutions

The Party has arranged matters so that the whole institutional landscape reflects its leadership. Thus the chairman of the Private Sector Association, the heads of other permitted political parties and recognised religions are chosen by and beholden to the Party. However, there are areas where Party leadership stumbles. One example is the media. Much effort is devoted to controlling the message which goes out so that it reflects the Party line. However, journalists seem consistently capable of expressing alternative messages, and the state media offer many detailed illustrations of contemporary society that differ sharply from the Party's message.[17] Another example is academic institutions. University professors often give outspoken critiques of contemporary society – whether criticising social issues, the legal system or political matters. And academic institutions often publish findings which contradict government statements. There is an academic term for this – 'institutional amphibiousness' – coined by Professor X. L. Ding at Hong Kong University of Science and Technology.[18]

Although official views dominate the print and broadcast media, there are increasing signs of public distrust of officials and national institutions. After the railways minister, who had championed rapid rail development, was sacked for corruption in 2011, there was public concern over rail safety. When finally there was a high-speed railway disaster polls revealed that 97 per cent of the public did not trust the railways ministry.[19] In 2012, Qiao Mu of Beijing Foreign Studies University said that there was more hostility to the national government than in 2006. The Party leaders are happy for there to be criticism of local officials – who can act as a lightning rod – but when it engulfs central leadership it affects the legitimacy of the system, so Qiao's observation is deeply worrying.

Contemporary China is such a complex and sophisticated society that it would be difficult to eliminate all these avenues for expression without enforcing a degree of control that would damage economic development. Individuals in authority who express views that differ from those of the leadership do not necessarily wish to destroy the government. They may simply favour changing some policies. Such expression might be seen as conducive to strengthening the state and social development.

There is a gulf between what the Party expects of officials and what they actually do. Former Premier Zhu Rongzhi said in 1996 that even written orders did not oblige his subordinates to act: many of these documents disappeared 'like a stone dropped into the sea'.[20] Central Party leaders are less powerful than is imagined. In terms of decision-making, expenditure and, particularly, practical implementation, China is quite a decentralised country: the state is not in full control. It is not that local officials contend overtly with Beijing, but in practice different provincial leaders emphasise different policy approaches.

The Party and the Army

Today's political leaders generally lack a military background; no Party leader since Deng has had military credentials. Thus the practical overlap that existed when the Party was fighting a revolutionary war (and in the years afterwards) no longer exists. It is widely believed that, following the Sichuan earthquake of 2008, Prime Minister Wen ordered the military to make planes available for rescue work and was refused, since he held no military rank. The order had to come from President Hu, as chairman of the Central Military Commission (CMC). The Ministry of Defence does not have authority over the military; the CMC does, and notionally it is meant to report to the Party. It is quite obvious who is military and who is in government.

This can cut two ways. It means that Jiang Zemin and Hu had no resonance with the military, and thus no special respect, beyond the fact that they occupied the top posts. However, conversely, no current military leader has led any successful campaign, as there haven't been any. The nearest to an exception was Bo Xilai, who lived on a military compound and cultivated ties with senior military officials. We should assume that Party rhetoric and discipline are weaker than in the 1960s and that military discipline and *esprit de corps* may have increased a little. It is debatable whether the military would follow an order from today's leadership to suppress a Tiananmen-style protest. Indeed, it is quite difficult to assert that the military is still fully under Party control. It is more likely that outcomes are a result of complex negotiation. The military leaders no longer sit on the Standing Committee of the Politburo but also there are no longer attempts to reduce military spending and it is not clear how much the political leaders interfere in how the military functions.

The Party, Friends and Enemies

The Party is rational. It does not wilfully antagonise the Chinese people as a whole: it tries to give them what they want. Wages may have been growing moderately, but it seems that even the poor are reasonably satisfied with their lot (unless disaster strikes). Those who actively contemplate destroying the state are few; those who want a more prosperous life, many. The latter form the Party's constituency. It is the comfortable and the would-be comfortable whom it represents. As, according to the 2012 Pew China Survey, 70 per cent feel they are better off than they were five years ago and apart from Brazil no other country comes within twenty points of that, the Party has quite a strong constituency. The leftist academic Wang Hui has written: 'Today, workers and peasants have wholly disappeared not only from the leadership bodies of party and state, but also from the National People's Congress, the sole legislative house in the PRC'.[21] This is a group that the Party is in danger of alienating in its drive to win the 'advanced' members of society. In a country where many describe themselves as 'middle class' (and we are told they are now the majority), the Party's political support base is not small; but ironically, it is vulnerable to any rise in political consciousness among the proletariat.

Nonetheless the 2011 and 2012 budgets were interesting: expenditure on public security now exceeds military expenditure. The clear message is that the Party believes it now has more enemies inside the country than outside.

The Party and its Sense of Mortality

How has the Party survived, when Western communism collapsed after 1989? Two points made by leftist commentators are, first, that the Chinese Communist Party always sought its own political path rather than slavishly following others (i.e. the Soviets), so China was able to select solutions which were based on actual national conditions; second, a surprise result of being sent to the countryside during the Cultural Revolution is that leaders became familiar with the needs of the people. This didn't happen in the Soviet Union and Eastern Europe.[22] In Chinese discourse there is frequent reference to history. One common observation is 'Without an exception, China's dynasties were wrecked by uprooted, migrant farmers'; and rural dwellers have been described as China's 'active volcano'.[23] The Party is all too aware of the danger to its very existence from natural disaster, rural unrest, inflation and corruption.

The relationship with the countryside is a complex one. Exploiting rural unhappiness proved an effective route to power, and yet, once in power, the Party found itself peculiarly threatened by developments in rural China. During the revolutionary years, there was both a desire to co-opt the turbulent history and folklore of the countryside and a fear of what it might do next. On victory, the Party moved almost immediately to benefit the cities at the expense of the countryside.

In 2012, a rare event occurred: the ejection of a Politburo member. However, even the fall of the controversial Bo Xilai as Party Secretary of Chongqing in 2012 was overshadowed by the trial of his wife. Reading the party's *Global Times* account of the sentencing of his wife and their servant for murdering a foreign businessman with cyanide conjured up images of a medieval Italian court or accounts of life under the Roman Emperor Nero.[24] In 1998 Chen Xitong, a Politburo member, was found guilty of corruption, and in 2008 another Politburo member, Chen Liangyu, was jailed for corruption. Even if the reality was, as observers suggested, that they had simply lost out in a factional struggle, the fact that the Party chose to label former leaders as highly corrupt weakens its image. So, in 2012, charging a Politburo member with discipline violations, usually taken to mean corruption, is a severe indictment of the Party's senior ranks. As its leaders admitted, the case 'badly undermined the reputation of the Party and the country'.[25] It might be that the Party should rethink its automatic policy of labelling those leaders to be removed as corrupt given that public antagonism to rampant corruption then diminishes the acceptability of the Party. This suggests that the long-term strategy of consistency and 'following the line' might be outweighed by an urgent need to be seen to make radical change.

Increasing integration into the world seems to be viewed with unease by some Party leaders. First, working with the WTO or the UN can entail a lot of transparency, which the Party instinctively finds uncomfortable. Second, while sometimes necessary, a mercantilist country such as China finds importing food a national security risk. There is a sense that these issues could lead to an erosion of national sovereignty. Aware of the dangers, in 2003–4 the Politburo held lengthy sessions on the rise and decline of states over the last six centuries.[26]

The Party and Reforms

China was the fastest-reforming major country in the 1980s and 1990s. But that has ended: there has been little reform since 2000. The national leaders in the reform era had tremendous charisma and determination. Having helped to win the civil war, Deng Xiaoping had legitimacy as a ruler, but subsequent leaders have lacked the endorsement of either bullets or ballots. This made them timid and able to focus only on stability and regime survival – 'big picture' reforms frightened them. The second problem they face is that the reforms the economy needs now if it is to move forward (e.g. property rights, liberalisation of banking and rule of law) all carry clear consequences for the economic interests of many in the leadership. This makes it difficult for nervous leaders to march determinedly forward. Of course even weak leaders can order suppression if they have no other strategy. President Xi announced certain reforms after the Third Plenum in 2013 but was careful to refer to the continued dominance of the state.

Zhou Enlai announced the 'four modernisations' – of industry, agriculture, science and technology, and defence – in 1964.[27] The dissident Wei Jingsheng added to this by advocating the 'fifth modernisation' – democracy – in 1979. However, for many of those who endured the upheavals of the Cultural Revolution it is hard to submit to the uncertainties of mass democracy. Party leaders baulk at leaping into the unknown – or worse, risking what they experienced before.

The Party and Its Identity

For Deng Xiaoping, the Party was an essential tool for maintaining control. The policies and – subtly – the principles might change, but the Party should be inviolate. Even the debunking of Mao was done with great sensitivity. The verdict of '70 per cent good, 30 per cent bad' has puzzled observers. It is an irony that this is the verdict that Mao is reported to have passed on Stalin as well as on his own Cultural Revolution.[28] Why such a positive summary of someone who, on a personal level, had driven Deng out of power and caused acute suffering to him and his family, as well as to tens of millions of Chinese? The answer comes in an aphorism of Deng's: 'To build up Mao's errors too much would only damage the image of our Party and our country, and harm the socialist system.'[29] Thus, the verdict was not what Deng thought, but what he believed necessary. Jettisoning Mao would weaken the Party's ability to control China, by undermining its legitimacy after its long association with Mao.

The intense desire by the leadership to retain power is not distinctively ideological; it is a normal trait of politicians. What the Chinese authorities do to maintain power – curbing free speech, avoiding most forms of elections, tapping telephones, jailing peaceful protesters and firing on their own unarmed young people – does not constitute ideology. There are many similar examples in the Middle East, South East Asia and even in the United States. This is method, not ideology; process, not principle.

The rewriting of history is a *feature* of communism, but not a distinguishing one – other regimes do it, too. But in China's case it has been so successful that today few people realise, for example, that the Communist Party was founded in 1920 by a group including Chen Duxiu, its leader for the first six years, rather than by Mao Zedong, who joined in 1921 and took over only in 1935 (and again in 1943). This rewriting is about power, memory and legitimacy, not about policy and ideology. The Party's method has been described as 'Consultative Leninism', referring simply to Lenin's organisational practices and the Party's concern with public opinion.[30] The depoliticisation of the Party can be seen as a natural reaction to the upheaval of the Cultural Revolution.[31] The continuing requirement to read Marxist texts at the Party schools should be seen less as ideological and more as a differentiating discipline – rather like the obligatory reading of classical texts for the imperial examination system. However, like classical texts, the Marxist texts can offer a degree of organisational discipline and acceptance of hierarchy.

The Party has reworked its wider self-description. Clearly it is no longer a proletarian vanguard – even capitalists are welcome. Moreover, it has subtly restated its case for power. The unnegotiated 'bargain' between party and people could be formulated as: 'We deliver rising prosperity and social stability; you let us stay in power.' Occasionally, this is called 'performance legitimacy', and that is why the leadership is deeply troubled by economic crises: a deteriorating economic performance and increasing unemployment and inflation not only undermine rising income but also encourage instability, thus breaking the 'contract'.

Other things can undermine perceived performance: during the severe drought of 2009–10, for example, Beijing's National Audit Office noted that money allocated to the water industry had not been appropriately spent, and Zhao Zhengyuan, a former official with the Ministry of Environmental Protection, was reported to have said that embezzlement of money for water treatment facilities was widespread.[32] This profoundly affected the drought-stricken south-west of China and directly echoes a comment made at the end of the eighteenth century, during the Qing dynasty: 'embezzlement of government funds destined for the upkeep of public works such as irrigation channels and dykes ... greatly exacerbated the natural disasters of drought and floods.'[33] Such corruption and complacency continued to weaken the Qing through the nineteenth century. The central Party leaders cannot afford to let self-indulgent local officials wreck their mandate.

The 'public perception of a lack of virtue and integrity among Chinese officials' is palpable.[34] Events such as the Sichuan earthquake and its aftermath have attracted public criticism. One Beijing professor has said that 'it is ridiculous to see the party trying to turn the calamity and people's sufferings into its own victory' and 'despite the talk of scientific development, Beijing remains obsessed with the most unscientific addiction to covering up truth and favouring lies in the name of maintaining stability and social harmony'.[35] Liu Changle, CEO of Hong Kong-based Phoenix TV, has said that de – often translated as 'virtue' – is lacking in society.[36] Virtue is, of course, a value particularly needed in officials.

Transformation of the Party is not new. In origin, the Party was an intellectual – if not a literary – force. It later forged itself into a disciplined and forceful revolutionary party. For thirty years it has been a developmental party. Of course, there isn't a 'Party way' to build a dam, or even to decide how many should be built. The performance being judged is now largely practical. An important recent change was the passing of the generation that fought to create the 'New China' of 1949. Leaders today came to adulthood after 1949; they didn't help win the victory. Officials have risen through the ranks by serving their bosses satisfactorily. It is not known what steel the new leaders have for dealing with future instability. Furthermore, given their institutionalised and collegial background, it is difficult to be sure how future dramatic change is to arise.

The Party's ideology has taken interesting directions in recent years. Jiang Zemin, frequently treated as a lightweight, contributed the idea of the 'Three Represents'. Initially seen as somewhat banal, this is increasingly being regarded as part of the justification for a retrospective makeover of the Party now that it has started co-opting entrepreneurs and the wider technical elite. It shifts the Party's self-description from a proletarian movement to one which incorporates the 'advanced forces' of society. Hu Jintao's contribution was 'The Harmonious Society', which represented a timely shift of emphasis from growth at all costs to consideration of social development, awareness of growing income disparities and environmental challenges although there was little practical application.

As Party members must study these formulations, they have been digested by 80 million important people countrywide. Communist Party ideology in China is not dated and unchanging rhetoric: some very talented people work hard to keep it relevant. However, the examples above are not about updating Marxism; they are essentially non-Marxist. Given China's established policies, updating Marxism is not easy. Yu Jianrong of CASS has said that he has reflected on the theory of a harmonious society and thinks that it 'must have clearly defined property rights, an authoritative judicial system, a truly representative system [of government], and it must have an open media'.[37] This may not be what President Hu originally meant, but the ideas advanced by the leaders do get more than cursory attention, and even non-members of the Party analyse them.

The purpose of ideology is to provide intellectual and emotional underpinning to the claim to power, and to suggest consistency and continuity. Although the Party has reason to feel optimistic, it lacks a language which is accurately self-definitional. It cannot articulate compellingly the characteristics which define CCP rule. This is another result of de-emphasising the rhetoric of communism. In the twenty-first century it is no longer accurate – or appropriate – to talk of communism or the values of a non-elected oligarchy. As a result, the CCP is a party which dare not speak its name.

The purpose of a political organisation is normally to seek and retain power. It usually has a distinctive ideology. Even as ancient and innately unideological an organisation as the British Conservative Party has developed variant political philosophies – from the kind of conservatism espoused by Edmund Burke, through One Nation to Thatcherism. Like all political parties, the CCP can discuss policy and good government, but is profoundly uncomfortable when required to describe and defend its particular distinguishing features. It is just as well there are no other parties from which it needs to distinguish itself. People may accept a government which does not hold national elections (indeed many certainly do); but as a battle cry, 'Support us to avoid elections' is singularly uninspiring.

The Party is largely quite successful at governing, yet has completely lost the ability to justify itself in terms of political philosophy. This is quite rare. In France, for example, ex-President Sarkozy's Union for a Popular Movement, though intellectually incoherent, could just about claim to be *not a socialist party*. The CCP does not say it is capitalist, yet it cannot accurately claim to be Marxist or even socialist. It is in a difficult situation. The Party urgently requires an articulate political philosophy. This lack of original mythology for the present century leads to the clumsy reiteration of words borrowed from other philosophies because they are deemed to be 'good'. Look at Premier Wen at the 2009 National People's Congress: 'We need to improve democratic institutions, enrich the forms of democracy, expand its channels, and carry out democratic elections.'[38]

What did he mean by that? He almost certainly didn't mean it literally. I once heard the Dean of Harvard Business School describe his audience of senior managers of multinationals as 'entrepreneurs'. In much the same way, Premier Wen was using the word 'democracy' as a way of conveying a positive feeling. Democracy (like entrepreneurialism) is regarded by many as a 'good' word – on a par with motherhood and apple pie – and so Wen used it in the context of China's institutions and procedures. Such unusual constructions and borrowings will inevitably continue until someone can endow the Party with an ideology. And this must be done. It would be a great mistake to believe the Party can permanently operate with no intellectual offering. That is the political equivalent of coasting on empty.

Critical to the Party's identity in the public mind is competence (hardly a *value* in any normal sense). It has an enviable record of delivery for the public, and the expectation that it will continue is widespread. One 2009 opinion poll investigating the level of confidence that each population had in its government's ability to resolve the financial situation was eloquent. The US scored 47 per cent, Britain 33 per cent – and China 72 per cent.[39] Such surveys are not rigged: they represent the respondents' genuine views.

When we consider the pragmatism as opposed to utopianism, the leading position in the Party of educated men, the representation of academics, military men and entrepreneurs, the emphasis on gradual change rather than radical initiatives, the rhetorical homage to the past, the foreign policy based on national interest not rights and ideology, and the avoidance of universal suffrage, we are in many respects observing Edmund Burke's pre-1832 England. China today has a conservative political system. In a general sense, those who have a stake in society are those who influence policy. China has even had its equivalent of the 1819 Peterloo Massacre, where people gathered to demand political reforms, only to be dispersed militarily, leaving several hundred dead and wounded.

So where does the Party go now? If it were to rename itself based on its current policies, something like 'National Development Party' would fit. However, it has found it easier to keep the rhetoric and redefine its meaning. 'Socialism with Chinese characteristics' is the term employed for what is, in certain respects, fairly unbridled capitalism. The fear of confronting realities through language is part of a desire to avoid radical change and to pursue incremental moves towards objectives. However, if domestic conditions deteriorate, we might yet see the Party change its name and rhetoric in a bid for relevance and continued power.

There are periodic warning calls for society to be grounded in something other than making money. This could take the form of a return to a 'purer' version of Marxism. We are seeing an increase in labour and social legislation, coupled with more intense union activity, but few advocate a more Marxist society. In 2010 a deputy director of the State Council research centre said 'during the past three decades, we prioritized . . . total GDP growth. But from now on, we have to focus on distributing wealth'.[40] The head of a research centre affiliated to the Ministry of Finance has proposed that 'high earners should contribute more in tax revenues'.[41] The wave of industrial suicides in 2010 (see Chapter 5), combined with rising labour unrest, led senior officials to propose further improvement in working conditions. The authorities could eventually readjust the economy from investment to consumption and curb environmental degradation. The Party would then have ruled a China which has been successively communist, almost capitalist and then almost socialist. Adherents would say that at each stage these approaches met the country's needs. The Party's capacity to reinvent itself in order to retain power is breathtaking. The new leadership of 2012 has the ability to lead it in new directions.

The purpose of the Party is power, and everything is subordinated to that. It has been one of the most successful political parties in history in achieving power and then retaining it.

Atheism, Morality and Religion

Officially the Communist Party is atheist. However a 2007 survey of 900 local cadres by the China National School of Administration found that 53 per cent had superstitious beliefs.[42] Many are turning to the ancient philosopher Zhou Gong for spiritual explanations of their dreams; other practices include physiognomy, astrology and *I Ching* (*Yi Jing*) divination. These are deeply embedded in Chinese culture and difficult to uproot: Zhou Gong, for example, was the brother of the founder of the Zhou dynasty, over three thousand years ago. If the vicious campaigning of the Cultural Revolution could not eradicate these traditions, we should not imagine that today's more emollient leadership will be more successful.

To develop a belief system, the Party could dive back into the treasure trove which is Chinese history and construct a new sociopolitical philosophy. Some suggest replacing or paralleling today's ageing Marxist heritage by returning to Confucian principles. The elegance of this is fourfold: Confucian thinking is Chinese; it is part of a long and venerable tradition in the nation's history; it has the advantage of a moral code (which all governments value) without the transcendental aspects of a religion (which can present mortal competition to the claims to ultimate authority of a atheistic authoritarian government); and it is not incompatible with a hierarchical society. Confucianism supports conceptions of benevolent rulers, obedience and harmony. Unfortunately many Chinese respect the past but yearn for the modern. Since at least 1900 there has been a strong current that rejects Confucianism as rooting China in meek, acquiescent decline. Many Party members see the May 4th Movement of 1919 as a patriotic forebear of the CCP, and the May 4th leaders loathed Confucianism. One approach might be to adapt Confucianism for today. A neo-Confucian construct could combine some traditional themes with the aspiration to create a modern and strong China.

China had by 2013 developed 440 Confucius institutes, which promote the Chinese language and culture abroad – and inevitably instil sympathy for China. These are the equivalent of Germany's Goethe Institute or Spain's Cervantes Institute.[43] Thus today's China finds Confucius' values sufficiently compelling to make him the national brand. Indeed, to coincide with his 2,560th birthday, 2009 saw the first update since 1937 of his family tree (2 million descendants are now recognized). Confucian thought could even be adopted centrally as a core value of the state: perhaps the early Ming version, which 'conspicuously lacked the sense of reciprocity between ruler and advisor or between ruler and people that Confucianism praised as an essential principle of good government'.[44]

In 2013, the Party had 85.1 million members. Another 80 million-plus 14–28-year-olds belong to the Communist Youth League. Many people join the Party for career reasons rather than from political convictions. On the other hand, an official survey conducted by East China Normal University for the Ministry of Education concluded that 300 million Chinese adhere to a religion.[45] 2013 estimates are of between 60 and 130 million practising Christians.[46] Even Party members are known to practise Christianity without being asked to resign.

The Party's attitude to religion has undergone a profound metamorphosis since the 1970s, when the rhetoric expected religion to expire. In 1982, Document 19 was issued as the basic paper on religion: 'the long-term influence of religion cannot be avoided [but] Religion will eventually disappear'.[47] In 2000–1 Jiang Zemin made a number of pronouncements, including: 'we respect the objective rules for the existence and development of religion . . . the final disappearance will take even longer than the final disappearance of class and state'. It was, he said, necessary 'to positively guide the adaptation of religion to socialist society'.[48]

As Professor F. T. Ying of the Chinese University of Hong Kong said in 2009: 'belief in the final extinction of religion has been marginalized'.[49] A few years ago, Christians were generally quite old. Today many are young, despite sixty years of atheist school teaching. China's attitude to religion has developed in a way that is similar to that of the former Soviet Union. There it was first stated that religion would inevitably disappear; later that the believers were the older and less educated; and then finally, in the 1970s, came a grudging acceptance that, particularly in the shape of Islam, religion was a problem 'not of the past but of the present and of the future'.[50]

The nihilism of the Cultural Revolution led first to a materialistic society, hungry to make money, and now to a deep need in the soul for values and beliefs transcending what the state can offer. Officials have been examining whether they can bring the underground (or 'house') churches (see Chapter 8) into a loose but formal relationship with the state. The danger is that this might open the door to student unions, trades unions and a host of other unwelcome organisations which would also insist on working independently of state supervision.

Ethnic Identity

Historically, there has been a confused comprehension of Chinese racial identity – what were the early ethnic components of the original Chinese state; exactly who ruled the country for centuries; how should distinctly non-Han peoples today become part of a Chinese monoculture; what is Chinese ethnicity? All these questions have been obfuscated and debate has been discouraged. Furthermore, there is a long-standing and important strand in Chinese culture of polygenism, or the belief that the Chinese race is unique (demonstrably true) and not linked genetically to the rest of humanity (distinctly controversial). The idea that the Chinese were a branch of universal humankind was denounced in the seventeenth century and disavowed in the nineteenth.[51] There is today apparently 'a powerful body of opinion in China that believes in polygenism and holds that the origins of the Chinese are discrete and unconnected with that of other branches of humankind. In other words . . . a widespread belief that the difference between the Chinese and other peoples is not simply cultural or historical but also biological.'[52]

As noted, Beijing receives strong criticism for restricting the rights and self-determination of minorities such as the Tibetans and the Uighurs in Xinjiang. It is interesting, then, to find the nationalists, exemplified by the *hanwang* movement,[53] strenuously advocating Han national (racial) identification, traditional Chinese clothing and complaining about government favouritism towards minorities, the hijacking of national education by unpatriotic elements, and the activities of Manchus (who are often likened to 'Jews'), stressing 'the paramount importance of racial righteousness' and trumpeting that the Han are 'one of the purest blooded races in the world'.[54] Specific complaints are that minorities get favourable treatment under the one-child policy and are advantaged for university entrance; patriotic figures are being downgraded in the school textbooks and historic alien rulers are being glorified.[55]

As we saw in Chapter 5, there is a (rarely expressed) belief by legal authorities that rural people are genetically and sexually disposed to backwardness and criminality. These nationalist, eugenic, racial and class views sit oddly with a society which is nominally socialist. Thus, whenever Beijing contemplates a moderate initiative in foreign (or sometimes domestic) policy, it must guard against being outflanked by a fervent nationalist movement.

Heighten Emphasis on National Issues

Having moved away from communism, and more recently socialism, and in effect having 'depoliticised', the Party could decide to emphasise nationalist thinking. This is not because the leaders are nationalistic but because powerful elements of the public are.

'Nationalism' and 'nationalistic' tend to be used as pejorative terms to suggest excessive publicly declared preference for the position, merits, claims and aspirations of one's own country or race over others. Objective assessment is rejected. Others simply see the attitude as patriotism. America is quite nationalistic, and so is China. 'Educated opinion' in China is far more nationalistic than in Japan, where overt nationalism is largely confined to noisy minorities. According to Steve Tsang: 'few Chinese citizens in fact know the history of their country well but they have all been indoctrinated in the greatness of China's long civilisation and unity . . . The historical narrative is outwardly a "pan-Chinese" one, but in reality it is a Han centric view of the history of greater China. The nationalism thus promoted is essentially xenophobic in nature'.[56]

Language and culture dominate the narrative of Chinese nationalism and the projection of a Chinese identity. After the Opium Wars, the language was seen as an ineffective tool of national identity and inappropriate for building a strong and modern country (see Chapter 3).[57] It was also believed to discourage literacy. Disillusion grew and exploded with the May 4th Movement. The desire for a modern Chinese national culture partially explains limiting the public space for minority cultures, such as that of the Uighurs, who, if handled differently, might be more passive. Contemporary ambivalence over the May 4th tradition – do we still want an enlightenment movement or do we prefer to cleave to Chinese tradition? – means that calls for rejection of the national past, such as language, have less resonance for many intellectuals.

Elsewhere, nationalism is often associated with yearning for a strong leader. Chinese nationalism can relate to Mao nostalgia, which is enhanced by the unexciting post-Deng leadership: the absence of style, drama and charisma saps public interest and enthusiasm.

If the economy erodes and unemployment swells, the government may face the evaporation of public approval and may try to turn attention to an overseas confrontation or shift the blame to external sources in order to harness nationalist sentiment. Tellingly, surveys show that a substantial number of Chinese regard certain major countries as enemies: Japan (38 per cent), America (34 per cent) and India (24 per cent).[58]

Nationalism in China goes back at least as far as the Boxer rising in 1899, and maybe even to the resistance to the Qing from 1644. Mass nationalistic demonstrations certainly date back to 1901 and Russia's initial refusal to honour its treaty commitment to withdraw from Manchuria. Chinese people think highly of themselves – not as individuals, but as Chinese. There is also a deep national feeling which tends to express itself more fiercely than in other countries. The Han Chinese are easily roused to anger against Japan, seventy years after the appalling events of the 1930s. They don't tend to sympathise with the Uighurs in Xinjiang; they consider the Tibetans ingrates for not appreciating the benefits of Chinese settlement; and they regard the Taiwanese as evil (or at least misguided in seeking independence) and see nothing wrong in issuing military threats. Unification is a strong passion. Even Chinese people who like the market economy, internet freedom and perhaps some political liberalisation are still likely to be fairly nationalistic. Beijing has been ambivalent about this, both stoking it through nationalistic school textbooks to enjoy the role of defender of the motherland and yet often discouraging rather than exacerbated it, since popular demonstrations could have unintended consequences.

The CCP uses nationalism as part of its claim to legitimacy: unlike the Guomindang, it is seen as having resisted – and partially defeated – Japanese invasion. Portraying itself as having put country before ideology was a winning card for the CCP in the 1940s, although this view is strongly challenged by many living outside China. Officials comb the internet for comment, but in most societies it is the people with strong views who speak out, and the internet encourages extreme opinions. Thus officials may miss the broad sense of public opinion.[59] Nationalism is widespread and is encouraged not only by the school textbooks but also by the official media. Since the 1970s, China has eschewed adventurism overseas and has maintained a public line of 'peaceful rise', 'peaceful development' and non-intervention. Now officials shy away from compromise on sensitive issues and largely follow the 'public'. However, if pressed economically, the regime may decide to ride the tiger, not restrain it.

China's leaders may make regular references to socialism, Marxism–Leninism and other universal themes, but in reality China's thinking (so far as it can be categorised ideologically) seems closest to nationalism. It is difficult to identify any universal political values to which China subscribes. Non-intervention in the affairs of other nations is scarcely a *value*; it is a policy. It has suited China's leaders. Although opposition to multilateral and unilateral intervention has hitherto been Chinese policy, this is showing some signs of change, as discussed in Chapter 15. Any overseas confrontation would need to be significant enough to divert attention from internal issues. That would justify terror alerts, the muzzling of critics, tolerance of economic hardship and many of the tactics employed by the second Bush administration to focus on security rather than internal socio-economic goals.

There are many points where extraterritorial conflict could arise. With Japan, there are the Diaoyu Islands; with India, Arunachal Pradesh; with the Philippines, the South China Sea; and with Vietnam, the Spratlys. Indeed, given China's current geographical claims – if one accepts the rhetoric – the case could be made that such confrontations would not even constitute inter-vention in other countries' affairs.

China's current nationalism is a work in progress. There are deep unan-swered questions. Is it a multinational empire's nationalism or will it become Han nationalism, as is ardently desired by many? While it might be a viable strategy to move from the current awkward formulation of 'a united multi-ethnic state'[60] to stress ethnic unity, nationalism and shared historical experi-ence, this does have a reverse side: Uighurs, Tibetans and other minorities cannot be expected to feel conjoined in an ethnic Chinese vision. Accordingly, ethnic nationalism has advantages and disadvantages as a future vision for the state.

A radical but not impossible twist would be to build on the view held in China that all Chinese are ultimately 'of China'. The extension would be that if any Chinese community is badly treated anywhere in the world someone should right the wrong. Theoretically, this could even apply to an individual. In 1850, the 'Don Pacifico Affair' saw Britain send a naval squadron to blockade the Greek port of Piraeus in protest at the ill-treatment of a Gibraltarian (and thus a British subject). Lord Palmerston declared at that time: 'a British subject, in whatever land he may be, shall feel confident that the watchful eye and the strong arm of England, will protect him against injustice and wrong'.

Potential targets for such an initiative would include Malaysia and Indonesia, where there are sizeable Chinese minority communities and a history of discrimination (and, in a recession, a potentially envious majority population). One reason China advanced for its 1979 invasion of Vietnam was the ill-treatment of the ethnic Chinese minority, most of whom had probably never seen China and were not Chinese citizens, and all of whom were presumably born in Vietnam.

What Should *China* Look Like?

This discussion has focused largely on the Party's future. Party and state are, of course, entwined – but this need not necessarily always be so. We should also consider whether the country of China will always remain the same. It has changed its shape and size – expanding and contracting – frequently during its history. It is an empire, not a nation. A question that is seldom raised is what China will prefer to be in future. As we have seen, the official description of China recognises the ethnic minorities, but popular discourse sees it as Han China. Can it be successful as a multiracial empire or would it be more successful as a Han Chinese nation state? Is it comfortable with embracing large (and growing) non-Han racial communities in return for possessing their lands and resources?

Sometimes it is worth indulging in blue-sky thinking. Will the time come when China feels it would be stronger with a culturally united, solely Han population in a smaller territory? Or would China prefer to accept potential instability from its ungrateful minorities in return for such natural resources as energy, minerals and the waters that rise on the Tibetan plateau? One can rule by force or one can rule by consensus. Consensus is cheaper and simpler – and it doesn't have to involve elections. It might occasionally look difficult to rule China in this way, but China can have the population she wants and can forge a consensus within a nation with shared values. Those who prefer not to share the country's destiny could be cut adrift.

If Islam is every year becoming more radical in most of the world, is the clock ticking for China in Xinjiang? Would its Muslims be any different? Why not just say goodbye? China does not need 1.35 billion people when it has a one-child policy to control births. China doesn't need 4 million square miles, when 1 million is desert. What is national interest as opposed to emotion?

There are practical issues involved in separation, but it is always possible for deals to be worked out (think of access to West Berlin stranded in the middle of East Germany in the 1960s). Presumably, for example, water resources could be shared – as they should be in any multinational riverine system. Nationalism is not always about aggrandisement and occupying the territories of others. Sometimes the objective is to create a strong monocultural nation state by shedding those who do not belong (for example Israel's unilateral cession of Gaza in 2005 or Malaysia's 1965 expulsion of Singapore). Perhaps the 22.5 million Uighurs and Tibetans do not need the 40 per cent of the land mass of the current China that they occupy: they could probably live happily on a tenth of that. China might need the nuclear facilities, access to Tibetan water and perhaps oil-sharing rights.

The issue here is: what is best for China? If the central government public security budget is half that for education, isn't something wrong? From an economic, social and security perspective, wouldn't it be better to humanely expatriate the unhappy people? After all, 'many of the world's problems stem from the fact that it has 5,000 ethnic groups but only 192 countries'. [61] It is a huge challenge to modernise and strengthen China and make it a great power, and a competitive one for the twenty-first century. Isn't it a distraction to have to spend time on people who are not ethnically Chinese, don't seem to want the same things and embroil one in a 'life and death struggle'? [62]

Reflections

There is the potential in China for further major change in Party, state and nation. The Party's ideology is likely to develop; the process of government will adapt either to enable the regime's survival or to reflect its departure; and national borders could change significantly to ensure a more secure future for the Han people.

The Party is likely to lurch towards nationalist and welfare policies, including a more effective environmental commitment. China has many opportunities to adopt a more nationalist stance. Some are more likely to be taken up than others, but circumstances and perceptions change. The combination of partially controlled media, a muted internet, low-level foreign language skills, highly partial official history books and a degree of innate nationalism derived from prolonged foreign occupation means the public might indeed fervently support military confrontation abroad. To galvanise public enthusiasm, the Party may need to end the grey collective leadership system and inject some glamour or charisma. An important geostrategic issue will be whether it is worth Beijing carving out some territory for the Tibetans and Uighurs and 'extra-territorialising' them, while at the same time preserving its resources and military interests in those regions. This could surgically remove the potential for an externally assisted Islamic war inside China. Bold decisions sometimes avert disasters.

Another necessity is a strong focus on social policy. Policy-makers may say there was no choice in the late 1970s but to focus on growth, but there is now such income disparity that it can probably be accommodated only by ensuring that the poorest are protected by elementary social provisioning, improved work conditions and greater attention to wages. If it goes down this road, China will have moved from ideologically led policy to economically led policy to socially led policy.

An amalgam could be created of nationalist, social welfare and Confucian thinking: a Confucian approach does not require a liberal democracy; however, rulers must govern justly. A key question is whether neo-Confucianism is intellectually conducive to the creation of the society and technology required for a superpower in the twenty-first century.

The nation's rulers need constantly to be sure that they are ruling for the greater good of the country – and that they are seen to be doing so. A disadvantage of the absence of democracy is that there are few platforms on which to articulate a philosophy of government under sharp public scrutiny. That means a greater burden on rulers to prove themselves to general satisfaction. A wise and benevolent government can provide public satisfaction for prolonged periods without recourse to democratic processes. Unfortunately, any type of benevolent government may eventually stumble. Here Japan provides a good example: for twenty years, in the 1960s and 1970s, its economic policy was almost universally admired; since 1990 it has been almost universally derided. In China the Party has been highly successful at governing, and that has earned it popular legitimacy. However, lack of an electoral mandate means that legitimacy relies upon its being right almost always. As issues become increasingly complex, it is not certain that the Party will always make the right decisions. To give one example, there may be substantial unintended consequences from the $2.6 trillion of bank lending sprayed into society during the 2008–10 crisis. That was a bold move, but it could lead to devastation of the banking system.

Ideology has changed from the Maoist years, when it was an uneasy blend of socialism and communism, to the reform years, when it has been national development through a mixed-economy strategy combined with strong state control over society. Beijing has thus refocused from politics to economics. The coming years will be marked by further pragmatic shifts, reflecting social considerations. China may steel itself to accept a measure of socialism in order to avoid instability. The Party keeps renewing and strengthening itself. History has no 'law of the inevitability of democracy'. If the Party keeps adapting, resumes reforming and delivers what most of the people want most of the time, it could govern for another century. But what is certain is that a profoundly unstable China will not continue its rise. There is much for the new leadership to contemplate.

CHAPTER TEN

America and China: Common Interests, Mutual Antagonisms

In order for China to ascend to superpower status, America must relinquish it. That is the *sine qua non*. It could be argued that the world does not at present have a superpower at all; if so, that would make China's ascent easier, but still not assured. To explore America's position in the world today, I draw some lessons from its recent wars, particularly in Afghanistan. For, after all, a great power at peace is somewhat like a racehorse in a stable. China will also be examining its behaviour, and what China sees will influence its policies and actions. The relationship is ambivalent: partnership or threat? Certainly, it is not friendship. America has an interest in strengthening Asia's security, but not in presenting a direct challenge to China. My argument will be that America is clearly weakened in its global position but is not fatally wounded. Furthermore, America does not have to be a superpower to remain more important than China.

The Sino-American relationship is understandably far and away the most important and interesting of all China's relationships. It is based on common interests and mutual antagonisms: China envies America. This is partly because of what America is, but more because of what it has. Because of China's exaggerated sense of humiliation, it longs for admiration and respect. China would like quietly to supplant America's position in the world and be respected by it. It would like to replace the US's soft power and better its technology. China is auditioning for a part for which no one is hiring. The future is wide open. Succession may happen peacefully, messily or not at all.

Jobs, Trade and Investment

One of the debates of 2011–12 was over 're-shoring' – whether the rising costs in China could lead to companies moving their manufacturing capacities out of the country. The proponents note trends towards fast-rising wages and further gradual exchange rate appreciation. The opponents cite the size of the experienced workforce in southern China and the importance of the existing supply chain. They also point out that comparisons with China's average wage are deceptive, as employers don't necessarily pay the average wage. There are inland areas of China where the wage is much lower than average (then again, wages have become quite flexible in the southern states of the US). On the other hand, although wages in the hinterland may be a lot lower than on the coast, many of those workers are not suited to international factory work.

Only half of American companies in China increased their profits in 2011, and 90 per cent said that higher costs were hurting. The World Bank suggests that a US worker is twelve times as productive as a Chinese worker, which covers a certain amount of wage differential. Also, the US 'jobless recovery' has been based largely on good productivity growth. Boston Consulting Group forecasts that net labour costs in the US and China will 'converge by around 2015' and it anticipates 'support' from some US state and local governments for new manufacturing plants.[1] Much recent US job growth has been in low-paid occupations: indeed those in low-wage jobs – earnings on the threshold of poverty for a family of four – have risen to 28 per cent of the workforce and the rise is likely to continue until 2020.[2] We also need to take account of the labour-force contraction in China. Since, by and large, other developing countries have neither the supply chains nor an experienced and abundant workforce, it seems unlikely that there will be any substantial re-shoring either in that direction (apart, perhaps, from Mexico) or to Europe (which lacks wage flexibility).

China needs to sell its goods to the huge market that is the US: that is true whether America is prospering or not. There are other, lesser needs – to acquire products, services and technologies from America and to have a relatively safe place to keep a great deal of money (China has been the largest holder of US government bonds – see Chapter 4). It would like to overtake the US in many respects, and that will mean mimicking certain of America's features, good and bad.

Washington complains vocally about currency rates and trade surpluses, despite the fact that nearly 60 per cent of all China's exports are from foreign-funded ventures (many of which are managed and owned by Americans). Furthermore, US consumers and the US inflation rate have benefited hugely from the decade-long waterfall of low-priced Chinese manufactured goods (Walmart has become the second largest employer in the world only because of cheap Chinese goods).

Or take another example: China's rising prosperity has made it an acquirer of overseas assets. The US (leading advocate of free markets that it is) blocked

China's oil giant CNOOC from buying the American energy company Unocal in 2005, prevented the Chinese telecoms company Huawei buying 3Com in 2008, and discouraged Anshan Iron and Steel from investing in 2010. Chinese nationalists see an American tendency to seek to humiliate China. The lessons America is teaching China are that a great power can espouse a doctrine, but avoid its practice whenever it proves inconvenient.

There is a recurring theme here: 'Please fund our profligacy but don't acquire our assets. Please manage your currency at rates that suit our over-priced workers rather than your economy. You mustn't hold your currency down, but we need to use low interest rate policies and quantitative easing to manipulate ours.'

We should be aware that such contra-investment-policy action by the US pushes China into the 'outer darkness', forcing it to acquire energy assets in Sudan or Iran simply because the US blocks it from free market acquisition in easier environments. The US and Australia may say that China does not play by the same rules as the host country and so it must not be allowed to buy, or that major Chinese state enterprises are but an arm of the government. They may reject acquisitions on the grounds of national security (such as the purchase of mines adjacent to the Woomera space rocket facility in Australia). These are good reasons, as long as the host countries do not apply double standards.

Certainly China could consider privatising its large state enterprises and challenging the Anglo-Saxon free economies directly, but Beijing sees these companies as strategic, and thus feels it necessary to keep them under state direction.

America's Political and Military Relationship with China

The political relationship is quite convoluted. America was a strong ally of the Chinese Republican, or Nationalist, government in the 1940s, during the war against Japan. In 1950, China attacked US troops that had pushed up into North Korea as part of the UN support for South Korea. By fighting US troops to a standstill and by achieving a stalemate truce with the world's strongest power, China felt it had boosted its prestige in the early days of Communist rule. Some in China believe the intervention cost Beijing an early takeover of Taiwan, but the challenge on its doorstep had been immediate and had to be confronted.

After Mao's rapprochement with Nixon, when both countries opposed Soviet hegemony, there was wary mutual sympathy. But by the 1990s, the Soviet threat had evaporated and Sino-American relations had become frosty again.

The NATO bombing of the Chinese Embassy in Belgrade in 1999 drew an understandably sharp response. Although it was denied by Washington, some leading Western newspapers reported that the bombing had been deliberate, as the Chinese were briefing the Serbian army on NATO attacks.[3] The bombing and US opposition to China hosting the 2000 Olympics coincided with (and encouraged) a new phenomenon of large-scale involvement by ordinary Chinese in overseas disputes, over the internet, in the print media and on the street, and paved the way for an understandable anti-Americanism.

A 1999 US House of Representatives report laid a number of charges at China's door, including spying and 'stealing' US nuclear technology,[4] though many American analysts criticised the report as poorly grounded. The rebarbative relationship continued with such incidents as the collision of a US surveillance plane with a Chinese fighter in 2001. Through all this, there were occasional moments of cooperation: China was willing, for pragmatic reasons, to support George Bush's call for a coalition against terrorism and managed to get the principal separatist group in Xinjiang – the East Turkestan Islamic Movement – blacklisted as 'terrorist' by Washington (see Chapter 8). Yet while America encourages China to back US diplomatic initiatives, the US Congress produces annual strategic reviews that are sharply critical of Chinese military spending, and America continues to engage in provocative military behaviour along China's perimeter (see below). Through its policy of 'strategic ambiguity', it sporadically arms Taiwan, eliciting carefully managed hysteria from China: a mixture of woe and threat.

Sino-American naval confrontation has lasted from the early 1990s until the present, and has even included action in third-party waters. In 1993, the US navy had the Chinese freighter *Yinhe* searched in port in Saudi Arabia, claiming (falsely, as it turned out) that it was carrying banned agents for the manufacture of mustard gas and nerve gas.[5] In 2009, five Chinese naval vessels approached 'dangerously close' to the USNS *Impeccable*, an ocean surveillance ship, 75 miles south of Hainan Island, which China is developing as a major submarine base. A Pentagon spokesman said, 'We expect Chinese ships to act responsibly and refrain from provocative activities.' The US subsequently made it clear that it would in future accompany unarmed surveillance ships with heavily armed destroyers.[6] It is the US history of maritime and aerial 'surveillance' off the Chinese coast that might more accurately be described as 'provocative'. China's military can only respond aggressively to an American entity if Washington puts it there in the first place.

The United States is one of the most important military powers in the Far East, and the American military has consistently adopted an aggressive policy towards China, which has – not wholly unexpectedly – responded in similarly aggressive terms. It seems that America is willing to anger China by taking military craft through its 'spheres of influence'. Chinese aircraft, in turn, regularly annoy Japan by flying into its airspace and the Chinese navy occasionally approaches US Pacific territory.

The South China Sea is of strategic importance to Washington, as over half the world's oil tankers pass that way. It is equally strategic to China, as most of its oil flows through there. America has been building its relationship with Vietnam, both politically and militarily. In fact, US military strategy in East Asia seems calculated to inflame relations with China. A couple of things are worth noting: America shows aggression towards China on Chinese frontiers; China has shown hostility on the margins of its own jurisdiction, but until 2013 there was no accusation of China taking its military capability into American waters. American provocation transcends presidencies: it was evident under Clinton and George W. Bush and it continues under Obama. It seems there is a bipartisan willingness to provoke China.

Obama's muted approach to human rights (he avoided the Dalai Lama early on in his administration and passed up photo opportunities in 2010, when the two men finally met, and he and his senior officials have omitted to raise the issue during visits to Beijing) suggests that America feels it cannot engage in controversial issues because China holds so much US debt.[7] Chinese officials have seemed exultant that they are somehow in the ascendant and that the balance of the Sino-American relationship is now satisfactory (even if the actual relations are not). American diplomats counter that they cannot prioritise everything and choose to focus on the environment, economy, security and finance.

Obama is accused of lacking interest in the human rights issue. The left wing of the Democratic Party is ultimately interested only in domestic public expenditure projects, and America now seems to be pursuing its interests rather than projecting its values. We seem to be getting conservative foreign policy from Obama, having had liberal policy from Bush. Where Obama has made an impact is in the extraordinary achievement that by 2011 he was simultaneously unpopular in both Middle Eastern Muslim countries *and* in Israel.[8]

From the Asian perspective, an important aspect has been America's low regional profile in recent years. Fighting serious wars has caused distractions. However, the previous invisibility of the US in Asian forums has increased the impact of China's growing regional presence. The fate of Georgia, a one-time NATO aspirant, will have chilled some smaller Asian countries: the long arm of America is not always available. In fact, China's ever-widening footprint now includes significant parts of the South Pacific, from Papua New Guinea and East Timor to Vanuatu and Fiji (whose rapprochement with China has been encouraged by its suspension from the British Commonwealth for lack of democracy). This evaporation of US influence has now been partially reversed; but it is unclear how great the appetite is for this reversal or how large the resources are. Washington plans to switch the balance of the US navy between the Atlantic and the Pacific from 50:50 to 40:60. This partly comes as a result of concern about potential 'area denial' in the western Pacific by China's navy.

The military relationship with Vietnam has gradually grown, with former Secretary of State Hillary Clinton echoing Hanoi's call for a multilateral settlement in the South China Sea. Several ASEAN members have quietly encouraged the US to raise its East Asian profile, as they do not wish to face a rising Chinese military and maritime force without a sizeable US presence.

The reduced standing of America in relationship to a rising China was sharply delineated in 2009, when Chinese leaders began publicly lecturing America on its poor economic management. The year ended with the climate change conference in Copenhagen, which saw the derailing of Barack Obama's policies. Still, at least America was in the room when the final deal was worked out: although uninvited, President Obama apparently accidentally arrived. That is more than can be said of the troubled European Union, which was neither invited nor present.

While the US military and diplomatic focus on Asia increased in 2010–12, the debilitating debate on confronting the American budget deficit underlined the need for reductions in at least the *growth* of military spending. Financial constraints could well mean sharp cuts in Washington's military programmes, which will have a strong impact on its force effectiveness. By late 2011, $465 billion of cuts were under way and another $600 billion looked likely. The navy, for example, was looking – according to former Defense Secretary William Cohen – at reductions that would 'impact the fleet for 20 to 50 years'.[9] The Defense Department anticipated the cut of $1 trillion in its budget and Secretary Leon Panetta said that in ten years the US would possess 'the smallest ground force since 1940, the fewest ships since 1915 and the smallest air force in its history'.[10]

The Chinese commitment to raising military expenditure and the likely cutting of US spending will reduce the difference considerably. Two points give some grounds for cautious optimism. First, Secretary of Defense Robert Gates said in 2010 that there was a mind-boggling degree of waste in the Pentagon budget; perhaps $300 billion a year can be saved by tightening up on efficiency, if politics allows. Second, perhaps America doesn't actually need so many ships, given that its battle fleet is larger than the next thirteen navies combined (eleven of which belong to allies and partners).[11]

America as a Superpower

There is some debate as to when America became the dominant world power. Some say it was after 1945, when it had gradually – between the two world wars – overtaken the British empire. This dominant position endured until the 1950s, when the Soviet Union managed, through the development of nuclear technology, to force a bipolar system in which America was the lead player. By the 1980s, the failing Soviet system could not sustain bipolarity. The Sino-Soviet split, the associated Sino-Vietnamese War, the Soviet failure in Afghanistan, the renaissance of Islam, the failing economy, the Vatican, the East German churches, the Polish unions and the 'Star Wars' missile system, all played a part. By the fall of the Berlin Wall, America was widely acknowledged as the world's only superpower.

What do we mean by a superpower? Some writers, rather feebly, use 'superpower' merely to mean 'world power' or 'great power'; in other words, one of a handful of leading states. Others feel it has to mean one of two at the pinnacle, as we saw the bipolar world of America and the Soviet Union. Many Chinese thinkers, for example, in a form of wish-fulfilment, like now to talk of a 'G2' of America and China as superpowers. A discussion I had with professors at the Communist Party Central School in 2009 revealed that there was no agreement – even among themselves – on what constitutes a superpower. With some Beijing academics one feels that the concept is synonymous with 'major power', while with others it is a euphemism for 'hegemony'.

I suggest that the term 'superpower' does not mean just a great power – or even the largest power with the greatest technology. It should mean a state that is so much more powerful than all others that it can largely (though not wholly) enforce its will and impose its values worldwide. A corollary of this is that there is only ever one superpower, and sometimes none at all.

The Shortest-lived Superpower?

A lesson the West learned in Korea, and again in Vietnam, is that the stronger player does not necessarily beat the weaker one.

The Afghanistan war is discussed elsewhere (Chapter 12), but I refer to it here because it offers illustrations of America's current status as a world power. It is often easier to observe a power during war, and this is America's principal war. The wars in Afghanistan and Iraq present a distinct problem: the opponents and the terrain were chosen by America, and yet, after several years of fighting technologically inferior enemies with a combined population of around 60 million people, these wars were not won.

A number of facts and figures illustrate the difficulties the US is encountering in Afghanistan. Particularly arresting has been the extraordinary inability on the part of America and its allies in Afghanistan – after over a decade of fighting – to hold even the 190-mile main military supply route from Peshawar to Kabul (which principally runs through the land of its ally, Pakistan). This has forced America to request its non-ally Russia to allow supplies to pass through its territory. In addition, three of the four roads out of Kabul have been under Taliban influence or control.[12] By the end of 2009, almost two-thirds of Afghanistan was too dangerous for aid workers to reach.[13]

Second, the US is aware that its resources are very stretched. Even back in 2007, Larry Wilkerson, former Chief of Staff to Colin Powell, told the *Financial Times* that the US was finding it ever harder to meet enlistment targets: 'Standards have been lowered too. The army is now enlisting recruits aged 40, paying recruitment bonuses of up to $40,000 and has lowered the mental threshold to "category three", which, according to Mr. Wilkerson, is "one level above imbecility"'.[14] The economic downturn subsequently improved recruitment somewhat, but didn't fundamentally change matters.

Third, at the 2011 peak, around 150,000 allied forces were stationed in Afghanistan, which had a population of around 28 million. Taking all American and allied troops currently in Afghanistan, there was a 'force density' of 0.4 per cent. The Russians had a troops-to-population ratio of 1 per cent when they admitted defeat and left Afghanistan. This compares with 2.3 per cent for the British in Northern Ireland, 3.5 per cent for the Thai army in the Muslim insurgency in southern Thailand, 6 per cent in the Sri Lankan civil war and 14 per cent for the Indian army in Kashmir. Whether one claims to be providing security for the population or admits that one is fighting them, the issue of force density is equally relevant. To match India's unsuccessful effort in Kashmir, America would have had to raise its troop level in Afghanistan to 4–5 million soldiers. That is the equivalent of the combined armies of America, India and China. It was not going to happen.

Fourth, between 2002 and 2012, the US provided roughly $17 billion in military aid to Pakistan, its ally.[15] According to Serge Michailof, an aid and reconstruction specialist, it is possible to gauge the level of support for the Taliban from the ISI (the Pakistan intelligence service) by the 'appearance of hundreds of four by four vehicles and satellite telephones among the Taliban forces'.[16] If it is not possible to manage (or even monitor) billions of dollars of military payments and prevent the money from being given to the enemy, it is difficult to emerge a winner from conflict.

Fifth, the shortage of soldiers available to both American and British armies has given rise to a huge industry of 'private contractors'. Both the American and British armies are under-manned for the role they have to play. They cannot guard diplomats, provide training programmes for local soldiers or protect aid workers. They seem unable even to operate missile and drone systems and other complex military equipment. As a result, contractors – perhaps 'mercenaries' would be the correct word – have replaced soldiers. America uses contractors for 'more than half of the U.S. presence in the contingency operations in Iraq and Afghanistan' and in 2010 their number exceeded 260,000.[17] American nationals make up less than a fifth of them. This extensive use of contractors has led to a culture of paying cash to warlords and enemy insurgents in return for safe passage.[18] It also obscures the human costs of war: if we add in the deaths of contractors in Iraq and Afghanistan, US military casualties increase by over 40 per cent.[19]

We might also question the general behaviour of the West's superpower. At the very least, we must recognise that it has now abandoned habeas corpus (prisoners held without charge for ten years and more), believes in torture (waterboarding) and practises deliberate and systematic assassination (drone attacks on targeted individuals). It is a surreal time in US history, when anything seems acceptable. Yet on entering the White House, President Obama said that if – in pursuit of your enemy – you offend against the basic values of the country, you have lost the fight.

No matter how alien or unsympathetic another society might seem to American eyes, playing superpower by breaking into that society's world and turning its culture upside down is probably not a game that will be pursued so enthusiastically in future.

In theory, military force and strong-arm policies are how a superpower might demonstrate and maintain its power. In the case of America, it has been more subtle. In 2009, former Prime Minister Mahathir of Malaysia stated that the US had not won a war since 1945, except for when it invaded the Caribbean island of Grenada.[20] That comment sums up its entire history as a superpower. One survey of unilateral American sanctions concludes that they were 80 per cent a failure.[21] We might say that the future of the Afghan War bears much similarity to the Vietnam War, not least in the consistent official avoidance of the term failure. Also in 2009, the then Russian ambassador to NATO, Dmitry Rogozin, said that NATO in Afghanistan had 'repeated all our mistakes, and have made a mountain of their own'.[22]

Its inability successfully to conclude the Afghanistan and Iraq wars means that the US can no longer realistically be regarded as the world's superpower. It is still the world's strongest power, but it is impossible to call it a superpower. Arguably, then, with a lifespan of 1989–2003 it was the shortest-lived superpower ever. This would hold true even if it had been a superpower continuously since 1945. In historical terms, that is the blink of an eye. Immersed in a culture that thinks in terms of millennia, Chinese strategists would find it unimaginable that their own superpower standing could last barely two decades. China needs to absorb every lesson from America's brief supremacy.

Can a Superpower be a Russian Hostage?

America's relationship with Russia offers a number of lessons in US decline. Russia told NATO members bluntly that, although in principle she might help supply their armies in Afghanistan, she would ration access to her supply routes, based on her view of each NATO member's foreign policy towards Moscow. Russia was not, of course, against the Afghanistan war: theoretically at least, it disrupted the vast heroin trade that costs Russia dear, without Russian soldiers having to do the fighting. However, what matters is that Russia is demonstrating its power in its 'near abroad'. It is uncertain how much power the Russians will have in future, and its neighbours are reminded that it would be unwise to be disrespectful of Moscow. Kazakhstan, Kyrgyzstan, Uzbekistan and Tajikistan are members of the Shanghai Cooperation Organisation (SCO), along with Russia and China. The SCO is a sort of anti-NATO, which functions partly to put a spoke in America's wheel, but also allows China and Russia to jockey for position in Central Asia. Andrei Sorokin, head of a Russian think tank, said in 2009: 'Russia is interested to the maximum extent possible, in making things difficult for the US – in making the transfer of American forces into Afghanistan be dependent on the will of the Kremlin.'[23]

Russia is in many ways a 'paper tiger': it could beat Georgia (once that country was shorn of allies), but could not send its navy to Venezuela without tugboats capable of rescuing its warships (see Chapter 11). That America needs to throw itself at Russia's feet and beg for a supply line demonstrates the utter military futility of the previous decade. That America cannot confront it or deter it shows that Russia has played its limited cards quite well and knows where it can successfully bring force to bear. It also demonstrates how America is retreating from its superpower status.

Did American Hegemony Ever Exist?

In fact, it is possible that American hegemony was only ever a myth that existed for a period after 1989 simply because the other power had left the field and no new power stepped up to present a challenge. After the September 11th, 2001 World Trade Center attack, few countries were going to object to a US invasion of Afghanistan. This gave another short burst of world support and sympathy for America, and it facilitated alliances. The way this sympathy was squandered explains the subsequent absence of sympathy. It also created a climate in which other powers felt able or eager to challenge Washington. For many people, America's new international wars were symbolised by the prisons of Abu Ghraib and Guantanamo. It is possible to lose superpower status without another country becoming the superpower. It is also possible to move from a bipolar to a multi-polar world. What we may have experienced was an interregnum, when America was the largest player, no one else was competing and so there arose the *illusion* of superpower status. The US has had the power to hurt peoples and countries and to make them angry, but it has not been able to beat them (apart from Grenada).

To be the world's superpower does not just mean having one of the largest armies and the best technology. It means being beyond challenge. We have seen US technology displayed superbly in the attack on Iraq, but then we have seen the US army bogged down in local fighting in Iraq and Afghanistan, where the advantage does not always lie with technology. Indeed, compensating for a shortage of troops by using imprecise bombing from unmanned predator drones exemplifies how technology is actually making more enemies for America. There are parallels with Varus' defeat by Arminius and the German tribesmen at the Teutoburger Wald in AD 9, which showed that, although Rome was very powerful, it could be defeated. The defeat did not mean the end of Rome, but it instantly dispelled its image as a superpower.

China has seen that America is stretched to fight in Iraq and Afghanistan simultaneously – let alone fight successfully – even with allies by its side. Beijing's top envoy to the Middle East noted in 2011 that 'US policies were losing the hearts of people in the region' (referring to Egypt) and went on: 'the US position on Palestine and its invasion of Iraq also disappointed people in the region and the damage was very difficult to undo'.[24] After Afghanistan and Iraq, the idea of America willingly waging a third war – against Iran or anyone else – is almost inconceivable.

If America were to embroil itself in a further war at a time of rapidly and massively rising indebtedness, it could experience the financial problems that contributed to Britain's loss of global leadership after 1941. The difference is that Britain's banker then was America. Although the USA had a separate and, at times, opposing foreign policy to that of the British empire, it was largely supportive of Britain's aims and ultimate survival. Now that China is a major banker to America, we must watch with interest how supportive she will be of America's aims and survival – certainly as a great power.

America's decision to make the long-term wars in Afghanistan and Iraq its principal military activity has caused some 'collateral damage'. In Britain there has always been hostility on the Left to the American alliance; but now there is widespread antipathy on the Right, too, owing to ill-thought-through wars and crass execution. This has weakened the traditional conservative view that whatever America does is generally for the best. Moreover, the wars against Muslim countries have made America look hostile to Islam; they weaken Washington by requiring it to ask favours from Russia and China; they have detached Iraq from Sunni influence and in so doing have provided Iran with an important Shia ally; they have undermined the already frayed Western alliance; and they limit America's ability to promote other aspects of its agenda militarily – such as defending self-determination in Taiwan. Though there was a need to respond immediately to the attack on the World Trade Center, the decision to engage in debilitating nation-building wars has perhaps undermined America's core international interests.

Whether America was the world's shortest-lived superpower or never was a superpower at all, evidently it is one no longer. There is a clear constellation of powers which require consideration in the new world order:

- Russia demands recognition of its spheres of influence, where the American writ will not run: it is co-opting Turkey; the Caucasus has been accepted in practice as a 'privileged interest' of Russia; and the US is obliged to accept Russia and China similarly in Central Asia.
- Turkey is becoming an increasingly important regional player in the Middle East, with extensive Central Asian interests.
- Increasingly, China is politely confronting US hegemony, and it is likely to continue to be America's banker.
- India regards its nuclear arrival as acceptance of its great power role.
- Any deal with Iran will involve recognition of its regional status, unpopular and destabilising as it will be in the Gulf States.

The countries that are out of the game for the moment are Britain, France, Germany, Brazil, Japan and Indonesia. China, India, Russia, Iran and France all wish to see the end of any lingering suggestion of US hegemony and are willing in various ways to work towards that goal (whatever they say publicly) and to see the world openly embrace multi-polarity.

That said, as a former Clinton adviser has claimed, America remains the only country capable of launching a war anywhere in the world at any time. Empires can have periods of weakness, followed by renewed rise: Britain, for example, beset by domestic insurgency in the fifteenth century, withdrew from its time-honoured pastime of beating the French, but later resumed its rise by building a maritime empire.

Reflections

China – like India – sees itself as a leading world power in the medium term. The official formulation is rather diffident: 'China's peaceful development'. The difference between China and India is that many in senior positions in Beijing see an inevitability about China's rise to be not one of several *great powers* but the world *superpower*. Furthermore, over 60 per cent of all Chinese believe that China has already, or will, become the world's superpower.[25] China will be observing and carefully drawing conclusions from the US initiatives. She has made opposition to any state's hegemony her fundamental foreign policy – at least so far. This should put Washington firmly on notice. China, like Russia, wants to be seen as a powerful state acting responsibly in difficult times. This means being seen to cooperate with America, where that country is demonstrably right. But it doesn't want to be seen as a lapdog. It will take rigorous analysis and planning if China is to become one of the world's great powers (or the next superpower). But that is something China does well.

In 2013, the favourable ratings of the US (63 per cent) were far higher than those of China (50 per cent), but China was understandably way ahead in the Muslim world, Greece and Russia.[26] In 2011, Europe and most of Asia had a more positive than negative view of US foreign policy.[27] America is better regarded in Europe, and less well regarded in Muslim countries, for fairly obvious reasons.

On Washington's part, it seems that its notions of changing the world by force, so that it better resembles America, will be allowed to fade away. America's lost superpower position broadly coincided with an economic downturn – and perhaps with a loss of belief in its omnipotence (or even righteousness).

American criticism of China now seems to be economic, rather than political or moral. It is paradoxical that the chorus of anti-Chinese rhetoric that sounded throughout America in 2011–12 focused almost entirely on trade and currency (where the Chinese have arguably done nothing wrong); more dispassionate observation would probably have censured China's behaviour in threatening its neighbours, its aggressive cyber hostility and its abuse of human rights. Either America does not currently feel up to being the 'world's policeman', or else its request for China to purchase its Treasury bills puts it in an awkward position.

President Bush comprehensively demonstrated that the US can no longer be seen as the world's superpower. Barack Obama was elected to manage not only the economy, but also America's transition from perceived sole superpower to member of a leading powers' club, with all the differences in behaviour which that suggests. From 2008, a more realist school of foreign policy emerged, after the utopian, turn-everything-upside-down, bring-democracy-to-the-Middle-East, don't-let-conventional-ethics-get-in-the-way-of-a-transcendent-strategy approach of George W. Bush.[28]

The Challenge of America

For China, convinced there is a real chance of gaining the coveted superpower status but aware that nothing is guaranteed, one challenge is to know how to work with America (when necessary, in everyone's interests), when to stand aside and when to destabilise Washington. It would, of course, be possible to hold to a strategy of benign neglect and minimal engagement while at the same time pursuing vigorous economic and financial success.

China's mercantilist natural resources policy appears to have fostered a diplomatic strategy of making friends in remote and inhospitable countries and of non-intervention in the internal affairs of nations. This seems to fit quite well with the policy, but there may eventually come another challenge – perhaps again issued by an American leader: on which side of history does China wish to stand? It is not certain that a friend of Sudan, Sri Lanka and Robert Mugabe's Zimbabwe will gain enough traction to rise effortlessly to accepted global leadership. America must not, of course, give the impression that it wishes to contain China's rise, but it should be willing to speak out on matters of global concern. While African leaders may gather in Beijing and receive Chinese trade and investment, even on that continent political change is stirring. No matter how successful China's tactics, the global response may be: 'I don't like America, but China is less attractive'. On the other hand, one way to become a superpower is for one's predecessor to abdicate. America's recent behaviour – financial and military – comes close to abdication without the announcement.

America is beginning to settle into a mentality of countdown. Every statistic, every announcement seems to be another amazing advance by China. The US administration continually talks of China's heavy military spending programme. Americans are displaying some of the signs that the British showed in the 1920s and 1930s as they became resigned to 'passing on the baton'. Imperial fatigue is showing. But things are not that clear-cut. Hegemony is not unitary: America may have lost its military superpower status in the sands of Iraq; it may have lost its banking hegemony in the 2008 Western crisis. But America is reasserting itself in Asia. Few foreigners are heard saying they want their country to resemble Russia or China, but many would like their countries in future to resemble America. Developing countries might want

Russia's arms or China's investment, but they don't want their education or their political systems. There may be global debate between pro- and anti-Americans, but there is no debate about Russia or China because there are, in the political sense, no pro-Russians or pro-Chinese.

The dollar is still the world's reserve currency. America has some of the most creative companies, rigorous universities, innovative technology, and by any reasonable criteria it has the largest middle class. It is as big as China's, but in a population that is currently one-fifth that of China. However, as we have noted, demography in China will take a hand in changing that ratio: by 2100, China will have maybe 1.5 times the population of America so it will have to put the emphasis on technology rather than scale. America – depending on immigration – will continue as a vigorous, relatively youthful, growing nation; meanwhile China will be visibly ageing and diminishing.

China may be obliged to reconsider its global sociocultural offering. Perhaps the prospect of world leadership makes it worth changing China's system to something more internationally attractive. Even people who don't like America seem to want some part of it – Disneyland, McDonald's, technology, free speech or democracy. Even Chinese leaders' children study there. While China offers something that many Chinese want, it is not yet clear that she offers the non-Chinese world much beyond trade, aid and investment. This will need to change. China must rise to the challenge of America. The US is down, but she certainly isn't out.

CHAPTER ELEVEN

Great Power Relationships

This chapter examines the extent to which the major powers surrounding China – India, Japan and Russia – present a threat to its rise. This requires some analysis of their domestic situation. I will argue that, although there is friction between China and each of these three countries, conflict is in the interests of none of the latter and would ensue only if China decides to prosecute aggressive policies.

India

India and China are populous, Asian-based, powers, with contiguous territory and ambiguous relationships with the West, and both feel their day is dawning. They invite further comparison: India has a 'blue water navy' and China plans to have one; both envisage having a number of aircraft carriers and nuclear submarines; both have the nuclear bomb. Over the last sixty years, India has probably forcibly annexed more external territories than any other country (including Soviet Russia). One might start with Hyderabad in 1948, going through Goa, Pondicherry, Sikkim and so on. China, on the other hand, formally claims Arunachal Pradesh, Taiwan and some essentially uninhabited ocean-based islands. China is a major donor to poorer countries but also receives aid; India both receives and gives aid.[1] There is a diaspora of over 25 million ethnic Indians in other countries; China, too, has a large diaspora (estimated at 40 million).

China has had an unresolved border dispute with India that dates back to the nineteenth century and the British Raj. It involves two territories – the Aksai Chin, or White Desert, in the West, north of Ladakh, between Pakistan and Tibet; and Arunachal Pradesh (AP), between Tibet and Assam. AP was under the Tibetan empire in the ninth century, the Mongol Yuan dynasty in the fourteenth century and Tibet again (by then under the sovereignty of the Manchu Qing dynasty) in the eighteenth century. There has been little of either Indian or Chinese control.

The borders were never properly demarcated. After Indian independence, in the 1950s New Delhi was spurred on by the popular media to take a wide view of its territorial rights, and by 1959 hostilities had broken out. Despite warnings from his military, Jawaharlal Nehru, the then Indian Prime Minister, adopted an aggressive 'Forward Policy' of provocation (despite his own observation that Aksai Chin was a place where 'no people live and no blade of grass grows').[2] Border talks ensued in 1962, but Nehru publicly denied them – which China interpreted as perfidy.[3] That year, China finally responded militarily, invading AP. India was routed. Afterwards, China withdrew from virtually all of AP. India has frequently been blamed for the war. The outbreak amply reflects the view that 'a leader's misperception of his adversary's power is perhaps the quintessential cause of war'.[4] Since then, India has treated its sizeable Chinese minority as potential spies, occasionally restricting their movements and even withdrawing citizenship from some.

By 2012, there had been fifteen rounds of talks, but a solution seemed no nearer. India wants the 15,000 square miles of the barren Aksai Chin (although it has never really been Indian) and the 'missing' pieces of AP. China seems to feel no great need to talk, but it maintains its claim to all 35,000 square miles of AP, which it has taken to calling 'South Tibet', and has an especial interest in the formerly Tibetan district of Tawang.[5]

Around 2000, China reached land border agreements with many of its other neighbours, such as Vietnam and the former Soviet territories of Central Asia. It also accepted pre-existing borders with Burma and Afghanistan. Since 1949, even when it has fought wars with its neighbours, it has usually agreed the frontiers subsequently. With Nepal, it signed the final protocol, including border demarcation, in 1963 – and reportedly even ceded some territory to reach conclusion. This makes India feel that China may prefer not to reach a definitive agreement with it – and China is the strongest ally of Pakistan, which is permanently on a semi-war footing with India.

China's strategic motivation towards South Asia can be analysed in two ways. The first is that it is avoiding reaching a permanent border agreement in order to assist its ally Pakistan. So long as there is no final agreement between India and China in the Himalayas, India has to deploy significant military forces there, and that weakens its potential manning of the western front with Pakistan. Another way of looking at things is that China sponsors Pakistan in order to oblige India to keep much of its army on its western frontier, away from China. A reasonable conclusion would be that both perspectives are right: a distracted opponent is a lessened opponent.

India granted AP statehood in 1987, leading to a troop build-up on the 'Line of Actual Control' and a statement from Beijing that it would 'teach India a lesson' if it continued encroaching on Chinese territory. In 2006, the Chinese ambassador to India stated the official view that AP belongs entirely to China. India felt this contradicted entirely the 2005 joint agreement that 'in reaching a boundary settlement, the two sides shall safeguard due interests of their settled populations in the border areas'.[6] India cancelled a 2007 'confidence-building' visit to China by top civil servants when one from AP was refused a visa (on the grounds that his home was in China, he was thus Chinese, and so didn't need a visa). Since then, China has insisted that normal visa arrangements are inapplicable to any resident of AP. In 2009, reflecting its support for Pakistan, it started to act similarly towards Kashmir residents. India finds this provocative and deeply frustrating. China has also developed a habit of breaching India's airspace over Kashmir with unmanned aerial vehicles, or drones, and has helped Pakistan with the technology so that it can do the same.[7] In 2012, China responded to what it saw as Indian provocation by staging a high-altitude live-ammunition simulated battle on the Tibetan plateau, with India as the unstated target.

China's concern over the Dalai Lama's international profile has led it to take a strong interest in how his successor will be chosen (see Chapter 8). The Dalai Lama has suggested that his reincarnated successor will be found outside Tibet. As the most important Tibetan Buddhist monastery outside China and Tibet is just over the Indian border at Tawang in AP, China has a special interest in reuniting the Tawang area with Tibet. Indeed, it has even said that, in seeking this, it is simply acting on the express will of the Tibetan people to reintegrate the alienated territory. As political ammunition, China can always cite the Asian Centre for Human Rights reports, which are highly critical of India's human rights practices in AP.

These are the facts of the border dispute but it would not be unreasonable to say that the dispute is a symptom of a broader struggle for standing and leadership in the Asian region.[8] Territory and even ideology do not adequately explain the hostility.

Asia Regional Policy

It is widely believed that India and China are racing to establish military facilities from the Middle to the Far East – what is known as 'the string of pearls'. China's bets are seen as Cambodia, Bangladesh, Sri Lanka, until recently, Burma and Pakistan, where it is already seriously involved in the strategic port of Gwadar (see Chapter 15). India is thought to be upgrading its 'regional' cooperation with Iran (helping to build Chabahar port), Oman, the Maldives, Australia, Singapore, Vietnam, the Philippines, Japan and – significantly – Taiwan.[9] It also operates the Farkhor Air Base in Tajikistan. This is without mentioning the US and Israel, which, with Russia and France, are the major arms suppliers to India. It has been noted that 'with a second landing platform and the appropriate air power, "India would be on the verge of possessing Asia's only viable expeditionary naval force".[10] Some in Delhi subscribe to the theory, but Beijing spokesmen hotly deny that China is putting together a 'string of pearls'.

There are some areas – notably Burma, Bangladesh, Nepal, the Seychelles and Iran – where China and India both appear to wish to exercise influence. From Burma, for example, China would like a route to the Indian Ocean, naval facilities and access to natural resources such as gas; India, on the other hand, buys Burmese natural resources (particularly oil and gas) and worked to prevent the Burmese junta from agreeing to Chinese bases. India is also one of the few countries to supply military equipment to Burma, and it assists the country in fighting rebels on its north-west frontier (which are also India's enemies); it has even offered joint military operations against dissidents inside Burma. It was growing Chinese influence in Burma in the mid-1990s that caused India to drop its pro-democracy stance towards Burma. Consequently we have not seen either the Chinese or the Indian government leading any international criticism of the Burmese regime. The reforms since 2010 in Burma have eased Delhi's discomfort and weaken links with Beijing.

Sri Lanka also represents a problem for India. It has been armed for several years by India's great enemy Pakistan, which also trains Sri Lankan pilots. In 2005 India was offered the project to develop the deepwater port of Hambantota in southern Sri Lanka, but it declined: it doesn't need a new port on a foreign island 20 miles from its shore, particularly when it is trying to develop its own domestic ports. Unfortunately it did not think ahead: despite India's efforts to persuade it otherwise, Sri Lanka then offered the project to China, which accepted, lent most of the money but the port seems largely empty. It is claimed that it is purely commercial, but many observers believe it will also have a military role.

China became Sri Lanka's biggest arms supplier in the 1990s, when India and the West declined to supply the country, owing to the civil war. Beijing increased supply further after 2007 and provided substantial amounts of arms, ammunition and radar equipment. Aid has followed the same pattern: the West has reduced its flow to negligible amounts, while China, Iran and Russia are pumping in huge sums. In 2009, Beijing lent Sri Lanka $1.2 billion – three times the amount provided by the second-biggest lender. And in 2010, China promised $290 million to upgrade the railways and build a new airport.[11] China has also shown interest in drilling for oil off the coast of north-east Sri Lanka. Meanwhile the Sri Lankan government, despite having brutally won the civil war, perpetuates a state of emergency; an opposition presidential candidate was jailed; journalists are frequently killed; and the presiding family shrugs off criticism by citing 'Asian culture'.[12]

India's great rival is thus positioned north, south, east and west of it. Encirclement is a feeling engendered in a country when its enemies establish alliances, bases or other strategic interests on various sides. It is a very uncomfortable feeling, particularly for a rising power, to have Chinese-originated facilities apparently surrounding it, and Indians, Americans and Japanese have all expressed concern at the apparent 'encirclement' of India. Now India is determined to do nothing to upset Sri Lanka for fear she will strengthen her relations with China and Pakistan.

Beijing has given Sri Lanka the same diplomatic cover as Burma, except that it has gone further. It has blocked UN resolutions censuring it, and has even secured a UN Human Rights Council motion *praising* it, by marshalling its competing new allies. Russia and China have been concerned about the increasing NATO activity in the Persian Gulf, the Indian Ocean and Pakistan. Thanks to its newly recognised strategic position in the Indian Ocean, Sri Lanka was invited by China and Russia in 2009 to become a 'dialogue partner' in the Shanghai Cooperation Organisation (described earlier as the 'anti-NATO').

With the agreements seemingly in place (though not developed) for many elements of the Chinese 'string of pearls' and with the 'encirclement' of India (however loose and seemingly unmilitary), we can now see the dawn of an era when the Indian Ocean will no longer be secured by Indian and US naval fleets. China has arrived and needs no support from either of the other two.

Water Access

By 2030, China is forecast to increase its demand for water to 818 billion cubic metres a year; its current supply is 25 per cent short of that. At the same time, India will increase its demand to 1.5 trillion cubic metres, and its supply is half of that.[13] These neighbours seem almost predestined to come into conflict. China's proposed diversion of the Brahmaputra (or Yalong Tsangpo in China), one of Asia's greatest rivers, deeply concerns India, through which it subsequently flows. The Tsangpo project not only features a hydroelectric facility, but also a substantial diversion, through three man-made rivers, to transport 38–48 billion cubic metres of water annually to China's dry northern region (see Chapter 6).[14] The Brahmaputra rises on the Tibetan plateau, as do ten of

Asia's largest rivers on which almost a third of the world's population depend for water. Indian Prime Minister Manmohan Singh raised his concerns about the project during his 2008 Beijing visit (Wen Jiabao replied that water shortage threatens the very 'survival of the Chinese nation'). China halted the project temporarily; but considering its genuine and urgent need for water, its resumption was not surprising. The Indian water specialist Brahma Chellaney observed in 2011 that 'while almost all of China's neighbors have water agreements among themselves, not one has a water agreement with China'.[15]

If the water flowing through the Brahmaputra in India and then Bangladesh is substantially reduced, it will threaten the livelihood (and lives) of tens of millions of people and is likely to exacerbate the already apparent migratory trends from Bangladesh into India. As early as 2003, the Indian defence minister claimed that there were 20 million Bangladeshis living in India and 100,000 crossing the border annually, 'altering the demographic character of the north-eastern states'.[16] That Bangladesh is Muslim adds to the concern of the authorities in secular India. There is a real prospect of escalating racial or religious violence as natural resource changes cause rising patterns of cross-border migration. One observer commented in 2008 that if the Chinese project continues 'it would practically mean a declaration of war against South Asia'.[17]

Paradoxically, this same charge is levelled against India by Pakistan over the Indian damming of the Indus to create the Baglihar Dam in Kashmir. It is claimed that this could turn Pakistan into 'a barren land' by 2014.[18] Bangladesh, too, is worried about Indian water diversion: the migration of millions of Bangladeshis into Assam in north-east India is partly ascribed to changing water patterns in the Ganges.

A further concern is that the dam at Baglihar – and indeed the Chinese one planned on the Tsangpo – could be used as a weapon to deliberately flood downstream neighbouring land, as appears to have been done by India against Pakistan in 2005. India has been used to holding the (stronger) upper riparian position vis-à-vis its neighbours; now, with China, it is in the reverse position, which weakens its traditional negotiating approach.

In general, this shows that environmental, socio-economic and demographic changes are causing governments to take actions in their own national interest that they know could have severe repercussions for their disadvantaged neighbours.

The Indian Diaspora

There are an estimated 25 million Indians living overseas, many of them foreign citizens. Large numbers of these non-resident Indians (NRIs) have become prosperous. Manmohan Singh has sought to engage them in Indian life by offering dual citizenship and an Indian citizenship card with many rights. In 2010 he went further, asking why more overseas Indians should not return home to join in politics and public life.[19] This suggests that NRIs may in future have all the rights of full Indian citizenship, including voting and even entering political life, without requiring a passport. This has several implications. First, it could give rise to concern in the host countries about the divided loyalties of Indian emigrants (should ethnic Indian citizens of, say, America not be allowed to participate in intelligence or sensitive scientific work?). It also gives the Indian authorities grounds to intervene to protect an NRI wherever he or she may be. This begins to justify global military intervention: there are sizeable ethnic Indian communities in East Africa, Guyana, Fiji and the Gulf.

But the main point is that China could play the same card: there are huge Chinese communities internationally, and signs that China is starting to develop similar policies.[20]

India and the Nuclear Club

At the time of the 1998 nuclear tests, Defence Minister George Fernandes claimed that China was a greater threat to India than Pakistan.[21] Indian nuclear expert Bharat Karnad has said that India has set 'the aim eventually of achieving near or at least notional parity with China as the basis for equitable security' and that its nuclear submarine and long-range missile projects are configured accordingly. He adds that the imports of 'American capital weapons and surveillance platforms are meant to beef up the Indian military for the coming strategic competition with China'. In time, Pakistan will 'become a sideshow'.[22] China's reaction to this strategy is not known, but it is unlikely to be happy.

Pakistan, too, will either have to keep spending in order to build up a 'second-strike capability', or resign itself to being unable to retaliate in the event of a first strike by India. It is not clear whether Pakistan currently possesses a second-strike capability, though privately Islamabad claims that it does. If it does not, then it may, if threatened, feel obliged to fire first. Whatever the facts, India's nuclear strategy is creating greater regional instability.

Pakistan has repeatedly proposed a negotiated denuclearisation with India. However, India is watching not Pakistan but China.[23] Unfortunately, Sino-Indian disarmament is not easily negotiated because nuclear diplomacy doesn't work unless each country sees the other as a material threat. India's self-regard requires it to be seen as an equal by China, but that is unrealistic. This leaves the region in a state of unresolved instability, where it is uncertain how far states will increase their armaments and how those which cannot keep up will respond.

India and the West

The West seems determined to accommodate India more than China. Both countries have oil interests in the Sudan, but only China is criticised for it. India and China invested in Burma and supported the Burmese government, yet again only China was condemned. India develops a nuclear weapons capability and America does a deal that allows it to avoid signing the Nuclear Proliferation Treaty yet still have access to US technology. China is criticised over Tibet, but India escapes censure over Kashmir. The West is willing to give India 'a free pass', but often excoriates China.

This is because India is a large democracy, has (of necessity) dropped its old pro-Soviet tendency, has become more market-oriented and globalising, does not call itself 'communist' – and is not China. And yet in 2007 India voted with America at the United Nations only 14.7 per cent of the time;[24] and both climate change and trade divide the two countries. India also has a distinct and independent foreign policy: it has been willing to defy American pressure on trade with Iran (for example in buying its oil) and has made it quite clear that it has no problem with that country. Washington supports India's rise as a regional power (though support is weaker under Obama than under Bush). No specific mention is made of using India to act as a check on China, nor is it acknowledged that India might also become a world – rather than a regional – power with its own agenda. In the long term, America and India do not necessarily share similar objectives.

Obama made a faux pas in 2009 by issuing a joint statement with China on South Asia, offering 'to work together to promote peace, stability and development in that region'.[25] This drew a predictably hostile Indian response for its implication that China (or indeed America) could interfere in South Asia: Delhi sees South Asia as its 'backyard' and wants no foreign interference. This creates another region where a superpower cannot easily operate. India is also, like Russia, cautious about NATO's objectives in Afghanistan.[26]

The West's attitude to India is as confused as its attitude to China. It is paradoxical that in 2011 India was receiving development aid from Britain and five other countries, and yet was developing aircraft carriers and a Moon mission and was itself handing out aid to Burma, Afghanistan and sub-Saharan Africa.[27]

The Uneasy Indo-China Relationship

Aside from the many political issues which complicate Sino-Indian relations there is a sense that these two rising powers could end up in serious competition. After a few short years of friendliness, India became one of the leaders of the 'non-aligned movement', which sought to distance the developing world from both the Communist powers and the West. Although heavily left-leaning, the non-aligned movement did seek to present itself as a third force. China, on the other hand, vied with the Soviet Union for leadership of the Communist world and regarded the non-aligned movement as a bogus conception. India developed good relations with the Soviet Union at a time when the Soviets and Chinese were quarrelling. This was the background for India falling into a Himalayan war with China.

China and India compete to influence Nepal. India has twice applied sanctions against Nepal. The first time, in 1988, was because Nepal sought to buy arms from China (after India refused it). The second time, in 2005, was nominally because of the termination of parliamentary democracy, but again happened at a time when Nepal was perceived as Sinophile. The Maoist guerrillas there have had very close military links with India's 'Maoist' Naxalite guerrillas, and reportedly the Indian intelligence service invested huge efforts in preventing a Maoist electoral victory in the 2008 elections (which, paradoxically, actually brought it about). In the last years of the 2000s, more than 500 businesses started up in Nepal with Chinese investment, and over four times as many Chinese as Indian officials visited the country. There has also been what amounts to an aid war going on, with India outbidding the Chinese after the departure of the Maoist premier in May 2009. However, it was reported in 2012 that owing to the aid provided, Beijing has the ability to instruct the Nepalese authorities on police deployment against anticipated Tibetan protests.[28]

Trade between India and China has, over the years, been a minor point of friction. Although generally rising, it has been somewhat one-sided: China exports manufactured goods to India, but buys fairly simple imports, predominantly iron ore, and China's trade surplus is up to $25 billion. India has complained about China 'dumping' underpriced products. The two countries are also in competition with each other in Africa for trade, energy and minerals.

Intelligence has been a continuing thorn in the Indians' side. In the mid-1990s, for example, India feared the presence of Chinese radar technicians in Burma's Coco Islands in the Andaman Sea. Later, China's increasingly intrusive cyber operations caused anger in Delhi. Former Indian Foreign Secretary Kanwal Sibal said in 2008 that China's intelligence activity in India is 'massive and intrusive'. This echoes the strong concerns of America and other states.

The two nations have common interests, although they may not always recognise it: they maintain 'close consultation' on environmental issues; both have been cautious about Western exhortations to make early commitments to curb emissions; they conduct joint research on the Himalayan glaciers; both are concerned (from their very different perspectives) about the impact on

Kashmir and Xinjiang of any negative developments in Pakistan or rise in radical Islamist activity.

The differential birth rates of India and its Muslim neighbours, Pakistan and Bangladesh, mean that the former's population dominance is gradually being eroded. India's own Muslim population is growing faster than the Hindu majority. Moreover, if we accept that there is significant Bangladeshi Muslim immigration and that the Muslim proportion of India's population is under-reported, then (on the basis of World Bank figures) by 2050 South Asia will be 45 per cent Muslim and 55 per cent Hindu, and India itself will be 25 per cent Muslim. If the clash of civilisations becomes more confrontational, there could be an argument for Sino-Indian rapprochement. Indeed, India, China and Russia could find common cause.

China's rise discomposes India in several ways. Earlier we looked at India's sense of Chinese 'encirclement'. But, for several reasons, Indians believe that China has long tried also to 'contain' them: Chinese military and nuclear support for their great enemy Pakistan; Chinese reluctance to agree the border; and particularly China's refusal to give firm backing to India's desire for a permanent seat on the UN Security Council and its unwillingness to support Indian nuclear ambitions. The Security Council seat became an even more difficult issue a few years ago, when India yoked its case to that of Japan. Given the continuing open antipathy to Japan, it was impossible for Beijing to support a combined approach.

India has seen itself and China as rising world powers, jostling for destiny. But China sees India merely as an important regional player. Interestingly, the Indian historian Ramachandra Guha has prepared a list of reasons why India could not become a superpower. These include corruption (with family politics at its heart), growing income inequality, weak media, dissatisfied regions and environmental degradation. Ironically, these reasons are pertinent to China as well.[29] A report prepared for the Asian Development Bank discusses India's 'inter-generational challenges', which include eliminating social disparities, improving education, innovation, public services, infrastructure and energy production, building a prosperous neighbourhood and becoming a responsible world power.[30]

Superficially India and China both appear to have quite extensive military reach; but in fact there is a wide gap in their budgets. In 1995 the two powers had roughly similar military budgets, but by 2011 China was spending almost three times as much as India. India acknowledges that it is behind China, but it oozes rather disconcerting confidence. The head of the air force said in 2010: 'With the capabilities that we have built up and are in the process of building, a repeat of 1962 [the Sino-Indian border conflict] can never happen.'[31]

Washington's apparent deference to Beijing worries some Indians. As a former ambassador to the UN said in 2009: 'we are not in a position to take them on militarily, economically and now not even politically . . . The only option we've got is diplomatic. At the moment, the US is of no help.'[32] Yet despite the continuing sensitivity and fear of being 'contained' by China, India refuses to enter alliances that are openly built on containing China. Unfortunately, this is the logic underlying discussions with Australia, Vietnam and Japan, which is a continually sensitive issue for Beijing. 'China was especially angered' that India participated in the 'Quadrilateral Initiative' war games in 2007 with America, Australia and Japan.[33]

The world has some shaky preconceptions about the two powers: India speaks English, China does not. China is potentially dangerous, India is democratic and so 'safe'. History will reveal the value of these observations. One fact is certain. China is currently the world's most populous country; in future India will be.

An Economic and Social Comparison between China and India

It is interesting to compare the prospects for China with those of India, particularly as almost 40 per cent of the world's population lives in one or the other. What factors might determine the future economic performance of the two countries? Eight drivers are government policy, education, infrastructure, cultural issues, economy, the legal system, social stability and demography.

Government policy is an issue that perhaps covers two separate political questions. First, which country has a greater chance of resuming reform, which has flagged in both? India has a strong lobby that is wary of substantial further reform. Moreover Singh and other Congress Party leaders have behaved maladroitly in announcing reforms without consulting their coalition partners, and subsequently have almost always had to retract. At the local level, too, populist provincial politicians are frequently able to obstruct reforms. As we have seen, China has moved from bold reformer before 2000 to timid tinkerer and, now, perhaps a reformer again. Neither country currently impresses in reform.

The second, and associated, political question is whether its authoritarian system gives China a strong competitive advantage in implementing growth policies. China's national government is a generally high-quality technocratic administration which studies issues in depth, decides and then firmly implements. Both India and China are highly decentralised countries, where provincial government can frustrate national policy. This is easier in India than it is in China because it can be done openly – in the daylight – as the local officials have a democratic mandate. Yes, power in China is monopolised by the Communist Party but the CCP is rather like the Church of England. It has traditionally been necessary to be a member to reach the top but, once a member, one's private beliefs don't matter too much. Until recently, China has probably largely benefited from its authoritarian government system – though we should not overestimate this. Now there are areas where China may suffer from its democratic deficit. Three examples are its inability to reform fully the weak Chinese banking system without freeing ownership and control from the Party and state; the difficulty of developing world-class innovation without freedom of inquiry; and the question of how one creates a consumer society while controlling, in some areas, freedom of choice. Neither China nor India currently shows reforming credentials, but Manmohan Singh launched a further attempt in 2012 which foundered and Xi Jinping in 2013 which anticipated results by 2020. From this it is hard to tell which will do better in the longer term.

Education is usually seen as a major indicator of a country's long-term ability to grow. China has over 90 per cent literacy, while India's figure is just 66 per cent (less than the Congo). China produced nearly 7 million university graduates in 2012; India generated about 3 million. However, in India employers regard only 10 per cent of generalist graduates as employable, and 25 per cent of engineering graduates. In China, according to McKinsey, multinational employers consider fewer than 10 per cent of graduates to be employable in any international context.[34] The reasons cited in both surveys are lack of critical thinking skills coupled with poor English.

Independent studies of global universities show similar results: 19 of the top 20 universities in the world are Anglo-Saxon and neither China nor India has a university in the world's top 100. These countries have not improved the quality of university education much; only the quantity of it. Graduates are essentially aspirational clerks, and the starting salaries of Chinese graduates, as we have seen, are now below those of migrant workers. Neither country comes out of this analysis well.

India has a large *infrastructure* deficit. For example, it is deficient in roads and railways, power and ports. China is ahead here. For example, each year it adds the equivalent of the entire British power supply. There is, however, concern about the safety implications of China's rapid development of high-speed rail and about the environment. It is said that the world will not invest in India because of the deficiency in infrastructure. In 2004, the world invested 10 times the amount of FDI in China as India, in 2009 only 2.5 times and by 2012 10 times again. It is a question of relative confidence. India needs to try harder. Investment in China is larger not entirely because China is a more attractive country for investment; much of it is because

China has the world's largest population, and so virtually every multinational company has a China strategy. However, by 2028 India will overtake China in terms of population.[35] Well before that time, virtually every multinational company will need to have an India strategy. The impact on India's infrastructure and industry is potentially enormous. But the country needs around $1 trillion – a huge sum for India. The capital flows which India has failed to attract in previous decades may start to flow dramatically in coming years, but this will happen only if Indian politicians can convince business that the opportunities and the framework are attractive. Not only can the new infrastructure create formal jobs, but the building of the infrastructure will itself create jobs. One concern is that, according to the World Bank, there are currently not even half the engineers needed to modernise the infrastructure over the next decade.[36] As a result, education really must be advanced. Superficially, then, China has the advantage; but there is a strong hidden positive factor for India.

A fourth question concerns what we might call *cultural issues*. Both countries have large and growing middle classes, hungry for consumer goods. China has witnessed the Japanese invasion, civil war, the communist revolution, the Great Famine, followed by the Cultural Revolution. Many of the traditional cultural and religious values of the Chinese undoubtedly perished in these events, although the post-1900 urbanisation of the elite possibly started this process.[37] Although spirituality shows great resurgence in China, many traditional values may have been replaced by the impulse to make money. Arguably, then, China is well placed to be a financial success.

India is the origin of and home to some of the world's most important religions. The Indian character has a strongly transcendental element. This could indicate that India may lack commercialism. However, India is said to have the largest number of entrepreneurs per capita of any country apart from Thailand. The caste system, which plays an important part in the Hindu religion, does mean that many able people are excluded from the business world for reasons of birth; on the other hand, it suggests that any mutation of the system could provide an invigorating influx of new ability beyond the growth of the population itself. The same could be said for a greater assimilation of Muslims into the mainstream Indian economy. Both countries are heavily corrupt, India more so than China on some measures. Although the societies are different, neither has an overwhelming cultural advantage.

Agriculture plays a much more important part in the Indian *economy* than in the Chinese – 17 per cent compared with 11 per cent. Surprisingly, 94 per cent of the Indian labour force works outside the corporate sector.[38] Indian agricultural production has always been affected by weather conditions, particularly the monsoon season, but this impact is becoming increasingly erratic, supposedly due to climate change. There are far more extreme events, including heavy rainfall, leading to floods and crop damage.[39] This creates a wild card for India's annual growth rate. Growth could be surprisingly low one year because of a bad monsoon.

The *legal system* is markedly different in the two countries. In India there is a long history of the rule of law and respect for property rights, but decades of neglect and underfunding have clogged the court system. By 2010, there was a backlog of as many as 30 million cases.[40] Until the Property Rights Law of 2007, there were few property rights in China and even now there is lack of clarity and a Party committee structure which guides the legal system in how to handle cases.[41] There has in recent years been a sustained effort to introduce a legislative system and an attempt to promote the rule of law, including the introduction of property rights and intellectual property protection. In 2009, for the first time, the number of legal cases in China hit 11 million. Locally, there is a distinct culture of mediation – the *heshilao* system – which helps to keep smaller disputes out of the courts. Both countries have weak legal systems: India was bequeathed a good system which has been allowed to corrode; China has had no system but is now starting to build one. This is important for companies doing business or investing.

Both countries have enjoyed *social stability* in recent decades. Now they face challenges. China has seen a continual rise in mass incidents (estimated at over 180,000 a year), and growing unemployment could cause an exponential increase in unrest. India is witnessing widespread Naxalite terrorist activity, which has been a force in 200 of the country's 600 administrative districts, from the north-east to the south-west. In both countries, there are an estimated 40 million guns in private hands. Both governments recognise the security challenge to the central state, though this is not emphasised overseas.

We have looked at China's *demographic problems* in detail above (see pp.142ff, 146ff), specifically ageing: only 17 per cent of the population is under 15. India has quite different demography: 40 per cent of its population is under 15. India will for decades remain a young society with an ample supply of low-cost labour. This is a huge advantage.

Conclusion

India may be hampered by a fragmented political elite, poor infrastructure and non-commercial cultural attitudes, but one should not underestimate the likelihood of multinationals pouring investment into India, the speed with which infrastructure can be built up, and the power of an open society to develop. As China is forced to tackle its huge social and environmental issues and as demographic pressures on wage costs begin to bite, the annual growth rate there could eventually slow to about 6 per cent. As we see more multinational inflows, India is likely to reduce its infrastructural deficit. If reform is revitalised, we could see several years of 8 per cent growth. But one of the biggest problems faced by both countries is the weakness of their university education: they can produce workers and technicians, but not enough leaders. The developing world has first to realise that engineering isn't leadership.

I offer two economic predictions for the next decade. First, India's growth rate will be higher than China's over the next ten years. Second, by the end of the decade, China will still be a more important economy and a richer society than India.

Some economists have developed the idea of 'Chindia', where – through happy symbiosis – India drives its economy forward through the service sector and China through its skills in manufacturing. The two can provide each other with what each does best. This is envisaging the future by extrapolating from the past and present. It misses the fundamental fact that both are large developing countries which fully intend to maximise their economies in every area. There will be no hanging back to allow a neighbour to develop his comparative advantage. However, China could change the relationship over the coming decade in order to bring India into a strategic partnership. It could offer India a 'grand bargain': settling the border issue, dropping support for Pakistan and demarcating regional spheres of influence, perhaps in return for a security partnership against radical Islam, India joining the SCO, expelling the Dalai Lama and surrendering Tawang district. The disadvantage is that such a bargain would cement India as No. 2 in the region. The range of outcomes for India and China is very wide: from outright confrontation between two rising powers to a close alliance based upon a shared animosity to militant Islam. A second conflict with India cannot be ruled out. Over 60 per cent of Chinese people have a negative view of India, and a quarter see it as an enemy.[42]

Demography flags up two issues for China. The first is that, as noted, by 2028 India should be the most populous country in the world. Any development of military and political muscle and modest global projection by India as the new No. 1 will make it difficult for a new superpower to emerge. A multipolar world would look much more likely. Second, any sustained economic success by India represents a mortal threat to the Chinese Communist Party's mantra that no very large developing country can have economic development and participatory politics without courting instability. These factors make India's future development of great significance to China.

Japan

China, Japan and Modern History

Japan made its presence felt in Korea and China in the first half of the twentieth century in a forceful and bloody manner. Not only was Japan an ally of Britain and America in the 1914–18 war (for which it received an additional concession in China afterwards), but it is alleged to have had covert encouragement from President Theodore Roosevelt in the opening years of the century to move into Korea and challenge Russia's position.[43] It is a source of continuing anger to both China and South Korea that Japan downplays the casualties of its aggression, at times ignores them and fails to apologise properly for them. The worst event was the 1937 Nanjing Massacre (the 'Rape of Nanjing') in what was then China's capital, in which up to 300,000 Chinese civilians were murdered.[44] Since 1945 Japanese politicians, officials and academics have largely closed ranks to ignore, minimise or deny details of the massacre,[45] and it has suited America – and even China – to ignore this concealment in their desire to work with post-war Japan.[46]

The Second World War finds little space in Japanese school textbooks, and any references to it are hazy and benign. In the 1980s and 1990s, Japanese politicians were frequently excoriated for denying aspects of the country's wartime behaviour; this led occasionally to outcry and resignation. But America after 1945 was absorbed in the Cold War and was keen to cement Japan as a firm ally, so it wasn't keen to reopen old wartime wounds. Taiwan and China were fighting for trade with Japan and the prize of diplomatic recognition. Neither rocked the boat by insisting on an apology: the demands of the Cold War took priority over any desire to oblige Japan to be candid.

If Japanese school textbooks are less than open about aspects of the country's history, the Chinese government, too, has been complicit in allowing extremely nationalistic material to circulate in schools as history. Professor Yuan Weishi of Zhongshan University noted as much in *Freezing Point* magazine in 2006:

Their [the textbooks'] common points are: 1. The current Chinese culture is superior and unmatched. 2. Outside culture is evil and corrodes the purity of the existing culture. 3. We should or could use political power or the dictatorship of the mob to violently erase all the evil in the field of cultural thinking. To use these kinds of logic in order to quietly exert a subtle influence on our children is an unforgivable harm no matter what the objective intent was.[47]

He gives examples of inaccurate descriptions of the Opium Wars, the Boxer rising and the sacking of the Summer Palace in Beijing. Yuan's point is that these distortions seriously affect the attitudes of young Chinese, and how they view foreign countries. China is today a conscious actor, not a victim, in contemporary Sino-Japanese hostility. As Yuan said, 'Our children are continuing to drink the wolf's milk'. The Chinese history writer and television celebrity Yuan Tengfei has stated that under 5 per cent of the material in China's history textbooks is truthful.[48] Many countries find objective analysis of their history hard, but Beijing might have less difficulty in executing its 'peaceful rise' over the next twenty years if it removed tendentious materials from the schools. In the midst of the dispute between Japan and China over the Senkaku (or, as they are called in China, Diaoyu) islands in the East China Sea in 2012, the Japanese education minister, Makiko Tanaka, said 'there were "flaws" in Japan's history curriculum because of an insufficient focus on contemporary history. "I've had doubts about that for a long time and I believe such education is problematic." '[49] No Chinese minister has made a similar admission.

China Looks at Japan

China's approach to Japan ranges through three attitudes: need, contempt and hatred. There is a need for its trade and investment now, contempt for its present status as a 'non-power', and a vocal hatred of its behaviour in the first half of the last century. The two countries' commingled cultural and ethnic heritage does not appear especially beneficial. To what extent does China face a threat from Japan?

Most of the early joint ventures in China after 1978 were Japanese – by some accounts around 90 out of the first 125 – and Japan is a major trade partner of China. However, for historical reasons, the relationship with Japan has been hostile and verbally confrontational, with a specific geographical dispute over the Diaoyu (or Senkaku) Islands, although there has been no recent fighting. China has expressed hostility over the content of Japan's history books, Japan's lack of apology for the war and its leaders' visits to the controversial Yasukinu Shrine, where 'Class A' war criminals are buried.

China used to take comfort from the US bases in Japan both as a substitute for Japan's needing an army and as a possible check on any rise by Japan. However, in recent years America has gently exhorted its allies in Europe and Asia to build up their military capability. Japan has questioned China's increasing military spending, and China has responded in kind. In late 1997 China helped America to derail the plans outlined by Japan and ASEAN for an Asian Monetary Fund; it then openly undermined Japanese attempts to gain a seat on the UN Security Council. The only two subjects consistently capable of making Chinese officials go red in the face are Taiwan and Japan.

Domestic public emotion affects China's diplomatic relationship with Taiwan, America and Japan: events may galvanise public opinion – a US maritime incursion, a Taiwanese statement on its international position or a Japanese politician visiting Yasukinu. Sometimes China's authorities facilitate and encourage public demonstrations; sometimes they feel the expressions are too violent or inconvenient and seek to dampen them. Indeed successful, violent, public demonstrations are a double-edged sword: if Chinese citizens become too accustomed to demonstrating, they may extend the practice in inconvenient directions – against pollution, unpaid wages or compulsory land acquisition. Additionally, these violent reactions can constrain officials' policy flexibility.

So, when China looks at Japan, it sees a country that could be a useful investor, a useful trade partner, and a supplier of advanced technology. But above all it sees a country that laid waste to Chinese territory for almost twenty years.

Japan Looks at China

After a period of dithering foreign policy under the Democratic Party of Japan between 2009 and 2012, the traditional ruling party, the Liberal Democrats returned to power. Prime Minister Shinzo Abe has taken a much firmer line in the conflicts with China earning criticism from Beijing and caution from Washington. Abe has been somewhat more hawkish than his party's predecessors in office at a time when the Chinese authorities have similarly hardened their stance. This has made conflict appear much more likely than in previous decades. The US Navy has claimed that China is training for a "short, sharp war" against Japan in the East China Sea with the intention of taking control of the Senkaku islands: "the PRC navy is focused on war at sea, and sinking an opposing fleet."[50] Washington stated in 2014 that China's actions were creating uncertainty, instability and insecurity in the region. Tokyo has stated that China's stance towards other countries and its military moves raise concern in Japan and the wider international community.

Japan's annual Defence White Paper has increasingly noted China's military development: in 2005 the Japanese Air Self-Defence Force scrambled against PLA aircraft on 191 times and in 2012 it reached 300 times.[51] The country has also remonstrated about Chinese oceanographic vessels operating in Japanese territorial waters. China often complains about US naval encroachments into its territorial waters (again often by 'oceanographic investigation

ships') but consistently adopts the same measures against Japan. In 2007 the
Defence White Paper was concerned about China's use of outer space for
military purposes and the combination of ballistic missile technology with
space rockets. Japan has also been concerned about air pollution stemming
from China: in 2007, 28 of Japan's 47 prefectures issued warnings of high
levels of ozone pollution, largely on the west coast. Tokyo cannot easily overlook the drumbeat of aggression from Chinese military strategists. Zhang
Songfeng from the PLA's Institute of International Relations has commented
that 'the maritime lifeline that Japan depends upon for its imports and
exports is also the only passageway for China's eastward entry into the
Pacific, the United States' westward entry into East Asia, and Russia's
southward movement'.[52]

China's strategic thinkers (often rather undiplomatically) make China's rise
appear a zero-sum game for Japan. As Professor Ni Leixiong of Shanghai
University said: 'As we obtain absolute security of our own maritime lifeline, it
also implies absolute control over Japan's maritime lifeline'.[53] When Japan
announced in 2012 that it would name four of the disputed Senkaku (or Diaoyu)
islets, over which it presently has authority, there was an outpouring of fervour
in China: of 6,000 respondents to a survey on Sohu, a Chinese website, 38 per
cent – the largest group – supported 'immediate military occupation' of the
islands by China.[54] Later the Tokyo government decided to purchase the islands
from their private Japanese owner, which caused further furore. Government
coastal vessels from Japan and China met around the islands. Amidst the
tension, Washington moved two carrier battle groups to the vicinity.[55]

Since 2000, surveys of Japanese public opinion towards China show a clear
deterioration with only 15 per cent of Japanese feeling an affinity with China
(down from about 55 per cent in 2002).[56] In considering Japan's ability to
respond to the increasing aggressiveness by China, some legitimate questions
could be raised. The Japanese military (or Self-Defence Forces, SDF) does not
convey an impression of professional competence: in January 2008 it lost
confidential data on the Aegis self-defence system, and in July it transpired that
it had lost a flash memory device holding secret information on the army's
joint US–Japan military exercises; then in November a navy destroyer failed in
an exercise to shoot down a mock ballistic space missile. Repeatedly, the
country has displayed breathtaking incompetence in dealing with nuclear
disasters and earthquakes. Speaking of the 2011 Fukushima nuclear accident,
the chairman of the investigating commission said the fundamental causes 'are
to be found in the ingrained conventions of Japanese culture: our reflexive
obedience; our reluctance to question authority; our devotion to "sticking with
the programme"; our groupism; and our insularity'.[57]

Diplomatically, as a major democracy and one of the world's largest economies, Japan is acutely aware of its absence from permanent membership of the UN Security Council. Accordingly, it actively uses its G8 membership, and at the summer 2009 meeting its criticism of China for its environmental dereliction and its partly export-fuelled economic model caused heated exchanges. Japan will be a major loser if the focus of attention shifts from the G8 to the G20.

When Japan looks at China, it sees a growing market for its exports, a low-cost base for its manufacturers, but a frustrating opponent in diplomatic terms and a rising threat to its supply lines. In spite of everything, though, Japan's recent annual overseas development grants to China have totalled over $1.2 billion, more than to any other country.[58]

Japan and Taiwan

Japan is well aware that if Sino-American conflict arises over Taiwan, the Americans will need to use their bases in Okinawa and perhaps the Ryukyu Islands, which could enmesh Japan. China's growing military might means it could more easily forcibly subjugate Taiwan, and this is deeply uncomfortable to Japan. Its own security directly affects its position on the Taiwan issue. As Rear Admiral McDevitt, who was previously responsible for East Asia policy at the US Defense Department, has said:

> Because a hostile power in possession of Taiwan could easily disrupt maritime traffic bound for Japan, Taiwan is strategically significant to Japan . . . the PRC annexation of Taiwan . . . would not only compromise the sea lanes upon which Japan's Middle Eastern oil imports travel (e.g., the Bashi Channel east of Taiwan), but also give China improved leverage in its relationship with Southeast Asia, which could have an indirect impact on Japan's significant economic interests in that region.[59]

In 2006, for the first time Japan sent a military official to its office in Taipei. The top Japanese official in the team then said: 'Now the Taiwanese can say that both the US and Japan are on their side.'[60]

Japan's unilateral decision in 2010 to assume full air control over Yonaguni, its westernmost island 60 miles from Taiwan, has raised many questions. Previously it had jointly managed air control with Taipei. Does Tokyo feel Taiwan President Ma is dangerously close to Beijing? Has Taiwan lost too much air and sea defence capability to be reliable? Or is the aim to protect the unoccupied Senkaku Islands? Some American analysts have referred to 'the growing rift between Taiwan and Japan'. However, it also demonstrates concern for the southern approaches, given China's rising military capability. Suggesting a divergence of interests is not very credible, given that in 2010 almost half the members of the Japanese parliament were members of Japan–Taiwan friendship organisations.[61]

Japan disliked former Taiwan President Chen Shui-bian's inflaming of Taiwan–China relations, and might be equally cautious of President Ma's opposite strategy. However, it prefers Taiwan's continuing independence to seeing China dominate the South and East China Seas.

Japan's sympathy for Taiwan has risen separately from, but in parallel with, a rising understanding that Taiwan's demise would represent a mortal threat to its own security. Against that is a fear of disavowing the 'one China' mantra, which it was required to avow when opening diplomatic relations with Beijing. In the 1970s, 'one China' was palatable because even the Republic of China government in Taipei talked of China as one country (the difference being that it felt it should run 'one China'). Now, however, the Taiwan issue has metamorphosed into one of self-determination for a functioning democracy of over 20 million people. This makes it increasingly difficult for Japanese or westerners to see why the 'one China' formula should be upheld in a very different environment.

The Japanese Response to China

Japan is not reacting as we might expect to the rising regional tensions. It is sensitive to wartime memories and has chosen not to emphasise military or security links in South East Asia. Instead, in the post-war period, it initially stressed foreign direct investment, trade and overseas aid; then increasingly it began to introduce non-traditional security issues, sometimes assisting with crime, narcotics and human trafficking issues. So concerned has it become by China's military build-up, however, that in 2011 and 2012 the country began upgrading its jet fighters and naval ballistic missile systems.

At home, Japan's role in Afghanistan was controversial, as was its decision to send vessels to Somalia and its attempts to increase domestic military manufacturing and reduce the burden of weapons research by cultivating overseas arms sales. Domestic critics often see such moves as an attempt to circumvent the pacifist framework enshrined in the country's US-written post-war constitution and to turn Japan into a more 'normal nation'.[62]

In 2007, Japan and Australia committed themselves to strengthening security ties, though they also stated that they had no intention of 'cornering' China either diplomatically or militarily. Alliance with India (and possibly Vietnam) is debated in Japan, but the benefits come with costs attached. Japan and India do not want an alliance that could be seen as targeting China; however, the reason for contemplating such an alliance is the rise of China. Parallel to this, Japan and China have military meetings and exchange visits which, theoretically, reduce tension. In 2012, Prime Minister Noda discussed maritime security with heads of the Pacific island states, reportedly 'in the face of China's growing regional influence'.[63]

Japan's annual military budget has been flat to falling for about fifteen years.[64] In 2013 the Abe government finally reversed this announcing five years of modestly rising expenditure. Japan is now the fifth-largest military power in the world. In terms of developing a strategy, it doesn't help that every prime minister is an interim one. Despite prodding from Washington, the response by Tokyo to events has been timid, but in some respects steady: eventual small increase in spending and a gradual building of alliances. So Japan's reaction to China's mounting provocative actions (and indeed to those of Russia) has been governed mainly by the pacifist social culture, falling population, decades without economic growth, high public debt and dysfunctional political system.

Reflections on the Relationship with China

Japan's public and both of its leading political parties are concerned about China and its military build-up and, within the Fukuda doctrine,[65] there is sympathy for military expansion. Japan is stumbling towards a more assertive international role and is no longer abashed and embarrassed about seventy-year-old events.

The business community is divided. It has much investment in, and trade with, China and has had some influence in moderating points of friction (such as visits by prime ministers to the Yasukinu Shrine), and yet there would be many commercial benefits from developing an American-style military-industrial complex. There are compelling economic reasons for having a stronger military research and production industry, which would foster technological development beneficial to other branches of industry, get the country into space, create employment and increase exports. This doesn't arise from aggressive or bellicose positioning in international affairs.

Japan presents no real challenge to China. It would be unfortunate if China's maritime and aerial brinkmanship causes an incident that obliges a strong response from Japan. Japanese nationalist opinion may gain more traction and encourage a sharp response to provocation, but at present its influence is weak. Nor is Japan – an ageing, shrinking and economically slowing power – likely to be able to stomach war. Both Beijing and Tokyo are sufficiently alert for a military clash over the Diaoyu/Senkaku Islands or Chinese overflights of Japan to occur. Tokyo is not minded to mount military adventures, and indeed it finds policy-making quite difficult. Any pressure is Chinese pressure on Japan, not the reverse, and that can be damped down by Beijing, subject to popular opinion.

Some Japanese analysis suggests that, as a society, China is too flawed to rise very far: the anti-Japanese rhetoric should be recognised as signifying entrenched intolerance and lack of freedom of expression, inappropriate in a future great power.

> There lies the basic and crucial issue of freedom of speech: that there is a weak notion of the importance of freedom of expression, and that freedom of expression does not socially apply to things relating to Japan. The process of becoming a major world power must be accompanied by Chinese society's opening its doors not only economically but also politically to the rest of the world. In reality, a somewhat parochial nationalism seems to be casting a shadow over China.[66]

China's retention of Maoist-style vilification of Japan makes overseas observers less confident that China has entirely abandoned the Cultural Revolution. There is always the possibility that the Chinese government might come under popular pressure to take aggressive military action following some perceived slight by Japan or by a particular group there. Beijing might feel unable to withstand such popular pressure. China may have suborned much of the world to subscribe to its mantra on Taiwan, however if it made a violent attack on Japan, things would be different. For seventy years Japan has been an exemplary world citizen. However, the US, while still Japan's major ally, clearly has limited appetite for confrontation with China.

The Japanese challenge to China is, in effect, an internal one: how will China manage its own domestic opinion? Furthermore, the Liberal Democratic Party's firm responses to China and raising military expenditure suggests that if feeling threatened, it could build further its security relationships in Asia, including Taiwan. That could result in something resembling the encirclement of China, which in turn could inspire a reaction within China that its leaders would find unstoppable. This risks China being seen as a harsh and belligerent power.

Russia

The impression one gets of Russia is of a large, powerful and somewhat belli-cose country. However, it has severe social issues that inevitably affect its economic, political and strategic position. When he became president for the first time, Vladimir Putin recognised many of Russia's weaknesses: the state lacked finance and had no governance; socially the country was in a mess; and foreigners did not respect it. His analysis was correct, but his performance has not been. Russia's relationship with China is embarrassing and has historically been marked by extremes. But Russia has no interest in getting into a conflict with China. It is only if Beijing pushed Russia on matters such as water diversion or access to the Russian Far East that tension would rise.

Demography

Russia's population is falling. In forty to fifty years' time its population may fall to 100 million. According to the head of the UN Population Fund's Russian office, the country lost between 400,000 and 650,000 people a year from 1992 to 2006. Male life expectancy is nearly twenty years lower than in Western Europe: '[We] do not share the optimism of government officials who claim that Russia will succeed in halting the population decline by 2015 and increase the population to 145 million by 2025.'[67] In 2009, the UNDP was predicting that the population could be as low as 90 million by 2050: 'It will not be possible to overcome negative demographic trends in the foreseeable future.'[68]

The likelihood of industrial accidents, violent encounters or alcohol-induced driving accidents makes life in Russia statistically similar to the worst of sub-Saharan Africa:

> There are no reasons as yet to think that Russia has even begun to address this crisis . . . Experts are certain that the 'alcohol factor' makes a very large contribution to the level of early deaths from circulatory diseases and external causes . . . According to data of an epidemiological survey, carried out in a typical Russian city [Izhevsk], 40% of deaths of men aged 25–54 are related to hazardous drinking.[69]

The difference between Chinese and Russian ageing patterns is that the Chinese population will remain static for a prolonged period but gradually age, whereas Russia's population will sharply decline. Russian males smoke and drink excessively, and the average male will barely survive to retirement age. A recent estimate for male life expectancy at birth is 62.8 years.[70] The country ranks below Bolivia, South America's poorest and most unhealthy country.

Fertility is extremely low and is blamed by Russian statisticians on a number of causes, including economic uncertainty and widespread drug taking by young people: the UN Office on Drugs and Crime reports that Russia has the highest national level of per capita heroin consumption.[71] In 2010 the Russian authorities put the drug addiction rate at virtually 1.8 per cent.[72] For comparison, it is estimated that in the 1820s Qing dynasty China had 1 million regular opium-users in a population of something over 300 million – a rate of 0.3 per cent.[73]

The national labour force is believed to have peaked in 2006 and to be declining rapidly. Repatriation of overseas Russians swamped emigration during the 1990s, obscuring the population reduction. Though it has diminished, repatriation still provides most immigrants. The only prospects for 'demographic repair' now are either improbable rates of future fertility or mass immigration into a society which is not notably welcoming of cultural diversity. The potential sources of immigration are controversial. By 2009, 68 per cent of young non-Russian immigrants were from Muslim countries.[74] Others could be Chinese and ethnic Korean minorities from China migrating into the Russian Far East. Official demographers, referring to immigration, speak of 'the possible threat to the territorial integrity of Russia'. The dependency rate, measured as the number of non-working-age people to working-age, is projected to rise from 0.61:1 in 2010 to 1.24:1 in 2050.

Domestic Russia: Society, Economy and Stability

> Russia's patterns of death from injury and violence [by whatever provenance] are so extreme and brutal that they invite comparison only with the most tormented spots on the face of the planet today. The five places estimated to be roughly in the same league as Russia as of 2002 were Angola, Burundi, Congo, Liberia, and Sierra Leone.[75]

There is a culture of inefficiency and neglect that can lead to the most appalling disasters. When the submarine *Kursk* sank with all hands in 2000, Putin pledged to rebuild not just the armed forces but the country itself.[76] Yet the disasters continue. In 2010 there were forest fires that exposed unmaintained or missing equipment and untrained firemen; hydroelectric turbine and coal mine explosions; in 2011 came the sinking of a passenger boat on the Volga. Blame has been placed on the 'hyper-centralisation of the Putin regime'.[77] What is clear is that in Russia negligence and irresponsibility are institutionalised.

Social trends can be deeply disturbing. Illegitimacy seems to have settled at over a quarter of births;[78] there are over 60 per cent more divorces than marriages;[79] over 700,000 children were in institutional care in 2010;[80] there are over a million homeless children, and possibly many more.[81] By extension, up to 200,000 children every year are abandoned by their parents, either deliberately or through gross incapacity.[82] If this calculation is correct, that amounts to an incredible 16 per cent of all Russian births.

Russia has an economy which is unhealthily based on volatile energy and mineral prices. A measure of Russia's need for immediate cash is the deal struck in 2009, when China undertook to pay $25 billion in return for 2.2 billion barrels of oil over twenty years. The effective price seemed like $17/barrel.[83] This compares with the then most distant futures contract price on the New York Mercantile Exchange (for December 2017) of $73.22. It is a good example of China needing resources and having money and of Russia, faced with imminent cash requirements, having to sell energy at historically low prices, although there have been subsequent disputes about the contract. Russia produces little the world wants. No serious attempt was made to diversify away from dependence on raw materials during the boom years. Foreign exchange reserves have been volatile and vulnerable. President Medvedev was explicit in 2009: 'It's a dead end . . . We will have to make decisions on the structure of the economy. Otherwise our economy has no future. The situation is outrageous and has been for a long time.'[84] At that time Russia's economy was contracting at an annualised rate of 11 per cent. But in late 2010 he was still saying 'it is unavoidable that we completely change our economic infrastructure'.[85] That same year, the authorities began to develop a Russian 'Silicon Valley' under the tutelage of President Medvedev's Deputy Chief of Staff, Vladislav Surkov, who has a largely unreformed view of modernisation: 'consolidated power in Russia is the instrument of modernisation. I would even insist it is the only one'.[86] Surkov describes the strategy as 'authoritarian modernization'.[87] With this approach, Russia's version of Silicon Valley should be problematic.

Stability is threatened continuously by the brutal wars in the Caucasus. Even local officials admit that police and military brutality causes citizens to support the rebels.[88] Putin's macho approach to the rebellion appeals to some voters, but many would prefer withdrawal. This is a war which is not just fought in the northern Caucasus but also in the streets of Moscow: regular terrorist incidents plague the lives of Muscovites, and there seems little that the state can do to prevent them.[89] Corruption, brutality, poverty, absence of economic development and an abiding Islamic faith which survived seventy years of communism all nourish the insurrections in the Caucasus. The familiar discussion of terrorism obscures the enduring nature of most asymmetrical warfare. Four centuries distinguishes this as one of the longest struggles for self-determination.

Somewhat similar to those in China, domestic polls put corruption and income inequality at the top of people's concerns.[90] Russia has amongst the worst international ratings for corruption and lack of innovation.[91] Nevertheless, Putin is enthusiastic about petrochemicals, plane-making, defence and nuclear power, and Russia is a leader in armaments and aerospace – fields where the state tends to be dominant. In Russia, the state budget is 40 per cent of GDP (compared with all Chinese government spending of just over 20 per cent). Putin and Medvedev say that a strong state is needed because of corruption and a weak economy. However, one could argue that corruption exists because of the strong state. It has become such an issue that 'government institutions have been taken over as conduits for private interests, some of them criminal. Property rights no longer exist, people who are supposed to enforce the law are breaking it, innocent people are victimised and courts have turned into political tools.'[92] 'At the top level, there is such limitless consumption that it is beginning to look like ancient Rome.'[93]

Putin has been prime minister, president, prime minister and president again for over a decade. When he became president in 2000, he planned to double GDP in ten years. He achieved perhaps half that target (partly as a result of the performance of the global economy). This is nowhere near China's performance following Hu Yaobang's aim in 1980 to quadruple the economy in twenty years. The impact of Putin and the Kremlin on the Russian economy appears to have been negligible. It is estimated that a $10 rise in the oil price creates $20 billion of extra revenue,[94] and that if Russia's variety of oil can reach $115–125 a barrel that would eliminate the budget deficit:[95] the country remains a roulette economy. However, the development of shale gas – particularly in the US – has sharply reduced the natural gas price and thus undermined Gazprom, once (in theory) the world's most profitable company, which uses oil-linked pricing. Meanwhile, in 2013 Russian media described it as 'the fifth largest victim of illicit capital flow in the world' based on figures from Global Financial Integrity in the US.[96] When events go well for Russia, it seems to be a matter of luck; when things go badly, it often seems to stem from incompetence.

Russia has a democratic system, and Putin and Medvedev have been democratically elected; until 2011 their approval ratings were high. There are two reasons for this: first, the television media are largely organised to be pro-government and the two-thirds of the overall population who live in provincial towns and villages receive news only from television stations that are heavily government-influenced.[97] Second, Putin's macho nationalism is genuinely popular. His pitch is to the lower- and middle-class television viewers.[98] Many are unaware there is any choice. And Russia is unsympathetic to a plural society: as a Russian journalist observed, 'Putin is more liberal in his views than 80 percent of the Russian population.'[99]

Russia in the World

Like France, Russia wants to be treated as a great power beyond its resources, and is willing to act aggressively to be recognised as having 'spheres of influence' in areas where the Tsarist empire and the Soviet Union once ruled and no new power relationships have arisen. Moscow refers to the former tributaries on its borders as its 'zone of privileged interest' or the 'near abroad'. Although Washington publicly denies it, Moscow believes that America has tacitly accepted this.[100] It maintains the Commonwealth of Independent States (CIS), a loose association of its former Soviet republics. However, it works closely with China in using the Shanghai Cooperation Organization, a kind of outsiders' NATO (see Chapter 10). The chairman of the CIS committee in the Russian parliament says that the country is 'realizing its mission to be the key player in the post-Soviet space'.[101] But this verdict ignores China's influence in Central Asia.

It is widely believed that Putin seeks to build a 'Third Empire', after the Tsarist and the Soviet empires. He has had some gains with Armenia and Georgia; there are hopes that former tributaries in Central Asia will project Russian influence – military and political – further. However, these countries, ossified though their political systems may be, have not stood still since formal independence. Their trade links with China have flourished: China has a serious economy, whereas Russia does not. They would not easily fit back into a wholly Russian environment. One might also note Turkmenistan's natural gas diplomacy with China.[102]

This is largely wishful thinking. Projection of Russian power diminishes the further afield it is aimed. The Russian navy, for example, put together a flotilla for the ceremonial 2008 visit to Venezuela comprising the nuclear-powered missile cruiser *Petr Velikiy*, the anti-submarine destroyer *Admiral Chabanenko*, the naval auxiliary tanker *Ivan Bubnov* – and the tugboat SB-406, in case the warships broke down.

Russia's behaviour is largely a reaction to the Soviet Union's collapse. Just as the George W. Bush administration's foreign policy was founded in contrast to President Clinton's perceived spineless performance towards North Korea and other pariah regimes, so the Putin administration has sought to rebuild Russia's international position after the perceived humiliations of the Yeltsin years. As Gilbert Rozman, professor of sociology at Princeton, noted as far back as the late 1990s, 'Russia's cognitive dissonance' in losing its status overnight as joint top world power without having found a new role or respect among the Western powers will not quickly fade.[103] Putin is a Russian nationalist and understandably regrets losing international standing. According to former US National Security Advisor Brent Scowcroft in 2009:

On Russia, we have tended, since the end of the Cold War, to benign neglect, except when we need them for some particular thing ... I think we have severely underestimated the humiliation that Russia and Russians felt at the demise of their position in the world.[104]

Putin's response to national humiliation has been to try to make Russia feared by acting as a 'spoiler', seeking to weaken America's world position while knowing that there will be no future Russian hegemony. As US Defense Under-Secretary Michele Flournoy said in 2010, there are aspects of Russia's nuclear doctrine and activity that 'we find very troubling ... They are actually increasing their reliance on nuclear weapons', while America is prioritizing arms control.[105] This is for several reasons. One is that Russia and America own 95 per cent of the world's known nuclear warheads and so here Moscow is still a leader.[106] Also, Russia's conventional military position has deteriorated since 1989. Military reforms announced in 2008 were billed as Russia's boldest since the Crimean War: the officer corps was to be slashed by over 40 per cent, conscription was to be ended and new, modern equipment was to be acquired (though the cuts seem to have preceded the acquisitions). Third, Russia's massive nuclear arsenal enabled it to have bilateral negotiations with Washington on a potential nuclear arms reduction treaty. Such pre-eminence endows Russia with huge status versus other powers. However, it is difficult for Russia to pursue this road too far, as its weak conventional position obliges it to see its strong nuclear capability as a balancing factor.

Russia has concentrated on its traditional spheres of influence, where they can be maintained and reinvigorated – whether on its western frontiers, in the Caucasus or in Central Asia. But its international friendships are not strong. When America procured the secession of Kosovo from Serbia, it persuaded over sixty countries to grant diplomatic recognition (though Spain and China refused for fear of encouraging secession in their own regions). When Russia marched into South Ossetia and Abkhazia and declared their independence as states from Georgia, just one country granted recognition: Nicaragua. Even Belarus declined. China was always unlikely to support secession.

After 2007, as the economy began to sink, Russian 'diplomacy' began a small resurgence: using a cold winter, it disciplined several European countries in the economics of gas supply. A new oil terminal at Kozmino in the Russian Far East and a 1,800-mile pipeline between there and Irkutsk assists Russia to decide how much oil to sell to Europe and how much to Asia.[107] The Gazprom investment in Nigerian gas in 2009 and the Trans-Sahara pipeline were seen as attempting to control gas reserves that might go to Europe.

When Russia invaded Georgia in 2008, the EU found its hands tied by the need to beg Russia for helicopters and pilots for a military mission to Chad. Then by late 2008, NATO needed Russia's help to move supplies to Afghanistan via Central Asia. Russia adopted the imperial tactic of divide and rule: those European countries which had shown themselves most biddable to Russia's wishes were given privileged access to supply routes. Any talk of the Ukraine and Georgia joining NATO – an idea abhorred by Moscow – dropped down the Western priority list. Putin's foreign policy has been described as one 'in which the organising emotions are grievance and belligerence'.[108] The drive for closer links with former Soviet republics is partly to compensate for Russia's deteriorating demography.

Also in 2009, Anders Fogh Rasmussen, the Secretary General of NATO, said he intended to send 'senior officials to visit Moscow to hear the Kremlin's views on how Nato should develop strategically in the long term'.[109] Suddenly, Russia was receiving serious respect.

In 2009, Russia, with China, argued at the UN against punitive sanctions on North Korea, though they accepted a degree of tightening after North Korea's second nuclear test. Both said they wished to avoid precipitating regime collapse and a refugee exodus. Neither state wants a collapse into chaos or the emergence of a unified and strongly nationalistic Korea, led by the southern elites. The delicate position of the empty Russian Far East already presents a potential challenge. North Korea's disappearance would create for Russia and China less stability, not more.

Russia's China Relationship

Russia has gone from being China's enemy in the Maoist period to being a counterfoil against America. It has a trade surplus with China, but there are fears in Moscow that increased trade is eviscerating Russia's steel and other industries, and energy prices are volatile. The only Russian products that most foreigners buy are oil, gas, timber and armaments. China buys Russian energy, although Russia accounts for only 6 per cent of China's oil imports.[110] Beijing has also bought many substantial military items. However, when it chose to upgrade the obsolete Ming class submarines with Russian-built Kilo class ships, at least two of the first four were reportedly returned because they malfunctioned. Russia is ambivalent about selling high-end equipment to China, as Beijing was discovered in the early 2000s to be copying Russian military equipment – jet fighters, radar and naval data link systems.[111] But it has been willing to sell China equipment that is less high-tech – provided the order is large enough. Russia wants the revenue, but fears supplying its rising neighbour with what – if it works – could be sophisticated equipment. As the Rand Corporation has said: 'The fact that Russia is willing to sell its most advanced weapon systems to India, but not to China, is not lost on Chinese leaders.'[112] But China is looking further afield for really high-technology armaments, and it is continuing to improve domestic production.

Bilateral trade is largely in Russian raw materials and Chinese manufactured goods. However, Russia's declining population will never be a highly important market for Chinese goods, nor does China wish to rely too heavily on one source for its energy supplies. As the arms trade diminishes in importance, in this classic trade of raw materials for manufactured goods, Russia, economically, is assuming the role of China's Third World 'colony'.

China and Russia both belong to the SCO, which suits their needs: it helps Russia (noisily) and China (stealthily) to damage America's Asian plans. It has co-opted Sri Lanka, and India, Pakistan, Iran and Turkey (a member of NATO) have all asked to join, which means its participants would then represent over 45 per cent of the world's population. With China as an equal partner in the SCO, Russia has much more to offer its ex-colonies than when it only had the CIS, or a remnant of the Warsaw Pact. Russia wants to keep its links with its former satellites because they boost its standing (much as Britain finds with the Commonwealth). Russia also wants an effective cordon sanitaire against the increasingly turbulent Islamic world. The Central Asian states fit the bill: their populations are Muslim, but not predominantly radical, with distinctly secular leaders. The governments of the client states of the SCO in turn benefit from security links with two important powers, where no uncomfortable political questions are asked and, in radical Islam, they share a common threat. Those leaders are in turbulent regions where it is good to have friends who are both strong and close.

The SCO does not formally provide a mutual security pact – a function offered only by the much smaller Collective Security Treaty Organisation (CSTO), which excludes China. Being more clearly dominated by Russia, it tends to be the CSTO that is proposed by Russia as an interlocutor for NATO. Though they have come a long way since the Amur Ussuri River military clash in 1969 which saw several hundred casualties, Sino-Russian friction can flare up: for example, in 2009 the 5,000-tonne Chinese-owned vessel *New Star* left Vladivostok in controversial circumstances and was later fired upon by Russian coastguard vessels. It sank in heavy waters and several crew members died. Blogs speculated that the captain had left without paying either some official fees or bribes. Both countries appear to have quickly embargoed news. In 2012 Chinese fishing vessels were fired on in Russian Far Eastern waters, with one sailor reportedly killed.[113]

Russia and China like to talk of non-intervention and they disdain external commentary on their human rights regimes. Neither country wants Western interference in its domestic affairs. China was therefore distinctly unhappy when Russia broke the unwritten code and recognised the secession of South Ossetia and Abkhazia from Georgia. This sets very unpleasant precedents for China. If small parts of a larger country – with different religious or racial features – can leave when they wish and be recognised as fully independent states, it could cause severe problems for Beijing.

China's energy deals in Central Asia, such as the 2006 Turkmenistan gas agreement, endanger Russia's energy strategy. The purchase and onward sale of a substantial part of Turkmenistan's gas reserves is an important part of Russia's energy policy, foreign revenues and force projection. Russia also has a significant anti-China lobby which is nervous and disinclined to partnership. Researchers have pointed out that both Beijing and Moscow planners often hold the view that the other country is potentially their top enemy. As far back as 1969, Washington noted Soviet provocation of China in Xinjiang.[114] Moscow has recently moved slowly in increasing its energy exports to China. It has also been a serial supplier of major arms to Vietnam and India, both of whose principal potential enemy is China.[115]

The Russo-Chinese relationship is not founded upon an ideologically coherent base of anti-liberal democratic ideas: it is based on convenience, although the conveniences are rather different on each side. It is no more a relationship based upon common values than George Bush's 'war on terror' alliance with Uzbekistan. Neither Russia nor China likes American interests promoting 'open society' values and 'colour revolutions' in Central Asia. Neither of them wants regime change, new leaderships emerging unbidden, and thus the creation of uncertainty.

The Sino-Russian relationship has changed since it was forged in the early 1990s. Then both China and Russia sought to deny hegemony to the US in favour of a tripolar world, in which all three would treat each other as peers rather than accept the US as *primus inter pares*. They did not wish to recognise Japan as being in the same club. At the end of the 1990s, Rozman presciently noted: 'Although Chinese and Russians often assume that they understand each other because of their common socialist past, in fact they do not show much comprehension of each other's search for a national identity.'[116] Like India, Russia aspires to be accepted in future as one of the world's leading powers, alongside the US and China. It might be said that China and Russia have a starkly different relationship to history: one seeks to make it and the other to recapture it.

The last fifteen years have seen a unilateral evolution in China's perceptions. It is not so wedded to multi-polar architecture, except as mere transition. Strategists in China now have two visions. One is to see China, informally and perhaps later formally, join a 'G2', comprising itself and the US. The other view is that ultimately China will replace America as the world's superpower.

'The two cornerstones of the [Sino-Russian] partnership over the past two decades – military and energy cooperation – are crumbling.'[117] Energy deals are announced but rarely happen.[118] Indeed, in many respects China and Russia compete with each other. The relationship is one in which broadly the partners get the results they want, but it does not fulfil all their needs. Russia's relationship with China helps to validate Russia's decision since 2000 to avoid constructive relations with the West in favour of an independent diplomacy more suited to an aspirant great power. Or, more charitably, it partially compensates Russia for the West's excluding Russia from the 'top table'.

China appears to be quietly confident of its own eventual rise and doesn't want to upset the proceedings. It would like to be seen by the other powers as responsible, without facilitating US objectives. Russia lacks confidence, as it confronts an ageing and declining population, a weak economy, an empty interior and an outdated military. As such, Russia's style is to play the brash adventurer demanding respect.

China is hoping for tomorrow. Russia is pining for yesterday. America is enjoying today.

The Border Issues with China

Russia's relationship with China began to form as it slowly occupied Siberia in the seventeenth century, principally in search of sable. The first formal contact was a letter from the Ming court inviting Russia to trade. However, the letter was written in such a recherché style that it took fifty-six years for it to be fully translated.[119] The 1689 Treaty of Nerchinsk reflected a period of Chinese military strength and halted Russian expansion for some time. By the nineteenth century Russia was on the march again and began a series of acquisitions of land from the Qing. Although the border is officially settled, there are potential issues. A substantial area of Far Eastern Russia was, for prolonged periods, ruled by the Jin, Yuan, Ming and Qing dynasties, particularly a part of the Amur River basin, north of Vladivostok. Ceded to Russia in 1858 and 1860, it covers 300,000 square miles and forms a sizeable part of the Russian Far East.

During the Jin dynasty (1115–1234), the Empire held the Amur basin. Under the Mongol Yuan dynasty (1271–1368), the Empire included Mongolia and extended halfway up both sides of Lake Baikal in contemporary Siberia. It also included Korea, virtually reached the mouth of the Amur and included almost the whole of the basin. During the Ming dynasty (1368–1644), the

Amur basin was held. The Qing dynasty (1644–1912) held Mongolia, part of current Siberia north-east of Mongolia and the Amur basin until it was progressively wrested away by the Russians under the 'unequal treaties'. Tannu Tuva (now known as the Tuva Republic), north of today's Mongolia, went to Russia in 1912 after the Qing dynasty collapsed.

China's view seems to be that anything once Chinese-ruled is fair game. This has been stretched to include anything ever ruled by China's Mongol or Manchu overlords; or areas owned by races which are now wholly or partially Chinese-ruled, such as the Tibetans or the Mongols. Various dynasties which ruled China have also ruled these Siberian areas and so, under the current thinking, claims could easily be advanced again. After the Sino-Soviet rift in the late 1950s, relations grew increasingly hostile. Throughout the 1960s China stated that the treaties granting lands to Russia in the nineteenth century were 'unequal'. By some accounts, over half a million square miles of land were appropriated from the Qing dynasty, almost all by Russia. Chairman Mao developed this point with a fairly strong hint for the future:

About a hundred years ago, the area to the east of Lake Baikal became Russian territory, since then Vladivostok, Khabarovsk, Kamchatka and other areas have been Soviet territories. We have not yet presented our account for this list.[120]

In 1969, China went further:

After the Opium War of 1840 . . . tsarist Russia forced China to sign a series of unequal treaties by which it annexed more than 1.5 million square kilometres of Chinese territory . . . The treaties relating to the present Sino-Soviet boundary are all unequal treaties . . . [and] should all be annulled.[121]

It is interesting to ponder how many treaties are concluded by parties that are evenly matched, rather than after one has been trounced by the other.

Early in 1969, the Damansky Island incident flared up into open conflict between China and Russia; over 300 troops are believed to have died. It spread along the Ussuri River and out to the Central Asian borders. It has been suggested that one of the reasons why the Soviet Union did not further industrialise Central Asia was a fear of attracting the interest of a China 'in search of rapid development'.[122] In 1978, Soviet troops moved into Chinese territory by boat; in 1979, Vietnam and China fought a Sino-Soviet war by proxy; in the 1980s mobilised troop levels continued to grow; and by 1990 Russia had a quarter of its army and air force and a third of its navy dedicated to the Chinese border.

Chinese commentators kept the issue simmering, presumably with senior-level support:

Mao Tse Tung declared in 1964 that 'Russia had taken too much land', citing among other areas the Priamur and the Primorye . . . After border clashes along the Ussuri River in 1969, Beijing openly called the Priamur and the Primorye 'historically Chinese possessions' . . . Taking a similar tack, the Xinhua News Agency in 1977 announced the discovery of 'close connections' between North China and the Amur Basin some 2,700 years ago that confirmed that the latter had been 'an integral part of our great motherland since ancient times.' The following year the Institute of Modern History of the Chinese Academy of Social Sciences published the first of a three-volume philippic against Russian encroachment on the Priamur, the Primorye, and Sakhalin. By 1981 the Arctic Ocean was being called China's northern frontier in the thirteenth century.[123]

Interestingly, Chinese tour groups to the Russian Far East now unceasingly mention that these lands were 'stolen', suggesting that the Chinese school system maintains these national claims, even though officially the book was closed with the signing of an agreement in 2008 on one of the last three undemarcated sections of border. Formally, the border has no unresolved disputes. The 1981 Arctic Ocean reference is particularly relevant, given the contemporary preoc-cupation in China with 'energy security' and the substantial estimates of the world's undeveloped reserves in the Arctic region. At present, nothing is being heard on this issue. Beijing academics said in the time of Hu Jintao that it would be 'difficult for this generation of Chinese leaders' to raise the issue with Moscow, presumably after the series of agreements leading up to 2008. However, if efforts were made in the 1980s to negotiate the return of Hong Kong (which had been ceded permanently in 1842 in an 'unequal treaty') and Macau (finally declared independent of China by the Portuguese in 1849), why should China not at some point decide, for example, to raise the issue of the more recent unequal treaty of 1860, which forcibly ceded the Amur basin?

Vladivostok is six time zones and seven hours removed from Moscow. Demography reappears here: there is secular depopulation of Siberia and the Russian Far East. Novosibirsk is centrally located in Russia. There is no Russian city to the east with over a million people: 'At present there is no reason to think that the western drift of population in Russia can be stopped or reversed.'[124] Some 85 per cent of China lies east of Novosibirsk; fifty-six cities have over a million people. The Russian Far East Federal District is the largest, by area, of the seven comprising Russia, but its population is below 7 million. The prin-cipal cities of Khabarovsk and Vladivostok are not large, and Vladivostok's population fell by 6 per cent between 1989 and 2010 (to 592,000 inhabitants). Khabarovsk's has also steadily fallen, and by 2010 stood at 578,000. As in eastern Germany, we can see 'large areas of the Russian Far East being virtually deserted by the able-bodied'.[125]

The Chinese claims are not currently being aired, but they lie in waiting. As the Russian population of the Far East ebbs, the Asian population is rising. China is short of agricultural land, Siberia may hold vast energy reserves, the north-east passage to Europe is reopening, and climate change may open up the Siberian wastes. The transnational greater Amur basin – the likely centre of future territorial claims – has 70 million people in today's China, 5 million in Russia and under 50,000 in Mongolia. We should not forget the (potentially) united Korea, where another 70 million people border Siberia. Another way of looking at the matter is that China has a population density of 356 people per square mile, compared to 3 per square mile in the Russian Far East.

Vladivostok was founded in 1860 only after Russia secured the area from the Qing dynasty. In the early twentieth century, Chinese reputedly outnumbered Russians there: the city lies less than 60 miles from the Chinese border. Vladivostok and Khabarovsk are seeing a growing Asian population of Chinese, Korean-Chinese and Koreans (registered and unregistered): there are believed to be over 100,000 Chinese in the region, and perhaps 250–400,000 in all Russia.[126]

The issue may possibly be raised under a commercial guise. At the end of the 1990s, some Russian regional government officials wanted to strike a deal with China over large tracts of the Russian Far East, but Putin reportedly blocked it.[127] Financial factors might very well lead to the idea being resurrected. The recent energy deals should be regarded as unfinished business: if energy prices fall again, or if oil shale really takes off, Russia's budgetary needs will be difficult to fulfil and we should anticipate further creative transactions, such as China buying areas of the Russian Far East. This would be hugely sensitive for Russia, but it might be financially unavoidable. It might be disguised as a long-term lease or a special economic zone, but it is likely to happen.

The Russian Far East could become the 'Third Alaska': following Russia's sale of Alaska to the US in 1868, and the loss of Eastern Europe, the Caucasus and Central Asia in 1989, the third step in the Russian march from empire to nation state could be the cession of the Far East. A long-term strategic target for China could be to have a sixth seat at the Arctic coastal states' table when an estimated 30 per cent of the world's unexplored gas and 13 per cent of its oil resources are carved up.

Where Does Russia Go?

Many would like to see Russia again become a great power: strong, modern, successful, respected – and happy. However, it seems that only part of the renaissance agenda has been addressed. There has perhaps been more interest in the symptoms of success, without focus on the causes. One cannot long project standing, power and purpose without a suitable underlying economy. This critical element has been woefully neglected. The state seems accordingly to live largely on its 'lottery winnings' from those years when energy prices were high. Meanwhile, the UNDP calculates that by 2050 Russia could have a population below that of Vietnam; it is difficult to have economic growth with a declining labour force and population.

Moscow believed it could again bestride the world as a Eurasian great power. Apart from the *opéra bouffe* when the Russian navy visited Venezuela, some shipyard investment in Vietnam and a naval base in Assad's Syria, there has been little attempt at global power projection. Increasingly it is clear that Russia's destiny is not to rebuild great power status. The 2010 decision to buy four French naval amphibious assault ships seems to confirm Russia's demise as a world-class naval shipbuilder. Even during the energy booms it could not adequately finance its military. Russia cannot command the world stage, and so it talks of spheres of influence on its marches: Belarus, the Caucasus and Central Asia. Its foreign policy seems based on the words imputed to Caligula; *oderint dum metuant* – let them hate me as long as they fear me. It is a country at bay. The death throes of an ex-world power may be lengthy and will reverberate with the fluctuations of the oil price.

The relationship between China and Russia is mutually important without being friendly. It could quite easily become hostile. The population of the Russian Far East is not overjoyed under Moscow's sovereignty. Apart from North Korea, this is the only part of the Far East to miss out on the long post-war Pacific economic boom, which alone is sufficient reason for bitter resentment. China might reopen the border issue, seek to infiltrate population into the Far East, challenge Russia's hold on Central Asian resources, or divert the headwaters feeding the Ob River. However, all these issues are for China to push. Russia has no inclination or stomach to challenge China, although it does not want to see China as the superpower, and can probably be counted on to demonstrate this. China is now self-confident and Russia is nervous. The 2008 border settlement was a relief for Moscow. The only challenge will come from China pushing Russia into a corner, but it is hard to see this happening soon. Pragmatic resolutions are more likely. China feels now that time is on its side. A future generation of leaders may revisit the issue of the unequal treaties and the Amur basin.

CHAPTER TWELVE

Central Asia

Sometimes the less remarked regions and trends have the potential for dramatic upheaval. What is happening in Central Asia poses two serious problems for China's future. First, Western military departure from Afghanistan will probably lead either to a coalition of the present government with the Taliban or to collapse of the regime, to be succeeded by a Taliban government. Survival of the Karzai regime in the teeth of Taliban opposition seems implausible. As Afghanistan borders China's Muslim Xinjiang province, this brings the real possibility of radicalism reaching restive Xinjiang.

Second, Pakistan's nuclear arsenal is the world's fastest growing, but its government is weak and is confronted by militant Islamic dissidence. Regime collapse threatens both the country and the region. Pakistan's alliance and common border with China not only present a clear threat, but also put huge pressure on China as a rising power to show responsible leadership. In addition, Central Asia's ex-Soviet republics, located between China and Russia, offer a tinderbox of fragmented Islamic movements and could explode at any moment. Collapse in Central Asia could be disastrous for China's rise, bringing with it nuclear risk and the threat of sustained insurgency across Xinjiang.

Central Asia is treated here as encompassing Pakistan, Afghanistan and the former Soviet republics of Kazakhstan, Kyrgyzstan, Tajikistan, Turkmenistan and Uzbekistan. The ex-Soviet states are not functional democracies and are largely run by intolerant and unattractive leaders. Afghanistan is scarcely a democracy, and Pakistan is a poor example. They are predominantly Muslim, and the Muslims are heavily Sunni. All are in the bottom – meaning worst – quartile of countries for corruption. They are also, with the exception of Kazakhstan and Turkmenistan (which enjoy the benefits of being energy producers), in the bottom third of countries for economic output per person.

All have low life expectancy. Poor states with weak or repressive governance, largely Sunni populations, exposure to radical ideas and short life expectancy are likely to provide both militants and targets for future Islamic struggles. It is a huge area with a small population, little respect for nationhood and poorly monitored frontiers. And this volatile region adjoins China's borders, sharing with it 2,100 miles of frontier.

Here, in the nineteenth century, Russia and Britain played 'the Great Game' for political and strategic advantage. Now four full powers and two half-powers concern themselves with Central Asia. First is the US, not wholly convinced of the wisdom of having intruded. Russia is active in its former republics and in Afghanistan, partly because of the huge drug trade into Russia. China is involved through being Pakistan's principal ally and a leader, with Russia, of the Shanghai Cooperation Organisation, which includes the former Soviet republics. It gives some aid and has invested over $3 billion in Afghanistan. It hopes profoundly that the Karzai administration will not collapse and leave chaos on its border, but it doesn't want to be involved in protecting it. India is an active player in Afghanistan and Pakistan with its ubiquitous, if not always successful, intelligence services, its trade with Afghanistan and its Cold War with Pakistan. It maintains an airbase in Tajikistan. Iran and Turkey are both active but smaller-scale regional players.

The uncertain future of Central Asia presents one of the greatest and most intractable threats faced by China. The collapse of some of these states is likely (Islam is not a religion that focuses on the nation state), and that could cause upheaval right on China's frontiers. Beijing's regional strategic objectives are political stability and energy security. It prefers to avoid a disastrous Islamic incursion, but has no clear plan. It may also have an interest in extending the encirclement of India.

Xinjiang

Xinjiang province represents a sixth of the land mass of the People's Republic of China but accounts for just 1.5 per cent of China's population. The territory is almost four times the size of California, but has only 22 million people. It hosts a nuclear weapons complex and is noted for its oil and gas. This huge and empty province shares a lengthy border with Afghanistan, Kazakhstan, Kyrgyzstan, Pakistan and Tajikistan. It is difficult to say what proportion of Xinjiang's people are Muslim, but those racial groups whose traditional religion is Islam – Uighur, Kazakh, Hui and others – constitute about 60 per cent of its population. Over 90 per cent of China's Muslims are believed to be Sunni, which provides a link with the Muslims of Central Asia. Xinjiang's proximity to the volatile Central Asian region presents Beijing with security challenges.

China would like religion – in this case Islam – to be under government supervision, and this brings Beijing into tension with believers. (The same situation arose in the Muslim areas of the Soviet Union, and the situation was not resolved there to the advantage of the Soviets.) Certain issues clearly generate resentment among some of the natives of this vast province. Like the Tibetans, the original inhabitants are linguistically and racially distinct from the Han, and they have a distinct religion. As in Tibet, there is a feeling that the continual increase in Han settlers is an attempt to change Xinjiang's demography: the Chinese authorities have 'begun a massive state-sponsored population migration . . . and claim the region may bulge with as many as 40 million new inhabitants'.[1] This would treble the existing population. Beijing continually asserts that every effort is being made to improve the economic situation of the territory. Unfortunately, some observers suggest that much of the improvement seems to assist the recent Han arrivals rather than the original Uighurs. Historically, Muslims held prominent roles in China (see Chapter 8), and Toynbee even claimed that there was a 'temporary political union, under Mongol rule, between China and Dar-al-Islam [Muslim lands or communities].'[2] But Muslims are much less prominent in today's China.

As Arienne Dwyer (writing for the East-West Center in Washington) notes, 'Multilingualism and cultural pluralism have been progressively curtailed' but the PRC should realise that 'supporting the maintenance of Uyghur language and identity is not antithetical to the Chinese goal of nation building.'[3] Perhaps more importantly, there is a fundamental issue as to whether a self-proclaimed atheistic government can take decisions that best meet the needs of a society which is very attached to its historical and religious culture. While people may appreciate tarmac roads, hospitals and schools, they may also desire religious freedom, greater opportunity to use their language and perhaps some genuine autonomy. Beijing may believe that giving the Uighurs what Han people appreciate is a benevolent strategy, but it may not always comport with the priorities of a different people with a distinct culture and more spiritual values. The issue is not just how the cake is divided up; it may also be that different peoples prefer different cakes.

The Chinese authorities have consistently sought to discourage religious practices outside approved places of worship, for reasons of effective oversight and supervision. However, the practices that occur away from mosques tend to be practices characteristic of the Sufi versions of Islam that are prevalent in Xinjiang. Such Sufi practices have been attacked by Muslims who have encountered other schools of Islam:

Religious figures who have travelled to Saudi Arabia and adopted religious ideologies that have emphasized and more stringently applied the concept of 'tawhid' [oneness of God] have been particularly instrumental in spearheading the critique of a range of local religious practices, such as attendance at the cemetery to pray on behalf of the deceased and the undertaking of ritual feasts, that have previously been seen in Xinjiang as being central to the Muslim faith.[4]

It is paradoxical, then, that the local Sufism is being attacked simultaneously by the Chinese authorities and by those with Wahhabi sympathies. Activity outside the mosque has understandably diminished.

Xinjiang separatists recall when the territory was independent and called East Turkestan. The leader of the secessionist East Turkestan Islamic Movement, Hasan Mahsum, was shot dead in Pakistan by the army in 2003 (possibly as a favour to China), but the conflict continued. The Chinese state media say many arrests are still made for endangering state security in Xinjiang. In 2009 there were serious riots in Ürümqi and other areas: according to the government, 136 Han Chinese and 46 Uighurs died. This sparked threats by an al-Qaeda affiliate in North Africa against Chinese interests in Algeria; al-Qaeda-affiliated websites threatened the same in the Middle East; Indonesian Muslims demanded a jihad against China; and frequent internet 'chatter' discussed attacking Chinese interests. In 2012, a Chinese woman was killed in Pakistan in revenge for Chinese state actions against Uighurs. In 2013 there were dozens of deaths in incidents, a bomb explosion in Tiananmen Square and the top Chinese general in Xinjiang was demoted.[5] As in Tibet, such incidents will probably continue. However, one marked difference between Xinjiang and Tibet is that Tibetans have no fiery cousins willing to wreak violent revenge on Chinese targets abroad.

State collapse in neighbouring Afghanistan or Pakistan would also create a major challenge. Thus both radical Islamic revenge and regional political collapse may be viewed as 'force multipliers', offering the prospect of transnational support and a higher media profile than purely internal dissidence could attract. Instead of home-grown riots and incidents, China could face an extensive, externally aided insurrection.

Since the disasters on the military supply routes from Pakistan to Afghanistan in 2008, NATO has been seeking alternatives. The Russian supply agreements have proved difficult. In 2009, Washington asked China to allow allied troops to be supplied through Xinjiang to the Wakhan Corridor in eastern Afghanistan. That border closed in 1949. The US proposal raises problems. According to the great explorer Sir Aurel Stein, in the Corridor 'winter lasts ten months and summer two'.[6] The border crosses one of the world's highest passes (16,150 feet) and lacks proper roads. Opening presumably requires some US military presence (which raises issues of sovereignty). China is trying to seal the border of Xinjiang from external Islamic influence but it might be too late. For China, the alluring aspect of the American request is that it obliges Washington to bargain. Possible bargaining chips may include the Dalai Lama and Taiwan. Beijing's dilemma is that while it prefers to maintain a sealed border with Afghanistan and to avoid the American war there, there are advantages: better access to its new copper mine at Aynak, south of Kabul, and the possible American concessions elsewhere to secure agreement.

Despite Wahhabist returnees from the Middle East, radical Islam does not bulk large in Xinjiang today. Back in 2003, China complained to Pakistan about the political activities of Uighur exiles, but there is little public evidence of regular cross-border incursions or of external involvement in Xinjiang disturbances. Paradoxically, it is conceivable that the tough supervision and suppression of Uighur and associated groups could now backfire. The point was made back in 2005:

> Beijing's new hard-line stance, which restricts even language and culture, has galled the many moderate Xinjiang citizens . . . The PRC government still has an opportunity to win back these people with a more pluralistic cultural policy that emphasizes support for Uyghur and other policy-relevant minority languages and that eases other cultural restrictions, particularly on religion. Without such a policy shift, as Beijing well knows, Xinjiang could become China's Kashmir.[7]

This may overstate matters, but, since it was written, incidents do seem to have been increasing. There may be a case for China to soften its policy; to identify what the Uighurs want and to seek some grand bargain involving free worship, use of language, etc. in return for loyalty to the state as it stands. It is a sad irony that Beijing's methods for governing the non-Han in Xinjiang seem almost predestined to create the feared radicalisation.

Pakistan

Pakistan has for decades been a firm ally of China's. Initially after independence there was discussion between Pakistan and India about reconciliation and cooperating against the menace of Mao's China. After the Tibetan revolt of 1959, President Ayub Khan of Pakistan presented a joint defence proposal to India. However, their differences were clearly difficult to resolve, and Pakistan approached China in 1960 to discuss outstanding border issues. In the 1960s, a strong Pakistani lobby developed which felt more overtures should be made towards China. Pakistan opened its airspace to Chinese flights during the 1960s and 1970s, at a time when neither Moscow nor Delhi had cordial relations with Beijing.

China is a major investor in Pakistan and an important trade partner. When China executes projects here it uses local labour, unlike in Africa. Pakistan also facilitated the Nixon–Mao talks (which led to the normalisation of US–China relations) and is the largest customer for Chinese military exports. The US and Indian intelligence services both maintain that China supplied Pakistan with the nuclear technology it needed. China officially denies this. Sino-Pakistan joint agreements have led to co-production of jet fighters and other aircraft.

The relationship endures despite Chinese engineers being murdered in Pakistan and Pakistani drug dealers being executed in China. One of the great benefits of the 'all-weather' Chinese alliance is that whereas US aid comes to Pakistan with onerous conditions, Chinese assistance tends to have no demands attached, which enables Pakistan to avoid accepting the full rigour of US demands. America would like to feel it has an alliance with Pakistan; China does have one.

China is indisputably Pakistan's strongest ally. Even Nawaz Sharif, the leader of Pakistan's opposition, said after the killing of Osama bin Laden that 'at this crucial juncture of history, I cannot say anybody is standing with Pakistan except for China.'[8] The Sino-Indian border dispute remains unresolved, and China is widely seen as contributing support to Pakistan by occupying Indian troops on the Sino-Indian frontier, rather than letting them confront Pakistan. A different view is that China stokes Pakistan's military capability in order to keep India's attention occupied in the west and discourage it from challenging China (see Chapter 11).

Washington's attitude to Pakistan is based on the premise, expressed in 2011 by a senior US official, that 'you can't have an antagonistic relationship with Pakistan and hope to win in Afghanistan.'[9] Unfortunately, many US actions have been highly antagonistic. The New American Foundation estimates that in 2004–10 there were 158 drone strikes on Pakistan, killing an average of three civilians each.[10] Pakistani sources suggest far more, and a 2012 Stanford University study maintains that Washington grossly understates civilian casualties.[11] On his arrival in office, President Obama substantially increased the number of strikes. Unsurprising, then, that the Pakistani population is one of the most anti-American worldwide.

The only compensation has been the billions of dollars that go to the Pakistan military (much of which appears to have been passed straight on to the Afghan Taliban – see Chapter 10). America would not even accept Pakistan's request for a free trade agreement (though it was willing to conclude one with Bahrain): Washington said it would need to exclude textiles, which is one of Pakistan's main products. This inability to conclude something commercially constructive nurtures Pakistani unhappiness. Cumulative American disdain for Pakistan's sovereignty is contributing to a humiliation of the government and the radicalisation of the people. Regime collapse and the Islamicisation of Pakistan will not benefit American strategic objectives.

Unfortunately, this region does not operate on principles of good neighbourliness and tension marks almost every substantial border. Iraq has assisted Pakistan against the interests of Iran; Iran cooperates with India against Pakistan; India cooperates with Afghanistan against Pakistan; Pakistan cooperates with China against India. However, India is no longer Pakistan's main problem.

The Fight against the Taliban

Islam in Pakistan and Kashmir has undergone considerable radicalisation. This has created a domestic Pakistan Taliban that has caused a continuing tide of violence from 2008 and that threatens the state itself. And yet Pakistan has continued to fund the Taliban in Afghanistan, in order to retain influence there. Pakistan army officers share a religion with the Taliban militants, but espouse US principles of democracy. It is understandable that, for many, the religious bonds should take priority.

The Pakistani elites have not reached consensus that the real enemy is no longer India, but is internal. There is a distinct possibility – although currently somewhat diminished – that the state of Pakistan will either fail (and disintegrate) or be consumed by an Islamicist movement. In addition to Islamicists, there are Baluchistan rebels fighting in the province around Gwadar, where China is financing development of the port (see p.286 above). Any destabilisation of Pakistan will oblige China to re-evaluate its regional strategy.

A Nuclear State

More importantly from a global point of view, Pakistan has an estimated 110 nuclear warheads.[12] US officials in 2009 described this as the world's fastest-growing nuclear weapons programme, and some expect it soon to overtake Britain and France to become the world's fourth-biggest nuclear power.

The regional nuclear situation is complicated because the actors gaze in different directions. Pakistan measures itself against India in nuclear and conventional strength and won't want any freeze on new weapons, even though it has more, since it is conventionally 'out-soldiered'. Pakistan regards the threat of 'first strike' as a real deterrent to India launching a large-scale attack.[13] India sees China as its target. China looks not at India, but at the US capability, particularly in Asia. America looks at what Russia is doing. As a result, the Indo-Pakistan nuclear balance is not easily susceptible to a rational standstill agreement.

Risks from the Nuclear Programme

The worry must be what will happen to Pakistan's nuclear arsenal if the state collapses or is co-opted into a new radical Muslim regime. Certain rather vague assurances have been given by both Pakistani and American leaders about the security of the arsenal, but US commanders continue to be deeply concerned. General David Petraeus, then Commander of the US Central Command, testified to Congress that 'Pakistani state failure would provide transnational terrorist groups and other extremist organizations an opportunity to acquire nuclear weapons and a safe haven from which to plan and launch attacks.'[14] It could be that President Musharraf's strategy in 2007 to disperse the nuclear arsenal to 'at least six secret new locations' was, in retrospect, not so wise if parts of the country eventually become alienated from Islamabad, the capital. There have been a number of terrorist attacks against (or in the vicinity of) some of these nuclear facilities. The Indian National Security Adviser has expressed confidence in the safety of the nuclear weapons in Pakistan, but Moscow has voiced its deep concern.[15]

Ahmed Rashid, a noted analyst, has said that during the 1980s Pakistan's army became deeply Islamicised at every level. Islamabad's role in supporting the Afghan resistance against the Soviet invasion seems to have built an entire web of militant and Taliban sympathies, loyalties and relationships in the military intelligence (ISI) and army, and it is difficult to jettison these overnight.

Nor should we think only of deliberate events affecting nuclear security. South Asia has an appalling record for safety, maintenance and security. Praful Bidwai and Achin Vanaik, two Indian journalists, have written of how even normal safety issues affect nuclear security:

> . . . the disaster-prone character of a good deal of Indian [and Pakistani] military, as well as civilian physical infrastructure and hardware, marked as it is by frequent accidents, component failures, substandard designs, poor maintenance and unsafe operational practices . . . a high occurrence of defects, [is]

rampant in Indian and Pakistani industries, especially in defence production factories, which are shielded from public scrutiny and safety audits . . . There are generic problems arising from a poor culture of safety in India and Pakistan . . . The frequency of industrial accidents in India is estimated to be four times higher than in the US . . . The important point about a generally poor safety culture is simply that if Indian and Pakistani engineers fail to control and reduce the frequency of mishaps in relatively less complex and loosely 'coupled' systems such as road traffic, then they do not inspire much confidence that they will be able to safely handle highly complex, 'tightly coupled' systems such as nuclear weapons and C3I [command, control, communications and intelligence] structures.[16]

Here, then, are echoes of the institutional and cultural incompetence we saw in, for example, Russia (Chapter 11).

A further risk from the Pakistan nuclear programme is international: the risk of proliferation. Nuclear technology was reportedly sold by the Pakistan military to Iran (not a particularly friendly neighbour) and possibly also to North Korea, although this has been denied at a senior level. The *New York Times* has stated as fact that A. Q. Khan, an engineer returned from Germany who become a leading figure in the national nuclear weapons programme, sold nuclear technology to Iran, North Korea and Libya.[17] It is also suggested in Western arms control circles that Pakistan may be giving nuclear assistance to Saudi Arabia.[18]

If Pakistan's military forces are to switch focus from confronting India to fighting the Taliban, it is likely to severely strain the much-vaunted unity of the military leadership.

Security Measures for the Nuclear Capability

There is a policy of secrecy and even 'deception' over issues such as the location of the facilities. An increase in security was mandated after the attacks on the nuclear bases and after the army's headquarters in Rawalpindi was occupied by terrorists in 2009. However, the fighting with the Taliban and in Baluchistan makes it operationally difficult to comply with the new levels of security. There seems to be a significant gap between the level of security ordered at the nuclear facilities and that being provided. In 2009, Hillary Clinton was quoted as saying in Baghdad that 'if the worst . . . were to happen, and this advancing Taliban . . . were to essentially topple the government . . . then they would have the keys to the nuclear arsenal of Pakistan . . . We can't even contemplate that.'[19] The successful incursion into the Rawalpindi HQ demonstrated that defective security is pervasive in even the most august locations. The official response was that the Army HQ is not nearly so well guarded as nuclear facilities.

In this context, Washington has understandably sought to take action to strengthen the security of the nuclear facilities and has allocated $100 million for this. Rather like the rest of its military aid programme, implementation has been left to the Pakistan military, which has taken the money but seems not to have given the Americans either access to the facilities or information on how the money is being spent.

We know that the US is training a Pakistani military unit to recover and reposition stolen warheads. There are about 10,000 people in the country with some involvement in the nuclear programme.[20] Especially with anti-American feeling gaining ground, it is quite possible that any misuse of nuclear weapons could be an 'inside job'. It has happened: the former head of the country's plutonium reactor, Bashir Mahmood, was arrested in 2001 on charges of being associated with Osama bin Laden and of visiting him with another senior nuclear scientist just before September 11th, 2001 for talks.[21]

One of Washington's concerns is that the nuclear weapons vetting process takes no account of Islamicist sympathies. According to the *The Times* in 2010, 'The US army is training a crack unit to seal off and snatch back Pakistani nuclear weapons in the event that militants, possibly from inside the country's security apparatus, get their hands on a nuclear device or materials that could make one.'[22] And yet General Tariq Majid has insisted that no information is passed to the Americans. According to him, they can only 'guess' the security arrangements for Pakistan's nuclear assets. The prospect of America deciding whether a political change in Islamabad justifies the deployment of an American military team to 'seal and snatch' the weapons is worrying. It is quite likely to find itself on the receiving end of even more widespread popular hostility, if that is possible. The Pakistani public which currently holds an 11 per cent favourable rating of the US might be forgiven for not being easily able to distinguish between America allying with it and declaring war on it.

Political Possibilities

In the event of a coup, we should not underestimate the capacity of senior officials to accept events: when the Shah fell in Iran, the generals decided that the army's role was to defend their country against foreign enemies, not to wage war on a new administration. Pakistan is an Islamic society, and Islam doesn't necessarily require a democratic mandate for governmental change. For over half of its history, Pakistan has been under military rule and even when the country has had an elected government the army has sometimes played a very active political role. There is, of course, continuing speculation that the army may again decide it has to intervene directly in political life. The previous army chief General Kayani admitted contemplating this in 2010.[23] The judiciary has raised its profile to constitute a third pole of political authority in the country, distinct from and often in conflict with the army and the politicians.

Afghanistan

The Taliban in Afghanistan receive possibly $1 billion annually from the drug trade. The World Bank estimates that opium revenues constitute a further 33 per cent on top of the official GDP of Afghanistan.[24] America is sometimes accused of allowing the drug trade to continue as a quid pro quo for the other side moderating its attacks on US troops. In 2013 the number of acres under opium production was at at least a 20-year high.[25] 2014 was forecast to be higher. This includes large numbers of very young children who have become addicted through passive exposure; they have been called a 'doomed generation'.[26] The drugs are causing global damage. For example, "more Russians die from Afghan drugs, per year, than the total number of Russian fatalities during the entire 10-year Soviet-Afghan war".[27]

Transparency International, the German-based NGO which monitors corruption worldwide, ranks the country 180th of the 182 countries it measures. As one Western resident of Kabul has said: 'The system is not corrupt. Corruption is the system.' The Reporters without Borders' Index of Press Freedom place Afghanistan 74th in 2012 – down from 35th in 2002.

President Obama openly admitted in 2009 that America was not winning the war in Afghanistan, and no assessment since then has been any more optimistic. The Afghanistan authorities admitted in 2009 that they had bribed the Taliban in certain provinces to allow the national elections to take place.[28] Zalmay Khalilzad, former US ambassador in Afghanistan, said in 2010: 'militarily, the insurgency has grown stronger in recent years while popular support for the government and the coalition has declined in areas where the insurgents are strong.'[29] The continuing attacks by American forces using drone predator planes have, as in Pakistan, caused many civilian deaths and created huge public animosity.

In 2011, the allies' latest strategic idea of securing the country and turning it over to domestic police and military was undermined by such issues as the violence in Kandahar, where, in one year, the top politician, the deputy governor, the mayor, police chief and head of the clerical council were all assassinated.[30] The UN announced that 2010 had been the most violent year since the war began in 2001: assassinations by insurgents were up 105 per cent to 462.[31] Oxfam reported in 2011 that 40,000 Afghan police had had no training for the role and that a tenth of all civilians killed in 2010 had been killed by their own domestic security forces.[32] Following a 2011 UN report that inmates were frequently tortured, NATO stopped sending people to prisons run by the police and intelligence services.[33] An Afghan police firearms instructor, Lt Ahmed Zay Mirweis, said, 'these guys wear the uniform of a policeman, but that is all that is police about them'.[34] These facts demolish any suggestion that a normalised country is being returned to self-rule.

As noted earlier, the US and its allies cannot hold the principal military supply route to Kabul: either it is closed by Pakistan because Americans have shot Pakistani soldiers or it is open to NATO but under Taliban assault. America has even had to ask Russia to allow supplies to transit (see Chapter 10), which has made it difficult to censure Russia on the Crimea.

The opinions of ordinary Afghans are not immediately apparent but there are some discouraging insights. The spokesman for Afghanistan's army, Major General Zahir Azimi, said in 2009: 'Where international forces are fighting, people think it is incumbent on them to resist the occupiers and infidels. This feeling is strong in the south and east and it may spread to other places.'[35] This cannot give much encouragement to the Afghan government's allies in NATO.

In late 2009, the Taliban wrote a letter to the Shanghai Cooperation Organisation asking for assistance in driving the infidel out.[36] The fact is that the West is reluctant to admit that the Taliban is seeking to reclaim Afghans' country. There is a clash between the values of the Western states in the coalition and the country's traditions. The Americans have criticised the Karzai government's Shia family law, which, human rights analysts say, encourages marital rape. President Obama even called it 'abhorrent'. The 2012 'Clerics' Code' on women not mixing with men and having a male guardian with them at all times caused feminist uproar in the West. Women's rights advocates protested against the Shia family legislation, but Afghan counter-protests in favour consisted of crowds several times larger.[37] The omens are not encouraging. It is not difficult to believe that, in order to survive the occupation years unscathed, many heads of families have reached some understanding with the Taliban. The nature of the compact doubtless varies, but it is likely to provide the Taliban with valuable intelligence.

When NATO troops first went into Afghanistan, shortly after the attack on the World Trade Center in New York in 2001, they met with early military success. But that was only part of the story. Soon after the 2001 US invasion, US

Congressman Jim Leach announced a grant of around $750 million to Afghanistan for the damage caused by America. At the time, Abdullah Abdullah, later the unsuccessful candidate in the 2009 Afghan presidential election, told me that he considered the UNDP's figure of $10 billion to be a reasonable estimate for the reconstruction of the country. There seems no connection between the damage wrought and the aid given. It has been estimated by the development aid specialist Serge Michailof that the money generated from the drug trade is perhaps $5–6 billion a year, which is more than the total international aid.[38]

When the victorious West summoned a *Loya Jirga*, or traditional gathering of Afghan tribal leaders and people of influence, in Bonn in 2002 to discuss the country's future, two-thirds of the Afghan delegates argued that the country's king should be made head of state.[39] America's contempt for national feeling was made quite clear by its refusal to countenance this and by its appointment instead of Hamid Karzai. It was the beginning of what many Afghans see as a continuing disdain for their culture and values. And this is what has built considerable support for the Taliban, which is seen in many quarters as a national resistance. Had the West been willing to have the king (who was of Pashtun tribal descent) as the country's leader, the Taliban (which is also generally Pashtun) would have been stripped of much ethnic and cultural justification for their existence.

Belatedly, it is being recognised that the most important public goods are security and justice. Security may be difficult to guarantee across the whole country, but more attention should have been given to it at the beginning. Justice is often provided by the Taliban in its rough and ready way. Plans to expand the domestic Afghan National Police, to bring security and justice to the cities and countryside, sound laudable, but there are a number of practical problems. An *International Herald Tribune* interview with the Italian police general who tried to train the police highlighted a few: the salary levels are lower than those offered by the Taliban; a fifth of all recruits test positive for drugs; less than one in ten can read and write (which is below even the national average of 15 per cent) and 'Many cannot even read a licence plate.'[40] After two months of training, one in twenty fails the firearms tests and is issued with a certificate stating he is not competent; then he is armed and posted on duty. There is a shortage of armoured vehicles, and so many die in ambushes: the death toll has been almost 70 per cent greater than among NATO troops.

Conflict of interest is a live issue, as the police are local to their area and many have relatives serving in the Taliban. There is a strong incentive to warn opposing forces of planned operations. Foreign police trainers have been shot by Afghan policemen, and other policemen appear to have defected with heavy weapons. In all, a quarter of the police leave every year. Some recent pay rises have helped but they still leave the police with income below the cost of living, which can only affect their loyalty. The situation is so bad that Afghan police have been described by Michailof as 'le premier racketteur du pays', the principal criminal in the country.[41]

The domestic financial system cannot actually support the security strategy that is used to justify the US withdrawal. The World Bank has forecast that by 2021–2 there will be 'an unmanageable fiscal gap' of 25 per cent of GDP. The likely size of force that can be funded at the time of US withdrawal – even if composed of competent men – is probably inadequate to maintain the current political system.[42] It is not surprising that, after a decade, President Karzai told the West, 'we will need your steadfast support for at least another decade'.[43] America has changed the way it evaluates Afghan military and police units. In 2011 not a single unit achieved the top category of 'independent' (which signified that it could operate independently of Western troops); the category was scrapped in 2012. Now the top category is simply 'independent with advisers', and only 8 per cent reached that standard in 2012.

On the bright side, since the overthrow of the Taliban, boys and girls have been able in many parts of the country to go to school. A study in 2011 estimated that infant mortality had been halved in two years and life expectancy had improved.[44] The Brookings Institution has published a number of polls from 2011 suggesting that public opinion believes the country is broadly going in the right direction.[45] (An earlier survey had found that, although there was strong opposition to the Taliban, less than half of those polled viewed the US favourably, and a quarter saw some justification for attacks on US troops.)[46] The point is the fragility of Western gains since the invasion of 2001.

Most analysts agree that a viable solution that allows the allies to take their soldiers home must be based on power-sharing with the 'moderate' or the 'more biddable' elements in the Taliban. (One might ask why the Taliban should negotiate if it feels it has won the war.) However, if a coalition is the future, then presumably there will have to be negotiations that would open the door to a lot more than the existing Shia family law, corruption, drugs and crooked elections. What could the Karzai government compromise on with the Taliban? Negotiation might serve to push Afghanistan further away from Western values. It is understandable that the West wants to come up with a target for closure in the Afghan war that is achievable, so that its troops can stop fighting and go home. But it does cast a shadow over the bravery of those men and women who have died along the way for a variety of different – and higher-sounding – objectives.

If the Taliban becomes an important element in the national government, the critical question for China will be whether the new government's reach extends further than the Taliban managed before 2001, when it could not govern the north-eastern part of the country owing to the strong presence of the Northern Alliance and its leader Ahmad Shah Massoud (who was assassinated in 2001). Without Massoud blocking the way, substantial Taliban activity has been seen in the north-east. Moreover Afghanistan is increasingly the principal drug supplier to China.

Taliban control of the Wakhan Corridor in eastern Afghanistan would bring radical Islam to the borders of Xinjiang province, and thus China. This explains China's heightened and uncharacteristic participation in diplomatic discussions about Afghanistan since 2011 and the interest being shown by the SCO.

The Former Soviet Republics

Allied with the prospect of instability in Pakistan and defeat in Afghanistan are the clear signs of fragility in the former Soviet states of Central Asia. Together, these five countries are eleven times the size of Germany but have less than three-quarters of its population. The West has shown little interest in them, except for America's needs in the context of the 'war on terror', which have led it to ally with the authoritarian rulers. The leaders are being wooed by the Russians and Chinese to form a non-Islamicist cordon sanitaire, and yet the people are poor – and Muslim. America, Russia and India have all managed to secure military bases in the region. In 2009, China's net trade with this region overtook that of Russia. As a result, Putin's attempt to re-knit the Soviet empire is effectively being contested by China. Debate over membership of the Eurasian Union is the focus.

Kyrgyzstan depends on 900,000 of its workers in Russia as remittances from overseas constitute one third of its GDP.[47] It had a bloody civil war in 2010 and Russia refused to send security troops. Uzbekistan, with 28 million inhabitants, is the population giant. Under Karimov, its repressive leader, it has waged a deadly internal war with Islamicist militants for years. Despite his human rights deficiencies, Karimov is courted by Washington for his country's strategic location as a conduit to Afghanistan. The al-Qaeda-linked Islamic Movement of Uzbekistan (IMU) announced in 2012 that its leader had been killed by a drone attack in Pakistan; presumably this was Washington seeking to please Karimov. All these countries are fragile. One analyst has suggested that Central Asian regimes will not in future fall through divisions within the elite but through popular uprisings. The strong men of Central Asia could be swept away by an Islamicist current.

There has been a tendency amongst authoritarian governments in Central Asia to be concerned about the potential growth of a Wahhabi-style Islam, which could generate opposition to the very existence of the post-Soviet republics and instead agitate for the restoration of a quasi-mythical Islamic 'Caliphate'. As a result Central Asian leaders have shown interest in encouraging Sufi Islam as a counterweight. However, the fragmentary nature of Islam in the region suggests that the danger is not of a unitary movement sweeping the authoritarian regimes from power. It is more likely that religion will be the banner raised by militant groups that are as much against the present regimes as in favour of any alternative: they might be opposed to corrupt and repressive existing governments and find in Islam an appealing rallying cry.

The Caliphate is the model of a unified movement to create change, sweep away the present infidel period and bring righteous government. There does not seem to be any one movement which enshrines this effectively on a regional basis; there are many separate, contrasting movements with differing objectives. It is more than an issue of favouring or opposing radical Islam; it is a matter of racial tension as well. This might suggest that the future is not the Caliphate, but chaos or obscurantist particularism. In other words, we are less likely to see a Wahhabi military victory over the entire region and more likely to see individual states collapse owing to local rebellions. As one observer has noted, the problem lies with the states, not the insurgents.[48] We need to get away from the post-1945 international fixation on propping up existing states, almost regardless of their viability. Non-state actors can at times be healthier forces than states. Any regional intervention is fraught as, for different reasons, all four neighbouring powers – Russia, China, India and Shia Iran – can be seen as infidel. Central Asia may go from comprising secular autrocities to resembling Somaliland rather than the Caliphate.

The governments and the peoples of the five former Soviet republics are essentially secular, so do not favour Islamic government. However, all are faced with highly motivated, militant minority groups that are influenced by radical Islam. All have adopted similar methods to repress radical tendencies and foster moderate Islam: they have instituted state control of religion; how it is taught, supervised and practised. Each government feels there is a clear danger of radical Islam subverting the regime. This fear of subversion is not unusual in the Islamic world – where most governments are authoritarian and seek to control their religion – particularly after the events in Egypt. Muslim countries usually control the practice of Islam more than non-Muslim countries control their major religions. Furthermore, Muslim countries have increased the amount of regulation significantly since 1990. The Central Asian states have just taken this further than most others.

Encirclement

Contemporary victims of encirclement include India, Pakistan and Russia. The world is trying hard to avoid giving China this feeling through Indo-Japanese or other regional security pacts. India feels that – with China on its Himalayan border; China's ally, Pakistan, on its western flank; and Chinese facilities planned or claimed to be in Burma, Bangladesh, Sri Lanka and Pakistan – it is well on the way to encirclement. Meanwhile Pakistan sees India to its east; a quietly hostile Afghanistan to its north; Indian-sponsored Baluchistan separatism in its south-west; and a trade route being constructed by India down its western border from Afghanistan, through Iran to the sea. Russia has seen NATO arrive on its western borders, Ukraine and Georgia – temporarily at least – 'go Western', a US presence in Central Asia and NATO links with Pakistan and Afghanistan. The sense of encirclement has become pervasive and almost universal in Central Asia.

Reflections

The fractured nature of Sunni Islam in Central Asia means that China is not facing a concerted push towards its borders but more likely the combination of intermittent regime collapses and an increasingly anarchic regional environment, where uncomfortable surprises are likely.

Dysfunctional borders will be more than overshadowed by quasi-existential questions, such as the fate of Pakistan's nuclear arsenal. Pakistan likes to reassure interested parties that its arsenal is both dispersed and under firm control. However, it is not clear under whose control it is or how firm that control is. In the event of regime collapse, there may have to be some foreign intervention in Pakistan to remove the nuclear capability. This could not be undertaken by India. It would be interesting to see if China is nominated on the grounds of contiguity, old alliance, the fact that it is not Indian or Shia – and the fact that it is believed to have supplied some of the technology.

On the other hand, both because it is on principle opposed to overseas 'adventures' and because it has witnessed the hostility that America has managed to provoke in its Asian sorties, Beijing is unlikely to be keen on any such intervention in Pakistan. China's response to Central Asian regime collapse will colour its suitability for superpower status – by choice or by peer acclaim – and even its status as a regional power.

America's difficulty in its Central Asian war constitutes a strategic dilemma for China. Beijing is deeply fearful of the spread of militant Islam in its direction, but it is publicly committed to opposing American hegemonism. In one sense, China would like America to win. Conversely, it wants a demonstration that America has feet of clay. It does not want the American army in Central Asia, but still less does it want the Taliban in Xinjiang. The last time the Taliban was in power in Afghanistan, it did not control the whole country. In particular, its writ did not extend to the eastern province of Badakhshan, on China's border, and there was no active hostility towards China or clear interference in Xinjiang. However, Badakhshan is now a war zone, featuring confrontation between the Taliban and the coalition. The fact that in this area there is no meaningful Pashtun community (which tends to provide recruits for the Taliban militants in other provinces) suggests that the Taliban has been able to broaden its ethnic catchment area. The suppression by China of recent disturbances in Xinjiang provoked a diplomatic slap from Premier Erdogan of Turkey (who called it 'a kind of genocide'), and also condemnation from al-Qaeda. If the Taliban succeeds in its struggle against America and its allies, jihad could be launched from beyond Xinjiang's borders. The Taliban today has real influence in Afghanistan's north-east, which it did not have before 2001.[49] China could be in a difficult position.

CHAPTER THIRTEEN

Undeclared War in the Fourth Dimension?

Among other attributes, a superpower needs a high level of technology and the ability to project itself militarily worldwide. These have recently only been the preserve of the United States; and not even of the USSR. In the relatively new, rather opaque but dramatic area of cyber power, China has developed as a world leader. It is difficult to see direct threats to China through this technology. What is interesting, however, is what it shows us about China's use of its increasing powers. This leads to a consideration of how the world may react to China's actions and what adverse consequences may arise.

Recent Chinese Development

Chinese strategists have shown increasing interest in incorporating cyber conflict into the country's military capability. Since 1997, cyber information warfare has featured in the People's Liberation Army doctrine and training. As early as in 2001, the US Congressional Research Service summarised China's commitment:

> China is moving aggressively toward incorporating cyberwarfare into its military lexicon, organization, training, and doctrine. In fact, if a Revolution in Military Affairs (RMA) is defined as a significant change in technology taken advantage of by comparable changes in military training, organization, and doctrine, then perhaps China of all nations is experiencing a true RMA in cyberspace. Several large annual training exercises have taken place since 1997. The Chinese have placed significant emphasis on training younger persons for these tasks.[1]

We could see cyber action as the twenty-first-century equivalent of guerrilla warfare, where a weaker power can defeat a stronger one by asymmetric warfare and better tactics. As Robert Gates, former Secretary for Defence, said in 2014, "they are investing selectively in capabilities that target our vulnerabilities, not our strengths".[2]

By 2003, the PLA had conducted numerous cyber warfare training exercises, and in 2010 Xu Caihou, vice chairman of China's Central Military Commission, urged 'continued efforts to transform military training based upon mechanized warfare to that based on information warfare';[3] In 2011, recognising a weakness in its officer corps, the Central Military Commission of the PLA said it would focus on four talents: specialisation in commanding joint military operations; information construction and management; cyber technology; and applying and maintaining new combat weapons.

A Decade of Malicious Attacks

China's cyber activity has drawn increasing criticism since at least 2002, and this links with American complaints of cyber intrusion from various sources. In the year to October 2006, 30,000 malicious attacks on US Defense Department computer networks were reported; by 2009 the number had reached 72,000 – one every seven minutes.[4] Attacks have been directed at, among others, the Pentagon, the intelligence services, the military, the State Department and the White House. The cost of defending against these attacks is huge and is expected to exceed $10 billion by 2014.

Military command and control systems are seen as particularly vulnerable. These have been attacked by groups linked to foreign governments, as well as by organised crime gangs and hackers. The US–China Economic and Security Review Commission of the US Congress (USCESRC) reports extensively on this area. Its 2008 report said that US authorities had

> detected a series of cyber intrusions in 2002 into unclassified U.S. military, government, and government contractor web sites and computer systems. This large-scale operation . . . was attributed to China . . . China downloaded 10 to 20 terabytes of data . . . In addition to seeking to acquire important information about military and government activities, the operation conducted reconnaissance of the U.S. command and control system.[5]

In 2011, one cyber attack stole 24,000 files, many of which involved highly sensitive defence systems.[6]

Washington believes many of the attacks it has suffered originated within China. Much of the discussion in this field revolves around identification of the sponsors of the attacks. Already China has tested a weapon that can destroy American satellites, and it has the ability to blind them with lasers. The 2009 USCESRC report clarified three points: Chinese cyber espionage activity against the US is continuing to expand; the PLA has created cyber warfare 'militia units' of civilians, including academics; and the case study used of an American defence technology company attacked from China left 'no doubt that that's state-controlled'.[7] The Commission asked Northrop Grumman, the global security company, to review this avalanche of malicious activity. Its analysis is clear:

> The depth of resources necessary to sustain the scope of computer network exploitation targeting the US and many countries around the world coupled with the extremely focused targeting of defense engineering data, US military operational information, and China-related policy information is beyond the capabilities or profile of virtually all organized cybercriminal enterprises and is difficult at best without some type of state sponsorship.[8]

A recent US government panel said that China – meaning the state – now has the capability to launch cyber attacks 'anywhere in the world at any time'.[9] A 2007 cyber attack on the Pentagon was believed to have been executed by the PLA. The hackers targeted a secure Pentagon system known as NIPRnet, which is fundamental to the mobilisation of US forces for any defensive action regarding Taiwan. Damaging this network could cause critical delay to the US military response. That same year, a Pentagon report by Larry Wortzel of the US Army War College stated that China had drawn up detailed plans to render harmless the US aircraft carrier battle fleet via a cyber attack. Major Laura Knapp at the US Air Command and Staff College wrote in 2008:

> Finjan, a private cyber security firm based in California, released an interim report in December 2007 stating, 'In the last three months, the attacks [from China] have almost tripled'. An official spokesman from the Naval Network Warfare Command asserted that computer 'attacks from China, probably with government support, far outstrip other attackers in terms of volume, proficiency, and sophistication'. Additionally, the Finjan report discovered a 'centralized group of activity based in China', with one website in the group belonging to a Chinese government office.[10]

Regarding the attack on the Pentagon, Major Knapp wrote:

> The 'Financial Times' referenced a former Pentagon official's comments that 'the PLA has demonstrated the ability to conduct attacks that disable our

system . . . and the ability in a conflict situation to re-enter and disrupt on a very large scale' . . . In the Pentagon penetrations, analysts traced the attacks back to twenty computer systems in China's Guangdong province, known to be the home of cyber units and the PLA 4 Department (responsible for Electronic Warfare/Signals Intelligence).[11]

Major Knapp quotes Alan Paller, then director of research at the Security Institute in Bethesda, Maryland:

> The precision in the attacks, the perfection in the methods, and the 24 by-seven operations over two and a half years, and the number of workstations involved are simply not replicated in the amateur criminal community . . .[12]

Major Knapp said Paller characterised the attacks as 'an order of magnitude more disciplined' than any others perpetrated by the civilian hacker community. Following a hacking at Oak Ridge National Laboratory in 2007, Knapp said:

> The hackers' selection of e-mail address books and passwords is significant because it allows them to develop the social network of their victims so that they can conduct follow-on attacks against more lucrative targets . . . These cyber exploitation attempts are noteworthy because computer experts have actually traced several of them back to the Chinese government.[13]

Subsequently she recorded:

> Not long after the Pentagon attack, the US State Department acknowledged that it also suffered massive Chinese cyber attacks that resulted in 'large-scale, network break-ins affecting operations worldwide'. The attacks seemed to target department headquarters and offices handling matters relating to North Korea and China. Additionally, the Rand Corporation reported that hackers targeted its Chinese scholars.[14]

In 2010, Google announced that it had been the victim of extensive hostile cyber attacks in China (Operation Aurora) and would cease censoring its service there (see Chapter 8). A security firm engaged in the subsequent investigations, iDefense, declared that both the source Internet Protocol addresses and the servers used in the attacks 'correspond to a single foreign entity consisting either of agents of the Chinese state or proxies thereof'.[15] Researchers 'traced the penetration to two schools in China, one of which has ties to the Chinese military'.[16] Leaked US diplomatic cables published by WikiLeaks said that the attack was directed by high-level officials in the Chinese government security apparatus.[17] The same year, MessageLabs Intelligence Report investigated the origins of targeted attacks and malicious emails that were intended specifically to access corporate data. The largest number, over 28 per cent, came from senders in China.[18] In 2011, Google stated that the email passwords of US officials and journalists had been stolen. The campaign originated in 'the city of Jinan in Shandong Province, the site of a vocational school associated with the Chinese military'.[19] In 2012 the White House Military Office was hacked into, reportedly from China.[20] In 2011, Deputy Secretary of State for Defense William Lynn said that 'now, the danger of cyberwarfare rivals that of traditional war'.[21] What is the ultimate threat?

Scott Borg, head of the US Cyber Consequences think tank, suggests that 'most countries can survive a major assault lasting two to three days, but if an enemy knocked out part of the critical infrastructure for eight to ten days, the accumulated economic and social damage would bring a country to its knees ... What constitutes an act of cyberwar? ... Is it the placing of sleeper viruses on a country's electric grid, as the Chinese have done in the US?'[22]

Over the course of a decade we have seen a mixture of malicious cyber attacks on the US, frequently blamed on China. Some have simply been spying; others have caused real damage. 'Malicious activity' peaked in early 2009, since when it has declined. However, as the US Defense Department explains, this is only because measures have been taken to 'mitigate threats before they reach the threshold that merits an incident log entry' – it does not mean the number of attempted attacks is falling.[23] As Rear Admiral Samuel Cox, intelligence director of US Cyber Command, said in late 2012 of Chinese attacks, 'their level of effort against the Department of Defense is constant'.[24]

Ten years after the attacks began, the US Department of Defense, in its *Quadrennial Roles and Missions Review Report* of 2009, claimed that: 'Although cyberspace presents unique challenges to military operations, the Department has made significant progress in defining its roles, missions, and objectives in cyberspace.'

Americans might prefer that the last decade of cyber attacks had focused its military more on defending than on defining.

Surprisingly, an American security researcher, Dillon Beresford, claims to have successfully hacked into many highly classified Chinese military facilities: aggressive behaviour is not always matched by proficient cyber security. Indeed, he states that China has 'an almost total lack of basic cyber defense.'[25]

In late 2010, William Lynn said that internet-based threats to intellectual property represented a threat to US national security. He went on: 'The power grid, the financial systems, the transportation network, all of those need to have a higher level of protection than I think we can currently provide them.'[26] The tone continues to be one of unpreparedness. That same year, General Michael Hayden, a former CIA director, said: 'As an intelligence professional, I stand back in absolute awe and wonderment at the Chinese espionage effort against the United States of America . . . It is magnificent in its breadth, its depth and its efficiency.'[27] And in 2011, Alan Paller, now of the SANS Institute in Washington, said that 'the attacks coming out of China are not only continuing, they are accelerating.'[28]

Not Only Practised by China

China is not, of course, alone in sanctioning hacking: there were rather amateurish Indonesian attacks on Malaysia in 2005 and a more professional Japan–Korea altercation that year. Russia and Israel sponsor hacker communities. Iran has responded fiercely to the 2010 attack.

Analysts have suggested that 2007 was the year cyber warfare really 'came of age': that year saw the (presumed) Russian attack on Estonia, and Israel is believed to have used cyber weapons to disable Syrian air defences. In 2008 Russia and Georgia carried out cyber attacks on one another while their troops were fighting. That same year Lithuania underwent a pro-Russian attack.[29] Seoul blamed North Korea in 2009 for a network crash that damaged South Korean and American government and private websites.

The attack on Estonia is the benchmark for cyber warfare so far: it lasted three weeks and disabled the websites of government ministries, political parties, newspapers, banks and communications companies. The method used was to create a wave of 'distributed denials of service' (DDoS), by overloading the servers. The idea that any future US naval operation to support Taiwan could be technologically thwarted naturally concerns the Pentagon. Similarly, crashing national communications or banking systems could be highly destructive commercially.

The technology continues to develop. In 2010, cyber specialists said they had 'identified the world's first known cyber super weapon designed specifically to destroy a real-world target – a factory, a refinery, or just maybe a nuclear power plant'.[30] The speculation was that the 'worm' (named Stuxnet) was a state-sponsored attack, probably Israeli and American, on an Iranian nuclear facility. It was described as the most important development in cyber warfare in a decade. This is the only (albeit a most serious) example of deliberate damage ascribable to the United States. It is arguably less serious than putting logic bombs on the American electricity grid which, if activated, could have caused power interruptions and thus loss of life (see p.343 above). However, it associates Washington with what it would, under other circumstances, call terrorism. Its precursor, the "Flame" malware, imitates Windows updates and thus undermines the integrity of a staple American IT product.

Not Only Experienced by America

Jonathan Evans, head of MI5, Britain's domestic security service, warned 300 leading British companies in 2007 that they were potential spying targets 'from Chinese state organizations'.[31] Angela Merkel, the Chancellor of Germany, confronted Wen Jiabao in 2007 after her own office and several ministries had been hacked into by what German security officials called 'Chinese state interests', and in 2008 the deputy head of German domestic intelligence blamed the Chinese government for malicious cyber attacks on the German government.[32] In 2008, Jo Vandeurzen, Belgian justice minister, stated that his country had been attacked by the Chinese government.[33] These statements go beyond the usual amorphous claim that entities in China have attacked a system: they attribute them firmly to the Chinese state.

The Institute of Peace and Conflict Studies in Delhi reported that Chinese hackers had 'defaced' 858 websites in one month in 2007. Then the French Embassy in Beijing saw its website brought down after President Sarkozy met the Dalai Lama.[34] In 2009, there was an extensive investigation by Cambridge and Toronto Universities into a massive espionage operation against the computers of the Dalai Lama's offices, which involved 1,295 computers being hacked into in 103 countries:

> Clearly this investigation and our analysis tracks back directly to the PRC, and to known entities within the criminal underground of the PRC. There is also an obvious correlation to be drawn between the victims, the nature of the documents stolen, and the strategic interests of the Chinese state. But correlations do not equal causation. It is certainly possible that the attackers were directed in some manner – either by sub-contract or privateering – by agents of the Chinese state, but we have no evidence to prove that assertion.[35]

Researchers said embassies and government communications systems in many countries had been affected, including the foreign ministries in Indonesia, Iran and the Philippines, the office of the Prime Minister of Laos and a single non-secure computer at NATO. The implication is, of course, that a civilian is unlikely to expend so much effort on complex cyber attacks on the Dalai Lama.

Japan and Taiwan have both complained of Chinese interference with their computer networks. In 2011, a South Korean opposition legislator said government officials had told him that Chinese hackers had accessed military procurement plans; a government legislator said that 37 per cent of all attempts to break into government computers came from China.[36] When the IMF was hacked into in 2011, the FBI investigated and concluded that the attack had originated in China and 'was probably connected to the government'.[37] 'Evidence pointing to China includes an analysis of the attack methods, as well as the electronic trail left by hackers.'[38]

On the other hand, according to a report ascribed by a well-known website to Beijing Rising, a Chinese computer security firm, there were some 10 million malicious attacks on China's classified websites in 2010 alone, of which 90 per cent originated overseas. The largest proportion (21 per cent) was alleged to be American.[39] The *People's Daily* says that 4,635 government websites were hacked into in 2010.[40] It is unclear how the figure of 10 million incidents is arrived at.

China's Response to Criticism

The combined attacks on government and private sector facilities in South Korea and the US in 2009 were interesting for two reasons. First, US officials said privately that they were the longest and most effective of any cyber attacks. Second, a White House official said, 'We can't accurately identify who an attacker is in cyberspace.'[41] This does not mean that the country where an attack originates cannot be identified, but that the actual attacking entity may be difficult to trace. Also, governments may prefer not to reveal what they can identify.

In the case of the 2009 infiltration of the Dalai Lama's communication systems, involving many governments and over 1,000 computers worldwide, a Chinese diplomat in New York denied that Beijing was responsible. 'These are old stories and they are nonsense,' said Wenqi Gao. 'The Chinese government is opposed to and strictly forbids any cybercrime.'[42] The Chinese Embassy in Washington described the charges in the 2009 USCESRC report as 'a product of cold war mentality'. 'Accusations of China conducting, or "likely conducting" as the commission's report indicates, cyberspace attacks or espionage against the US are unfounded and unwarranted.'[43] In 2010, the official mantra developed further. A spokesman said:

> The Chinese government firmly opposes cyber attacks in any form and Chinese law clearly states that any hackers will be held liable for their actions

. . . China itself is a major victim of cyber attacks and network viruses . . . and has laws in place to deal with hackers . . . In 2009, Chinese law enforcement authorities investigated about 48,000 cases.[44]

None of those 48,000 investigations appears to have concerned a Chinese hacking into an overseas computer. China's official definition of cyber crime embraces attempts to navigate government internet controls in order to access publicly held information from overseas or to make unofficial political comment. The standard response from Beijing to charges of involvement in offensive cyber activity overseas has been a mixture of ignorance, denial and insistence that 'rogue civilians' are to blame. A rare exception was when Chancellor Angela Merkel confronted Wen Jiabao in public in 2007, blaming China for hacking into her office: he is reported not to have denied it but to have said that the activity should cease.[45]

On the other hand, President Xi will probably have greatly enjoyed his meeting in 2014 in the Netherlands with President Obama where he reportedly asked for a clear explanation of reports of America's National Security Agency spying on the leading Chinese telecoms company, Huawei.

Whether there are 300,000 internet police or 30–40,000 (as others say), China clearly WITH State media made clear in 2013 there are two million internet police and China clearly has the most sophisticated internet control system.[46] The American company Cisco has provided it with routers and switches for the explicit purpose of monitoring internet traffic and controlling unapproved activity.[47] As Sami Saydjari, an ex-US Defense Department computer security veteran, has pointed out: 'it's highly unlikely there are hacker groups that have any substantial level of capability they [the Chinese] don't control'.[48]

The implication is straightforward. Beijing believes government should monitor aspects of citizens' lives: it makes a public virtue of internet monitoring. If China has so much power over its internet traffic – it certainly monitors and limits undesirable political discussion and claims to control pornography – it could surely prevent destructive internet practices overseas by its citizens if it wished to.

Furthermore, there are charges that the PLA actually sponsors the hacking; that they organise 'hacking competitions' with prizes, and give money to hackers ('techie mercenaries') with targets to fulfil.[49] Interviews with Western journalists partly confirm these charges, and technologically capable units are reported to have been established in China's 8 million-strong military reserves.[50] This is said to create 'deniability', as they are not employees. China is said to have the world's largest capacity for DDoS attacks.

China is not publicly proven guilty. We simply have assertions from a long list of officials from democratic governments that it is a fact (or that they have evidence, or that the clues strongly point that way). We must either believe the statements of Western officials or believe the case is not proven. The Western case is somewhat weakened by statements such as the one quoted above that 'We can't accurately identify who an attacker is in cyberspace.' However, we should ask why so many governments are apparently comfortable about specifically attributing the crime to China, and no one else, if they have no evidence.

It appears reasonable to assume that the attacks occurred. If we adopt the old approach of means, motive and opportunity, criminal gangs are unlikely to have much interest in the State Department, the Pentagon or the Indian Prime Minister's office. The parties are more likely to be state actors, or people acting on behalf of the state. Presumably they are reasonably technically advanced. Who hates the Dalai Lama?

Cyber Sabotage Is a Serious Threat

Most countries are involved in cyber intelligence activity. Israel is reported to use it against the US; France against its EU partners; and the US against China. However, we must see if we can differentiate. The US protests that its massive, intrusive and unwelcome spying operation at home and abroad is qualitatively better than that of China because – although it gathers highly diverse material – it does not use the results to benefit its commercial sector. China is accused of stealing R&D and other hard-won commercial secrets. 'The activities of the two sides, however, are vastly different in scope and intent. The United States engages in widespread electronic espionage, but that classified information cannot legally be handed over to private industry. China is using its surveillance to steal trade secrets, harm international competitors and undermine American businesses.'[51] However, it is not universally agreed that spying for a state is morally superior to spying for commercial reasons.

According to James Mulvenon, director of the Center for Intelligence and Research in Washington: 'The Chinese are the first to use cyberattacks for political and military goals . . . Whether it is battlefield preparation or hacking networks connected to the German chancellor'. Here the definition of an 'attack' is important. It is difficult to believe that the US and Israel do not seek to understand the military capabilities of countries they deem enemies. And the US taxpayer might be aggrieved to think that none of the $600 billion Pentagon budget was spent in checking its enemies' plans. Perhaps 'exfiltration' is OK, but smashing internet capabilities for military or political goals is an 'attack' – wilful damage.

The growing dependence of telecoms infrastructure on software rather than hardware makes it more vulnerable to cyber attack. This is a repetitive theme. General Deptula testified to the USCESRC in 2011 that China had 'identified the U.S. military's reliance on information systems as a significant vulnerability that, if successfully exploited, could paralyze or degrade U.S. forces to such an extent that victory could be achieved'.[52]

US legislators have lamented the tendency towards secrecy by attack victims, including Washington, and have demanded greater transparency in order to draw lessons and limit future damage. The Senate Committee said that America 'cannot presume a clear-cut technology advantage in this field'. This may be political-speak for 'in some areas we do not have the lead' – which is credible, because the report recommended a programme of long-term 'high-risk' research aimed at achieving 'revolutionary breakthroughs', to be financed despite short-term budgetary pressures.[53]

Washington deliberately downplays Chinese cyber activities. In 2009, Joel Brenner, then the most senior US counter-intelligence coordinator, said there were minimal concerns about a Chinese cyber attack on US banking networks because 'they have too much money invested here . . . Our electricity grid? No, not now. But if there were a dust-up over Taiwan, these answers might be different.'[54] He went on to say that aggressive Chinese computer hacking had been long known, but Washington preferred not to give details. The CIA had sponsored research in the late 1990s that sought to minimise Chinese cyber warfare capabilities, believing that highlighting them would hype the threat.[55]

So Washington knowingly understates Chinese activity (much of which is, of course, spying rather than destruction). According to Mike McConnell, head of US Intelligence, in 2007 both Russia and China were spying on the USA at close to Cold War levels.[56]

Attribution

Attribution is one of the most difficult issues in cyber conflict. If we can attribute responsibility for an attack, it allows retaliation. Publicly, states tend to downplay this for political and technical reasons. Though it might be hard to trace the perpetrators, often there is some evidence. However, politics often intrudes to make it unhelpful to announce where the evidence points. China appears to employ the resources of young domestic hackers extensively, as a form of mercenary auxiliary, to obfuscate attribution and permit deniability.

It is not enough for critics to imply who the perpetrator is by saying that the activity comes from Guangdong (which is the base of PLA Signals Unit 4) or

Sichuan (where the office monitoring the Dalai Lama is based). Sichuan has the same population as Germany; and if it were a country, Guangdong would be the world's twelfth most populous. Together they have 176 million people. China has millions of dedicated hackers; extreme nationalism is rife; skills are rising rapidly; and many people work in the IT industry. However, investigators do know much more than is publicly stated. Occasionally this becomes clear, as when Britain's MI5 or Germany's state security organisation specifically mention actions by Chinese state organisations. In 2013 the US leadership decided to go public with attribution in an attempt to rally global support to stop Chinese cyber hostility. Ironically this coincided with Edward Snowden's disclosure of massive intrusive US spying on its public and foreign publics and leaders which effectively left the US initiative stillborn.[57]

What is known about aggressive cyber activities? We know they happen at nationally important locations worldwide. President Obama believes the 'threat is one of the most serious economic and national security challenges we face'.[58] We know that frequently they require sophisticated skills which are largely only governmental. We are told that the countries of origin can be traced, and sometimes the region, though often not the entity itself. We have heard that US policy has been to downplay evidence of Chinese involvement, even when available. We know that US State Department cables, published without authorisation on WikiLeaks, admit traceability to the Chinese state, and even to specific units.[59]

Specialists suggest that it might be difficult to marshal the resources to track all attacks to the origination points, as there are so many. However, several maintain that, if enough forensic resources are mustered for a specific incident, it should be possible to identify precisely where an attack was initiated. It is hard to imagine that Western governments have not deemed some of the most egregious attacks worthy of such an exercise. If it is possible to attribute an attack to a specific computer in a secure government location, that entity should be held responsible for its personnel and its access policies. Resources of such value and sophistication are unlikely to be unguarded. The excuse of 'rogue civilians' ceases then to have even a shred of credibility.

The Rand Corporation's 2009 cyber warfare report (by Martin Libicki) says it is difficult to respond to a cyber attack aggressively, as responsibility is unclear.[60] It stresses the likely responsibility of third-party hackers and suggests that their involvement can escalate inter-governmental hostility. Libicki also suggested that if a perpetrator believes there is no clear evidence, he can deny responsibility and condemn any retaliation. Attribution is vital. In fact, the 'international community' may reject the retaliation.[61]

As we have seen, China polices the internet closely. If the twenty computer systems in Guangdong that attacked the Pentagon in 2007 were privately owned, it beggars belief that domestic intelligence services were not fully aware of the activity. If they were hijacked, it is likely to have been by a sponsored group. Computer security specialists have consistently stressed the sophistication of the cyber attacks from China. It is unlikely that unemployed IT graduates would have access to the necessary resources. China knows such overseas incidents have happened and is capable of investigating them; but no individuals have been apprehended. While hackers are prosecuted for circumventing domestic security systems, the servers used in the assaults on the West or on Google have not been identified or – it seems – even sought. This suggests that the authorities either condone or sponsor them. Reports of PLA assessment, encouragement and sponsorship of hackers for the convenience of 'deniability' suggest the latter.

In short, there are so many indications that cyber attacks frequently originate 'somewhere in China' that the assumption must be that this is the case. Substantial resources are required, and China is not the kind of society where those resources can be utilised without state agencies being aware. Add to that the fact that much of what is stolen or damaged really only benefits one particular entity. The source of individual attacks can be pinpointed (at considerable cost and effort), and democratic governments are unlikely to name the Chinese state specifically as the perpetrator if they have no convincing evidence. The circumstantial and forensic evidence seems to point unequivocally to Chinese state responsibility.

Reflections

What conclusions should be drawn from this?

Hacking is a relatively new activity and lacks mutually agreed protocols. There is probably a clear distinction to be made between taking information while leaving data and facilities intact, and temporarily shutting down or damaging facilities and data. The former is spying; the latter is arguably an act of sabotage or state terrorism. The US will say that there is a difference between states stealing state secrets and states stealing business secrets to use them in business.

As with conventional espionage, it is difficult to have overt regulation of covert activities. But how will the victims of such attacks respond? India has stated that it regards cyber attacks as 'terrorist acts'. Russia has debated a similar formulation. What retaliation does that allow these countries against those deemed perpetrators, and how much evidence is required, is not clear. While most significant countries engage in cyber spying, only a few appear to inflict damage or disable systems. It is sometimes said that this isn't cyber *warfare*, as no one dies.[62] However, damage to critical infrastructure is central to warfare, and this is deliberate damage. Certain countries, including China, Russia,

North Korea and Israel, seem to play by different rules. But we don't know what those rules are. What is acceptable behaviour and what is considered unacceptable? America arrived late but, widely held responsible with Israel for the Stuxnet cyber attack on Iran, is now the prime example of hostile action which has had three results: it spurred counter attacks from Iran, it cast doubt on the integrity of US IT and legitimised offensive cyber action.[63]

In 2009, the US Senate Intelligence Committee called for 'an international framework on cyber war'.[64] Others have proposed a new Geneva Convention, or at least a code of conduct. Certainly there needs to be a definition of when hostility becomes war. It must be clearly laid down what targets should be exempt from attack and what evidence permits what retaliation. What is the etiquette in cyber war? If you 'crash' my air traffic control system for a week, can I divert my river from flowing downstream to your agriculture? The boundaries of cyber war have no agreed definition. This is important to bear in mind.

We live in a world of alliances. If war is declared on an ally, an allied response may be required. If you crash my bank payments system, can I ask my ally – who is your neighbour – to stop rail traffic into your country? Mutual defence treaties will in future probably need to stipulate how signatories should react to a vicious cyber attack when the perpetrator can be identified. Cyber warfare should be recognised, acts of war should be redefined and what triggers the right (and, for an ally, the duty) to respond militarily needs clarification. NATO, for example, must reform Article 5 of its Treaty, which defines when a threatened member should receive armed support.

China is a leading power in the cyber field. It reportedly perpetrates hostile acts in the virtual world which, if undertaken in the real world, would probably require a declaration of war. However, China has rejected the criticisms made against it by many national governments since 2000. The environment is so new that, although China seems the technological leader, we don't know what it intends as the boundaries to this activity, nor whether major Western states will adopt its approach and expand their activities in this sphere.

If America was responsible for Stuxnet, we don't know if it was unique or if Washington will now employ cyber terrorism wherever it feels its interests require this. It is not known whether China's political leaders have discussed the subject with its military leaders: this in itself raises issues about the nature of government there. We know the Chinese Ministry of Defence does not run the military: that is the role of the Central Military Commission (see Chapter 9). Nominally it is divided into a party commission and a state one, but the party commission seems the dominant one. Do the civilian authorities – the

President and the Premier – set the military objectives, including its apparently hostile cyber activity overseas? Probably not. If not, are they informed? Or do they not interfere in 'military matters'? Former Premier Wen Jiabao told Angela Merkel that the cyber attacks should stop. They have not. Does the Party still control the military? Is it solely a Party matter? If so, should we assume that the President, as Party leader, is agreeing the strategy? Or is the military free to do anything it likes, short of formally declaring a conventional war? Each Chinese leader might well have a different relationship with the military. Such possibilities give us contrasting pictures of how China is run.

The principle of undertaking cyber sabotage in peacetime should be approved at the very top of the state. If, for example, civilian leaders are not consulted or involved in military matters, then that suggests a parallel state structure where even actions that affect foreign states can be decided by the military authorities. Conversely, if the President and Premier are involved in approving these actions, that rather undermines their claims of China's 'peaceful development'. (We should not forget that Afghanistan's hosting of al-Qaeda at the time of 9/11 justified the American invasion of that country and the toppling of its government.) Such issues may condition how different countries react to China's rise. After all, Chinese computers have broken into the facilities not only of perceived rivals, such as the US, but also of friends, such as Laos. Similarly, the US has been exposed as spying on the leader of Germany.

The Challenge

China may now be the leading cyber power. That presents it with a challenge: how will other countries react if they believe that China is acting increasingly belligerently?

There are two possible points of view. One is that China habitually employs cyber terrorism, whereas most countries do not. The other is that China is simply far more aggressive than any other country. China risks tarnishing its international image. Do its leaders think a demonstration of strength can smooth the path of an aspiring power? Other countries might recoil at such opaque and unpredictable aggressiveness.

Growing evidence that America is using cyber violence could well lead to a general acceptance of the practice as normal behaviour. It is therefore surprising that China has produced no such credible evidence – it would certainly be in its interests to do so. Otherwise, China risks being branded as the power that goes too far. If the world takes that view, it can only damage the prospects for China's rise.

CHAPTER FOURTEEN

Nervous Neighbours

This chapter discusses the territories bordering mainland China, excluding India, Russia, Central Asia, Afghanistan and Pakistan. The emphasis is on those that could become a focus of conflict. An element of uncertainty about Beijing's future policy in the area is injected by Chinese policy analysts' suggestions that 'destabilising factors' in the 'near abroad' might call for 'pre-emptive measures to promote regional stability'.[1] This is precisely the language that India has used about South Asia and that has accompanied its active intervention in Nepal and Afghanistan and its occupation of independent territories such as Hyderabad and Sikkim. Such actions by China would represent a rupture with its traditional mantra of non-intervention, but we saw an indication of the future in its exasperated call in 2010 to Thailand to get its domestic house in order. China's strong support for Sri Lanka's government during the civil war could be seen as a form of interventionism, as could its financing of weak Central Asian states, which comes close to blocking Russia's influence in the neighbourhood. There is sometimes a thin line between supporting whoever is in power and intervening.

Many countries would see any intervention in, or conflict with, a neighbour as a cessation of China's 'peaceful development'. That could lead to a reassessment of its attractiveness as the future superpower. Chinese claims to disputed neighbouring territory present a predicament.

The world has witnessed China's more aggressive stance on the South China Sea and the East China Sea, more missiles aimed at Taiwan, and a steadily rising Chinese military budget; one (albeit contested) forecast is that by 2015 China's military budget will be larger than the next twelve biggest in the region, including Japan's.[2] China is also the world's sixth-largest arms exporter (although two-thirds of the arms go to Pakistan). There is a growing nervousness among China's neighbours about all of this, and America has responded by 'pivoting' from the Atlantic to the Pacific.

Asian arms budgets are rising rapidly, and South East Asian military spending is forecast almost to double from 2010 to 2016. The five largest arms importers in the world in 2007–11 were Asian; in fact, almost half the world's arms imports in that period went to the Asia-Pacific region.[3] Ni Leixiong, a prominent scholar at Shanghai University of Political Science and Law, was quoted in 2012 as saying that this was happening 'because of fears about China's rapid military build-up'.[4] Although undesired, there are signs of a potential conflagration in the region.

Vietnam

Historically, the Vietnamese have blocked Chinese attempts to dominate South East Asia. Except during the Vietnam War, the two countries have been more antagonistic than comradely. Even in 1969, during that war, French Foreign Minister Maurice Schumann claimed that the North Vietnamese government had made it clear to him that it 'wanted to find some way to defend itself from the Chinese'.[5] Brecher and Wilkenfeld put it bluntly: 'China and Vietnam were hostile neighbours for a thousand years.'[6] China strongly supported Hanoi during the Vietnam War, but relations soured after victory. And before then, in 1974, China had taken control from South Vietnam of the western part of the Paracel Islands in the South China Sea.

The deterioration in relations between the former allies culminated in the Sino-Vietnamese War of 1979. The Chinese invasion of Vietnam lasted less than thirty days and cost up to 70,000 casualties. It has been viewed by analysts as variously a strategic victory and a complete failure for China. When China declared war it noted the Vietnamese occupation of some of the Spratly Islands in the South China Sea and Vietnamese ill-treatment of ethnic Chinese (see Chapter 15). China was also wary of Vietnam's alliance with the Soviet Union and objected to its invasion of Cambodia. The best explanation is that the invasion was a strike at Soviet 'hegemonism'. One Chinese scholar called it 'a gift to America' from Deng Xiaoping, who was then visiting the USA.

The invasion undermines the assertion that China does not invade foreign territories. However, some analysts maintain that the attack was technically not an invasion, as there was no intention of annexing Vietnamese territory. They suggest the strategy was 'active defence': China wanted to degrade Soviet standing and ambitions by demonstrating that Russia could not effectively assist an ally in South East Asia. The Soviets indeed huffed and puffed, but did not intervene. It is difficult to say which side 'won' the war. China could not prevent Vietnam from toppling the Khmer Rouge in Cambodia, and was not seen to have 'punished' it. However, Beijing did demonstrate that being a Soviet ally meant little. Active defence is designed to ensure that other countries do not compromise China's interests. The Korean War and the Sino-Indian War have both also been placed in this context. However, academics note that active defence can cause more conflict than other strategies.

After the war, intermittent fighting, sabotage and cross-border shelling continued until at least the late 1980s. In 2010, the border was still littered with unexploded landmines. The Spratly Islands continue to cause Sino-Vietnamese incidents. Occupied by troops from five armies, they are claimed by six countries. China believes the 650 reefs and islets hold more gas reserves than Kuwait. In 1988, the dispute escalated into a fight between the two navies at Johnson Reef. Several Vietnamese ships were reportedly sunk and more than seventy sailors lost their lives. This century, the conflict has mutated into a proxy war fought through fishing fleets: in the first quarter of 2010, thirty Vietnamese boats with over 200 fishermen were captured by Chinese vessels in disputed seas. This continued into 2013 with Hanoi stating that a Chinese government vessel fired at a Vietnamese fishing boat in waters claimed by the Philippines.

China's vast South–North Water Diversion Project, which intends to divert water from the Tibetan plateau for the benefit of northern China, potentially reduces flow from China to the Mekong and thus raises the prospect of further substantial tension (see Chapter 6). Vietnam is usually regarded as a country that is 'wary' of China, and thus a potential partner for those who are not entirely Sinophile. Joining ASEAN provided it with convenient protection, and tensions relaxed for a while owing to China's interest in engaging more closely with that organisation. Vietnam hopes its membership will lead to multilateral settlement, and America has been enlisted to reinforce the approach. However, China understandably prefers to engage with each country separately, as it is then the dominant interlocutor. Furthermore, this prevents countries 'ganging up' against it.

The Vietnam–Burma relationship is intriguing. Despite not having engaged with democratisation itself, Hanoi has encouraged Burma to move in that direction: at a 2010 ASEAN gathering under Vietnamese chairmanship, the Prime Minister urged the Burmese to ensure that their 'elections should be free and democratic with the participation of all parties'.[7] It has also supported the thawing of relations between America and Burma, for which it received recognition from US Assistant Secretary of State Kurt Campbell: 'it was Vietnam who quietly urged us to continue to talk directly to the government'.[8] In 2012, two Burmese navy ships paid a visit to Vietnam and a subsequent communiqué stressed the need for 'securing peace and stability in the South China Sea'.[9] This will have puzzled China, which built the warships.

In a sense, Vietnam has been repairing relations with China. It offered Beijing strong support over Tiananmen Square in 1989; and in 2008 the land border was finally officially demarcated. Talks are theoretically under way to demarcate the waters between the Chinese island of Hainan and Vietnam. Many Chinese academics believe Vietnam's historical relationship with China and their shared experiences in the recent past create strong bonds of mutual sympathy between a 'big brother' and a 'little brother'. Some Western observers think likewise. However, history can as easily be read the other way, to suggest centuries of unease and antipathy in Vietnam towards China. Although they have shared some recent experiences, and have a mutual interest in regime survival now, it seems as if race and history are dominant and rebarbative factors. These tendencies intermingle, but antipathy seems stronger.

China is now Vietnam's largest trade partner, although Hanoi has a substantial deficit; but the top foreign investors in Vietnam are South Korea, Singapore and Japan. Relations with Korea and Japan in particular are being fostered by the Vietnamese government. US investment in Vietnam has been rising rapidly since the country joined the WTO, and the USA is Vietnam's biggest export destination. Vietnam is building a relationship with America based on trade, investment, security and military cooperation. Yet escalating incidents between US navy vessels and the Chinese have followed a heightened American concern for security in the South China Sea. America is encouraging a military build-up by Vietnam. US companies have been discussing oil exploration, although any US exploration in contested areas around the Spratly Islands would cause tension with China.

The long-standing dispute with Beijing over the Spratlys is a thorn in Vietnam's side. BP secured a concession from Hanoi and started work in 2007 to extract gas, but Beijing applied pressure on BP, which then suspended operations in 2009. In 2008, Exxon Mobil was also reported to have experienced Chinese pressure. In 2010, China elevated its extensive claims in the South China Sea to one of 'six primary concerns' which inter alia implies non-negotiability; this new and strong language has caused deeper concern to Vietnam, its maritime neighbours and its potential energy partners.[10] Retired Chinese army Major General Luo Yuan said in 2012 that 'China's patience has been tested to its limits, and there is no room for further tolerance.'[11] No country wants to be on the receiving end of any Chinese statement that contains the phrase 'non-negotiable'. The leaders now have a 'hotline' installed to handle disputes. Good as that sounds, it does imply that there are and will be disputes.[12]

In 2003, US naval vessels started a continuing programme of visiting ports the length of the Vietnamese coast. Speaking in Hanoi in 2009, not long after the USS *Impeccable* tangled with Chinese vessels off Hainan, Senator John McCain said 'we see new security challenges in this region'.[13] He stated that the US wants an open South China Sea, a peaceful resolution to the dispute between Vietnam and China over the Spratlys and indeed the Paracel Islands (which many thought had passed irretrievably to China), and encouraged Vietnam to work with America's other regional allies to 'explore a multitude of ways to expand our ties'.[14]

In early 2010, the USNS *Richard E. Byrd* was sent to Vietnam for repair. Although civilian-crewed, this was the first time the US navy had had a ship repaired in a country which is not technically a strategic ally or partner. By 2012 there had been six joint US-Vietnamese naval exercises just off Chinese waters. By 2011 the CIA had a liaison office in Hanoi.[15] In 2012 Leon Panetta, Secretary for Defense, visited Vietnam and said: 'We need to obviously build a stronger defense relationship with countries like Vietnam, and elsewhere so that we can help provide them the training, assistance, whatever they need to improve their capabilities.'[16] He made it clear that Washington would like to have regular access to the strategic port of Cam Ranh Bay, as it had during the Vietnam War.

The 1998–2004 Bharatiya Janata Party (BJP) government in India pushed strongly for a partnership with Vietnam which was based not only on trade and investment but also on security and military cooperation. The Indian defence minister visited in 2000 and signed a wide-ranging cooperation agreement covering joint naval training, anti-sea piracy exercises in the South China Sea, jungle warfare training, counter-insurgency training and closer relationships between the countries' air forces and defence industries.[17] India's Congress administration was more cautious, but quietly continued the relationship. India supported Vietnam's bid to become a non-permanent member of the UN Security Council in 2008, and Vietnam has for some years supported India's campaign to become a permanent member. A Vietnamese alliance logically benefits India. One South Asian analyst observed:

> Strategically, to put it more bluntly, Vietnam offers India a long range option of developing and sustaining a vital strategic counter-pressure point against China. If China persists and can have a Pakistan in South Asia as a pressure point, then India too needs a strategic counter-pressure on China's periphery, and Vietnam should be wooed for this purpose.[18]

China is reportedly seeking naval facilities on the coast of Cambodia, Vietnam's long-standing rival. Hanoi might therefore move closer to Delhi, which is seeking naval facilities in the South China Sea in its quest to build a 'blue water navy'. In 2012 India was reported to be training Vietnamese submarine crews.[19]

Russia's Gazprom agreed in 2012 to take on the two exploration blocks in the South China Sea which had been dropped by BP in 2009 under pressure from Beijing. This bold decision seems to indicate that Moscow has decided to defy Beijing pressure for international operators to accept Chinese sovereignty in the South China Sea. Vietnam has bought diesel-electric submarines, frigates, corvettes, fast attack craft and patrol boats from Russia, and is one of the largest buyers of Russian jet fighters.[20] Vietnam entered an agreement with Russia in 2009 that included a commitment to upgrade the facilities in Cam Ranh Bay to enable berthing and ship repair to be offered to international fleets. There will reportedly also be a submarine base.[21] As one Russian diplomat has said, 'the Russian Pacific Fleet is once again an important part of Russia's regional presence'.[22] In 2012, it was reported that Vietnam would begin joint production with Russia of a subsonic anti-ship missile.[23]

Vietnam is in the middle of what has been described as an Asian arms race. The extensive overhaul of Hanoi's naval capability is particularly important, as it is right on China's South China Sea oil and trade route. The corvette purchase programme will in future focus on anti-submarine warfare, which is significant given that China's major submarine base on Hainan Island adjoins Vietnamese waters. In 2010 the Vietnamese President went to one of the disputed islands and informed naval officers that the country was prepared to 'fight for the sovereignty of the fatherland in any situation'.[24]

The relationship with China is multifaceted and explains most other policies. China is sharply increasing its tourism and trade with Vietnam. The two countries share party-to-party discussions on their common interest in internal security. On the other hand, Vietnam now has twenty bases in the Spratly Islands – more than China.[25] China is believed to maintain an extensive espionage operation in Vietnam. The Vietnamese dissidents put on trial in October 2009 requested not only human rights and multi-party democracy, but measures to protect Vietnam's islands in the South China Sea from China. Observers are suggesting that 'previously disparate groups of dissidents such as Buddhist monks, Catholic priests and political bloggers appear to be coalescing around certain issues, notably opposition to China's growing influence in Vietnam'.[26] Vietnamese public opinion is even more Sinophobic than the government; this could lead to hostility towards the million-odd ethnic Chinese who represent 1 per cent of the population and are prominent in private enterprise. Harsh treatment of ethnic cousins might exacerbate relations with China. On the other hand, if the governments do become hostile, these communities could be seen as having divided loyalties, which could make them potential victims. It is arresting that in Vietnam, China and Russia popular opinion is even more nationalistic than the government and so pressures the authorities to be firm. Indeed, Hanoi is afraid to allow too much anti-Chinese public sentiment because it could, like anti-Japanese activity in China, provide a training ground for anti-regime militancy. With internet usage growing faster in Vietnam than almost anywhere in the world, belatedly Hanoi has the tools to police dissident activities. Anti-Chinese sentiment too is growing rapidly, with issues such as the Chinese arrest of Vietnamese fishermen, Chinese mining plans in Vietnam and, of course, China's damming and diversion of the Mekong. Bloggers' concerns are both environmental, and overtly Sinophobic. Meanwhile the state media themselves highlight the plight of the arrested fishermen.

If it can solve its economic problems, Vietnam may become a regional power. Its economy has grown by about 7 per cent annually on average for a decade, though it has slowed recently. There are structural weaknesses in the economy which reflect those of China. The Vinashin scandal highlighted a state-owned shipbuilding company with $4 billion of debt and management, which was out of its depth. This resulted in the country's sovereign debt being downgraded in 2010.[27] Such issues of credit expansion without quality control need to be addressed. However, the country has significant energy reserves and occupies a prime strategic location on the major international oil route between the Malacca Straits and the South China Sea.

In 2000, Vietnam had half the population of Russia; by 2050, it will conceivably be more populous. At about the same time it will overtake Japan. Many countries will wish to befriend it because of where it is, what it is and what it is not – viz. China. Its future alliances are likely to make China feel very uncomfortable. If other countries plan to contain or encircle China, Vietnam would be a priceless strategic element. According to one American think tank in 2012, 'it holds the key to the balance of power in the South China Sea . . . If Vietnam doesn't resist China's rise to power, feebler and less decisive countries, such as the Philippines, have no chance of blocking Chinese hegemony.'[28] Beijing's extraordinary continued provocation of Hanoi in the South China Sea demonstrates a defective strategic vision.

Laos

Laos and China have some tension – both currently and historically. In the years around 1980, China was hostile towards the Lao government because of its friendliness with Hanoi, and sponsored exiled Hmong anti-Communist militias. Since the late 1980s, Beijing has sought to compete with Hanoi for the goodwill of the Lao Communist regime. China gives aid, training and investment to Laos but several issues cloud Sino–Lao relations. The construction projects which benefit the Lao economy bring the collateral damage of long leases on Lao property and demands for resettlement of Chinese workers in Laos. Chinese business interests have controversially tried to bring casinos to Laos, with all the social impact that would have. And the Chinese cyber operation against the Dalai Lama's communications system compromised the Laotian Prime Minister's office (see Chapter 13). Chinese damming of the Mekong also causes apprehension, since Laos depends upon the Mekong and itself generates hydropower from it, so any flow reduction would be a threat.

The Obama administration slowly raised the US profile in Laos, but still it trails behind China. Beijing trains hundreds of military officers and government officials, whereas the American International Military Education and Training programme has had places for just eight Lao officers. Laos receives around $400 million of overseas aid each year, much of it from China. In 2009, the US provided $5 million (of which over 60 per cent was to deal with unexploded bombs it had dropped in the 1960s and 1970s). The US State Department criticises Vientiane in its annual human rights review, whereas Chinese aid is based on non-interference in Laotian affairs.

Washington's advantage lies in advising Vientiane on the Mekong issue. If America is adroit and China is not, China could become more unpopular. China's only potential challenge is regional hostility to its water plans, which would be exacerbated by any drought. In the worst case, Thailand, Laos and Vietnam might decide to engage in hostilities; but without support from a greater power their totally disproportionate resources would make them vulnerable.

Burma

China is concerned to rebuild its relationship with Burma. Its strategic goals are to build transport links to modern port facilities on the Indian Ocean, to exploit energy reserves, build up commercial interests, and, reportedly, to establish naval and intelligence bases (see also Chapter 15). However, China did not welcome the thousands of ethnic refugees from Burma who crossed its border in 2009, and it issued a rare rebuke to Burma to solve its problems. China is also worrying the Burmese by damming the upper reaches of the Salween River.

In 2010–11, China invested $10 billion, or two-thirds of total inward foreign investment.[29] Although their mutually beneficial relationship seemed, until 2011, untroubled, there have been occasional hints that Burma doesn't want to rely unconditionally on Chinese goodwill. In 2011, it announced it was putting a $3 billion Chinese dam project on hold owing to popular concerns. US sanctions had driven Burma closer to China, and some might argue that Beijing has ensured the junta's survival (though India and ASEAN also trade with Burma). Recently America has been eyeing Burmese links, although with some frustration. Since 2011 much has changed: several reforms have been introduced.

This cuts both ways for China. It is good because a less demonised Burma relieves pressure on Beijing to apply sanctions; but conversely, a more acceptable Burma is a potential business partner for much of the world, which is to China's disadvantage. US–Burma relations clearly improved in 2012, and the burgeoning Burma–Vietnam friendship looks ominous to Chinese eyes. Japan is also now gearing up its involvement, spurred by a $3.7 billion debt-forgiveness deal and expectation that Burma will become one of the biggest Japanese aid destinations.[30] It is uncertain whether a liberalising Burma would become closer to Beijing. Indeed – after all the effort Beijing has made – in 2012 one prominent Chinese academic called Burma a 'potential opponent'.[31]

Bhutan and Nepal

Bhutan, with a population of around 700,000, is in an uncomfortable position as a buffer state between China and India, and Beijing has claimed four areas in its north. Apart from India, Bhutan is the only neighbour whose land border with China is still not demarcated: 2013 saw the twenty-first round of frontier talks. Reportedly, China has made military incursions, and Bhutan has protested about China building roads approaching the border. Indian media state that China has occupied the Himalayan peak of Kula Kangri and it is reported that ownership has been ceded.

For its part, India has pressed Bhutan to expel militant Indian dissidents, and has even conducted joint military operations with the Bhutanese army to achieve this. Given India's post-independence record of military expansion, Bhutan's position is unenviable. It must maintain constructive relations with both great powers while preserving its integrity.

It was somewhat surprising when, in 2012, the prime ministers of Bhutan and China were reported as saying that they were progressing diplomatic recognition and border demarcation. India has some influence over Bhutan's foreign policy. The *Times of India* declared, 'China's coziness with Bhutan rings security alarm for India', suggesting that Sino-Indian relations are a zero-sum game.[32] Bhutan later denied the report, though it is quite possible that a deal will be reached, as it seems to benefit both parties. This would probably involve a land swap, whereby China might receive part of the Chumbi Valley, which would expose India in a sensitive area. According to the *Indian Express*,

> The Chumbi salient – where India, China and western Bhutan meet – is like a dagger pointed at the narrow Siliguri Corridor that connects India with its northeastern states. Any border settlement between China and Bhutan that alters the currently disputed Chumbi trijunction in Beijing's favour will have

a negative bearing on Delhi's military plans for the defence of its northern frontiers.[33]

China and India are deeply engaged in Nepal and both have a reasonable relationship with Kathmandu. With the Maoist ex-guerrillas extensively represented in parliament, Nepal's future is unclear. China has invested substantially and gave $19 million of military aid in 2011. During Wen Jiabao's visit to Kathmandu in 2012, it was noted that 'the Nepalese side expressed its firm support for China on its efforts to uphold state sovereignty, national unity and territorial integrity. Nepal does not allow any forces to use its territory for any anti-China or separatist activities.'[34] This means Tibetan exiles are discouraged. Indian intelligence is extensively involved in Nepalese politics. Yet the Sino-Indian scramble for influence is unlikely to lead to war.

There may be nervousness, but neither Bhutan nor Nepal harbours strong ill will towards China, and neither justifies Indo-Chinese conflict. India's expansionist ambitions may eventually embrace Bhutan and Nepal; indeed, history suggests it. However, towards China, India feels defensive, not offensive.

Mongolia

China's longest border, of almost 3,000 miles, is with Mongolia – a very large country with very few people. Mongolia is the same size as the whole of the northern European continent from Poland to Portugal, yet it has a population that is scarcely more than that of metropolitan Lisbon.

China's relationship with Mongolia has been complex and volatile. Mongolia declared independence from China in 1911, at the fall of the Qing dynasty, with strong support from Tsarist Russia. The dominant power in the region during the twentieth century was the Soviet Union, until its 1989–90 collapse. The new Mongolian People's Republic (recognised by the USSR in 1924) encompassed what is called Outer Mongolia, while the Chinese Nationalists (and later the Communists) held Inner Mongolia. The nationalist Republic of China only recognised the Mongolian People's Republic as an independent state in 1945, and its Taiwan successor retained Mongolia as Chinese territory on its maps until the twenty-first century. Mongolia, perhaps understandably, felt closer to the PRC and recognised it early on – in 1949. Taiwan blocked Mongolia's UN membership until Moscow forced the issue in 1960. Sino-Mongolian relations have suffered from Chinese references to 'lost territories' and Mongolian concern about possible expansion by a populous China. Since 2001, though, China has tried to improve the relationship and is now Mongolia's largest trade partner and investor.

China's interest in Mongolia lies in ensuring its own security, thwarting any tendency towards pan-Mongolism (which seeks to unite the Mongol populations of Mongolia, Chinese Inner Mongolia and Buryatia and Kalmykia in Russia) and looking out for mining opportunities. Pan-Mongolism particularly concerns China, as its border with Mongolia consists almost entirely of Inner Mongolia and Xinjiang. Inner Mongolia has just 24 million inhabitants in almost half a million square miles, although less than a fifth are classified as Mongol. Nonetheless, that is a lot more Mongols than there are in Mongolia. There are dissidents, websites are blocked and arbitrary arrests are made. In addition, a specific environmental tension arises from the perception that herdsmen's livelihoods and culture are being lost because of degradation of the grasslands.

All border disputes have been officially settled. However, there could be a future Chinese territorial claim to this underpopulated country, as China's (foreign-originated) imperial dynasties ruled both China and Mongolia (see Chapter 1). This would be something of an inversion of history, rather as if France claimed Prussia because France had once been under German rule. Mongolians prefer the Russians to the Chinese. Concern about China leads to economic inefficiency: 'Mongolians dislike China and suspect it of having inappropriate territorial intentions. These fears have already impeded the construction of a railway needed to export coal and triggered an ill-thought-out foreign investment law.'[35] Lack of friendliness towards China partly stems from Mongolia's Buddhist links with the exiled Tibetan community in Dharamsala, where Mongolian lamas often go to study. Mongolian troops have also fought alongside the Americans and their allies in Iraq. The country desires friendships outside the stifling embrace of its two sole neighbours – China and Russia.

The Koreas

Both North and South Korea are, in a sense, neighbours of China: North Korea by land and sea, and South Korea by maritime proximity (it disputes with China a claim to ownership of Socotra Rock), by having a rival air identification zone and by having a future cultural and practical claim to all Korea.

China has downgraded North Korea from an ally to a problem. Chinese people are largely unsympathetic to the country, seeing it as a state where the population is undernourished – three inches shorter than South Koreans[36] – and the government engages in crazy military gestures. China, abhorring instability, would hate to see it collapse. Washington feels China has helped in the six-power talks on Korea, even if it won't freely share its thoughts with America, and Beijing seemed to revel in chairing these sensitive multilateral discussions. China was 'resolutely opposed' to North Korea's nuclear test in 2009 and to its attempted proliferation. (Iran's long-range Shahab-4 missile is believed to be modelled on Pyongyang's Nodong missile, and North Korea is supposed to have briefed Iran on its 2006 nuclear test.) The late Kim Jong-il – the 'Dear Leader' – was probably a quite rational person with weak cards; owing to the absence of conventional strengths, he relied heavily on the effects of making extreme threats. One plausible analysis of his nuclear adventure in 2009 is that he wished to prove his hard-line instincts to his lieutenants, so that they would feel secure in their political longevity and would accept his youngest son, Kim Jong-un, as his successor.

North Korea and China have long had border disagreements involving both a mountain with sacred Korean associations and some river courses. Then in 2012, Chinese media reported that twenty-eight of China's fishermen had been kidnapped in Chinese waters, beaten and robbed by what were described as uniformed North Korean sailors; apparently this was not the first such incident.[37] The reports died down without explanation. Where there are personal relationships between North Koreans and Chinese, there is such a Korean obsession with racial purity that the families are stigmatised and often there are forced abortions or infanticide.[38] North Korea's unpredictable military behaviour – whether with guns or missiles – makes it an uncomfortable and unruly neighbour for China.

China's strategic view is clear. It doesn't like nuclear-armed neighbours issuing threats; nor does it like rockets and nuclear tests in the neighbourhood, even if the missiles are directed towards Japan or the Pacific. However, it prefers not to see a collapse of the North Korean state for several reasons. First, it already has a 2 million-strong ethnic Korean population in the border area and does not want several million refugees flocking into the country, especially when unemployment is high.

Second, it does not want a strong and united nationalistic or pro-American Korea to emerge on its border. It would particularly abhor US troops on its frontier for the first time since the Korean War: Beijing would regard that as a threat to its sovereignty, and would give high priority to countering it. A united Korea would initially be preoccupied with reconstruction (estimated by Seoul at $1 trillion).[39] But later the innate nationalism of the Koreans could well lead to frontier frictions with Russia, and that would have implications for China, which sees itself as the default player in that region. After all, a 'United Korea' would have around 60 per cent of the population of Russia by 2025 (rising to 70 per cent), all of whom would be just across the border from Russia's underpopulated Far East, which has just 7 million people and is several time zones removed from Moscow. South Korea has an economy nearly the same size as Russia's, and healthier. If unified today, a 'United Korea' would have a population of over 70 million and very low labour costs, and be the sixth most densely populated significant country in the world. It would have a nuclear capability, a nationalist attitude and a spirit of expansion.

Third, if North Korea disappeared, there is always the concern that America's restless and uncertain moral imperative would pick some other target on which to fixate. Who might it be next? Laos? Cambodia? Sri Lanka?

Finally, North Korea plays a useful role for China: in American eyes it exemplifies bad behaviour (worse than China's) and thus diverts attention from China, while also demonstrating that America isn't all-powerful in Asia. China even gains kudos by chairing the multinational committee handling the North Korea problem. If China eventually decides that a solution is needed, it will suit her to find one which avoids an untidy collapse.

It is a paradoxical that the status quo represents instability for America, but stability for China and Russia (and a tense stability for Japan). Change could generate greater security for America, but more insecurity for Russia and China. Either a stream of millions of refugees or a successfully united nation-alistic Greater Korea would represent a bad outcome for Beijing and Moscow. Ironically, despite having been threatened by Pyongyang's nuclear weapons, even Japan prefers to avoid a united Korea emerging as a new challenger as its own population collapses to 85 million.

In South Korea, there are mingled attitudes to China. There is resentment at the pollution which arrives from China, and concern about resource competition. Many in the south do not believe that China should have any of the Baekdu San, the sacred Korean mountain on the North Korea–China border. The Northeast Project of the Chinese Academy of Social Sciences (2002–6) caused considerable Korean public offence, being seen as suggesting that parts of Korea were really China.

President Lee said in 2012 that he wanted to scrap the agreement with Washington that South Korean missiles should have a range no greater than 200 miles, as strategic circumstances had changed. This would make Seoul a more independent player, and Beijing apprehensive. The BBC 2013 Country Ratings Poll shows that of all major countries, South Korea is one of the least sympathetic to China. Nonetheless, it is one of the countries which have managed to enjoy a growing trade surplus with China, and it is nervous of any threats to that trade. There are tensions in the relationship, but nothing too serious yet.

Taiwan

The island state of Taiwan enjoys a unique status. As President Ma said in his inauguration speech in 2008: 'Taiwan is the sole ethnic Chinese society to complete a second democratic turnover of power. Ethnic Chinese communities around the world have laid their hopes on this crucial political experiment.'[40]

The acceptance by Western democracies of the mainland dictum that there is only one China, and thus Taiwan cannot be recognised, is surprising. Across the globe, politicians who profess a commitment to human rights, freedom and democracy have happily accepted this, perhaps influenced by a closer relationship with the world's most populous country or by trade in Boeings. The terms of the Nixon–Kissinger opening to China might have been tactically appropriate during the Cold War, but tomorrow's realities may cause reassessment of the formula.

China has painted itself into a corner: students are taught that Taiwan inarguably belongs to China, the people are Chinese, the island is currently detached through perfidy, the situation perpetuates a highly humiliating history, and anyone who supports the status quo – let alone formalisation of the current detachment – is effectively a traitor to China. The message is repeated in the media, both official and commercial, and is magnified on the internet. Yet China and Taiwan are among each other's top trading partners. Even by 2007, Taiwanese business had invested $100 billion in China; it does not want a destabilising, independence-oriented Taipei government. There is a strong belief that growing economic interdependence will moderate politics. This is true, but it only works in one direction: the Taiwanese business community calls openly for its government to adopt moderate policies, but the mainland Chinese business community has no corresponding public voice. The Taiwanese are divided on China: some would like to formalise an independent sovereign status; others prefer to keep quiet and continue leading their own – separate – lives, and then there are those who would prefer closer links with China.

Surveys tend to emphasise separation rather than association. In the five years from 2006 to 2011, those wanting unification fell from 29 per cent to 16 per cent, and those wanting eventual independence rose from 44 per cent to over 49 per cent. The remaining 35 per cent want either no change to the current separate status or have no opinion. Only once since 2006 has unification been the choice of more than 20 per cent.[41] A 2013 poll found that 66 per cent wanted the status quo, 24 per cent wanted independence and 7 per cent preferred unification. If the status quo is ruled out, 71 per cent would prefer independence and only 18 per cent would favour unification. An overwhelming 78 per cent view themselves as Taiwanese while 13 per cent see themselves as Chinese.[42]

In days gone by, it was suggested that time would resolve the issue, as economic links with China grew. But anecdotal evidence suggests that younger people are even less interested in unification than average: each year sees a waning interest in China. At the same time, there is a rising Taiwanese younger generation that knows little of mainland life: they might be said to face

California and have their backs to China. This suggests that although businessmen might invest more money in China each year, electorally they are eclipsed by ordinary voters.

Against the wishes of Beijing and Washington, the Taiwan government called a referendum in 2008 on the question of applying to join the UN as Taiwan. Although less than half of eligible voters participated (and so the vote was scrapped), virtually a third of *all registered voters* (so not just those who turned out on the day) voted yes to a proposition that was effectively a declaration of independence.

A poll in 2006 found that the countries most admired by Taiwanese people were Japan (47 per cent), the USA (40 per cent) and China (16 per cent).[43] Politicians, particularly from the Democratic Progressive Party (DPP), have been assiduously trying to build relationships with Japan as a counterbalance to China. In Taiwan, Japanese actions that have caused annoyance in China have tended to be overlooked. DPP leaders have called for tripartite missile defence systems with Japan and the US, a permanent seat on the UN Security Council for Japan, and faster militarisation. There are disputes with Japan, but they are muted: for example, fishing in the East China Sea and the issue of the Diaoyu (Senkaku) Islands. Some politicians have even proposed that the islands should be traded for a strong Japanese security deal. Political realist academics, such as Kenneth Waltz at Columbia, see an increasing contest between China and Japan for Taiwan as a prize strategic asset. The year 2005–6 saw some significant developments:

> In early 2005, in a strategic dialogue held in Washington, both US and Japanese governments agreed to include Taiwan into 'strategic common interest' of the US and Japan. This means the Japanese government formally agreed to adjust its policy toward Taiwan by including the Taiwan Strait into the sphere of concern in the Japan–US Security Treaty. In February 2006, in a controversial speech, Japan's foreign minister Taro Aso called Taiwan a 'country'.[44]

This was described by some commentators as the most significant diplomatic development for Taiwan since the passage of the Taiwan Relations Act by the US in 1978. Furthermore, 'it involved a quietly stated commitment to the security of the Taiwan Strait that was beyond Taiwan's wildest dreams three months ago'.[45]

It has frequently been said that pro-Japanese sentiment in Taiwan dates back to the era of Japanese colonial rule, between 1895 and 1945, when there were positive contributions in infrastructure, economic growth, health and education. While once unsayable, today reference to colonial history has become a basis for closer understanding between Taiwan and Japan. The relationship of Japan with the authorities on Taiwan has become warmer and warmer since the 1990s. Indeed Professor Jing Sun has coined an expression for the Japan–Taiwan relationship – 'unofficial in name only'.[46]

A military balance between the two states needs, of course, to incorporate America's ambiguous policy of support for Taiwan. Although America has a huge military and technological lead over China, certain factors have changed. For several years Washington let its presence in the Far East diminish. Under Obama, it started to engage again. The process is accelerated by a chorus of requests from South East Asia, yet is undermined by calls from Washington analysts to sacrifice Taiwan for a better relationship with China, which has been growing its military and (especially) its naval capability. Recent developments include the introduction of laser capability to blind satellites (see Chapter 13), anti-ship ballistic missiles, and silent diesel submarines. Used in conjunction with information gleaned from hacking into the Pentagon command and control systems, these augment Beijing's ability to neutralise US involvement in a conflict and to enforce 'area denial' in the Western Pacific.[47] Any US defence cuts, of course, only serve to bolster that capability. Despite disproportionate US armament, the odds are narrowing.

A report from the US–China Economic and Security Review Commission states that the PLA has held a military exercise each year on Dongshan Island which concentrates on joint military exercises, practising the subjugation of Taiwan. Three options have been under consideration: military invasion, missile attack or naval blockade. American observers think that China has about 1,000 missiles aimed at Taiwan, though Taipei officials say the number is more like 1,500. China appears unconcerned that every increase in the number of rockets aimed at Taiwan is likely to weaken further the sympathies of the island's inhabitants. Indeed the threats virtually guarantee that there can be no satisfactory solution for Beijing other than through military force.

Beijing may have fashioned a rod for its own back by propagating extreme views on Taiwan in schools. So embedded are they in the minds of young and middle-aged Chinese that they might be difficult to adjust. Policy may be straitjacketed by the appeasement of popular nationalism and a failure to rectify the school textbooks. If Taiwan is treated as the litmus test of national honour for a politician, Chinese leaders are vulnerable to being dragged into conflict by the extreme public sentiment in the streets and on the internet. Otherwise they may be seen as the heirs to the 1919 Chinese government, unable to prevent concessions to Japan. This could cast Taiwan as Serbia in 1914 and China as a juggernaut with no contemporary politician powerful enough to withstand the siren calls to mobilisation.

The Philippines

Manila, too, has a mixed relationship with China. There is a large ethnic Chinese minority, which is prominent in the business community, and there are growing trade links. In 2006, China was the third-largest source of bilateral development assistance, and in 2007 the Philippines was apparently the largest recipient of PRC loans in South East Asia. However, there is a major dispute over islets in the South China Sea, particularly the Scarborough Shoal. The dispute has a long history, but in 2011 it led to a Chinese warship firing on a Philippine fishing vessel, and in 2012 there was a series of confrontations between Chinese and Philippine vessels, which often involved Chinese warships. The Philippine authorities seem to be deliberately understating the scale of incidents and the involvement of Chinese naval vessels. The Philippine Defence Secretary, Voltaire Gazmin, has admitted that his military is incapable of halting these confrontations: 'We are in no position to confront the forces that are intruding in our territory simply because we don't have the capability.'[48] The Chinese Communist Party's *Global Times* carried an editorial in 2011 entitled 'Time to teach those around South China Sea a lesson'. It made the suggestion that as 'The tension of war is escalating second by second but the initiative is not in our hand . . . out there could just be an ideal place to punish them. Such punishment should be restricted only to the Philippines and Vietnam, who have been acting extremely aggressive these days.'[49] Rear-Admiral Yin Zhuo of the PLA navy said in 2012 that China's naval troops should board and search Philippine government ships found in the disputed area. He also said China would not hesitate to use deadly force against its enemies.[50]

It is not surprising that the Philippine government doubled its arms budget in 2011. That same year, Prime Minister Noda of Japan and President Aquino of the Philippines reaffirmed their 'vital interests' in the South China Sea, agreed to step up military exchanges, cooperate on maritime security and strengthen links between their navies. Noda talked of their shared strategic interests and basic values. The US, Japan, Korea and Australia have all discussed supplying arms or supplying materiel. Unfortunately for the Philipines, an archipelago, it seems that the US–Philippines mutual defence treaty does not cover disputes in the South China Sea.

Water Wars

The desertification sweeping across China, the associated pollution, the disappearance of water sources and recently the increased likelihood of severe drought all affect Beijing's relations with its neighbours. Chinese households, industry and agriculture require additional water, and there has been a sharp influx of Chinese settlers into the sparsely populated territory of Xinjiang, particularly since 2000, and an expansion in oil drilling there, both of which further increase the water requirement.

As has been noted, China is fortunate to control the sources of many of the world's great rivers: the Mekong, the Brahmaputra, the Salween, the Indus, the Ob . . . It is engaged in many projects to harness these sources in order to reverse desertification and declining water availability, but such projects inevitably reduce the flow downstream to China's neighbours (see especially Chapter 11). The Mekong supplies Burma, Thailand, Laos, Cambodia and Vietnam – almost all of South East Asia. The Yalong Tsangpo supplies the Brahmaputra, which traverses India and Bangladesh. The Ili River supplies Lake Balkhash, which provides water in Kazakhstan. The Black Irtysh River supplies Kazakhstan, then Russia, joining the Ob River, which empties into the Arctic Ocean.

A fifth of Kazakhstan's water comes from Lake Balkhash, which sources well over half its water in China. A recently constructed 200-mile Chinese canal takes water from the Black Irtysh River to Karamay, the oil and gas centre of Xinjiang. Chinese officials downplay the impact of rising water demand and the need to access increasing amounts from Chinese rivers that flow into neighbouring countries. But Kazakhstan and Russia are alarmed by the effects of upstream Chinese actions on water flow. Reportedly, half of the Kazakh population drinks water that is below international standards.

The Chinese ambassador to Kazakhstan said in 2004 that China anticipated using 40 per cent of the Irtysh flow.[51] The Russian media forecast that China would take between a quarter and a fifth of the river water, and the Russian authorities expressed concern about the diversion of so much water from the Irtysh, and thus the Ob. However, in 2012 a Russian university reported that China's off-take has actually increased by 400 per cent.[52] According to Yuri Vinokurov of the Novosibirsk Institute of Economics, to take even 6 per cent of the Ob water could damage the Russian fisheries.[53] Alexey Yablokov, of the Russian Academy of Sciences, said in 2006 that environmentalists and the Russian authorities were anxiously following the case. He noted that China was taking increasing amounts of the Black Irtysh water for irrigation purposes. 'Now, the amount of water flowing [into Russia] seems to be half as much as [it used to be]. It has affected not only Kazakhstan, but also Russia.'[54] Shallowing, salinisation and degradation around Omsk in the Russian basins was noted in 2012.[55]

The Yalong Tsangpo project to dam the river before it feeds the Brahmaputra in India has caused huge concern in India and Bangladesh, as it provides a third of the Brahmaputra's water. It is unclear which will be greater – external pressure from China's neighbours against the project, or the internal need to revive the parched landscape. The UN projects up to 50 million 'environmental refugees' in China from desertification and the disappearance of water; they are expected to constitute a mass migration eastwards. Political leaders might well feel obliged to take strong action to get water to them and try to keep them in place, rather than have angry millions flooding the cities. The price for this could be frontier confrontation. Any reduction in water flows or increase in natural droughts will make water provision a zero-sum game.

Reflections

China has fourteen land and six maritime neighbours (counting South Korea). On land, it is seeking to divert water flows currently going to Russia, Kazakhstan, India, Burma, Laos and Vietnam; it has land border issues with India, Bhutan and North Korea; and it has territorial disputes with all its maritime neighbours, but particularly Vietnam, Japan and the Philippines. Thus it is in disagreement with well over half of its twenty neighbours. Some disagreements are low-key, such as with Laos (over water) or with North Korea (over the Tumen and Yalu rivers), but most are heated: with Japan, its South China Sea neighbours and India. Such disputes have led Japan and South East Asia to encourage Washington to resurrect its military presence in the region. The abandonment of ideology and the avoidance of a values-based system in contemporary China mean that Beijing will struggle to find genuine allies overseas. As Asia heats up, the fact that China has been openly cultivating overseas Chinese communities threaten them all – from India to Australia – with charges of split loyalties.

As Gopalaswami Parthasarathy, a former Indian diplomat, said in 2011, 'Beijing is upping the assertiveness towards all its neighbours. The Chinese are carefully testing the waters to see how far they can go.'[56] There are potential conflicts along China's frontiers, but by showing goodwill it should be possible to solve most issues. The greatest prospects for conflict lie in a nationalistic escalation with Vietnam and a deterioration in the water situation. Beijing could also face a problem in any Taiwan crisis if it is unable to defuse nationalist rhetoric. The collapse of Afghanistan or Pakistan would render it difficult to ensure stable frontiers. Each of these risks – self-inflicted and exogenous alike – is a distinct threat to the economy, to stability, to China's image – and thus to China's rise.

CHAPTER FIFTEEN

China in the World

Overseas, China faces critical threats to its rise. I have mentioned the risk of regime collapse in neighbouring Afghanistan and Pakistan, the threats arising from Beijing's massive investment in volatile regions of the developing world and also the risks from antagonising a large number of neighbouring countries over either territorial disputes or the threat of water diversion. Another area of risk is how the world views China's rhetoric and actions as it becomes more powerful. I have examined this so far principally through Beijing's belligerence in the cyber world, but I will argue that China is not paying enough attention to the risk it runs of endangering its rise by its aggressiveness overseas.

Beijing has taken the view that the global environment is favourable to the country's rise. Wars between great powers are unlikely; free markets and globalisation beneficial. However, many in China's government and policy elite feel that China is not yet ready to replace a weakening America. Most wish to continue adhering to Deng Xiaoping's advice and keep a low profile during the country's rise.[1] Some prefer to be seen as America's interlocutor in dealing with the world's issues, a sort of G2, which Western analysts have christened 'Chimerica' (overlooking the fact that this smacks of 'chimerical', or 'fanciful'). And yet the prospect of a G2 looks increasingly irrelevant with the rise of phenomena such as Putin's foreign policy, Iranian international diplomacy (oxymoron or not), Korean space projects and Indian global military projection.[2] To those in Beijing who await the prospect of a G2, the world – and China – would be better if America were no longer the superpower.

China is becoming more economically and militarily powerful, and more influential in global organisations. Over time it has reluctantly softened its firm non-intervention strategy, when confronted by global reaction to the Sudan situation and the reality of the secession of oil-producing Southern Sudan and thus the need to broaden its friendships for economic reasons. There are now different and independent factors influencing Beijing's policy. Aversion to foreign intervention in the affairs of sovereign states remains but is joined now by economic interests, global perception of China as a power and domestic reaction to the possibility of Chinese lives at risk, as in Libya. This has created a more complex prism through which to formulate foreign policy and thus creates the impression of a less principled and less predictable policy reponse. Although it has vetoed UN action on Burma and Zimbabwe, we should antici- pate further softening. It has agreed actions on Iran, North Korea, Burma, Libya and Sudan, from which it had previously recoiled. It has followed its poli- cies of no military bases overseas and no foreign wars (except against the Vietnamese); but the attractiveness of bases is being debated internally. Chinese money, arms and diplomacy have already created semi-client relations with Sri Lanka, Cambodia and Pakistan. No internal political strings are attached, and for many states this explains the appeal. In engaging with the world, the only political topics China seems interested in discussing are opposing hegemony and now supporting its 'core interests', which – currently – means Taiwan, Tibet, Xinjiang and the South China Sea.

The 2008 Olympics were regarded in China as international acknowledge- ment that it had emerged as a leading nation. Some people admired the magnificent stadium and wonderful showmanship of the opening ceremony – not so different in concept from American college marching bands, but vastly superior in execution. For others, the spectacle evoked images of North Korea or the 1936 Berlin Olympics. In fact, Zhang Yimou, the director of the Olympic opening, observed that he could only have organised it in China or North Korea.[3] It is not clear what international impact the opening ceremony had; it probably projected the image of a strong power, rather than of creative indi- viduals. During the games themselves, celebrities in their special boxes saw an admirably organised production. The public in the stands, however, noted certain features, such as rows of empty seats (owing to official ticket misalloca- tion) and the absence of food after about 10 a.m.

If we examine global opinions of China and America through the findings of the Pew Centre and BBC country ratings polls, there is a broadly similar view. Amongst the twenty or so countries polled, China was substantially more popular than the US in 2005. This reversed to preference for the US by 2013. The 2008 Olympics did not improve China's standing. The broad differences are that China is more popular in Africa, particularly in Islamic countries, and less popular with its neighbours and in Western Europe. It is tragic that in 2013 China was liked less than an America that had recently fought two controver- sial wars and was widely disliked throughout the Muslim world. Globally, most believe that China already has replaced America – or soon will – as the major world power. The US and Western Europe think China is now the world's economic superpower, and believe that to be bad. The rest of the world thinks America is still the economic superpower and believes that is good (again with the exception of the Islamic world).[4]

For its part, China feels vulnerable to separatism (it worries that foreign NGO activity could exacerbate this) and encirclement: Russia and even Burma are now described as 'potential opponents'.[5] Beijing feels threatened by the fact that foreign countries receive the Dalai Lama, send ambassadors to events honouring Chinese Nobel Prize winner Liu Xiaobo or arm Taiwan.[6] The progress of the Olympic torch in 2008 was marred in several countries by protests supporting Tibetan independence. It feels as though the West unreasonably criticises China over pollution, has been reluctant to share technology and is unfairly biased against the work of its scientists.[7] For all its rising international status, China feels vulnerable.

Military Issues

Military modernisation was first promoted by Zhou Enlai in 1964 and was later pursued by Deng Xiaoping. China scored early successes with its nuclear and ballistic missile programme, but not in other military areas. In the 1980s, in order to allow funding to be diverted to economic growth, the PLA budget was cut. For the next twenty years there was virtually no growth in real terms. In return, Beijing allowed the military to develop businesses to provide incremental revenue, and in the early 1990s the PLA was permitted to export arms.[8] Most military equipment was either bought overseas or employed foreign technology. However, things have changed: 'Indigenous Innovation with Chinese Characteristics . . . has become a core aspiration for China's leaders, scientific community and defense economy since the early years of the twenty-first century.'[9] Unfortunately, the spirit of scientific inquiry is quite limited: 'One of the biggest challenges in nurturing the innovative spirit of the defense economy is to overturn an insular and conservative institutional mindset shaped by decades of central planning. This has meant a strong aversion to risk, a lack of competitive instincts, poor motivation, and weak disciplinary practices.'[10] This seems pervasive in science and technology. The international powers have effectively embargoed Chinese acquisition of defence technology. The exception has been Russia, which has been willing to sell selected modern weapons and military technology to China, while appreciating – and compensating for – the risks of reverse engineering.

China's priorities here are to be a modern and strong world power, an aspirant superpower. It must be militarily overwhelming vis-à-vis Taiwan. It

chooses to project itself in East Asia: to assert its maritime claims and to safeguard its oil supply routes from the Gulf and Africa. The growth of overseas
interests and China's concern about the security of energy routes leads it to
prioritise its navy. Here Beijing must take note of India, which in 2008
announced plans for a navy of over 160 ships, including three aircraft carriers,
and close to 400 aircraft by 2022.[11] This presents Beijing with a challenge.
Soviet Russia is seen as having been ruined in an arms race with America, so
China is trying to pursue a more balanced course of building its military capability while prioritising the navy. Cheaper asymmetric warfare, such as cyber
activity, offers great potential. China also has at least twenty-five types of
unmanned aerial vehicle (used for incursions into India). Despite some budgetary restraint, there has been a steady increase in military expenditure. China's
aviation industry corporations have accumulated over 5,000 patents in recent
years, and the Chengdu Aircraft Industry Group is developing the J-20 fighter
aircraft, which on completion should bring China to less than twelve years
behind the Western powers in military aircraft capability.[12]

How China conducts itself as a nuclear power has been much discussed.
Beijing often cites its attachment to (and efforts in) non-proliferation. However,
its nuclear development has had a controversial history. It received some technical knowledge from Moscow before the Sino-Soviet split, and also gained
significant input from ethnic Chinese US scientists. Such scientists and technicians continue to be put on trial in America on charges of supplying secret
information to China.[13]

Beijing is accused of deliberately deciding in 1982 'to flood the developing
world with atomic weapons knowhow'; its clientele allegedly included Algeria,
North Korea and Pakistan.[14] It is also said to have secretly provided facilities at
Lop Nor in Xinjiang to the French. China publicly denies supplying knowledge
which reached Libya and Iran, though the US Congressional Research Service
has detailed many US claims that China has supplied nuclear-related goods to
Iran.[15] Early on, Beijing was probably rather cavalier with its nuclear exports,
but it now seems much more disciplined. There is, for example, clearly a deep
reservation about Iran developing nuclear weapons and little tolerance of
Pyongyang issuing nuclear threats. Estimates of China's nuclear arsenal differ
widely, from 80 to 3,000 missiles.[16] Whichever figure is correct, it is much lower
than the arsenals of America and Russia, at 5,000 and 8,000, respectively.

The space programme occasionally attracts foreign attention, as China
launches more satellites annually than America. Whereas America, Russia,
Japan, Canada and the Europeans share the cost of a satellite station, China is
building its own. President Obama's cancellation of George W. Bush's decision
to resume a manned lunar programme leaves China as the only country with a

definite medium-term commitment.[17] The Chinese space programme serves three purposes: it showcases Chinese technology and satellite-launching capability; it suggests that China is approaching superpower status; and it shows the Chinese that the Party is delivering on the country's international standing. Of course, this leaves it vulnerable if disaster should strike the project.

Foreign specialists have assessed the PLA's military capability critically. Its contribution to a 2008 snowstorm crisis that left 100 million people stranded was described as 'woefully inadequate'. But it was the Sichuan earthquake of that same year that really tested its preparedness, and the US National Defense University suggested that the PLA underperformed. The logistical requirements closely resembled those of war conditions, and its poor performance caused analysts to downgrade their estimates of the PLA's current military preparedness and effectiveness. A report noted that 'exposure of these shortcomings provides a unique insight into China's capability to project power using its ground forces in large-scale contingency operations that require expensive logistics, planning and inter-service cooperation'.[18]

The weak military response was ascribed to a poorly integrated command structure, ageing equipment and lack of personnel experienced in large-scale disaster relief operations. The dire shortage of airlift capability to ferry heavy equipment to affected areas was exposed, and it was left to America, Russia and Pakistan to provide transport planes. Even the courier company Federal Express contributed one.[19] The PLA deployed 140,000 troops in its largest single operation since the 1979 Vietnam War. Scathing reference was made to the PLA's 'antiquated ground capabilities', and strong doubt was expressed as to whether it had really experienced the 'revolution in military affairs' that would transform it into an agile and high-technology fighting force. Naval performance off the Somali coast has also been criticised. On the other hand, the PLA is clearly proud of its performance in the evacuation of Chinese citizens from Libya in 2011. As Major General Luo Yuan said afterwards, 'our people can still count on the PLA wherever they go'.[20] However, even this operation was viewed by some as exposing the age of the Russian-built military aircraft and the small size of the guided-missile frigate that was dispatched.[21]

China has refitted an old ex-Ukrainian aircraft carrier and intends to build two new ones. Their purpose is not to patrol inshore. Through its cyber activity, China has shown that it can hack into the US military command and control system. The plan to build aircraft carriers and the deployment of two destroyers to deter piracy in the Gulf of Aden can be seen as part of China's drive to project itself as a global military power (though unfortunately, the bluster of vowing to rescue captured Chinese vessels soon gave way to ransom payments being dropped by helicopter on to their decks).

According to an Australian White Paper:

> China will be the strongest Asian military power, by a considerable margin. Its military modernisation will be increasingly characterised by the development of power projection capabilities . . . But the pace, scope and structure of China's military modernisation have the potential to give its neighbours cause for concern if not carefully explained, and if China does not reach out to others to build confidence regarding its military plans . . . particularly as the modernisation appears potentially to be beyond the scope of what would be required for a conflict over Taiwan.[22]

The naval drive in the east comes as Russia talks of an armament build-up and Japan has launched a helicopter-carrying destroyer which seems carefully calibrated to fall just below the category of aircraft carrier – a class of vessel it has vowed not to have. India, Australia, Vietnam and South Korea are all expanding their military capabilities. Asia aims to spend $60 billion on naval armament alone up to 2015 – more than all NATO members (bar America) combined.[23] There is strong interest in increasingly sophisticated equipment and a change of focus from patrolling regional waters to operating a 'blue water navy', or to projecting military force into international waters far beyond the countries' neighbourhoods. Anxiety about this development explains Australia's decision to massively expand its own capability, by spending $50 billion over twenty years. China's capacity is even said to exceed that needed 'to deter American intervention' in any future China–Taiwan conflict.[24] This may be somewhat exaggerated; however, while American strategy has been enmeshed in its Iraq and Afghanistan wars, China has been developing a global perspective.

Looking at execution as opposed to armament, there seems to be some question over China's capability in terms of conventional military action. However, much has probably been learned from its extensive examination of sensitive US military computer networks. Given the country's strong position in cyber activity, we should perhaps not be surprised if two Pacific-based carrier strike forces find themselves unable to communicate or if the lights one day go out in the Pentagon.

The 'String of Pearls'

Several analysts have claimed there is a strategic drive by China to secure naval bases running from Hainan, past Cambodia to the Middle East, and to enhance its Asian land presence through a series of footsteps which have been described as a 'string of pearls'. This supposedly fulfils the dual purpose of extending the country's maritime reach and encircling India (see Chapter 11). The idea has given rise to an extensive literature imputing aggressive motivation to Beijing. It is important to point out that China disputes any such strategy, and currently there is not enough evidence to substantiate the theory. Despite this, the steps China has taken in the South China Sea, the Himalayas and the Indian Ocean are being used to create a negative image of China's rising power.

The phrase 'string of pearls' appears to have originated in this controversial context in a 2005 Booz Allen report for the US Department of Defense.[25] The individual 'pearls' vary markedly in size (and in some cases it is not even certain that they actually exist). Different analysts have their own lists, encompassing ports, airfields and other facilities that allow access to strategic areas. Countries which feel enmeshed in such a 'string of pearls' strategy find it distinctly uncomfortable.

China's targeted locations are said to be 'the South China Sea', Thailand, Cambodia, Burma, Bangladesh, Sri Lanka and Pakistan. The projects are meant to combine commercial developments with the upgrading of airstrips and introduction of naval or military facilities. Beijing's South China Sea strategy is not entirely clear. The extensive claims in this area were, in 2011, declared a 'core interest', which makes the issue close to non-negotiable. The domestic Hainan Island submarine base has been completed, and there appear to be developments on some of the many small islands where sovereignty is (often hotly) contested. Even ten years ago accounts suggested a chain of fortress-like structures being built by China from the Paracel Islands to the Spratlys – right across the South China Sea. China reportedly began operating a signals intelligence facility in 1995 on Rocky Island in the Paracels, capable of monitoring maritime activity as far away as the Malacca Straits.

Thailand is hedging its bets by replacing a wholly American-oriented defence policy with one finely balanced between different relationships: although the US–Thailand Cobra Gold military operation is the world's largest annual field exercise, it has been overshadowed by the development of Sino-Thai trade and military linkages. Bangkok has also discouraged the Dalai Lama and Falun Gong. Thailand is not an immediate neighbour of China and thus has no territorial disputes; the only sensitive issue involves any diversion of Mekong water. However – echoing China and Xinjiang – Thailand has a serious domestic separatist threat in the Muslim south, and has had historic disputes with the Vietnamese and Cambodian alliances, which predisposes it to support China in South East Asia.

Cambodia is seen as a critical step in China's possible military extension; this could perhaps involve the provision of naval facilities, given Cambodia's historic wariness of Vietnam. The country has a $320-million special economic zone financed by China, and in 2008 a joint venture was announced between a Cambodian enterprise and a state-linked Chinese enterprise from Jiangsu that would occupy more than 11 square miles around Sihanoukville. Hun Sen, Cambodia's Premier, said it could even rival Sihanoukville itself, the country's deepest port. Speculation suggests that this could become a Chinese-managed deep-water port with naval facilities, but little has transpired.

Cambodia is a major recipient of Chinese commercial attention and is the South East Asian country which tries hardest to accommodate China's political requirements. For example, the 2012 ASEAN meeting in Phnom Penh ended without a joint concluding statement – for the first time in forty-five years – reportedly because of Chinese pressure on Cambodia. This suggests that China uses its power aggressively and is an important player inside ASEAN without actually being a member.

Indian strategists note that if India is to become the leader in the Asian region, it must assume pre-eminence in the Indian Ocean.[26] China and India have been vying for the affections of Burma. What China gained militarily from its previously strong links was not evident, but it reportedly helped Burma modernise its naval bases at various ports, such as Hianggyi, Akyab, Zadetkyi Kyun, Mergui, Kyauk Phyu, and in the Coco Islands in the Bay of Bengal. This might have led to the Chinese navy receiving some berthing facilities. China was also reportedly building a port or naval base at Kyauk Phyu on Ramree Island and it was rumoured that it had installed naval reconnaissance and signals intelligence facilities on Great Coco Island. Though this rumour is now discredited, there may be Chinese-supplied signals intelligence facilities on Sittwe, close to the Bangladesh border, and on Zadetkyi Kyun, an island off the tip of Victoria Point, Burma's southernmost point, at the entrance to the Malacca Strait.

In 2008 there were reports of an agreement for China to establish helipads and upgrade the 'communications' facilities on the Cocos. These islands are particularly sensitive from India's point of view, as they are near to the regional naval Far East command in the Andaman and Nicobar Islands and to its nuclear, rocket and space facilities on the Bay of Bengal coast. In 2010 Indian media reported that a senior air force source had confirmed the Chinese presence. As a result, India made plans to increase its air capability in the Andamans.

In 2008, China appeared to beat the Indians to part of Burma's gas reserves, when it concluded a deal for a gas pipeline from Sittwe to Yunnan (complementing a previous deal on gas field exploration). However, India is continuing the development of Sittwe port to counter Chinese influence. There is a

Chinese-built road from Yunnan province to Bhamo on the Irrawaddy, from which all points south are navigable.

Despite all this activity, Burma's generals avoided choosing definitively between China and India. It has been satisfactory to have two such large and influential neighbours diplomatically neutralised: 'Myanmar does not lean towards China or India. It makes best [*sic*] of the competition between China and India . . . for Myanmar's resources.'[27]

Meanwhile, since 2010 America has increasingly engaged with Burma. In 2012 it resumed diplomatic relations and later relaxed sanctions. China and India will find competition in their quest for Burma's natural resources – not only from the US, but also from Japan and others that will follow. Moreover, whatever military arrangements China might have in Burma are not guaranteed to continue after a US–Burma thaw.

Muslim Bangladesh has a history of border, migration and water quarrels with India; but it also has an ambivalent relationship with China. While it wants closer links with Muslim countries, it is not friendly with Pakistan, its former master and China's staunch ally. It dislikes Chinese attempts to divert the Brahmaputra, which flows into the Ganges (see Chapter 11). Dhaka is described as sympathetic to India, but it appears more interested in China; The right word is probably 'opportunistic'. China has armed Bangladesh's military, offered nuclear plants and asked to participate in the gas fields. It is building a container port at Chittagong and is reportedly seeking maritime facilities. There was an indication of China's influence in 2009, when – in the face of Bangladeshi protests about freedom of speech – armed police broke up a photography exhibition organised by Tibetan activists. In 2011 the Bangladesh army chief claimed that the relationship with China was not strategic and did not affect India–Bangladesh ties. However, in 2012 the Chinese said the proposed deep-sea port in Bangladesh at Sonadia Island was strategic.[28] China's influence in Bangladesh seems extensive, stronger than India's and currently under no pressure.

In Sri Lanka, Beijing's role has attracted international criticism. It has given the government financial, military and diplomatic support, helping it avoid international censure for the bloody ending of the long-running civil war and the undermining of press freedom. China has helped build the Sri Lankan port of Hambantota, the first phase of which opened in late 2010 (see Chapter 11). According to the Port Authority, bunkering, or refuelling, will be the main revenue from the port and analysts suggest that Chinese naval vessels will bunker there while stepping up their patrolling of the Indian Ocean. The Sri Lankan relationship allows China a friendly haven in one of the Indian Ocean's finest natural harbours, and in return provides Sri Lanka with regular and substantial foreign aid and arms supplies.

The Sri Lankan defence ministry, which is often outspoken, has thanked countries such as China, Russia, India and Japan for their support, and has expressed considerable criticism of the West. China is very influential in this country, which is not even a neighbour. In 2008, it gave the country $1 billion in aid. The amount of American aid is a relatively small amount ($22 million in 2012) because of human rights abuses and lack of accountability. By 2013, China was Sri Lanka's biggest lender, totalling over 43 billion.[29] Despite membership of the Commonwealth, the predominant influences on Sri Lanka are no longer Western.

With Pakistan, as we have seen (Chapter 12), there is a major long-term port project at Gwadar in the Indian Ocean, near the the Persian Gulf, which theoretically offers a strategic link with Central Asia, Afghanistan, and China's own province of Xinjiang. China and Pakistan both insist that China's interest in Gwadar is purely commercial, and yet it is reported that China has installed electronic maritime surveillance facilities there to monitor traffic entering and leaving the Persian Gulf, and that there will be berthing for Chinese nuclear submarines. The port has not been very successful; its main merit seems to be as an insurance policy against another Indian blockade of Karachi.

China has 'toe prints' across South East Asia and the Indian Ocean. But it is not proven that a network of military and intelligence facilities unites those toe prints in a credible way, and some of the suggested elements in the 'string of pearls' evaporate on closer inspection. The Chinese view seems to be that it is itself 'encircled' by 'potential opponents' – Vietnam, Burma, the Philippines, India, Japan, the US, and even Russia.[30] This might be seen as further justification for military expansion.

Taiwan

Taiwan should only constitute a military flashpoint if China chooses to escalate tension and loose the hounds. Taipei is not going to declare war on China. Taiwan's only real forms of defence are politics and diplomacy. The authorities on both sides of the strait have a broad understanding of the rules of engagement, with Washington's ambiguous protective role towards Taiwan a vital part of the equation. Frequent Chinese cyber attacks on US command and control capabilities are assumed to be for the purpose of understanding American systems and then disabling them in any conflict. Given the extent of US reliance on networks, even thirty minutes of signals interruption could give Chinese forces the edge in an attack on Taiwan. If Beijing used force to occupy Taiwan, it would send a very powerful signal worldwide that self-determination is not respected and coercion is the principal tool for conflict resolution.

Ethnic Issues and the Chinese Diaspora

Over the centuries, large numbers of Chinese have emigrated to neighbouring countries or to the other side of the world: today it is estimated that there are 40 million ethnic Chinese abroad.

The existence of overseas Chinese gave China a major comparative advantage in its rapid development post-1979. When investment became possible, thousands responded, and the capital flows, expertise and contacts they provided gave China an early advantage. The authorities have cultivated this source of finance and sought to build strong links with the overseas communities. When he met the Congress of Returned Overseas Chinese and their Relatives in 2009, Politburo member Wang Zhaoguo referred to 'blood lineage', exhorted them to think of ethnic unity and to 'do a better job of uniting the force of the circle of overseas Chinese around the Party and the Government'.[31] This is all very stirring, but it is language that can harm Chinese communities in volatile overseas countries. It also raises such questions as: Where do ultimate loyalties lie? Are they with the country whose passport they carry or are they with China – and the Party? In 2012 a proposal was made in the CCPCC in Beijing that there should be a special identity card for overseas Chinese to have permanent residence, simplified entrance–exit procedures and equal rights in education and buying property (compare the Indian citizenship card mentioned in Chapter 11).[32]

The 1979 invasion of Vietnam occurred well after Mao was dead and the Cultural Revolution over. Reforms had begun, albeit timidly, and Deng was installed as leader. Hence it was a war waged by 'reform China'. One of the causes was anger at Vietnam's treatment of its Chinese inhabitants. China made it clear numerous times during 1978 that it would not accept their ill-treatment. It cancelled aid projects in Vietnam and diverted the funds to assist fleeing ethnic Chinese refugees. Beijing said it would hold Hanoi responsible for the refugees' fate and sent two ships to assist the refugee vessels and rescue 'persecuted Chinese'. Note that it called them Chinese: China said it opposed any foreign government which forced ethnic Chinese to adopt foreign citizenship. Such opposition to the integration of overseas Chinese communities in their host society suggests that all ethnic Chinese are effectively, throughout all time, 'of China'. It also appears that racial solidarity trumps inhibitions regarding 'non-intervention in the affairs of other countries'. While not the only reason, it was a clear contributory factor in the invasion. This should be a good guide to China's thinking and propensity to act. Assuming that China's policy is not capricious, we should find the reasons for starting the 1979 war helpful in understanding China's decisions in the future.

Another instance was the evacuation of over 300 Chinese from the Solomon Islands during riots in 2006. Beijing chartered planes to fly them to Guangdong province. Most had been in the Solomons for decades; many did not have PRC Chinese identity papers, and the Solomon Islands have diplomatic relations not with the PRC, but with Taiwan.[33] This was obviously not a case of repatriating PRC citizens in trouble, but of intervening to help those who had emigrated or fled China and had no plans to return. Again Beijing has a wide definition of who its citizens are, and it is essentially race-based.

Concern over the ill-treatment of ethnic cousins abroad is understandable. However, as a contributory argument for war – as in Vietnam – it should be put in context. There is a huge Chinese diaspora. If the race card is deemed acceptable, even imperative, the chances of conflict multiply. Beijing has hinted at deploying the expanded military beyond East Asia, including more escort missions, as in the Gulf of Aden, assuring the security of the oil route through the Malacca Strait and improving 'the navy's abilities to cross the ocean [to] escort, rescue and evacuate Chinese nationals abroad'.[34] Overseas cousins can be used as a *casus belli* if required. Looking back to the last century in Europe, we might call this the Sudetenland gambit. It risks worrying, for example, South East Asian countries with substantial Chinese minority communities.

Policy Implications of Overseas Investment and Trade

China espouses a strongly neo-mercantilist foreign economic policy, based on securing natural resources – energy, minerals and food – in the ground rather than relying on markets. In a 2007 meeting with the US ambassador to Brazil, executives of the mining company Vale said America 'would need to pay greater attention to where its raw materials would come from as China hoped to lock up both South America and Africa as its suppliers'.[35] For example, also in 2007, a Chinese company announced a large project in the Democratic Republic of the Congo to grow oil palms to create biofuel.[36]

It is not at all certain that such a strategy will work in the event of drought and failed harvests. How, for example, might an impoverished host nation react to the trucks loading up with food crops for investor countries? Distant, underdeveloped and volatile countries might well renege on agreements reached in happier times. China will need to consider how to respond to threats to its raw materials supply. To protect assets in distant and unstable areas might eventually require Chinese security units. Increasingly, China is an active participant in UN peacekeeping missions, which gives its military invaluable operating experience worldwide.

China has long pursued a self-restraint policy in not having overseas military bases. But there is now an emerging debate. The first manifestation was Colonel Dai Xu's 2009 article in *Global Times*, advocating overseas bases for security and supply in order for China to 'assume the responsibility of a great power'.[37] If Beijing is reluctant to use the PLA to defend its interests overseas, there is the precedent of the Vietnam War, when the PLA sent tens of thousands of 'volunteers' to man engineering and anti-artillery units. There are hints of a potential quagmire here. When the Seychelles offered China a base in 2011, *Global Times* said: 'It is absolutely necessary [for China] to establish overseas military bases; we must break obsolete concepts and self-restriction.'[38]

The likelihood of future dispute is heightened by the reported tendency of China's enterprises to draft contracts that disadvantage the host country and then secure official acceptance with bribes. The IMF and the World Bank have privately expressed concern at the unilateral nature of some contracts. This became public in the case of some Congolese contracts in 2009. Indeed I have been told that the IMF threatened the cessation of Western aid if they were not renegotiated, as they finally were in December 2009. Notably, the victim was pressured, not the perpetrator: multilateral organisations appear reluctant to confront Beijing directly.

President Hu Jintao noted the Malacca dilemma, where Chinese oil imports traverse vulnerable waterways. Military officials have commented that the expanded naval power will assist in escort duties. Sir John Beddington, chief scientist to the British government, has forecast a 'perfect storm' by 2030 of three key dangers: to energy security, water security and food security. It is not difficult to anticipate China's plan to escort its imported oil being extended to all forms of imports sourced from regions such as Africa.

The Rand Corporation has said that China's state energy companies are driving Chinese foreign policy. This is difficult to support, however. Energy executives do not appear to derive significant personal income – beyond high salaries – from the posts they occupy and they are rotated between posts by the authorities. Senior government officials can be appointed to run a state enterprise, and later sent to a ministry. The heads of all three major Chinese oil companies hold vice-ministerial rank; they are not entrepreneurs or even businessmen in the accepted sense. We cannot really talk of 'corporate interests' in China in this way. However, the head of a major SOE would certainly lobby for interests of his company because its growth promotes his career. It would be more accurate to say that there is an elite preoccupation with energy security across government and state enterprises. This is despite the fact that for some years it seems little of the oil generated overseas actually came to China. Instead, it was sold on the world market.

The heads of state energy enterprises would no doubt enjoy being compared with the chief executives of Shell or Exxon. However, neither corporate power nor remuneration allows them to set the foreign policy agenda. If they make large profits, it is because of their oligopolistic position, not their abilities. Their influence stems from their Party position. It is the domestic shortage of energy, certain minerals and agricultural land, coupled with pessimism over future market functioning, which is driving resource policy. Less clear is whether the chosen path and methods will deliver the desired result.

China's aid budget to Africa is now bigger than the World Bank's.[39] Many people value the highways and bridges they receive in return for natural resources, but the use of Chinese workers for everything can cause disappointment and even hostility. Li Ruogu has defended this by saying that African labourers prefer to work only during the daytime, whereas Chinese workers can support triple shifts. It is not always appreciated that Chinese manual labour is relatively cheap in Africa for two reasons. First, many of the workers cannot get a job at home and so will take low-paid work overseas. Second, workers are frequently convicts.[40] Twenty-five of them can be crammed into a four-bedroom house on three sleeping shifts a day. The incremental cost is scarcely more than the security guards needed to control them. After four years' rental, an African friend told me, his house was unusable, but the rent had been enough to demolish and rebuild it. The convicts are apparently often left in Africa after project completion; China does not want them to return. Many become entrepreneurs and import cheap Chinese goods, which can hamper the rise of African manufacturing. Some have become very rich.

A curious parallel is to be found in the problem facing Britain, which has many thousands of illegal Chinese immigrants, driven to emigrate by poverty. British attempts to repatriate them meet with no Chinese cooperation.[41] People who have broken the law overseas and are not an economic asset are effectively blocked from being forcibly returned. Thus the practical result of China's policies and actions is to expatriate the unattractive and criminal classes.

Western observers are dismayed at China's Africa policies and its 'politics-blind' commercial policy, which lead it to invest in countries with unsavoury leaders. They are similarly critical of its aid policy. Be that as it may, this policy has helped to fuel a seventeen-fold rise in Sino-African trade in a decade – to $198 billion by 2012.[42] It is difficult to take the Western paroxysms of guilt seriously: America willingly allies with an Uzbek president who is accused of killing an opponent in boiling oil, and it extracts petroleum in Equatorial Guinea, where President Obiang has been accused of cannibalism.[43] Yet the US won't invest in Sudan because of Darfur. France, on the other hand, invests in Sudan, but not Guinea. China invests in all countries in the belief that investment and trade are better than sanctions.[44] It has suffered considerable criticism for investing in Sudan, and yet Sudan has almost twice the African average number of bilateral investment treaties, so China is not alone.

A second aspect of Chinese projects in Africa and elsewhere is the habit of relying on imported Chinese products. Although this does not immediately assist African businessmen it may force them eventually to increase competitiveness. China's concentration in its aid on infrastructure and its use of Chinese contractors are said to minimise corruption. Combined with limited use of expert consultants, these projects are praised for their cost-effectiveness.[45] Where China is invited to adopt projects it tends to evaluate them professionally, and occasionally declines them as unhelpful to the host country. Western notions of aid over the last fifty years have definitely not solved Africa's problems. Arguably China's development model may do better.

The Asia-Pacific Region

Koreans are generally wary of China: former President Lee Myung-bak showed concern over Beijing's military expenditure; polls show the public to be very unsympathetic towards China; there are regular violent disputes over fishing; and the Finance Ministry sees growing economic competition from China – for example, in 2009 it issued a report entitled *The Beijing Consensus*, which envisaged competition with China in both exports and overseas energy acquisition.[46] South Korea is a leader in the $60 billion upgrading of Asian naval power and has naval ships patrolling as far as the Gulf of Aden.

And yet Korea has enjoyed a growing trade surplus with China, 20,000 Korean companies operate in China and large numbers of each country's population reside in the other. Analysts have speculated that because of its size, China will eventually absorb the South Korean economy. But that ignores two points: the deeply nationalist nature of Koreans, and the eventual prospect of a united Korea in which the reduced need for such a large military and security apparatus would stimulate the economy.

China uses the Asia Pacific Space Cooperation Organisation (APSCO) to bring other countries under its leadership – Bangladesh, Iran, Pakistan, Thailand, Peru and Mongolia. Indonesia and Turkey have signed the agreement, but have not joined the organisation. It is interesting that a hitherto staunch US ally like Turkey has signed up for space research with China; Mongolia has had troops in Iraq supporting the Americans; and Pakistan used to have good NATO links.

Little seems to have happened with APSCO, but its existence offers states the chance to develop non-American relationships. China has used it to build

influence with Middle Eastern, Asian and South American countries – its position as one of the few independent space actors helps build friendships in quite
unlikely quarters. It is also a low-cost centre for launching commercial and
governmental satellites for regions without a rocketry capacity; for example it
is helping Nigeria. Two overseas satellite tracking stations have been opened:
one in Karachi (Pakistan) and the other in Dongara (Western Australia).[47] In
2011, Beijing announced that over five years it would create a space laboratory,
take samples from the Moon and develop its global positioning system further.[48]
This is at a time when America has virtually halted its space programme for
financial reasons.

In Asia in 2007 there were reportedly 277 multilateral intergovernmental
meetings on security.[49] China has prioritised two organisations: the ten
members of ASEAN Plus China, Korea and Japan and the Shanghai Cooperation
Organisation. ASEAN Plus Three allows it to work closely with the increasingly important countries of South East Asia, including Indonesia, Malaysia,
Thailand and Burma, in a privileged way shared only with Japan and Korea.
The SCO gives Russia and China special entrées and interests in a strategically
interesting region, certainly for energy. Both these organisations (and thus
the areas they cover) are effectively closed to Australia and the US. The more
they grow, the more China isolates its non-friends in the Asian sphere. (That
said, owing to Russian friendship, India has managed to reach the fringes of
the SCO.)

China has increasingly become an international donor and yet it still
receives aid. (Only in 2011 did Britain cease giving aid.) Not only is the country
Sri Lanka's biggest donor, but as early as 2002 its aid to Indonesia was double
that of America; in 2009 Chinese aid to Cambodia was reported to be eleven
times that of the US, and to the Philippines four times.[50] As Freedom House in
Washington says: 'Chinese aid now outstrips that of democratic donor countries in a range of Southeast Asian and Central Asian states.'[51] It gives more aid
than America to South East Asia – quite a change since the days of the Vietnam
War. Beijing has been highly successful at making friendships and buying
influence in South East Asia. Significant elites there now appear comfortable
with China and supportive of many of its objectives – and not just because of
ethnic links. Beijing has, for example, lavished attention on the Thai royal
family: in 2011 'Princess Sirindhorn, the second most beloved Thai royal, has
made a reported 28 trips to China since 1981 – including three in 2009.'[52] In
2010, Cambodia did its largest financing ever to acquire Huawei's telecoms
equipment, and in parallel China's influence in the country seems to grow.[53]

However, South East Asian defence officials complained in 2011 that
'Beijing has been evading dialogue on conflict prevention in disputed waters'.[54]

This is similar to the criticism by Russia and Kazakhstan that China avoids discussion of water issues. Beijing's position, understandably, is that it would rather discuss South China Sea conflicts one-to-one, and is evading all suggestions of a multilateral settlement. It has made major efforts in diplomacy, aid, trade and investment. Helpfully, this has coincided with a decade in which America has had a low profile there. America's return coincides with rising friction.

Nevertheless, not unconscious of maritime tensions, ASEAN may choose to refocus from ASEAN Plus Three to the broader, newer idea of the East Asia Summit (EAS), which brings in India, Australia and New Zealand. There are further plans to involve Russia and America. These developments are probably driven by an Asian desire not to be dominated by China.

Clash with America?

China and America are likely to continue having minor regional clashes. They will also pursue the major agenda of trade and finance, and occasionally America will raise human rights points. But good bilateral relations are important to both. Lobbies in Washington are calling for a less confrontational stance towards China, to be achieved by easing up on the defence of Taiwan in order to build a more constructive business relationship.

It will be interesting to see for how long China maintains its large-scale, regular cyber attacks on the American state (see Chapter 13). This is so close to an undeclared war that it would be reasonable to expect the US to take action to force China to desist. For neither of them is there any incentive to engage in military conflict – unless China chooses to attack Taiwan. Beijing seems to be preparing for that eventuality by expanding naval deployment in the West Pacific and testing missiles which can shoot down satellites, missiles which can take out warships and cyber weapons which can interrupt America's military command and control systems. But whether it is preparing for a fight or just discouraging America from intervening is not clear.

Global Projection and Soft Power

While causing anxiety amongst its neighbours as far away as Australia, China's military build-up does not yet impress analysts. Indeed, there is a school of thought amongst Chinese academics that there should be less focus on military expenditure and more on social issues. Even reasonable goals, such as protecting the freedom of the seas and energy and food security in the Indian Ocean and elsewhere, could, they argue, be reached by others; in other words, by free-riding on America. This seems to be a minority view, but that may change if budgetary constraints bite.

Foreign analysts may note with concern the emergence of a new, assertive (if not aggressive) China, yet Beijing is regularly excoriated in the Chinese print media and over the internet for its spinelessness in standing up for national interests. The leaders need to placate their domestic constituency more than foreign parties, and there is a long history of Chinese governments being castigated by the public for failing to uphold national honour.

The very size of China is both an advantage and a disadvantage. Because there are over a billion people, the economy has become one of the largest in the world, and yet large numbers of citizens live in poverty. Theoretically, this constrains the policy options of leaders, who must give some priority to poverty alleviation. Put another way, China can influence the world, yet still be unable to solve its own problems.

China has become much more effective in multilateral organisations, and it sees the UN as playing a major role: by bolstering the UN's role and standing, it weakens America's ability to act unilaterally. It also opposes the idea of inviting other large powers to become permanent members of the Security Council, thus entrenching its relative status versus theirs. As a permanent member of the Council, China has the power of veto, and it has been willing to use its influence, for example, to protect its client state, Sri Lanka, from criticism. However, it was interesting to see China vote at the UN to refer Colonel Gaddafi to the International Criminal Court (ICC) for treating his people badly; Beijing said this was something the African and Arab people wanted.[55] But China does not recognise the ICC (which has the potential to infringe its sovereignty), and Beijing would prefer not to have the precedent of Tiananmen Square raised.

In cultivating other countries through its UN work, China seems well ahead of America: it manages to operate satisfactorily and seldom has to employ its veto (from 1971 until 2008, it used it six times, while America used its veto 81 times).[56] It has been suggested that China can achieve its goals simply by threatening to use its veto; however, that argument could be applied to all the veto-holding powers. If there is any country that uses its UN influence regularly to obstruct widely held values, it is America. Of course, China probably finds large and heterogeneous bodies like the UN useful, as Beijing's policy is generally to stop initiatives it does not like, rather than to push those it wants. When China wants to achieve something, it is more likely to look to a small forum, or eventually to the much-anticipated 'G2'.

China has emerged from being wary of UN missions to becoming one of the most enthusiastic participants. In fact, it has become the most active permanent Security Council member in UN peacekeeping operations, contributing about 1,800 troops in late 2012.[57] These missions provide operational military experience in all terrains and climates. A charming result of this sustained engagement is that a Chinese general, Zhao Jingmin, was appointed in 2007 as military commander of MINURSO, a UN operation to facilitate a popular referendum in Western Sahara. The objectives were to 'identify and register qualified voters and organize and ensure a free and fair referendum and proclaim the results'.[58]

China has worked within the IMF, and at the same time has demonstrated its rising power outside the organisation. In 2007 China offered a loan, on generous terms, which enabled Angola to terminate its negotiations with the IMF.[59] China has seen its views on currency noticeably sway the G20 and the IMF. This demonstrates international reaction, outside the US, to the economic rise of China, its emergence – seemingly unscathed – from the Western downturn, and its increasing presence in global trade and finance. One unintended consequence of Dominique Strauss-Kahn's precipitate departure from the IMF is that China later received a deputy managing directorship for the first time. There is a sense of inevitability regarding institutional change. As one policy organisation wrote in 2011: 'Attempting to cling to institutional power structures that reflect the state of the world at the end of World War Two . . . would put the US on the wrong side of history.'[60]

The US, Canada, Denmark and, particularly, Russia are expanding their occupation of Arctic territory. Apart from Russia, the world largely ignored it for decades, but now it is believed that a fifth of the world's undiscovered oil and gas lies there. Furthermore, with possibly warmer climates, a number of fishing grounds might move northwards to these waters and shorter trade routes might open. Since 2004, China has had the Yellow River Research Station on the Norwegian island of Spitsbergen. As an aspiring world power, China may seek a way to share in the Arctic's rich resources. Despite having no Arctic shoreline, it has one operating ice breaker (the same as America). Interestingly, in 1981 China claimed that it had Arctic shore just eight hundred years ago.[61]

Meanwhile some 67 per cent of Chinese think China will replace America as the world's superpower; 47 per cent of Americans and many others agree, but many who believe it do not like it.[62] This dislike potentially builds a lobby against China. The facts that it is large, that it has the world's second-largest military budget and that it is not a democracy together build a presumption that China is ill-intentioned. This frustrates Chinese citizens, who don't entirely grasp how fashionable the assumption of liberal democratic formats now is globally. When Nigeria, Russia, Pakistan, Indonesia, Brazil – and even Iran – operate forms of democracy, China seems increasingly isolated.

Chinese people are inherently nationalistic. They have a high sense of self-worth and an innate view that certain countries have not behaved kindly to them. Many might sympathise with democratisation but are antagonistic to Tibetan autonomy or Taiwanese independence. Favouring Tibet or Taiwan in China is like enjoying cricket in America: not only is it a minority sport, but it is also seen as alien (at the very least). In the 2012 Pew China Survey, Chinese respondents made it clear which countries were perceived as enemies: India (24 per cent), America (26 per cent) and Japan (41 per cent). Issues involving Taiwan, America or Japan can lead to spontaneous internet outbursts or public demonstrations that the government struggles to temper. This is one area where the authorities nervously follow public feeling rather than leading it. Everyone knows that what brought down previous regimes was the failure to deliver economic well-being and to defend China's honour, sentiments which go back at least to 1905.[63]

Beijing is concerned to ensure that other states support most of its positions. However, the rising powers often have diverging interests or policies. Within the BRICS grouping of Brazil, Russia, India, China and South Africa, Russia will not sell China the most modern fighter planes but will sell to India; Brazil plans to prevent China buying up its agricultural land; and India is distressed by China's reluctance to finalise a border agreement and its determination to press on with gigantic water diversion plans. China must be careful not to alienate or worry too many countries.

China's Behaviour as a Rising Power

Since the 1990s academics have used quantitative means to assess the tendency of countries to employ violence in diplomacy. Chinese historical strategic culture has been extensively analysed. There is a Western misconception that Chinese military strategy is conflict-averse. Harvard's Professor Alastair Johnston says this results from overemphasis on (and under-analysis of) Sun Tzu's *Art of War*. The research suggests there has been a historic tendency to favour violent options when resources permitted: China fought 3,790 internal and external wars in the three thousand years to 1911 (or 1.25 per annum, which is rather a lot).[64]

According to Johnston:

> once in a militarized dispute, China will tend to escalate to a relatively high level of force. With doctrinal changes in recent years that stress the offensive, even pre-emptive, use of military power, and in the absence of alternative forms of crisis management, [China's] preference may well be to use this force

in a militarily offensive manner and further beyond China's 'gates' than in past disputes, even if for politically 'defensive' purposes.[65]

This sounds similar to the theory that China engages in 'active defence', with such examples as the Korean War, the Sino-Indian War and the invasion of Vietnam. It is interesting that Johnston wrote this in 1998, before Washington unveiled its theory of pre-emptive war.[66]

Scholars have concluded that modern China also has a high propensity to use force-based solutions to solve disputes. Academic analysis of the Mao years up to 1985 (a good representation of the 'New China') calculates that China was involved in eleven foreign policy disputes and resorted to violence in eight (72 per cent). The comparable figures for the US, USSR and UK are 18 per cent, 27 per cent and 12 per cent, respectively. Chinese violence was called 'high intensity'.[67] China has frequently stated that it does not invade other countries or take aggressive action outside its own territories. It usually refines that to imply 'after the death of Mao, in 1976, and the initiation of reforms'. However, China did impose a form of sanctions on both Vietnam and Albania in 1978, invade Vietnam in 1979 and fight seriously with it throughout the 1980s. In this sense it has paralleled some of the unilateral tools of the US, such as sanctions. Brecher et al. state that historically 'these uses of force tended to occur on issues that Chinese leaders perceived to be high value and zero sum. Territorial disputes, for instance, were crucial drivers in many . . . due in part to a historical sensitivity to threats to the territorial integrity of the state.'[68] Thus old China used violence extensively, and modern China has been far more likely to use force to resolve a foreign policy crisis than the United States, Britain or the Soviet Union. This illustrates the old Chinese saying, 'resort to peace and friendship when temporarily obliged to do so; use war and defence as your actual policy'.[69]

A tool regularly deployed is the announcement that an action or expression of some party overseas has 'hurt the feelings of China' or of 'the Chinese people'. Considering how large and powerful China is becoming, it is extraordinary how often its people's sensitivities are disturbed. This didn't seem to happen much under Mao, but since then it appears to be a steeply rising trend: by 2009, eighteen countries had offended the Chinese people.[70] These included Guatemala, Denmark, the Vatican and Iceland. France managed to do it six times, India nine times, the US 27 times and Japan a royal 58 times. The Chinese people were also deeply offended by the EU, the Nobel Prize committee and the Melbourne Film Festival (which screened a documentary that China objected to).

In 2010, Colonel Liu Mingfu, a professor at the National Defence University, launched *The China Dream*, a book which called on China to become the world's No.1 power, economically and militarily. A general and an admiral were asked to comment by *Global Times*. The general said it was a grand dream, but not necessarily a reality; the admiral said that China should continue keeping a low profile. So they were not completely antagonistic to the idea. What was not carried in the English-language edition of the newspaper was the fact that, according to an opinion poll on its website, of the 4,000 or so people who responded, 80 per cent said the country should aim to become the leading military power; when asked whether this goal should be expressed in public, 52 per cent thought it should and 48 per cent thought not.[71]

There are various signs of China's aggressive use of its power. When President Sarkozy insisted on meeting the Dalai Lama in 2008, despite Chinese protests, China cancelled the scheduled China–European Union summit. This was no real sacrifice for China, which does not take the EU very seriously; it was a cost-free way of punishing the Europeans. If there were a similar dispute with the US, it is less likely that a China–US summit would be cancelled. However, Obama's decision to upgrade Taiwan's armaments and meet the Dalai Lama in 2010 certainly provoked reactions that were more hostile than usual, including threats to boycott US companies and cancel military exchanges.

When South East Asian countries complained in summer 2010 about China's extensive claims in the South China Sea, 'China's foreign minister, Yang Jiechi, worked himself into a rage: "All of you remember how much of your economic prosperity depends on us," he reportedly spat back.'[72] In 2011, shortly after Japan and the Philippines agreed to increase military ties to protect their regional interests, China's official *People's Daily* declared that

> certain countries think as long as they can balance China with the help of US military power, they are free to do whatever they want . . . We don't deny that some Asian countries have a certain feeling of insecurity in the face of China's rapid rise, particularly that the development of China's military power will destroy the balance long meticulously maintained by the US . . . But today's Asia has changed . . . no country wants to give back their ticket for the high speed train of China's economic development.[73]

The analogy with high-speed rail travel was unfortunate, coming so soon after the Wenzhou train disaster, but the hectoring tone was unmistakable. It is sometimes difficult to know what impression Beijing feels it is conveying to the world.

Visa denial is used as a means of managing foreign academics and journalists. Though it is rather ineffective, some may feel that their work would be harder and less credible if they could no longer visit China, and so might 'self-censor' their output. As China increases in prominence, more intellectuals are likely to visit, and presumably this 'opinion management' will continue. Whether it builds goodwill towards China in the wider world might be debated. ('Banned in China' could become a useful marketing slogan for an author.) Foreign diplomats and officials of multilateral institutions in Hong Kong have noted that Beijing adopted a tougher visa regime after the Nobel Peace Prize was awarded to Liu Xiaobo in 2010.[74] On the other hand, America retaliated to hostile Chinese action against Obama's first ambassador to Beijing by suspending some of the visa privileges usually granted to Chinese leaders' children in the US.

China's reluctance to follow the West's lead in condemning and sanctioning reviled regimes has been much criticised. China broadly shares the West's concerns over a nuclear Iran, but differs in its tactical response; similarly it has gradually come to recognise Sudan's unpleasant behaviour, but is only slowly dropping non-interventionism. Furthermore – and not unlike the US vis-à-vis China – it has trade interests which tend to trump human rights concerns. It was principally the independence of oil-rich Southern Sudan which contributed to a greater neutrality towards Sudan.

China is also a victim of history. There is perhaps another analogy with late nineteenth-century Germany: it was a newly formed power that was becoming increasingly strong; it had no legacy colonies and had missed out on most of the 'scramble for Africa' so could only pick up a few crumbs from the floor. China in the twenty-first century, having come late to the global 'scramble' for natural resources, feels pushed into regions which are naturally or politically desolate.

At the Asian Development Bank (ADB) in 2009, China used its power to postpone a $2.9 billion development loan to India, the ADB's largest borrower. It objected that part would be spent in Arunachal Pradesh, a province occupied by India, where sovereignty is disputed by China. Beijing's objection came despite the ADB charter stating that loans are judged on economic grounds. We can speculate on how China will use its increased power in multilateral institutions. After all, America opposed World Bank and IMF loans to India when the latter tested a nuclear bomb in 1998. If the US sees a conflict between its ethical causes and its national and political interests, it usually follows the latter. This is a more traditional foreign policy and quite recognisable from the nineteenth century. Not surprisingly, China shows evidence of following the same path.

Analysts continue the analogy with Imperial Germany before 1914 when they look at China's rapid armament. While some commentators see trade as a deterrent to war, we should remember that Britain was then Germany's largest export market. Furthermore, in 1913 almost half of Russia's trade was with Germany.[75] It might also be worth considering comparisons with pre-1939 Germany. To what extent we can rely on statements of peaceful intention is a moot point. The only current explicit threat is to Taiwan, where China declines to disavow force. However, the ramming and arrest of neighbours' ships is low-intensity conflict, and party media openly call for China's neighbours to be 'taught a lesson'. The situation has been likened to 1907 Europe.[76] We should hope it is not more like 1938 Europe.

Among Western liberals, there is some anxiety that 'a strong China may not be so good for the world'.[77] Professor Alan Dupont of Sydney University refers to 'perceptions of a new and ugly assertiveness in Beijing'.[78] This is a combination of many factors, including the vituperative foreign affairs language, the elevation of the South China Sea claims to the high status of a 'core interest', the aggressive behaviour at Copenhagen, the lecturing of America and the snarling at ASEAN members. Foreigners might begin to ask if a pattern is emerging.

China's past use of threat and force have exceeded the rhetoric of peaceful development. Beijing seems oblivious to the cold fact that 'peaceful' doesn't only mean no declaration of war; it describes a manner of speech and behaviour towards other parties. In several respects China's behaviour is not 'peaceful'. The most likely opportunity China has – if it wishes – to demonstrate hostile intent overseas is on Taiwan. It is irrelevant to foreigners what are the legal rights and wrongs of the Taiwan issue. Nor is the adherence by various governments to complex diplomatic formulae about China's unity of any import. The sight of a small, democratic territory being militarily crushed (or even cowed into submission) by the world's largest – and non-democratic – state is likely to convince many that China is a danger to the world and no respecter of individual self-determination. This may not appear legal, right or fair to Chinese people, but it is likely. A country may survive one hostile minority (as Spain has with the Basques), but to have angry Tibetans, rioting Uighurs and frightened Taiwanese would be too much for China's image. What the world and its media will see is one country (with two unhappy minorities) threatening another. That would considerably increase the odds of a hostile reception to China's rise.

Perhaps China should consider the lessons of the former Yugoslavia: the component parts were not happy together, and so they split up and the world recognised the dissolution. This would be one solution. If, on the other hand, Tibet and Xinjiang were to become calm and happy, and if the Taiwan issue were left to mutual agreement or for future generations, the world might regard China's rise as a welcome alternative to the recent unilateralist approach of

America. This would be another solution. The issue is a challenge for China's foreign strategy, but the prize is worthwhile.

Risk of Confrontation

China's international presence is growing. It talks of peace, but it is slowly developing global military power and speaking belligerently. That it has facilities which could have a military application doesn't *ipso facto* mean it has any intention of using them confrontationally. However, as China develops its reach, particularly towards the Gulf, it causes concern to Asian neighbours. Any extension of China's naval capability to protect its oil routes could easily look to these countries like a potential threat to their own supplies. That might lead Japan to abrogate its post-1945 pacifist constitution; it is likely to lead India to step up its efforts to strengthen itself militarily. China, America, Japan, India – any of them could trigger an unplanned incident. At present, it would be unlikely to lead any further. But if China comes under intense domestic nationalist pressure, pragmatic responses to blunders may not remain the norm.

There have been several tense incidents in recent years (not all involving China): the US aircraft close to Hainan Island in 2001; the Chinese ship sunk by 500 rounds of fire outside Vladivostok in 2009; or the US ships entering the Chinese 'exclusion zone', also in 2009. Then there have been Chinese oceanographic ships skirting Japanese waters; Russian bombers overflying Canada; and the Japanese air force scrambling against Chinese and Russian aircraft 567 times in 2012. It seems we inhabit a world where politicians allow armies to engage in brinkmanship. One result of this is that an 'incident' becomes more likely – and greater domestic public awareness may make it difficult for China to back down.

There are so many potential sources of friction and dispute (covered at length in preceding chapters), such rebarbative language and behaviour employed by China, and such a fiercely nationalistic domestic public that it is hard to believe that conflict will not arise eventually, either by choice or by accident. Even a minor clash would be damaging to the entire message of China's 'peaceful development'. If the world becomes less sympathetic to Beijing, it could impede China's rise in a host of ways.

CHAPTER SIXTEEN

Outcomes

Many of the challenges which China confronts appear to an international audience to have clear solutions. However, they must be viewed in the context of a government which is driven by the desire to stay in power and yet has a sense of fragility. Many obvious policy solutions are avoided as they carry political costs or risk. This creates a sense of impotence or stasis amongst policy-makers. Will the threats to growth and stability be sufficient to damage China's rise? The answer is yes. China can continue to rise but the threats are so serious and so widespread, and the domestic policy response so timid, that it is inconceivable that China will overtake the United States this century.

There are demographic trends which no government can now change: the extreme gender disparity, wholesale ageing, impending labour force decline and above all a sharp population contraction. Other very serious issues that could be solved but are not being tackled include lack of social welfare, a low-tech economy, environmental disaster and a growing number of large-scale riots. China's leaders treat the threats as if they have centuries; in fact they have at most perhaps a decade.

Little about China's future is certain, except for the looming adult gender imbalances and declining population. Rather than offer predictions, it is more realistic to demonstrate the likely outcomes and to propose some policy options that Beijing has (probably) not yet considered but could adopt.

Most projections are a continuation of existing trends. Similarly, deviation from the recent past is seen as aberrant and temporary. In China, in the 1980s and even 1990s, many expected the market reforms to be reversed as part of a return to an earlier socialist economy. From the late 1990s onwards a consensus started to develop that the reforms would endure and grow. By the time the consensus prevailed, the reforms had essentially ended. Since the early 2000s, there have been competing projections as to when China will overtake the US economy, but these projections fail to take account of the fact that reform has stopped. Other analysts note China's transition from Maoism to authoritarianism and assume democracy is the destination. Straight-line extrapolation is a convenient forecasting tool for many; this might partly explain the fate of so many of the risk models used recently in the Western banking industry.

It is fashionable for economists to pose the question: when will China overtake the US to become the world's No. 1 economy? This is reminiscent of the 1950s to the 1980s, when observers asked the same first of Germany, then Japan. Neither has done so, not least because history does not usually operate by iterative steps. Venice and the France of Louis XIV were once leading states; both eventually flirted with bankruptcy and disappeared from history. Societal extinction is more common than survival, let alone dominance. We must look at the future with a humble sense of the difficulty of the art of looking forward.

It has been clear since at least 2006 that the engines of China's recent phenomenal growth would one day falter. A liquidity-induced boom is not necessarily a sustainable response to this. Neither are high debt levels. Several of China's problems are, remarkably, also American issues: structural unemployment, the lack of SME loans and even questions about the quality of graduates and pervasive poverty. There are not necessarily common answers to the common problems. Other Chinese problems do not exist in America, such as technological weakness and tens of thousands of mass riots annually.

Is China Strong or Weak?

It is widely believed that China is close to becoming the dominant power. However, a number of observers have in recent years seen it as a weak power. It is fashionable amongst foreigners to cite Sun Tzu's *The Art of War*. One piece of advice offered there is, if weak, then appear strong, and if strong, appear weak. The late Gerald Segal said in 1999, 'China matters far less than it and most of the West think, and it is high time the West began treating it as such.'[1]

On the other hand, as far back as 1997, 'fashionable comparisons [were] being made between present day China and militarist Wilhelmine Germany'.[2] Ten years later, in 2007, Hisahiko Okazaki, a noted Japanese strategist, also saw China as a rising threat, similar to Germany before the First World War: 'like China today . . . both wariness about Germany's growing strength and hopes for its peaceful development existed'.[3] Fears about Germany a century ago came to a head, he says, in 1907, when the international psychological state changed from 'anxiety' to 'nightmare'. He traces China's development in precisely the same terms and focuses particularly on the economic growth and military build-up.[4] The analogy will recur. How to deal with China's looming presence is a vital question for Japan's security policy, as it will be for the world.

In 2009, China was declared 'a truly global actor' but not yet a global power.[5] Academics have commented that it is a much weaker state than is thought,[6] and analysts suggest that imbalances in the economy, environmental blight or racial tensions might destabilise its rise. As to whether China really is a weak or a strong state, there is an interesting set of arguments in a best-selling Chinese book published in 2009. The authors of *Unhappy China* argue that the country 'has the power to lead the world and the necessity to break away from Western influence'.[7] They feel China should have the ambition to establish its preeminence and create a new world order. However, the authors also criticised the Beijing leaders for their obsession with the Olympics, which betrayed a 'weak nation's psychology'. Furthermore, the inability to deal with the widespread scandal of tainted milk (the 'melamine affair' – see Chapter 3) 'reflects the decline and fall of Chinese civilization'. Thus, though popular, the book sends out mixed messages. Despite being dubbed the 'new masters of the world'[8] and in spite of the frequent adulation heaped on it, China stresses its position as simply a developing country with many poor inhabitants. Contradictions, as always, abound.

China is replacing America as the principal donor in many parts of the world, yet it still accepts international aid. It aims for G2 status with the US, but has not been paying its fair share of the costs of the UN. The world is transfixed by China's $3 trillion of reserves without considering that there is a domestic monetary cost to every dollar held. When asked about increasing its contribution to IMF capital, China's response has often been that it should be assessed on the basis of its per capita wealth. That would put it outside the top 100 countries, and would thus – by self-definition – exclude it from making a more meaningful contribution. If per capita wealth is the criterion, we should be looking to Luxembourg, Norway, Switzerland and Qatar to fund the IMF. But that's not the way it works.

An impending workforce decline, combined with rising wage costs and welfare spending, high domestic debt levels and some signs of reduced productivity growth, suggests that China's long-term economy could shadow Europe's low growth rather than America's usual buoyancy. This reduces the logic behind a G2, and many rising nations will flatly reject a Sino-American G2. Furthermore, if we look at population trends to 2100, it might be more important to consider the future of Africa – resource-rich, economically buoyant, urbanising rapidly, gradually more market-oriented and increasingly populous. It will be paradoxical if, over the next fifty years, China's investment serves to propel Africa to a more prominent position than China itself.

China is the world's second-largest economy, but not long ago its budget was half that of Britain and 40 per cent that of France. If China earns a handful of dollars from every $300 iPod manufactured onshore (see Chapter 3), it is unsurprising that tax revenue is so low. If a Taiwanese company in China employs 1.2 million people and produces the iPad, who has a high-tech economy: China or Taiwan? Almost 60 per cent of China's exports and over 80 per cent of its high-tech products are produced by foreign companies. Is China again a colony, commercially exploited for its cheap labour and low-cost engineers? If the currency appreciates, costs rise or the general environment deteriorates, these companies may decamp. What has China gained?

In late 2009, eyebrows were raised at the rolling over (rather than redemption) of tens of billions of dollars' worth of ten-year government bonds issued to state banks a decade ago to lift a previous generation of bad loans off balance sheets. Could the state not afford to redeem the bonds? In 2011, there was a flicker of concern when state shipping company COSCO reneged on charter contracts with overseas shipowners. Increasingly, it is looking as if China cannot increase its military capability at the rate it would like, develop a large-scale internal security apparatus and at the same time introduce an adequate welfare system. Analysts have suggested that China was stretched in 2009 when it sent a small naval detachment to deter piracy in the Gulf of Aden.

Forgetting actual numbers (because they will always sow confusion in the Chinese context), the country has a reducing labour force, a rapidly ageing and eventually declining population, and a worryingly high percentage of men who will never have the chance to marry. It may not be as dystopic as Russia, but it has serious problems. It is unclear whether the continuing ecological devastation, allied to climate change, will consign the country to geopolitical catastrophe. There might come a time when China's neighbours will simply not permit it to divert rivers to quench the outsized, ill-used and underrestrained national thirst. Climate change, environmental abuse and natural disaster are, sadly, frequent visitors to China; we should not forget that they helped to undermine the Tang dynasty, the Yuan, the Ming, the Qing and Guomindang rule.

How important is it for China to overtake America as the largest economy? It has 1.3 billion citizens; America has 300 million. Eventually, it is likely that Chinese citizens will produce a quarter of the economic output per head that America does, and thus become the No. 1 economy in aggregate. But so what? Using very basic arithmetic – and leaving aside currency forecasts – if China grew at 8 per cent annually and America at 3 per cent, China would overtake the US as the world's biggest economy before 2030. (These numbers are of course simply illustrative. In practice both countries are likely to underperform those growth rates.) However, this would give China a per capita income of just over $17,000, while the figure for America would be about $68,000. The agglomeration of many poor people in one economic area nominally creates a large economy, but it is one which would have difficulty meeting its people's expectations. This is before we look out to 2100 by which time there should be 50 per cent more Americans and between a third and two-thirds fewer Chinese (see Chapter 5).

How will China spend its money as its economy grows? It will still be making tough decisions between welfare and the military. China might choose to resemble Sparta, while America emulates Athens. However, unless there is a structural decision that the accumulating value of China's economic output should accrue not to its citizens but to projection of the state, China will continue to have a disproportionately small state relative to the size of its economy. So, even when (or if) it overtakes the US by size of economy, it will probably still be unable to combine a first-rank military, a large-scale public security apparatus and a comprehensive social security system.

China often enacts admirable legislation, but it has great difficulty in implementing it. It has a very weak and decentralised financial and governing system. Beijing reports unusually high economic results (whether accurately or not), but has failed in its objectives to raise the education budget, to meet the environmental goals, to deal with the water and desertification issues, to provide healthcare, to make pensions work, to achieve research targets or to reduce corruption while violent riots continue to multiply. There have been many great achievements in areas such as the economy and poverty reduction, but there must be systemic weaknesses for this degree of implementation failure. If China cannot improve implementation, it is in grave danger of going from being a sunrise state to a sunset state without ever having had its day in the sun.

A further point is how desirable a strong state is. Clearly, to implement beneficial legislation, it is important that the state should be functional. But strength is a different question. The writer Xiao Jiansheng notes that 'China, throughout its long history, was most prosperous when it had a pluralistic society, and often divided into smaller states and kingdoms. This division allowed competing ideas and cultures to flourish.'[9] I believe China is *both* a strong *and* a weak power. In some respects it is weaker than the world imagines; in other senses it has deep strengths on which to draw. Indeed we could go further and suggest that China is weak where it should be strong and strong where it should be weak. For example, it needs to temper strong government with constitutional restraints, and yet it needs to strengthen government in policy implementation.

Many foreign people would like China to become a power in the world, although most hope it would become a power for good. Belligerence is not power. The question is whether it can exercise power beneficially: lift its people fully out of poverty, put in place a comprehensive social security system, successfully participate in international security, mediate in global disputes, clean up its environment, build technological power and really create a harmonious society, where differences of opinion can be peacefully reconciled.

The Future Economy

Lending should be more focused, and structural reform is needed to open up the economy. Government can play a direct role in this by borrowing modestly and spending. Despite substantial domestic off-balance-sheet liabilities, government is in the fortunate position of at least being under-borrowed externally. The public and the state-owned industries are both savings-rich, but that could be changed by further reform. China can modestly increase its small overseas borrowing in order to expand the welfare system and possibly give further substantial boosts to the domestic economy. The cost of the swollen public security apparatus is beginning to dwarf social programmes. In future, leaders might decide it is cheaper to please people than to control them.

The range of potential outcomes must include for some the possibility of an eventual recovery in China's export-driven economy, based on the old low-cost manufacturing model (although that is highly unlikely). If domestic manufacturers really want the past to return, several changes are required, including a deliberate currency depreciation, a conscious abatement of environmental controls, a strong recovery in Western demand for manufactured goods, a recovery in the currencies of China's main export competitors, ideally a halt in the one-child policy with new incentives to produce more children, and a slowdown in Western-style labour legislation. These are not all within the government's power to effect, even if it so desired; but a sufficiently potent cocktail of many of them is essential if the past is to be regained. There is a case for some of these changes, but it is unlikely we shall see any such comprehensive trend. Appealing though it may seem to many factory owners, it only addresses the present, not the future. It would be a short-term fix, regressive for the country and counter-productive.

Responding to economic challenge is one of the government's major roles. If the low-cost export model has ended and funding for state industrial dinosaurs is ending, then the challenges will be twofold: how to build a more dynamic domestic economy and how to become a high-quality, more innovative, export economy. There are two routes out of the current situation. One is to spur the domestic economy on by recycling more effectively the large cash surpluses within state enterprises and persuading the citizenry to reduce their savings in order to consume. The other is to upgrade the export economy to compete at prices well above the level to which costs are rising and leave surplus revenue for further research and development to maintain competitiveness.

Household savings can be mobilised by tackling the causes of excess savings: exiguous welfare support; newly-weds' expectation of an apartment; low interest rates; and lack of financial products, such as private pensions and health insurance. The situation could be substantially improved by ending so-called 'financial repression', in which the country's consumers subsidise its producers. Expansion of services, rather than manufacturing, not only creates more jobs but raises wages as a percentage of GDP. Raising the cost of capital would discourage excess manufacturing investment and return more revenue annually to household depositors, who could spend it. Appreciating the currency would weaken inflation, encourage higher-quality exports and overall (on past record) doesn't damage exports too much. It would drive productivity increases. However, as noted, it does cause huge losses on the country's US Treasury bonds. Labour should be encouraged into the service sector rather than manufacturing, but this requires skills which are not currently taught. Excess corporate savings in the state sector could be drained by encouraging greater dividend payments to shareholders – and making sure the funds reach the state. This creates a dual benefit: increasing government revenue and discouraging profligate investment.

Mobilising personal savings to create domestic spending is problematic: there is still nervousness about unemployment and jobs are not created in line with economic growth; there is a need for savings against social costs in the future; large-scale purchase of consumer goods is environmentally damaging; and household savings are not as substantial as is often suggested. Finally, the rate of interest on household deposits is artificially low, which reduces potential income. Raising interest rates would reduce corporate profit and increase losses for the central bank in holding US Treasury bonds. It would also hit government finances, as virtually all public debt is domestic. The real drive to consume should come when there is enough confidence that the holes in the state welfare umbrella can be plugged and unemployment reduced. Unfortunately, high unemployment means that, even if welfare issues are solved, there is probably still too much public nervousness to spend. A poll by CASS at the end of 2008 found that over a third of all families said they knew people who had suffered redundancy. However, semi-official figures estimated the urban jobless rate in mid-2012 at over 8 per cent.[10] Unemployment is too close to too many. Beijing needs to ask itself whether the whole economy could be developed to balance the interests of the consumer with those of the producer. It seems that no current policy initiative will accelerate private consumption fast enough to push the economy. The gathering challenges will need to be addressed via the alternative route – of upgrading innovation and knowledge skills (as discussed in Chapter 3).

The currency needs to be permanently under review. If the dollar were to break decisively downwards, China might no longer be willing to use it as its benchmark. As much as currency realignment, America should (for as long as trade surpluses last) hope for Beijing to continue to increase its holding of US Treasury bonds, risky though this is. Axiomatically, every rise in the *renminbi* is a loss on US dollar bond holdings. It is excessive for America to request both. Were China to become a less competitive exporter and were its budget to come under greater pressure, it might ultimately be saved from this dilemma by its currency naturally starting to depreciate.

Providing local government debt and non-performing loans don't spin out of control, China may eventually increase its foreign borrowing to finance further large-scale requirements. This could be facilitated by fund-raising through some genuine privatisation among major SOEs. Bond interest is currently notionally less than 2 per cent of the budget. The principal use of funds should be for social welfare and high-quality education: there is a real need to transform the educational base, to introduce elite universities and encourage critical thinking and innovation.

However – further out – there is the real risk that events might erode confidence in China's ability to service public debt, and then declining confidence and adverse demography could combine to cause a debt crisis. China's sources of capital do, at the moment, include foreign borrowing but this window can close if perceptions of debt service ability weaken. An alternative is genuine privatisation of major state-owned companies. This could mitigate the impact of a slowing economy. So far we have largely seen minority stakes sold in SOEs, which has had no effect on their management and strategy. Genuine privatisation could benefit China substantially by obliging such companies to accept market disciplines and become properly competitive. Better business performance from privatised SOEs could generate a substantial increase in fiscal revenue for the state. Privatisation proceeds and any overseas borrowing will need to be directly focused on improved education, creating an innovative economy, cleaning up the environment and then on social expenditure, to maintain civil stability.

China's economic future is likely to embrace a substantially bigger service sector, which, outside banking, insurance, transport and communications, tends to be dominated by smaller companies, predominantly in the private sector. We have already seen evidence, through corrections to GDP data, even in 2011, that the service sector is not well understood by the authorities, mainly because it is relatively new and significantly private. The focus of increased lending in 2009–10 was the state-linked sector: in 2011, only 15 per cent of SMEs got loans from banks and financial institutions.[11] Private sector difficulty in borrowing from the state banks suggests a need for a far stronger government policy of making credit available to the economy's growth sectors, regardless of ownership. Perhaps the Party committees in the major state banks should be directed to prioritise disbursals of credit to private companies. There could also be a mandatory improvement in auditing standards for private companies. The facts that employment growth has historically been generated by the private sector, that manufacturing is becoming increasingly capital (rather than labour) intensive, that the service sector is labour intensive and private sector dominated, should inspire policy-makers to make certain choices. Until then, the economy may have liquidity bursts but lack sustainable growth.

Even in 1925, it was noted that 'property is insecure. In this one phrase the whole history of Asia is contained.'[12] Although there has been a great expansion in entrepreneurial activity, we could reasonably expect it to grow even faster if property rights and wealth were more secure, if arbitrariness were ended and if the rule of law were entrenched. Such reform presents political challenges and threats to the system that need consideration. Now that private sector activity gets more recognition (and indeed entrepreneurs can join the Party), the logic must be to encourage such activity. Service sector reform could create far more competition. Beijing must end the Jekyll and Hyde approach to the private sector. It is time to salute Jekyll and shoot Hyde. The challenge of reorienting and invigorating China's dated economic model is achievable, but it needs to be tackled soon.

Social Security

The key social issues Beijing should tackle first are healthcare and pensions, ideally through some form of insurance. If this is swiftly implemented and understood, there should be early confidence, which could translate into rising spending levels. Official initiatives on social security issues are more powerful than money spent on infrastructure. There is the additional – and substantial – benefit that, at a time of continuing unemployment, a social safety net reduces the potential for instability.

However, on the question of pensions, for instance, we have to look not only at coverage (the proportion of the country that is participating) but also depth (what the cover buys versus what is needed), portability and funding. Some of the early pension fund accounts were raided by local authorities within less than five years, which raises the question of sustainability. So far the proposals put forward have been either opaque or clearly lack the reach and approach to allow effectiveness. The programmes should be as close to self-funded as possible, although they may require some state funding at the outset.

For many years now, the authorities have discussed the need to improve social security. Targets were announced but frequently missed during the boom. It is unclear why this has lacked priority. To accelerate the process, one possibility would be to copy what China has done with the banking system and allow tripartite competition: Sino-international joint ventures in social provision, insurance, etc.; a limited opportunity for foreign firms to operate in the market; and domestic firms, which would absorb the trickle-down of expertise (they might perhaps hire foreign professionals or take in some overseas shareholders) and compete using their own skills and market positioning. This is a market with potentially explosive opportunity. Encouraging domestic and foreign institutions to provide basic financial products could meet the obvious public need, while the chance to sell health insurance, pensions, etc. in China would be a major opportunity for financial services companies worldwide. There will be ample chance to stack the cards a little in favour of domestic or state providers, if that is deemed economically desirable.

Success will not come overnight, and will depend upon two things. First, large-scale overseas funding is required to finance a universal healthcare scheme, which could perhaps be amortised through obligatory – but modest – individual subscriptions. This could be planned, funded and then introduced within two years. Second, foreign providers need to be brought in to introduce new skills, experience and ideas across healthcare, unemployment and pension insurance. This should raise the standards of all participants – and thus the offer to the public and their confidence in it. The allure of buying into an oligopolistic role to provide social products to tens of millions of Chinese for, say, a set period could be irresistible to foreign financial services companies. There is the added benefit of new streams of taxable income; namely, the profit of the service providers and the possible auctioning of operating licences.

If anxiety over social security can be banished, then we should see the release of savings into consumption. But with unemployment a continuing feature, it will not be easy for the extension of social programmes to create less saving and more spending. Indeed, right now the opposite seems to be the case. If the right measures are not taken, the factors that will emerge are severe constraints on growth. A falling labour force, rising old-age dependency and falling productivity gains, coupled with the existing low consumption and poor educational attainment, would suggest a sharp deceleration of growth over the next twenty years and the possibility of the country being locked for a long period in a 'middle income trap'.

Education and Innovation

The upgrading of the export economy depends upon innovation, either through technical invention, more innovative process engineering or branding. Each of these requires behavioural changes for business, both in method and mentality. New inventions require research spending, then good decisions on the targets and bright, original results which can lead to patentable and commercial products. This is not so easy for the private sector, where margins have been thin in the good times and are currently problematic. The 'guerrilla' or *shanzhai* innovation which is emerging in China could become a basis for this (see Chapter 3). The creation of branded goods means a change in thinking from contract manufacturing to identifying, or creating, the market for a new product, and then concentrating on the marketing proposition and reiterating it endlessly, while continually emphasising quality and customer service. Indeed, manufacturing might even be divorced from the process and contracted out, within or outside China. However, if any country can remain an integrated manufacturer, this is it.

A further area for China to exploit is innovation in other countries. This could be licensed to Chinese companies to deploy within China or even to market across the whole of Asia. Japan did this in the 1970s, when the US and Germany were bigger innovators: it bought a product, maybe improved it, got it to market first and sold it. Brands can be truly innovative without comprising inventions. Later, on the strength of this, Japan increased its own innovation and patent grant. However, we should not expect early successes in this area. The innovative skills required to unleash a wave of successful research and development are not yet being created by China's educational system (see Chapter 3). However, I am optimistic that China can gradually increase the level of innovation in industry, if it makes the necessary reforms.

China's recent culture has not stressed marketing and customer service. Government attempts to turn hundreds of loss-making state enterprises into a few dozen profitable monopolies run counter to the need to focus on customer preference or service. Yet the remorseless rise of Chinese people as buyers of luxury branded goods suggests that there is easily enough comprehension of the differences between good products and poor ones, good brands and less good ones, to guide companies into the world of branding, quality, marketing and service. If China is priced permanently out of the low-cost goods market it must produce goods which allow it to compete effectively in the middle ranks. It is not good enough for China to be an assembler and final shipper. The biggest margins come from producing high-quality items in China – or, indeed, in Cambodia or Burma – putting its brand names on the goods and finding the customers, not from producing for others. Success will come when the message the world understands changes from 'Chinese products are cheap' to 'Chinese products are good'.

Frequently consideration of economics and society returns to issues of culture and morality. When Hegel discussed the Chinese character at the time of the Qing occupation, he said, 'Its distinguishing feature is, that everything which belongs to Spirit, – unconstrained morality, in practice and theory, Heart, inward Religion, Science and Art properly so called, – is alien to it.'[13] It is perhaps necessary to enjoy certain freedoms to develop a degree of spirituality and ethics. A recurring theme throughout this narrative has been the need for honesty and objectivity in China. This book cites many authoritative Chinese noting that the culture is not strongly oriented towards self-reflection or integrity. One prominent intellectual, the late Li Shenzhi, criticised the Tiananmen Square suppression and the nervousness of officials to reveal official documents regarding that and other events. 'The cost', Li said, 'is the national loss of memory and the loss of the ability to think logically among the people.'[14] Professor Yuan Weishi points out how notions of patriotism are allowed to subsume critical thinking in analysis of historical events:

> The current history textbooks are using this concept to guide thinking. It is obvious that we must love our country. But there are two ways to love our country. One way is to inflame nationalistic passions . . . The other choice is this: we analyze everything rationally; if it is right, it is right and if it is wrong, it is wrong; calm, objective and wholly regard and handle all conflicts with the outside.[15]

Sadly, the Chinese magazine which carried this essay in 2006 was soon after closed down. We constantly run up against an unwillingness to face facts and frankly acknowledge truths: Deng Xiaoping's famous exhortation to 'seek the truth from facts' is not universally applied. Vladimir Putin has said of Stalin's Russia 'the positives that undoubtedly existed were achieved at an unacceptable price'.[16] No Chinese politician can yet be so honest.

There are a number of reasons for choosing to publish fabricated nationalist history. One is that in an authoritarian society such as China it is relatively easy to conjure the idea that to love the country is to love the government and the Party. If young people are made to feel that their country has been treated even more shabbily by foreign countries than is actually the case, this may create a sense of solidarity with the authorities. Beijing sees value in inculcating the narrative that China has been egregiously ill-treated by foreigners, because it positions the Party as China's bulwark and undermines sympathy for alien influences, such as democracy and liberal values: 'China is caught … in a prison of history'.[17]

Another reason is that it provides China with a 'golden age', in which its relationship with the world, and particularly its neighbours, was harmonious and mutually satisfactory. This era was smashed by foreign armies. The subtext is that the world will improve if China rightly resumes its place as a major power. The suggestion that China represents a different set of principles and practices which are more respectful of other countries is defensible. However, attempting to bolster it through historical inaccuracy will not be cost-free. The domestic price for this portrayal is the avoidance of objectivity, which will take its toll in several ways. Some costs will inevitably be commercial.

The measures required to foster economic innovation include better – not more – education, with a culture of analysis, challenge and debate. This applies particularly to Chinese universities, where the critical faculty needs to be developed. The state must also find ways to encourage private companies to finance their own research, possibly through tax incentives. What the state should not do is to pick the projects. There could be prizes and cash sums for successful international patent applications, but that is not the same as the alleged practice of the Chinese patent office receiving bonuses for granting patents.

Tax incentives to encourage research amongst SMEs, and maybe outright grants, soft loans or matched funding for private sector R&D investment, could help. Perhaps there should be further funding for start-ups. Then there is the whole area of national honours to be considered: a system of honours and decorations, which are seen to be objective – not politicised – and awarded on merit, is a relatively cost-free way of motivating people and can be invested with dignity. Perhaps the President or Premier could have lunch once a year with the top prize-winning inventors and innovators of China?

It can be argued that sending thousands of students abroad to study each year is a way of outsourcing critical thinking, because Chinese universities are simply not equipped to perform this role. However, there are two drawbacks: many of the overseas universities chosen have no more idea of critical appraisal than do Chinese institutions, and China goes on to make inadequate use of the students' skills on their return. There is a distinct nervousness about using students who have learned to think overseas in positions of sensitivity, although this has applied less to engineers. Scientists who have studied or lived abroad report considerable collegial hostility and jealousy when they take up positions at home. Nonetheless, more encouraging signs are now emerging of a greater willingness to tap this source of national talent. The state should also scrap restrictions on the establishment of foreign schools and universities in China for Chinese people. This could lead to a flourishing of healthy competition with the state system, generating a rise in the quality of education.

No one wants China to stagnate like the Islamic world in a scientific void. Many of us would like China's future to be as glorious as its past. Destiny will not favour China if it cannot engender an environment of independent thought. Wen Jiabao called for critical thinking to boost innovation; but it is difficult to have 'critical thinking' in science if it is banned in history and politics. One fears that his use of the term is similar to his use of 'democracy' (see p.258ff above). Meanwhile there is plenty of energy left in the US. America will continue to enjoy the technological lead for as long as it invests generously in research and development and cultivates freedom of thinking and the curious spirit.

Stability and Identity

If stark confrontation does come to China again, as it did to almost the entire communist world in 1989, what might happen differently? Last time, the Politburo Standing Committee, theoretically the most senior organ of authority, could not make a decision. The plan was formulated by the old and largely retired leaders – the 'Immortals' – meeting in Deng's home. They were all Long March veterans, who had fought in the revolution and whose experience and history gave them overwhelming authority with government officials. The rule of law had not settled; that of men still held sway. Will it be the same for each generation of leaders if they have neither won a war nor faced the electorate and won a mandate? Will the lack of electoral (or other) mandate sap the authority and thus engender uncertainty in future difficult times? Who will step in the next time the Politburo cannot decide?

In the downturn of 2008–9, the ripples of economic pain were more pronounced and widespread than during the slowdown of 1989. Then there was serious inflation, widespread complaints of corruption, and it was a struggle to afford basic provisions. In 2008–9, with tens of millions out of work, it was much worse. Throughout China, almost every soldier and policeman will have had a cousin or friend whose family suffered. The government may decide that the last economic downturn was sufficiently structural and the recovery sufficiently disconnected from long-term employment creation for it no longer to be able to deliver rising prosperity amid stability. If so, it will need to engage in further deep reform – or even consider another basis for its legitimacy. There are several options for re-grounding the party, some of them complementary. The overall competence of the authorities has been outstanding for several decades, and the analysis and planning which underpins their decisions highly impressive. The Party will probably choose some form of 'makeover' to accommodate changing times.

One possibility, although not highly desirable, is to play the nationalist card – but with an added twist, acknowledging the need for a more nationalist and socialist ideology. Growth will slow and unemployment will be a serious problem for some years. Welfare and the environment are probably more important now to the public than is high growth. However, these negative factors could be obscured by some foreign distraction, such as a dispute with Japan, India, Russia, Vietnam or Islamists in Xinjiang. This is unlikely to mean war, but might result in a war footing. It could mean militarisation of the unemployed, and perhaps a lot of the young, single men. After all, national security seemed to work as a re-election issue for George Bush in 2004. However, we should not forget that one of the lessons China drew from the Soviet Union's fall was that it should avoid overseas military adventures.

A military showdown with Taiwan could explode at any time. This would not necessarily be planned by either side, but any incident could spark the nationalistic passions of the mainland public in a manner that it would be dangerous for Beijing not to endorse. As with the First World War, this might lead all the way to (an undesired) war. Beijing might gamble that the world has been conditioned to accept that Taiwan is an 'internal' matter and no country will respond to any attack – beyond keeping its head down. Then again, the potential damage to China's international image could temper any tendency to hasty action.

One risk of an adventurist attack on Taiwan is that it could embroil China in a war with America. Wars can be limited – or they can become total. One distinct feature of liberal democracies at war is that they have such a strong sense of their own righteousness that they are reluctant to talk peace with their opponents. This was evident in both the First and the Second World Wars. Democracies thus have a tendency to wage total war rather than limited war and, believing they are morally right, they resist negotiating with their enemy. One hopes that China will not slip into a limited conflict with America only to find itself enmeshed in a global military morass. Whether or not America does come to Taiwan's aid, if China snuffs out the light on Taiwan's democracy it will sharply illuminate the world's impression of a future Chinese world order. Under the scholar's robe, there might be the glimpse of a jackboot.

China already shows a surprisingly adventurist streak in the field of cyber hostility. The risk calculus of Chinese decision-makers is unknown. Washington may have broken the norms of peacetime behaviour with Stuxnet (Chapter 13), but China's sponsored hackers cause cyber violence every week. Considering the PLA's less than dazzling performance during the Guangzhou railway crisis and the Sichuan earthquake, there must inevitably be some reservations about China's likely performance in a conventional external military conflict, but asymmetric warfare such as cyber activity could generate spectacular results. It is to be hoped this will not be put to the test.

Returning to the domestic arena (and thinking the unthinkable), perhaps China would be economically, socially, culturally and politically stronger and more stable if it unilaterally dropped Tibet, Inner Mongolia and Xinjiang (or parts of them) and possibly parts of Gansu, Qinghai and Sichuan. After all, Israel ultimately felt it would benefit by ceding Gaza. If the local people essentially want to go, it may not be worth the financial, political, diplomatic and social costs involved in preventing them. It is not clear that Turkey is better off with its share of Kurdistan, France with Corsica, Israel with large parts of Palestine, Russia with Chechnya – or England with Scotland. Academic work suggests that large-scale ethnic diversity saps economic growth. For China, huge security spending is a massive burden, preventing other more congenial options.

Thinking radically, China might be richer, more powerful, more stable, more respected, more modern, more secure and happier as a Han Chinese nation state with a cohesive view of itself, its history, its values and its goals – and, let's say, with 90–95 per cent of its current land mass. In other words, China could go back towards the borders of the Ming dynasty, rather than stick with most of those of the foreign and multiracial Qing empire. There would be complications over the waters rising on the Tibetan plateau and over the mineral and energy resources of Xinjiang (and its nuclear base). However, deals could be struck. There would be no need for existing provinces to go in their entirety – just those areas that would allow communities to live satisfactorily. Ethnic and political unity could be an important prize for China and well worth some detailed planning. Chinese leaders like to talk about the importance of unity: this is one clear route to achieving it.

If funding the growing international military projection and having an ever bigger domestic security apparatus to manage instability are preventing the full implementation of social programmes, it creates a vicious circle, since the weak social welfare then stokes further instability. Measures such as expatriating minority ethnic communities could help break this unfortunate symbiosis.

Having considered the minorities within, it might be useful to consider briefly the minorities from without. It is both a strength and a weakness that foreign people generally do not seem to wish to live in China. The Population Reference Bureau estimated that in 2009 there were 39 million immigrants in the US of whom almost 6 million were in low-paid work and 11 million were illegal;[18] in China the comparable figure was less than 600,000.[19]

A China-based migrant is likely to be an executive rather than a cleaner. China does not welcome unskilled labour. The fact that China can maintain strong ethnic unity, principally has executive and temporary immigrants and does not presently require cheap foreign labour are largely strengths. The disadvantage might be the shortage of better-educated foreign residents for technology transfer and other benefits.

Ironically, the all too evident Han nationalist elements in the country might conclude that China's national interest requires ending the excessive internal security costs (thus the ditching of the minorities), building a fair society for Chinese and creating a unitary cultural state; in other words, the opposite of what is seen as domestic nationalism today. This means the Party may one day be under pressure from those who feel that China's slender financial resources should be devoted to the Chinese. The 'de-repression dividend' could be a large cut in the $100 billion security budget. Perhaps surprisingly for those overseas, the effective opposition to current policy might not be the liberal democrats, but intransigent nationalists who choose an end to empire and the creation of a nation state.

The Party might adopt a neo-Confucian model, which could even be coupled with a 'Constantinian moment' in which religion is (in some shape) adopted officially. However, if Confucianism is not to be the sole model, there would need to be a multi-faith approach, as Christianity is spreading quite rapidly, as are the traditional religions of Buddhism and Daoism. The initiative could go further by offering large-scale religious recognition, on the basis that the interests of Church and State can be kept separate and in the twenty-first century do not need to be antagonistic. This has parallels with Putin's use of religion and adoption of the Russian Orthodox Church as a national bond; it could be an interesting model.

If religion continues to grow strongly – and if it can stand alongside the authorities rather than be seen as subversive – it might lend significant credibility to the state. We might find that a Chinese Christian is as much a Chinese as he is a Christian and thus possessed of a pronounced ethnocentric worldview. Here the 'house churches' of the Protestant sects (Chapter 8) lend themselves better to an accommodation with the nation state than the universal Catholic Church, which will always owe loyalty to Rome. If the PLA representatives in the National People's Congress are in future joined by delegates from the Christian churches, the Buddhist community and others, the Chinese legislature will increasingly resemble the British House of Lords, the Hong Kong Legco, or Mussolini's national assembly. It would continue Jiang Zemin's strategy of co-opting into the system all the key components of the community. Perhaps in 2022 the next president of China will visit the home of Confucius, a

Buddhist temple, Beijing's South Cathedral for a mass and a Protestant mega-church as part of his inauguration.

The authorities might eventually feel they should take an outrageous bet and seek some form of electoral mandate. The Party could co-opt those calling for greater participation in the civil process. It is quite possible that, if the ground was prepared carefully and the media used dextrously, that mandate would be resoundingly given. For example, democracy works in Singapore without threatening the ruling party – the media and the courts tend conveniently to follow the government's perspective on controversial issues. Despite the fact that the scale is so completely different, this could offer a model for China.

The Chinese authorities pay considerable attention to monitoring public opinion and try to be as attuned as any Western politician. This influences their decision-making. Leaders would do well to consider the historic British system of five-year terms, with the right of the government to call early elections on a date of its choosing. This, combined with the normal benefits of incumbency, tilts the balance of advantage significantly towards continuity. We may see a 'grand bargain' where the Party finally drops the historic rhetoric and rebrands itself as the national party. Dissidents might be offered greater civil participation. Many Chinese do not want revolving party government. Most might be satisfied with greater responsiveness from the existing system. One possible grand bargain would be a proposal for a loose association of Taiwan and China, in return for the introduction of universal suffrage on the mainland and the replacement of both flags with something new. It might not be hugely popular in Taiwan, but it could work if it promised an end to the continual threats from the PRC.

The authorities always stress the need for Chinese to love their country, with the implication that this is the same as loving the government and Party. But there should be a difference. To be a patriotic Chinese should mean loving one's country but discriminating between good and bad governments, good and bad policies. China's identity will never be satisfactorily resolved until the government respects truth.

The first thirty years of the PRC – from 1949 until 1979 – were objectively disastrous. There were some achievements in health and, of course, China became a nuclear power. It defeated India and Russia militarily and started a relationship with the US. Yet it was domestically bleak. If Mao had successfully purged Deng Xiaoping, and if his chosen successor Hua Guofeng had lasted in power, China would be a failure today. The Party is likely in future to find it a strength to reassess modern history in order to boost its credibility and enhance its popularity. Professor Jiang Mingan of Peking University noted in

2012: 'We are going through a peak period of social conflicts.'[20] It would be a prudent strategy for the Party to seek to unite the people around a platform of recognition of historic tragedies, reference to recent achievements and credible plans to continue China's rise. Truth and reconciliation broadly worked in South Africa. It is not correct that the Party's legitimacy relies on the denial of truth. Without courage and honesty it will be difficult for China to establish its identity this century. There should be no continuation of the denial seen during SARS, the Songhua River contamination (Chapter 6) or the death of children in the Sichuan earthquake. If the Party cannot unite in acceptance of recognition and renewal, it opens itself to the possibility of a Yeltsin-like senior defection which will reject the past and embrace the future.

Not only is it a debilitating waste of money to have a huge intelligence and security apparatus to stifle dissent, but more importantly it makes it difficult for the state to engage with its citizens on any discussion of moral values, since such debate will stray into uncomfortable areas. Just as the Soviet system had an uneasy ethical base – embracing localised ethics (such as condemning crime), yet unable to articulate generalised ethical standards such as human rights, free speech or rule of law – so China wobbles ambiguously in the face of moral issues. This has at least three disadvantages: there is a disorientation born of moral inconsistency, which leads to increased youth crime, drug use and other social disorders; countries become friends with China only because of trade and investment, not shared values; and when government officials have either to lie about something (e.g. the existence of 'black jails' for petitioners, or torture in detention) because it conflicts with the laws or the constitution or to justify it as being in conformity, they undermine respect both for themselves and for the state.

If the Party risks initiating and leading a moral renovation of China, with all the collateral aspects that this implies, it will have the opportunity to open doors to a far greater destiny for the country – and the Party – in the wider world. It also makes it far more likely that it will achieve the much-longed-for reunification with Taiwan. If the Guomindang and the PRI in Mexico could successfully transform themselves from presiding over a dictatorship to ruling on democratic mandates, then it is not beyond the ability of a highly competent CCP. However, perhaps the best models are Singapore, Russia or Iran where opposition is a theoretical concept.

The Party is likely to adapt to the challenging new environment by co-opting some of the disaffected and by developing new strategies, in order to secure its overlapping objectives of maintaining social stability and retaining power. It will need to reconsider the requirements of 'performance legitimacy', for social stability and rising prosperity (if still maintainable) will no longer be enough.

The Party must deal with the additional issues of healthcare, environment and corruption. This is possible, but it will require serious changes in the way political power is exercised. The other challenge will be the extent to which it has the courage to revisit its national frontiers and acknowledge its history.

Conditions which exist elsewhere cause severe distress when present in China: for example, levels of income inequality which in America are regarded as inequitable are felt in China to be insupportable. Clumsy or insensitive behaviour in Japan or America (e.g. visits to the Yasukinu Shrine) can cause paroxysms of fury in China. The problem is that when young Chinese are educated in the importance of egalitarianism, they believe it. Of course, if young people are told they live in a socialist state based on equality and justice, they are offended not only by the inequality but by a widespread perception that those who enjoy greater wealth have achieved it improperly. Worse, though, is the fact that wealth is seen by the Chinese public as arising not from enterprise but from systemic corruption.

Many Chinese, through no fault of their own, look back through a fog of science, literature and economics and believe – with Henry Kissinger, but against all historical evidence – that China once 'had its moment' on the world stage and somehow will regain that moment. It is to the Party's credit that notions of superpower status take a much lower priority than the potentially more achievable objective of remaining in power. The latter may lead, for example, to a strategic shift from military to social spending. And if the real enemy is internal insecurity rather than external, the focus could change in a different way.

While considering issues of identity, we should note the point that Ian Morris has raised, that developments in global science may come to affect much of what we have discussed: 'The new technologies . . . might also have the effect of putting us into a passive, sensory-laden state where our personalised brains – our minds – become less relevant'.[21] If in future 'brains may merge man and machine' or humans may be able to live for 150 years through the use of artificial chips as medical monitors, any considerations of which society will eventually dominate may not be a simple choice between China and America.[22] Indeed, perhaps mankind in the last one or two millennia has been enjoying living in a brief interlude between being dominated by nature and being dominated by science. What is clear is that identity is contested and stability is weak.

Central Asia and Xinjiang

China has assiduously built regional links with Muslim states. The Central Asian Muslim states, except Turkmenistan, are in the SCO. Pakistan is closely allied to China, and Bangladesh is being armed by China. However, if trouble spreads amongst the 8 million Uighurs in remote Xinjiang province and the scale of fighting intensifies, we could easily see far more bloody incidents like the ones in Kashgar in 2008 and Urumqi in 2009. Xinjiang Muslims are Sunni, and so many of their neighbours might support them. Today, in gratitude for Chinese support, Pakistan swears to eliminate Uighur training camps; tomorrow the government could have other priorities. For example, in 2011, Kazakhstan's surprising plans to send troops to Afghanistan were ended by radical Islamic violence. The same goes for the rest of the region. As America and its allies wind down in Afghanistan, China may need to offer recognition to the forces which are de facto in control of much of the country. A Karzai truce with the Taliban would free them to export their ideas to neighbouring territories. It would be unfortunate if Beijing's own domestic policies caused radicalisation of the hitherto quietist Muslims in Xinjiang. It would be undesirable for China to be on the front line of a radical Islamic advance; but if it were to be, it could offer a stronger response if it had a united Han nation behind it. That is one reason for dissociating itself from the Uighurs and Tibetans (see pp.266–7).

If Pakistan collapses into the hands of Islamists they will receive nuclear weapons and a large conventional army. We saw how quickly the process can play out with the fall of the Shah of Iran in 1979. There might then be a reluctant scramble by India, Iran, America and China to intervene – on some humanitarian pretext or with world support – to secure the nuclear facilities. As China supplied some of the technology and is Pakistan's closest ally, there is a certain logic in China assuming the role. However, such intervention might be as popular as that of the British, the Soviets and the Americans in Afghanistan. Furthermore, China is currently unenthusiastic about foreign adventures.

This sets the issue squarely on the table: is China a superpower, or even a regional power? Bangladesh may find that its love affair with China is dimmed by any reduction in the flow of the Brahmaputra (and by its own rising interest in a 'Muslim' foreign policy). Although Dhaka has assisted Beijing on Tibetan issues, it might not be helpful in the longer term. Tibet scarcely features here because we are discussing important challenges to China. Tibet is a large territory with a very small population and no potential allies abroad. Even Buddhist countries such as Thailand, Sri Lanka and Bhutan are neutralised on the Tibet question. There are few signs of foreign resistance to China's presence and actions there. Britain's nuanced declaration of accepting China's 'suzerainty', as opposed to sovereignty, has been dropped. If India changes its position it is more likely to agree a frontier deal, and maybe even a closer relationship with Beijing, at the price of a cession of Tawang to China (see Chapter 11). Tibet's situation is very different from Xinjiang's, as the Uighurs might well find foreign assistance and wage an effective struggle. For Tibet, that possibility appears closed. The situation is not precisely as depicted in the West. Tibetans and Chinese regard each other with mutual incomprehension: Chinese cannot understand why Tibetans are so ungrateful for the modernisation they bring, while Tibetans don't understand why the Chinese are there.

Any act that heightens conflict in Central Asia could transform Xinjiang from the scene of a low-intensity conflict to the venue for a full-fledged war. Given the failure of the US war in Afghanistan, the possibility of the collapse of its ally Pakistan, and perhaps even an Islamist insurrection throughout Central Asia, China may face serious problems in Xinjiang. Blessed with one of the most peaceable Muslim communities in the world, the surprise is that Beijing has adopted policies in Xinjiang in recent decades which have encouraged radicalisation. If Islamist challenges markedly increase on China's borders and within, or if Pakistan collapses, Beijing might just consider building an alliance with its rival – India – to meet new circumstances with a new strategy. China could make a grand bargain with India, reverse their mutual coolness and form a joint alliance against the Islamist tide. This would have the perverse effect of bringing about a rapprochement between Asia's two contending superpowers.

China has only one choice for a strong ally in Asia. For historical and practical reasons it is unlikely to choose Russia or Japan. This renders a volte-face on the Sino-Indian relationship not entirely unimaginable. It might look like a cynical rerun of the Molotov–Ribbentrop pact, but it would be logical. If the price of such an alliance was final settlement of the Sino-Indian border issue, both countries would be free to deploy their troops where they might soon need to fight some real wars. The next phase of the Sino-Indian encounter could involve a real clash of cultures and values. Alliance with China might be a marriage of convenience; but those can often be stronger – and longer lasting – than romances.

Governance

As mentioned above, China has good laws but poor implementation. This applies, for example, in intellectual property rights, which Cao Cong of the State University of New York has said are 'as perfect as those promulgated in other countries'.[23] There is good, sensible environmental legislation. The problem is implementation failure. SOEs have often made profits, frequently through their quasi-monopoly positions or privileged low interest rates, but those limited dividends they have paid have not normally arrived in government income. As a result, the national budget is squeezed, corporate savings are excessive and investment is often profligate and ineffective. Better corporate governance by the state over state enterprises is vital. Appropriate governance could also arrest the abysmal degree of managerial corruption through asset diversion, and thus more effectively protect public finances. There are extensive regulations and laws against corruption but state leaders imply the situation has deteriorated. China has subscribed to human rights declarations and has various rights built into its constitution, but several officials, even in 2009, said there is torture in jails and 'black jails' where abuses take place (see Chapter 8). So there is a chasm in China between law and practice. What is the problem with implementation? Is it that economic development is so important that, to this day, no one has the energy for anything else? Or is there a culture that passing legislation is an end in itself, while acting on it is unnecessary? Or an argument that China is such a large country that observing the law is bound to be optional?

A counter-intuitive disadvantage of China's diverse and decentralised governing structure is that it is sometimes difficult to achieve things. The current system, by which officials are deployed to their posts, monitored and promoted, does not, in practice, generate accountability. Relationships, or *guanxi*, are important in careers and it is difficult to combine genuine performance appraisal with a relationship culture (see Chapter 7). According to Chinese media, there is a widespread culture of officials buying their posts and thus needing to recoup their 'investment' by all possible means. A target-based promotion system for officials has several defects: the wrong targets get priority, there are too many targets, and the statistics are fudged to reach targets; it also leads to short-term thinking and can encourage unlawful activity in order for the targets to be met. It might be the best of the options, but it certainly has to be managed much more carefully.

The fall of Chongqing Party Secretary Bo Xilai in 2012 may have dealt a blow to the emergence of a 'communicating politics', where politicians build a public profile and rapport as part of staking their claim to power within the system. While populism might be controversial, cultivating popularity and communicating directly with the people need not be. Bo's demise may have shored up the grey collectivity of contemporary Party politics. If he had achieved partial success, others with different politics might have been encouraged to step forward using similar methods.

Whither Hegemony?

China may not seek hegemony, but – along with Russia, Islam and France (and, in its wake, the European Union) – it does desire to end American hegemony.

India wants only to be taken seriously, eventually, as one of the great powers. Each of the first four aspiring powers has its own way of looking at the world.

Islam is confused in the twenty-first century about what its world-view is, and is also largely paralysed logistically. Traditional Muslims are obliged to live in a world where American values are imposed unilaterally which conflict with their values. They would prefer to see American hegemony end. However, there is no single Islamic global power. Neither Saudi Arabia, nor Iran, nor Indonesia is inclined (or able) to challenge America and make the world more suited to Islamic life. Extremists may fight asymmetrical wars, but there is currently no rising power that holds to Islamic values and can offer an alternative world vision to that of America. Most importantly, Islam is not really a nation-state religion.

France has always had an idea of itself as distinct from the 'Anglo-Saxon world' and its values. It has a distinct conception of society based on a state-controlled economy, high taxation, 'solidarity', rigid labour markets and 'social partnerships'. It is deeply conscious that its attempts in earlier centuries to attain global leadership failed conspicuously. Accepting that its contrary values cannot prevail globally through the agency of France alone, it has adopted a strategy of promoting some form of 'European global leadership' to replace the United States – and, to a much lesser extent, Britain. Despite recently increasing its links, this involves gently sidelining NATO and promoting a European army, a diplomatic service, bending before Russia as a supplicant, enlarging its boundaries until the combined notional economy becomes more important than that of the US, and supervising it in a *dirigiste* manner to the taste of the Western Europeans. This vision is irrespective of political party (indeed most major political parties in continental Western Europe are of the Centre Left, whatever they may call themselves). The weakness of the strategy is that it relies on enlargement to challenge America, but the price of enlargement is to hold together a supremely unsympathetic British public, a market-oriented Eastern Europe, and later possibly even an increasingly eastward-looking and Muslim Turkey. This house is unlikely to be sustainable, let alone capable of unseating America. Indeed its security depends on America.

Russia would dearly like to see the end of American hegemony. However, the Russian leadership is sufficiently realistic to know that its best realisable goal is to retain dominance in the former Soviet sphere and, if all goes well, to further develop its 'influence' over the European Union. Russia may regain the Caucasus, including Georgia, assisted by President Obama's need for support on Iran. Putin can apply the new Russo-Turkish 'Monroe Doctrine' against America in the Caucasus and the Black Sea. The 2010 Ukrainian elections provided a good opportunity. However, Russia is losing out to China in parts of

Central Asia. Russia's destiny, if it does well, is to become a top regional power; but not to challenge for hegemony.

The only rising power which has economic strength, political unity and clear purpose is China. Certainly, economic strength can be sapped, unity can be compromised and purpose can wane, but China is currently the most likely country to be effective in challenging America's perceived hegemony. However, it has been asserted that since 1500 'no rising challenger, however capable, has ever succeeded, at least thus far, in supplanting any prevailing hegemony through cold or hot war'.[24] It has tended to be the leading powers in winning coalitions. This means retaining more power than its allies, as well as its enemies. It also means having key allies, which in China's case is not at present evident.

With the clear rise of international influence in distant continents, from Brazil, Turkey and Iran, the obvious superiority of America and the potential rise of China over all others, we may say the world today is beginning to take on a new shape. That would be what the academics call polycentric: 'with two preeminent centres of military power and multiple centres of political decision'.[25]

A Rising Power

Sir Robert Hart was Inspector General of China's Maritime Customs from 1868 until 1907. This was perhaps the period of the country's maximum prostration; nonetheless he forecast that the Chinese would one day be 'armed, drilled, disciplined and animated by patriotic – if mistaken – motives' and would 'take back from foreigners everything that foreigners have taken from them and pay off old grudges with interest': 'They will carry the Chinese flag and Chinese armies into many a place that even fancy will not suggest today, thus preparing for the future, upheavals and disasters never even dreamt of'.[26] This may be a little gloomy, but it does demonstrate that, even in the worst of times, observers have believed in China's capacity to recover.

What would it actually mean for China to become the world's superpower? In terms of the financial architecture, it would mean supplying the lion's share of the funding for multilateral institutions – if it retains them. It would be in a position to appoint the senior officials in the World Bank, the IMF and the ADB, and would help to guide their policies. A step forward was taken in 2011 when the widely respected Zhu Min was appointed a deputy managing director of the IMF. One issue is how easy it would be for a Chinese official to cease to be a national spokesman and adopt a truly independent role. If China eventually takes the helm of the financial system, in the broader sense of exercising leadership, it might entail changing the world's reserve currency arrangements. It could mean restructuring the UN Security Council, although that body currently seems to suit Beijing well. Perhaps, as we have seen with the UN Human Rights Council, countries will not be elevated because of their adherence to human rights and democracy, but because of their capability and willingness to play a role and give mutual support. If Iran could give $1 billion in aid, and Gaddafi's Libya $500 million, to a small country like Sri Lanka, perhaps it will be the scale of states' munificence that will raise them to a more influential role in a new dispensation. China is currently being quite sparing with its funding for international organisations. This may be because it refuses to fund in excess of its voting weight. At the same time, in the private sector, a Chinese company official was chosen in 2011 as the President of the World Steel Association, prompting the *Financial Times* to call it 'one of the first incidences of a Chinese manager taking the helm of a big global industry body'.[27]

Its new status might imply a Chinese military presence overseas. Having recognised that the fall of the Soviet empire underlined the futility of overseas military adventures, China could be obliged to change this stance either because of the peril posed by a collapse of nuclear Pakistan or because superpower responsibility requires increased intervention in the world's conflicts, either as peacekeeper or participant. Or it might arise because the scale of China's investments in volatile countries eventually requires a defensive military presence to ensure security of trade routes, contracts and investments or to cement alliances with political leaders. This is not so different from British policy in the eighteenth and nineteenth centuries or French policy in Africa after 1960.

It could also mean China going beyond its UN participation and acting as arbiter or peacekeeper in many regional conflicts, as American troops did in Serbia and Somalia. We will know China has arrived on the world stage when it engages in arbitrating problems in the Caribbean or becomes a fifth member of the Quartet on the future of Palestine.

The neo-mercantilist policy China is pursuing on energy and food resources is not unique: several Middle Eastern countries are behaving likewise, while Daewoo and other private investors have similar strategies. China, for environmental reasons, would like to reduce its reliance on its abundant but low-quality domestic coal and replace it with the cleaner fuels with which it is less well endowed. It has not succeeded in rolling back the overall level of desertification. Thus it does not expect to produce either enough clean energy or food to meet its needs through the century. Furthermore, the world will probably witness millions of climate refugees, interruptions to supply routes, and market pricing that is volatile and rising. All this encourages Chinese officials to invest now or commit to long-term financial contracts to secure direct access to oilfields, gas supplies and food acreage. However, this strategy has led China to some of the most remote and unstable regions and has involved deals with some of the most controversial regimes. In 2012, total Chinese direct investment worldwide – concentrated in the developing world – was estimated at over $400 billion; it is forecast to reach $1-2 trillion by 2020.[28]

There are four problems with the strategy: the investments are often unprofitable; state enterprises executing it are unlikely to be chosen for privatisation, thus blocking economic reform; the very disruptions anticipated – climatic, economic and political – are likely to imperil delivery of the production which is acquired; and political change in volatile regions can hamper contract enforcement. In an increasingly volatile world, governments may lose control of society and become failed states or they may rise to the challenge of change. Even in the more benign outcome, there is no guarantee that such governments will prioritise the law of contract over feeding their own people. Adopting foreign policy realism, one can befriend governments rather than their publics – providing the strategy is sustainable. Unfortunately, in a politically volatile region, any upheaval could easily endanger such a long-term and high-cost strategy. And any contracts signed by those later deemed to be 'dictators' might not be honoured.

Would turmoil in remote, resource-rich nations cause China to consider enforcing its contracts militarily? American troops can look somewhat crass in a traditional Islamic society; what reactions would be evoked by a Chinese military detachment arriving in Zambia to enforce delivery of copper or – worse – food? Could Beijing meet its Afghanistan in the 2020s? It seems unlikely that there is enough fondness for China in Africa to allow non-military solutions to contract enforcement. The picture of smiling Congolese cleaning the windscreens of Chinese lorries as they take the last food supplies out of Kinshasa is inherently implausible. The financial problem arising from China's direct investment overseas is that the sums are very large – and are rising rapidly. This makes it increasingly difficult, if events go badly, to put them down to misfortune. It may prove necessary to contest any regime change that leads to expropriation.

A further dimension is human. As China's commercial interests spread internationally, Chinese citizens have been harmed or threatened in recent years in at least twenty-seven countries. There have been kidnappings and killings, protests and riots. One example is the Chinese-built Ramu mine in Papua New Guinea, where local workers protested violently against conditions which Labour Minister David Tibu described as 'not fit for pigs or dogs'.[29] This was perhaps a result of somewhat 'retro' labour practices, but the Chinese do frequently display a degree of racial disdain. With every additional investment abroad, such incidents become more likely. Beijing leaders, being politicians, are much more focused on domestic than on foreign opinion. This may eventually result in Beijing feeling obliged to pursue military initiatives. Furthermore, we should not ignore the ethnocentric perception of many Chinese that all Chinese are in some sense 'citizens of China', whatever passport they may happen to carry. As noted earlier, this was one cause of the 1979 war against Vietnam. It allows China to be pressured to intervene in race riots in Indonesia or disturbances in Calcutta if people of Chinese origin are seen to be in danger.

China could nowadays have a challenge sprung on it almost anywhere in the world. If the giant cruise ship *Oasis of the Seas* with 6,000 Chinese tourists on board were captured or sunk off the Zanzibar coast by Islamist militants based in Somalia, in response to a crackdown on Xinjiang Muslims, would public opinion oblige Beijing to order military action against the Somali bases? Since al-Qaeda's North African affiliate condemned China and declared it a target for its behaviour in Xinjiang in 2009, the scenario cannot be ruled out. This gives China a global security requirement. To depend for security on the Congolese or Zimbabwean army is perhaps optimistic. But the possession of global force projection is a double-edged sword: taxpayers and 'netizens' may demand that it be occasionally unsheathed.

Being outside the 100 richest countries per capita is an impediment to China's becoming the world's superpower. While enormous steps have been taken against poverty – the country's poverty rate has fallen (1990–2010) from 62 per cent to 12 per cent – China's poor are still an eighth of the world's poor.[30] Although the Party may use nationalist sentiment to trump Han social unrest, the income inequality gap might eventually put such pressure on social spending that the state will be unable to maintain its military expenditure.

Undoubtedly China observes and analyses America closely. If America behaves in certain ways, China will feel perfectly free to do the same when the time comes. It will not accept that there is one law for America and a different one for China. Thus an issue for the world to consider may be the future unintended consequences of US unilateralism. To give one example, the US has pursued a policy of targeted assassination of resistance leaders in Pakistan and Afghanistan using Predator drones. Civilians have been disproportionately killed as collateral damage.[31] Israel has used similar tactics against Palestinian fighters with similar results. Israeli politicians and generals are accordingly finding it difficult to travel for fear of arrest under international warrants for war crimes charges.[32] There has been discussion of whether similar action should be taken against US officials for their actions in Iraq and Afghanistan.

While America is likely to be able to shrug off this threat thanks to its international position, it is unclear what lessons Beijing will learn from this.

Two parallel tendencies are evident. Beijing appears to be increasingly willing to take unilateral actions which are not popular with the leading developed nations (e.g. its negotiating stance at the Copenhagen climate conference in 2009 or the jailing of Nobel Prize-winning dissident Liu Xiaobo). On the other hand the world seems less willing to hold China publicly accountable for its actions. The IMF's response to unfair African contracts was to bully the African government concerned, not the country that drafted the contracts. America, while willing to be provocative in the South China Sea with its naval manoeuvres, chooses not to say anything publicly about the preservation of Taiwanese democracy, which might be considered by some a core US value under threat.

China's willingness to slight Western sentiment seems to be growing *pari passu* with the decline in Western censoriousness. We may be moving into a new phase in history, where states are reorienting their behaviour in anticipation of an as yet unannounced new world order. No one has used the word 'appeasement' – yet. Some governments may have unconsciously decided that placatory behaviour is now more appropriate than censure, as certain milestones have been reached in the rise of China. This does not mean that passivity will inevitably dominate their behaviour from now on: China *may* take steps that are so threatening to other powers that they adopt an active response. But nothing in that sentence is certain. The world could consider engaging with rising China on the basis of equality. That is, neither to disdain her for being not entirely a cultural or technological leader, nor propitiate her and accept her demands without deep reflection.

There is a well-funded Beijing campaign to win hearts and minds in the West through intense media activity. Chinese culture, language and cuisine are all brought to bear. However, in the West it is possible to distinguish between traditional culture and contemporary government. It is possible to enjoy good Chinese food and yet deplore the jailing of dissidents. What this campaign overlooks is the fact that it is not *ignorance* of China that causes unease, but *knowledge* of it: for many people overseas, the more they know of China, the more unease they feel about its current path.

The return of America to Asia, combined with the success (albeit at a high price) of US drone technology, might suggest to Beijing a strategy within East Asia of building friendships. However, despite suggestions of a revived tributary system, the reality is that amongst China's neighbours there are today more countries which are nervous than friendly. If it is difficult to cultivate friendships with neighbours, will it be difficult to become accepted as the world's superpower? Beijing's strategy towards its neighbours leads many to encourage a greater US regional presence.

Influential countries may start to ponder the nature of China's values and character as it rises. Hitherto, since the 'Nixon breakthrough', the tendency has been to see certain issues through China's prism. It was a condition of establishing relations that Taiwan should be expelled from the formal global community: the PRC would not accept its recognition as a distinct political entity – a state. This occasionally causes problems, but international leaders have largely acquiesced. However, as China continues to flex its muscles on the global stage, some may start to reflect on the desirability of aiming over 1,000 warheads at this vibrant democracy. Foreign leaders may begin to ask whether – if they accepted self-determination in Kosovo – they should tolerate coercion in the Taiwan Strait. When they try to assess the outlook for a world cohabiting with a 'risen China', they may wonder whether they acted too hastily in acceding to demands which, in retrospect, conflict with their values, and without China making similar sacrifices. Will China's relationship with the world, on close analysis, look unilateral? If so, will it stay like that?

There may well be aspects of today's China that, if magnified through projection into a new world order, could cause dismay to other countries. However, little in this world is certain. Considering how much the country has changed in the last thirty years, it would be an unwise observer who believes that China in 2040 will be just like China in 2010. If a Chinese-dominated world does emerge, it may not be informed by the virtues, vices or appetites of today.

We can see that there are some countries whose success is not helpful to China. Japan – a democracy and until recently the second-largest economy in the world – is regarded by many Chinese with a mixture of dislike, envy and contempt. Taiwan's imprisonment of its previous independence-leaning President was leaped on by the Chinese state media (see Chapter 7), but the notions that an ethnic Chinese society could pursue corruption to the top, that no one is above the law and that in a democracy all must be accountable, have come as revelations to the Chinese public which Beijing may in time regret. India is the world's largest democracy. If it delivers consistently high growth with political stability, it is a threat to China's political model because it suggests that developing countries could have both prosperity and democracy. These are three states that will not go out of their way to smooth the path of China's rise.

Earlier, we noted that China, Russia, France and Iran would all like to see the end of American hegemony and its replacement by a multi-polar world led by several great powers. Yet this in itself creates difficulty for the idea of China's rise beyond a point of acceptable parity. After that, any additional projection of force and accretion of authority is likely to generate hostility from the other world powers. The 'sunset powers' such as Russia and France are likely to be defensive of their prerogatives in the face of the 'sunrise powers' of India and (arguably) China. This leads to the conclusion that China's rise, insofar as it needs external assistance, will come from its growing links with developing countries, or client states, in Africa, South East Asia and Latin America. However, it is still important for Beijing not to antagonise so many countries that there is a move to 'check China'. In particular, China cannot afford to alienate the bigger developing countries of Brazil, Indonesia, South Africa, Turkey and, of course, India. They have certain policy imperatives in common with China, but also important issues which divide them: in 2010, India and Brazil publicly criticised China's currency policy. The dividing lines are not democracy versus autocracy, but are much more subtle and are likely to shift. Even smaller countries which come into contact with China do not all become Sinophile.

We might observe in passing that modern crisis research suggests that a bipolar world is the most stable; a multi-polar one less so; and that 'polycentrism' – with two great powers and a number of lesser centres – involves the greatest stress, crisis and violence. We may be heading for this third option.[33]

China should consider how it is viewed during the interregnum between the American past and its own possibly enhanced future status. If it is regarded as needlessly provocative towards Japan and threatening to Taiwan, as arms dealer to the world's dictatorships, as antagonistic to a border treaty with India, and as the latest neo-colonial power in Africa, few states are likely to rally to its cause. Muslim countries may initially stay quiet about Xinjiang riots for reasons of trade and diplomacy; but when the issue is no longer one of 10 million co-religionists, but one of who will lead the world, they may develop greater activism. After all, China's superior popularity over America in the Islamic world is not Beijing's success but Washington's failure. China's apparently uninhibited use of advanced cyber power against other countries raises real questions as to how comfortable and congenial a superpower it would be. America, with its close link with Israel, may be a flawed leader for the world, but China would probably be even less acceptable to many.

To the outside world, China expresses no remorse or timidity; it is supremely confident in the rightness of its behaviour. However, it has engaged in, and is continuing to perform, many activities at home and abroad which other countries and people find offensive and frightening.

We might ask how far others can reasonably go in criticising China. Observers may say it is offensive for China to 'bully' Australia or India, but isn't

Table 16.1: **China Takes a Hard Line in Foreign Policy**

- 'punishing' France for meeting the Dalai Lama
- shielding Sri Lanka diplomatically from war crimes criticism
- pressuring the Melbourne Film Festival to drop a film China didn't like
- shielding Burma from criticism and sanctions
- aiming over 1,000 missiles at Taiwan
- denying India loans from the Asia Development Bank
- training Central Asian police and judges in its idea of judicial procedures
- applying pressure to change the guest list of authors at the Frankfurt Book Fair
- training and arming paramilitary police for African dictatorships
- increasing its non-negotiable 'core interests' in East Asia

that what the United States does by threatening to withdraw military support from Pakistan if Islamabad belatedly follows Washington into the nuclear club? When other countries bribe or torture, they usually say it is for 'national security' reasons. The means are felt to justify the end. Some may see a moral equivalence between US methods of interrogating terrorism suspects and elements of the Chinese judicial system. One can probably compare China only with the US, because other powers are less able to take equivalent actions.

China's behaviour in persuading and preventing might be more blatant than America's, but it has stopped short of declaring war on countries (since Vietnam in 1979). Unlike America, China has not announced a doctrine of pre-emptive war (though it could be argued that the Battle of Johnson Reef against Vietnam in 1988 or the cyber activity since 2000 constitute undeclared war). It could also be argued that China's actions are less harmful – in scope and scale – than America's invasions. America's period of hegemony was marked by many features which others found distasteful. Now it looks as if China is capable of provoking concern as well. The problem may be that, in its decline, America has littered the diplomatic world with justifications for dubious tactics.

China provided some interesting comparative material in 2010, when it berated Japan for arresting a Chinese trawler crew who approached the contested Senkaku (Diaoyu) islands and became enmeshed in conflict. Nationalist emotion was inflamed. China demanded an apology from Japan and the Japanese ambassador was called into the Chinese foreign ministry six times to receive protests. Yet, in a different island dispute, in the South China Sea, China regularly rams and sinks Vietnamese fishing vessels and once held several hundred fishermen for over a year, demanding money from their families. Unilateralism is not unique to America. If China believes that the preceding superpower – America – has shown loose ethical standards and decides to follow suit, it is not creating a specifically Chinese world order, merely filling a vacuum by behaving like America. We still know almost nothing about the texture of a Chinese-led new world order. Some modern Chinese philosophers have suggested that China's lack of religion leads to an absence of transcendence and thus an inability to contemplate universal values. Whatever the values of China in coming decades, in projecting them the state may declare fewer wars than America, because of concern about domestic fragility and weakness. The world might prefer leadership by a power which, though belligerent, is unable to declare wars owing to deep internal fissures. America may have projected itself more successfully because it is not an ethnic empire and so can co-opt others to its value system. For better or worse, it is difficult to imagine any Chinese leader echoing then US Defense Secretary Robert Gates: 'I am very much an American exceptionalist and I believe that we are, as a country, the greatest force for good in the history of the world.'[34]

In the Republican period, China was involved in multilateral diplomacy, and Mao's China espoused sympathy for the Third World and international communism. We don't know what today's China may later propose, but since 1979 it has never shown any values beyond the interests of an ethnic nation state.

One of the differences between America and China is the mode of decision-making. Washington often appears to take decisions relatively lightly, without detailed consideration and often with no sense of the historical background. China is likely to use its habitual approach, which Li Ruogu has called the 'gradual decision-making' model.[35] In this sense, a Chinese world order is likely to be less radical and developments are likely to be more considered. There will be the opportunity to adjust if the results are unsatisfactory. This is not to disagree with Alastair Johnston's analysis of China as a country that is historically prone to take the aggressive road rather than the pacific one, providing it has the strength and funding.[36] Thus the last thirty years (or even 200 years) of a poorer and weaker China are no guide to its strategy once it is strong. The likelihood is that China will be fully open to the option of war, but, before acting, will give greater consideration than America to all the issues.

There are contradictions in many areas of Chinese society, such as a mixed economy with elements of state domination and elements of laissez-faire.

Social life is also divided: some areas are tightly supervised, others are free. Politics is restricted, but one can freely express one's views on social matters. The vocal elements of China's public are quite nationalist, while the government is more restrained. China is officially atheist yet there are more Christians than members of the Communist Party. China runs an interventionist state domestically but has generally favoured non-interventionism overseas.

The world will want to know the future shape of a Chinese-influenced world order. What are China's distinctive values? Should we judge China by the countries to which it is close? Which are those? Are they in the SCO – Russia and the Central Asia republics? Or are they Pakistan, Venezuela, Sri Lanka and Cambodia? China's friends are not generally open societies. An aspiring power's choice of friends – and enemies – could give us insights into what it thinks, likes and believes. Indeed it might be thought curious to suggest that any country has values rather than interests. Perhaps the choice of friends and enemies is the closest we can get to ascribing values to a country.

However, reference to values is not a westerner being somewhat precious. America will find that after Guantanamo, Abu Ghraib, extraordinary rendition, torture and assassination, it is taken less seriously on the subject of values – particularly after 2010, as its actions then were seen to be sanctioned by both the Bush and Obama administrations. However, from a pragmatic viewpoint, this is America in its decline. When America was rising, many felt its values were clear and noble. It might be hard for China to rise by copying America in its decline.

It is easier to become the superpower if no one is occupying that position. It is also easier to succeed if yesterday's global leader has no strong army of consistent friends. America has smoothed the path for China by weakening or damaging many of its international friendships and by not making enough new ones amongst other powers. Beijing, by rarely using its UN veto, demonstrates that it is broadly on the same wavelength as a large proportion of the world, whether nice or nasty. However, by blocking Brazil, Japan and India from permanent membership of the Security Council, it is creating antipathy amongst rising powers. There is some contradiction here with its environmental diplomacy, which saw it hammer out a deal at Copenhagen with large developing powers such as India and South Africa, which was seen as inimical by some of the smaller and poorer powers. There seems to be inconsistency in China's alliance-building.

There are three ways for China to become the world's superpower. The first is by military force. The second is because the world welcomes the arrival of non-American leadership and has decided China is desirable. The third is if China becomes so financially strong and America so weak that only China can fulfil the role and responsibilities, and therefore its rise is inevitable. The first is a long way off. The second doesn't seem on the cards for the moment. The third condition hasn't arrived yet.

Culture and Society

During this inquiry, several cultural or social issues have arisen which illuminate aspects of the Chinese character. The 2008 Pew Survey noted that over one-fifth of all Chinese believed that China was then the world's leading economic power. Only a third completely agreed with the statement that to succeed today's children must learn English. Premier Wen estimated that 300 million might be learning English, but we should assume that many will drop it and many others will not become proficient. China is not about to become an anglophone society.

Pew in 2008 asked how Chinese people believed they were perceived and compared that with how they actually were. It was noted in Chapter 15 that Chinese people are not aware that they are not universally admired. The point here is not the country's unpopularity (which can always change) but the Chinese lack of sensitivity to the outside world. Self-absorption appears to overshadow self-awareness.

This self-absorption was reinforced when, in 2009, *Chinese History Revisited* was banned. The book 'reflects on how traditional Chinese teaching, with its emphasis on obedience to authority, and the centralisation of power had caused the decline of Chinese civilisation – and its need of diversity, openness and an outward-looking environment'.[37] Of course, this was not the first book to be banned in modern China. Other examples are *River Elegy* and *The Ugly Chinese*. As Professor Hu Xingdou of Beijing University of Technology says: 'Chinese civilisation lacks self-reflection. That's why books like *The Ugly Chinese* and *River Elegy* were banned.'[38]

The education system is frequently criticised for using history textbooks which demonise foreign involvement in China's history and lionise acts by Chinese. The celebrated best-selling Chinese historian and history video producer Yuan Tengfei is characteristically blunt about this: 'There is maybe only 5 per cent truth in Chinese [history] textbooks.'[39] This breeds nationalism and weakens the ability to come to a dispassionate view of international problems.

Another example of Chinese self-absorption is the shrill official denunciations of perceived hostile behaviour overseas. Those who came up with *serpent* and *prostitute* to describe former Hong Kong Governor Chris Patten or *a jackal with a wolf's heart* for the Dalai Lama have reintroduced political badinage scarcely seen since Georgian England. When the world regards nascent China, is it seeing a state incarnating the wisdom and balance of four millennia of civilisation?

While noting earlier in this chapter China's domestic policy timidity, its diplomacy is a world apart. China's foreign policy is littered with demands for people to 'justify' themselves and to 'be punished'; these demands are often used in conjunction with the adverb 'sternly'. The woolly liberals on the 2010 Nobel Prize committee were probably surprised to be described as 'clowns' and to have their decision to award the Peace Prize to Liu Xiaobo branded an 'obscenity'. When four recent award-winners demanded that Liu be released, a Chinese foreign ministry spokesman said rather illogically that 'this is an obscenity against the Peace Prize'. China threatened that 'ties with Norway would suffer'. Their arbitrary change of focus caused an explosion in Scotland's bemused salmon industry.

When Asian countries bordering China's Pacific claims discussed security cooperation, Beijing declared that 'certain countries . . . think as long as they can balance China with the help of US military power, they are free to do whatever they want'.[40] When, in 1999, the then President of Taiwan, Lee Teng-hui, described his policy of engagement with the mainland as 'state-to-state relations' he was called 'a rat' and 'the sinner of 1,000 years'.[41] Such language is less that of a venerable elder statesman and more that of the newest street gang leader. Either Chinese officials are autistically oblivious of the effect of such outbursts of diplomatic rap music, or they speak externally for the sole benefit of a domestic audience. This latter interpretation might be understandable, but the impression given is of China blending hyperbole and apoplexy to create diplomacy.

If we consider the environmental degradation, the industrial manufacture of counterfeit goods, the return of extreme markets (where anything can be bought), the cyber hostility and the careful avoidance of historical truth, we must wonder whether China is building a society devoid of culture or moral standards.[42] Is China the country that goes too far?

Earlier, in Chapter 3, we saw how the writer Lu Xun and some of his contemporaries considered the Chinese personality to lack integrity and honesty. Ai Weiwei says that, owing to the Cultural Revolution, 'humanity' is the quality most lacking in modern China. Earlier in this chapter, Professor Hu Xingdou tells us that 'Chinese civilisation lacks self-reflection'. All races have their personality characteristics or attributes, and these help to differentiate them. Usually some general characteristics are good, and some less so. America is often accused of isolationism and of not being attuned to the outside world. However, in the case of contemporary China the issue is probably greater. If differentiating features include a lack of self-reflection and frankness, we should ponder whether this might make it harder to develop technologically and in the service sector, and whether it will hinder the country's ability to analyse well the challenges to its rise.

Outlook

China's continuing rise faces many challenges; several are serious. Some can be solved and others, principally demography, cannot. There appears to be lethargy in addressing the issues which are soluble; this makes the outlook bleak.

Many factors influence China's future, but none is as important as demography. China will still have a smaller proportion of elderly than Britain until 2040. But the UK economy has higher per capita wealth, and so it can better support a burgeoning elderly population. The trebling in China between 2010 and 2030 of the over-65s (to more than 300 million) means either that families must accommodate unprecedented numbers of elderly per adult, at a time when property prices are very high compared with wages, or alternatively that the government must handle a growth in the number of people in institutional care (from the current 2 million to perhaps over 150 million), which will create severe budgetary pressure. The PLA might have to scrap plans for a second aircraft carrier so that Beijing can build care homes for well over 100 million people.

The population should peak before 2030, and then fall by one- to two-thirds by the end of the century. Although there can be per capita GDP growth, sustained high growth rates for the overall economy will be difficult after 2030–40. This outlook is prejudicial to China's overtaking the US economy. In 2030 China's population will still be over a third rural and poorly educated. Per capita growth from that level is not the same as per capita growth in ageing Japan's more advanced economy. China has had a window of opportunity to reorient itself and move to higher growth in order to reach a more developed status before 2030. Much will depend on where China has reached by that turning point. Indeed the window could be narrower, as some economists think everything hinges not on the overall population, but on the labour force, which is due to peak and then decline much sooner. In this context it is unhelpful that economic growth is already slowing.

There is the risk that the narrowing of China's window for advancing to the top rank of powers will cause some senior leaders to break out and adopt confrontational measures rather than see the chance lost for another century. They could justify military adventurism by patriotism.

China's wounds in the twenty-first century are mostly self-inflicted and treatable. Experts say the one-child policy has had no arithmetical impact on birth rates; nonetheless it has undermined the state's relationship with millions of its citizens. Externally, too many people and countries do not want China to become the superpower. Lack of respect for farmers' land, decades of environmental abuse, poor education, severe income inequality and careless policies towards Islam have created a destructive cocktail which threatens to poison the Party and the nation. Systemic corruption is interesting, as (both in China and elsewhere in the developing world) it can coexist with rapidly improving living standards. Furthermore, on some surveys the levels in China appear lower than in comparative countries. Yet it is in China that public anger reaches boiling point. I suggest that this is for two reasons: first, corruption is contradictory to the rhetoric of a socialist and egalitarian society; second, according to Xinhua it reaches right to the top of the Party, involving at least three members of the Politburo in just over a dozen years. It begins to look as if corruption is the system.

Solutions to such challenges exist; the problem is the sense of stasis. Even where threats could be defused, there is insufficient vitality and purpose. Laws are passed but not implemented; problems noticed but not addressed; and there is sheer inattention. It is as if reforms and serious policy-making are in conflict with the patronage machine. China today shows some of the seething concern, the sense that the wheels are coming off the train, that emerged in the late eighteenth century before the country was racked to near disaster in the nineteenth century. We are seeing the emergence of a China brittle at home and brusque overseas.

Time is short if the supertanker is to be set on a different course. There is little sense that within the large collective leadership there are yet alternative visions of the future or a sense of urgency. The new 2012 leadership under Xi Jinping may be the last generation to have any freedom of choice in how to address China's challenges. Interest has been shown in reforms but – on the evidence of recent years – there is reason to believe that the big issues will not be urgently addressed. Unless there is deep, rapid and structural reform, China is likely to be caught in the 'middle-income trap' and will fail to achieve super-power status this century. America may have receded, but China will not replace it.

Notes

Introduction: Facing Multiple Challenges

1. I suggest there can be only one 'superpower' at a time (as opposed to a 'world power' or 'great power'). The word superpower is used here to refer to a country that exercises more than global leadership or hegemony: it can impose its will on a significant proportion of the world in a large number of spheres most of the time, while not actually running the world. In a multipolar world, for example, it seems difficult to have a superpower.
2. Angus Maddison, *The World Economy: A Millennial Perspective*, p.261.
3. Henry Kissinger, *On China*, p.493.
4. *Global Language Monitor*, Austin, Texas, 050511 http://www.languagemonitor.com/top-news/bin-ladens-death-one-of-top-news-stories-of-21th-century/.
5. http://www.pewglobal.org/2013/09/19/environmental-concerns-on-the-rise-in-china/.

1 The Making of Today's China

1. See the foreword of Xiao Jiansheng, *Chinese History Revisited*, http://chinahistoryrevisited. blogspot.com/search?updated-min=2010-01-01T00:00:00%2B08:00&updated-max=2011-01-01T00:00:00%2B08:00&max-results=3.
2. Ray Huang, *China: A Macro History*, p.149.
3. Fairbank and Goldman, *China*, pp.113–14.
4. Huang, *China*, p.127.
5. Fairbank, *China*, pp.85, 114.
6. Huang, *China*, pp.130, 141–2.
7. There are stories that the ancestors of the Jin might have given arrowheads as tributary gifts in the time of the ancient Zhou dynasty (1046–221 BC). So perhaps tribute travelled both ways at different points in China's history.
8. Jasper Becker, *City of Heavenly Tranquillity*, p.16.
9. One could also note that one reason Beijing was not often chosen was that it was not at that time within the borders of Han Chinese rulers.
10. Ian Morris, *Why the West Rules, – For Now*, p.389.
11. Peter Lorge, *War, Politics and Society in Early Modern China, 900–1795*, p.80.
12. ibid., pp.78, 79.
13. Fairbank, *China*, p.122.
14. See James C. Y. Watt, *The World of Khubilai Khan: Chinese Art in the Yuan Dynasty*. Introductory coverpiece.
15. See Alastair Johnston, *Cultural Realism: Strategic Culture and Grand Strategy in Chinese History*, p.27.
16. See ibid., p.xi.

17. Until recently, no one had thought to argue that the Great Wall extended into Xinjiang: maps and books showed the Great Wall's westward construction ending in what is today Gansu province. Autonomists and separatists have used this as an effective argument that China did not pretend to encompass the Xinjiang area in the far west. But in 2001, China's state media reported that the Great Wall had been found by Chinese archaeologists to extend 300 miles further westward than previously believed – into Xinjiang. Now the claim is taken by many tour groups and much travel literature to be true. Given the political sensitivity as to whether Xinjiang is Chinese or not, we should be cautious about such announcements.

18. Fairbank and Goldman, *China*, p.110.

19. ibid., pp.88, 124.

20. The repetitive and entrenched misattribution of trade as tribute has been described by several writers, for example Morris, *Why the West Rules*, p.406.

21. See the observations of Dominicus Parrenin and David Hume in Liu Dun, 'A New Survey of the Needham Question'.

22. Shawn Ni and Pham Hoang Van, 'High Corruption Income as a Source of Distortion and Stagnation', pp.5–8.

23. Timothy Brook, *The Troubled Empire*, p.71.

24. ibid., p.29.

25. Paul John Bailey, *China in the Twentieth Century*, p.18.

26. The same agricultural tools described at the time of Khubilai Khan, in 1315, were in use 600 years later, in the twentieth century, even if some new crops had been introduced (Jonathan Spence, *The Search for Modern China*, p.95: Huang, *China* p.164).

27. Bailey, *China in the Twentieth Century*, pp.17–18.

28. Fairbank, *The Great Chinese Revolution*, p.49.

29. Fox, Elvin and Wen 'Qing Demographic History: Lower Yangzi Valley in the Mid-Qing', 2007 http://gis.rchss.sinica.edu.tw/QingDemography/.

30. Spence, *The Search*, pp.45, 95.

31. ibid., pp.123–4.

32. Fairbank and Goldman, *China*, p.122.

33. ibid., p.151.

34. ibid., p.148.

35. Edward J. M. Rhoads, *Manchus and Han*, p.37.

36. Spence, *The Search*, p.94.

37. Bailey, *China in the Twentieth Century*, p .20.

38. Frank Ching, *Ancestors*, p.317. However, be aware of Barend ter Haar's view that the term White Lotus had little value after 1600 as it was no longer self-referential and was virtually entirely used by others in denigration. See Valerie Hansen's review of ter Haar's book 'The White Lotus Teachings in Chinese Religious History': http://www.yale.edu/history/faculty/materials/hansen-white-lotus-review.pdf.

39. Jean Chesneaux, *Peasant Revolts in China 1840–1949*, p.17.

40. Ching, *Ancestors*, p.302.

41. Chesneaux, *Peasant Revolts*, pp.16–17; for the arguments in favour, Esherick, *The Origins of the Boxer Uprising*, pp.219–21, against.

42. Fairbank, *The Great Chinese Revolution*, p.64.

43. See Woei-lien Chong, ed., *China's Great Proletarian Cultural Revolution*, p.40.

44. ibid., p.23. Bailey stresses the ethnic aspect.

45. Byron Farwell, *Armies of the Raj*, p.74.

46. F. L. Hawks Pott, *A Short History of Shanghai*, pp.47–8.

47. ibid., pp.59–60.

48. It has been calculated that between 108 BC and the end of the dynasty in 1912 there were 1,828 natural calamities. Walter H. Mallory, 'China: Land of Famine', 1926, cited by Cormac Ó Gráda in *Famine: A Short History*, 2009, p.40, http://press.princeton.edu/chapters/s8857.html.

49. Chesneaux, *Peasant Revolts*, p.66.

50. Maddison, 'Chinese Economic Performance in the Long Run', Ch. 2, p.9.

51. Hawks Pott, pp.47, 172–3; An Chunggun, p.9, fn 32.

52. Niv Horesh, *Shanghai's Bund and Beyond: British Banks, Bank Note Issuance, and Monetary Policy in China, 1842–1937*, p.46.
53. Fairbank, *The Great Chinese Revolution*, p.73.
54. Bailey, *China in the Twentieth Century*, p.23.
55. Chesneaux, *Peasant Revolts*, p.35.
56. ibid., pp.51–2.
57. George T. Yu, *Party Politics in Republican China*, p.22.
58. ibid., p.30.
59. ibid., p.46.
60. Bailey, *China in the Twentieth Century*, p.25.
61. Frank Dikotter, *Things Modern, passim.*
62. Fairbank and Goldman, *China*, pp.115, 117.
63. Mark C. Elliott, *The Manchu Way*, p.xvii.
64. Bailey, *China in the Twentieth Century*, p.18.
65. Book review in *Journal of Historical Biography* by Xiuyu Wang. Washington State University Vancouver, http://www.ufv.ca/jhb/Volume_4/Volume_4_Wang.pdf.
66. Fairbank and Goldman, *China*, p.122.
67. ibid., p.118.
68. Rhoads, *Manchus and Han*, p.75.
69. ibid., p.41.
70. http://www.chss.iup.edu/chr/CHR-2004Fall-11-WANG-research%20notes-final.pdf.
71. R. Mitter, *Modern China: A Very Short Introduction*, pp.25, 26.
72. Rhoads, *Manchus and Han*, p.70.
73. Professor William A. Lyell, trans., in the introduction to *Diaries of a Madman*, p.xxxi.
74. Rhoads, *Manchus and Han*, pp.187–205.
75. ibid., p.191.
76. Robert Gamer (ed.), *Understanding Contemporary China*, p.98.
77. Andrew Simpson (ed.), *Language and National Identity in Asia* p.148. There are an estimated 30,000 speakers of the related Xibo language in Xinjiang, and Manchu are now starting to use this to refresh their language. *WSJ* 031009 http://online.wsj.com/article/SB125452110732160485.html.
78. See James Leibold 'More than a Category: Han Supremacism on the Chinese Internet', *China Quarterly* 203 Vol. 3 (September 2010), p.549. http://tlweb.latrobe.edu.au/humanities/profiles/ss/leibold/Liebold_More_Than_a_Category_China_Quarterly.pdf, p.554.
79. It can, of course, be argued that the war left Turkey with little that was not Turkish. However, Kemal Atatürk gave a clear ideology to the new nation, which was not notionally multi-ethnic like China but clearly that of a nation state. This is despite Atatürk coming from near Albania and possibly being Albanian. Turkey encouraged undesirable populations to emigrate.
80. Elliott, *The Manchu Way*, p.67. Elliott refers to the end of the ban.
81. An Chunggun, 'A Treatise on Peace in the East', trans. by Han Jieun and Franklin Rausch, http://www.utoronto.ca/csk/A_Treatise_on_Peace_in_the_East.pdf, p.12, fn; John Stephan, *The Russian Far East: A History*, pp.58, 60 and 61.
82. Madame Chiang, Kai-shek, 'Conversations with Mikhail Borodin', p.4.
83. Horesh, *Shanghai's Bund*, p.107.
84. ibid., p.65.
85. Frank Dikotter, *The Age of Openness* and *Things Modern, passim.*
86. Dikotter, *Age of Openness*, p.90 and *passim*.
87. ibid., p.94.
88. Dikotter, *Age of Openness*, p.42.
89. Maddison, *Chinese Economic Performance*, ch. 2, p.11.
90. Horesh, *Shanghai's Bund*, p.34.
91. Carl Crow, *400 Million Customers* (1938).
92. Thomas Rawski, *Economic Growth in Pre-war China*, citing K.C.Yeh. P. . . . . . .
93. Maddison, Chinese Economic Performance, Ch. 2, p.9.
94. Dikotter, 'Age of Openness', p.5.
95. Horesh, *Shanghai's Bund*, p.65.

96. ibid., p.118.

97. ibid., p.30.

98. ibid.

99. Maddison, *Chinese Economic Performance*, Ch. 2, p.11.

100. Horesh, *Shanghai's Bund*, pp.6, 63, 166.

101. Professor Steve Tsang of Nottingham University writing in *SCMP* 220909.

102. In terms of public health we should note the work on adults' height as a proxy for nutrition. It rose steadily through the Republican period but then stagnated from the 1940s until the 1990s. This suggests that the Communist era was in certain respects not a time of great progress. Dikotter, 'Age of Openness', pp.88–9, cites the work of Stephen L. Morgan in *Economics and Human Biology*, No. 2, 2004.

103. Kang Chao, *Man and Land in Chinese History*, pp.92, 93,105 and 240.

104. Dikotter, *Age of Openness*, p.86.

105. ibid., pp.86–7.

106. Paul G. Pickowicz, 'Rural Protest Letters: Local Perspectives on the State's Revolutionary War on Tillers, 1960–1990', in Ching Kwan Lee and Guobin Yang, eds, *Re-visioning the Chinese Revolution: The Politics and Poetics of Collective Memories in Reform China* (Stanford, CA: Stanford University Press, 2007), pp.21–49.

107. Lee and Yang (eds), *Re-envisioning the Chinese Revolution*, p.26.

108. World Bank, *Re-envisioning*, 'From Poor Areas to Poor People' (2009), p.viii.

109. Lee and Yang, p.33.

110. ibid., p.46.

111. ibid., p.47.

112. ibid., p.45. Pickowicz, 'Rural Protest Letters: Local Perspectives on the State's Revolutionary War on Tillers, 1960–1990,' p.47.

113. http://usa.chinadaily.com.cn/china/2013-10/29/content_17067582.htm.

114. Lee Shu-ching, 'Agrarianism and Social Upheaval in China', *American Journal of Sociology* 56, no. 6 (May 1951) http://www.jstor.org/pss/2772468.

115. Y. C. Wang, *Chinese Intellectuals and the West* (1966), *passim*.

116. *Looking at China through a Third Eye* was published pseudonymously [by Luoyi Ningge'er] in Beijing in 1994 and believed to have been written by Wang Shan. Joseph Fewsmith, *China Since Tiananmen*, p.148.

117. Li Ruogu, *Institutional Suitability and Economic Development*, p.152.

118. Recent work drawing on government archives suggests that this is reasonably accurate. See Frank Dikotter, *Mao's Famine*.

119. ibid., *passim*.

120. Yang Jisheng in the introduction to his book *Tombstone* (2009). http://www.pen.org/viewmedia.php/prmMID/4400/prmID/1873.

121. O'Grada, *Famine*, p.244.

122. ibid., pp.242–3.

123. Dikkoter, *Mao's Famine*, *passim*.

124. Li Changyu, 'Mao's Killing Quotas', p.2. Frank Dikotter corroborates this by citing annotations on key documents.

125. Jeremy Brown, 'Terrible Honeymoon' (2004).

126. See, for example, Tariq Ali in the *New Left Review* 66, November–December 2010, http://www.newleftreview.org/?view=2874.

127. Jorge Castaneda, 'Companero: The Life and Death of Che Guevara', p.226 and *passim*.

128. Andrew Scobell, *China's Use of Military Force*, p.114.

129. ibid., p.107.

130. ibid., Chapter 5, *passim*.

131. Christopher Hibbert, *The Dragon Wakes*, frontispiece.

132. Gamer, *Understanding Contemporary China*, p.76.

133. See Wang Fei-ling, *Organising through Division and Exclusion: China's Hukou System* (2005), p.33.

134. ibid., pp.33–4.

135. Gamer, *Understanding Contemporary China*, p.70.

136. Spence, *The Search*, pp.123–4.

137. McGregor, pp.78–9.
138. Morris, *Why the West Rules*, p.338.
139. Waley, p.23. The example given was for the suppression of opium consumption. Also Morris, *Why the West Rules*, p.265.
140. Barend ter Haar in Woei-lien Chong (ed.), *China's Great Proletarian Cultural Revolution*, p.28.
141. Essay by Barend J ter Haar in Chong, *China's Great Proletarian Cultural Revolution*, p.28.
142. David S. G. Goodman, *Beijing Street Voices*, p.32.
143. Resolution on certain questions in the history of our party since the founding of the People's Republic of China *(Adopted by the Sixth Plenary Session of the Eleventh Central Committee of the Communist Party of China on June 27, 1981)* http://www.marxists.org/subject/china/documents/cpc/history/01.htm.
144. Clause 27 of the 1981 Resolution.
145. Li Ruogu, *Institutional Suitability*, p.402.
146. Herbert Butterfield, *The Whig Interpretation of History*, pp.16–17.
147. John Gray, *Black Mass*, p.30.
148. Carl Riskin, China Human Development Report 1999: Transition and the State.UNDP http://www.undp.org.cn/downloads/nhdr/nhdr1999.pdf.
149. Mobo Gao, *The Battle for China's Past*, *passim*.
150. *FT* 130509.
151. PlayFair 2008, p.8.
152. *SCMP* 081011, http://www.scmp.com/portal/site/SCMP/menuitem.2af62ecb329d3d77334 92d9253a0a0a0/?vgnextoid=655fd9b697ed2310VgnVCM100000360a0a0aRCRD&ss=China&s-ews.
153. *SCMP* 070510.
154. *Beijing News* cited by BBC 101208.
155. http://www.pewglobal.org/files/2013/09/Pew-Global-Attitudes-Project-China-Report-FINAL-9-19-132.pdf.
156 Tu Wei-ming cited in a paper by Wang Yuting and Yang Fenggang in *Sociology of Religion* 67, no.2 (2006) http://www.purdue.edu/crcs/itemPublications/articles/Wang-Yang.pdf.
157. *FT* 180411.
158. chinaeducationblog 260310 http://www.chinaeducationblog.com/university/2010-03-26/npc-and-cppcc-delegates-suggest-measures-to-incrementally-advance-chinas-education-sector/.

2 The Broken Economic Model

1. Zhao Ziyang, *Prisoner of the State*.
2. James C. Mulvenon, 'Soldiers of Fortune: the Rise and Fall of the Chinese Military Business Complex 1978–98', Bonn International Centre for Conversion (1999), p.6.
3. ibid., p.121.
4. *Newsweek* 261009.
5. For an interesting discussion of this see Jorg Mayer, 'Global Rebalancing', p.7ff.
6. CESifo Forum February 2007, p.31. http://www.ifo.de/pls/guestci/download/CESifo%20 Forum%202007/CESifo%20Forum%202/2007/forum2–07-focus5.pdf.
7. *China Daily* 040809.
8. Quoted in *FT* 040809.
9. Quoted in *China Daily* 040809.
10. *FT* 301209.
11. http://papers.ssrn.com/sol3/papers.cfm?abstract_id=2307054.
12. *FT*   140512,   http://www.ft.com/intl/cms/s/0/f7cf01fe-9db7–11e1–9a9e-00144feabdc0. html#axzz1v8AbeMNF.
13. A twenty-year experiment in remote Guizhou province to see if fertility would be slowed if land was no longer reallocated based on family size. http://www.sosc.ust.hk/faculty/detail/jk/2006_Do_Secure_Land_Use_Rights_Reduce_Fertility.pdf.
14. Zhang Weiying's paper on China's transformation at the University of Chicago in July 2008, 'The Reallocation of Entrepreneurial Talent', p.39.
15. Well discussed in ibid., p.39.

16. ibid., pp.22–4.
17. Cai, Du and Wang 'Migration and Labour Mobility in China' (UNDP, 2009), p.6.
18. Mayer, 'Global Rebalancing', p.8.
19. *China Daily* 190211, http://europe.chinadaily.com.cn/china/2011–02/19/content_12045877_2.htm.
20. Cai, Du and Wang, 'Migration and Labour Mobility in China', p.6.
21. Li Ruogu, *Institutional Suitability*, p.228ff., p.258ff., p.229ff.
22. Zhao Ziyang, *Prisoner of the State*, p.108.
23. *Daily Telegraph* 160910.
24. See the discussion in McGregor, p.199.
25. Fan Gang in *Business Week* 220805.
26. Zhang Weiying, 'The Reallocation', p.36.
27. Minister of Industry and Information Technology (MIIT) Li Yizhong quoted in *Xinhua News* 301209, http://english.mofcom.gov.cn/aarticle/counselorsreport/europereport/201001/20100106721756.html.
28. Hou Junchun, Deputy Director of the State Council's Development Research Centre, quoted in *SCMP* 151011, http://www.scmp.com/portal/site/SCMP/menuitem.2af62ecb329d3d7733492d9253a0a0a0/?vgnextoid=6b1abea2fe203310VgnVCM100000360a0a0aRCRD&ss=China&s–ews.
29. *SCMP* 151011, http://www.scmp.com/portal/site/SCMP/menuitem.2af62ecb329d3d7733492d9253a0a0a0/?vgnextoid=6b1abea2fe203310VgnVCM100000360a0a0aRCRD&ss=China&s–ews.
30. Private sector growth of 21 per cent is simply the residual of moving from 3 per cent of the economy to 70 per cent in the context of overall GDP growth of 10 per cent annually.
31. Chris Hall writing in CESifo Forum February 2007, 'When the Dragon Awakes', p.30.
32. Ferri and Liu, 'Honour thy Creditors'; Deepak Lal, 'Continuing the Chinese Economic Miracle'.
33. He, Zhang and Shek, 'How Efficient has been China's Investment? Empirical Evidence from National and Provincial Data' Hong Kong Monetary Authority 2006, p.27, http://www.info.gov.hk/hkma/eng/research/RM19–2006.pdf.
34. http://www.reuters.com/article/2013/11/19/us-china-smallbusiness-analysis-idUSBRE9AI08V20131119.
35. http://www.imf.org/external/pubs/ft/weo/2012/02/weodata/weoseladv.aspx?a=&c=924%2c158&s=NGDPD.
36. *Der Spiegel* online 2/020/, http://www.spiegel.de/international/spiegal/0,1318,463007–3,00.html.
37. Jin Zhong, editor of *Kaifeng* (Open) magazine in Hong Kong quoted in *SCMP* 260910 (Wang Hui, *The End of the Revolution*, pp.27–8).
38. Wang Hui, 'China: Improving Unemployment Insurance', pp.27–8.
39. Vodopivec and Tong, p.2.
40. ibid., p.2.
41. *SCMP* 110311.
42. Economist 210113, http://www.economist.com/blogs/analects/2013/01/chinas-workforce.
43. *Beijing Review* Autumn 2006.
44. Booz & Co., *The 12th Five-year Plan*, April 2011, p.10.
45. *FT* 300912, http://www.ft.com/intl/cms/s/0/62eb2ea8–06e1–11e2–92b5–00144feabdc0.html#axzz283KiNUN7.
46. CASS, 'Migration and Labour Mobility in China', 2009, p.3.
47. McKinsey China Skills Gap, p.7 http://mckinseyonsociety.com/downloads/reports/Education/china-skills-gap.pdf.
48. International Organisation for Migration website 2010 www.iom.int.
49. CASS, 'Migration and Labour Mobility in China'.
50. Xinhua (China View.cn) 071208.
51. BBC 021010.
52. A-15 in US Labour Bureau Statistics, http://www.bls.gov/news.release/empsit.t15.htm.
53. Professor Hu Angang of Tsinghua University's Centre for the Study of China is quoted in *SCMP* 080702. His estimate was three times the then official figure.

54. See the article in *China Economic Weekly* online in Southcn.com 190606 http://big5.southcn.com/gate/big5/www.southcn.com/news/china/zgkx/200606190022.htm.
55. See *FT* 161011, http://www.ft.com/intl/cms/s/0/8533566e-f582–11e0–94b1–00144feab49a.html#axzz1b01KJBpp.
56. http://pluto.huji.ac.il/~ebenstein/Ebenstein_Jennings_HIV_in_China_March_2008.pdf.
57. This is because there are no social costs or regulations; no holiday pay or premium for over-time pay (*SCMP* 230410). Apart from the demographic implications, China is not culturally attuned to imported labour. Executives are one thing, but factory workers are quite another. There have already been riots in Guangdong involving Uighur industrial workers, and other incidents involving African traders.
58. *Daily Telegraph* 281108.
59. See *Wall Street Journal* 070212, http://articles.marketwatch.com/2012–02-07/markets/31040945_1_new-jobs-jobless-data-state-run-xinhua-news-agency.
60. *Time* 100809.
61. Wei Jianing in *SCMP* 260909; 20 per cent official estimate in *Daily Telegraph* 120809.
62. Interview with the *FT* 040410.
63. See IMF, 'Targets, Interest Rates and Household Savings in Urban China', 2011, http://www.imf.org/external/pubs/ft/wp/2011/wp11223.pdf.
64. It is interesting to note that in the many areas where there is a notable male child surplus, families with sons save more, as their boys will need to compete for wives (Wei Shang-Jin, 'The Mystery of Chinese Savings', 2010).
65. Zhao Ziyang, *Prisoner of the State*, p.131.
66. Professor John Ross at Shanghai Jiaotong University 030510, http://ablog.typepad.com/key_trends_in_the_world_e/2010/05/key-determinants-of-the-different-gdp-growth-rates-in-india-and-china.html.
67. David Beim, 'The Future of Chinese Growth', New America Foundation 2011, http://newamerica.net/publications/policy/the_future_of_chinese_growth and see Currensee 270112 (The foreign exchange traders' weblog)http://blog.currensee.com/tag/icor/.
68. CASS, 'Migration and Labour Mobility in China'.
69. CCTV 240114, http://english.cntv.cn/program/newsupdate/20140124/104182.shtml.
70. Vodopivec and Tong, 'China: Improving Unemployment Insurance', p.2.
71. Kang Chao, *Man and Land in Chinese History*, pp.92, 93.
72. Xiangzheng Deng and Jikun Huang, 'Cultivated Land Conversion', p.39.
73. Yan, Liu *et al.*, 'Assessing the Consequence of Land Use Change', pp.16–17.
74. Liu and Tian, 'China's Land Cover and Use Change', p.1.
75. Liu and Tian state that cropland reduced between 1980 and 2005, ibid., p.1.
76. Franklin L. Ho, and Ministry of Agriculture, Beijing, http://english.agri.gov.cn/sa/ca/ooa/201003/t20100304_1661.htm Using populations of 500 million in 1935 and 1.328 billion in 2008.
77. *FT* 200309.
78. Zhang Weiying, 'The Reallocation', p.5 and *passim*.
79. The Asian Development Bank, http://www.adb.org/Documents/Books/ADO/2010/Update/ado2010-upd.
80. *SCMP* 020410; *FT* 240310.
81. Professor Bardhan in Yale Global online 250909; *FT* 160110.
82. *FT* 260310.
83. Eichengreen, Park and Shin, 'When Fast Growing Economies Slow Down: International Evidence and Implications for the People's Republic of China', ADB Working Paper Series 262 (2011), http://www.adb.org/Documents/Working-Papers/2011/Economics-WP262.pdf.
84. China Daily 160114, http://www.chinadaily.com.cn/business/2014-01/16/content_17240588.htm.
85. See, for example, *FT* weblog, 141011, http://blogs.ft.com/the-world/2011/10/chinas-fear-of-the-talent-show/#axzz1b7iT7GCY.
86. *Global Times* 020611, http://opinion.globaltimes.cn/commentary/2011–06/661483.html.
87. *Le Figaro* 190210.

88. *FT* 030610.
89. http://www.theguardian.com/world/2009/may/21/chinese-companies-investment-africa.
90. Thomas J. Christensen, Deputy Assistant Secretary for East Asian and Pacific Affairs, and James Swan, Deputy Assistant Secretary for African Affairs, testifying to the US Senate 040608, http://www.africom.mil/getArticle.asp?art=1786.
91. Hanlong Mining, http://www.hanlongmining.com/.
92. http://www.tralac.org/files/2013/08/Africa-China-trading-relationship-Synopsis.pdf.
93. Richard F. Grimmett, 'Conventional Arms Transfers to Developing Nations, 2001–2008', CRS 2009, p.37.
94. Ben Simpfendorfer, *The New Silk Road*, p.137.
95. BBC 080114, http://www.bbc.co.uk/news/world-africa-25654155.
96. United Nations Radio 231210, http://www.unmultimedia.org/radio/english/detail/109843.html.
97. 121110 Chinese Academy of Sciences (CAS) http://english.cas.cnEshNe/CASE/201011/t20101112_61341.shtml.
98. Maplecroft, the global risk consultant, http://www.maplecroft.com.
99. Li Ruogu, *Institutional Suitability*, p.3.
100. *FT* 240410.
101. *Guardian* 031109.
102. *FT* 240410.
103. *Time* 230309.
104. *FT* 020610.
105. *FT* 040610.
106. Tai Ming Cheung, 'The Chinese Defense Economy's Long March from Imitation to Innovation', p.345, http://dx.doi.org/10.1080/01402390.2011.574976.

3 The Elusive Knowledge Economy

1. Dushko Josheski and Cane Koteski, 'The Causal Relationship between Patent Growth and Growth of GDP with Quarterly Data in the G7 Countries: Cointegration, ARDL and Error Correction Models', Goce Delcev University-Stip, Macedonia 2011, http://mpra.ub.uni-muenchen.de/33153/1/MPRA_paper_33153.pdf.
2. Chen Yutian in a University of Oregon interview, April 2000.
3. *Daily Telegraph* 180810.
4. Tai Ming, Cheung, 'The Chinese Defense Economy's Long March from Imitation to Innovation', p.345.
5. *Newsweek* January 2006.
6. Danny Breznitz, *The Run on the Red Queen*, *passim*.
7. PricewaterhouseCoopers, 'Global Reach', pp.1–2ff.
8. OECD Factbook 2008, *Economic, Environmental and Social Statistics*.
9. Frank Gannon of the European Molecular Biology Association writing in EMBO Rep. 2002 15 August, 3(8): 701. doi: 10.1093/embo-reports/kvf163 http://www.ncbi.nlm.nih.gov/pmc/articles/PMC1084217/.
10. https://www.gov.uk/government/uploads/system/uploads/attachment_data/file/246231/13-499-set-statistics-2013A.pdf.
11. http://usa.chinadaily.com.cn/business/2013-10/22/content_17051049.htm.
12. UNDP, Human Development Report, 2007–8.
13. http://www.weforum.org/reports/global-competitiveness-report-2013-2014.
14. http://www.wipo.int/export/sites/www/freepublications/en/economics/gii/gii_2013.pdf.
15. http://www.imd.org/uupload/IMD.WebSite/wcc/WCYResults/1/scoreboard.pdf.
16. www.oecd.org/document/44/0,3343,en_2649_34273_41204780_1_1_1_1,00.html.
17. Michael Schrage of MIT writing in the *FT* 071105.
18. ibid.
19. Birdsall and Rhee, 'Does Research and Development Contribute to Economic Growth in Developing Countries?', 1993.

20. P. D. Hien, 'A Comparative Study of Research Capabilities of East Asian Countries and Implications for Vietnam' Vietnam Atomic Energy Agency, http://www.vaec.gov.vn/Portals/0/Images/Document/25_3_2010_1.pdf.
21. *SCMP* 180310.
22. Felipe Larrain, 'Innovation in Latin America', Santiago, October 2008.
23. http://infoproc.blogspot.com/2006/03/china-research-and-development.html.
24. NSF, *Science and Engineering Indicators 2010*, Chapter 4 (Arlington, Virginia), http://www.nsf.gov/statistics/seind10/, shows 2006 US R&D expenditure in China at $804 million. The Chinese Ministry of Science and Technology in *China Science and Technology Statistics Data Book 2007* states that total R&D expenditure in 2006 was RMB300 billion ($37.5bn).
25. US–China Business Council, *Bringing R&D to China*, April 2008.
26. http://milexdata.sipri.org/files/?file=SIPRI+milex+data+1988-2012+v2.xlsx.
27. NSF, *Science and Engineering Indicators 2010*, Chapter 4.
28. NBS 2009 20–46, http://www.stats.gov.cn/tjsj/ndsj/2009/indexeh.htm.
29. Xinhua 100110, http://news.xinhuanet.com/english/2010-01/10/content_12786073.htm.
30. Florida, Mellander, 2008.
31. In the report, mentioned in the bibliography, WB, DRC 'China 2030' (2012), p.176.
32. *SCMP* 180310.
33. Cited by the *Economist* 141010, http://www.economist.com/node/17257940.
34. http://www.europeanchamber.com.cn/en/publications-patent-policy-innovation-in-china-study.
35. *Economist* 141010, http://www.economist.com/node/17257940.
36. UNESCO Science Report 2010.
37. Altbach, Reisberg, 'Trends in Global Higher Education', p.i.
38. PricewaterhouseCoopers, 'Global Reach', p.5.
39. Juliane Bielinski, 'Globalisation of R+D to China'.
40. David Zweig, ILO 2006.
41. *SCMP* 180310.
42. Tai Ming Cheung, 'The Chinese Defense Economy's Long March from Imitation to Innovation'.
43. *Caixin* 121110, http://english.caixin.com/2010-11-12/100198348.html.
44. Milan Brahmbhatt and Albert Hu, 'Ideas and Innovation in East Asia', p.37.
45. US–China Business Council, *Bringing R&D to China*.
46. Yuqing Xing and Detert Neal, 'How the iPhone Widens the United States Trade Deficit with the People's Republic of China', Asian Development Bank Institute, 2010, http://www.adbi.org/files/2010.12.14.wp257.iphone.widens.us.trade.deficit.prc.pdf.
47. Tai Ming Cheung, 'The Chinese Defense Economy's Long March from Imitation to Innovation', p.331.
48. *Economist* 160110.
49. Tai Ming Cheung, 'The Chinese Defense Economy's Long March from Imitation to Innovation', p.344.
50. China Organic Growth Fund 130213.
51. *Yale Daily News* 281207.
52. Reported by China News Service cited by *SCMP* 220910.
53. *China Daily* 170111.
54. Fairbank and Goldman, *China*, p.100.
55. Harley Farnsworth McNair (ed.), 'China', p.398. For a quotation from Confucius, see Morris, *Why the West Rules*, p.257.
56. G. W. F. Hegel, *Lectures on the Philosophy of History*, p.144.
57. Arnold Toynbee, *A Study of History*, p.59.
58. Fairbank, *The Great Chinese Revolution*, p.65.
59. Morris, p.379.
60. ibid., p.380.
61. Joseph Needham, *Science in Traditional China*, p.121.
62. See the foreword to Xiao Jiansheng's *China History Revisited*. In English: http://chinahistoryrevisited.blogspot.com/search?updated-min=2010-01-01T00:00:00%2B08:00&updated-max=2011-01-01T00:00:00%2B08:00&max-results=3.

63. See the interview with the Xiao Jiansheng 310110: http://asiancorrespondent.com/28252/chat-with-chinese-author-xiao-jiansheng/University of California, Irvine.
64. Morris, *Why the West Rules*, p.392.
65. Liu Dun, 'A New Survey'.
66. Toynbee, *A Study*, p.63.
67. Wang, *Chinese Intellectuals and the West*, p.497.
68. Oswald Spengler, *The Decline of the West*, Vol. II, p.501.
69. Hegel, *Lectures on the Philosophy of History*, pp.140–1.
70. Christian Wolmar, *Blood, Iron and Gold*, p.210.
71. David Pong, 'Confucian Patriotism', p.647.
72. Wolmar, *Blood, Iron and Gold*, pp.210, 211.
73. Kenneth Pomeranz, *The Great Divergence*, p.43ff.
74. ibid., Introduction, *passim* and pp.7–8.
75. Horesh and Landes, pp.17–20.
76. Wang Hui, pp.82–3.
77. Wang, *Chinese Intellectuals and the West*, pp.26–7.
78. Morris, *Why the West Rules*, p.619.
79. ibid., p.35.
80. Fairbank, *The Great Chinese Revolution*, p.49.
81. http://www.interbrand.com/en/best-global-brands/2013/Best-Global-Brands-2013-Brand-View.aspx.
82. http://www.millwardbrown.com/BrandZ/Top_100_Global_Brands.aspx Millward Brown.
83. 2011 R&D EU Scoreboard, http://iri.jrc.ec.europa.eu/research/docs/2011/SB2011_World_top_1400.pdf.
84. http://www.marketingweek.co.uk/analysis/essential-reads/the-top-100-most-valuable-global-brands-2013/4006682.article.
85. WIPO IP Facts and Figures, 2012 edn, see Data and Graphs Figure B.3, http://www.wipo.int/ipstats/en/.
86. *Medical News Today* 250507, http://www.medicalnewstoday.com/articles/72220.php.
87. Alan Vandemolen of Edelman quoted in *FT* 190111.
88. *Guardian* 021208.
89. United Nations Radio 260908, http://www.unmultimedia.org/radio/english/detail/35865.html.
90. *Guardian* 170707.
91. *SCMP* 270311.
92. *SCMP* 280911, http://www.scmp.com/portal/site/SCMP/menuitem.2af62ecb329d3d7733492d9253a0a0a0/?vgnextoid=5b6259a49faa2310VgnVCM100000360a0a0aRCRD&ss=China&s-ews.
93. Lu Xun, *Diary of a Madman and Other Stories,* trans. and introduced by William A. Lyell (1990), p.xxx.
94. Hegel, *Lectures on the Philosophy of History*, p.137.
95. Lu Xun, *Diary of a Madman and Other Stories,* p.xxxi.
96. *SCMP* 080309.
97. *Global Times* 211011, http://www.globaltimes.cn/NEWS/tabid/99/ID/680288/Voices.aspx.
98. See   http://www.booz.com.global/home/what_we_think/global-innovation-1000/top-innovators-spenders/51180614.
99. Adam Segal writing in the CNN weblog 100311. http://globalpublicsquare.blogs.cnn.com/2011/03/10/why-american-innovation-will-beat-out-china/.
100. *Economist* 150410, http://www.economist.com/node/15879359.
101. *FT* 161011, http://www.ft.com/intl/cms/s/2/0b05d818-de75-11e0-a2c0-00144feabdc0.html#axzz1b01KJBpp.
102. Tai Ming Cheung, The Chinese Defense Economy's Long March from Imitation to Innovation', p.334.
103. Book review of Karl Gerth, *As China Goes, So Goes the World*, http://www.globalforesightbooks.org/Book-of-the-Month/as-china-goes-gerth.html.
104. Reuters 140411, http://www.reuters.com/article/2011/04/14/us-china-usa-cyberespionage-idUSTRE73D24220110414?pageNumber=1.

105. http://issa.house.gov/wp-content/uploads/2014/01/final-nsa-reforms-letter-01-23-2014-2. pdf.
106. Zorina B. Khan, *The Democratisation of Invention* (2005), Preface.
107. China.org.cn 151011, http://www.china.org.cn/opinion/2011-10/15/content_23626282_2. htm.
108. Adam Segal writing in the CNN weblog 100311, http://globalpublicsquare.blogs.cnn. com/2011/03/10/why-american-innovation-will-beat-out-china/.
109. Addressing multinational executives in Guangzhou, *FT* 301111.
110. Gerth, p.155.
111. 280711 BBC, http://www.bbc.co.uk/news/business-14321131.
112. BBC 280711, http://www.bbc.co.uk/news/world-asia-pacific-14321787.
113. *Global Times* 280911, http://www.globaltimes.cn/NEWS/tabid/99/ID/677381/The-signal-of-Shanghai-subway-crash.aspx.
114. *World Affairs* March/April 2011, http://www.worldaffairsjournal.org/articles/2011-MarApr/full-Morais-MA-2011.html.
115. See the discussion in Chapter 11 above about India, Japan and Russia.
116. *Global Times* 261011, http://www.globaltimes.cn/NEWS/tabid/99/ID/680930/Public-trust-is-withering-on-Chinas-bigger-projects.aspx.
117. Fairbank, *The Great Chinese Revolution*, pp.61, 66.
118. See *China Daily* 190712, http://www.chinadaily.com.cn/business/2012-07/19/content_15601041.htm.
119. IPS News 040811, http://ipsnews.net/news.asp?idnews=56741.
120. *China Daily* 280108, http://www.chinadaily.com.cn/cndy/2008-01/28/content_6424054. htm.
121. *People's Daily* 220201, http://english.peopledaily.com.cn/english/200102/22/eng20010222_63087.html.
122. Morris, *Why the West Rules*, p.201.
123. For example, Douglas J. Keenan, 'Astro-Historiographic Chronologies of Early China are Unfounded', *East Asian History* 23 (2002), http://www.informath.org/pubs/EAH02a. pdf.
124. China.org.cn 151011, http://www.china.org.cn/opinion/2011-10/15/content_23626282_2. htm.
125. Pan Su-yan, *University Autonomy, the State and Social Change in China*, pp.61–2.
126. ibid., p.162.
127. See Marie-Carine Lall and Edward Vickers, *Education as a Political Tool in Asia*, pp.67–77.
128. Huan Xin, President of the Mainland Students Association at Shue Yan University, quoted in *SCMP* 231011, http://www.scmp.com/portal/site/SCMP/menuitem.2af62ecb329d3d773 3492d9253a0a0a0/?vgnextoid=3f27c26117523310VgnVCM100000360a0a0aRCRD&ss=Ed ucation&ss=Lifestyle.
129. *SCMP* 310312, http://www.scmp.com/portal/site/SCMP/menuitem.2af62ecb329d3d77334 92d9253a0a0a0/?vgnextoid=d7cf231fe3466310VgnVCM100000360a0a0aRCRD&ss=Colu mns+%26+Insight&s=Opinion.
130. Tai Ming Cheung, 'The Chinese Defense Economy's Long March from Imitation to Innovation', p.335.
131. 'Why Half a Nobel Prize Again?' on a website dated 010109, http://www.21pinglun. com/?p=285.
132. *FT* 040110, http://www.ft.com/cms/s/0/c67477f4-f8cf-11de-beb8-00144feab49a.html #axzz1GB5SReVY.
133. *SCMP* 011011, http://www.scmp.com/portal/site/SCMP/menuitem.2af62ecb329d3d77334 92d9253a0a0a0/?vgnextoid=62e2893c4ab2310VgnVCM100000360a0a0aRCRD&ss=Chi na&s–ews.
134. Stanislas Dehaene, *The Number Sense*, pp.102–3.
135. *China Daily* 250707.
136. *People's Daily* online 120309, http://english.people.com.cn/90001/90776/90883/6612934.html.
137. http://www.mla.org/pdf/06enrollmentsurvey_final.pdf.

138. http://www.mla.org/pdf/2009_enrollment_survey_pr.pdf.

139. Scott McGinnis, 'Heritage as a Gateway: Chinese as a Heritage Language', p.3.

140. Ali Allawi, *The Crisis of Islamic Civilisation,* p.134.

141. Private conversation with Wally Olins in London, 2011.

142. Hegel, *Lectures on the Philosophy of History*, p.142.

143. Andrew Simpson (ed.), *Language and National Identity in Asia*, pp.151–2.

144. ibid., p.152.

145. *From State to Nation: The Forging of the Han through Language Policy in the PRC and Taiwan* (2005), p.394, http://www.law.nyu.edu/ecm_dlv3/groups/public/@nyu_law_website__journals__journal_of_international_law_and_politics/documents/documents/ecm_pro_059617.pdf.

146. Simpson (ed.), *Language and National Identity in Asia*, p.155.

147. Gernet, p.330.

148. Spengler, *The Decline*, Vol. II, p.145.

149. See work by the researcher Patrick Hassell Zein, http://www.zein.se/patrick/3000en.html.

150. *Economist* 230409.

151. *LA Times* 120710, http://articles.latimes.com/2010/jul/12/world/la-fg-china-characters-20100712.

152. Private conversation with Thomas Rawski, 2010.

153. *NYT* 160489.

154. NRC, Office of Scientific and Engineering Personnel, 'Foreign and Foreign-Born Engineers in the United States', 1988, http://books.nap.edu/openbook.php?record_id=1525&page=5.

155. NSF, National Center for Science and Engineering Statistics (NCSES), 'Doctorate Recipients from U.S. Universities: Summary Report 2007–08', Table 11, http://www.nsf.gov/statistics/nsf10309/pdf/tab11.pdf.

156. *SCMP* 040411.

157. Damian Harper and David Elmer, *Shanghai City Guide*, p.32.

158. *Global Times* 230911, http://www.globaltimes.cn/NEWS/tabid/99/ID/676549/1-of-Shanghais-population-from-overseas.aspx. The fabled 400,000 Russians in Beijing are largely traders who travel in and out.

159. NBS of the People's Republic of China 290411, http://www.stats.gov.cn/english/newsandcomingevents/t20110429_402722638.htm.

160. Moses Abramovitz, 'Catching Up, Forging Ahead, and Falling Behind', *Journal of Economic History*, 46, No. 2, The Tasks of Economic History (June 1986), pp.405–6, http://www.cenet.org.cn/userfiles/2007-9-25/20070925002223921.pdf.

4 Finance

1. C. Fred Bergsten, 'A Proposed Strategy to Correct the Chinese Exchange Rate', Congressional Testimony Peterson Institute for International Economics, 2010, http://www.iie.com/publications/testimony/bergsten20100916.pdf.

2. *SCMP* 150311. In May 2008, the economist John Greenwood estimated that 85 per cent of foreign exchange reserves appeared to be balanced by commercial bank reserves at the PBC and bank purchases of PBC bonds.

3. John Greenwood, 'The Costs and Implications of PBC Sterilisation', 2008, Cato, http://www.cato.org/pubs/journal/cj28n2/cj28n2-4.pdf.

4. *Time* 100809.

5. Estimates of interest received and paid were made in Gagnon, Lardy and Borst, 'The Internal Cost of China's Currency Policy' (Peterson Institute, 2011). Published on a weblog, http://www.piie.com/blogs/china/?p=422.

6. See *Daily Telegraph* 100512, http://www.telegraph.co.uk/finance/financialcrisis/9258317/Chinese-sovereign-wealth-fund-stops-buying-European-government-debt.html.

7. See http://www.treasurydirect.gov/govt/reports/pd/mspd/2013/opds122013.pdf.

8. Professor John Taylor, Stanford University 260712, http://johnbtaylorsblog.blogspot.hk/2012_07_01_archive.html.

9. *Sunday Telegraph* 190910.

10. *SCMP* 131009.

11. *Newsweek* 200910.
12. *Newsweek* 111010; such policies come with severe social cost, as we note in Japan with the doubling in old-age poverty and the trebling in shoplifting by the elderly.
13. Booz & Co., *The 12th Five-year Plan*, April 2011, p.5.
14. See the work of Wang Shaogang and Ha Angang.
15. The Open Budget Survey 2008, p.7.
16. *Economic Observer* 110411, http://www.eeo.com.cn/ens/2011/0519/201661.shtml.
17. *Economist* 201110, http://www.economist.com/node/17528136?story_id=17528136.
18. For example, with the Zhejiang bond issue. See *SCMP* 071011. http://www.scmp.com/portal/site/SCMP/menuitem.2af62ecb329d3d7733492d9253a0a0a0/?vgnextoid=74986ef0a1ad2310VgnVCM100000360a0a0aRCRD&ss=Companies+%26+Finance&s=Business.
19. Reuters 030810, http://www.reuters.com/article/idUSTRE6721D320100803.
20. Reuters 301213, http://www.reuters.com/article/2013/12/30/us-china-economy-debt-idUS-BRE9BT09M20131230.
21. *SCMP* 240310.
22. *FT* 300912, http://www.ft.com/intl/cms/s/3/b4d68d96-0981-11e2-a424-00144feabdc0.html#axzz283KiNUN7.
23. Wang Xiaolu, deputy director of the national economic research institute under the China Reform Foundation in 2007. Cited in *China Daily* 120510.
24. http://www.sipri.org/research/armaments/milex/milex_database/milexdata1988-2012v2.xsls/view.
25. Bloomberg 040309.
26. http://milexdata.sipri.org/files/?file=SIPRI+milex+data+1988-2012+v2.xlsx.
27. See the debate in the 2011 NPC, reported in *SCMP* 100311.
28. See Nicholas Borst PIIE 110512, http://www.piie.com/blogs/china/?p=1258.
29. Li Ruogu, *Institutional Suitability*, pp.258, 260.
30. The Agricultural Development Bank of China, the China Development Bank and the Export–Import Bank of China.
31. Detailed analysis in *WSJ* 090311, http://online.wsj.com/article/SB10001424052748703883504576186252054344030.html.
32. *SCMP* 280912, http://www.scmp.com/news/china/article/1048977/boom-city-dongguan-faces-bankruptcy.
33. Gagnon and Hinterschweiger, *The Global Outlook for Government Debt over the Next 25 Years* (Peterson Institute, 2011), p.30, http://www.piie.com/publications/chapters_preview/6215/iie6215.pdf.
34. *FT* 220910.
35. Including Credit Suisse analysts, reported in *SCMP* 131011, http://www.scmp.com/portal/site/SCMP/menuitem.2af62ecb329d3d7733492d9253a0a0a0/?vgnextoid=dd2d4eeb409f2310VgnVCM100000360a0a0aRCRD&ss=Companies+%26+Finance&s=Business.
36. ibid.
37. Survey by US law firm Pillsbury Winthrop Shaw Pittman in 2011, cited in *SCMP* 050311.
38. A report from China's National Bureau of Economic Research cited in *SCMP* 170311.
39. Richard Podpiera, *Progress in China's Banking Sector Reform: Has Bank Behavior Changed?* (IMF, 2006).
40. Deputy Governor Hu Xiaolian cited on the PBC website 310510 http://www.pbc.gov.cn/english//detail.asp?col=6500&ID=191.
41. *FT* 310311.
42. Estimated by researchers GaveKal and quoted in *SCMP* 101011, http://www.scmp.com/portal/site/SCMP/menuitem.2af62ecb329d3d7733492d9253a0a0a0/?vgnextoid=28538b95b19e2310VgnVCM100000360a0a0aRCRD&ss=Columns&s=Business.
43. *FT* 091011, http://www.ft.com/intl/cms/s/0/a83e5cf4-f02c-11e0-977b-00144feab49a.html#axzz1aLUTKtMO.
44. A survey by the firm Alibaba and Peking University cited in *SCMP* 151011, http://www.scmp.com/portal/site/SCMP/menuitem.2af62ecb329d3d7733492d9253a0a0a0/?vgnextoid=6b1abea2fe203310VgnVCM100000360a0a0aRCRD&ss=China&s–ews.
45. *FT* 091011, http://www.ft.com/intl/cms/s/0/a83e5cf4-f02c-11e0-977b-00144feab49a.html#axzz1aLUTKtMO.

46. Ferri and Liu, 'Honour thy Creditors'.
47. *SCMP* 260909.
48. *SCMP* 131011, http://www.scmp.com/portal/site/SCMP/menuitem.2af62ecb329d3d773349 2d9253a0a0a0/?vgnextoid=190d4eeb409f2310VgnVCM100000360a0a0aRCRD&ss=Compa nies+%26+Finance&s=Business.
49. *SCMP* 200910.
50. China Organic Growth Fund 130213.
51. *SCMP* 180409.
52. See Erica Downs and Michal Meidan, 'Business and Politics in China: The Oil Executive Reshuffle of 2011', *China Security*, Issue 19.
53. *SCMP* 150311.
54. Reported by *China Daily* 110311 on People's Forum website, http://www.peopleforum.cn/ viewthread.php?tid=77163.
55. IMF, *People's Republic of China: Financial System Stability Assessment* (2011), http://www.imf. org/external/pubs/ft/scr/2011/cr11321.pdf, p.7.

5 Social Welfare: Missing Umbrella

1. *SCMP* 240310 and *Times* 101210.
2. See World Bank, 'From Poor Areas to Poor People' (March 2009).
3. ibid., pp.iv–viii.
4. For example, Dr Hu Biliang, deputy director of the China Centre for Rural Governance Research, cited in *SCMP* 060311.
5. Professor Zheng Fengtian of Renmin University and Shen Wen CPPCC delegate, cited in *SCMP* 010411.
6. Global Hunger index IFPRI 2010, http://www.ifpri.org/sites/default/files/publications/ ghi10.pdf.
7. ADB Key Indicators for Asia and the Pacific 2010, http://www.adb.org/documents/books/ key_indicators/.
8. Parekh, MacInnes and Kenway, 'Monitoring Poverty and Social Exclusion 2010' (Joseph Rowntree Foundation), http://www.jrf.org.uk/sites/files/jrf/poverty-social-exclusion–2010-full.pdf.
9. http://www.fns.usda.gov/pd/34SNAPmonthly.htm.
10. *Economist* 091010.
11. Ding Ning Ning, 'Conceptions, Policies and Challenges Arising from Daily Life'.
12. World Bank *Meeting the Challenges of Secondary Education*, p.260.
13. Ding Ning Ning, 'Conceptions, Policies and Challenges'.
14. China.org.cn 151011. http://www.china.org.cn/opinion/2011–10/15/content_23626282_2.htm.
15. *SCMP* 021010.
16. OECD, *Review of Tertiary Education, China* (2009), p.83.
17. China.org.cn 151011, http://www.china.org.cn/opinion/2011–10/15/content_23626282_2.htm.
18. University World News 100711, http://www.universityworldnews.com/article. php?story=20110708162827633.
19. China Daily 290811, http://usa.chinadaily.com.cn/china/2011-08/29/content_13207511.htm.
20. *SCMP* 130309.
21. The UK's *Daily Mail* in 2012 carried a photograph of dozens of Chinese students studying for the *gaokao* while receiving intravenous drips of energy supplement: *Daily Mail* 070512, http://www.dailymail.co.uk/news/article–2140719/Education-bosses-hook-Chinese-high-school-students-IV-drips-energy-boosts-help-graduate.html.
22. AEI Research on the *gaokao*, 2009.
23. MGI, 'Addressing China's Looming Talent Shortage' (2005), http://www.google. ch/#hl=en&sugexp=gsihc&cp=53&gs_id=3&xhr=t&q—GI+%E2%80%9CAddressing+Chin a%E2%80%99s+Looming+Talent+Shortage%E2%80%9D+2005&pf=p&sclient=psy&site=& source=hp&rlz=1W1GGLL_en&pbx=1&oq—GI+%E2%80%9CAddressing+China%E2%80 %99s+Looming+Talent+Shortage%E2%80%9D+2005&aq=f&aqi=&aql=&gs_sm=&gs_ upl=&bav=on.2,or.r_gc.r_pw.&fp=e38e133e1426acae&biw=1280&bih=541.

24. See also Kumar Goldman and Liu, 2008. Interestingly, a survey by the Indian Manufacturers' Council of domestic businessmen, at about the same time, came to almost the same conclusion – 75–90 per cent unsuitable – for similar reasons.

25. See Shanghai Jiaotong University, http://www.shanghairanking.com/ARWU2011.html.

26. *SCMP* 130309.

27. A McKinsey quarterly survey published in 2008, cited by *FT* 070509, http://www.ft.com/cms/s/0/2c827696–3a9d–11de–8a2d–00144feabdc0.html#axzz1GB5SReVY.

28. OECD, *Education at a Glance* (2010), http://www.oecd.org/dataoecd/45/39/45926093.pdf.

29. See *WSJ* 220812, http://online.wsj.com/article/SB10000872396390443545504577566752847208984.html.

30. It appears at first sight that there is more cheating in the SATS in the US. However, on closer examination, the cheating in US exams seems substantially to be associated with Asian students.

31. *SCMP* 070510.

32. See work by the UN's Population Division, statisticians at the University of Washington and Cai Yong at the University of North Carolina cited in BBC 190912, http://www.bbc.co.uk/news/world-asia–19630110. See also Gu Baochang and Cai Yong, 'Fertility Prospects in China', UN Population Division, 2011.

33. *Daily Telegraph* 040709.

34. Gu Baochang and Cai Yong, 'Fertility Prospects in China'.

35. Gavin W. Jones, 'Recent Fertility Trends, Policy Responses and Fertility Prospects in Low Fertility Countries of East and Southeast Asia', UN Population Division 2011.

36. Gu Baochang and Cai Yong, 'Fertility Prospects in China'.

37. Li Shuzhuo, 'Imbalanced Sex Ratio at Birth and Comprehensive Intervention in China', *Daily Telegraph* 310510. http://www.telegraph.co.uk/news/worldnews/asia/china/7787661/Chinese-hiding-three-million-babies-a-year.html.

38. Chen Wei, 'Sex Ratios at Birth in China'.

39. See Frank Dikotter's *Sex, Culture and Modernity in China: Medical Science and the Construction of Sexual Identities in the Early Republican Period* (1995) and the review, http://www.galtoninstitute.org.uk/Newsletters/GINL9703/dikotter_review.htm.

40. *SCMP* 260310.

41. Those who can currently benefit from this liberalisation are few and they must be parents with no siblings.

42. Jones, 'Recent Fertility Trends'.

43. *Economist* 220811, http://www.economist.com/blogs/dailychart/2011/08/populations.

44. UN Population Division 2011, http://esa.un.org/wpp/P-WPP/htm/PWPP_Total-Population.htm.

45. See Avraham Ebenstein and Ethan Jennings, '"Bare Branches", Prostitution, and HIV in China', p.8 http://pluto.huji.ac.il/~ebenstein/Ebenstein_Jennings_HIV_in_China_March_2008.pdf.

46. For an alternative view that the economic effect of population ageing can be mitigated, see David E. Bloom, David Canning and Günther Fink, 'Implications of Population Aging for Economic Growth', Harvard Initiative for Global Health 2011, http://www.hsph.harvard.edu/pgda/WorkingPapers/2011/PGDA_WP_64.pdf.

47. http://esa.un.org/wpp/unpp/panel_population.htm.

48. Liu Zhifeng, Vice Minister of Construction, in *People's Daily* 090802.

49. See Huang Youqin and Chengdong Yi, 'Second Home Ownership in Transitional Urban China' (forthcoming in *Housing Studies* in 2011, Vol. 26 No. 3) 2010 http://www.albany.edu/~yhuang/Second%20Home_HS_V2_WithTables.pdf.

50. Joyce Yanyun Man, *Affordable Housing in China* (2011). This compares with 67 per cent (and falling) in America, 70 per cent in Britain and 57 per cent in France, http://www.lincolninst.edu/pubs/PubDetail.aspx?pubid=1871&URL=Affordable-Housing-in-China&Page=5.

51. See GCIS 250512, http://www.gcis.com.cn/GCiS%20Commentary/China%20Home%20Ownership%20Rate%20–%20Misleading%20Statistics.htm.

52. A CASS Blue Paper quoted in *People's Daily* 081209, http://english.peopledaily.com.cn/90001/90782/90872/6835669.html.

53. A JP Morgan analyst writing in *SCMP* 011010.
54. Heikki Oksanen, 'The Chinese Pension System', p.3.
55. ibid., p.3.
56. *Beijing Review* 230511, http://www.bjreview.com.cn/print/txt/2011–05/23/content_359562.htm.
57. BBC 160512, http://www.bbc.co.uk/news/world-asia-china–18091107.
58. BBC 160512, http://www.bbc.co.uk/news/world-asia-china–18091107.
59. *SCMP* 091010.
60. *New York Times* 220307.
61. *SCMP* 091010.
62. Richard Jackson, 'China's Long March to Retirement Reform', 2009, CSIS.
63. *Shanghai Daily* 150612, http://www.china.org.cn/business/2012–06/15/content_25654231.htm.
64. Aviva, *Mind the Gap. Quantifying Europe's Pensions Gap* (2010), http://www.aviva.com/europe-pensions-gap/downloads/regional_uk.pdf.
65. See *Beijing Review* 230812, http://www.bjreview.com.cn/print/txt/2012-08/20/content_477184.htm.
66. *FT* 130509.
67. ibid.
68. See Pew Global Attitudes China Report 2012, http://www.pewglobal.org/files/2012/10/Pew-Global-Attitudes-China-Report-FINAL-October-10-2012.pdf.
69. *FT* 130509.
70. Herd, Hu and Koen, *Improving China's Health Care System* (OECD, 2010), http://www.oecd-ilibrary.org/docserver/download/fulltext/5kmlh4v2fv31.pdf?expires=1295569444&id=0000&accname=guest&checksum=F2E2CF276D191AF460FAD3D230254D3A P15.
71. WHO, *World Health Statistics* (2007). http://www.who.int/whosis/whostat2007.pdf.
72. See BBC 221012, http://www.bbc.co.uk/news/world-asia-pacific-11861919.
73. SCMP 140311.
74. Oxfam, 'Blind Optimism' (2009), p.20, note 69, citing W. C. Hsiao, *Harvard China Review* 5: 64–70 (2004).
75. Yu, Meng *et al.*, 'How Does the New Cooperative Medical Scheme Influence Health Service Utilization?'
76. *FT* 130509.
77. *SCMP* 090410.
78. GE's http://www.healthymagination.com/blog/health-of-nations/
79. *The Lancet* 081108.
80. Huffington Post 040913, http://www.huffingtonpost.com/2013/09/04/china-diabetes_n_3867778.html.
81. The George Institute 250510, http://www.georgeinstitute.org.cn/news-and-events-china/news/unmasking-china-s-secret-killer.
82. *Guardian* 200509 and Frank Lu, Liu and Shen, 'The Impact of Mental Health on Labour Market Outcomes in China'. See Abstract.
83. Phillips, Zhang, Shi *et al.* 'Prevalence, Treatment, and Associated Disability of Mental Disorders in Four Provinces in China during 2001–05: an Epidemiological Survey', *The Lancet* 373, No. 9680, pp.2041–53 (13 June 2009).
84. Xiao Park *et al.* 'Mental Health Care in China: Recent Changes and Future Challenges', *Harvard Health Policy Review* 6, No. 2 (Fall 2005), http://www.hcs.harvard.edu/~hhpr/currentissue/park.pdf.
85. Oxfam, 'Blind Optimism', (2009) citing Blumenthal and Hsiao *NEJM* 353 (2005): 1165–7.
86. See Siwan Anderson, 'The Economics of Dowry and Brideprice', *Journal of Economic Perspectives* 21, No. 4 (Fall 2007), 151–74, http://faculty.arts.ubc.ca/asiwan/documents/siwan-jep.pdf.
87. SCMP 151011, http://www.scmp.com/article/981931/business-brink-smes-say.
88. PlayFair 2008, http://www.playfair2008.org/docs/playfair_2008-report.pdf.
89. *SCMP* 210910.
90. *FT* 140410.
91. *SCMP* 070510.

92. BBC 301011, http://www.bbc.co.uk/news/world-asia-pacific–15510423 and Bloomberg 311011 http://www.businessweek.com/news/2011–10–31/china-mining-accident-deaths-near–100-may-boost-coal-imports.html.

93. *Guardian* 270709.

94. *IHT* 011009.

95. The most recent Korean figure is in *FT* 300511. The others are from OECD, *Society at a Glance 2009: OECD Social Indicators* (2009), http://puck.sourceoecd.org/pdf/societyataglan ce2009/812009011e–08–04.pdf.

96. Freedom House, *The Global State of Workers' Rights* (2010), http://www.freedomhouse.org/ uploads/special_report/92.pdf.

97. CASS, 'Migration and Labour Mobility in China'.

98. *IHT* 080109.

99. *FT* 121208.

100. *SCMP* 250311.

101. *SCMP* 051010.

102. CASS, *Migration and Labour Mobility in China*, p.27.

103. *China Daily* 120510, http://www.chinadaily.com.cn/china/2010–05/12/content_9837073. htm http://www.census.gov/hhes/www/income/data/historical/inequality/taba2.pdf.

104. *Economist* 151212, http://www.economist.com/news/finance-and-economics/21568423-new-survey-illuminates-extent-chinese-income-inequality-each-not?frsc=dg%7Ca.

105. *SCMP* 260910.

106. Song Xiaowu, President of the China Society for Economic Reform, and Zhang Dongsheng, Director of the Income Department of the National Development and Reform Commission, quoted in *China Daily* 020310, http://www.chinadaily.com.cn/china/2010–03/02/content_ 9521611.htm.

107. *SCMP* 261011, http://www.scmp.com/portal/site/SCMP/menuitem.2af62ecb329d3d77334 92d9253a0a0a0/?vgnextoid=7baecf3f1cb33310VgnVCM100000360a0a0aRCRD&ss—arkets&s=Business.

108. *SCMP* 291011, http://www.scmp.com/portal/site/SCMP/menuitem.2af62ecb329d3d77334 92d9253a0a0a0/?vgnextoid=43f92dda07b43310VgnVCM100000360a0a0aRCRD&ss=Chi na&s–ews.

109. China Daily 010313, http://www.chinadaily.com.cn/china/2013-03/01/content_16265552.htm.

110. CNTV 251111, http://english.cntv.cn/program/china24/20111125/103154.shtml.

111. The Ministry of Public Security quoted in *SCMP* 260910.

112. See Pew Global Attitudes China Report 2012, http://www.pewglobal.org/files/2012/10/ Pew-Global-Attitudes-China-Report-FINAL-October-10-2012.pdf.

113. See report in *Global Times* 081211, http://www.globaltimes.cn/NEWS/tabid/99/ID/687701/ Wealth-gap-widely-felt-in-China-newspaper.aspx.

114. J. R. Logan (ed.), *Urban Transition in China*, Notes, p.2.

115. *Guardian* 200509.

116. See Das Gupta, Ebenstein and Sharygin, 'China's, Marriage Market and Upcoming Challenges for Elderly Men', World Bank 2010, http://paa2011.princeton.edu/papers/110036.

117. Lou and Jiwei, *Public Finance in China*, p.204. Essay by Dahlman, Zeng and Wang 'Financing Lifelong Learning'.

118. Frank Dikotter, 'Reading the Body: Genetic Knowledge and Social Marginalization in the People's Republic of China', p.13, http://web.mac.com/dikotter/Dikotter/Publications_files/ Reading%20the%20Body.pdf.

6 The Environment

1. World Bank, 'Addressing China's Water Scarcity' 2009 Pxx http://www-wds.worldbank.org/ external/default/WDSContentServer/WDSP/IB/2009/01/14/000333037_20090114011126/ Rendered/PDF/471110PUB0CHA0101OFFICIAL0USE0ONLY1.pdf.

2. Blacksmith Institute, 'The World's Worst Polluted Places' (2007), p.6.

3. World Bank and the Chinese State Council's Development Research Centre in the report *China 2030* (2011), p.70, n. 30, http://www.citymayors.com/environment/world_pollution.html.

4. See Micah Muscolino, *Global Dimensions of Modern China's Environmental History* (University of Illinois, 2009). http://worldhistoryconnected.press.illinois.edu/6.1/muscolino.html.

5. Mark Elvin, *The Retreat of the Elephants*, p.xvii.

6. Elizabeth Economy, *The River Runs Black*, p.45.

7. See Tu Wei-ming, for example, on Qian Mu, Tang Jungyi and Feng Youlan. http://www.amacad.org/publications/fall2001/weiming.aspx.

8. See IEA 2 IEA 'Global carbon-dioxide emissions increase by 1.0 Gt in 2011 to record high' 240512, http://www.iea.org/newsroomandevents/news/2012/may/name,27216,en.html.

9. Vennemo, Aunan *et al.*, 'Environmental Pollution in China', p.210.

10. *SCMP* 030312, http://www.scmp.com/portal/site/SCMP/menuitem.2af62ecb329d3d773349 2d9253a0a0a0/?vgnextoid=3b378d30d63d5310VgnVCM100000360a0a0aRCRD&ss=Chi na&s-ews.

11. Vennemo, Aunan *et al.*, 'Environmental Pollution in China', p.211.

12. Yunnan's Child Lead Prevention and Cure Office cited in *SCMP* 180310.

13. Vennemo, Aunan *et al.*, 'Environmental Pollution in China', p.211.

14. 2030 Water Resources Group.

15. Lijin Zhong and Arthur P. J. Mol, *Water Price Reforms in China: Policy-making and Implementation*, Water Resources Management 220509, p.377, http://www.wri.org.cn/files/wri/documents/water%20tariff%20reform_fulltext_2010Issue2.pdf.

16. *SCMP* 010411.

17. *SCMP* 060311.

18. Reported on the respected science website Physorg citing local Chinese media referring to Rizhao city in Shandong province: http://www.physorg.com/news/2011-02-china-drought-global-impact.html.

19. *NYT* 080211, http://www.nytimes.com/2011/02/09/business/global/09food.html.

20. Norwegian Refugee Council, *Future Floods of Refugees* (2008). See diagram on p.15.

21. McKinsey Climate Change, *From Bread Basket to Dust Bowl* (2009), p.13, http://209.172.180.99/locations/chinatraditional/From_Bread_Basket_Dust_Bowl_EN.pdf.

22. *SCMP* 010411.

23. See AFP 121011, http://www.google.com/hostednews/afp/article/ALeqM5gG5jnCXw_sZSiyVs5jI1EkaADpXA?docId=CNG.d9529d7f75a4ac19ba01d71e2ca6c731.401.

24. Timothy Brook, *The Troubled Empire*, p.59.

25. Zhong and Mol, *Water Price Reforms in China*, p.383, http://www.wri.org.cn/files/wri/documents/water%20tariff%20reform_fulltext_2010Issue2.pdf.

26. ibid., p.387.

27. Xinhua 010211, http://news.xinhuanet.com/english2010/china/2011-02/01/c_13716274.htm.

28. Associated Press cited in *SCMP* 180411.

29. *Guardian* 240510, http://www.guardian.co.uk/environment/2010/may/24/chinese-hydroengineers-propose-tibet-dam and Professor Brahma Chellaney writing in SCMP 181011 http://www.scmp.com/portal/site/SCMP/menuitem.2af62ecb329d3d7733492d9253a0a0a0/?vgnextoid=2f52984a4b113310VgnVCM100000360a0a0aRCRD&ss=Columns+%26+Insight&s=Opinion.

30. Associated Press cited in *SCMP* 180411 and see the thinking of Isabel Hilton 090212, http://chinawaterrisk.org/opinions/diverting-the-brahmaputra-much-ado-about-nothing/.

31. Gong Jing, Cui Zheng, writing in Caixin's *New Century Weekly*, reproduced 100112, http://www.chinadialogue.net/article/show/single/en/4722-China-s-thirst-for-water-transfer.

32. OECD cited in *Observer/Guardian* 170707.

33. Hu Siyi, Vice Minister of Water Resources, cited by CCTV 160212, http://english.cntv.cn/20120216/115325.shtml.

34. Vennemo, Aunan *et al.*, 'Environmental Pollution in China', p.212.

35. *NYT* 030611 citing the Ministry of Environmental Protection, http://www.nytimes.com/2011/06/04/world/asia/04china.html?_r=1&ref=waterpollution.

36. Qu and Fan, 'The Current State of Water Quality and Technology Development', p.519.

37. Lijin Zhong and Cy Jones, *China Needs Comprehensive and Cost-effective Strategies to Address Water Pollution* (World Resources Institute, 2011), http://www.wri.org/stories/2011/06/china-needs-comprehensive-and-cost-effective-strategies-address-water-pollution.

38. WB, *Addressing China's Water Scarcity* (2009), p.14, http://www-wds.worldbank.org/external/default/WDSContentServer/WDSP/IB/2009/01/14/000333037_20090114011126/Rendered/PDF/471110PUB0CHA0101OFFICIAL0USE0ONLY1.pdf.

39. The 2012 *Good Beach Guide* reviewed in *Guardian* 030512. http://www.guardian.co.uk/environment/2012/may/03/rain-water-quality-uk-beaches?INTCMP=SRCH.

40. See, for example, BBC 231105. http://news.bbc.co.uk/2/hi/asia-pacific/4462760.stm.

41. *Caixin* 140212. http://english.caixin.com/2012-02-14/100356513.html.

42. Vennemo, Aunan *et al.*, 'Environmental Pollution in China', pp.210–11.

43. Xinhua 130511, http://news.xinhuanet.com/english2010/china/2011-05/13/c_13873675.htm.

44. Qu and Fan, 'The Current State of Water Quality', p.521.

45. ibid., p.520.

46. Xue, Zhang, Ye *et al.*, 'Land Subsidence in China', p.713.

47. Xu, Shen and Cai, 'The State of Land Subsidence and Prediction Approaches', 2007.

48. Li, Huang and Zhou, 'Land Subsidence Prediction by Various Grey Models', abstract.

49. Yin, Zhang and Li, 'Urbanisation and Land Subsidence in China', p.1.

50. ibid., p.5.

51. Xue, Zhang, Ye *et al.*, 'Land Subsidence in China', p.719.

52. Xu, Zhang, Shen *et al.*, 'Geo-hazards with Characteristics and Prevention Measures', p.482.

53. Xue, Zhang, Ye *et al.*, 'Land Subsidence in China', p.716.

54. Xu, Zhang, Shen *et al.*, 'Geo-hazards with Characteristics and Prevention Measures', p.495.

55. Xue, Zhang, Ye *et al.*, 'Land Subsidence in China', p.719.

56. ibid., p.720.

57. But not only: the humble potato is also to blame. Since its arrival (but particularly in the seventeenth and eighteenth centuries), farmers have gravitated to ever more remote – and higher – regions of the country, where new land could be found suitable for the new crop. The result of such upland land clearance and then cultivation was often erosion. The soil was washed downwards and silted up the rivers. Micah S. Muscolino, 'Global Dimensions of Modern China's Environmental History', *World History Connected*, 6 (2009), http://worldhistoryconnected.press.illinois.edu/6.1/muscolino.html.

58. Huang and Chan, 'Human-induced Landslides', p.2766.

59. ibid., p.2771.

60. *SCMP* 080509.

61. The minister, was quoted in AFP 121011, http://www.google.com/hostednews/afp/article/ALeqM5gG5jnCXw_sZSiyVs5jI1EkaADpXA?docId=CNG.d9529d7f75a4ac19ba-01d71e2ca6c731.401.

62. *SCMP* 080509.

63. Yan Tan, *Resettlement in the Three Gorges Project*, p.1.

64. Yang, Milliman *et al.*, '50,000 Dams Later', p.14.

65. *SCMP* 080509.

66. *China Daily* 121007; Peter H. Gleick, *The Three Gorges Dam Project, Yangtze River, China*, Water Brief 3, The World's Water (2008–9), p.145 http://www.worldwater.org/data20082009/WB03.pdf. http://www.chinadaily.com.cn/china/2007-10/12/content_6167689.htm.

67. Yan Tan, *Resettlement in the Three Gorges Project*, p.75ff.

68. Dai, Yao *et al.*, 'A Study on the Relationship between Water Levels and Seismic Activity in the Three Gorges Reservoir', Institute of Seismology, China Earthquake Administration, Wuhan (trans. and published in English by Probe International 2011), http://probeinternational.org/library/wp-content/uploads/2011/06/3-Gorges-Report-26-5.pdf.

69. L. M. High Land, 'Geographical Overview of the Three Gorges Dam and Reservoir, China – Geologic Hazards and Environmental Impacts: US Geological Survey Report 2008-1241', Slide 12 http://pubs.usgs.gov/of/2008/1241/pdf/OF08-1241_508.pdf.

70. Peter H. Gleick, 'The Three Gorges Dam Project, Yangtze River, China', Water Brief 3, The World's Water 2008–9, pp.144–5, http://www.worldwater.org/data20082009/WB03.pdf.

71. *Nature News* 250511, http://www.nature.com/news/2011/110525/full/news.2011.315.html.

72. See *SCMP* 190412.

73. Probe International, 'Seismic Regions always a Risk' 160410, http://journal.probeinternational. org/2010/04/16/building-dams-in-china%E2%80%99s-seismic-regions-always-a-risk/.

74. *Nature News* 250511, http://www.nature.com/news/2011/110525/full/news.2011.315.html.

75. For example Ban Gu (AD 32–92) Shi, Yan, Yuan *et al.* 'Wind Erosion Research in China', p.366.

76. National Meteorological Bureau of China cited in ibid.

77. Elvin, *The Retreat of the Elephants*, p.9.

78. Yancheva, Nowaczyk, Ingram, 'Influence of the Intertropical Convergence Zone'. However, Zhang and Lu and Zhang, Tian *et al.* disagree about the dry conditions before the fall of the Tang but agree about the cold.

79. Xinhua 170612 said 27.33 per cent, http://news.xinhuanet.com/english/china/2012--06/17/c_131658899.htm. However, strangely, X. Y. Zhao of the Chinese Academy of Sciences gave the same data twelve years earlier, in 2000. Has the desert grown or contracted? Both statements are made. As always in China statistics can mislead. http://www.klter.org/ EVENTS/Conference00/html/Xueyong%20Zhao.htm. State Forestry Administration figures cited by Chinese Embassy Botswana website 2007 http://bw.china-embassy.org/eng/xwdt/ t366582.htm.

80. Liu, Zhang, Wang *et al.*, 'Soil Degradation', p.87.

81. e.g. Elizabeth Economy in *Foreign Affairs* 070907 reproduced on http://yaleglobal.yale.edu/ content/great-leap-backward and Food and Agriculture Organisation 'Drylands development and combating desertification' 1997 http://www.fao.org/docrep/W7539E/w7539e03.htm.

82. See Al Jazeera 081212, http://www.aljazeera.com/indepth/features/2012/12/ 2012126123056457256.html.

83. BBC 040111.

84. Shi, Yan, Yuan *et al.* p.366.

85. The growth of the cashmere market has been identified as a major contributor to over-grazing. While America keeps 9 million goats and sheep, China reportedly has 366 million on the same land area, and these herds have devastated much of China's grassland.

86. CAS, http://english.cas.cn/Ne/CASE/201011/t20101112_61341.shtml.

87. Probe International 200710, http://journal.probeinternational.org/2010/07/20/beijings-water-crisis-unabated-neighbours-pay-the-price/.

88. Probe International 2008, p.12, http://www.probeinternational.org/files/Beijing%20 Water%20Report%20Update%202010.pdf.

89. See Probe International 221112, http://journal.probeinternational.org/2012/11/22/sucking-beijing-dry/.

90. *SCMP* 290212, http://www.scmp.com/portal/site/SCMP/menuitem.2af62ecb329d3d773349 2d9253a0a0a0/?vgnextoid=aee4974b674c5310VgnVCM100000360a0a0aRCRD&ss= China&s–ews.

91. Probe International 150709, http://journal.probeinternational.org/2009/07/15/beijings-water-crisis-and-economic-collapse/.

92. See Ministry of Water Resources (accessed 060113) http://www.mwr.gov.cn/english/swcc. html.

93. See Reuters 211108, http://www.reuters.com/article/2008/11/21/us-china-erosion-idUSTRE4AK1J220081121.

94. Shi, Yan, Yuan *et al.*, 'Wind Erosion in China', p.375.

95. Cao, Chen, Shankman *et al.*, p.240.

96. John McKinnon of EU–China Biodiversity Programme quoted in *Guardian* 110309.

97. Shi, Yan, Yuan *et al.*, 'Wind Erosion in China', p.381.

98. See Yale University's 'environment 360' 170112, http://e360.yale.edu/feature/chinas_ reforestation_programs_big_success_or_just_an_illusion/2484/.

99. Cao, Chen, Shankman *et al.*, 'Excessive Reliance on Afforestation', p.241.

100. ibid., p.241.

101. Treehugger weblog 060607 Living, Green Wall Fends Off Encroaching Desert: TreeHugger Via ::'Green Wall of China' Aims to Hold Back Desert. http://www.treehugger.com/ files/2007/06/living_green_wall.php.

102. Cao, Chen, Shankman *et al.*, p.240.
103. *Daily Telegraph* 040308.
104. US EPA cited in LA *Daily Times* 290706.
105. Article Elizabeth Economy in a 2007 edition of *Foreign Affairs*.
106. See Yale University's 'environment 360', 170112http://e360.yale.edu/feature/chinas_reforestation_programs_big_success_or_just_an_illusion/2484/.
107. Tian Yanfang, China's Imports of Russian Timber', p.3.
108. With the development of the Tarim and Daqing basins, China is now Asia's largest oil producer, but this is unfortunately not significant.
109. Vennemo, Aunan *et al.*, 'Environmental Pollution in China', p.212.
110. BBC 150909.
111. *Daily Telegraph* 100109.
112. Water issues have certainly arisen elsewhere: they led to the temporary closure in 2003 of nuclear power plants supplying three-quarters of France's electricity, and to anger about excessive water consumption by solar facilities in California and Nevada. See *IHT* 011009, *Times* 300511 and *SCMP* 270311.
113. Energy Information Administration, USA, May 2011, http://www.eia.gov/cabs/china/Full.html.
114. *SCMP* 280910.
115. Tao and Watson, 'China's Energy Transition', 2009.
116. Li Ruogu, *Institutional Suitability*, p.403.
117. http://www.pnas.org/content/110/32/12936.full.pdf.
118. Economy, Elizabeth, p.75.
119. FT 170113 http://www.ft.com/intl/cms/s/0/e048f7e4-6083-11e2-a31a-00144feab49a.html#axzz2PltdlHJE.
120. William P. Alford, and Benjamin L. Liebman, 'Clean Air, Clear Processes?', *Hastings Law Journal* 52, No. 3 (2001), pp.9, 29, http://www.wcfia.harvard.edu/sites/default/files/676__CLEAN_AIR_5_03.pdf.
121. Vennemo, Aunan *et al.*, 'Environmental Pollution in China', p.224.
122. Ho and Vermeer (eds), *China's Limits to Growth*, p.39.
123. See Greenpeace 131009, http://www.greenpeace.org/eastasia/news/stories/toxics/2009/silent-giants-news/.
124. Vennemo, Aunan *et al.*, 'Environmental Pollution in China', p.221.
125. Reuters 060111; Zhang Ping of NDRC speaking to Xinhua, http://www.reuters.com/article/2011/01/06/us-china-energy-intensity-idUSTRE7051OE20110106.
126. Professor Tang Hao of South China Normal University 161210, http://www.chinadialogue.net/article/show/single/en/4008-Relic-of-a-planned-economy.
127. W. P. Alford and B. L. Liebman, 'Clean Air, Clean Processes?', p.31.
128. *China Daily* 310109, www.chinadaily.com.cn/china/2009-01/31/content_7433211.htm.
129. Zhong and Mol, 'Water Price Reforms in China: Policy-making and Implementation', p.388.
130. *SCMP* 080411.
131. Zhao Dagong, 'The Xiamen Demonstrations and Growing Civil Consciousness', *Human Rights in China* (2007), http://www.hrichina.org/sites/default/files/oldsite/PDFs/CRF.3.2007/CRF-2007 3_Xiamen.pdf; Xinhua 151207, http://www.china.org.cn/english/environment/235761.htm; *China Daily* 300507, http://www.chinadaily.com.cn/china/2007-05/30/content_882936.htm.
132. NDRC, 'China's Climate Change Programme' (2007), p.19.
133. Pew Survey 2009, p.87.
134. *Guardian* 231209.
134. *SCMP* 300409.
136. *SCMP* 161009.
137. McGregor, p.75.
138. Pew Survey 2009.
139. *SCMP* 220308.
140. *US–China Economic and Security Review Report* (2007), p.173.

141. See *FT* 280211. http://www.ft.com/intl/cms/s/0/3671a476-4359-11e0-8f0d-00144feabdc0. html#axzz1obk8Gl33.

142. Ho and Vermeer, *China's Limits to Growth*, p.21.

143. *Asia Sentinel* 261107, http://www.asiasentinel.com/index.php?option=com_content&task= view&id=898&Itemid=31.

144. *SCMP* 100509.

7 Threats to Social Stability

1. Xinhua 080409.

2. *People's Daily* 140311, http://english.peopledaily.com.cn/90001/90776/90785/7318786.html.

3. *FT*   100712.   http://www.ft.com/intl/cms/s/0/86a82f3e-bc69-11e1-a470-00144feabdc0. html#axzz20Pwvk96E.

4. BBC 080110.

5. BBC 081012, http://www.bbc.co.uk/news/world-asia-china-19843176.

6. See   www.chinaview.cn   100309,   http://news.xinhuanet.com/english/2009-03/10/ content_10987127.htm.

7. For example, see *SCMP* 160409 and *NYT* 250810, http://www.nytimes.com/2010/08/26/ world/asia/26corrupt.html.

8. See   www.chinaview.cn   100309,   http://news.xinhuanet.com/english/2009-03/10/ content_10987127.htm.

9. *China Daily*'s blog 060110, http://bbs.chinadaily.com.cn/redirect.php?gid=2&tid=657246&goto =lastpost.

10. See *Daily Telegraph* 261112, http://www.telegraph.co.uk/news/worldnews/asia/china/9702910/ Chinese-sex-tape-scandal-unearths-corruption-in-Bo-Xilais-Chongqing.html.

11. See   www.chinaview.cn   100309,   http://news.xinhuanet.com/english/2009-03/10/ content_10987127.htm.

12. *Caixin* 080212, http://english.caixin.com/2012-02-08/100354426.html. It has been noted in the CCPCC that government administrative spending, including cars, receptions and overseas travel total 18.6 per cent of government spending (compared to 2.8 per cent in Japan): *SCMP* 030312 http://www.scmp.com/portal/site/SCMP/menuitem.2af62ecb329d3d7733492d9253a 0a0a0/?vgnextoid=3bf931b8954d5310VgnVCM100000360a0a0aRCRD&ss=China&s–ews.

13. *FT* 210911, http://www.ft.com/intl/cms/s/0/a5f7a660-e421-11e0-b4e9-00144feabdc0. html#axzz1Ye4vRF6u.

14. Lemos, *The End of the Chinese Dream*, p.32.

15. Gong Ting, *The Politics of Corruption in Contemporary China*, p.135.

16. In Ann Elliott, Kimberly (ed.), *Corruption and the Global Economy*, p.72.

17. *Der Spiegel* 270207, http://www.spiegel.de/international/spiegel/0,1518,465007-5,00.html.

18. *SCMP* 180410.

19. ibid.

20. *SCMP* 110399.

21. *SCMP* 160409.

22. *Global Times* 261011, http://www.globaltimes.cn/NEWS/tabid/99/ID/680930/Public-trust-is-withering-on-Chinas-bigger-projects.aspx.

23. http://cpi.transparency.org/cpi2013/results/.

24. CEIP, 'Corruption Threatens China's Future' 2007.

25. Gong and Shi, 'Management Corruption in China's Industrial Restructuring', 2009.

26. Wang Hui, *The End of Revolution* (2011 edn), p.27.

27. Zhao Ziyang, *Prisoner of the State*, p.157.

28. *China Daily* 170310.

29. It has even been suggested that some members of the CCPCC – the Chinese parliament's upper house – had bought their memberships: *SCMP* 090312, http://www.scmp.com/portal/ site/SCMP/menuitem.2af62ecb329d3d7733492d9253a0a0a0/?vgnextoid=1645bd404e2f531 0VgnVCM100000360a0a0aRCRD&ss=Hong+Kong&s–ews.

30. Bloomberg   060311,   http://www.bloomberg.com/news/2011-03-06/china-s-spending-on-internal-police-force-in-2010-outstrips-defense-budget.html.

31. See Dr Theresa Hesketh, 'Ratio of Males to Females in China', *British Medical Journal* 090409, http://www.bmj.com/content/338/bmj.b483.full.
32. One wonders if this might be another example of failed statistics.
33. Gu and Roy 'Sex Ratio at Birth in China' (1995).
34. Gerth, *As China Goes*, p.160.
35. http://news.bbc.co.uk/2/hi/asia-pacific/7002201.stm.
36. *Beijing Today* 140610, http://www.beijingtoday.com.cn/outlook/sex-ratio-discrepancy-declines-baby-steps-to-narrow-gender-imbalance.
37. See the Population Reference Bureau, Washington DC, http://www.prb.org/Articles/2012/china-census-excess-males.aspx. For the growing crime rate, see NBC News 140904, http://www.msnbc.msn.com/id/5953508/ns/world_news/t/china-grapples-legacy-its-missing-girls/. Also see 'Sex Ratios and Crime' 2007, pp.4 and 16, ftp://ftp.iza.org/RePEc/Discussionpaper/dp3214.pdf; Li Shuzhuo, 'Imbalanced Sex Ratio at Birth and Comprehensive Intervention in China' UN Family Planning Association 2007 p.8, http://www.unfpa.org/gender/docs/studies/china.pdf.
38. See Zhang et al 2007 http://ftp.iza.org/dp3214.pdf.
39. Institute of Child Health, UCL press office 280806.
40. VOA 240111, http://blogs.voanews.com/breaking-news/2011/01/24/experts-say-chinas-gender-ratio-contributes-to-human-trafficking/.
41. Extreme markets embrace a wide range of unorthodox produce from rare species for consumption or rejuvenation to prisoners' organs for transplants (which he writes about), to other areas such as arms and drugs: Gerth, *As China Goes*, Ch. 7 'Extreme Markets'.
42. Chen, Zhang *et al.*, 'Syphilis in China', *The Lancet.*
43. Tucker, Chen *et al.*, 'Syphilis and Social Upheaval in China', *NEJM* 060510.
44. Das Gupta, Chung and Li, 'Is There an Incipient Turnaround in Asia's "Missing Girls" Phenomenon?', 2009.
45. *People's Daily* 210602.
46. *International Narcotics Control Strategy Report* Vol. 1 (US State Department, 2011), p.188.
47. *International Narcotics Control Strategy Report* Vol. 1 (US State Department, 2009), p.193.
48. China Daily 070114 http://usa.chinadaily.com.cn/epaper/2014-01/07/content_17220890.htm.
49. http://www.silkroadstudies.org/new/docs/CEF/Quarterly/February_2006/Niklas_Swanstrom.pdf, page 128.
50. Q. Deng, Q Tang, R. S. Schottenfeld, W. Hao and M. C. Chawarski, 'Drug Use in Rural China: a Preliminary Investigation in Hunan Province', http://www.ncbi.nlm.nih.gov/pubmed/21906200.
51. *SCMP* 311011, http://www.scmp.com/portal/site/SCMP/menuitem.2af62ecb329d3d7733492d9253a0a0a0/?vgnextoid=5c3ec1bb18553310VgnVCM100000360a0a0aRCRD&ss=China&s–ews.
52. Logan, *Urban China in Transition*, pp.272–3.
53. *SCMP* 091107.
54. Reuters 290308.
55. *SCMP* 101009.
56. *SCMP* 110410.
57. *SCMP* 260910.
58. Serious Organised Crime Agency cited in *London Evening Standard* 290108.
59. 'Organised Crime Threats Assessment (OCTA) 2009', Europol.
60. Roberto Saviano, *Gomorrah: Italy's Other Mafia*, pp.7 and 43.
61. Dr Joel Brenner interviewed by the *Daily Telegraph* 101008.
62. See GunPolicy.org, http://www.gunpolicy.org/firearms/region/china. They cite the Small Arms Survey 2007, p.67.
63. ibid.
64. *Jane's* 210508.
65. BBC 030810.
66. *Pakistan Daily Times* 020406.
67. SIPRI, http://armstrade.sipri.org/armstrade/page/values.php.

68. Internet Business Law Services citing *People's Daily* online. http://www.ibls.com/internet_law_news_portal_view.aspx?s=latestnews&id=1689.
69. *China Daily* 150109.

8 Threats to Civil Stability

1. Wang Hui, *The End of the Revolution*, p.12.
2. *Daily Telegraph* 240308, http://www.telegraph.co.uk/news/worldnews/1582645/Chinese-intellectuals-call-for-talks-with-Tibet.html.
3. Yu Jianrong, part 4. Yu Jianrong gave a lecture at the Ministry of Finance to the Beijing Lawyers' Association in December 2009. A detailed transcript appears on Berkeley University's 'China Digital Times' news website: http://chinadigitaltimes.net/2010/03/yu-jianrong-maintaining-a-baseline-of-social-stability-part-4/.
4. *China Daily* 100311, http://www.chinadaily.com.cn/bizchina/2011-03/10/content_12151446.htm.
5. *FT* 070311, http://www.ft.com/intl/cms/s/0/f70936b0-4811-11e0-b323-00144feab49a.html.
6. Quoted in *NYT* 081208, http://www.nytimes.com/2008/12/09/world/asia/09china.html.
7. Office of the High Commission on Human Rights 251209, http://www.ohchr.org/EN/NewsEvents/Pages/Media.aspx.
8. *FT* 281209.
9. *Le Figaro* 261209.
10. *IHT* 060109; *Daily Telegraph* 120310, http://www.telegraph.co.uk/news/worldnews/asia/china/7425759/China-arrests-more-than-1000-people-for-endangering-state-security.html.
11. Bloomberg 290110.
12. ibid., 170809.
13. *SCMP* 040410.
14. A detailed transcript appears on Berkeley University's 'China Digital Times' news website, which is the source of the quotations: http://chinadigitaltimes.net/2010/03/yu-jianrong-maintaining-a-baseline-of-social-stability.
15. *Washington Post* 140108, http://www.washingtonpost.com/wp-dyn/content/article/2008/01/13/AR2008011302383.html.
16. http://chinadigitaltimes.net/2010/03/yu-jianrong-maintaining-a-baseline-of-social-stability-part-i/, *passim*.
17. *FT* 121205.
18. Human Rights Watch 010606.
19. *China Daily* 010708.
20. *SCMP* 250410.
21. Susan Shirk, *China: Fragile Superpower*, p.35 citing sources.
22. Wang Hui, *The End of the Revolution*, p.23.
23. *FT* 290512, http://www.ft.com/intl/cms/s/0/897c10b6-a983-11e1-9972-00144feabdc0.html#axllzwBV9podm.
24. McGregor, pp.109–10.
25. Mulvenon, 'Soldiers of Fortune', pp.9–10, n. 28, citing Baum, 'Burying Mao: Chinese Politics in the Age of Deng Xiaoping', pp.304–6.
26. Quoted in *The Times* 070608.
27. Myron Weiner, and Sharon Stanton Russell (eds), *Demography and National Security*, p.289.
28. Eric Teichman, *Journey to Turkistan*, p.18.
29. James A. Millward, *Eurasian Crossroads: A History of Xinjiang*, p.45.
30. ibid.
31. It is hard to be more specific about the causes of unrest, as the opinions of dissidents in Urumqi and Kashgar are not widely accessible.
32. Adrienne M. Dwyer, 'The Xinjiang Conflict: Uyghur Identity, Language Policy, and Political Discourse', p.x.
33. *IHT* 060109.
34. *NYT* 181008, http://www.nytimes.com/2008/10/19/world/asia/19xinjiang.html.
35. *Cib* magazine 100209, http://www.cibmagazine.com.cn/Features/Focus.asp?id=819.

36. *FT* 250511.
37. *SCMP* 081009.
38. Quilliam Foundation 290310.
39. See *SCMP* 190910, http://www.scmp.com/article/725199/hong-kong-beacon-culture.
40. Hegel, *Lectures on the Philosophy of History*, p.138.
41. See *Economist* 021003, http://www.economist.com/node/2102073.
42. *SCMP* 051010.
43. *SCMP* 010411.
44. ibid.
45. O'Brien (ed.), *Popular Protest in China*, p.116.
46. *China Aid News* 150811 see notes 104, 105 http://www.chinaaid.org/2011/10/excerpts-from-cecc-report-freedom-of.html.
47. Wang Zuoan, deputy director of the State Administration for Religious Affairs, cited in *SCMP* 251011, http://www.scmp.com/portal/site/SCMP/menuitem.2af62ecb329d3d7733492d9253 a0a0a0/?vgnextoid=03897cd47d633310VgnVCM100000360a0a0aRCRD&ss=China&s–ews.
48. *NYT* 270409.
49. Thomas Lum, 'China and Falan Gong', p.3.
50. Nick Couldry and James Curran (eds), *Contesting Media Power: Alternative Media in a Networked World*, p.212.
51. Fairbank, *The Great Chinese Revolution*, p.22.
52. Lum, 'China and Falan Gong', p.7.
53. ibid., p.1.
54. CBC News 120709.
55. *FT* 240410.
56. BBC 021205.
57. ibid., 070510.
58. Report to the UN General Assembly by the Special Rapporteur on Torture 050210.
59. *SCMP* 140309.
60. *SCMP* 110412. It is disturbing to note that disabled dissidents seem capable of becoming disabled while in police custody, which theoretically should be the safest environment in all China: http://www.scmp.com/portal/site/SCMP/menuitem.2af62ecb329d3d7733492d 9253a0a0a0/?vgnextoid=b246f07f75c96310VgnVCM100000360a0a0aRCRD&ss=China&s–ews.
61. *FT* 250410.
62. ibid.
63. *China Daily* 161009, 290709, 170507, 240409, 290509, 310709. http://www.chinadaily.com.cn/china/2009-10/16/content_8801506.htm, http://www.chinadaily.com.cn/china/2009-07/29/content_8484166.htm, http://www.chinadaily.com.cn/opinion/2007-05/17/content_874453.htm, http://www.chinadaily.com.cn/cndy/2009-05/29/content_7951683.htm.
64. *The Times* 280711.
65. *Global Times* 031110, http://china.globaltimes.cn/society/2010-11/588872.html.
66. WSJ blog 080311, http://blogs.wsj.com/chinarealtime/2011/03/08/chinas-foreign-minister-to-foreign-press-don%e2%80%99t-believe-your-lying-eyes-jasmine-protests/.
67. *SCMP* 031010.
68. *Independent*   200412,   http://www.independent.co.uk/news/world/asia/investigations-surrounding-death-of-briton-bring-state-funding-into-focus-7661517.html?printService=print.
69. Berkman Centre 090507, http://opennet.net/research/profiles/china.
70. BBC 140110.
71. A Survey by Nature magazine. *Nature* 463, 1012–1013 (2010) published online 240210 doi:10.1038/4631012a, http://www.nature.com/news/2010/100224/full/4631012a.html.
72. Cited by Yang Guobin in O'Brien (ed.), *Popular Protest in China* (2008), p.131. Sourced from Kevin J. O'Brien, 'Collective Action in the Chinese Countryside', *China Journal* 48 (2002), p.144.
73. CASS, *Surveying Internet Usage and Impact in Twelve Chinese Cities* (2003), p.13, http://www.policyarchive.org/handle/10207/bitstreams/15539.pdf.
74. BBC 041013, http://www.bbc.co.uk/news/world-asia-china-24396957.

75. Estimate of the US State Department cited by *Daily Telegraph* 230711.
76. The World Economic Forum survey for 2009–10 reckons that China has more judicial independence than a quarter of the member countries of the European Union. However, this probably relates more to commercial cases (and perhaps says more about the EU than it does about China).
77. CNN 180912 citing Chinese Supreme People's Court http://edition.cnn.com/2012/09/17/world/asia/china-wang-trial-starts/index.html.
78. Zhou Ruijin, a deputy editor-in-chief of the *People's Daily*, reported in *SCMP* 051011, http://www.scmp.com/portal/site/SCMP/menuitem.2af62ecb329d3d7733492d9253a0a0a0/?vgnextoid=e4f138cd67fc2310VgnVCM100000360a0a0aRCRD&ss=China&s–ews.
79. Quoted in *Daily Telegraph* 271109.
80. A survey by Yu Jianrong at CASS cited in HRW, 'An Alleyway in Hell' (2009), p.8.
81. Chen, Xi, 'Collective Petitioning and Institutional Conversion', in O'Brien, *Popular Protest in China*, pp.54–70.
82. Of course, there is not one unambiguous form of Western democracy: it ranges from Switzerland (where politicians might be accused of contracting out much decision-making to the public rather than taking responsibility themselves) to Britain (where politicians feel their role is not to reflect public opinion but to 'lead' it). In the latter, legislation is passed which the MPs know is opposed by a majority of the public (but not all at the same time, so it does not necessarily affect the result of the next election). We have recently seen the appearance of a new idea – the European Union. There, citizens of different countries are asked to vote on seemingly important issues, such as constitutions; but if an infelicitous response is given by a constituent country, the electorate is told by the unelected leadership to go away and think again. The embryonic 'state' is by its nature committed to a strategic policy of ever deeper union, and so alternative choices by the electorate, axiomatically, require rejection. If the acceptable answer is given, the opportunity to opine never recurs. The European Union is founded on an institutionalised contempt for public opinion and an innate fear of democracy.
83. Hegel, *Lectures on the Philosophy of History*, p.126.
84. Aristotle, *Politics*, trans. J. E. C. Welldon (1897), p.145.
85. *SCMP* 280912, http://www.scmp.com/news/china/article/1048977/boom-city-dongguan-faces-bankruptcy.
86. Fishkin, He, Luskin and Siu, 'Deliberative Democracy in an Unlikely Place: Deliberative Polling in China', B.J.Pol.S., p.1 of 14 Copyright r Cambridge University Press, 2010, http://cdd.stanford.edu/research/papers/2010/fishkin-bjps-china.pdf.
87. Samuel Huntington, The Clash of Civilizations and the Remaking of World Order (1996), p.310.
88. David Shambaugh, *China's Communist Party*, p.37.

9 Identity: Future of State and Party

1. Using the Gini coefficients from the UNDP and the CIA, albeit in different years.
2. China Daily 010313, http://www.chinadaily.com.cn/china/2013-03/01/content_16265552.htm.
3. See the Hurun Rich List 2012, http://www.hurun.net/usen/NewsShow.aspx?nid=349.
4. See Hélène Carrère d'Encausse, *L'Empire éclaté, passim*.
5. Rebecca Karl's preface to Wang Hui, p.ix.
6. See the search of the *Yinhe* in Chapter 10 above.
7. *FT* 160110.
8. McGregor, pp.31–2.
9. *FT* 120210.
10. Wang Hui, p.13.
11. *WSJ* 010609.
12. *NYT* 251012, http://www.nytimes.com/2012/10/26/business/global/family-of-wen-jiabao-holds-a-hidden-fortune-in-china.html?pagewanted=all&_r=0.
13. Fairbank, *The Great Chinese Revolution*, p.63.
14. Shirk, *China: Fragile Superpower*, p.66, citing Pei Minxin and see http://www.chinatoday.com/org/cpc.

15. Shambaugh, *China's Communist Party*, pp.35–6.
16. Zhou Ruijin's article in *Yanhuang Chunqiu*, cited in *SCMP* 051011. http://www.scmp.com/portal/site/SCMP/menuitem.2af62ecb329d3d7733492d9253a0a0a0/?vgnextoid=e4f138cd67fc2310VgnVCM100000360a0a0aRCRD&ss=China&s-ews.
17. An example of this might be Hu Jiwei, former chief editor of the Communist Party's *People's Daily*, who, in 2010, called for the release of arrested Nobel Prize-winner Liu Xiaobo.
18. See his essay in O'Brien (ed.), *Popular Protest in China*.
19. *The Times* 280711.
20. Quoted in O'Brien (ed.), *Popular Protest in China*, p.66.
21. Wang Hui, p.10.
22. See discussion in Wang Hui, pp.xviii–xix.
23. 'The Third Eye' pseudonymously authored by a 'Luoyi Ningge'er', cited in *SCMP* 100894.
24. *Global Times* 200812, http://www.globaltimes.cn/DesktopModules/DnnForge%20-%20NewsArticles/Print.aspx?tabid=99&tabmoduleid=94&articleId=727926&moduleId=405&-PortalID=0.
25. *Global Times* 290912, http://www.globaltimes.cn/content/736020.shtml.
26. *Economist* 061210, http://www.economist.com/node/17601499.
27. Goodman, *Beijing Street Voices*, p.5.
28. Remarks on successive drafts of the Resolution on Certain Questions in the History of our Party since the Founding of the People's Republic of China (Remarks by Deng Xiaoping) March 1980–June 1981, http://english.peopledaily.com.cn/dengx p/vol2/text/b1420.html.
29. Deng Xiaoping on 25 October 1980 cited by *People's Daily*, http://english.peopledaily.com.cn/dengxp/vol2/text/b1420.html.
30. Steve Tsang, 'Consultative Leninism: China's New Political Framework', *Journal of Contemporary China* (2009), p.868.
31. Wang Hui, p.7.
32. *SCMP* 250310.
33. Bailey, *China in the Twentieth Century*, p.19.
34. Economy, Elizabeth, p.268.
35. *SCMP* 151011, http://www.scmp.com/portal/site/SCMP/menuitem.2af62ecb329d3d7733492d9253a0a0a0/?vgnextoid=a803bea2fe203310VgnVCM100000360a0a0aRCRD&ss=China&s-ews.
36. *SCMP* 251011, http://www.scmp.com/portal/site/SCMP/menuitem.2af62ecb329d3d7733492d9253a0a0a0/?vgnextoid=03897cd47d633310VgnVCM100000360a0a0aRCRD&ss=China&s-ews.
37. Yu Jianrong, Part 8.
38. *FT* 290509.
39. *Guardian* 200809.
40. *People's Daily* online 170810 citing Ba Shusong, http://english.people.com.cn/90001/90778/90862/7106935.html.
41. *People's Daily* 030311, http://english.peopledaily.com.cn/90001/90778/7306287.html.
42. *Southern Weekly* 170507, English trans.: http://www.zonaeuropa.com/20070519_1.htm.
43. The choice of Confucius in the name is interesting, and would have been unthinkable forty years ago. Mao was vitriolic in his condemnation of Confucianism. Presumably this now forms part of the 30 per cent of his thinking and action which was deemed bad. Never in the history of mathematics has 30 per cent represented so large a proportion.
44. Brook, *Troubled Empire*, pp.87–8.
45. *Guardian* 070207.
46. http://www.economist.com/news/china/21584057-even-death-popular-pastor-makes-authorities-nervous-lamb-god.
47. Lecture by F. T. Ying of Chinese University Hong Kong 230309.
48. ibid.
49. ibid.
50. Carrère d'Encausse, *L'Empire éclaté*, p.246.
51. Frank Dikötter, *The Discourse of Race in Modern China*, pp.72–5.

52. Martin Jacques, *When China Rules the World*, p.421.
53. The *hanwang* movement is an ethnic nationalist movement seeking to uphold the position (even including the clothing) of the Han race as opposed to, say, the Manchu or Mongol citizens of the PRC. See: Leibold, 'More Than a Category: Han Supremacism on the Chinese Internet'.
54. ibid.
55. ibid.
56. Tsang, 'Consultative Leninism', p.876.
57. Simpson (ed.), *Language and National Identity in Asia*, pp.149, 150.
58. Pew Survey 2008.
59. Shirk, *China: Fragile Superpower, passim*.
60. See 'Regional Autonomy for Ethnic Minorities in China' (2005), http://english.gov.cn/official/2005-07/28/content_18127.htm.
61. Cited in William Easterly 'The Middle Class Consensus and Economic Development' WB 2001 P2 http://williameasterly.files.wordpress.com/2010/08/34_easterly_middleclassconsensus_prp.pdf.
62. Wang Lequan, former Party Secretary of Xinjiang, describing the friction there. Rodger Doyle in *Scientific American* (September 1998) *NYT* 181008; http://www.nytimes.com/2008/10/19/world/asia/19xinjiang.html.

10 America and China: Common Interests, Mutual Antagonisms

1. See FT 301011, http://www.ft.com/intl/cms/s/0/bd30c094-0151-11e1-b177-00144feabdc0.html#axzz1cM9PxArJ Boston Consulting Group press release 050511. http://www.bcg.com/media/PressReleaseDetails.aspx?id=tcm:12-75973.
2. *Think Progress* 020812, http://thinkprogress.org/economy/2012/08/02/627021/workers-low-wage-jobs/?mobile=nc.
3. *Observer* 171099, jointly investigated with Politiken of Copenhagen, http://www.guardian.co.uk/world/1999/oct/17/balkans.
4. ibid.
5. Di Hua at Stanford University, http://news.stanford.edu/pr/94/940218Arc4432.html.
6. According to the UN Convention on the Law of the Sea, countries must seek prior consent from maritime countries before conducting scientific investigation, including surveillance activities inside their 'economic exclusion zone'. The US has so far declined to ratify this convention, although this will probably change – not least because it also governs claims over the Arctic waters, where there is a scramble for energy resources.
7. This should be set in context: in mid-2011, China held 8 per cent of total US public debt; thus 92 per cent was supplied either domestically or from other foreign investors.
8. Pew Global Attitudes Survey 2011, http://pewglobal.org/files/2011/07/Pew-Global-Attitudes-Balance-of-Power-U.S.-Image-Report-FINAL-July-13-2011.pdf.
9. William S. Cohen, former Secretary of State for Defence, writing in *IHT* 231111.
10. *Economist* 261111.
11. ibid.
12. International Council on Security and Development, 'The Struggle for Kabul' December 2008.
13. *Economist* 220809.
14. FT 060107, http://www.ft.com/intl/cms/s/0/929cf220-9d2a-11db-8ec6-0000779e2340.html#axzz27TSZwCN0.
15. Congressional Research Service 270712, http://www.fas.org/sgp/crs/row/pakaid.pdf.
16. Serge Michailof, 'Sortir du piège afghan', *Commentaire* (2009).
17. Commission on Wartime Contracting in Iraq and Afghanistan, *Transforming Wartime Contracting*, Final Report to US Congress (2011), Foreword and p.2, www.wartimecontracting.gov.
18. ibid., p.4.
19. ibid., p.31.
20. Remarked at a Forbes conference in Kuala Lumpur in September 2009.
21. Gary Hufbauer, *Economic Sanctions Reconsidered, passim*.
22. *NYT* 220209.

23. ibid.
24. Wu Sike cited in *SCMP* 110311.
25. Pew Survey, 2008.
26. See the Pew Global Attitudes Survey 130612.
27. Pew Global Attitudes Survey, 2011.
28. It is difficult to understand how the Republican Party of traditional conservatives like Bob Taft, Barry Goldwater and Ronald Reagan got hijacked by a morality-light, big government utopian like George W. Bush.

11 Great Power Relationships

1. *FT* 150910, http://www.ft.com/cms/s/0/80292cc2-c0f7-11df-99c4-00144feab49a. html#axzz1GB5SReVY.
2. Rose Fisher and Huttentuck, p.5.
3. Katherine Villers, 'Is the Border Dispute a Symptom or a Cause of the Antagonism between India and China?', unpublished paper.
4. John George Stoessinger, *Why Nations go to War*, p.409.
5. *Guardian* 271111, http://www.guardian.co.uk/world/2011/nov/27/china-india-dalai-lama-border-row.
6. An article in *The Hindu* cited in Shashank Joshi, *China and India: Awkward Ascents* (2011) p.4, http://shashankjoshi.files.wordpress.com/2011/02/sino-indian-relations-pdf.pdf.
7. A. K. Anthony, Indian Defence Minister, and others cited in *FT* 161210, http://www.ft.com/cms/s/0/2bafc45c-093c-11e0-ada6-00144feabdc0.html#ixzz1KVKIVzj2.
8. Villers, 'Border Dispute'.
9. Joshi, *China and India: Awkward Ascents*, p.11.
10. Walter Ladwig's 'Delhi's Pacific Ambition: Naval Power' cited in Joshi, *China and India: Awkward Ascents*, p.11.
11. *FT* 210510, http://www.ft.com/cms/s/0/833aca0e-646f-11df-8cba-00144feab49a. html#axzz1GB5SReVY.
12. *Economist* 181110, http://www.economist.com/node/17527970?story_id=17527970.
13. 'Charting our Water Future' (2009), 2030WaterResourcesGroup@mckinsey.com.
14. Rohan D'Souza, 'How Not to Discuss Water with China' 180112, http://www.chinadialogue.net/article/show/single/en/4730-How-not-to-discuss-water-with-China.
15. See Carnegie Endowment, 'A Crisis to Come? China, India, and Water Rivalry' 130911, http://carnegieendowment.org/2011/09/13/crisis-to-come-china-india-and-water-rivalry/54wg.
16. George Fernandes in *Tribune of India* 270903.
17. Lt. Col. J. S. Kohli in the *Journal of the United Service Institution of India*, 138, No. 571 (January–March 2008).
18. *The Dawn* 240210.
19. BBC 080110.
20. *SMH* 270709, http://www.smh.com.au/world/rally-around-flag-china-tells-diaspora-20090726-dxin.html.
21. J. Mohan Malik, *India-China Relations* (Berkshire Publishing Group LLC, 2009), http://www.apcss.org/core/BIOS/malik/India-China_Relations.pdf.
22. Bharat Karnad, *India's Nuclear Policy* (Westport, Conn.: Praeger Security International, 2008), cited in Joshi, *China and India: Awkward Ascents*, p.12.
23. ibid., p.1.
24. Teresita Schaffer in *FT* 100809.
25. http://www.whitehouse.gov/the-press-office/us-china-joint-statement 171109.
26. Joshi, *China and India: Awkward Ascents*, p.22.
27. *FT* 150910, http://www.ft.com/cms/s/0/80292cc2-c0f7-11df-99c4-00144feab49a. html#ixzz1KE8ntAIj.
28. See *Economist* 170312, http://www.economist.com/node/21550315.
29. *FT* 160709, http://www.ft.com/cms/s/0/d78a3788-71a0-11de-a821-00144feabdc0. html#ixzz1KVS9mfZC.

30. *India 2039: An Affluent Society in One Generation*, Report prepared by the Centennial Group for the ADB cited in *FT* 080709, http://www.ft.com/cms/s/0/2739f53e-6b57-11de-861d-00144feabdc0.html#ixzz1KEimuFmx.
31. P. V. Naik quoted in *FT* 161210, http://www.ft.com/cms/s/0/2bafc45c-093c-11e0-ada6-00144feabdc0.html#ixzz1KVKIVzj2.
32. Arundhati Ghose quoted in *FT* 130709.
33. Joshi, *China and India: Awkward Ascents*, p.7.
34. MGI, 'Addressing China's Looming Talent Shortage', pp.5–6.
35. http://esa.un.org/wpp/Documentation/pdf/WPP2012_HIGHLIGHTS.pdf.
36. *FT* 151009, http://www.ft.com/cms/s/0/08e50726-b923-11de-98ee-00144feab49a.html#ixzz1KW6faWIL.
37. See, for example, Wang, *Chinese Intellectuals and the West 1872–1949*.
38. Pranab Bardhan, Professor of Economics at the University of California, Berkeley, in Yale Global online, cited in *SCMP* 240410.
39. See *Time Science and Space* 310712 lhttp://science.time.com/2012/07/31/how-climate-change-and-the-monsoons-affect-indias-blackouts/.
40. http://thediplomat.com/2013/12/justice-delayed-is-justice-denied-indias-30-million-case-judicial-backlog/.
41. See Eva Pils, 'Chinese Property Law as an Image of PRC History' (2010), http://papers.ssrn.com/sol3/papers.cfm?abstract_id=1564448.
42. See Pew China Survey 2012, http://www.pewglobal.org/files/2012/10/Pew-Global-Attitudes-China-Report-FINAL-October-10-2012.pdf.
43. See James Bradley in *NYT* 051209 and surrounding debate, e.g. Jonathan Tremblay in History News Network 120809, http://hnn.us/articles/121196.html.
44. See Iris Chang, *The Rape of Nanjing*. No one seems to recall the Nanjing Massacre of 1912, just twenty-five years previously, when Han slaughtered 'an incalculable number' of Manchu men, women and children and the Manchu city was reduced to 'scorched earth' (Rhoads, *Manchus and Han*, p.198).
45. In 1988 the Japanese distributor of Bertolucci's film *The Last Emperor* cut the brief scene depicting the Rape of Nanking: Chang, *The Rape of Nanjing*, p.210.
46. ibid., *passim*.
47. Reproduced from *Freezing Point* by Ming Pao, a Hong Kong newspaper, 270106.
48. *Korea Times* 080510, http://www.koreatimes.co.kr/www/news/nation/2011/04/113_65556.html.
49. *SCMP* 031012 and AFP, http://www.scmp.com/news/china/article/1052588/six-chinese-ships-return-waters-near-diaoyus-overs-tokyos-protests.
50. http://www.ft.com/intl/cms/s/0/687e31a2-99e4-11e3-91cd-00144feab7de.html#axzz2u3ttonQW.
51. http://www.mod.go.jp/e/d_act/ryouku/index.html.
52. See Yoshihara and Holmes 'The Japanese Archipelago through Chinese Eyes'.
53. ibid.
54. *SCMP* 310112, http://www.scmp.com/portal/site/SCMP/menuitem.2af62ecb329d3d7733492d9253a0a0a0/?vgnextoid=7b02d32ca4f25310VgnVCM100000360a0a0aRCRD&ss=China&s–ews.
55. *Washington Free Beacon* 300912, http://freebeacon.com/white-house-hack-attack/.
56. See Pew Global Survey 2012, http://www.pewglobal.org/files/2012/06/Pew-Global-Attitudes--U.S.-Image-Report-FINAL-June-13-2012.pdf.
57. *IHT* 060712.
58. Foreign Policy blog 280910, http://blog.foreignpolicy.com/posts/2010/09/28/japan_sends_china_12_billion_in_aid_every_year.
59. Michael McDevitt, *Asia Policy* No. 1 (January 2006), p.74.
60. Jason J. Blazevic, 'The Taiwan Dilemma', p.155.
61. ibid., p.145.
62. *FT* 140309.
63. Yomiuri 270512, http://www.yomiuri.co.jp/dy/national/T120526002703.htm.
64. *Defense Programs and Budget of Japan: Overview of FY2011 Budget* (Ministry of Defence, Tokyo, 2011), p.29, http://www.mod.go.jp/e/d_budget/pdf/230401.pdf.
65. The Fukuda doctrine – enunciated on Premier Fukuda's 1977 tour of South East Asia – begins 'Japan would never become a military great power.' This was reaffirmed by his son, Prime Minister Yasuo Fukuda, in 2007.

66. Professor Kazuo Ogoura in *Japan Times* 230908.
67. Karl Kulessa, reported by Reuters 290408.
68. UNDP *Russia Facing Demographic Challenges* (2009), p.184.
69. ibid., pp.13, 67, 71.
70. UNICEF and Rosstat, *Youth in Russia* (2010), p.21, http://www.unrussia.ru/en/public.html.
71. US State Department's International Narcotics Control Strategy Report Vol. 1 (2009), p.464, http://www.state.gov/documents/organization/156575.pdf.
72. Spence, *The Search*, pp.94, 129; UN World Drug Report 2012, p.23, http://www.unodc.org/documents/data-and-analysis/WDR2012/WDR_2012_web_small.pdf. In fact official estimates range up to 3.6 per cent (Russian Federal Drug Service, March 2008, cited by the US State Department's International Narcotics Control Strategy Report Vol. 1, 2009, p.494), http://www.state.gov/documents/organization/120054.pdf.
73. Spence, p.129.
74. UNICEF and Rosstat, *Youth in Russia*, p.29.
75. Nicholas Eberstadt, 'Drunken Nation: Russia's Depopulation Bomb', *World Affairs* 090409.
76. *FT* 110810, http://www.ft.com/cms/s/0/cfd28a08-a57b-11df-a5b7-00144feabdc0.html#ixzz1JkMvxj5Q.
77. Lilia Shevtsova of the Carnegie Institute cited in *FT* 130810, http://www.ft.com/cms/s/0/5d8e8594-a6fe-11df-90e5-00144feabdc0.html#ixzz1JkHkBc54.
78. UNICEF and Rosstat, *Youth in Russia* p.25.
79. ibid., p.27.
80. Pavel Astakhov, head of the Russian parliamentary commission on children's rights, interviewed by *Moscow Times* 240810.
81. The Russian government is quoted as saying a million or more in a video on the Russia Today website 221007. The highest estimate is 5 million (RIA-Novosti 020607).
82. This is a combination of those sent to orphanages (around 120,000 annually) and the unknown numbers going to live on the streets. If the minimum number of street children is only 1 million and children are aged 3–15, it suggests 80,000 annually. For the numbers going to orphanages, see Boris Altshuler, a member of the Public Chamber of the Russian Federation, writing for the Open Democracy website 310510, http://www.opendemocracy.net/od-russia/boris-altshuler/children-in-care-russian-orphan-industry.
83. *NYT* 190209.
84. *Daily Telegraph* 120809.
85. *FT* 100910, http://www.ft.com/cms/s/0/b67770fe-bcfb-11df-954b-00144feab49a.html#ixzz1JkACPM00.
86. *Time* 190410.
87. *FT* 140410.
88. e.g. President Magomedov of Daghestan cited in *FT* 220510, http://www.ft.com/cms/s/0/e490b8ca-6539-11df-b648-00144feab49a.html#ixzz1Jk9Kr2ru.
89. Lucian Kim, the author, writing in *NYT* 300111, http://www.nytimes.com/2011/01/31/opinion/31iht-edkim31.html?sq=cracks in the russian regime&st=cse&adxnnl=1&scp=1&adxnnlx=1296572274-f+Uwv8YoahtXZUk6xKbK8g.
90. Lev Gudkov, director of the Levada Centre, an independent pollster, *FT* 150311, http://www.ft.com/cms/s/0/7dd04742-4f29-11e0-9038-00144feab49a.html#ixzz1JgBfKCrC.
91. From Transparency International and the World Economic Forum.
92. William Browder, a prominent critic of Russia, writing in *FT* 060709, http://www.ft.com/cms/s/0/2172e246-6a53-11de-ad04-00144feabdc0.html#ixzz1JkwHWEcw.
93. Igor Yurgens, head of a liberal think tank, advising Mr Medvedev, *FT* 150311, http://www.ft.com/cms/s/0/7dd04742-4f29-11e0-9038-00144feab49a.html#ixzz1JgBfKCrC.
94. *FT* 230311, http://www.ft.com/cms/s/0/76647ffa-5569-11e0-a2b1-00144feab49a.html#ixzz1IhiG2AXi.
95. RIA Novosti 051212 http://en.rian.ru/business/20121205/177936835.html.
96. Russia Today 220213, http://rt.com/business/russian-capital-outflow-study-olympics-297/.
97. *FT* 130810, http://www.ft.com/cms/s/0/5d8e8594-a6fe-11df-90e5-00144feabdc0.html#ixzz1JkHkBc54.
98. *FT* 041209, http://www.ft.com/cms/s/0/41ae3176-e075-11de-8494-00144feab49a.html#ixzz1JkOJ0uRL.

99. Victor Erofeyev writing in *IHT* 260911, http://www.nytimes.com/2011/09/27/opinion/27iht-ederofeyev27.html.

100. *FT* 160810, http://cachef.ft.com/cms/s/0/948014ac-a968-11df-a6f2-00144feabdc0.html #ixzz1JkPZgwCX.

101. *FT* 030809.

102. *Natural Gas Daily* 150612, http://interfaxenergy.com/natural-gas-news-analysis/russia-and-the-caspian/curtain-rises-on-turkmen-gas/.

103. G. Rozman, *Sino-Soviet Relations*, p.412.

104. *WSJ* 040509.

105. *FT* 190310.

106. *FT* 050709, http://www.ft.com/cms/s/0/9817e45e-698c-11de-bc9f-00144feabdc0.html #ixzz1JkqARiJQ.

107. *FT* 281209, http://www.ft.com/cms/s/0/1b48d786-f351-11de-a888-00144feab49a.html# ixzz1JkFRyqZn.

108. *FT* 200809, http://www.ft.com/cms/s/0/ef405120-8db4-11de-93df-00144feabdc0.html #ixzz1JkRX8v7j.

109. *FT* 170909.

110. Jakobson, Holtom *et al.*, *China's Energy and Security Relations with Russia* (SIPRI, 2011), p.vi. http://books.sipri.org/files/PP/SIPRIPP29.pdf.

111. Tai Ming Cheung, 'The Chinese Defense Economy's Long March from Imitation to Innovation', p.341.

112. Evan S. Medeiros, 'China's International Behaviour', Rand (2009), p.109.

113. *Washington Times* 010812, http://www.washingtontimes.com/news/2012/aug/1/inside-china-aide-to-consulate-defector-charged/?page=all.

114. Allen Whiting's note to Henry Kissinger 160869, http://www.gwu.edu/~nsarchiv/NSAEBB/NSAEBB49/sino.sov.9.pdf.

115. *People's Daily* 110210, http://english.peopledaily.com.cn/90001/90777/90853/6893082.html.

116. Rozman, *Sino-Soviet Relations*, p.411.

117. Jakobson, Holtom *et al.*, *China's Energy and Security Relations with Russia*.

118. See Dr Richard Weitz in RIA Novosti 140411, http://en.rian.ru/valdai_op/20110414/163523421.html.

119. Dmytryshyn, p.lx.

120. Byron Tzou, *China and International Law*, p.80.

121. ibid., p.81.

122. Carrère d'Encausse, *L'Empire éclaté*, p.113.

123. Stephan, *The Russian Far East*, p.18.

124. UNDP, *Russia Facing Demographic Challenges*, p.80.

125. Dennis Donahue, *The Future of Work in Russia: Population Projections and the Labor Force* (2004), p.12.

126. Bobo Lo, 'Ten Things Everyone should Know about the Sino-Russian Relationship' (2008), p.4.

127. Information from an academic in Beijing, April 2009.

12 Central Asia

1. Jeremy Allouche, 'The Governance of Central Asian Waters: National Interests versus Regional Cooperation' (2007), UNIDIR, p.52, quoting the *IHT* 080307.

2. Toynbee, *A Study*, p.284.

3. Dwyer, 'The Xinjiang Conflict', p.x.

4. Edmund Waite, Post-Communism 2008: 'Islam and Post-Communism', p.2.

5. BBC 031113, http://www.bbc.co.uk/news/world-asia-china-24793887.

6. Sir Aurel Stein, *On Ancient Central-Asian Tracks*, p.42.

7. Dwyer, 'The Xinjiang Conflict', p.xi.

8. *SCMP* 160511.

9. See *Guardian* 301111.

10. http://counterterrorism.newamerica.net/drones#2012chart.

11. Stanford Law School and NYU School of Law, *Living Under Drones* (2012), pp.32–3, http://livingunderdrones.org/wp-content/uploads/2012/09/Stanford_NYU_LIVING_UNDER_DRONES.pdf.
12. SIPRI 030613, http://www.sipri.org/media/pressreleases/2013/YBlaunch_2013.
13. Joshi, *China and India: Awkward Ascents*, p.14.
14. ibid., p.1.
15. ibid., p.8.
16. Bidwai and Vanaik, *New Nukes: India, Pakistan and Global Nuclear Disarmament*, pp.175, 177.
17. *NYT* 281109.
18. Private conference in Switzerland, 2010.
19. *Global Asia* 300609.
20. ibid.
21. *The Times* 110809.
22. *The Times* 170110.
23. http://www.theguardian.com/world/2010/nov/30/wikileaks-cables-pakistani-leadership-wrangle.
24. *FT* 180312, http://www.ft.com/intl/cms/s/0/a888d1fc-6f12-11e1-afb8-00144feab49a.html#axzz1pXI6hkTt.
25. BBC 131113, http://www.bbc.co.uk/news/world-asia-24919056.
26. Afghan Ministry of Counter-Narcotics cited by IRIN. http://www.drugaddictiontreatment.com/addiction-in-the-news/addiction-news/drug-addiction-growing-in-afghanistan/.
27. Open democracy 241112, http://www.opendemocracy.net/daniel-nguyen/geopolitics-of-drug-trafficking-in-afghanistan.
28. *Guardian* 170809.
29. *NYT* 180210.
30. *Daily Telegraph* 280711.
31. *FT* 030911.
32. Oxfam *Afghanistan: No Time to Lose* (2011), http://www.oxfam.org/sites/www.oxfam.org/files/afghanistan-no-time-to-lose-20110510-en.pdf.
33. BBC 060911, http://www.bbc.co.uk/news/world-south-asia-14809579.
34. *IHT* 020210.
35. *Economist* 220809.
36. *Times of India* 161009.
37. *NYT* 150409.
38. Private conversation with the author, January 2010.
39. See *The Times* 251111.
40. *IHT* 020210.
41. Serge Michailof, 'Commentaire', p.344.
42. See *Guardian* 021211.
43. See CNN 051211, http://edition.cnn.com/2011/12/05/world/asia/afghanistan-bonn-conference/index.html?eref—rss_igoogle_cnn.
44. A report sponsored by UNICEF, WHO and the American and British governments, cited in *Guardian* 011211.
45. Brookings Institution 160512, http://www.brookings.edu/~/media/programs/foreign%20policy/afghanistan%20index/index20120516.
46. *Washington Post* 220209.
47. http://www.universalnewswires.com/centralasia/kyrgyzstan/viewstory.aspx?id=13932.
48. Ahmed Rashid, *Jihad: The Rise of Militant Islam in Central Asia* (2002), p.245.
49. See BBC 051211, http://www.bbc.co.uk/news/world-south-asia-15132461.

13 Undeclared War in the Fourth Dimension?

1. Steven Hildreth, 'Cyberwarfare', CRS (2001), p.12.
2. Bloomberg 140114 http://www.bloomberg.com/news/2014-01-13/gates-says-china-s-xi-has-firmer-grip-on-army-than-hu-did.html.

3. *SCMP* 200411.

4. USCESRC 2010, p.237, http://www.uscc.gov/annual_report/2010/10_annual_report.php.

5. USCESRR 2008, p.162, http://www.uscc.gov/annual_report/2008/08_annual_report.php.

6. William Lynn III, 'The Pentagon's Cyberstrategy, One Year Later: Defending against the Next Cyberattack', *Foreign Affairs* (2011), http://www.foreignaffairs.com/articles/68305/william-j-lynn-iii/the-pentagons-cyberstrategy-one-year-later.

7. Larry Wortzel quoted in *WSJ* 231009, http://online.wsj.com/article/SB125616872684400273.html.

8. USCESRR 2009, p.169, http://www.uscc.gov/annual_report/2009/09_annual_report.php.

9. See USCESR 2007 cited in the *Guardian* 201108, http://www.guardian.co.uk/technology/2008/nov/20/china-us-military-hacking.

10. Laura Knapp, 'Interpreting Chinese Cyber Attacks of 2007', p.7.

11. ibid., pp.7, 12.

12. ibid., p.12.

13. ibid., pp.11–12.

14. ibid., p.8.

15. USCESRR 2010, p.239, http://www.uscc.gov/annual_report/2010/10_annual_report.php.

16. ibid.

17. Bloomberg, *Business Week* 130611, http://www.businessweek.com/news/2011-06-13/imf-state-backed-cyber-attack-follows-hacks-of-lab-g-20.html.

18. http://www.infosecurity-us.com/view/8386/symantec-reveals-china-and-rar-files-are-a-rising-threat/ 260310.

19. Bloomberg, *Business Week* 130611.

20. *Washington Free Beacon* 300912, http://freebeacon.com/white-house-hack-attack/.

21. Lynn III, 'The Pentagon's Cyberstrategy, One Year Later'.

22. *Guardian* 260609.

23. USCESRR 2010, p.237.

24. *Washington Free Beacon* 300912.

25. *Threat Post* 270411. http://threatpost.com/en_us/blogs/glass-dragon-chinas-cyber-offense-obscures-woeful-defense-042711.

26. *FT* 091210.

27. Bloomberg 230711, http://www.bloomberg.com/news/2011-07-21/spies-connected-to-china-said-to-have-carried-out-hacking-of-imf-computers.html.

28. Reuters 140111, http://www.reuters.com/article/2011/04/14/us-china-usa-cyberespionage-idUSTRE73D24220110414?pageNumber=1.

29. *Washington Post* blog 030708, http://voices.washingtonpost.com/securityfix/2008/07/lithuania_weathers_cyber_attac_1.html.

30. *CSM* 210910, http://www.csmonitor.com/USA/2010/0921/Stuxnet-malware-is-weapon-out-to-destroy-Iran-s-Bushehr-nuclear-plant.

31. See *FT* 081108 and see: Government Executive 041207, http://www.govexec.com/defense/2007/12/us-british-officials-target-chinese-as-source-of-cyberattacks/25874/.

32. *Der Spiegel* 100409, http://www.spiegel.de/international/world/0,1518,618478,00.html.

33. UPI 030508, http://www.upi.com/Top_News/2008/05/03/Is-China-attacking-Belgian-computers/UPI-70831209790694/.

34. AFP 131208, http://www.france24.com/en/20081211-france-claims-cyber-attack-its-beijing-embassy-website-.

35. Shadows in the Cloud: Investigating Cyber Espionage 2.0. 060410, http://www.scribd.com/doc/29435784/SHADOWS-IN-THE-CLOUD-Investigating-Cyber-Espionage-2-0.

36. AFP 070311, http://gadgets.ndtv.com/others/news/china-hacked-into-secret-south-korea-military-files-226801.

37. *Irish Times* 230711 citing the *FT*.

38. Bloomberg 230711, http://www.bloomberg.com/news/2011-07-21/spies-connected-to-china-said-to-have-carried-out-hacking-of-imf-computers.html.

39. Dark Visitor 110311, http://www.thedarkvisitor.com/2011/03/us-1-perp-attacking-chinas-classifed-networks/ http://www.rising-global.com/About-Us/About-Us/About-Us.html.

40. *People's Daily* 140311, http://english.peopledaily.com.cn/90001/98649/7319285.html.

41. *FT* 090709.
42. *NYT* cited in *SCMP* 300309.
43. Julian Spencer citing Reuters in *CSM* 040308, http://www.csmonitor.com/World/terrorism-security/2008/0304/p99s01-duts.html, and the website netlexfrance.net on 290309, http://www.netlexfrance.net/29/03/2009/the-snooping-dragon; *Washington Times* 120509.
44. *China Daily* 060510.
45. Cited in *CSM* 140907, http://www.newsmax.com/Newsfront/china-cyberwar/2007/09/14/id/321684.
46. http://www.bbc.co.uk/news/world-asia-china-24396957
47. R. McMahon, 'U.S. Internet Providers and the "Great Firewall of China"', (CFR) 2011.
48. Cited in *CSM* 140907, http://www.newsmax.com/Newsfront/china-cyberwar/2007/09/14/id/321684.
49. Knapp, 'Interpreting Chinese Cyber Attacks', p.27.
50. *FT* 121011, http://www.ft.com/intl/cms/s/0/33dc83e4-c800-11e0-9501-00144feabdc0.html#axzz1adwXUjr9.
51. *Newsweek* 011113, http://www.newsweek.com/how-edward-snowden-escalated-cyber-war-1461.
52. USCESRR 2011, http://www.uscc.gov/annual_report/2011/annual_report_full_11.pdf, p.50.
53. US Senate Intelligence Committee Report 220709, http://www.fas.org/irp/congress/2009_rpt/srpt111-55.pdf.
54. Office of the Director of National Intelligence, 'Remarks by the National Counterintelligence Executive Dr. Joel F. Brenner' 030409, https://www.hsdl.org/?view&did=37389.
55. *Washington Times* 120509.
56. BBC 180907, http://news.bbc.co.uk/2/hi/americas/7001856.stm.
57. http://www.newsweek.com/how-edward-snowden-escalated-cyber-war-1461.
58. *IHT* 010609.
59. Reuters 140411, http://www.reuters.com/article/2011/04/14/us-china-usa-cyberespionage-idUSTRE73D24220110414?pageNumber=1.
60. Martin Libicki, *Cyberdeterrence and Cyberwar*, (Rand, 2009).
61. NATO and Cyber Defence 2009, http://www.nato-pa.int/default.asp?SHORTCUT=1782.
62. Bruce Schneier, chief security officer of BT, cited by the BBC 160211.
63. Vanity Fair July 2013, http://www.vanityfair.com/culture/2013/07/new-cyberwar-victims-american-business.
64. US Senate Intelligence Committee Report, pp.50ff., http://www.fas.org/irp/congress/2009_rpt/srpt111-55.pdf.

14 Nervous Neighbours

1. e.g. Chen Xiangyang of the Chinese Institute of Contemporary International Relations cited in *SCMP* 040510.
2. *IHS* Jane's 2012, reported in *SCMP* 260212.
3. The SIPRI *Yearbook 2012* contains much valuable information in this field, http://www.sipri.org/yearbook/2012/06.
4. A.F.P. Bloomberg, cited in *SCMP* 200312, http://www.scmp.com/portal/site/SCMP/menuitem.2af62ecb329d3d7733492d9253a0a0a0/?vgnextoid=d82aa5d1edb26310VgnVCM1000003 60a0a0aRCRD&ss=China&s–ews.
5. The Nixon–Schumann meeting, New York, 180969, http://www.gwu.edu/~nsarchiv/NSAEBB/NSAEBB49/sino.sov.22.pdf.
6. Michael Brecher and Jonathan Wilkenfeld, *A Study of Crisis*, p.158.
7. Prime Minister Nguyen Tan Dung quoted in *SCMP* 100410.
8. *SCMP* 200312, http://www.scmp.com/portal/site/SCMP/menuitem.2af62ecb329d3d773349 2d9253a0a0a0/?vgnextoid=db3fb414f0b26310VgnVCM100000360a0a0aRCRD&ss=Asia+ %26+World&s–ews.
9. *SCMP* 200312, http://www.scmp.com/portal/site/SCMP/menuitem.2af62ecb329d3d773349 2d9253a0a0a0/?vgnextoid=db3fb414f0b26310VgnVCM100000360a0a0aRCRD&ss=Asia+ %26+World&s–ews.
10. *Economist* 061210, http://www.economist.com/node/17601499.

11. *Daily News and Analysis* 080812, http://www.dnaindia.com/analysis/column_high-stakes-and-rising-tension-in-the-south-china-sea_1725204.

12. *SCMP* 200409.

13. US Embassy, Hanoi, 070409, http://vietnam.usembassy.gov/mccain_dav040709.html.

14. ibid.

15. Richard Halloran writing in the (Honolulu) *Star Advertiser* 200311, http://www.staradvertiser.com/editorials/guesteditorials/20110320__A_long_reconciliation.html.

16. *WSJ* 030612, http://online.wsj.com/article/SB10001424052702303918204577443961224587928.html.

17. Dr Subhash Kapila, South Asia Analysis Group 010605, http://saag.org/papers14/paper1397.html.

18. ibid.

19. See SCMP 020509 Naval training from 2000 See: 01. 06. 2005 South Asia Analysis Group.

20. *Defense Industry Daily* 290312, http://www.defenseindustrydaily.com/Vietnam-Reportedly-Set-to-Buy-Russian-Kilo-Class-Subs-05396/.

21. The deepwater harbour of Cam Ranh Bay has had a chequered history: it was a Russian base in 1905 and from the late 1970s until 2002; it was an American base in the late 1960s and early 1970s (and may be again in the 21st century); it was a Japanese base in the 1940s; it might be a Russian and an Indian base in the 21st century.

22. *SCMP* 290411, http://www.scmp.com/portal/site/SCMP/menuitem.2af62ecb329d3d7733492d9253a0a0a0/?vgnextoid=ce5195a790c9f210VgnVCM100000360a0a0aRCRD&ss=Asia+%26+World&s–ews.

23. *Defense Industry Daily* 150212 (accessed 290312), http://www.defenseindustrydaily.com/Vietnam-Reportedly-Set-to-Buy-Russian-Kilo-Class-Subs-05396/.

24. *SCMP* 040410.

25. *SCMP* 280409.

26. *Economist* 151009.

27. *FT* 270312, http://www.ft.com/intl/cms/s/0/84ed5296-77e5-11e1-b437-00144feab49a.html?ftcamp=rss#axzz1qTh6ddSv.

28. The Centre for a New American Security, cited in *Le Figaro* 040612.

29. *FT* 011011, http://www.ft.com/intl/cms/s/0/520bcdb2-eb4f-11e0-9a41-00144feab49a.html#axzz1ZQz5wm2y.

30. *FT* 300912, http://www.ft.com/intl/cms/s/0/62eb2ea8-06e1-11e2-92b5-00144feabdc0.html#axzz283KiNUN7.

31. Zhuang Guotu, director of the Center for Southeast Asian Studies at Xiamen University, interviewed in *Global Times* 110612, http://www.globaltimes.cn/content/714263.shtml.

32. *Times of India* 230612, http://articles.timesofindia.indiatimes.com/2012-06-23/india/32381541_1_sino-bhutanese-jigme-y-thinley-thimphu.

33. *Indian Express* 280612, http://www.indianexpress.com/news/bhutan-buffer/967453/3.

34. Xinhua 140112, http://news.xinhuanet.com/english/china/2012-01/14/c_131360593.htm.

35. *FT* 300512, http://www.ft.com/intl/cms/s/0/717c28fc-a979-11e1-9772-00144feabdc0.html#axzz1x67jRFMd.

36. Its people are three inches shorter than South Koreans.

37. *Global Times* 210512, http://www.globaltimes.cn/NEWS/tabid/99/ID/710439/NK-frees-all-Chinese-crew.aspx and also BBC 210512 http://www.bbc.co.uk/news/world-asia-china-18141009.

38. *Economist* 120512, http://www.economist.com/node/21554582.

39. *FT* 160810, http://www.ft.com/cms/s/0/7c2afef8-a855-11df-86dd-00144feabdc0.html#axzz1GB5SReVY.

40. K. Brown, 'Options for a Democratic Taiwan' (2009), p.2.

41. Global Views Survey Research Center 2504–11, http://www.taiwansecurity.org/2011/GVMaApproval_Independence-042511.pdf.

42. Taipei Times 311013, http://www.taipeitimes.com/News/front/archives/2013/10/31/2003575806.

43. A poll in June 2006, by the magazine *Global Views Monthly*: Chen Mumin, 'The Taiwan Factor in China–Japan Relations' 2007.

44. BBC 090306 http://news.bbc.co.uk/2/hi/asia-pacific/4789072.stm.

45. *Asia Times* 190305.

46. *Asian Survey* 47, No. 5 (Sept–Oct 2007) pp.790–810; Jing Sun Assistant Professor, University of Denver, http://www.jstor.org/discover/10.1525/as.2007.47.5.790?uid=3738032&uid=2129&uid=2&uid=70&uid=4&sid=21101128567207.

47. *FT* 301209, http://www.ft.com/cms/s/0/d4ba7782-f4e2-11de-9cba-00144feab49a.html#axzz1GB5SReVY.

48. ABS-CBN News 030611, http://www.abs-cbnnews.com/-depth/06/02/11/china-fired-filipino-fishermen-jackson-atoll.

49. *Global Times* 290911, http://www.globaltimes.cn/NEWS/tabid/99/ID/677717/Time-to-teach-those-around-South-China-Sea-a-lesson.aspx.

50. ABS-CBN 230612, http://www.abs-cbnnews.com/-depth/06/23/12/chinese-navy-admiral-targets-philippine-ships.

51. Allouche, 'The Governance of Central Asian Waters: National Interests versus Regional Cooperation', p.52.

52. Ksenia Muratshina, Ural Federal University 290512, http://russiancouncil.ru/en/inner/?id_4=437.

53. Zherelina Vinokurov *et al.*, 'Transboundary Water Problems in the Basin of the Irtysh River' (NATO workshop, 2003); cited frequently in the *Caucasus Times*.

54. Radio Free Europe 130706, http://www.rferl.org/content/article/1069833.html.

55. Ksenia Muratshina, Ural Federal University 290512.

56. *Guardian* 281111.

15 China in the World

1. The widely cited, but unreferenced, '24 character strategy' which reads 'Observe calmly; secure our position; cope with affairs calmly; hide our capacities and bide our time; be good at maintaining a low profile; never claim leadership; make some contributions'.

2. *FT* 210510, http://www.ft.com/cms/s/0/e3af4fd6-646f-11df-8cba-00144feab49a.html#axzz1GB5SReVY.

3. Brown, *Friends and Enemies*, p.152.

4. Pew Global Attitudes Survey 2011 http://pewglobal.org/files/2011/07/Pew-Global-Attitudes-Balance-of-Power-U.S.-Image-Report-FINAL-July-13-2011.pdf.

5. Zhuang Guotu, director of the Center for Southeast Asian Studies at Xiamen University, interviewed in *Global Times* 110612, http://www.globaltimes.cn/content/714263.shtml.

6. Though ten years ago it would not have expected the Iraqi and Afghan ambassadors to Norway to have heeded its request for them not to attend the Nobel Prize ceremony.

7. *SCMP* 090412, http://www.scmp.com/portal/site/SCMP/menuitem.2af62ecb329d3d773349 2d9253a0a0a0/?vgnextoid=2bee126d09396310VgnVCM100000360a0a0aRCRD&ss=China&s–ews.

8. Gamer (ed.) *Understanding Contemporary China*, p.86, citing Mulvenon, 'Soldiers of Fortune'.

9. Cheung, 'The Chinese Defense Economy's Long March from Imitation to Innovation', p.326.

10. ibid., p.348.

11. Joshi, *China and India: Awkward Ascents*, p.11.

12. Tai Ming Cheung writing in the *WSJ* blog 130111, http://blogs.wsj.com/chinareal-time/2011/01/13/what-the-j-20-says-about-chinas-defense-sector/.

13. Israel is also known to have covertly transferred American technology to China, including that for killer drones in 1994–2004, but it is not proven that nuclear technology was transferred: John J. Mearsheimer and Stephen M. Walt, *The Israel Lobby and US Foreign Policy*, pp.75–6.

14. Thomas C. Reed and Danny B. Stillman, *The Nuclear Express* (2008).

15. Carl E. Behrens, 'Nuclear Non-proliferation Issues' (CRS, 2006); p.14; Shirley A. Kan, *et al.*, 'China and Proliferation of Weapons of Mass Destruction and Missiles: Policy Issues' (CRS, 2006), and Reed and Stillman, 'Nuclear Express'. See discussion in *NYT* 081208, http://www.nytimes.com/2008/12/09/science/09bomb.html?pagewanted=all&_moc.

semityn.www. At an early stage, Beijing officials privately acknowledged proliferation of nuclear weapons but said rather disarmingly that the quality was not very good. (Private conversation with a British official, 2011.)

16. See for example the report sponsored by Professor Phillip Karber of Georgetown University, cited in *Washington Post* 301111, http://www.washingtonpost.com/world/national-security/georgetown-students-shed-light-on-chinas-tunnel-system-for-nuclear weapons/2011/11/16/gIQA6AmKAO_story.html.

17. Professor Michael Sheehan of Swansea University writing in BBC 290911, http://www.bbc.co.uk/news/world-asia-pacific-15089720.

18. Nirav Patel, 'Chinese Disaster Relief Operations' (2009).

19. See Fedex website: http://news.van.fedex.com/intl/cn?node=10345.

20. *SCMP* 160311.

21. Song Xiaojun, a defence specialist, cited in *SCMP* 050311.

22. 'Defending Australia in the Asia Pacific Century 2009', p.34.

23. AFP 120509.

24. *Economist* 041210.

25. Christopher J. Pehrson, p.24.

26. Professor Brahma Chellaney cited in *FT* 210510, http://www.ft.com/cms/s/0/833aca0e-646f-11df-8cba-00144feab49a.html#axzz1GB5SReVY.

27. P. Chacko Joseph, 'China's "String of Pearls" Strategy around India in Tatters', *Frontier India* (2009). http://frontierindia.org/chinas-string-of-pearls-strategy-around-india-in-tatters/.

28. *Daily Star* 230112, http://www.dredgingtoday.com/2012/01/23/sonadia-island-port-is-of-strategic-importance-china-says/.

29. Reuters   220513,   http://www.reuters.com/article/2013/05/22/srilanka-china-loan-idUSL3N0E338B20130522.

30. Zhuang Guotu, director of the Center for Southeast Asian Studies at Xiamen University, interviewed in *Global Times* 110612, http://www.globaltimes.cn/content/714263.shtml.

31. *SMH* 270709.

32. Xinhua 110312, http://english.cntv.cn/20120311/110556.shtml.

33. *China Daily* 250406, http://wenku.baidu.com/view/5064f317866fb84ae45c8d14.html.

34. Xinhua 220409.

35. Cited in *FT* 030311.

36. Professor Brautigam of American University discusses this in 'China in Africa: The Real Story' http://www.chinaafricarealstory.com/2010/03/china-and-african-land-grab-drc-oil.html.

37. Jamestown Foundation, 'Changes in Beijing's Approach to Overseas Basing?' 240909.

38. Quoted in *Washington Times* 071211, http://www.washingtontimes.com/news/2011/dec/7/inside-china-818785095/?page=all.

39. US–China Commission, *The Evolving Role of China in International Institutions*, p.89, http://www.uscc.gov/researchpapers/2011/TheEvolvingRoleofChinainInternationalInstitutions.pdf.

40. Author's conversation in 2009 with a house owner in East Africa who let out his house.

41. Author's conversation with an official in the UK Home Office, December 2009.

42. http://www.tralac.org/files/2013/08/Africa-China-trading-relationship-Synopsis.pdf.

43. *Guardian* 281003.

44. It seems to arm Mugabe's police in Zimbabwe and yet the anti-government demonstrators in Cairo's Tahrir Square were wearing Chinese-manufactured gas masks: *Economist* 261111.

45. Fang Cheng et al., *China's International Aid Policy and its Implications for Global Governance* (Research Center for Chinese Politics & Business, Indiana University, 2012), pp.23–4, http://www.indiana.edu/~rccpb/pdf/Cheng%20RCCPB%2029%20Aid%20June%202012.pdf.

46. *FT*   070509,   http://www.ft.com/cms/s/0/57d45a62-3a84-11de-8a2d-00144feabdc0.html#axzz1GB5SReVY.

47. *SCMP* 051111, http://www.scmp.com/portal/site/SCMP/menuitem.2af62ecb329d3d773349 2d9253a0a0a0/?vgnextoid=6a249c5a29e63310VgnVCM100000360a0a0aRCRD&ss=Chi na&s–ews.

48. *IHT* 301211.

49. Calculated by the Japan Centre for International Exchange: *Economist* 061210.

50. Freedom House, *Undermining Democracy* (2009), pp.24–5, http://old.freedomhouse.org/uploads/special_report/83.pdf.
51. Freedom House *Undermining Democracy* (2009), pp.24–5. http://old.freedomhouse.org/uploads/special_report/83.pdf.
52. US dispatch published by Wikileaks, cited by *FT* 030311.
53. *FT* 051110, http://www.ft.com/cms/s/0/4b89e260-e7ec-11df-b158-00144feab49a.html#axzz1GB5SReVY.
54. *FT* 090311.
55. Wu Sike, China's senior Middle East envoy cited in *SCMP* 110311.
56. 'Changing Patterns in the Use of the Veto in the Security Council', http://www.globalpolicy.org/component/content/article/102/32810.html.
57. See Contributors to UN Peace-keeping Operations, 30 November 2012, http://www.un.org/en/peacekeeping/contributors/2012/Nov12_1.pdf.
58. The MINURSO mandate established by the UN 290491.
59. Jacques, *When China Rules the World*, p.327.
60. US–China Commission, *The Evolving Role of China in International Institutions*, p.84.
61. Stephan, *The Russian Far East*, p.18.
62. http://www.pewglobal.org/topics/global-balance-of-power/2013/.
63. I refer here to the anti-American riots. See Horesh, *Shanghai's Bund*, p.46, and F. L. Hawks-Pott, *A Short History of Shanghai*, p.147.
64. Johnston, *Cultural Realism*, pp.26–7.
65. Alastair Iain Johnston, 'China's Militarized Interstate Dispute Behaviour 1949–1992: A First Cut at the Data,' *China Quarterly* 153, No. 1 (1998), p.29, http://www.ou.edu/uschina/texts/Johnston.98.CQ.pdf.
66. Alastair Johnston cited in Joshi, *China and India: Awkward Ascents*, p.16.
67. Brecher, Wilkenfeld and Moser's work *Crises in the Twentieth Century*, Vol. 2 cited in Johnston, *Cultural Realism: Strategic Culture and Grand Strategy in Chinese History*, p.256.
68. ibid.
69. Fairbank, *The Great Chinese Revolution*, p.107.
70. Research by Feng Kacheng: http://www.fangkc.com/2010/10/hurt-the-feelings-of-chinese-people/.
71. ABC News 020310.
72. *Economist* 061210, http://www.economist.com/node/17601499.
73. *FT* 280911, http://www.ft.com/intl/cms/s/0/873843be-e9bd-11e0-bb3e-00144feab49a.html#axzz1ZQz5wm2y.
74. *SCMP* 180411.
75. Professor Dominic Lieven writing in *FT* 140510, http://www.ft.com/cms/s/0/5bcb205c-5eef-11df-af86-00144feab49a.html#ixzz1JkCjbKnQ.
76. An essay written in 250507: Okazaki Institute, http://www.okazaki-inst.jp.
77. Professor Alan Dupont in *The Australian* 120410, http://www.theaustralian.com.au/news/opinion/many-shared-interests-but-few-shared-values-with-china/story-e6frg6zo-1225852475053.
78. ibid.

16 Outcomes

1. *Foreign Affairs* October 1999.
2. Eric Jones, 'Agenda', p.502.
3. An essay written in 250507: Okazaki Institute.
4. ibid.
5. Medeiros, 'China's International Behaviour'.
6. e.g. Shirk, *China: Fragile Superpower*.
7. 'China's Unhappy Neo-Leftists', *Diplomatic Courier* 220409, http://www.diplomaticourier.org/kmitan/articleback.php?newsid=361, *Unhappy China* is a collection of essays by five authors who argue that China has been too deferential to a Western world that is hostile towards it: http://economistonline.muogao.com/2009/03/unhappy-china.html. The writer

team is composed of famous media persons, cultural workers and scholars: Song Qiang (宋強), one of the authors of 'China Can Say No', has experience as a journalist, editor and TV script writer. Song Xiao Jun (宋小軍) is a commentator on CCTV and Phoenix TV, a well-known nationalist leader with military training. Wang Xiaodong (王小東)was sent to Japan to study Business Management after he decided to stop his study of Mathematics in Beijing University. He is famous for his criticism on 'reversed racism' (逆向種族主義), meaning the self-criticism of Chinese towards their own behaviour. Huang Jisu (黃紀蘇)is a sociologist and editor of the Chinese version of *Journal of International Social Science*. Liu Yang (劉仰) is an experienced media worker in issues related to culture, history and economy: http://globalvoicesonline.org/2009/03/13/china-is-unhappy/.

8. *Le Point* 231209, translation by the author.

9. See the interview with Xiao Jiansheng, http://asiancorrespondent.com/28252/chat-with-chinese-author-xiao-jiansheng/ University of California, Irvine.

10. See Bloomberg 091212, http://www.bloomberg.com/news/2012-12-09/china-s-wealth-gap-soars-as-xi-pledges-to-narrow-income-divide.html.

11. Ministry of Industry and Information Technology cited by *Caixin* 090312, http://english.caixin.com/2012-03-09/100366407.html.

12. Eric, *The European Miracle: Environments, Economies and Geopolitics in the History of Europe and Asia*, p.165.

13. Hegel, *Lectures on the Philosophy of History*, p.144.

14. Fewsmith, *China Since Tiananmen*, p.222.

15. Yuan Weishi in *Freezing Point* 110106.

16. *FT* 041209, http://www.ft.com/cms/s/0/41ae3176-e075-11de-8494-00144feab49a.html#ixzz1JkOJ0uRL.

17. J. W. F. Jenner in 'Tyranny of History' cited by Peter Hays Gries in *China's New Nationalism: Pride, Politics and Diplomacy*, p.45.

18. See http://www.prb.org/pdf10/immigration-update2010.pdf.

19. See National Bureau of Statistics 290411, http://www.stats.gov.cn/english/newsandcomingevents/t20110429_402722638.htm.

20. *SCMP* 110412, http://www.scmp.com/portal/site/SCMP/menuitem.2af62ecb329d3d7733492d9253a0a0a0/?vgnextoid=f036f07f75c96310VgnVCM100000360a0a0aRCRD&ss=China&s–ews.

21. See the preface to Susan Greenfield's, *Tomorrow's People*, p.xi. Ian Morris discusses this in his book *Why the West Rules – for Now*.

22. For a discussion of the science see Greenfield *Tomorrow's People* (*passim*). For the implications see for example *Why the West Rules*, Morris, pp.617–19.

23. Cao Cong Wilson Institute, May 2008.

24. Ashley J. Tellis. 'Preserving Hegemony: The Strategic Tasks Facing the United States', *Global Asia* (Spring 2009).

25. Brecher and Wilkenfeld, *A Study of Crisis*, p.80.

26. Hibbert, *The Dragon Wakes*, p.367.

27. *FT* 101011, http://www.ft.com/intl/cms/s/0/482df932-f324-11e0-8383-00144feab49a.html#axzz1aWsRSsLc.

28. Reported in the *FT* weblog 141011, http://blogs.ft.com/the-world/2011/10/chinas-fear-of-the-talent-show/#axzz1b7iT7GCY.

29. *Time* 071209.

30. http://www.worldbank.org/content/dam/Worldbank/document/State_of_the_poor_paper_April17.pdf.

31. Admission by David Kilcullen, adviser to Gen. Petraeus: *FT* 130509, http://www.ft.com/cms/s/0/46c20ab0-3f59-11de-ae4f-00144feabdc0.html.

32. One Israeli minister estimated that potentially 1,000 international war crimes lawsuits might be outstanding against military and security officials for such incidents: Avigdor Lieberman quoted in *Times* online 061009, http://www.timesonline.co.uk/tol/news/uk/article6862322.ece.

33. Brecher and Wilkenfeld, *A Study of Crisis*, p.85.

34. *Time* 150210.

35. Li Ruogu, *Institutional Stability*, pp.189, 190.

36. Alastair Johnston, *Cultural Realism*, p.230 *et passim*.
37. *SCMP* 240909.
38. ibid. 'The legendary six-part CCTV miniseries *River Elegy* . . . in June of 1988. . . . the docu-
    mentary . . . hit academic circles like an atomic bomb. The series' content – a sweeping,
    brutally painful critique of the deep structure of Chinese culture . . . informal discussion
    sessions on the topics of the program were organized at Tsinghua other universities
    throughout China.' http://www.thechinabeat.org/?p=3607 Bo Yang 'The Ugly Chinaman and
    the Crisis of Chinese Culture'. The Taiwanese-resident author criticises Chinese culture and
    the book was banned in China. http://www.amazon.com/Ugly-Chinaman-Crisis-Chinese-
    Culture/dp/1863731164.
39. *SCMP* 070510.
40. *FT*   031011,   http://www.ft.com/intl/cms/s/0/7885de20-edab-11e0-a9a9-00144feab49a.
    html#axzz1ZhorvPCY.
41. *SCMP* 051011, http://www.scmp.com/portal/site/SCMP/menuitem.2af62ecb329d3d773349
    2d9253a0a0a0/?vgnextoid=e00438cd67fc2310VgnVCM100000360a0a0aRCRD&ss=Chi
    na&s–ews.
42. For a description of the extraordinary development of Chinese consumer society, see Gerth,
    As China Goes.

Bibliography

Books

Adshead, S. A. M. *Province and Politics in Late Imperial China: Viceregal Government in Szechwan, 1898–1911*, 1984

Allawi, Ali A. *The Crisis of Islamic Civilisation*, 2009

Aristotle *Politics*, tr. J. E. C. Welldon, 1897

Bailey, Paul John *China in the Twentieth Century*, 2001

Baumler, Alan *The Chinese and Opium under the Republic: Worse Than Floods and Wild Beasts*, 2007

Becker, Jasper *City of Heavenly Tranquillity: Beijing in the History of China*, 2008

Bekerman, Zvi and Ezra Kopelowitz (eds) *Cultural Education – Cultural Sustainability: Minority, Diaspora, Indigenous, and Ethno-religious Groups in Multicultural Societies*, 2008

Bidwai, Praful and Anchin Vanaik *New Nukes: India, Pakistan and Global Nuclear Disarmament*, 1999

Brecher, Michael and Jonathan Wilkenfeld *A Study of Crisis*, 1997

Breznitz, Danny and Michael Murphree *The Run of the Red Queen. Government, Innovation, Globalization, and Economic Growth in China*, 2011

Brook, Timothy *The Chinese State in Ming Society*, 2005

—— *The Troubled Empire. China in the Yuan and Ming Dynasties*, 2010

Brown, Kerry *Friends and Enemies: The Past, Present and Future of the Communist Party in China*, 2009

Brzezinski, Zbigniew *Strategic Vision: America and the Crisis of Global Power*, 2012

Butterfield, Herbert *The Whig Interpretation of History* (1931), 1973

Carrère d'Encausse, Hélène *L'Empire éclaté*, 1978

Castaneda, Jorge *Companero: The Life and Death of Che Guevara*, 1997

Chang, Iris *The Rape of Nanking*, 2012

Chao, Kang *Man and Land in Chinese History*, 1986

Chesneaux, Jean *Peasant Revolts in China 1840–1949*, tr. C. A. Curwen, 1973

Chiang, Madame Kai Shek, *Conversations with Mikhail Borodin*, 1978

Ching, Frank *Ancestors*, 1988

Chong, Woei-lien (ed.) *China's Great Proletarian Cultural Revolution: Master Narratives and Post-Mao Counternarratives*, 2002

Connaughton, Richard *The War of the Rising Sun and the Tumbling Bear: A Military History of the Russo–Japanese War, 1904–5*, 1988

Couldry, Nick and Curran, James (eds) *Contesting Media Power: Alternative Media in a Networked World*, 2003

Dardess, John W. *Governing China 150–1850*, 2010

Dehaene, Stanislas *The Number Sense: How the Mind Creates Mathematics*, 1999

DeLong-Bas, Natana J. *Wahhabi Islam: From Revival and Reform to Global Jihad*, 2007

Diamond, Jared *Collapse: How Societies Choose to Fail or Survive*, 2005

Di Cosmo, Nicola *Ancient China and its Enemies: The Rise of Nomadic Power in East Asian History*, 2002

Dikotter, Frank *The Age of Openness: China before Mao*, 2008

—— *Crime, Punishment and the Prison in Modern China*, 2002

—— *The discourse of race in modern China*, 1992

—— *Mao's Famine: The History of China's Most Devastating Catastrophe*, 2010

—— *Things Modern: Material Culture and Everyday Life in China*, 2006

Dmytryshyn, Basil, E. A. P. Crownhart-Vaughan and Thomas Vaughan *Russia's Conquest of Siberia 1558–1700: A Documentary Record*, 1985

Economy, Elizabeth C. *The River Runs Black: The Environmental Change to China's Future*, 2004

Elliott, Kimberly Ann (ed.) *Corruption and the Global Economy*, 1997

Elliot, Mark C. *The Manchu Way: The Eight Banners and Ethnic Identity in Late Imperial China*, 2001

Elvin, Mark *The Retreat of the Elephants: An Environmental History of China*, 2006

Esherick, Joseph W. *The Origins of the Boxer Uprising*, 1987

—— and Mary Backus Rankin (eds) *Chinese Local Elites and Patterns of Dominance*, 1990

Fairbank, John King *The Great Chinese Revolution 1800–1985*, 1986

—— and Merle Goldman *China: A New History*, 1998

Farwell, Byron *Armies of the Raj: From the Mutiny to Independence, 1858–1947*, 1989

Fewsmith, Joseph *China since Tiananmen: The Politics of Transition*, 2001

Fisher, Margaret W., Leo E. Rose and Robert A. Huttenback *Himalayan Battleground: Sino-Indian Rivalry in Ladakh*, 1963

Fitzgerald, C. P. *China. A Short Cultural History*, 1954

Foster, Paul B. *Ah Q Archaeology: Lu Xun, Ah Q Projeny and the National Character Discourse in Twentieth-century China*, 2007

Friedman, Edward, Paul Pickowicz and Mark Selden *Revolution, Resistance and Reform in Village China*, 2007

—— and Kay Ann Johnson *Chinese Village, Socialist State*, 1993

Gamer, Robert E. (ed.) *Understanding Contemporary China*, 2008

Gao, Mobo *The Battle for China's Past: Mao and the Cultural Revolution*, 2008

Gaury, Guy de and H. V. F. Winstone (eds) *The Road to Kabul: An Anthology*, 1981

Gernet, Jacques *A History of Chinese Civilisation* (1970, tr. (1982)), 1996

—— *Chine et Christianisme: action et réaction, 1982*

Gerth, Karl *As China Goes, So Goes the World: How Chinese Consumers are Transforming Everything*, 2011

Gladney, Dru C. *Muslim Chinese: Ethnic Nationalism in the People's Republic* (1991), 1996

Gong, Ting *The Politics of Corruption in Contemporary China: An Analysis of Policy Outcomes*, 1994

Goodman, David S. G. *Beijing Street Voices: The Poetry and Politics of China's Democracy Movement*, 1981

Gray, John *Black Mass: Apocalytic Religion and the Death of Utopia*, 2007

Greenfield, Susan *Tomorrow's People: How Twenty First Century Technology is Changing the Way We Think and Feel*, 2004

Gries, Peter Hays *China's New Nationalism: Pride, Politics and Diplomacy*, 2004

Hammond, Kenneth and Kristin Stapleton (eds) *The Human Tradition in Modern China*, 2008

Harper, Damian and David Elmer *Shanghai: City Guide*, 2008

Harvey, Robert *The Undefeated: The Rise, Fall and Rise of Greater Japan*, 1944

Hegel, G. W. F. *Lectures on the Philosophy of History*, ed. and tr. J. Sibree (1857), 1894

Hibbert, Christopher *The Dragon Wakes: China and the West, 1793–1911* (1970), 1984

Ho, Peter and Eduard B. Vermeer (eds) *China's Limits to Growth: Greening State and Society*, 2006

Horesh, Niv *Shanghai's Bund and Beyond: British Banks, Banknote Issuance, and Monetary Policy in China, 1842–1937*, 2009

Huang, Ray *China. A Macro History* (1988), rev. edn 1997

Huc, Régis-Evariste *Lamas of the Western Heavens*, tr. Charles de Salis, 1982

Hufbauer, Gary *Economic Sanctions Reconsidered: History and the Current Policy*, 2007

Jacques, Martin *When China Rules the World: The Rise of the Middle Kingdom and the End of the Western World*, 2009

Johnston, Alastair Iain *Cultural Realism: Strategic Culture and Grand Strategy in Chinese History*, 1995

Jones, Eric *The European Miracle: Environments, Economies and Geopolitics in the History of Europe and Asia*, 2003

Khan, B. Zorina *The Democratization of Invention: Patents and Copyrights in American Development, 1790–1920*, 2005

Kissinger, Henry *On China*, 2003

Kuhn, Dieter *The Age of Confucian Rule: The Song Transformation of China*, 2011

Lagerwey, John *China: A Religious State*, 2010

Lall, Marie-Carine and Vickers, Edward *Education as a Political Tool in Asia*, 2009

Landau, Jacob M. (ed.) *Ataturk and the Modernisation of Turkey*, 1984

Lee, Ching Kwan and Guobin Yang (eds) *Re-envisioning the Chinese Revolution: The Politics and Poetics of Collective Memories in Reform China*, 2007

Lemos, Gerald *The End of the Chinese Dream: Why Chinese People Fear the Future*, 2012

Li Huaiyin *Village China under Socialism and Reform: A Micro History, 1948–2008*, 2009

Li Ruogu *Institutional Suitability and Economic Development: Development Economics Based on Practices in China*, 2008

Logan, J. R. (ed.) *Urban China in Transition*, 2008

Lorge, Peter *War, Politics and Society in Early Modern China 900–1795*, 2005

Lou, Jiwei and Shuilin Wang (eds) *Public Finance in China: Reform and Growth for a Harmonious Society*, 2008

Lu Xun, *The True Story of Ah Q*, 1921

——*Diary of a Madman and Other Stories*, tr. William Lyell 1990

Luo yi ning ge 'er (Wang Shan) *Looking at China through a Third Eye*, 1994

Macgregor, Richard *The Party. The Secret World of China's Communist Rulers*, 2010

Macnair, Harley Farnsworth *China*, 1946

Maddison, Angus *Chinese Economic Performance in the Long-Run*, 2007

——*The World Economy: A Millennial Perspective*, 2001

Mao Zedong *Poems* (1958), 1976

——*Quotations from Chairman Mao Tse-Tung*, 1964

Marx, Karl and Friedrich Engels *The Communist Manifesto* (1848), tr. 1888

Mearsheimer, John J. and Stephen M. Walt *The Israel Lobby and U.S. Foreign Policy*, 2007

Millward, James A. *Eurasian Crossroads: A History of Xinjiang*, 2010

Mitter, Rana *Modern China. A Very Short Introduction*, 2008

Morris, Ian *Why the West Rules – for Now: The Patterns of History, and What They Reveal About the Future*, 2011

Mote, F. W. *Imperial China 900–1800*, 1999

Myron, Weiner and Sharon Stanton Russell, (eds) *Demography and National Security*, 2001

Needham, Joseph *Science in Traditional China: A Comparative Perspective*, 1982

O'Brien, Kevin J. (ed.) *Popular Protest in China*, 2008

Ó' Gráda, Cormac *Famine: A Short History*, 2009

Pan, Su-Yan *University Autonomy, the State, and Social Change in China*, 2008

Perdue, Peter C. *China Marches West. The Qing Conquest of Central Asia*, 2005

Peyrefitte, Alain *The Collision of Two Civilisations: The British Expedition to China in 1792–4*, tr. Jon Rothschild, 1993

Pomeranz, Kenneth *The Great Divergence: China, Europe and the Making of the Modern World*, 2000

Pott, F. L. Hawks *A Short History of Shanghai: Being an Account of the Growth and Development of the International Settlement* (1928), 1973

Qian Gang *The Great China Earthquake*, 1989

Rashid, Ahmed *Jihad: The Rise of Militant Islam in Central Asia*, 2002

—— *Descent into Chaos: The United States and the Failure of Nation Building in Pakistan, Afghanistan and Central Asia*, 2008

Rawski, Thomas G. *Economic Growth in Pre-war China*, 1989

Reed, Thomas C. and Stillman, Danny B. *The Nuclear Express: A Political History and its Proliferation*, 2009

Rhoads, Edward J. M. *Manchus and Han: Ethnic Relations and Political Power in Late Qing and Early Republican China, 1861–1928*, 2000

Richards, D. S. *The Savage Frontier: A History of the Anglo-Afghan Wars*, 1990

Salisbury, Harrison E. *The New Emperors: Mao and Deng: A Dual Biography*, 1992

Saviano, Roberto *Gomorrah: Italy's Other Mafia*, tr. Virginia Jewiss, 2008

Scobell, Andrew *China's Use of Military Force: Beyond the Great Wall and the Long March*, 2003

Shambaugh, David *China's Communist Party: Atrophy and Adaptation*, 2008

Shapiro, Judith *Mao's War against Nature: Politics and the Environment in Revolutionary China*, 2001

Sheridan, James E. *China in Disintegration: The Republican Era in Chinese History, 1912–1949*, 1977

Shirk, Susan L. *The Political Logic of Economic Reform in China*, 1993

—— *China: Fragile Superpower*, 2007

Silcock, Arnold *Introduction to Chinese Art and History*, 1936

Simpfendorfer, Ben *The New Silk Road: How a Rising Arab World is Turning Away From the West and Rediscovering China*, 2011

Simpson, Andrew (ed.) *Language and National Identity in Asia*, 2007

SIPRI *Yearbook 2010: Armaments, Disarmaments and International Security*, 2010

Sorel, Georges *Reflections on Violence* (1908), tr. T. E. Hulme and J. Roth, 1961

Spence, Jonathan D. *The Search for Modern China*, 1990

Spengler, Oswald *The Decline of the West*, tr. C. F. Atkinson, 1947

Stein, Sir Aurel *On Ancient Central-Asian Tracks: Brief Narrative of Three Expeditions in Innermost Asia and Northwestern China*, 1974

Stephan, John *The Russian Far East: A History*, 1996

Stiglitz, Joseph E. and Linda J. Bilmes *The Three Trillion Dollar War: The True Cost of the Iraq Conflict*, 2008

Stoessinger, John G. *Why Nations Go To War*, 1993

Subramaniam, Arvind *Eclipse: Living in the Shadow of China's Economic Dominance*, 2011

Talbott, Strobe *Engaging India: Diplomacy, Democracy, and the Bomb*, 2004

Tan, Yan *Resettlement in the Three Gorges Project*, 2008

Tang Xiaobing *Chinese Modern: The Heroic and the Quotidian*, 2000

Teichman, Eric *Journey to Turkistan*, 1988

Thompson, J. Eric S. *The Rise and Fall of Maya Civilization*, 1993

Toynbee, Arnold. *A Study of History* (1961), one-volume edition, 1972

Trofimov, Yaroslav *The Siege of Mecca: The Forgotten Uprising in Islam's Holiest Shrine and the Birth of al Qaeda*, 2007

Turnbull, Stephen R. *Siege Weapons of the Far East: AD 300–1300*, 2001

Tyler, Christian *Wild West China: The Taming of Xinjiang*, 2003

Tzou, Byron N. *China and International Law: The Boundary Disputes*, 1990

Waldron, Arthur *The Great Wall of China: From History to Myth*, 1990

Wang Fei-ling *Organising through Division and Exclusion: China's Hukou System*, 2005

Wang, Hui *China's New Order: Society, Politics, and Economy in Transition*, ed. Theodore Huters, 2003

—— *The End of the Revolution: China and the Limits to Modernity*, 2009

Wang Ke-wen (ed.), *Modern China: An Encyclopedia of History, Culture, and Nationalism*, 1998

Wang Y. C. *Chinese Intellectuals and the West 1872–1949*, 1966

Wasserstrom, Jeffrey N. *Global Shanghai, 1850–2010: A History in Fragments*, 2009

Watt, James C. Y. *The World of Khubilai Khan: Chinese Art in the Yuan Dynasty*, 2010

Wolmar, Christian *Blood, Iron and Gold: How the Railways Transformed the World*, 2010

Xiao Jiansheng *Chinese History Revisited* (2006), 2009

Yu, George T. *Party Politics in Republican China: The Kuomintan, 1912–1924*, 1966

Zachman, Urs Matthias *China and Japan in the Late Meiji Period: China Policy and the Japanese Discourse on National Identity, 1895–1904*, 2009

Zhao Ziyang, *Premier Prisoner of the State*, 2009

Papers

Abbreviations (and see also pp.viii and ix)

AEI	Australian Education International
ASPI	Australian Strategic Policy Institute
BIS	Bank for International Settlements
CASS	Chinese Academy of Social Sciences
CEIP	Carnegie Endowment for International Peace
CFR	Council on Foreign Relations
CRS	Congressional Research Service
CSIS	Center for Strategic and International Studies
DIIS	Danish Institute for International Studies
DOD	US Department of Defense
DRC	Development Research Centre, under the State Council, Beijing
ECB	European Central Bank
FLA	Fair Labor Association
HKIMR	Hong Kong Institute for Monetary Research
HRW	Human Rights Watch
IEA	International Energy Agency
IFPRI	International Food Policy Research Institute
ILO	International Labour Organisation
MGI	McKinsey Global Institute
NCIX	Office of the National Counter Intelligence Executive
NDU	National Defence University
NEJM	*New England Journal of Medicine*
NSF	National Science Foundation (USA)
Pew	Pew Research Center
RAND	Rand Corporation
RIIA	Royal Institute for International Affairs, or Chatham House
SIPO	State Intellectual Property Office of the PRC
UN	United Nations
UNAMA	United Nations Assistance Mission in Afghanistan
UNHCR	United Nations High Commission for Refugees
UNIDIR	United Nations Institute for Disarmament Research
USCESRR	US–China Economic and Security Review Report
WB	World Bank
WWICS	Woodrow Wilson International Center for Scholars

2030WaterResourcesGroup@mckinsey.com 'Charting our Water Future' 2009

Abramovitz, Moses 'Catching Up, Forging Ahead, and Falling Behind' *The Journal of Economic History*, Vol. 46, No.2, The Tasks of Economic History. (June 1986), pp.385–406, http://www.cenet.org.cn/userfiles/2007-9-25/20070925002223921.pdf

ADB 'Addressing Climate Change and Migration'. 2012, http://beta.adb.org/sites/default/files/pub/2012/addressing-climate-change-migration.pdf

ADB Key Indicators for Asia and the Pacific 2010, http://www.adb.org/documents/books/key_indicators/

AEI 'Research on China's National College Entrance Examination (the Gaokao)' 2009, https://221.121.69.112/AEI/PublicationsAndResearch/Publications/AEIGaokaoReport_310809_pdf.pdf

Afghan Independent Human Rights Commission 'Afghanistan Annual Report on Protection of Civilians in Armed Conflict, 2010', http://www.aihrc.org.af/2010_eng/Eng_pages/Reports/Thematic/Executive_Summary_Final.pdf

Alford, William P. and Liebman, Benjamin L. 'Clean Air, Clear Processes?' *Hastings Law Journal* Vol. 52, No.3, 2001, http://www.wcfia.harvard.edu/sites/default/files/676__CLEAN_AIR_5_03.pdf

Allouche, Jeremy 'The Governance of Central Asian Waters: National Interests versus Regional Cooperation' 2007 UNIDIR, http://www.unidir.org/pdf/articles/pdf-art2687.pdf

Altbach, Reisberg and Rumbley 'Trends in Global Higher Education: Tracking an Academic Revolution' 2009 UNESCO, http://unesdoc.unesco.org/images/0018/001831/183168e.pdf

An Chunggun 'A Treatise on Peace in the East', tr. Han Jieun and Franklin Rausch, http://www.utoronto.ca/csk/A_Treatise_on_Peace_in_the_East.pdf

Anderson, Siwan 'The Economics of Dowry and Brideprice' *Journal of Economic Perspectives*— Vol. 21, No.4, Fall 2007; pp.151–74, http://faculty.arts.ubc.ca/asiwan/documents/siwan-jep.pdf

Asian Centre for Human Rights 'India Human Rights Report 2009', http://www.achrweb.org/reports/india/AR09/AR2009.pdf

ASPI 'Southeast Asia Patterns of Security Cooperation' 2010, http://www.aspi.org.au/

Association of Chief Police Officers 'Commercial Cultivation of Cannabis' 2010

Attali, Jacques 'The West and the Tyranny of Public Debt' (An essay published in *Newsweek* Special Edition: 2011), reproduced in http://www.thedailybeast.com/newsweek/2010/12/27/the-west-and-the-tyranny-of public-debt.html

Aviva 'Mind the Gap. Quantifying Europe's Pensions Gap' 2010, http://www.aviva.com/europe-pensions-gap/downloads/regional_uk.pdf

Bedeski *et al.* 'Small Arms Trade and Proliferation in East Asia' University of British Columbia 1998

Behrens, Carl E. 'Nuclear Non-proliferation Issues' CRS 2006

Beim, David 'The Future of Chinese Growth' New America Foundation 2011, http://newamerica.net/publications/policy/the_future_of_chinese_growth

Beukel, Erik 'Popular Nationalism in China and the Sino-Japanese Relationship: The Conflict in the East China Sea. An Introductory Study' DIIS 2011, http://www.diis.dk/graphics/publications/reports2011/rp-2011–01-china-japan_web.pdf

Bielinski, Juliane 'Globalisation of R+D to China' Leibniz University 2009

Birdsall and Rhee 'Does Research and Development Contribute to Economic Growth in Developing Countries?' 1993 WB

Blacksmith Institute 'The World's Worst Polluted Places' 2007

Blank, Stephen 'China's Water Policies in Central Asia' Central Asia Caucasus Institute 2009

Blazevic, Jason J. 'The Taiwan Dilemma: China, Japan, and the Strait Dynamic', *Journal of Current Chinese Affairs*, Vol.39, No.4, 2010, pp.143–73, http://hup.sub.uni-hamburg.de/giga/jcca/article/viewPDFInterstitial/360/358

Bloom, David E. Canning, David and Fink, Günther 'Implications of Population Aging for Economic Growth' Harvard Initiative for Global Health 2011, http://www.hsph.harvard.edu/pgda/WorkingPapers/2011/PGDA_WP_64.pdf

Borthwick, Alistair 'A Century of Change: The Environment and China' (read at a Library of Congress conference Autumn 2009)

Boston Consulting Group 'Innovation 2008'

Brahmbhatt, Milan and Hu, Albert 'Ideas and Innovation in East Asia' World Bank 2007

Brookings Institution, Livingston and O'Hanlon, 'Afghanistan Index' 2012 http://www.brookings.edu/~/media/programs/foreign%20policy/afghanistan%20index/index20120516

Brown, Jeremy 'Terrible Honeymoon' 2004 University of Southern California, San Diego http://ucsdmodernchinesehistory.org/2010/05/01/1045/

Brown, Kerry 'Options for a Democratic Taiwan' RIIA (Chatham House) 2009

Cao, Chen, Shankman *et al.* 'Excessive Reliance on Afforestation in China's Arid and Semi-arid Regions: Lessons in Ecological Restoration' *Earth-Science Reviews* 104 (2011) 240–5

Carpenter, Ted Galen 'Is Japan Tilting Toward China?' Cato Institute 2001, http://www.cato.org/pub_display.php?pub_id=4272

CEIP 'Corruption Threatens China's Future' 2007

Cai, Du and Wang 'Migration and Labour Mobility in China' UNDP 2009, http://hdr.undp.org/en/reports/global/hdr2009/papers/HDRP_2009_09.pdf

CEIP 'Will Central Asia Have Another 'Second Chance?' 'Olcott, Kaiser and Sestanovich Discussion Transcript 2005, http://www.carnegieendowment.org/2005/09/15/will-central-asia-have-another-second-chance/398u

CASS 'Surveying Internet Usage and its Impact' 2007

CASS 'Surveying Internet Usage and Impact in Twelve Chinese Cities' 2003, http://www.policyarchive.org/handle/10207/bitstreams/15539.pdf

Chamon, Marcos and Prasad, Eswar 'Why are Saving Rates of Urban Households in China Rising?' IMF 2008, http://www.imf.org/external/pubs/ft/wp/2008/wp08145.pdf

Chang, G. Andy and Wang, T. Y. 'Taiwanese or Chinese? Independence or Unification? An Analysis of Generational Differences in Taiwan' *Journal of Asian and African Studies* April Vol.40, No.1, 2005, pp.29–49, http://jas.sagepub.com/content/40/1–2/29.full.pdf

Chen, Gong, Li *et al.* 'Risk Assessment on the Land Subsidence in Beijing' 2009, http://adsabs.harvard.edu/abs/2009SPIE.7471E..56C

Chen Wei 'Sex Ratios at Birth in China' 2005, http://www.cicred.org/Eng/Seminars/Details/Seminars/FDA/PAPERS/18_ChenWei.pdf

Chen, Zhang *et al.* 'Syphilis in China: Results of a National Surveillance Programme' The Lancet 130107

Chen Mumin 'The Taiwan Factor in China–Japan Relations' Taiwan 2007

Cheng, Fang *et al.* 'China's International Aid Policy and Its Implications for Global Governance' Research Center for Chinese Politics & Business, Indiana University 2012, http://www.indiana.edu/~rccpb/pdf/Cheng%20RCCPB%2029%20Aid%20June%202012.pdf

Cheung, Kwok Wah and Pan, Suyan 'Transition of Moral Education in China: Towards Regulated Individualism' Citizenship Teaching and Learning Vol. 2, No.2, December 2006, http://www.citized.info/pdf/ejournal/Vol%202%20Number%202/022.pdf

Cheung, Tai Ming 'The Chinese Defense Economy's Long March from Imitation to Innovation', Journal of Strategic Studies, Vol. 34, No.3, 2001, pp.325–54, http://dx.doi.org/10.1080/0140239 0.2011.574976

'China Science and Technology Statistics Data Book 2007', Ministry of Science and Technology, http://www.most.gov.cn/eng/statistics/2007/200801/P020080109573867344872.pdf

Ci, Yang and Zhang. UNDP conference paper 2005

Cotula, Vermeulen *et al.* 'Land Grab or Development?' 2009 International Institute for Environment and Development, http://www.ifad.org/pub/land/land_grab.pdf

Commission on Wartime Contracting in Iraq and Afghanistan 'Transforming Wartime Contracting' Final Report to US Congress 2011, www.wartimecontracting.gov

Dai, Yao *et al.* 'A Study on the Relationship between Water Levels and Seismic Activity in the Three Gorges Reservoir' Institute of Seismology, China Earthquake Administration, Wuhan (tr. and pub in English by Probe International 2011), http://probeinternational.org/library/wp-content/uploads/2011/06/3-Gorges-Report-26-5.pdf

Das Gupta, Chung and Li 'Is There an Incipient Turnaround in Asia's "Missing Girls" Phenomenon?' World Bank 2009, http://www-wds.worldbank.org/external/default/WDSContentServer/IW3P/IB/2009/02/24/000158349_20090224084450/Rendered/PDF/WPS4846.pdf

Das Gupta, Ebenstein and Sharygin 'China's Marriage Market and Upcoming Challenges for Elderly Men' WB 2010, http://paa2011.princeton.edu/papers/110036

Defence, of Japan Report 2011 Part 1, Chapter 2. China. Ministry of Defence, Tokyo. 2011, http://www.mod.go.jp/e/publ/w_paper/pdf/2010/11Part1_Chapter2_Sec3.pdf

'Defending Australia in the Asia Pacific Century 2009' Australian Government, Department of Defence, http://www.defence.gov.au/whitepaper/docs/defence_white_paper_2009.pdf

'Defense Programs and Budget of Japan: Overview of FY2011 Budget' Ministry of Defense, Tokyo 2011, http://www.mod.go.jp/e/d_budget/pdf/230401.pdf

Deng, Q., Tang, Q., Schottenfeld, R.S., Hao, W., Chawarski, M.C. 'Drug use in rural China: a preliminary investigation in Hunan Province' *Addiction*, Vol. 107, No.3, 2012, pp.610–3, http://www.ncbi.nlm.nih.gov/pubmed/21906200

Deng, Xiangzheng, Huang, Jikun, *et al.* 'Cultivated Land Conversion and Potential Agricultural Productivity in China 2005', http://iisdb.stanford.edu/pubs/21642/cultivated_land_conversion_and_bioproductivity_final_version_draft3.pdf

De Salle, Appleby, Caputo 'China's South-to-North Water Diversion Project' 2008

Dikotter, Frank 'Forging National Unity: Ideas of Race in China' *Global Dialogue* Vol. 12, No.2, Summer/Autumn 2010—Race and Racisms, http://www.worlddialogue.org/content.php?id=489

——'Reading the Body: Genetic Knowledge and Social Marginalization in the People's Republic of China', http://web.mac.com/dikotter/Dikotter/Publications_files/Reading%20the%20Body.pdf

Dillon, Michael 'Muslim Communities in Contemporary China: The Resurgence of Islam after the Cultural Revolution' Journal of Islamic Studies Vol. 5, No.1, 1994, http://jis.oxfordjournals.org/content/5/1/70.full.pdf

Ding, Ning Ning 'Conception, Policies and Challenges Arising from Daily Life' DRC 2009

Dobija, Mieczyslaw 'Accounting for Growth of the China Economy along with an Unorthodox Methodology' Cracow University of Economics 2009

DOD 'Military and Security Developments Involving the People's Republic of China' 2010, http://www.defense.gov/pubs/pdfs/2010_CMPR_Final.pdf

Donahue, Dennis 'The Future of Work in Russia: Population Projections and the Labor Force' 2004 http://paa2004.princeton.edu/download.asp?submissionId=41088

Downs, Erica and Michal Meidan 'Business and Politics in China: The Oil Executive Reshuffle of 2011' China Security, 19, http://www.chinasecurity.us/images/stories/DownsMeidanCS19.pdf

Duckett and Hussain 'Tackling Unemployment in China: State Capacity and Governance Issues' 2008 http://www.gla.ac.uk/media/media_113311_en.pdf

Duda, Zhang and Dong 'China's Homeownership-Oriented Housing Policy' Joint Center for Housing Studies, Harvard University 2005, http://www.jchs.harvard.edu/publications/international/w05-7.pdf

Dwyer, Adrienne M. 'The Xinjiang Conflict: Uyghur Identity, Language Policy, and Political Discourse' East-West Center, Washington DC, 2005

Easterly, William 'The Middle Class Consensus and Economic Development,' WB 2001 http://williameasterly.files.wordpress.com/2010/08/34_easterly_middleclassconsensus_prp.pdf

Easterly and Levine 'Africa's Growth Tragedy: Policies and Ethnic Divisions' 1997, http://www.nyu.edu/fas/institute/dri/Easterly/File/africas%20growth%20tragedy.pdf

Ebenstein, Avraham and Jennings, Ethan ' "Bare Branches", Prostitution, and HIV in China: A Demographic Analysis' Hebrew University of Jerusalem 2008, http://pluto.huji.ac.il/~ebenstein/Ebenstein_Jennings_HIV_in_China_March_2008.pdf

Eberstadt, Nicholas Spring 2009 'Drunken Nation: Russia's Depopulation Bomb', World Affairs: http://www.worldaffairsjournal.org/articles/2009-Spring/full-Eberstadt.html

ECB 'The Accumulation of Foreign Exchange Reserves' 2006, http://www.ecb.int/pub/pdf/scpops/ecbocp43.pdf

Eichengreen, Park and Shin 'When Fast Growing Economies Slow Down: International Evidence and Implications for the People's Republic of China', ADB Working Paper Series No.262, 2011, http://www.adb.org/Documents/Working-Papers/2011/Economics-WP262.pdf

European Commission Joint Research Centre 'The 2010 EU Industrial R&D Investment Scoreboard', http://iri.jrc.ec.europa.eu/research/docs/2010/SB2010_final_report.pdf

European Commission 'The 2008 EU Industrial R+D Investment Scoreboard'

Eurostat. EU27 FDI in Brics 2008

Ferri and Liu 'Honour Thy Creditors Beforan Thy Shareholders' 2009 HKIMR

Finnegan, Michael 'Managing Unmet Expectations in the US–Japan Alliance' National Bureau of Asian Research, 2009

Fishkin, He, Luskin and Siu 'Deliberative Democracy in an Unlikely Place: Deliberative Polling in China' B.J.Pol.S., Page 1 of 14 Copyright r Cambridge University Press, 2010, http://cdd.stanford.edu/research/papers/2010/fishkin-bjps-china.pdf

FLA 'Independent Investigation of Apple Supplier, Foxconn: Report Highlights' 2012, http://www.fairlabor.org/sites/default/files/documents/reports/foxconn_investigation_report.pdf

Florida, Mellander, Qian 'Creative China?' 2008

Fox, Elvin and Wen 'Qing Demographic History: Lower Yangzi Valley in the Mid-Qing' 2007, http://gis.rchss.sinica.edu.tw/QingDemography/

Freedom House 'Undermining Democracy' 2009, http://old.freedomhouse.org/uploads/special_report/83.pdf

Furman, Nelly, Goldberg, David, and Lusin, Natalia 'Enrollments in Languages Other Than English in United States Institutions of Higher Education, Fall 2009' 2010, http://www.mla.org/pdf/2009_enrollment_survey.pdf

Gagnon and Hinterschweiger 'The Global Outlook for Government Debt over the Next 25 Years', Peterson Institute, 2011, http://www.piie.com/publications/chapters_preview/6215/iie6215.pdf

Gagnon, Lardy and Borst 'The Internal Cost of China's Currency Policy' Peterson Institute, 2011, http://www.piie.com/blogs/china/?p=422

Ge, Li, Chang *et al.* 'Impact of Ground Subsidence on the Beijing–Tianjin High-speed Railway as Mapped by Radar Interferometry' 170910, http://www.gmat.unsw.edu.au/snap/publications/ge_etal2010b.pdf

Gewirtz, Paul 'The US–China Rule of Law Initiative' 2003

Ghosh, Jayati 'Poverty Reduction in China and India: Policy Implications of Recent Trends' UN.org 2010, http://www.un.org/esa/desa/papers/2010/wp92_2010.pdf

Gleick, Peter H. 'The Three Gorges Dam Project, Yangtze River, China' Water Brief 3, The World's Water 2008–9, http://www.worldwater.org/data20082009/WB03.pdf

Goldman, Kumar and Liu 'Education and the Asian Surge: A Comparison of the Education Systems in India and China' RAND 2008, http://www.rand.org/pubs/occasional_papers/2008/RAND_OP218.pdf

Gong and Shi 'Management Corruption in China's Industrial Restructuring' 2009

Gosset, David 'The Dragon's Metamorphosis' 2006, http://www.ceibs.edu/ase/Documents/dragon.htm

Gregory, Shaun 'The ISI and the War on Terrorism' Bradford University 2008

Grimmett, Richard F. 'Conventional Arms Transfers to Developing Nations, 2001–2008' CRS 2009 http://www.fas.org/sgp/crs/weapons/R40796.pdf

Gu Baochang and Cai Yong 'Fertility Prospects in China' UN Population Division 2011 Expert Paper No.2011/14, http://www.un.org/esa/population/publications/expertpapers/2011-14_Gu&Cai_Expert-paper.pdf

Gu and Roy 'Sex Ratio at Birth in China with Reference to Other Areas in East Asia' Asia-Pacific *Population Journal* Vol. 10, No.3, 1995

Guo, Yan and Liu 'China's Evolving Reserve Requirements' BIS 2011, http://www.bis.org/publ/work360.pdf

Hall, Chris 'When the Dragon Awakes' 2007

——CESifo Forum February 2007 Institute for Economic Research, Munich, http://www.ifo.de/pls/guestci/download/CESifo%20Forum%202007/CESifo%20Forum%202/2007/forum2-07-focus5.pdf

He, Zhang and Shek 'How Efficient has been China's Investment? Empirical Evidence from National and Provincial Data' Hong Kong Monetary Authority 2006, http://www.info.gov.hk/hkma/eng/research/RM19-2006.pdf

Headey, Derek and Fan Shenggen 'Reflections on the Global Food Crisis' IFPRI, 2010, http://www.ifpri.org/sites/default/files/publications/rr165.pdf

Heeks, Richard 'Real-World Production in Developing Countries for the Virtual Economies of Online Games' University of Manchester Development Informatics Working Paper Series Paper No.32 2008, http://www.sed.manchester.ac.uk/idpm/research/publications/wp/di/documents/di_wp32.pdf

Heggelund, Gorild 'Resettlement Programmes and Environmental Capacity in the Three Gorges Dam Project' Development and Change Vol. 37, No.1, 2006, http://www.fni.no/doc&pdf/gmh-dc-2006.pdf

Heilig, Gerhard K.'Rural Development or Sustainable Development in China: Is China's Rural Development Sustainable?' International Institute for Applied Systems Analysis (IIASA) 2003, http://www.iiasa.ac.at/Research/SRD/pdf/IR-03-007.pdf

Herd, Hu and Koen 'Improving China's Health Care System' 2010 OECD, http://www.oecd-ilibrary.org/docserver/download/fulltext/5kmlh4v2fv31.pdf?expires=1295569444&id=0000&accname=guest&checksum=F2E2CF276D191AF460FAD3D230254D3A

Hesketh, Therese with Zhejiang University 'The Effects of the One-Child Policy after 25 Years' 2008 UCL, London

Hien, P. D. 'A Comparative Study of Research Capabilities of East Asian Countries and Implications for Vietnam' Vietnam Atomic Energy Agency, http://www.vaec.gov.vn/Portals/0/Images/Document/25_3_2010_1.pdf

Highland, L. M. 'Geographical Overview of the Three Gorges Dam and Reservoir, China – Geologic Hazards and Environmental Impacts: US Geological Survey Report 2008–1241', http://pubs.usgs.gov/of/2008/1241/pdf/OF08-1241_508.pdf

Hildreth, Steven 'Cyberwarfare' CRS 2001

Ho, Franklin L. 'The Land Problem of China' *The Annals of the American Academy of Political and Social Science* Vol. 276, No.1, 6–11, http://ann.sagepub.com/content/276/1/6.extract

HRW 'An Alleyway in Hell' 2009, http://www.hrw.org/sites/default/files/reports/china1109we-bwcover_1.pdf

Huang Youqin and Chengdong Yi 'Second Home Ownership in Transitional Urban China' (Forthcoming in Housing Studies in 2011, Vol. 26 No.3) 2010, http://www.albany.edu/~yhuang/Second%20Home_HS_V2_WithTables.pdf

Huang and Chan 'Human-induced Landslides in China: Mechanism Study and its Implications for Slope Management' *Chinese Journal of Rock Mechanics and Engineering*, Vol. 23, No.16, 2004, pp.2766–77

IEA 'CO2 Emissions from Fuel Combustion 2010', http://www.iea.org/co2highlights/co2high-lights.pdf

——'Global Carbon-Dioxide Emissions Increase by 1.0 Gt in 2011 to Record High' 240512, http://www.iea.org/newsroomandevents/news/2012/may/name,27216,en.html

IMD 'World Competitiveness Yearbook Rankings 2011', http://www.imd.org/research/publications/wcy/upload/scoreboard.pdf

IMF 'People's Republic of China: Financial System Stability Assessment' 2011, http://www.imf.org/external/pubs/ft/scr/2011/cr11321.pdf

——'Targets, Interest Rates and Household Savings in Urban China' 2011, http://www.imf.org/external/pubs/ft/wp/2011/wp11223.pdf

INSEAD 'Global Innovation Index 2009–10', http://www.globalinnovationindex.org/gii/main/reports/2009–10/FullReport_09–10.pdf

——'The Global Innovation Index 2011', 2011. http://www.globalinnovationindex.org/gii/GII%20COMPLETE_PRINTWEB.pdf

International Council on Security and Development 'The Struggle for Kabul' 2008

International Institute for Environment and Development 'Land Grab or Development?' 2009

International Narcotics Control Strategy Report Vol. 1, 2009. US State Department. http://www.state.gov/documents/organization/120054.pdf

International Narcotics Control Strategy Report Vol. 1, 2010. US State Department, http://www.state.gov/documents/organization/137411.pdf

International Narcotics Control Strategy Report Vol. 1, 2011. US State Department, http://www.state.gov/documents/organization/156575.pdf

Jackson, Richard 'China's Long March to Retirement Reform' 2009 CSIS

Jakobson, Holtom *et al.* 'China's Energy and Security Relations with Russia' SIPRI 2011, http://books.sipri.org/files/PP/SIPRIPP29.pdf

Johnston, Alastair Iain 'China's Militarized Interstate Dispute Behaviour 1949–1992: A First Cut at the Data' *China Quarterly* 1998, http://www.ou.edu/uschina/texts/Johnston.98.CQ.pdf

Johnston, Michael 'Corruption in China' UN Public Administration Network, http://unpan1.un.org/intradoc/groups/public/documents/apcity/unpan024539.pdf

Jones, Eric 'Agenda' Vol. 4, No.4, 1997, pp 495–504

—— 'China's Strategic Preferences' 1997

Jones, Gavin W. 'Recent Fertility Trends, Policy Responses and Fertility Prospects in Low Fertility Countries of East and Southeast Asia' UN Population Division Expert Paper No.2011/5 2011, http://www.un.org/esa/population/publications/expertpapers/2011–5_Jones_Expert-Paper_FINAL_ALL-Pages.pdf

Jones, Seth G. 'Reintegrating Afghan Insurgents' Rand Corp 2011, http://www.rand.org/content/dam/rand/pubs/occasional_papers/2011/RAND_OP327.pdf

Joseph, P. Chacko 'China's "String of Pearls" Strategy around India in Tatters' *Frontier India* 2009, http://frontierindia.org/chinas-string-of-pearls-strategy-around-india-in-tatters/

Josheski, Dushko and Koteski, Cane 'The Causal Relationship between Patent Growth and Growth of GDP with Quarterly Data in the G7 Countries: Cointegration, ARDL and Error Correction Models' Goce Delcev University-Stip, Macedonia 2011, http://mpra.ub.uni-muenchen.de/33153/1/MPRA_paper_33153.pdf

Joshi, Sharad 'Nuclear Proliferation and South Asia: Recent Trends' www.nti.org 2007

Joshi, Shashank 'China and India: Awkward Ascents', http://shashankjoshi.files.wordpress.com/2011/02/sino-indian-relations-pdf.pdf

Kan, Shirley A. 'China and Proliferation of Weapons of Mass Destruction and Missiles: Policy Issues' CRS 2009

Kaseda, Yoshinori 'Economic Motivations behind Japan's Military Expansion' 2005, http://citation.allacademic.com//meta/p_mla_apa_research_citation/0/7/0/9/3/pages70936/p70936-1.php

Keenan, Douglas J. 'Astro-Historiographic Chronologies of Early China are Unfounded' *East Asian History* 23, 2002, http://www.informath.org/pubs/EAH02a.pdf

Kerr, and Nikitin 'Pakistan's Nuclear Weapons:Proliferation and Security Issues' CRS 2009

Kerr, Rollins and Theohary 'The Stuxnet Computer Worm: Harbinger of an Emerging Warfare Capability' CRS, 2010, http://www.fas.org/sgp/crs/natsec/R41524.pdf

Kim, Samuel 'China's Quest for Security in the post-Cold War World' 1996

Knapp, Major Laura 'Interpreting Chinese Cyber Attacks of 2007', http://www.au.af.mil/au/aul/bibs/cyberspace2010.htm

Kung, James Kai-sing 'Do Secure Land Use Rights Reduce Fertility? The Case of Meitan County in China' Land Economics Vol. 82, No.1, 2006, http://www.sosc.ust.hk/faculty/detail/jk/2006_Do_Secure_Land_Use_Rights_Reduce_Fertility.pdf

Lal, Deepak 'Continuing the Chinese Economic Miracle' UCLA 2004, http://www.econ.ucla.edu/Lal/others/china.pdf

Lancet 'Emergence of Chronic Non-communicable Diseases in China' 111108

Lardy, Nicholas 'Financial Repression in China' Peterson Institute 2008

Larrain, Felipe 'Innovation in Latin America' 2008

Lee Shu-ching 'Agrarianism and Social Upheaval in China' The American Journal of Sociology Vol. LVI, No.6, May 1951, http://www.jstor.org/pss/2772468

Leibold, James 'More Than a Category: Han Supremacism on the Chinese Internet' *China Quarterly* 203 Vol. 3 (September 2010) p.549. http://tlweb.latrobe.edu.au/humanities/profiles/ss/leibold/Leibold_More_Than_a_Category_China_Quarterly.pdf

Li Changyu 'Mao's Killing Quotas' China Rights Forum 2005, http://www.hrichina.org/public/PDFs/CRF.4.2005/CRF-2005-4_Quota.pdf

Li, Huang and Zhou 'Land Subsidence Prediction by Various Grey Models' *Environmental Informatics Archives* Vol. 3 2005 International Society for Environmental Information Sciences

Li Shuzhuo 'Imbalanced Sex Ratio at Birth and Comprehensive Intervention in China' UN Family Planning Association 2007, http://www.unfpa.org/gender/docs/studies/china.pdf

Libicki, Martin 'Cyberdeterrence and Cyberwar' Rand 2009

Linton, Katherine 'China's R&D Policy for the 21st Century: Government Direction of Innovation' US International Trade Commission. 2008

Liu Dun 'A New Survey of the Needham Question' *Studies in the History of Natural Sciences* Vol.19, No.4, 2000, http://sourcedb.cas.cn/sourcedb_scr_cas/zwqkk/kxwhzl/kxjss/jxdkjs/201001/P020100103620918556729.pdf

Liu Peng 'The Achilles Heel of China's Rise: Faith' 2009, http://gsw.mvidc.com/lundianinfo.asp?id=977

Liu and Tian 'China's Land Cover and Land Use Change from 1700 to 2005: Estimations from High-resolution satellite data and historical archives' *Global Biogeochemical Cycles* Vol. 24, 16 July 2010

Liu Yingqiu 'Development of Private Entrepreneurship in China: Process, Problems and Countermeasures' The Maureen and Mike Mansfield Foundation (undated, post-2002)http://www.mansfieldfdn.org/backup/programs/program_pdfs/ent_china.pdf

Liu, Zhang, Wang et al. 'Soil Degradation: A Problem Threatening the Sustainable Development of Agriculture in Northeast China' *Plant, Soil and Environment*, Vol. 56, No.2, pp.87–97, 2010, http://journals.uzpi.cz/publicFiles/16435.pdf

Lo, Bobo 'Ten Things Everyone Should Know about the Sino-Russian Relationship' Centre for European Reform 2008

Lu, Frank, Liu and Shen 'The Impact of Mental Health on Labour Market Outcomes in China' Journal of Mental Health Policy and Economics, September 2009, http://www.ncbi.nlm.nih.gov/pubmed/19996477

Lum, Thomas 'China and Falun Gong' CRS 2006

Lum, Fischer et al. 'China's Foreign Aid Activities' CRS 2009, http://www.fas.org/sgp/crs/row/R40361.pdf

Lynn III, William 'The Pentagon's Cyberstrategy, One Year Later: Defending Against the Next Cyberattack'. *Foreign Affairs* 2011, http://www.foreignaffairs.com/articles/68305/william-j-lynn-iii/the-pentagons-cyberstrategy-one-year-later

Mainland Affairs Council 'Background Information: The Frequent Occurrence of Mass Incidents in China Pushes it into Becoming a "Risky Society"' Taiwan 2007

Makin, John H. 'China: Bogus Boom?' American Enterprise Institute 2009

Malik, J. Mohan 'India–China Relations' Berkshire Publishing Group LLC 2009, http://www.apcss.org/core/BIOS/malik/India-China_Relations.pdf

Man, Joyce Yanyun 'Affordable Housing in China' Lincoln Institute of Land Policy 2011, http://www.lincolninst.edu/pubs/PubDetail.aspx?pubid=1871&URL=Affordable-Housing-in-China&Page=5

Matsuda, Yasuhiro 'Japanese Assessments of China's Military Development', http://www.asian-perspective.org/articles/v31n3-g.pdf

Mayer, Jorg 'Global Rebalancing: Effects on Trade Flows and Employment' UNCTAD 2010, http://www.unctad.org/en/docs/osgdp20104_en.pdf

McGinnis, Scott 'Heritage as a Gateway: Chinese as a Heritage Language' Defence Language Institute 2008, http://www.docin.com/p-55937510.html

McKinsey Climate Change 'From Bread Basket to Dust Bowl' 2009, http://209.172.180.99/locations/chinatraditional/From_Bread_Basket_Dust_Bowl_EN.pdf

McMahon, Robert and Isabella Bennett 'U.S. Internet Providers and the "Great Firewall of China"' CFR 2008, http://www.cfr.org/china/hs-internet-providers-great-firewall-china/p9856

Medeiros, Evan S. 'China's International Behaviour' Rand 2009, http://www.rand.org/pubs/monographs/2009/RAND_MG850.pdf

Michailof, Serge 'Sortir du piège afghan' *Commentaire*, 2009

Ministry of Defence (UK) 'Security and Stabilisation' 2009

Ministry of Foreign Affairs, Beijing. 'National Report of the People's Republic of China on the Implementation of the United Nations Programme of Action to Prevent, Combat and Eradicate the Illicit Trade in Small Arms and Light Weapons in All Its Aspects, and of the International Instrument to Enable States to Identify and Trace, in a Timely and Reliable Manner, Illicit Small Arms and Light Weapons' 2010, http://www.poa-iss.org/CASACountryProfile/PoANationalReports/2010@42@POA-China-2010-E.PDF

MGI 'Addressing China's Looming Talent Shortage' 2005, http://www.mckinsey.com/insights/mgi/research/labor_markets/addressing_chinas_looming_talent_shortage

Mulvenon, James C. 'Soldiers of Fortune: The Rise and Fall of the Chinese Military-Business Complex, 1978–98'. Bonn International Center for Conversion, 1999, http://www.bicc.de/uploads/pdf/publications/papers/paper15/paper15.pdf

Muscolino, Micah S. 'Global Dimensions of Modern China's Environmental History,' *World History Connected* 6, 2009, http://worldhistoryconnected.press.illinois.edu/6.1/muscolino.html

National Development and Reform Commission 'China's National Climate Change Programme' 2007, http://www.ccchina.gov.cn/WebSite/CCChina/UpFile/File188.pdf

National Research Council, Office of Scientific and Engineering Personnel, 'Foreign and Foreign-Born Engineers in the United States', 1988, http://books.nap.edu/openbook.php?record_id=1525&page=5

National Science Foundation, National Center for Science and Engineering Statistics (NCSES) 'Doctorate Recipients from U.S. Universities: Summary Report 2007–08', http://www.nsf.gov/statistics/nsf10309/pdf/tab11.pdf

NCIX 'Foreign Spies Stealing US Economic Secrets in Cyberspace: Report to Congress on Foreign Economic Collection and Industrial Espionage, 2009–11', http://www.ncix.gov/publications/reports/fecie_all/Foreign_Economic_Collection_2011.pdf

NDRC 'China's Climate Change Programme' 2007

Ni, Shawn and Pham Hoang Van 'High Corruption Income as a Source of Distortion and Stagnation: Some New Evidence from Ming and Qing China' 2003, http://www.ucdenver.edu/academics/colleges/CLAS/Departments/economics/Documen/van.pdf

Norwegian Refugee Council 'Future Floods of Refugees' 2008 http://www.nrc.no/arch/_ing/9268480.pdf

NSF 'Science and Engineering Indicators 2010' Arlington, Virginia, http://www.nsf.gov/statistics/seind10/

OECD 'Compendium of Patent Statistics 2008'

——'Governance in China' 2005–6

——'Is Informal Normal? Towards More and Better Jobs in Developing Countries' 2009, http://www.oecd.org/document/54/0,3343,en_2649_33935_42024438_1_1_1,00&&en-USS_01DBC.html

——'Measuring China's Innovation System' 2009

——'Education at a Glance 2010, OECD Indicators', http://www.oecd.org/dataoecd/45/39/45926093.pdf

——Review of Tertiary Education, China 2009, http://browse.oecdbookshop.org/oecd/pdfs/free/9109031e.pdf

——'Society at a Glance 2009: OECD Social Indicators', 2009, http://puck.sourceoecd.org/pdf/societyataglance2009/812009011e-08–04.pdf

Office of the Director of National Intelligence 'Remarks by the National Counterintelligence Executive Dr. Joel F. Brenner' 030409, https://www.hsdl.org/?view&did=37389

Office of the Secretary of Defense (USA) 'Military Power of the Peoples Republic of China 2009'

OHCHR Resolution S-11/1 'Assistance to Sri Lanka in the Promotion and Protection of Human Rights' 270509

——'Urgent International Scrutiny Needed in Sri Lanka, Say UN Human Rights Experts' 080509

Oksanen, Heikki 'The Chinese pension system: First results on assessing the reform options' European Commission 2010, http://ec.europa.eu/economy_finance/publications/economic_paper/2010/pdf/ecp412_en.pdf

Open Budget Survey 2008

'Organised Crime Threats Assessment 2009'. Europol

O'Rourke 'China Naval Modernization' CRS 2012, http://www.fas.org/sgp/crs/row/RL33153.pdf

Oxfam 'Afghanistan: No Time to Lose' 2011, http://www.oxfam.org/sites/www.oxfam.org/files/afghanistan-no-time-to-lose-20110510-en.pdf

——'Blind Optimism' 2009, http://www.oxfam.org.uk/resources/policy/health/downloads/bp125_blind_optimism_private_health_care.pdf

Parameters 'Good Anthropology, Bad History' Summer 2007

Parekh, MacInnes and Kenway 'Monitoring Poverty and Social Exclusion 2010' Joseph Rowntree Foundation, http://www.jrf.org.uk/sites/files/jrf/poverty-social-exclusion-2010-full.pdf

Park, Cai et al. 'Can China Meet Its Employment Challenges?'

Park, Xiao et al. 'Mental Health Care in China: Recent Changes and Future Challenges' *Harvard Health Policy Review* Vol. 6, No.2, Fall 2005, http://www.hcs.harvard.edu/~hhpr/currentissue/park.pdf

Parliamentary Office of Science and Technology 'International Migration of Scientists and Engineers' 2008 http://www.parliament.uk/documents/post/postpn309.pdf

Patel, Nirav 'Chinese Disaster Relief Operations' *Joint Force Quarterly*, NDU 2009 Q1 pp.111–17, https://digitalndulibrary.ndu.edu/cdm4/document.php?CISOROOT=/ndupress&CISOPTR=20972&REC=8

Pehrson, Christopher J. 'String of Pearls: Meeting the Challenge of China's Rising Power' 2006, http://www.strategicstudiesinstitute.army.mil/pdffiles/pub721.pdf

Pew Global Attitudes China Report 2012, http://www.pewglobal.org/files/2012/10/Pew-Global-Attitudes-China-Report-FINAL-October-10-2012.pdf

Pew '2008 Pew Global Attitudes Survey'

Pew '2009 Pew Global Attitudes Survey'

Pew '2010 Pew Global Attitudes Survey'

Pew Forum 'Religion in China on the Eve of the 2008 Beijing Olympics', http://www.pewforum.org/Importance-of-Religion/Religion-in-China-on-the-Eve-of-the-2008-Beijing-Olympics.aspx

Phillips, Li and Zhang 'Suicide Rates in China, 1995–99' *Lancet* 090302 Vol. 359, pp.835–40, http://filer.case.edu/users/pxc26/020328213247225627.pdf

Pils, Eva 'Chinese Property Law as an Image of PRC History' 2010, http://papers.ssrn.com/sol3/papers.cfm?abstract_id=1564448

PlayFair 2008. Olympic Report June 2008, http://www.playfair2008.org/docs/playfair_2008-report.pdf

Podpiera, Richard 'Progress in China's Banking Sector Reform: Has Bank Behavior Changed?' IMF 2006, http://imf.org/external/pubs/ft/wp/2006/wp0671.pdf

Pong, Professor David 'Confucian Patriotism and the Destruction of the Woosung Railway, 1877' *Modern Asia Studies* Vol. 7, No.4, 1973, pp.647–76

PricewaterhouseCoopers 'Global Reach. China's Impact on the Semiconductor Industry 2010 Update', http://www.pwc.com/gx/en/technology/assets/china-semicon-2010.pdf

Probe International 'Beijing's Water Crisis 1949–2008 Olympics' 2008 with 2010 Update, http://www.probeinternational.org/files/Beijing%20Water%20Report%20Update%202010.pdf

Przystup James J. 'Japan–China Relations: All's Well that Ends Well' 2010 CSIS, http://csis.org/files/publication/1001qjapan_china.pdf

Qazi, Shehzad H. 'An Extended Profile of the Pakistani Taliban' Policy Brief 44 2011 Institute for Social Policy and Understanding. Washington DC, http://ispu.org/pdfs/ISPU%20Policy%20Brief%20Extended%20Profile%20of%20Pakistani%20Taliban.pdf

Qu and Fan 'The Current State of Water Quality and Technology Development for Water Pollution Control in China' *Critical Reviews in Environmental Science and Technology* Vol. 40, 2010, pp.519–60

Ravallion, Martin 'The Developing World's Bulging (but Vulnerable) Middle Class ' WB 2009, http://www.iadb.org/intal/intalcdi/PE/2009/02510.pdf

Robertson, Susan L. 'Market Multilateralism, the World Bank Group and the Asymmetries of Globalising Higher Education: Toward a Critical Political Economy Analysis' http://www.bris.ac.uk/education/people/academicStaff/edslr/publications/27slr

Rozman, G. Demokratizatsiya: Sino-Soviet Relations 1997–8

Segal, Adam 'Innovation, Espionage, and Chinese Technology Policy' Testimony to the House Foreign Affairs Subcommittee on Oversight and Investigations Council on Foreign Relations 2011, http://www.cfr.org/china/innovation-espionage-chinese-technology-policy/p24686

Seib and Powers 'China in the News' 010710 USC Centre on Public Diplomacy, the Annenberg School, http://uscpublicdiplomacy.org/media/China_in_the_News_Report.pdf

Setser, Brad 'Sovereign Wealth and Sovereign Power' CFR 2008

Schiere, Ndikumana *et al.* (eds) 'China and Africa: an Emerging Partnership for Development?' African Development Bank, http://www.afdb.org/fileadmin/uploads/afdb/Documents/Publications/text%20Anglais%20China.pdf

Shaplak, Orletsky *et al.* 'A Question of Balance' Rand Corp 2009

Shearman, Peter 'Decision-Making and the Iraq War: Misperceiving Saddam' 2008, http://www.isisthailand.org/asp/ASP_document/Decision-Making_and_the_Iraq_War_Misperceiving_Saddam_A4.pdf

Shelley, Louise 'The Drug Trade in Contemporary Russia' *China and Eurasia Forum Quarterly* 2006

Shi, Yan, Yuan *et al.* 'Wind Erosion Research in China: Past, Present and Future' Progress in Physical Geography Vol. 28, No.3, 2004, pp.366–86

Stanford Law School and NYU School of Law 'Living Under Drones' 2012, http://livingunder-drones.org/wp-content/uploads/2012/09/Stanford_NYU_LIVING_UNDER_DRONES.pdf

State Council 'China–Africa Economic and Trade Cooperation' Beijing 2010, http://news.xinhuanet.com/english2010/china/2010-12/23/c_13661632.htm

Steil and Duan 'Policies and Practice in Three Gorges Resettlement' *Forced Migration Review* 12, 2002, http://www.fmreview.org/FMRpdfs/FMR12/fmr12full.pdf

Strick von Lischoten, Alex and Kuhn, Felix 'Separating the Taliban from al-Qaeda' Center on International Cooperation, New York University 2011, http://www.cic.nyu.edu/afghanistan/docs/gregg_sep_tal_alqaeda.pdf

Tao and Watson, 'China's Energy Transition' Tyndall Centre 2009.

Tellis, Ashley J. 'Preserving Hegemony: The Strategic Tasks Facing the United States' *Global Asia*, Spring 2009

Tian Yanfang 'China's Imports of Russian Timber' Institute for Global Environmental Strategies March 2008

Transatlantic Partners against AIDS 'Abandoned Children born to HIV-positive Women: Analysis of the Situation in Russia' 2004, http://www.gbcimpact.ru/files/upload/publications/836.pdf

Transparency International 'Corruption Perceptions Index' 2009

Tsang, Steve 'Consultative Leninism: China's New Political Framework' *Journal of Contemporary China*, Vol. 18, No.62, November 2009, pp.865–80

Tucker, Chen *et al.* 'Syphilis and Social Upheaval in China' NEJM 060510

UN 'World Population Prospects: The 2008 Revision. Highlights.' 2009

UNAMA Human Rights 'Arbitrary Detention in Afghanistan' 2009, http://www.ohchr.org/Documents/Countries/ADVC_Vol_I_UNAMA.pdf

UNDP Human Development Report 2007–8, http://hdr.undp.org/en/media/HDR_20072008_EN_Complete.pdf

UNDP Human Development Report 2009, UNDP 'Russia Facing Demographic Challenges' 2009, http://www.undp.ru/documents/NHDR_2008_Eng.pdf

UNESCO 'Raising Quality and Strengthening Equity' 2009

UNESCO Science Report 2010, http://www.unesco.org/science/psd/publications/usr_2010.pdf

UNICEF and Rosstat, 'Youth in Russia' 2010, http://www.unrussia.ru/en/public.html

UN World Drug Report 2008, http://www.unodc.org/documents/wdr/WDR_2008/WDR_2008_eng_web.pdf

UN World Drug Report 2012, http://www.unodc.org/documents/data-and-analysis/WDR2012/WDR_2012_web_small.pdf

USCESRR 2007, http://www.uscc.gov/annual_report/2007/07_annual_report.php

USCESRR 2008, http://www.uscc.gov/annual_report/2008/08_annual_report.php

USCESRR 2009, http://www.uscc.gov/annual_report/2009/09_annual_report.php

USCESRR 2010, http://www.uscc.gov/annual_report/2010/10_annual_report.php

USCESRR 2011, http://www.uscc.gov/annual_report/2011/annual_report_full_11.pdf

US–China Commission 'The Evolving Role of China in International Institutions', http://www.uscc.gov/researchpapers/2011/TheEvolvingRoleofChinainInternationalInstitutions.pdf

Vennemo, Aunan *et al.* 'Environmental Pollution in China: Status and Trends' *Review of Environmental Economics and Policy*, Vol. 3, issue 2, Summer 2009, pp.209–30

Verburga, P. H., Veldkampb, A., Frescoa, L. O. 'Simulation of Changes in the Spatial Pattern of Land Use in China' *Applied Geography* 19, 1999, pp.211–33, http://lab.geog.ntu.edu.tw/course/luc/7/Simulation%20of%20changes%20in%20the%20spatial%20pattern%20of%20land%20use%20in%20China.pdf

Villers, Katherine 'Is the Border Dispute a Symptom or a Cause of the Antagonism Between India and China?' (unpublished thesis) Oxford University 2011

Vinokurov, Zherelina *et al.* 'Transboundary Water Problems in the Basin of the Irtysh River' NATO Workshop 2003

Vodopivec and Tong 'China: Improving Unemployment Insurance' 2008 World Bank, http://siteresources.worldbank.org/SOCIALPROTECTION/Resources/SP-Discussion-papers/Labor-Market-DP/0820.pdf

Waite, Edmund 'Post-Communism 2008: Islam and Post-Communism', http://www.indiana.edu/~reeiweb/events/2008/Waite_response.pdf

Waller, Michael and Millard, Frances 'Environmental Politics in Eastern Europe' *Environmental Politics* Vol. 1, Issue 2, 1992, pp.159–85, http://www.informaworld.com/smpp/content~db=all~content=a784194184

Wang, Cao *et al.* 'Trends and Numerical Simulation of Land Subsidence Caused by Groundwater Exploitation in the North China Plain' American Geophysical Union 2010, http://adsabs.harvard.edu/abs/2010AGUFM.H23E1255W

Wang and Yang 'More than Evangelical and Ethnic: The Ecological Factor in Chinese Conversion to Christianity in the United States' *Sociology of Religion* Vol. 67, No.2, 2006, http://socrel.oxfordjournals.org/cgi/reprint/67/2/179.pdf

Watson, Amy Beth 'How Many People Can China Feed? Assessing the Impact of Land and Water Constraints' MIT 2004, http://dspace.mit.edu/bitstream/handle/1721.1/29394/56131807.pdf?sequence=1

WB, DRC 'China 2030: Building a Modern, Harmonious, and Creative High-Income Society' 2012, http://www.worldbank.org/content/dam/Worldbank/document/China-2030-complete.pdf

WB 'Addressing China's Water Scarcity' 2009, http://www-wds.worldbank.org/external/default/WDSContentServer/WDSP/IB/2009/01/14/000333037_20090114011126/Rendered/PDF/471110PUB0CHA0101OFFICIAL0USE0ONLY1.pdf

WB 'China Quarterly Update: Sustaining Growth' April 2012, http://www.worldbank.org/content/dam/Worldbank/document/cqu_apri_2012_en.pdf

WB 'From Poor Areas to Poor People' March 2009, http://siteresources.worldbank.org/
    CHINAEXTN/Resources/318949-1239096143906/China_PA_Report_March_2009_eng.pdf

WB 'Meeting the Challenges of Secondary Education in Latin America and East Asia' 2006

WB and OECD 'Pensions at a Glance' 2009

WB 'Effective Discipline with Adequate Autonomy: the Direction for Further Reform China's
    SOE Dividend Policy' (53254) 2010, http://www-wds.worldbank.org/external/default/
    WDSContentServer/WDSP/IB/2010/03/02/000333038_20100302031054/Rendered/PDF/532
    540ESW0P11310final0Nov27020090En.pdf

WEF 'The Global Competitiveness Report 2011–2012' 2011, http://www3.weforum.org/docs/
    WEF_GCR_Report_2011–12.pdf

Wei Shang-Jin 'The Mystery of Chinese Savings' 2010, http://www.voxeu.org/index.
    php?q=node/4568

WHO 'World Health Statistics' 2007, http://www.who.int/whosis/whostat2007.pdf

Windrow, Hayden 'From State to Nation: The Forging of the Han through Language Policy in the
    PRC and Taiwan' 2005, http://www.law.nyu.edu/ecm_dlv3/groups/public/@nyu_law_
    website__journals__journal_of_international_law_and_politics/documents/documents/
    ecm_pro_059617.pdf

WIPO '2008 Patent Report'

——'World Intellectual Property Indicators' 2010, http://www.wipo.int/export/sites/www/ipstats/
    en/statistics/patents/pdf/941_2010.pdf

——'World Intellectual Property Indicators' 2009

Wittchen, Jacobi et al. 'The Size and Burden of Mental Disorders and Other Disorders of
    the Brain in Europe 2010' European Neuropsychopharmacology, Vol. 21, 2011, pp.655–79,
    http://www.ecnp.eu/~/media/Files/ecnp/communication/reports/ECNP%20EBC%20Report.
    ashx

WWICS China Environment Series 10 2008/9, http://www.healtheffects.org/International/
    CES10.pdf

Xing, Yuqing and Detert, Neal 'How the iPhone Widens the United States Trade Deficit with the
    People's Republic of China' Asian Development Bank Institute, 2010, http://www.adbi.org/
    files/2010.12.14.wp257.iphone.widens.us.trade.deficit.prc.pdf

Xu, Shen and Cai et al. 'The State of Land Subsidence and Prediction Approaches Due to
    Groundwater Withdrawal in China' Natural Hazards Vol. 45, No.1, 2007, pp.123–35, http://
    www.springerlink.com/content/p8672415538711t5/

Xu Yishuang 'The Rural Land Ownership Problem in China: Lessons from the Organizational
    Structure of REITs' 2009, http://www.universitas21.com/GRC/GRC2009/Xu.pdf

Xu, Zhang, Shen et al. 'Geo-hazards with Characteristics and Prevention Measures along the
    Coastal Regions of China' Natural Hazards Vol. 49, 2009, pp.479–500

Xue, Zhang, Ye et al. 'Land Subsidence in China' Environmental Geology Vol. 48, 2005,
    pp.713–20

Yancheva, Nowaczyk, Ingram Letters. 'Influence of the Inter-tropical Convergence Zone on the
    East Asian Monsoon', Nature vol. 445, 2007

Yan, Liu et al. 'Assessing the Consequence of Land Use Change on Agricultural Productivity in
    China' Chinese Academy of Sciences, 2009, http://www.igsnrr.cas.cn/xwzx/jxlwtj/200905/
    W020090715581531697576.pdf

Yang Guobin 'China's Zhiqing Generation' 2003

Yang, Milliman et al. '50,000 Dams Later: Erosion of the Yangtze River and its Delta' Global and
    Planetary Change Vol. 75, 2011, pp.14–20

Yang, W. and others 'Prevalence of Diabetes among Men and Women in China' NEJM 250310

Yin, Zhang and Li Geological Society of London 'Urbanisation and Land Subsidence in China'
    2006

Yoshihara and Holmes 'The Japanese Archipelago through Chinese Eyes' 2010 Jamestown
    Foundation, http://www.jamestown.org/uploads/media/cb_010_78.pdf

Yu Chaoqing 'China's Water Crisis Needs More than Words' Nature 470, 307, 2011, http://www.
    nature.com/news/2011/110216/full/470307a.html

Yu Jianrong. Talk to Beijing Lawyers at the Ministry of Finance 261209, http://chinadigitaltimes.
    net/2010/03/yu-jianrong-maintaining-a-baseline-of-social-stability-part-i/

Yu, Meng *et al.* 'How does the New Cooperative Medical Scheme Influence Health Service Utilization?' BMC Health Services Research 2010, http://www.biomedcentral.com/1472-6963/10/116

Zhang, D. and Lu, L. H. 'Anti-correlation of Summer/Winter Monsoons?' *Nature* 450, 2007, E7–E8, http://www.climategeology.ethz.ch/news/reply_Yancheva_2007.pdf

Zhang, David D., Lee, Harry F. *et al.* 'The Causality Analysis of Climate Change and Large-scale Human Crisis' *Proceedings of the National Academy of Sciences* (PNAS) 060911, http://www.pnas.org/content/early/2011/09/29/1104268108.full.pdf+html

Zhang Weiying 'The Reallocation of Entrepreneurial Talents and Economic Development in China' Guanghua School of Management, Peking University. Private paper presented at the University of Chicago in July 2008

Zhang Zhibin, Tian Huidong *et al.* 'Periodic Climate Cooling Enhanced Natural Disasters and Wars in China during AD 10–1900' The Royal Society 2010, http://rspb.royalsocietypublishing.org/content/277/1701/3745.full

Zhao Dagong 'The Xiamen Demonstrations and Growing Civil Consciousness' Human Rights in China 2007, http://www.hrichina.org/sites/default/files/oldsite/PDFs/CRF.3.2007/CRF-2007-3_Xiamen.pdf

Zhao Yuezhi 'Media and Elusive Democracy in China' *The Public* Vol. 8, 2001, No.4, pp.21–44, http://www.javnost-thepublic.org/media/datoteke/2001-2-zhao.pdf

Zheng Yongnian and Chen Minjia 'China's Recent State Owned Enterprise Reform and its Social Consequences' 2007

Zhong Lijin and Jones, Cy 'China Needs Comprehensive and Cost-effective Strategies to Address Water Pollution' World Resources Institute 2011, http://www.wri.org/stories/2011/06/china-needs-comprehensive-and-cost-effective-strategies-address-water-pollution

Zhong, Lijin and Mol, Arthur P. J. 'Water Price Reforms in China: Policy-making and Implementation' Water Resources Management 220509, http://www.wri.org.cn/files/wri/documents/water%20tariff%20reform_fulltext_2010Issue2.pdf

Zhou and Stembridge 'Patented in China: The Present & Future State of Innovation' Thomson-Reuters 2008, http://ip.thomsonreuters.com/media/pdfs/WIPTChina08.pdf

Zubir, Mokhzani 'Maritime Disputes and Cyber Warfare' 2006

Zweig, David 'Competing for Talent: China's Strategies to Reverse the Brain Drain', in: *International Labour Review,* special issue: migration, Vol. 145/1–2 ILO 2006, http://www.ilo.org/global/About_the_ILO/Media_and_public_information/Press_releases/lang en/WCMS_080665/index.htm

Index